PMP: Project Management Professional Study Guide, Deluxe Edition

Project Management Professional Objectives

OBJECTIVE	CHAPTER
Initiating the Project	
Conduct Project Selection Methods	2
Define Scope	2
Document Project Risks, Assumptions, and Constraints	2
Identify and Perform Stakeholder Analysis	2
Develop Project Charter	2
Obtain Project Charter Approval	2
Planning the Project	
Define and Record Requirements, Constraints, and Assumptions	3
Identify Project Team and Define Roles and Responsibilities	6
Create the WBS	4
Develop Change Management Plan	3
Identify Risks and Define Risk Strategies	5
Obtain Plan Approval	7
Conduct Kick-off Meeting	2
Executing the Project	
Execute Tasks Defined in Project Plan	8
Ensure Common Understanding and Set Expectations	8, 9
Implement the Procurement of Project Resources	8
Manage Resource Allocation	8
Implement Quality Management Plan	9
Implement Approved Changes	9
Implement Approved Actions and Workarounds	9
Improve Team Performance	8

SYBEX

OBJECTIVE	CHAPTER

Exam objectives are subject to change at any time without prior notice and at PMI's sole discretion. Please visit PMI's web site (www.pmi.org) for the most current listing of exam objectives.

SYBEX

PMP®:
Project Management Professional
Study Guide
Deluxe Edition

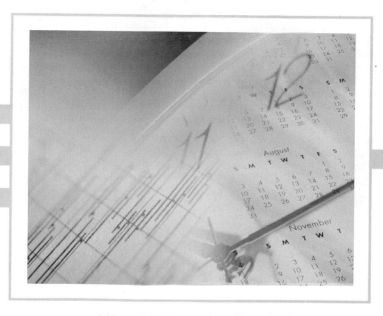

Kim Heldman, PMP

Claudia Baca, PMP

Patti Jansen, PMP

Wiley Publishing, Inc.

SYBEX

To Our Valued Readers:

Thank you for looking to Sybex for your PMP exam prep needs. Since publishing the first edition of our *PMP: Project Management Professional Study Guide* in April 2002, Sybex has earned the respect of tens of thousands of PMP candidates for providing accurate and accessible instruction on the skills and knowledge demanded by companies worldwide. Now with the update to the PMBOK (Project Management Body of Knowledge) in early 2005 and the recent revision to the PMP exam, the Project Management Institute has raised the standard by which project managers will be assessed in an increasingly competitive marketplace.

The author and editors have worked hard to ensure that the new edition you hold in your hands is comprehensive, in-depth, and pedagogically sound. We're confident that this book will exceed the demanding standards of the certification marketplace and help you, the PMP certification candidate, succeed in your endeavors.

As always, your feedback is important to us. If you believe you've identified an error in the book, please visit the Customer Support section of the Wiley web site. And if you have general comments or suggestions, feel free to drop me a line directly at nedde@wiley.com. At Sybex we're continually striving to meet the needs of individuals preparing for certification exams.

Good luck in pursuit of your PMP certification!

Neil Edde
Vice President & Publisher
Sybex, an Imprint of John Wiley & Sons

Acquisitions and Developmental Editor
Jeff Kellum

Technical Editor
Jodi Grossman

Production Editor
Elizabeth Campbell

Copy Editor
Judy Flynn

Production Manager
Tim Tate

Vice President & Executive Group Publisher
Richard Swadley

Vice President and Publisher
Joseph B. Wikert

Vice President and Publisher
Neil Edde

Media Development Specialists
Kevin Ly
Kit Malone

Book Designer
Judy Fung

Compositor and Illustrator
Jeffrey Wilson, Happenstance Type-O-Rama

Proofreader
Nancy Riddiough

Indexer
Nancy Guenther

Cover Design and Illustration
Richard Miller, Calyx Design

Cover Image
Getty Images, Duncan Smith, Comstock Images

Wiley Publishing Inc End-User License Agreement

To BB, my forever love.

—Kimmie

Acknowledgments

Thank you to the thousands of readers who have read previous editions of the *PMP Study Guide* and recommended it to their friends and co-workers. Because of your success using the book in passing the PMP exam, we are able to continue to upgrade and refresh the *Study Guide* with tips and hints from readers and with the changes made by PMI. Thank you also to all of the instructors and PMI chapters who use this book in their classes.

As always, a very special thank you to Neil Edde, Associate Publisher, for taking a chance on the first edition of this book and for giving me the opportunity to write it. Thank you again for the opportunity to revise and update it.

This book clearly fits the definition of a project and the team at Sybex is the best project team on earth to work with. I appreciate all the hard work and dedication everyone on the team put into producing this book. First, a special thanks to Jeff Kellum, Acquisitions Editor, for overseeing this project and for his many suggestions that helped improve and strengthen the text. Thank you also, for keeping everyone focused on the quick turn around time even though we faced some uncertainties in the midst of the project.

Thank you to Elizabeth Campbell for all her help managing the many, many activities that must be coordinated in order to finish on schedule. She was very helpful throughout the process and didn't scream when we found out close to the end of the project that some changes were needed to match up with newly published PMI materials.

Thanks to Judy Flynn, copyeditor, who did an outstanding job of helping me with all my grammatical blunders. (She'll probably even find some in this sentence!) She's the best copyeditor I've ever worked with. I appreciate her eye for detail and that she never told me "doh" after her suggestions.

Thanks also to all the behind the scenes team members including proofreader Nancy Riddiough, and the compositors at Happenstance Type-o-rama!

I again had the pleasure of working with Claudia Baca who served as the technical editor for this edition. Claudia was invaluable when helping me decipher areas of *A Guide to the PMBOK* that I questioned or weren't clear to me. Thank you, Claudia, for your help, suggestions, and contribution. Thanks also to Jodi Grossman for her work on the Workbook Exercises!

None of this would have been possible without the continued support and encouragement from my best friend in the whole world, BB. I love you and there's no one else I'd rather spend the rest of my life with. Thank you to Bob and Terri, our best friends in all the earth, for your support and prayers—they're always coveted. Thanks to my sister Jill and hubby John and to Sam, Promise, and Destiny for their cheerleading behind the scenes. Thank you mom and dad for giving me the love of reading; some of my best memories are story time. And thanks also to the greatest children on the planet: Jason and Leah (our soon to be daughter-in-law), Noelle, and Amanda. And I can't forget the two best grandchildren anywhere in the universe, Kate and Juliette. Thank you for your understanding of my limited availability and for your encouragement and support.

Contents at a Glance

Contents

Introduction

This book was designed for anyone thinking of taking the Project Management Professional (PMP) exam sponsored by the Project Management Institute (PMI). This certification is growing in popularity and demand in all areas of business. PMI has experienced explosive growth in membership over the last few years, and more and more organizations are recognizing the importance of project management certification.

While this book is written primarily for those of you taking the PMP exam, you can also use this book to study for the Certified Associate in Project Management (CAPM) exam. The exams are similar in style and the information covered in this book will help you with either exam.

This book has been updated to reflect the latest edition of *A Guide to the Project Management Body of Knowledge, (PMBOK Guide) Third Edition*. It assumed you have knowledge of general project management practices, although not necessarily specific to *A Guide to the PMBOK*. It's written so that you can skim through areas you are already familiar with, picking up the specific *Guide to the PMBOK* terminology where needed to pass the exam. You'll find that the project management processes and techniques discussed in this book are defined in such a way that you'll recognize things you've always done and be able to identify them with *A Guide to the PMBOK* process names or methodologies.

PMI offers the most recognized certification in the field of project management, and this book deals exclusively with its procedures and methods. There are many methods of project management, each with its own terminology, tools, and procedures. If you're familiar with another organized project management methodology, don't assume you already know the *Guide to the PMBOK* processes. I strongly recommend that you learn all of the processes—their key inputs, tools and techniques, and outputs. Take the time to memorize the key terms found at the end of every chapter as well. Sometimes just understanding the definition of a term will help you answer a question. It might be that you've always done that particular thing or used the methodology described but called it by another name. Know the name of each process and its primary purpose.

What Is the PMP Certification?

PMI is the leader and the most widely recognized organization in terms of promoting project management best practices. PMI strives to maintain and endorse standards and ethics in this field and offers publications, training, seminars, chapters, special interest groups, and colleges to further the project management discipline.

PMI was founded in 1969 and first started offering the Project Management Professional (PMP) certification exam in 1984. PMI is accredited as an American National Standards Institute (ANSI) standards developer and also has the distinction of being the first organization to have its certification program attain International Organization for Standardization (ISO) 9001 recognition.

PMI boasts a worldwide membership of over 150,000, with members from 150 different countries. Local PMI chapters meet regularly and allow project managers to exchange information and learn about new tools and techniques of project management or new ways to use established techniques. I encourage you to join a local chapter and get to know other professionals in your field.

Why Become PMP Certified?

The following benefits are associated with becoming PMP certified:

- It demonstrates proof of professional achievement.
- It increases your marketability.
- It provides greater opportunity for advancement in your field.
- It raises customer confidence in you and in your company's services.

Demonstrates Proof of Professional Achievement

PMP certification is a rigorous process that documents your achievements in the field of project management. The exam tests your knowledge of the disciplined approaches, methodologies, and project management practices as described in *A Guide to the PMBOK*.

You are required to have several years of experience in project management before sitting for the exam, as well as 35 hours of formal project management education. Your certification assures employers and customers that you are well grounded in project management practices and disciplines. It shows that you've got the hands-on experience and a mastery of the processes and disciplines to manage projects effectively and motivate teams to produce successful results.

Increases Your Marketability

Many industries are realizing the importance of project management and its role in the organization. They are also seeing that simply proclaiming a head technician to be a "project manager" does not make it so. Project management, just like engineering, information technology, and a host of other trades, has its own specific qualifications and skills. Certification tells potential employers you've got the skills, experience, and knowledge to drive successful projects and ultimately improve the company's bottom line.

A certification will always make you stand out above the competition. If you're certified and you're competing against a project manager without certification, chances are you'll come out as the top pick. As a hiring manager, all other things being equal, I will usually opt for the candidate who has certification over the candidate who doesn't have it. Certification tells potential employers you have gone the extra mile. You've spent time studying techniques and methods as well as employing them in practice. It shows dedication to your own professional growth and enhancement and to adhering to and advancing professional standards.

Provides Opportunity for Advancement

PMP certification displays your willingness to pursue growth in your professional career and shows that you're not afraid of a little hard work to get what you want. Potential employers will interpret your pursuit of this certification as a high-energy, success-driven, can-do attitude on your part. They'll see that you're likely to display these same characteristics on the job, which will help make the company successful. Your certification displays a success-oriented, motivated attitude that will open up opportunities for future career advancements in your current field as well as in new areas you might want to explore.

Raises Customer Confidence

Just as the PMP certification assures employers that you've got the background and experience to handle project management, it assures customers that they have a competent, experienced project manager at the helm. Certification will help your organization sell customers on your ability to manage their projects. Customers, like potential employers, want the reassurance that those working for them have the knowledge and skills necessary to carry out the duties of the position and that professionalism and personal integrity are of utmost importance. Individuals who hold these ideals will translate their ethics and professionalism to their work. This enhances the trust customers will have in you, which in turn will give you the ability to influence them on important project issues.

How to Become PMP Certified

There are several requirements you need to fulfill in order to sit for the PMP exam. PMI has detailed the certification process quite extensively at its website. Go to www.pmi.org and click the Professional Development and Careers tab to reveal the Certifications selection and get the latest information on certification procedures and requirements.

As of the date this book was published, you are required to fill out an application to sit for the PMP exam. You can submit this application online at PMI's website. You also need to document 35 hours of formal project management education. This might include college classes, seminars, workshops, and training sessions. Be prepared to list the class titles, location, date, and content.

In addition to filling out the application and documenting your formal project management training, there is one additional set of criteria you'll need to meet to sit for the exam. These criteria fall into two categories. You need to meet the requirements for only one of these categories:

- Category 1 is for those who hold a baccalaureate degree. You'll need to provide proof, via transcripts, of your degree with your application. In addition, you'll need to complete verification forms—found at the PMI website—that show 4,500 hours of project management experience that spans a minimum of three years and no more than six years.

- Category 2 is for those who do not hold a baccalaureate degree but do hold a high school diploma or equivalent. You'll need to complete verification forms documenting 7,500 hours of project management experience that spans a minimum of five years and no more than eight years.

The exam fee at the time this book is being published is $405 for PMI members in good standing and $555 for non-PMI members. Testing is conducted at Thomson Prometric centers. You can find a center near you at the PMI website. You have six months from the time PMI receives and approves your completed application to take the exam. You'll need to bring a form of identification such as a driver's license with you to the Thomson Prometric center on the test day. You will not be allowed to take anything with you into the testing center. You will be given a calculator, pencils, and scrap paper. You will turn in all scrap paper, including the notes and squiggles you've jotted during the test, to the center upon completion of the exam.

The exam is scored immediately, so you will know if you've passed at the conclusion of the test. You're given four hours to complete the exam, which consists of 200 randomly generated questions. Only 175 of the 200 questions are scored. A passing score requires you answer 141 of the 175 questions correctly. 25 of the 200 questions are "pretest" questions that will appear randomly throughout the exam. These 25 questions are used by PMI to determine statistical information and to determine if they can or should be used on future exams. The questions on the exam cover the following process groups and areas:

- Initiating
- Planning
- Executing
- Monitoring and Controlling
- Closing
- Professional Responsibility

All unanswered questions are scored as wrong answers, so it benefits you to guess at an answer if you're stumped on a question.

After you've received your certification, you'll be required to earn 60 professional development units (PDUs) every three years to maintain certification. Approximately one hour of structured learning translates to one PDU. The PMI website details what activities constitute a PDU, how many PDUs each activity earns, and how to register your PDUs with PMI to maintain your certification. As an example, attendance at a local chapter meeting earns one PDU.

How to Become CAPM Certified

If you find you don't have quite enough experience or education to sit for the PMP exam, you should consider sitting for the Certified Associate in Project Management (CAPM) exam. The CAPM exam is structured like the PMP exam only the requirements are not as strict as they are for the PMP. CAPM candidates typically work in a supporting role with a project manager or as a subproject manager. Like the PMP, CAPM has two categories of requirements; each category requires 23 hours of project management education.

Category 1 is for those who hold a baccalaureate degree. You'll need to provide proof, via transcripts, of your degree with your application. In addition, you'll need to complete verification forms that show 1,500 hours of project management experience that spans a minimum of two years and no more than three years.

Category 2 is for those who do not hold a baccalaureate degree but do hold a high school diploma or equivalent. You'll need to complete verification forms documenting 2,500 hours of project management experience that spans a minimum of two years and no more than three years.

The CAPM exam fee at the time of this publication is $225 for PMI members in good standing and $300 for non-PMI members.

Included on the CD with this book is a sample CAPM exam. If you're sitting for the CAPM exam, I encourage you to answer all of the end-of-chapter questions and take the Bonus Exams in addition to the sample CAPM exam. You'll get a much broader sense of the types of questions and the topics you'll encounter on the actual exam by using all of the sample questions provided in this book and on the CD.

Who Should Buy This Book?

If you are serious about passing the PMP exam (or the CAPM exam for that matter), you should buy this book and use it to study for the exam. This book is unique in that it walks you through the project processes from beginning to end, just as projects are performed in practice. When you read this book, you will benefit by learning specific *Guide to the PMBOK* processes and techniques coupled with real-life scenarios that describe how project managers in different situations handle problems and the various issues all project managers are bound to encounter during their career. This Study Guide describes in detail the exam objective topics in each chapter and has attempted to cover all of the important project management concepts.

How to Use This Book and CD

We've included several testing features, both in the book and on the companion CD. Following this introduction is an Assessment Test that you can use to check your readiness for the actual exam. Take this test before you start reading the book. It will help you identify the areas you may need to brush up on. The answers to the Assessment Test appear after the last question of the test. Each answer includes an explanation and a note telling you in which chapter this material appears.

An Exam Essentials section appears at the end of every chapter to highlight the topics you'll most likely find on the exam and help you focus on the most important material covered in the chapter so that you'll have a solid understanding of those concepts. However, it isn't possible to predict what questions will be covered on your particular exam, so be sure to study everything in the chapter.

Like the exam itself, this Study Guide is organized in terms of process groups and the natural sequence of events a project goes through in its life cycle. By contrast, in other study guides, material is organized by knowledge area— Human Resource Management, Communications Management, and so on— and it can be confusing when studying for the exam to map the processes in each knowledge area to process groups.

Review Questions are also provided at the end of every chapter. You can use these to gauge your understanding of the subject matter before reading the chapter and to point out the areas in which you need to concentrate your study time. As you finish each chapter, answer the Review Questions and then check to see if your answers are right—the correct answers appear on the pages following the last question. You can go back to reread the section that deals with each question you got wrong to ensure that you answer the question correctly the next time you are tested on the material. If you can answer at least 80 percent of the Review Questions correctly, you can probably feel comfortable moving on to the next chapter. If you can't answer that many correctly, reread the chapter, or the section that seems to be giving you trouble, and try the questions again. You'll also find 200+ flashcard questions on the CD for on-the-go review. Download them right onto your Palm PocketPC device for quick and convenient reviewing.

> Don't rely on studying the Review Questions exclusively as your study method. The questions you'll see on the exam will be different than the questions presented in the book. There are 200 randomly generated questions on the PMP exam and 150 on the CAPM, so it isn't possible to cover every potential exam question in the Review Questions section of each chapter. Make sure you understand the concepts behind the material presented in each chapter and memorize all the formulas as well.

In addition to the Assessment Test and the Review Questions, you'll find Bonus Exams on the CD. Take these practice exams just as if you were actually taking the exam (i.e., without any reference material). When you have finished the first exam, move on to the next exam to solidify your test-taking skills. If you get more than 85 percent of the answers correct, you're ready to take the real exam.

> If you purchased the Standard Edition of this book, there are a total of two bonus PMP exams and two additional CAPM exams. If you purchased the Deluxe Edition, there are a total of eight bonus PMP exams and two additional CAPM exams.

Finally, you will notice various Real World Scenario sidebars throughout each chapter. These are designed to give you insight into how the various processes and topic areas apply to real-world situations.

Additionally, if you are going to travel but still need to study for the PMP exam and you have a laptop with a CD drive, you can take this entire book with you just by taking the CD. This book is in PDF (Adobe Acrobat) format, so it can be easily read on any computer.

For those of you who purchased the Deluxe Edition, you'll find a series of scenarios and exercises that map to each chapter. These workbook exercises are designed to help you put the theories you've learned in each chapter into practice.

The Exam Objectives

Behind every certification exam, you can be sure to find exam objectives—the broad topics in which the exam developers want to ensure your competency. The official PMP exam objectives are listed in this section.

 Exam objectives are subject to change at any time without prior notice and at PMI's sole discretion. Please visit the Certification page of PMI's website, www.pmi.org, for the most current listing of exam objectives.

Domain 1.0: Initiating the Project

The objectives for the Initiating the Project domain are as follows:

1. Conduct Project Selection Methods
2. Define Scope
3. Document Project Risks, Assumptions, and Constraints
4. Identify and Perform Stakeholder Analysis
5. Develop Project Charter
6. Obtain Project Charter Approval

Domain 2.0: Planning the Project

The objectives of the Planning the Project domain are as follows:

1. Define and Record Requirements, Constraints, and Assumptions
2. Identify Project Team and Define Roles and Responsibilities
3. Create the WBS
4. Develop Change Management Plan
5. Identify Risks and Define Risk Strategies
6. Obtain Plan Approval
7. Conduct Kick-off Meeting

Domain 3.0: Executing the Project

The objectives of the Executing the Project domain are as follows:

1. Execute Tasks Defined in Project Plan
2. Ensure Common Understanding and Set Expectations
3. Implement the Procurement of Project Resources
4. Manage Resource Allocation
5. Implement Quality Management Plan

6. Implement Approved Changes

7. Implement Approved Actions and Workarounds

8. Improve Team Performance

Domain 4.0: Monitoring and Controlling the Project

The objectives of the Monitoring and Controlling the Project domain are as follows:

1. Measure Project Performance.

2. Verify and Manage Changes to the Project

3. Ensure Project Deliverables Conform to Quality Standards

4. Monitor all Risks

Domain 5.0: Closing the Project

The objectives of the Closing the Project domain are as follows:

1. Obtain Final Acceptance for the Project

2. Obtain Financial, Legal, and Administrative Closure

3. Release Project Resources

4. Identify, Document, and Communicate Lessons Learned

5. Create and Distribute Final Project Report

6. Archive and Retain Project Records

7. Measure Customer Satisfaction

Domain 6.0: Professional and Social Responsibility

The objectives for the Professional and Social Responsibility domain are as follows:

1. Ensure Individual Integrity.

2. Contribute to the Project Management Knowledge Base.

3. Enhance Professional Competence

4. Promote Interaction Among Stakeholders

Tips for Taking the PMP Exam

Here are some general tips for taking your exam successfully:

- Get to the exam center early so that you can relax and review your study materials.

- Read the exam questions very carefully. Make sure you know exactly what each question is asking and don't be tempted to answer too quickly.

- Unanswered questions score as wrong answers. It's better to guess than to leave a question unanswered.

- If you're not sure of an answer, use a process of elimination to identify the obvious incorrect answers first. Narrow the remaining choices down by referring back to the question, looking for key words that might tip you off to the correct answer.

- You'll be given scratch paper to take with you to the exam station. As soon as you get to your place, write down all the formulas and any other memory aids you used while studying before starting the exam. That way, you can relax a little because you won't have to remember the formulas when you get to those questions on the exam—you can simply look at your scratch paper.

- Visit the PMI website at `www.pmi.org` for the latest information regarding certification and to find a testing site near you.

Assessment Test

1. What is one of the most important skills a project manager can have?

    A. Negotiation skills

    B. Influencing skills

    C. Communication skills

    D. Problem-solving skills

2. Project managers have the highest level of authority and the most power in which type of organizational structure?

    A. Projectized

    B. Strong matrix

    C. Functional

    D. Balanced matrix

3. The Project Management Knowledge Areas _____.

    A. Include Initiation, Planning, Executing, Monitoring and Controlling, and Closing.

    B. Consist of nine different areas that bring together processes that have things in common.

    C. Consist of five different processes that bring together phases of projects that have things in common.

    D. Include Planning, Executing, and Monitoring and Controlling processes because these three processes are commonly interlinked.

4. The project sponsor has approached you with a dilemma. The CEO announced at the annual stockholders meeting that the project you're managing will be completed by the end of this year. The problem is that this is six months prior to the scheduled completion date. It's too late to go back and correct her mistake, and stockholders are expecting implementation by the announced date. You must speed up the delivery date of this project. Your primary constraint before this occurred was the budget. What actions can you take to help speed up the project?

    A. Hire more resources to get the work completed faster.

    B. Ask for more money so that you can contract out one of the phases you had planned to do with in-house resources.

    C. Utilize negotiation and influencing skills to convince the project sponsor to speak with the CEO and make a correction to her announcement.

    D. Examine the project plan to see if there are any phases that can be fast tracked, and then revise the project plan to reflect the compression of the schedule.

5. Which of the following describes the Executing process group?

   A. Project plans are put into action.

   B. Project performance measurements are taken and analyzed.

   C. Project plans are developed.

   D. Project plans are published.

6. You have been assigned to a project that will allow job seekers to fill out applications and submit them via the company website. You report to the VP of human resources. You are also responsible for screening applications for the information technology division and setting up interviews. The project coordinator has asked for the latest version of your changes to the online application page for his review. Which organizational structure do you work in?

   A. Functional organization

   B. Weak matrix organization

   C. Projectized organization

   D. Balanced matrix organization

7. According to *A Guide to the PMBOK*, the project manager is identified and assigned during which process?

   A. Prior to beginning the Develop Project Charter process

   B. At the conclusion of the Develop Project Charter process

   C. Prior to beginning the Planning processes

   D. Prior to beginning the Preliminary Scope Statement process

8. You are refining the product description for your company's new line of ski boots. Which of the following statements is true?

   A. You are in the Initiating processes of your project and know that the product description will contain more detail in this stage and that a decreasing amount of detail will be added to it as the project progresses.

   B. You are in the Planning processes of your project and know that the product description will contain less detail in this stage and greater detail as the project progresses.

   C. You are in the Planning processes of your project and know that the product description should contain the most detail possible at this stage, because this is critical information for the Planning process.

   D. You are in the Initiating process of your project and know that the product description will contain less detail in this stage and greater detail as the project progresses.

9. The business needs, strategic plan, and product scope description all describe elements of which of the following:

   A. Organizational process assets

   B. Tools and techniques of the Initiating processes

   C. The project statement of work

   D. The project charter

10. You are a project manager for Waterways Houseboats, Inc. You've been asked to perform a cost-benefit analysis for two proposed projects. Project A costs $2.4 million, with potential benefits of $12 million and future operating costs of $3 million. Project B costs $2.8 million, with potential benefits of $14 million and future operating costs of $2 million. Which project should you recommend?

    A. Project A, because the cost to implement is cheaper than Project B.

    B. Project A, because the potential benefits plus the future operating costs are less in value than the same calculation for Project B.

    C. Project B, because the potential benefits minus the implementation and future operating costs are greater in value than the same calculation for Project A.

    D. Project B, because the potential benefits minus the costs to implement are greater in value than the same calculation for Project A.

11. What is the purpose of the project charter?

    A. To recognize and acknowledge the project sponsor

    B. To recognize and acknowledge the existence of the project and commit organizational resources to the project

    C. To acknowledge the existence of the project team, project manager, and project sponsor

    D. To describe the selection methods used to choose this project over its competitors

12. Which of the following are tools and techniques of the Preliminary Scope Statement process?

    A. Project management methodology, project management information system, expert judgment

    B. Project selection methods and expert judgment

    C. Constraints, assumptions, and expert judgment

    D. Project charter, project management information system, project selection methods

13. You are a project manager for Swirling Seas Cruises food division. You're considering two different projects regarding food services on the cruise lines. The initial cost of Project Fish'n for Chips will be $800,000, with expected cash inflows of $300,000 per quarter. Project Picnic's payback period is six months. Which project should you recommend?

    A. Project Fish'n for Chips, because its payback period is two months shorter than Project Picnic's.

    B. Project Fish'n for Chips, because the costs on Project Picnic are unknown.

    C. Project Picnic, because Project Fish'n for Chips' payback period is four months longer than Project Picnic's.

    D. Project Picnic, because Project Fish'n for Chips' payback period is two months longer than Project Picnic's.

14. What are decision models?

    A. Project selection criteria

    B. Project selection methods

    C. Project selection committees

    D. Project resource and budget selection methods

15. You've been assigned as a project manager on a research and development project for a new dental procedure. You're working in the Scope Planning process. What is the purpose of the project scope management plan?

   A. The project scope management plan describes and documents a scope baseline to help make future project decisions.

   B. The project scope management plan decomposes project deliverables into smaller units of work.

   C. The project scope management plan describes how project scope will be developed and how changes will be managed.

   D. The project scope management plan describes how cost and time estimates will be developed for project scope changes.

16. You are the project manager for Lucky Stars Candies. You've identified the deliverables and requirements and documented them where?

   A. In the project scope statement, which will be used as an input to the Create WBS process.

   B. In the project scope management document, which is used as an input to the Scope Definition process.

   C. In the product requirements document, which is an output of the Scope Definition process process.

   D. In the project specifications document, which is an output of the Scope Planning process.

17. Each of the following statements describes an element of the Develop Project Management Plan process except for which one?

   A. Project management methodology

   B. Project specifications

   C. Configuration management system

   D. Expert judgment

18. What are the Scope Definition process tools and techniques?

   A. Cost benefit analysis, templates, and expert judgment

   B. Product analysis, cost benefit analysis, alternatives identification, and expert judgment

   C. Product analysis, alternatives identification, expert judgment, stakeholder analysis

   D. Alternatives identification, stakeholder analysis, and expert judgment

19. Which of the following statements is true regarding constraints and assumptions?

   A. Constraints restrict the actions of the project team, and assumptions are considered true for planning purposes.

   B. Constraints are considered true for planning purposes, and assumptions limit the options of the project team.

   C. Constraints consider vendor availability and resource availability to be true for planning purposes. Assumptions limit the project team to work within predefined budgets or timelines.

   D. Constraints and assumptions are inputs to the Initiation process. They should be documented, because they will be used throughout the project Planning process.

20. You've just completed the WBS. Which of the following statements is true?

    A. The WBS breaks the project deliverables down to a level where alternatives identification can be used to determine how level two assignments should be made.

    B. The WBS breaks the project deliverables down to a level where project constraints and assumptions can be easily identified.

    C. The WBS breaks the project deliverables down to the work package level, where product analysis can be documented.

    D. The WBS breaks the project deliverables down to the work package level, where cost and time estimates can be easily determined.

21. You are the project manger for Xylophone Phonics. It produces children's software programs that teach basic reading and math skills. You are performing the Quality Planning process and are identifying nonproductive activities. Part of this involves capturing information such as process boundaries, process configurations, and process metrics. Which of the following does this describe?

    A. The process improvement plan

    B. The quality management plan

    C. The quality metrics

    D. The cost of quality

22. Failure costs are also known as which of the following?

    A. Internal costs

    B. Cost of poor quality

    C. Cost of keeping defects out of the hands of customers

    D. Prevention costs

23. All of the following statements are true regarding Ishikawa diagrams in the Risk Identification process except which one?

    A. Ishikawa diagrams are also called cause-and-effect diagrams.

    B. Ishikawa diagrams are also called fishbone diagrams.

    C. Ishikawa diagrams are a tool and technique of this process.

    D. Ishikawa diagrams show the steps needed to identify the risk.

24. All of the following statements are true regarding risk events except which one? Choose the least correct answer.

    A. Project risks are uncertain events.

    B. If risks occur, they can have a positive or negative effect on project objectives.

    C. Unknown risks are threats to the project objectives, and nothing can be done to plan for them.

    D. Risks that have more perceived rewards to the organization than the consequences of the risk should be accepted.

25. You are a project manager working on a software development project. You've developed the risk management plan, identified risks, and determined risk responses for the risks. One of the risks you identified occurs, and you implement the response for that risk. Then, another risk occurs as a result of the response you implemented. What type of risk is this called?

A. Trigger risk

B. Residual risk

C. Secondary risk

D. Mitigated risk

26. Your team is developing the risk management plan. Which tool and technique of this process is used to develop risk cost elements and schedule activities that will be included in the project budget and schedule?

A. Planning meetings and analysis

B. Strategies for both threats and opportunities

C. Information gathering techniques

D. Risk data quality assessment

27. Monte Carlo analysis can help predict the impact of risks on project deliverables. This is an element of one of the tools and techniques of which of the following processes?

A. Risk Response Planning

B. Quantitative Risk Analysis

C. Risk Identification

D. Qualitative Risk Analysis

28. All of the following statements are true regarding risks except for which one? Choose the least correct answer.

A. Risks might be threats to the objectives of the project.

B. Risks are certain events that may be threats or opportunities to the objectives of the project.

C. Risks might be opportunities to the objectives of the project.

D. Risks have causes and consequences.

29. Which of the following contracts should you use for projects that have a degree of uncertainty and require a large investment early in the project life cycle?

A. Fixed price

B. Cost reimbursable

C. Lump sum

D. T&M

30. All of the following statements are true regarding the ADM method except which one?

   A. The ADM method is a tool and technique of Activity Sequencing.

   B. The ADM method uses one time estimate to determine durations.

   C. The ADA method is also called AOA.

   D. The ADA method is rarely used today.

31. You are the project manger for Xylophone Phonics. This company produces children's software programs that teach basic reading and math skills. You are ready to assign project roles, responsibilities, and reporting relationships. Which project Planning process are you working on?

   A. Resource Planning

   B. Human Resource Planning

   C. Acquire Staff

   D. Human Resource Acquisition

32. Which of the following compression techniques increases risk?

   A. Crashing

   B. Resource leveling

   C. Fast tracking

   D. Lead and lag

33. You are the project manager for Heartthrobs by the Numbers Dating Services. You're working on an updated Internet site that will display pictures as well as short bios of prospective heartbreakers. You have your activity list and resource requirements in hand and are planning to use parametric estimates and reserve analysis to determine activity durations. Which of the following statements is true?

   A. You are using inputs of the Activity Duration Estimating process.

   B. You are using tools and techniques of the Cost Estimating process.

   C. You are using tools and techniques of the Activity Duration Estimating process.

   D. You are using inputs of the Cost Estimating process.

34. You are working on a project that will upgrade the phone system in your customer service center. You have used bottom-up estimating techniques to assign costs to the project activities and have determined the cost baseline. Which of the following statements is true?

   A. You have completed the Cost Estimating process and now need to complete the Cost Budgeting process to determine the project's baseline.

   B. You have completed the Cost Estimating process and established a project baseline to measure future project performance against.

   C. You have completed the Cost Budgeting process and now need to complete the Schedule Development process to establish a project baseline to measure future project performance against.

   D. You have completed the Cost Budgeting process, and the cost baseline will be used to measure future project performance.

35. You are the project manger for Xylophone Phonics. It produces children's software programs that teach basic reading and math skills. You're performing cost estimates for your project and don't have a lot of details yet. Which of the following techniques should you use?

A. Analogous estimating techniques, because this is a form of expert judgment that uses historical information from similar projects

B. Bottom-up estimating techniques, because this is a form of expert judgment that uses historical information from similar projects

C. Monte Carlo analysis, because this is a modeling technique that uses simulation to determine estimates

D. Parametric modeling, because this is a form of simulation used to determine estimates

36. You are a project manager who has recently held a project team kickoff meeting where all the team members were formally introduced to each other. Some of the team members know each other from other projects and have been working with you for the past three weeks during the Planning processes. Which of the following statements is true?

A. Team building begins once all the members of the team are identified and introduced to each other. This team is in the storming stage of team development.

B. Team building begins in the Planning process group. This team is in the storming stage of team development.

C. Team building begins once all the members of the team are identified and introduced to each other. This team is in the forming stage of team development.

D. Team building begins in the Planning process group. This team is in the forming stage of team development.

37. Project managers spend what percentage of their time communicating?

A. 90

B. 85

C. 75

D. 50

38. People are motivated by the need for achievement, power, or affiliation according to which theory?

A. Expectancy Theory

B. Achievement Theory

C. Contingency Theory

D. Theory X

39. During your project meeting, a problem was discussed and a resolution to the problem was reached. During the meeting, the participants started wondering why they thought the problem was such a big issue. Sometime after the meeting, you received an e-mail from one of the meeting participants saying they've changed their mind about the solution reached in the meeting and need to resurface the problem. The solution reached during the initial project meeting is a result of which of the following conflict resolution techniques?

    A. Confrontation

    B. Forcing

    C. Smoothing

    D. Storming

40. You are the project manager for Heartthrobs by the Numbers Dating Services. You're working on an updated Internet site that will display pictures as well as short bios of prospective heart-breakers. You've just completed your project staff assignments and published the project team directory. Which process are you in?

    A. Human Resource Planning

    B. Direct and Manage Project Execution

    C. Develop Project Team

    D. Acquire Project Team

41. You need to convey some very complex, detailed information to the project stakeholders. What is the best method for communicating this kind of information?

    A. Verbal

    B. Vertical

    C. Horizontal

    D. Written

42. This process applies evaluation criteria to the bids and proposals received from potential vendors.

    A. Request Seller Responses

    B. Contract Administration

    C. Select Sellers

    D. Quality Assurance

43. The project manager has the greatest influence over quality during which process?

    A. Quality Planning

    B. Quality Assurance

    C. Quality Control

    D. Quality Change Control

44. There are likely to be team loyalty issues in a matrixed environment. All of the following are true regarding this situation as it pertains to the Manage Project Team process except for which one?

A. Two of the tools and techniques you might use to manage these relationships effectively are communications methods and issue logs.

B. In this type of structure, team members report to both a functional manager and a project manager.

C. The project manager is generally responsible for managing this relationship.

D. The effective management of these reporting relationships is often a critical success factor for the project.

45. The inputs of the Performance Reporting process include all of the following except for which one?

A. Work performance information

B. Performance measurements

C. Forecasted completion

D. Performance reviews

46. As a result of a face-to-face meeting you recently had to discuss the items in your issues log, you have resolved issues and come away with an approved corrective action and an update to the project management plan. Which process does this describe?

A. Manage Stakeholders

B. Performance Reporting

C. Information Distribution

D. Manage Project Team

47. Which performance measurement tells you how much more of the budget is required to finish the project?

A. ETC

B. EV

C. AC

D. EAC

48. All of the following statements are true regarding configuration management except which one?

A. Configuration management requires acceptance decisions for all change requests to be made through the CCB.

B. Change control systems are a subset of the configuration management system.

C. Configuration management describes the physical characteristics of the product of the project.

D. Configuration management controls changes to the product of the project.

49. Which performance measurement tells you what the projected total cost of the project will be at completion?

  A. ETC

  B. CPI

  C. SPI

  D. EAC

50. You know that PV = 470, AC = 430, EV = 480, EAC = 500, and BAC = 525. What is VAC?

  A. 70

  B. 20

  C. 25

  D. 30

51. All of the following are outputs of the Integrated Change Control process except for which one?

  A. Approved corrective actions

  B. Validated defect repair

  C. Requested changes

  D. Project scope statement updates

52. Every status meeting should have time allotted for Risk Monitoring and Control. Which of the following sentences is not true?

  A. Risk identification and monitoring should occur throughout the life of the project.

  B. Risk audits should occur throughout the life of the project and are specifically interested in measuring the team's performance in the Risk Identification and Risk Monitoring and Control processes.

  C. Risks should be monitored for their status and to determine if the impacts to the objectives have changed.

  D. Technical performance measurement variances may indicate that a risk is looming and should be reviewed at status meetings.

53. These diagrams rank-order factors for corrective action by frequency of occurrence. They are also a type of histogram.

  A. Control charts

  B. Process flowcharts

  C. Scatter diagrams

  D. Pareto charts

54. The primary function of the Closing processes is to perform which of the following?

   A. Formalize lessons learned and distribute this information to project participants.

   B. Perform audits to verify the project results against the project requirements.

   C. Formalize project completion and disseminate this information to project participants.

   D. Perform post-implementation audits to document project successes and failures.

55. You are the project manager for a construction company that is building a new city and county office building in your city. You recently looked over the construction site to determine if the work to date was conforming to the requirements and quality standards. Which tool and technique of the Perform Quality Control process are you using?

   A. Defect repair review

   B. Inspection

   C. Sampling

   D. Quality audit

56. Which of the following statements is true regarding Close Project?

   A. Close Project occurs at the end of a project phase and at the end of the project.

   B. Close Project occurs at the end of the project phase only.

   C. Close Project occurs at the end of the project only.

   D. Close Project is performed after Contract Closure.

57. What type of organization experiences the least amount of stress during project closeout?

   A. Projectized

   B. Functional

   C. Weak matrix

   D. Strong matrix

58. All of the following statements are true of the project Closing processes except for which one?

   A. Probability for success is greatest in the project Closing processes.

   B. The project manager's influence is greatest in the project Closing processes.

   C. The stakeholders' influence is least in the project Closing processes.

   D. Risk is greatest in the project Closing processes.

59. You are the project manager for a construction company that is building a new city and county office building in your city. Your CCB recently approved a scope change. You know that scope change might come about as a result of all of the following except which one?

   A. Schedule revisions

   B. Product scope change

   C. Changes to the agreed-upon WBS

   D. Changes to the project requirements

60. Inspections are also called each of the following except for which one?

   A. Reviews

   B. Assessment

   C. Walkthroughs

   D. Audits

61. You are a project manager working in a foreign country. You observe that some of your project team members are having a difficult time adjusting to the new culture. You provided them with training on cultural differences and the customs of this country before arriving, but they still seem uncomfortable and disoriented. Which of the following statements is true?

   A. This is the result of working with teams of people from two different countries.

   B. This condition is known as culture shock.

   C. This is the result of jet lag and travel fatigue.

   D. This condition is known as global culturalism.

62. Your project involves the research and development of a new food additive. You're ready to release the product to your customer when you discover that a minor reaction might occur in people with certain conditions. The reactions to date have been very minor, and no known long-lasting side effects have been noted. As project manager, what should you do?

   A. Do nothing because the reactions are so minor that very few people will be affected.

   B. Inform the customer that you've discovered this condition and tell them you'll research it further to determine its impacts.

   C. Inform your customer that there is no problem with the additive except for an extremely small percentage of the population and release the product to them.

   D. Tell the customer you'll correct the reaction problems in the next batch, but you'll release the first batch of product to them now to begin using.

63. You have just prepared an RFP for release. Your project involves a substantial amount of contract work detailed in the RFP. Your favorite vendor drops by and offers to give you and your spouse the use of their company condo for your upcoming vacation. It's located in a beautiful resort community that happens to be one of your favorite places to go for a getaway. What is the most appropriate response?

   A. Thank the vendor but decline the offer because you know this could be considered a conflict of interest.

   B. Thank the vendor and accept. This vendor is always offering you incentives like this, so this offer does not likely have anything to do with the recent RFP release.

   C. Thank the vendor, accept the offer, and immediately tell your project sponsor so they're aware of what you're doing.

   D. Thank the vendor but decline the offer because you've already made another arrangement for this vacation. Ask them if you can take a rain check and arrange another time to use the condo.

64. As a PMP, one of your responsibilities is to ensure integrity on the project. When your personal interests are put above the interests of the project or when you use your influence to cause others to make decisions in your favor without regard for the project outcome, this is considered which of the following?

  A. Conflict of interest

  B. Using professional knowledge inappropriately

  C. Culturally unacceptable

  D. Personal conflict issue

65. Name the ethical code you'll be required to adhere to as a PMP.

  A. *Project Management Policy and Ethics Guide*

  B. *Project Management Professional Standards and Ethics*

  C. *Project Management Code of Professional Ethics*

  D. *Project Management Professional Code of Professional Conduct*

Answers to Assessment Test

1. C. Negotiation, influencing, and problem-solving skills are all important for a project manager to possess. However, good communication skills are the most important skills a project manager can have. For more information, please see Chapter 1.

2. A. Project managers have the highest level of power and authority in a projectized organization. They also have high levels of power and authority in a strong matrix. However, a matrix organization is a blend of functional and projectized organizations. Therefore, the project manager does not have quite the same level of authority as they would in a projectized organization. For more information, please see Chapter 1.

3. B. The project management knowledge areas bring processes together that have commonalities. For example, the Project Quality Management Knowledge Area includes the Quality Planning, Perform Quality Assurance, and Perform Quality Control processes. For more information, please see Chapter 1.

4. D. Fast tracking is the best answer in this scenario. Budget was the original constraint on this project, so it's highly unlikely the project manager would get more resources to assist with the project. The next best thing is to compress phases to shorten the project duration. For more information, please see Chapter 1 and Chapter 7.

5. A. The Executing process group takes published project plans and turns them into actions to accomplish the goals of the project. For more information, please see Chapter 1.

6. B. Functional managers who have lots of authority and power working with project coordinators who have minimal authority and power characterizes a weak matrix organization. Project managers in weak matrix organizations are sometimes called project coordinators, project leaders, or project expeditors. For more information, please see Chapter 1.

7. C. According to *A Guide to the PMBOK*, the project manager should be identified prior to beginning the Planning processes and is named and authorized in the project charter. For more information, please see Chapter 2.

8. D. Product descriptions are used during the Initiating process group and contain less detail now and more detail as the project progresses. For more information, please see Chapter 2.

9. C. These elements are part of the project statement of work used as an input to both of the Initiating processes. For more information, please see Chapter 2.

10. C. Project B's cost-benefit analysis is a $9.2 million benefit to the company, compared to $6.6 million for Project A. Cost-benefit analysis takes into consideration the initial costs to implement and future operating costs. For more information, please see Chapter 2.

11. B. The purpose of a project charter is to recognize and acknowledge the existence of a project and commit resources to the project. The charter names the project manager and project sponsor, but that's not its primary purpose. For more information, please see Chapter 2.

12. A.   Preliminary Scope Statement has three tools and techniques: project management methodology, project management information system expert judgment. For more information, please see Chapter 2.

13. D.   The payback period for Project Fish'n for Chips is eight months. This project will receive $300,000 every three months, or $100,000 per month. The $800,000 will be paid back in eight months. For more information, please see Chapter 2.

14. B.   Decision models are project selection methods used as tools and techniques in the Develop Project Charter process. Decision models include benefit measurement methods and mathematical models. For more information, please see Chapter 2.

15. C.   The scope management plan outlines how project scope will be managed and how changes will be incorporated into the project. For more information, please see Chapter 3.

16. A.   The project scope statement contains an exhaustive list of the project deliverables, their requirements, and the measurable criteria used to determine project completion. The scope statement is an output of the Scope Definition process and is used as an input to the Create WBS process. For more information, please see Chapter 3.

17. B.   The tools and techniques of the Develop Project Management Plan include: project management methodology, project management information system of which the configuration management system is a component, and expert judgment. Project specifications are an element of the project scope statement. For more information, please see Chapter 3.

18. C.   The tools and techniques of the Scope Definition process include Product analysis, alternatives identification, expert judgment, stakeholder analysis. For more information, please see Chapter 3.

19. A.   Constraints limit the options of the project team by restricting action or dictating action. Scope, time, and cost are the three most common constraints and each of these has an affect on quality. Assumptions are presumed to be true for planning purposes. Always validate your assumptions. For more information, please see Chapter 3.

20. D.   The work package level is the lowest level in the work breakdown structure. Schedule and cost estimates are easily determined at this level. For more information, please see Chapter 4.

21. A.   This describes the process improvement plan, which is a subsidiary of the project management plan and an output of the Quality Planning process. For more information, please see Chapter 4.

22. B.   Failure costs are associated with the cost of quality and are also known as cost of poor quality. For more information, please see Chapter 4.

23. D.   Cause-and-effect diagrams—also called Ishikawa or fishbone diagrams—show the relationship between the effects of problems and their causes. Cause-and-effect diagrams were developed by Kaoru Ishikawa. For more information, please see Chapter 5.

24. C.   Unknown risks might be threats or opportunities to the project, and the project manager should set aside contingency reserves to deal with them. For more information, please see Chapter 5.

25. C. Secondary risks occur as a result of the implementation of a response to another risk. For more information, please see Chapter 5.

26. A. Planning meetings and analysis is the only tool and technique of the Risk Management Planning Process. For more information, please see Chapter 5.

27. B. Monte Carlo analysis is a modeling and simulation technique which is a tool and technique of the Quantitative Risk Analysis process. For more information, please see Chapter 5.

28. B. Risks are uncertain events that may be threats or opportunities to the objectives of the project. For more information, please see Chapter 5.

29. B. Cost reimbursable contracts are used when the degree of uncertainty is high and when the project requires a large investment prior to completion of the project. For more information, please see Chapter 6.

30. B. The arrow diagramming method (ADM)—also called activity on arrow (AOA)—uses more than one time estimate to determine project duration. For more information, please see Chapter 6.

31. B. The Human Resource Planning process identifies project resources, documents roles and responsibilities of project team members, and documents reporting relationships. For more information, please see Chapter 6.

32. C. Fast tracking is a compression technique that increases risk and potentially causes rework. Fast tracking is starting two activities previously scheduled to start one after the other at the same time. For more information, please see Chapter 7.

33. C. Parametric estimates and reserve analysis are two of the tools and techniques of the Activity Duration Estimating process. The other tools are expert judgment and analogous estimating. For more information, please see Chapter 7.

34. D. The Cost Budgeting process establishes the cost baseline, which is used to measure and track the project throughout the remaining process groups. For more information, please see Chapter 7.

35. A. Analogous estimating—also called top-down estimating—is a form of expert judgment. Analogous estimating can be used to estimate cost or time and considers historical information from previous, similar projects. For more information, please see Chapter 7.

36. D. Team building begins in the Planning processes of your project. In this question, the team members have just been formally introduced to each other, so they are still in the forming stage of Develop Project Team. For more information, please see Chapter 8.

37. A. Project managers spend about 90 percent of their time communicating through status meetings, team meetings, e-mail, verbal communications, and so on. For more information, please see Chapter 8.

38. B. Achievement Theory conjectures that people are motivated by the need for achievement, power, or affiliation. For more information, please see Chapter 8.

39. C. The smoothing technique does not usually result in a permanent solution. The problem is downplayed to make it seem less important than it is, which makes the problem tend to resurface later. For more information, please see Chapter 8.

40. D. The Acquire Project Team outputs include the project staff assignments, and the project team directory is part of this output. For more information, please see Chapter 8.

41. D. Information that is complex and detailed is best conveyed in writing. A verbal follow-up would be good to answer questions and clarify information. Vertical and horizontal are ways of communicating within the organization. For more information, please see Chapter 8.

42. C. The Select Sellers process is where bids and proposals are received from potential vendors and evaluation criteria are applied to them to make a selection. For more information, please see Chapter 9.

43. B. Quality Assurance is the process where project managers have the greatest amount of influence over quality. For more information, please see Chapter 9.

44. A. Communications methods are a tool and technique of the Manage Stakeholders process. The tools and techniques of the Manage Project Team process are observation and conversation, project performance appraisals, conflict management, and issue log. For more information, please see Chapter 9.

45. D. Performance reviews are not an input of the Performance Reporting process. The remaining inputs of this process are quality control measurements, project management plan, approved change requests, and deliverables. For more information, please see Chapter 9.

46. A. The two clues in this question are the face-to-face meetings (a communication method) and the resolved issues, which is an output of the Manage Stakeholders process. For more information, please see Chapter 9.

47. A. Estimate to completion (ETC) calculates how much more of the budget is needed to complete the project if everything continues at the current level of performance. For more information, please see Chapter 10.

48. A. Change control systems are a subset of the configuration management system. Change requests should be approved by the CCB, but in the case of an emergency, change requests may be approved by the project manager in accordance with the process outlined in the configuration management system. The project team may have discretion to approve changes within certain parameters without CCB approval. Configuration management also describes the physical characteristics of the product, it controls changes to the product, and tracks the changes requests and their status. For more information, please see Chapter 10.

49. D. Estimate at completion (EAC) estimates the total cost of the project at completion based on the performance of the project to date. For more information, please see Chapter 10.

50. C. VAC is calculated this way: VAC = BAC − EAC. Therefore, 525 − 500 = 25. For more information, please see Chapter 10.

51. C. Approved change requests are an output of this process, not requested change requests. The other tools and techniques of this process are rejected change requests, project management plan updates, approved preventive actions, approved defect repair, and deliverables. For more information, please see Chapter 10.

52. B.   Risk audits should be performed throughout the life of the project and are specifically interested in looking at the implementation and effectiveness of risk strategies. For more information, please see Chapter 10.

53. D.   Pareto charts rank-order important factors for corrective action by frequency of occurrence. For more information, please see Chapter 11.

54. C.   The primary function of the Closing processes is to formalize project completion and disseminate this information to the project participants. For more information, please see Chapter 11.

55. B.   Inspection involves physically looking at, measuring, or testing results to determine if they conform to your quality standards. For more information, please see Chapter 11.

56. A.   Close Project occurs at the end of the project phase and at the end of the project itself. Close Project is performed after Contract Closure. It is the last process performed on your project. For more information, please see Chapter 11.

57. C.   Weak matrix organizational structures tend to experience the least amount of stress during the project closeout processes. For more information, please see Chapter 11.

58. D.   Risk is lowest during the Closing processes because you've completed the work of the project at this point. For more information, please see Chapter 11.

59. A.   Scope changes will cause schedule revisions, but schedule revisions do not change the project scope. Project requirements are part of the project scope statement, and therefore D is one of the correct responses. For more information, please see Chapter 11.

60. B.   Inspections are also called reviews, peer reviews, walkthroughs, and audits. For more information, please see Chapter 11.

61. B.   When people work in unfamiliar environments, culture shock can occur. Training and researching information about the country you'll be working in can help counteract this. For more information, please see Chapter 12.

62. B.   Honesty and truthful reporting are required of PMPs. In this situation, you would inform the customer of everything you know regarding the problem and work to find alternative solutions. For more information, please see Chapter 12.

63. A.   The best response is to decline the offer. This is a conflict of interest, and accepting the offer puts your own integrity and the contract award process in jeopardy. For more information, please see Chapter 12.

64. A.   A conflict of interest is any situation that compromises the outcome of the project or ignores the impact to the project to benefit yourself or others. For more information, please see Chapter 12.

65. D.   The *Project Management Professional Code of Professional Conduct* is published by PMI, and all PMPs are expected to adhere to its standards. For more information, please see Chapter 12.

What Is a Project?

Congratulations on your decision to study for and take the Project Management Institute (PMI) Project Management Professional (PMP) certification exam. This book was written with you in mind. The focus and content of this book revolve heavily around the information contained in *A Guide to the Project Management Body of Knowledge (PMBOK, Guide) Third Edition,* published by PMI. I will refer to this guide throughout this book and elaborate on those areas that appear on the test. Keep in mind that the test covers all the project management processes, so don't skip anything in your study time.

When possible, I'll pass on hints and study tips that I collected while studying for the exam myself. Your first tip is to familiarize yourself with the terminology used in *A Guide to the PMBOK.* Volunteers from differing industries worked together to come up with the standards and terms used in the guide. These folks have worked hard to develop and define standard project management terms, and these terms are used interchangeably among industries. For example, *resource planning* means the same thing to someone working in construction, information technology, or telecommunications. You'll find *A Guide to the PMBOK* terms explained throughout this book. Even if you are an experienced project manager, you might find you use specific terms for processes or actions you regularly perform but *A Guide to the PMBOK* calls them by another name. So, step one is to get familiar with the terminology.

This chapter lays the foundation for building and managing your project. We'll address project and project management definitions as well as organizational structures. Good luck!

Is It a Project?

Consider the following scenario: The VP of marketing approaches you with a fabulous idea—"fabulous" because he's the big boss and because he thought it up. He wants to set up kiosks in local grocery stores as mini offices. These offices will offer customers the ability to sign up for new wireless phone services, make their wireless phone bill payments, and purchase equipment and accessories. He believes that the exposure in grocery stores will increase awareness of the company's offerings. After all, everyone has to eat, right? He told you that the board of directors has already cleared the project and he'll dedicate as many resources to this as he can. He wants the new kiosks in place in 12 stores by the end of next year. The best news is he's assigned you to head up this project.

Your first question should be, "Is it a project?" This may seem elementary, but confusing projects with ongoing operations happens often. Projects are temporary in nature, have definite start and end dates, result in the creation of a unique product or service, and are completed when their goals and objectives have been met and signed off by the stakeholders.

When considering whether or not you have a project on your hands, there are some things to keep in mind. First, is it a project or an ongoing operation? Next, if it is a project, who are the stakeholders? And third, what characteristics distinguish this endeavor as a project. We'll look at each of these next.

Projects versus Operations

Projects are temporary in nature and have definitive start dates and definitive end dates. The project is completed when its goals and objectives are accomplished. Sometimes projects end when it's determined that the goals and objectives cannot be accomplished or when the product or service of the project is no longer needed and the project is canceled. Projects exist to bring about a product or service that hasn't existed before. This may include tangible products, services such as consulting or project management, and business functions that support the organization. Projects may also produce a result or an outcome, such as a document that details findings of a research study. In this sense, a project is unique. However, don't get confused by the term *unique*. For example, Ford Motor Company is in the business of designing and assembling cars. Each model that Ford designs and produces can be considered a project. The models differ from each other in their features and are marketed to people with various needs. An SUV serves a different purpose and clientele than a luxury model. The design and marketing of these two models are unique projects. However, the actual assembly of the cars is considered an operation—a repetitive process that is followed for most makes and models.

Determining the characteristics and features of the different car models is carried out through what *A Guide to the PMBOK* terms *progressive elaboration*. This means the characteristics of the product or service of the project (the SUV, for example) are determined incrementally and are continually refined and worked out in detail as the project progresses. This concept goes along with the temporary and unique aspects of a project because when you first start the project, you don't know all the minute details of the end product. Product characteristics typically start out broad based at the beginning of the project and are progressively elaborated into more and more detail over time until they are complete and finalized. Keep in mind that product characteristics are progressively elaborated but the work of the project itself stays constant.

Exam Spotlight

Progressive elaboration is a concept you may encounter on the exam. Know this concept as it's described in *A Guide to the PMBOK*.

Operations are ongoing and repetitive. They involve work that is continuous without an ending date and you often repeat the same processes and produce the same results. The purpose of operations is to keep the organization functioning while the purpose of a project is to meet its goals and to conclude. Therefore, operations are ongoing while projects are unique and temporary.

Stakeholders

A project is successful when it achieves its objectives and meets or exceeds the expectations of the stakeholders. *Stakeholders* are those folks (or organizations) with a vested interest in your project. They are the people who are actively involved with the work of the project or have something to either gain or lose as a result of the project.

Key stakeholders can make or break the success of a project. Even if all the deliverables are met and the objectives are satisfied, if your key stakeholders aren't happy, nobody's happy.

The *project sponsor,* generally an executive in the organization with the authority to assign resources and enforce decisions regarding the project, is a stakeholder. The customer is a stakeholder, as are contractors and suppliers. The project manager, project team members, and the managers from other departments in the organization are stakeholders as well. It's important to identify all the stakeholders in your project up front. If you leave out an important stakeholder or their department's function and don't discover the error until well into the project, it could be a project killer.

Figure 1.1 shows a sample listing of the kinds of stakeholders involved on a typical project.

FIGURE 1.1   Project stakeholders

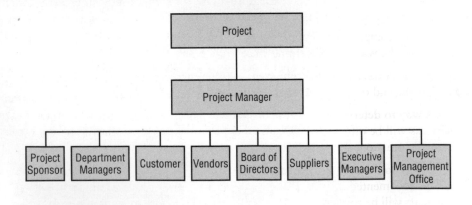

Many times, stakeholders have conflicting interests. It's the project manager's responsibility to understand these conflicts and try to resolve them. It's also the project manager's responsibility to manage stakeholder expectations. Be certain to identify and meet with all key stakeholders early in the project to understand all their needs and constraints. And when in doubt, stakeholder conflicts should always be resolved in favor of the customer.

We'll talk more about stakeholders and their needs in Chapter 3, "Developing the Project Scope Statement."

Project Characteristics

We've just learned that a project has several characteristics:

- Projects are unique.

- Projects are temporary in nature and have a definite beginning and ending date.

- Projects are completed when the project goals are achieved or it's determined the project is no longer viable.

- A successful project is one that meets or exceeds the expectations of your stakeholders.

Using these criteria, let's examine the assignment from the VP of marketing to determine if it is a project:

Is it unique?   Yes, because the kiosks don't exist in the local grocery stores. This is a new way of offering the company's services to its customer base. While the service the company is offering isn't new, the way it is presenting its services is.

Does the project have a limited time frame?   Yes, the start date of this project is today, and the end date is the end of next year. It is a temporary endeavor.

Is there a way to determine when the project is completed?   Yes, the kiosks will be installed, and services will be offered from them. Once all of the kiosks are intact and operating, the project will come to a close.

Is there a way to determine stakeholder satisfaction?   Yes, the expectations of the stakeholders will be documented in the form of requirements during the planning processes. These requirements will be compared to the finished product to determine if it meets the expectations of the stakeholder.

Houston, we have a project.

What Is Project Management?

You've determined that you indeed have a project. What now? The notes you scratched out on the back of a napkin at coffee break might get you started, but that's not exactly good project management practice.

We have all witnessed this scenario—an assignment is made and the project team members jump directly into the project, busying themselves with building the product or service requested. Often, careful thought is not given to the project-planning process. I'm sure you've heard co-workers toss around statements like "That would be a waste of valuable time" or "Why plan when you can just start building?" Project progress is rarely measured against the customer requirements. In the end, the delivered product or service doesn't meet the expectations of the customer! This is a frustrating experience for all those involved. Unfortunately, many projects follow this poorly constructed path.

Project management brings together a set of tools and techniques—performed by people—to describe, organize, and monitor the work of project activities. *Project managers* are the people responsible for managing the project processes and applying the tools and techniques used to carry out the project activities. All projects are composed of processes, even if they employ a haphazard approach. There are many advantages to organizing projects and teams around the project management processes endorsed by PMI. We'll be examining those processes and their advantages in depth throughout the remainder of this book.

Project management involves applying knowledge, skills, and techniques during the course of the project to accomplish the project requirements. It is the responsibility of the project manager to ensure that project management techniques are applied and followed.

Exam Spotlight

Know the term *project management* as it's described in *A Guide to the PMBOK.*

Project management is a process that includes planning, putting the project plan into action, and measuring progress and performance. It involves identifying the project requirements, establishing project objectives, balancing constraints, and taking the needs and expectations of the key stakeholders into consideration. Planning is one of the most important functions you'll perform during the course of a project. It sets the standard for the rest of the project's life and is used to track future project performance. Before we begin the planning process, let's look at some of the ways the work of project management is organized.

Programs

Programs are groups of related projects that are managed using the same techniques in a coordinated fashion. When projects are managed collectively as programs, they capitalize on benefits that wouldn't be achievable if the projects were managed separately. This would be the case where a very large program exists with many subprojects under it—for example, building a new shopping mall. Many subprojects exist underneath this program, such as excavation, construction, interior design, store placement, marketing, facilities management, and so on. Each of the subprojects is really a project unto itself. Each subproject has its own project manager, who reports to a project manager with responsibility over several of the areas, who in turn reports to the head project manager over the entire program. All of the projects are related and are managed together so that collective benefits are realized and controls are implemented and managed in a coordinated fashion. Sometimes programs involve aspects of ongoing operations as well. After the shopping mall in our example is built, the management of the facility becomes the ongoing operations part of this program. The management of this collection of projects is called program management. *Program management* involves centrally managing and coordinating groups of related projects to meet the objectives of the program.

Portfolios

Portfolios are collections of programs and projects that meet a specific business goal or objective. Let's say our company is in the construction business. There are several business units within our organization: retail, single family residential, and multifamily residential. All projects and programs associated with the retail business unit belong to the retail portfolio. The program we talked about in the preceding section (the collection of projects associated with building the new shopping mall) is one of the programs that belongs to the retail portfolio. There could be other programs and projects within this portfolio as well. The objective of any program or project in this portfolio is to meet the strategic objectives of the portfolio, which in turn should meet the objectives of the department and ultimately the corporation. *Portfolio management* encompasses managing the collections of programs and projects in the portfolio. This includes weighing the value of each project, or potential project, against the portfolio's strategic objectives. It also concerns monitoring active projects for adherence to objectives, balancing the portfolio among the other investments of the organization, and assuring the efficient use of resources. Portfolio management is generally performed by a senior manager in the organization.

Project Management Offices

The concept of a *project management office,* sometimes referred to as the PMO, has been around for several years. You'll find that many organizations are establishing PMOs in many different forms. PMOs may also be called project offices or program management offices. The PMO is usually a centralized organizational unit that oversees the management of projects and programs throughout the organization. The most common reason a company starts a project management office is to establish and maintain procedures and standards for project management methodologies. In some organizations, project managers and team members might report directly to the PMO and are assigned to projects as they are initiated. In other organizations, the PMO only provides support functions for projects and trains others in project management procedures and techniques. Still others, depending on their size and function, have experts available that assist project managers in project planning, estimating, and business assumption verification tasks. They serve as mentors to junior-level project managers and act as consultants to the senior project managers.

A PMO can exist in all organizational structures, functional, matrix, or projectized. It may have full authority to oversee projects, including the authority to cancel projects, or it may serve only in an advisory role.

The PMO usually has responsibility for maintaining and archiving project documentation for future reference. This office compares project goals with project progress and gives feedback to the project teams. It also measures the project performance of active projects and suggests corrective actions. The PMO evaluates completed projects for their adherence to the project plan and asks questions like the following: Did the project meet the time frames established, did it stay within budget, and was the quality acceptable?

Project management offices are becoming more common in organizations today, if for no other reason than to serve as a collection point for project documentation. Some PMOs are fairly sophisticated and prescribe the standards and methodologies to be used in all project phases across the enterprise. Still others provide all these functions and also offer project management consulting services. However, the establishment of a PMO is not required in order for you to apply good project management practices to your next project.

Defining Skills Every Good Project Manager Needs

Many times, organizations will knight their technical experts as project managers. The skill and expertise that made them stars in their technical fields are mistakenly thought to translate into project management skills. This is not necessarily so.

Project managers are generalists with many skills in their repertoire. They are also problem solvers who wear many hats. Project managers might indeed possess technical skills, but technical skills are not a prerequisite for sound project management skills. Your project team should include a few technical experts, and these are the people whom the project manager will rely on for technical details. Understanding and applying good project management techniques, along with a solid understanding of general management skills, are career builders for all aspiring project managers.

Project managers have been likened to small-business owners. They need to know a little bit about every aspect of management. General management skills include every area of management, from accounting to strategic planning, supervision, personnel administration, and more. General management skills are called into play on every project. But some projects require specific skills in certain application areas. Application areas are made up of categories of projects that have common elements. These elements, or application areas, can be defined several ways: by industry group (automotive, pharmaceutical), by department (accounting, marketing), by technical (software development, engineering) or management (procurement, research and development) specialties. These application areas are usually concerned with disciplines, regulations, and the specific needs of the project, the customer, or the industry. For example, most governments have specific procurement rules that apply to their projects that wouldn't be applicable in the construction industry. The pharmaceutical industry is acutely interested in regulations set forth by the Food and Drug Administration, whereas the automotive industry has little or no concern for either of these types of regulations. Having experience in the application area you're working in will give you a leg up when it comes to project management. While you can call in the experts who have application area knowledge, it doesn't hurt for you to understand the specific aspects of the application areas of your project.

The general management skills listed in this section are the foundation of good project management practices. Your mastery of them (or lack thereof) will likely affect project outcomes. The various skills of a project manager can be broken out in a more or less declining scale of importance. We'll look at an overview of these skills now and discuss each in more detail in subsequent chapters.

Communication Skills

One of the single most important characteristics of a first-rate project manager is excellent communication skills. Written and oral communications are the backbone of all successful projects. Many forms of communication will exist during the life of your project. As the creator or manager of most of the project communication (project documents, meeting updates, status reports, etc.), it's your job to ensure that the information is explicit, clear, and complete so that your audience will have no trouble understanding what has been communicated. Once the information has been distributed, it is the responsibility of the person receiving the information to make sure they understand it.

There are many forms of communication and communication styles. I'll discuss them more in depth in Chapter 8, "Developing the Project Team."

Organizational and Planning Skills

Organizational and planning skills are closely related and probably the most important, after communication skills, a project manager can possess. Organization takes on many forms. As project manager, you'll have project documentation, requirements information, memos, project reports, personnel records, vendor quotes, contracts, and much more to track and be able to locate at a moment's notice. You will also have to organize meetings, put together teams, and perhaps manage and organize media release schedules, depending on your project.

Time management skills are closely related to organizational skills. It's difficult to stay organized without an understanding of how you're managing your time. I recommend you attend a time management class if you've never taken one. They have some great tips and techniques to help you prioritize problems and interruptions, prioritize your day, and manage your time.

Planning is discussed extensively throughout the course of this book. There isn't any aspect of project management that doesn't first involve planning. Planning skills go hand in hand with organizational skills. Combining these two with excellent communication skills is almost a sure guarantee of your success in the project management field.

Budgeting Skills

Project managers establish and manage budgets and therefore need some knowledge of finance and accounting principles. Especially important in this skill area is the ability to perform cost estimates for project budgeting. There are different methods available to determine the project costs. They range from estimating individual activities and rolling the estimates up to estimating the project's cost in one big chunk. These methods will be discussed more fully in later chapters.

After a budget is determined, you can start spending. This sounds more exciting than it actually is. Reading and understanding vendor quotes, preparing or overseeing purchase orders, and reconciling invoices are budgeting skills that will be used by the project manager on most projects. These costs will be linked back to project activities and expense items in the project's budget.

Conflict Management Skills

Show me a project, and I'll show you problems. All projects have some problems, as does, in fact, much of everyday life. Isn't that what they say builds character? But I digress.

Conflict management involves solving problems. Problem solving is really a twofold process. First, you must define the problem by separating the causes from the symptoms. Often when defining problems, you end up just describing the symptoms instead of really getting to the heart of what's causing the problem. To avoid that, ask yourself questions like, "Is it an internal or external problem?" and "Is it a technical problem?" and "Are there interpersonal problems between team members?" and "Is it managerial?" and "What are the potential impacts or consequences?" These kinds of questions will help you to get to the cause of the problem.

Next, after the problem has been defined, you have some decisions to make. It will take a little time to examine and analyze the problem, the situation causing it, and the alternatives available. After this analysis, the project manager will determine the best course of action to take and implement the decision. The timing of the decision is often as important as the decision itself. If you make a good decision but implement it too late, it may turn into a bad decision.

Negotiation and Influencing Skills

Effective problem solving requires negotiation and influencing skills. We all utilize negotiation skills in one form or another every day. For example, on a nightly basis I am asked, "Honey, what do you want for dinner?" Then the negotiations begin, and the fried chicken versus swordfish discussion commences. Simply put, negotiating is working with others to come to an agreement.

Negotiation on projects is necessary in almost every area of the project, from scope definition to budgets, contracts, resource assignments, and more. This may involve one-on-one negotiation or it might involve teams of people, and it can occur many times throughout the project.

Influencing is convincing the other party that swordfish is a better choice than fried chicken, even if fried chicken is what they want. It's also the ability to get things done. Influencing requires an understanding of the formal and informal structure of all the organizations involved in the project.

Power and politics are techniques used to influence people to perform. *Power* is the ability to get people to do things they wouldn't do otherwise. It's also the ability to change minds and the course of events and to influence outcomes.

We'll discuss power further in Chapter 8.

Politics involve getting groups of people with different interests to cooperate creatively even in the midst of conflict and disorder.

These skills will be utilized in all areas of project management. Start practicing now because, guaranteed, you'll need these skills on your next project.

Leadership Skills

Leaders and *managers* are not synonymous terms. Leaders impart vision, gain consensus for strategic goals, establish direction, and inspire and motivate others. Managers focus on results and are concerned with getting the job done according to the requirements. Even though leaders and managers are not the same, project managers must exhibit the characteristics of both during different times on the project. Understanding when to switch from leadership to management and then back again is a finely tuned and necessary talent.

Team-Building and Motivating Skills

Project managers will rely heavily on team-building and motivational skills. Teams are often formed with people from different parts of the organization. These people may or may not have worked together before, so there may be some component of team-building groundwork that will involve the project manager. The project manager will set the tone for the project team and will help them work through the various team-forming stages to become fully functional. Motivating the team, especially during long projects or those experiencing a lot of bumps along the way, is another important role the project manager fulfills during the course of the project.

An interesting caveat to the team-building role is that project managers many times are responsible for motivating team members who are not their direct reports. This has its own set of challenges and dilemmas. One way to help this situation is to ask the functional manager to allow you to participate in your project team members' performance reviews. Use the negotiation and influencing skills I talked about earlier to make sure you're part of this process.

A Mile Wide and an Inch Deep

Project managers are an interesting bunch. They know a little bit about a lot of things and are excellent communicators. Or, as one person said, they're "a mile wide and an inch deep." They have the ability to motivate people, even those who have no reason to be loyal to the project, and they can make the hard-line calls when necessary. Project managers can get caught in sticky situations that occasionally require making decisions that are good for the company (or the customer) but aren't good for certain stakeholders. These offended stakeholders will then drag their feet, and the project manager has to play the heavy in order to motivate and gain their cooperation again. Some organizations hire contract project managers to run their large, company-altering projects, just because they don't want to burn out a key employee in this role. Fortunately, that doesn't happen often.

Now that you've been properly introduced to some of the skills you need in your tool kit, you'll know to be prepared to communicate, solve problems, lead, and negotiate your way through your next project.

Understanding Organizational Structures

Just as projects are unique, so are the organizations in which they're carried out. Organizations have their own styles and cultures that influence how project work is carried out. One of the keys to determining the type of organization you work in is measuring how much authority senior management is willing to delegate to project managers. While uniqueness abounds in business cultures, all organizations are structured in one of three ways: functional, projectized, or matrix. Variations and combinations exist among these three structures, such as a projectized structure within a functional organization and weak matrix, balanced matrix, and strong matrix organizations.

It pays to know and understand the organizational structure and the culture of the entity you're working with. Companies with aggressive cultures that are comfortable in a leading-edge position within their industry are highly likely to take on risky projects. Project managers who are willing to suggest new ideas and projects that have never been undertaken before are likely to receive a warm reception in this kind of environment. Conversely, organizational cultures that are risk averse and prefer the follow-the-leader position within their industry are highly unlikely to take on risky endeavors. Project managers with risk-seeking, aggressive styles are likely to receive a cool reception in a culture like this.

The level of authority the project manager enjoys is denoted by the organizational structure. For example, a project manager within a functional organization has little to no formal authority. And their title may not be project manager; instead they might be called a project leader, a project coordinator, or perhaps a project expeditor.

Let's take a look at each of these types of organizations individually to better understand how the project management role works in each one.

Functional Organizations

One common type of organization is the *functional organization*. Chances are you have worked in this type of organization. This is probably the oldest style of organization and is therefore known as the traditional approach to organizing businesses.

Functional organizations are centered on specialties and grouped by function, hence the term *functional organization*. As an example, the organization might have a human resources department, finance department, marketing department, etc. The work in these departments is specialized and requires people who have the skill sets and experiences in these specialized functions to perform specific duties for the department. Figure 1.2 shows a typical organizational chart for a functional organization.

FIGURE 1.2   Functional organizational chart

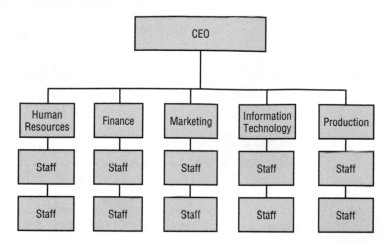

You can see that this type of organization is set up to be a hierarchy. Staff personnel report to managers who report to department heads who report to vice presidents who report to the CEO. In other words, each employee reports to only one manager; ultimately, one person at the top is in charge. Many companies today, as well as governmental agencies, are structured in a hierarchical fashion. In organizations like this, be aware of the chain of command. A strict chain of command may exist, and the corporate culture might dictate that you follow it. Roughly translated: *Don't talk to the big boss without first talking to your boss who talks to their boss who talks to the big boss.* Wise project managers should determine if there is a chain of command, how strictly it's enforced, and how the chain is linked before venturing outside of it.

Each department or group in a functional organization is managed independently and has a limited span of control. Marketing doesn't run the finance department or their projects, for example. The marketing department is concerned with their own functions and projects. If it were necessary for the marketing department to get input from the finance department on a project, the marketing team members would follow the chain of command. A marketing manager would speak to a manager in finance to get the needed information and then pass it back down to the project team.

Human Resources in a Functional Organization

Commonalities exist among the personnel assigned to the various departments in a functional organization. In theory, people with similar skills and experiences are easier to manage as a group. Instead of scattering them throughout the organization, it is more efficient to keep them functioning together. Work assignments are easily distributed to those who are best suited for the task when everyone with the same skill works together. Usually, the supervisors and managers of these workers are experienced in the area they supervise and are able to recommend training and career enrichment activities for their employees.

Workers in functional organizations specialize in an area of expertise—finance or personnel administration, for instance—and then become very good at their specialty.

There is a clear upward career path for people in a functional organization. An assistant budget analyst may be promoted to a budget analyst and then eventually to a department manager over many budget analysts.

The Downside of Functional Organizations

Functional organizations have their disadvantages. If this is the kind of organization you work in, you probably have experienced some of them.

One of the greatest disadvantages for the project manager is that they have little to no formal authority. This does not mean that project managers in functional organizations are doomed to failure. Many projects are undertaken and successfully completed within this type of organization. Good communication and interpersonal and influencing skills on the part of the project manager are required to bring about a successful project under this structure.

In a functional organization, the vice president or senior department manager is usually the one responsible for projects. The title of project manager denotes authority, and in a functional structure, that authority rests with the VP.

Managing Projects in a Functional Organization

Projects are typically undertaken in a divided approach in a functional organization. For example, the marketing department will work on their portion of the project and then hand it off to the manufacturing department to complete their part, and so on. The work the marketing department does is considered a marketing project, while the work the manufacturing department does is considered a manufacturing project.

Some projects require project team members from different departments to work together at the same time on various aspects of the project. Project team members in this structure will more than likely remain loyal to their functional manager. The functional manager is responsible for their performance reviews, and their career opportunities lie within the functional department—not within the project team. Exhibiting leadership skills by forming a common vision regarding the project and the ability to motivate people to work toward that vision are great skills to exercise in this situation. As previously mentioned, it also doesn't hurt to have the project manager work with the functional manager in contributing to the employee's performance review.

Resource Pressures in a Functional Organization

Competition for resources and project priorities can become fierce when multiple projects are undertaken within a functional organization. For example, in my organization, it's common to have competing project requests from three or more departments all vying for the same resources. Thrown into the heap is the requirement to make, for example, mandated tax law changes, which automatically usurps all other priorities. This sometimes causes frustration and political infighting. One department thinks their project is more important than another and will do anything to get that project pushed ahead of the others. Again, it takes great skill and diplomatic abilities to keep projects on track and functioning smoothly. In a later chapter, we'll discuss the importance of gaining stakeholder buy-in and of prioritization and communication distribution to avert some of these problems.

Project managers have little authority in functional organizations, but with the right skills, they can successfully accomplish many projects. Table 1.1 highlights the advantages and disadvantages of this type of organization.

TABLE 1.1   Functional Organizations

Advantages	Disadvantages
Enduring organizational structure.	Project manager has little to no formal authority.
Clear career path with separation of functions, allowing specialty skills to flourish.	Multiple projects compete for limited resources and priority.
Employees have one supervisor with a clear chain of command.	Project team members are loyal to the functional manager.

Projectized Organizations

Projectized organizations are nearly the opposite of functional organizations. The focus of this type of organization is the project itself. The idea behind a projectized organization is to develop loyalty to the project, not to a functional manager.

Figure 1.3 shows a typical org chart for a projectized organization.

FIGURE 1.3   Projectized organizational chart

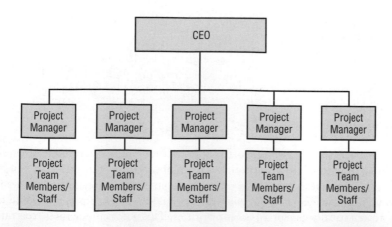

Organizational resources are dedicated to projects and project work in purely projectized organizations. Project managers almost always have ultimate authority over the project in this structure and report directly to the CEO. In a purely projectized organization, supporting functions like human resources and accounting might report directly to the project manager as well. Project managers are responsible for making decisions regarding the project and acquiring and assigning resources. They have the authority to choose and assign resources from other areas in the organization or to hire them from outside if needed. For example, if there isn't enough money in the budget to hire additional resources, the project manager will have to come up with alternatives to solve this problem. This is known as a constraint. Project managers in all organizational structures are limited by the triple constraints commonly known as: project scope, schedule, and cost (or budget). Quality is sometimes considered a constraint and it's generally affected by scope, schedule, and/or cost. We'll talk more about constraints in Chapter 2, "Creating the Project Charter and Preliminary Scope Statement."

Teams are formed and often *collocated,* which means that team members physically work at the same location. Project team members report to the project manager, not to a functional or departmental manager. One obvious drawback to a projectized organization is that project team members may find themselves out of work at the end of the project. An example of this might be a consultant who works on a project until completion and then is put on the bench or let go at the end of the project. Some inefficiency exists in this kind of organization when it comes to resource utilization. If you have a situation where you need a highly specialized skill at certain times throughout the project, the resource you're using to perform this function might be idle during other times in the project.

In summary, projectized organizations are identified in several ways:

- Project managers have ultimate authority over the project.
- The focus of the organization is the project.
- The organization's resources are focused on projects and project work.
- Team members are collocated.
- Loyalties are formed to the project, not to a functional manager.
- Project teams are dissolved at the conclusion of the project.

Matrix Organizations

Matrix organizations came about to minimize the differences between, and take advantage of, the strengths and weaknesses of functional and projectized organizations. The idea at play here is that the best of both organizational structures can be realized by combining them into one. The project objectives are fulfilled and good project management techniques are utilized while still maintaining a hierarchical structure in the organization.

Employees in a matrix organization report to one functional manager and to at least one project manager. It's possible that employees could report to multiple project managers if they are working on multiple projects at one time. Functional managers pick up the administrative portion of the duties and assign employees to projects. They also monitor the work of their employees on the various projects. Project managers are responsible for executing the project and giving out work assignments based on project activities. Project managers and functional managers share the responsibility of performance reviews for the employee.

In a nutshell, functional managers assign employees to projects, while project managers assign tasks associated with the project in a matrix organization.

Matrix organizations have unique characteristics. We'll look at how projects are conducted and managed and how project and functional managers share the work in this organizational structure next.

Project Focus in a Matrix Organization

Matrix organizations allow project managers to focus on the project and project work just as in a projectized organization. The project team is free to focus on the project objectives without distractions from the functional department.

Project managers should take care when working up activity and project estimates for the project in a matrix organization. The estimates should be given to the functional managers for input before publishing. The functional manager is the one in charge of assigning or freeing up resources to work on projects. If the project manager is counting on a certain employee to work on the project at a certain time, the project manager should determine their availability up front with the functional manager. Project estimates might have to be modified if it's discovered that the employee they were counting on is not available when needed.

Balance of Power in a Matrix Organization

As we've discussed, a lot of communication and negotiation takes place between the project manager and the functional manager. This calls for a balance of power between the two or one will dominate the other.

In a strong matrix organization, the balance of power rests with the project manager. They have the ability to strong-arm the functional managers into giving up their best resources for projects. Sometimes, more resources than necessary are assembled for the project, and then project managers negotiate these resources among themselves, cutting out the functional manager altogether, as you can see in Figure 1.4.

FIGURE 1.4   Strong matrix organizational chart

FIGURE 1.5   Weak matrix organizational chart

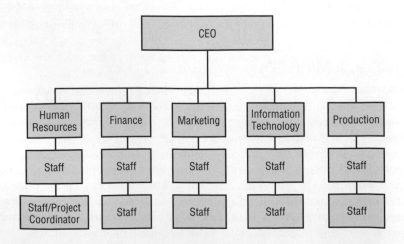

FIGURE 1.6   Balanced matrix organizational chart

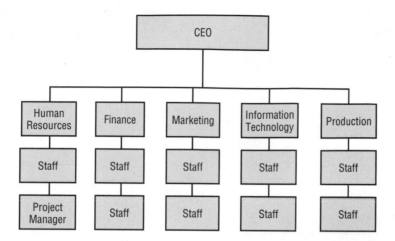

On the other end of the spectrum is the weak matrix (see Figure 1.5). As you would suspect, the functional managers have all the power in this structure. Project managers are really project coordinators or expeditors with part-time responsibilities on projects in a weak matrix organization. Project managers have little to no authority, just as in the functional organization. On the other hand, the functional managers have a lot of authority and make all the work assignments. The project manager simply expedites the project.

In between the weak matrix and the strong matrix is an organizational structure called the *balanced matrix* (see Figure 1.6). The features of the balanced matrix are what we've been discussing throughout this section. The power is balanced between project managers and functional managers. Each manager has responsibility for their parts of the project or organization, and employees get assigned to projects based on the needs of the project, not the strength or weakness of the manager's position.

Matrix organizations have subtle differences, and it's important to understand their differences for the PMP exam. The easiest way to remember them is that the weak matrix has many of the same characteristics as the functional organization, while the strong matrix has many of the same characteristics as the projectized organization. The balanced matrix is exactly that—a balance between weak and strong, where the project manager shares authority and responsibility with the functional manager. Table 1.2 compares all three structures.

Most organizations today use some combination of the organizational structures described here. They're a composite of functional, projectized, and matrix structures. It's rare that an organization would be purely functional or purely projectized. For example, projectized structures can coexist within functional organizations.

In the case of a high-profile, critical project, the functional organization might appoint a special project team to work only on that project. The team is structured outside the bounds of the functional organization and the project manager has ultimate authority for the project. This is a workable project management approach and ensures open communication between the project manager and team members. At the end of the project, the project team is dissolved and the project members return to their functional areas to resume their usual duties.

TABLE 1.2   Comparing Matrix Structures

	Weak Matrix	Balanced Matrix	Strong Matrix
Project Manager's Title:	Project coordinator, project leader, or project expeditor	Project manager	Project manager
Project Manager's Focus:	Split focus between project and functional responsibilities	Projects and project work	Projects and project work
Project Manager's Power:	Minimal authority and power	Balance of authority and power	Full authority and power
Project Manager's Time:	Part-time on projects	Full-time on projects	Full-time on projects
Organization Style:	Most like functional organization	Blend of both weak and strong matrix	Most like a projectized organization
Project Manager Reports to:	Functional manager	A functional manager, but shares authority and power	Manager of project managers

---

Exam Spotlight

Organizational structure is a topic you may encounter on the exam. Know this topic as it's described in *A Guide to the PMBOK*.

Organizations are unique, as are the projects they undertake. Understanding the organizational structure will help you, as a project manager, with the cultural influences and communication avenues that exist in the organization to gain cooperation and successfully bring your projects to a close.

Understanding Project Life Cycles and Project Management Processes

Project life cycles are similar to the life cycle that parents experience raising their children to adulthood. Children start out as infants and generate lots of excitement wherever they go. However, not much is known about them at first. So you study them as they grow and assess their needs. Over time, they mature and grow (and cost a lot of money in the process), until one day the parents' job is done.

Projects start out just like this and progress along a similar path. Someone comes up with a great idea for a project and actively solicits support for it. The project, after being approved, progresses through the intermediate phases to the ending phase, where it is completed and closed out.

Project Phases and Project Life Cycles

All projects are divided into phases, and all projects, large or small, have a similar life cycle structure. At a minimum, a project will have a beginning or initiation phase, an intermediate phase or phases, and an ending phase. The number of phases depends on the project complexity and the industry. For example, information technology projects may progress through phases such as requirements, design, program, test, and implement. All the collective phases the project progresses through in concert are called the *project life cycle.*

The end of each phase allows the project manager, stakeholders, and project sponsor the opportunity to determine if the project should continue to the next phase. In order to progress to the next phase, the deliverable from the phase before it must be reviewed for accuracy and approved. As each phase is completed, it's handed off to the next phase. We'll look at handoffs and progressions through these phases next.

Handoffs

Project phases evolve through the life cycle in a series of phase sequences called *handoffs,* or technical transfers. The end of one phase sequence typically marks the beginning of the next. However, the completion of one phase does not automatically signal the beginning of the next phase. For example, in the construction industry, feasibility studies often take place in the beginning phase of a project.

The purpose of the *feasibility study* is to determine if the project is worth undertaking and whether the project will be profitable to the organization. A feasibility study is a preliminary assessment of the viability of the project, the viability or perhaps marketability of the product or service of the project, and the project's value to the organization. It may also determine if the product or service of the project is safe and meets industry or governmental standards and regulations. The completion and approval of the feasibility study triggers the beginning of the requirements phase, where requirements are documented and then handed off to the design phase, where blueprints are produced. The feasibility may also show that the project is not worth pursuing and the project is terminated; thus, the next phase never begins.

Phase Completion

You will recognize phase completion because each phase has a specific *deliverable,* or multiple deliverables, that marks the end of the phase. A deliverable is an output that must be produced, reviewed, and approved to bring the phase or project to completion. Deliverables are tangible and can be measured and easily proved. For instance, a hypothetical deliverable produced in the beginning phase of our construction industry example would be the feasibility study. Deliverables might also include things like design documents, project budgets, blueprints, project schedules, prototypes, etc. This analysis allows those involved with the opportunity to determine if the project should continue to the next phase. The feasibility study might show that environmental impacts of an enormous nature would result if the construction project were undertaken at the proposed location. Based on this information, a go or no-go decision can be made at the end of this phase. The end of a phase gives the project manager the ability to discover, address, and take corrective action against errors discovered during the phase.

 A Guide to the PMBOK states that phase ending reviews are also known by a few other names: phase exits, phase gates, or kill points.

There are times when phases are overlapped to shorten or compress the project schedule. This is called *fast tracking*. Fast tracking means that a later phase is started prior to completing and approving the phase, or phases, that come before it. This technique is used to shorten the overall duration of the project.

Most projects follow phase sequences within a project life cycle and, as a result, have the following characteristics in common: In the beginning phase, which is where the project is initiated, costs are low and there are few team members assigned to the project. As the project progresses, costs and staffing increase and then taper off at the closing phase. The potential that the project will come to a successful ending is lowest at the beginning of the project; its chance for success increases as the project progresses through its phases and life cycle stages. Risk is highest at the beginning of the project and gradually decreases the closer the project comes to completion. Stakeholders have the greatest chance of influencing the project and the characteristics of the product or service of the project in the beginning phases and have less and less influence as the project progresses. This same phenomenon exists within the project management processes as well. We'll look at those next.

Project Management Process Groups

Project management processes organize and describe the work of the project. *A Guide to the PMBOK* describes five process groups used to accomplish this end. These processes are performed by people and, much like project phases, are interrelated and dependent on one another.

A Guide to the PMBOK documents five project management process groups:

- Initiating
- Planning
- Executing
- Monitoring and Controlling
- Closing

All of these process groups have individual processes that collectively make up the group. For example, the Initiating process group has two processes called Develop Project Charter and Develop Preliminary Project Scope Statement. Collectively, these process groups—including all their individual processes—make up the project management process. Projects start with the

Initiating process and progress through all the processes in the Planning process group, the Executing process group, and so on until the project is successfully completed or it's canceled. All projects must complete the Closing processes, even if the project is killed. Phase handoffs (the design phase handoff to manufacturing, for example) also occur within these life cycles.

> Don't confuse project phases and life cycles with the project management process groups. *A Guide to the PMBOK* makes a strong point of this. Project phases and life cycles describe how the work associated with the product of the project will be completed. For example, a construction project may have phases such as feasibility study, design, build, inspection, turnover. The five project management process groups (Initiating, Planning, Executing, Monitoring and Controlling, Closing) organize and describe how the project activities will be conducted in order to meet the project requirements. These processes are generally performed for each phase of a large project. The five process groups are the heart of *A Guide to the PMBOK* and the exam. As you progress through this book, be certain you understand each of these processes as they're described in *A Guide to the PMBOK*.

Let's start with a high-level overview of each process group. The remainder of this book will cover each of these processes in detail. If you want to peek ahead, Appendix A lists each of the process groups, the individual processes that make up each process group, and the Knowledge Area they belong in. (I'll cover knowledge areas in the section titled "The Project Management Knowledge Areas" later in this chapter.)

Initiating

The *Initiating* process group, as its name implies, occurs at the beginning of the project and at the beginning of each project phase for large projects. Initiating acknowledges that a project, or the next project phase, should begin. This process group grants the approval to commit the organization's resources to working on the project or phase and authorizes the project manager to begin working on the project. The outputs of the Initiating process group, including the project charter and preliminary project scope statement, become inputs into the Planning group.

Planning

The *Planning* process is the process group of formulating and revising project goals and objectives and creating the project management plan that will be used to achieve the goals the project was undertaken to address. The Planning process group also involves determining alternative courses of action and selecting from among the best of those to produce the project's goals. This process group is where the project requirements are fleshed out and stakeholders are identified. Planning has more processes than any of the other project management process groups. The Executing, Monitoring and Controlling, and Closing process groups all rely on the Planning processes and the documentation produced during the Planning processes in order to carry out their functions. Project managers will perform frequent iterations of the Planning processes prior to project completion. Projects are unique and, as such, have never been done before. Therefore, Planning must encompass all areas of project management and consider budgets, activity definition, scope planning, schedule development, risk identification, staff acquisition, procurement planning, and more. The greatest conflicts a project manger will encounter in this process group are project prioritization issues.

Executing

The *Executing* process group involves putting the project management plan into action. It's here that the project manager will coordinate and direct project resources to meet the objectives of the project plan. The Executing process keeps the project plan on track and ensures that future execution of project plans stays in line with project objectives. This process group is typically where approved changes are implemented. The Executing process group will utilize the most project time and resources, and as a result, costs are usually highest during the Executing process. Project managers will experience the greatest conflicts over schedules in this cycle.

Monitoring and Controlling

The *Monitoring and Controlling* process group is where project performance measurements are taken and analyzed to determine if the project is staying true to the project plan. The idea is to identify problems as soon as possible and apply corrective action to control the work of the project and assure successful outcomes. For example, if you discover that variances exist, you'll apply corrective action to get the project activities realigned with the project plan. This might require additional passes through the Planning processes to adjust project activities, resources, schedules, budgets, and so on.

Closing

The *Closing* process group is probably the most often skipped process group in project management. Closing brings a formal, orderly end to the activities of a project phase or to the project itself. Once the project objectives have been met, most of us are ready to move on to the next project. However, Closing is important because all the project information is gathered now and stored for future reference. The documentation collected during the Closing process group can be reviewed and utilized to avert potential problems on future projects. Contract closeout occurs here, and formal acceptance and approval are obtained from project stakeholders.

Exam Spotlight

The project manager and project team are responsible for determining which processes within each process group are appropriate for the project you're working on. This is called *tailoring*. You should take into consideration the size and complexity of the project and the various inputs and outputs of each of the processes when determining which processes to implement and perform. Small independent projects may not require the rigor of each of the processes within a process group, but every process should be addressed and its level of implementation determined. Use your judgment when deciding which processes to follow, particularly for small projects.

Characteristics of the Process Groups

The progression through the project management process groups exhibit the same characteristics as progression through the project phases do. That is, costs are lowest during the Initiating processes and few team members are involved. Costs and staffing increase in the Executing process group and then decrease as you approach the Closing process group. The chances for success are lowest during Initiating and highest during Closing. The chances for risks occurring are higher during Initiating, Planning, and Executing, but the impacts of risks are greater during the later processes. Stakeholders have the greatest influence during the Initiating and Planning processes and less and less influence as you progress through Executing, Monitoring and Controlling, and Closing. To give you a better idea of when certain characteristics influence a project, refer to Table 1.3 and Table 1.4. A recap of the characteristics in the beginning and ending process groups are shown here.

TABLE 1.3   Characteristics of the Initiating and Planning Process Groups

Low Impact or Probability	High Impact or Probability
Costs	Risk occurrences
Staffing levels	Stakeholder influence
Chance for successful completion	

TABLE 1.4   Characteristics of the Monitoring and Controlling and Closing Process Groups

Low Impact or Probability	High Impact or Probability
Stakeholder influence	Chance for successful completion
Staffing levels	Risk impact
Risk probability	

Remember that costs and resources are usually highest during the Executing phase.

The Process Flow

The five process groups should not be thought of as one-time processes that are performed as discrete elements. Rather, these processes interact and overlap with each other. They are *iterative* and may be revisited and revised throughout the project's life several times as the project is refined. *A Guide to the PMBOK* calls this process of going back through the process groups an *iterative process*. The conclusion of each process group allows the project manager and stakeholders to re-examine the business needs of the project and determine if the project is satisfying those needs. And it is another opportunity to make a go or no-go decision.

Figure 1.7 shows the five process groups in a typical project. Keep in mind that during phases of a project, the Closing process group can provide input to the Initiating process group. For example, once the feasibility study discussed earlier is accepted or closed, it becomes input to the Initiating process group of the design phase.

FIGURE 1.7   Project management process groups

Project Management Process Groups

Inputs		Outputs
	Initiating →	Planning
Initiating → Monitoring and → Controlling	**Planning** →	Executing
Planning → Monitoring and → Controlling	**Executing** →	Monitoring and Controlling
Executing →	**Monitoring and Controlling** →	Planning Executing Closing
Monitoring and → Controlling	**Closing**	

It's important to understand the flow of these processes for the exam. If you remember the processes and their inputs and outputs, it will help you when you're trying to decipher an exam question. The outputs of one process group become the inputs into the next process group (or the outputs may be a deliverable of the project). Sometimes just understanding which process the question is asking about will help you determine the answer. One trick you can use to memorize these processes is to remember syrup of ipecac. You probably have some of this poison antidote in your medicine cabinet at home. If you think of the Monitoring and Controlling process group as simply "Controlling," when you sound out the first initial of each of the processes, it sounds like "ipecac"—IPECC (Initiating, Planning, Executing, *Monitoring and* Controlling, and Closing).

As I stated earlier, individual processes make up each of the process groups. For example, the Closing life cycle process group consists of two processes: Close Project and Contract Closure. Each process takes inputs and uses them in conjunction with various tools and techniques to produce outputs.

NOTE   It's outside the scope of this book to explain all the inputs, tools and techniques, and outputs for each process in each process group (although each is listed in Appendix A). You'll find each input, tool and technique, and output detailed in *A Guide to the PMBOK,* and I highly recommend you get familiar with them.

There are test questions regarding inputs, tools and techniques, and outputs of many of the processes within each process group. One way to keep them all straight is to remember that tools and techniques usually require action of some sort, be it measuring, applying some skill or technique, planning, or using expert judgment. Outputs are usually in the form of a deliverable. Remember that a deliverable is characterized with results or outcomes that can be measured, are tangible, and are provable. Last but not least, outputs from one process sometimes serve as inputs to another process.

Process Interactions

We've covered a lot of material but there's one more concept I want to explain before we move on to the next section. As stated earlier, project managers must determine the processes that are appropriate for effectively managing a project based on the complexity and scope of the project, available resources, budget, and so on. As the project progresses, the project management processes may be revisited and revised to update the project management plan as more information becomes known. Underlying the concept that process groups are iterative is a cycle *A Guide to the PMBOK* describes as the "Plan-Do-Check-Act" cycle that was originally defined by Walter Shewhart and later modified by Edward Deming. The idea behind this concept is that each element in the cycle is results oriented. The results from the Plan cycle become inputs into the Do cycle and so on, much like the way the project management process groups interact. The cycle interactions can be mapped to work in conjunction with the five project management process groups. For example, the Plan cycle maps to the Planning process group. Before we go any further, let's do a brief refresher.

- Project phases describe how the work required to produce the product of the project will be completed

- Project management process groups organize and describe how the project activities will be completed in order to meet the goals of the project

- The Plan-Do-Check-Act cycle is an underlying concept that shows the integrative nature of the process groups

Figure 1.8 shows the relationships and interactions of the concepts we've learned so far. Please bear in mind that a simple figure can't get across all the interactions and iterative nature of these interactions; however, I think you'll see that the figure ties the basic elements of these concepts together.

FIGURE 1.8   Project management process groups

The Project Management Knowledge Areas

There is one more way to classify the processes from each project management process group. *A Guide to the PMBOK* groups these processes into nine categories that they call the *Project Management Knowledge Areas*. These groupings, or knowledge areas, bring together processes that have characteristics in common. For example, the Project Cost Management knowledge area involves all aspects of the budgeting process, as you would suspect. Therefore, processes such as Cost Estimating, Cost Budgeting, and Cost Control belong to this knowledge area. Here's the tricky part—these processes don't belong to the same project management process groups (Cost Estimating and Cost Budgeting are part of the Planning process group and Cost Control is part of the Monitoring and Controlling process group). Think of it this way: knowledge areas bring together processes by commonalities, whereas project management process groups are more or less the order you perform the project management processes (although remember you can come back through these processes more than once). The nine knowledge areas are as follows:

- Project Integration Management
- Project Scope Management
- Project Time Management
- Project Cost Management
- Project Quality Management
- Project Human Resource Management
- Project Communications Management
- Project Risk Management
- Project Procurement Management

Let's take a closer look at each knowledge area so you understand how they relate to the process groups. Included in each of the following subsections is a table that illustrates the processes that make up that knowledge area and the project management process group that each process belongs to. This will help you to see the big picture in terms of process groups compared to knowledge areas. We'll be discussing each of the processes in the various knowledge areas throughout the book, but for now, let's take a high-level look at each of them.

Exam Spotlight

The PMP exam will most likely have a question or two regarding the processes that make up a knowledge area. Remember that knowledge areas bring together processes by commonalities, so thinking about the knowledge area itself should tip you off to the processes that belong to it. Projects are executed in process group order, but the knowledge areas allow a project manager to think about groups of processes that require specific skills. This makes the job of assigning resources easier because team members with specific skills might be able to work on and complete several processes at once. To broaden your understanding of the knowledge areas, cross-reference the purposes and the processes that make up each knowledge area with *A Guide to the PMBOK*.

Project Integration Management

Project Integration Management (see Table 1.5) comprises seven processes:

- Develop Project Charter
- Develop Preliminary Project Scope Statement
- Develop Project Management Plan
- Direct and Manage Project Execution

- Monitor and Control Project Work
- Integrated Change Control
- Close Project

The Project Integration Management knowledge area is concerned with coordinating all aspects of the project plan and is highly interactive. This knowledge area involves identifying and defining the work of the project and combining, unifying, and integrating the appropriate processes. This knowledge area also takes into account satisfactorily meeting the requirements of the customer and stakeholder and managing their expectations.

Project planning, project execution, monitoring project work, and change control occur throughout the project and are repeated continuously while working on the project. Project planning and execution involve weighing the objectives of the project against the alternatives to bring the project to a successful completion. This includes making choices about how to effectively use resources and coordinating the work of the project on a continuous basis. Monitoring the work of the project involves anticipating potential problems and issues and dealing with them before they reach the critical point. Change control impacts the project plan, which in turn impacts the work of the project, which in turn can impact the project management plan, so you can see that these processes are very tightly linked. The processes in this area, as with all the knowledge areas, also interact with other processes in the remaining knowledge areas. For example, the Close Project process uses outputs from the Contract Administration process and produces inputs to the Contract Closure process.

The Project Integration Management knowledge area has two tools for assisting with process integration: Earned Value Management and project management software. Earned Value Management (EVM) is a project-integrating methodology used in this knowledge area to integrate the processes and measure project performance through a project's life cycle. We'll further define EVM and talk more about project management software tools in Chapter 7, "Creating the Project Schedule and Budget."

TABLE 1.5   Project Integration Management

Process Name	Project Management Process Group
Develop Project Charter	Initiating
Develop Preliminary Project Scope Statement	Initiating
Develop Project Management Plan	Planning
Direct and Manage Project Execution	Executing
Monitor and Control Project Work	Monitoring and Controlling
Integrated Change Control	Monitoring and Controlling
Close Project	Closing

Project Scope Management

Project Scope Management (see Table 1.6) has five processes:

- Scope Planning
- Scope Definition
- Create WBS
- Scope Verification
- Scope Control

Project Scope Management is concerned with defining all of the work of the project and only the work needed to successfully meet the project goals. These processes are highly interactive. They define and control what is and what is not part of the project. Each process occurs at least once—and often many times—throughout the project's life.

Project Scope Management encompasses both product scope and project scope. *Product scope* concerns the characteristics of the product or service or result of the project. It's measured against the product requirements to determine successful completion or fulfillment. The application area usually dictates the process tools and techniques you'll use to define and manage product scope. *Project scope* involves managing the work of the project and only the work of the project. Project scope is measured against the project management plan, the project scope statement, the work breakdown structure (WBS) and the WBS dictionary.

 To ensure a successful project, both product and project scope must be well integrated. This implies that Project Scope Management is well integrated with the other knowledge area processes.

Scope Planning, Scope Definition, Create WBS, Scope Verification, and Scope Control involve the following:

- Detailing the requirements of the product of the project
- Verifying those details using measurement techniques
- Creating a project scope management plan
- Creating a work breakdown structure
- Controlling changes to these processes

TABLE 1.6   Project Scope Management

Process Name	Project Management Process Group
Scope Planning	Planning
Scope Definition	Planning
Create WBS	Planning

TABLE 1.6   Project Scope Management *(continued)*

Process Name	Project Management Process Group
Scope Verification	Monitoring and Controlling
Scope Control	Monitoring and Controlling

Project Time Management

The *Project Time Management* knowledge area, shown in Table 1.7, has six processes:

- Activity Definition
- Activity Sequencing
- Activity Resource Estimating
- Activity Duration Estimating
- Schedule Development
- Schedule Control

This knowledge area is concerned with estimating the duration of the project plan activities, devising a project schedule, and monitoring and controlling deviations from the schedule. Collectively, this knowledge area deals with completing the project in a timely manner. Time management is an important aspect of project management because it concerns keeping the project activities on track and monitoring those activities against the project plan to ensure that the project is completed on time.

While each process in this knowledge area occurs at least once in every project (and sometimes more), in many cases, particularly on small projects, Activity Sequencing, Activity Duration Estimating, and Schedule Development are completed as one activity. Only one person is needed to complete these processes for small projects, and they're all worked on at the same time.

TABLE 1.7   Project Time Management

Process Name	Project Management Process Group
Activity Definition	Planning
Activity Sequencing	Planning
Activity Resource Estimating	Planning
Activity Duration Estimating	Planning
Schedule Development	Planning
Schedule Control	Monitoring and Controlling

Project Cost Management

As its name implies, the *Project Cost Management* knowledge area centers around costs and budgets. The processes that make up this knowledge area are as follows:

- Cost Estimating
- Cost Budgeting
- Cost Control

You can see how they work together in Table 1.8.

The activities in the Project Cost Management knowledge area establish cost estimates for resources, establish budgets, and keep watch over those costs to ensure that the project stays within the approved budget. This knowledge area is primarily concerned with the costs of resources, but other costs should be considered as well. For example, make certain to examine ongoing maintenance and support costs for software you're considering for the project.

Depending on the complexity of the project, these processes might need the involvement of more than one person. For example, the finance person might not have expertise about the resources documented in the staffing management plan so the project manager will need to bring in a staff member with those skills to assist with the activities in this process.

Two techniques are used in this knowledge area to decide among alternatives and improve the project process: life-cycle costing and Value Engineering. The life-cycle costing technique considers a group of costs collectively (such as acquisition, operations, disposal, and so on) when deciding among or comparing alternatives. The Value Engineering technique helps improve project schedules, profits, quality, and resource usage and optimizes life-cycle costs, among others. These techniques can improve decision making, reduce costs, reduce activity durations, and improve the quality of the deliverables. Some application areas require additional financial analysis to help predict project performance. Techniques such as payback analysis, return on investment, and discounted cash flows are a few of the tools used to accomplish this.

We'll discuss these techniques and others in further detail in Chapter 2.

TABLE 1.8 Project Cost Management

Process Name	Project Management Process Group
Cost Estimating	Planning
Cost Budgeting	Planning
Cost Control	Monitoring and Controlling

Project Quality Management

The *Project Quality Management* knowledge area assures that the project meets the requirements that it was undertaken to produce. This knowledge area focuses on product quality as well as on the quality of the project management process used during the project. These processes measure overall performance and monitor project results and compare them to the quality standards set out in the project-planning process to assure the customer will receive the product or service they commissioned.

As you can see from Table 1.9, Project Quality Management is composed of the following three processes: Quality Planning, Perform Quality Assurance, and Perform Quality Control.

TABLE 1.9   Project Quality Management

Process Name	Project Management Process Group
Quality Planning	Planning
Perform Quality Assurance	Executing
Perform Quality Control	Monitoring and Controlling

Project Human Resource Management

Project Human Resource Management involves all aspects of people management and personal interaction, including leading, coaching, dealing with conflict, performance appraisals, and more. These processes ensure that the human resources assigned to the project are used in the most effective way possible. Some of the project participants whom you'll get to practice these skills on include stakeholders, team members, and customers. Each requires the use of different communication styles, leadership skills, and team-building skills. A good project manager knows when to enact certain skills and communication styles based on the situation.

Projects are unique and temporary and so usually are project teams. Teams are put together based on the skills and resources needed to complete the activities of the project, and many times project team members may not know one another. Because the makeup of each team is different and the stakeholders involved in the various stages of the project may change, you'll use different techniques at different times throughout the project to manage the processes in this knowledge area.

The Project Human Resource Management knowledge area contains the following processes:

- Human Resources Planning
- Acquire Project Team
- Develop Project Team
- Manage Project Team

Take a look at Table 1.10 to see a visual overview of Project Human Resource Management.

TABLE 1.10   Project Human Resource Management

Process Name	Project Management Process Group
Human Resource Planning	Planning
Acquire Project Team	Executing
Develop Project Team	Executing
Manage Project Team	Monitoring and Controlling

Project Communications Management

The following processes make up the *Project Communications Management* knowledge area:

- Communications Planning
- Information Distribution
- Performance Reporting
- Manage Stakeholders

The processes in the Project Communications Management knowledge area are related to general communication skills, but they encompass much more than an exchange of information. Communication skills are considered general management skills that the project manager utilizes on a daily basis. The processes in the Process Communications Management knowledge area seek to ensure that all project information—including project plans, risk assessments, meeting notes, and more—is collected, documented, archived, and disposed of at the proper time. These processes also ensure that information is distributed and shared with stakeholders, management, and project members at appropriate times. When the project is closed, the information is archived and used as a reference for future projects. This is referred to as *historical information* in several project processes.

Everyone on the project has some involvement with this knowledge area because all project members will send and/or receive project communication throughout the life of the project. It is important that all team members and stakeholders understand how communication affects the project.

Table 1.11 shows the Project Communications Management process in progress.

TABLE 1.11   Project Communication Management

Process Name	Project Management Process Group
Communications Planning	Planning
Information Distribution	Executing

TABLE 1.11   Project Communication Management *(continued)*

Process Name	Project Management Process Group
Performance Reporting	Monitoring and Controlling
Manage Stakeholders	Monitoring and Controlling

Project Risk Management

Project Risk Management, as seen in Table 1.12, contains six processes:

- Risk Management Planning
- Risk Identification
- Qualitative Risk Analysis
- Quantitative Risk Analysis
- Risk Response Planning
- Risk Monitoring and Control

Risks include both threats to and opportunities within the project. The processes in this knowledge area are concerned with identifying, analyzing, and planning for potential risks, both positive and negative, that may impact the project. This means minimizing the probability and impact of negative risks while maximizing the probability and impact of positive risks. These processes are also used to identify the positive consequences of risk and exploit them to improve project objectives or discover efficiencies that may improve project performance.

Organizations will often combine several of these processes into one step. For example, Risk Identification, Qualitative Risk Analysis, and Quantitative Risk Analysis might be performed at the same time. The important thing about the Project Risk Management knowledge area is that you should strive to identify all the risks and develop responses for those with the greatest consequences to the project objectives.

TABLE 1.12   Project Risk Management

Process Name	Project Management Process Group
Risk Management Planning	Planning
Risk Identification	Planning
Qualitative Risk Analysis	Planning
Quantitative Risk Analysis	Planning

TABLE 1.12   Project Risk Management *(continued)*

Process Name	Project Management Process Group
Risk Response Planning	Planning
Risk Monitoring and Control	Monitoring and Controlling

Project Procurement Management

The *Project Procurement Management* knowledge area includes the processes involved with purchasing goods or services from vendors, contractors, suppliers, and others outside the project team. When discussing the Project Procurement Management processes, it's assumed that the discussion is taking place from your perspective as a buyer while sellers are external to the project team. Interestingly, the seller may manage their work as a project, particularly when the work is performed on contract, and you as the buyer become a key stakeholder in their project.

The processes in the Project Procurement Management knowledge area, shown in Table 1.13, are as follows:

- Plan Purchases and Acquisitions
- Plan Contracting
- Request Seller Responses
- Select Sellers
- Contract Administration
- Contract Closure

TABLE 1.13   Project Procurement Management

Process Name	Project Management Process Group
Plan Purchases and Acquisitions	Planning
Plan Contracting	Planning
Request Seller Reponses	Executing
Select Sellers	Executing
Contract Administration	Monitoring and Controlling
Contract Closure	Closing

The remainder of this book will deal with processes and process groups as they occur in order (i.e., Initiating, Planning, Executing, Monitoring and Controlling, and Closing), as this is the way you will encounter and manage them during a project.

Summary

Phew! We covered a lot of ground in this chapter. We learned that projects exist to bring about a unique product, service, or result. Projects are temporary in nature and have definite beginning and ending dates.

Stakeholders are those people or organizations that have a vested interest in the outcome of the project. Stakeholders include people like the project sponsor, the customer, key management personnel, the project manager, contractors, suppliers, and more. Projects are considered complete when the project meets or exceeds the expectations of the stakeholders.

Project management is a discipline that brings together a set of tools and techniques to describe, organize, and monitor the work of project activities. Project managers are the ones responsible for carrying out these activities. Projects may be organized into programs or portfolios and may be managed centrally by a PMO.

Project managers have a wide variety of skills. Not only should they be versed in the field they're working in, but in general management skills as well. Communication is the most important skill a project manager will use in the course of a project.

Organizational structures come in variations of three forms: functional, projectized, and matrix organizations. Functional organizations are traditional with hierarchical reporting structures. Project managers have little to no authority in this organization. Projectized organizations are structured around project work, and staff personnel report to project managers. Project managers have full authority in this organizational structure. Matrix organizations are a combination of the functional and projectized. A project manager's authority varies depending on the structure of the matrix, be it a weak matrix, a balanced matrix, or a strong matrix.

Projects progress through phases along a life cycle path to complete the product of the project. The project management process groups are performed throughout the project's life cycle. The process groups described in *A Guide to the PMBOK* are Initiating, Planning, Executing, Monitoring and Controlling, and Closing. Additionally, there are nine knowledge areas that bring together processes that have characteristics in common.

Exam Essentials

Be able to describe the difference between projects and operations.   A project is temporary in nature with a definite beginning and ending date. Projects produce unique products, services, or results. Operations are ongoing and use repetitive processes that typically produce the same result over and over.

Be able to denote some of the skills every good project manager should possess. Communication, budgeting, organizational, problem solving, negotiation and influencing, leading, and team building are skills a project manager should possess.

Be able to differentiate the different organizational structures and the project manager's authority in each. Organizations are usually structured in some combination of the following: functional, projectized, and matrix (including weak matrix, balanced matrix, and strong matrix). Project managers have the most authority in a projectized organization and the least amount of authority in a functional organization.

Be able to name the five project management processes. The five project management processes are Initiating, Planning, Executing, Monitoring and Controlling, and Closing.

Be able to name the nine Project Management Knowledge Areas. The nine Project Management Knowledge Areas are Project Integration Management, Project Scope Management, Project Time Management, Project Cost Management, Project Quality Management, Project Human Resource Management, Project Communications Management, Project Risk Management, and Project Procurement Management.

Key Terms

You've learned a lot of new key words in this chapter. PMI has worked hard to develop and define standard project management terms that apply across industries. Here is a list of some of the terms you came across in this chapter:

balanced matrix	program management
Closing	programs
Collocated	progressive elaboration
Deliverable	Project Communications Management
Executing	Project Cost Management
fast tracking	Project Human Resource Management
feasibility study	Project Integration Management
functional organization	project life cycle
Handoffs	project management
historical information	Project Management Knowledge Areas
Initiating	project management office
Iterative	project managers
Leaders	Project Procurement Management
Managers	Project Quality Management
matrix organizations	Project Risk Management
Monitoring and Controlling	project scope
Operations	Project Scope Management
Planning	project sponsor
Politics	Project Time Management
portfolio management	projectized organizations
Portfolios	projects
Power	stakeholders
product scope	tailoring

Review Questions

1. Which organization has set the de facto standards for project management techniques?

   A. PMBOK

   B. PMO

   C. PMI

   D. PMA

2. The VP of marketing approaches you and requests that you change the visitor logon screen on the company's website to include a username with at least six characters. This is considered
   _____.

   A. Project initiation

   B. Ongoing operations

   C. A project

   D. Project execution

3. Your company manufactures small kitchen appliances. They are introducing a new product line of appliances in designer colors with distinctive features for kitchens in small spaces. These new products will be offered indefinitely starting with the spring catalog release. Which of the following is true?

   A. This is a project because this new product line has never been manufactured and sold by this company before.

   B. This is an ongoing operation because the company is in the business of manufacturing kitchen appliances. Introducing designer colors and features is simply a new twist on an existing process.

   C. This is an ongoing operation because the new product line will be sold indefinitely. It's not temporary.

   D. This is not a project or an ongoing operation. This is a new product introduction not affecting ongoing operations.

4. Your company manufactures small kitchen appliances. It is introducing a new product line of appliances in designer colors with distinctive features for kitchens in small spaces. These new products will be offered indefinitely starting with the spring catalog release. In order to determine the characteristics and features of the new product line, you will have to perform which of the following?

   A. Fast tracking

   B. Consulting with the stakeholders

   C. Planning the project life cycle

   D. Progressive elaboration

5. A project is considered successful when _____.

   A. The product of the project has been manufactured.

   B. The project sponsor announces the completion of the project.

   C. The product of the project is turned over to the operations area to handle the ongoing aspects of the project.

   D. The project meets or exceeds the expectations of the stakeholders.

6. The VP of customer service has expressed concern over a project you're involved in. His specific concern is that if the project is implemented as planned, he'll have to purchase additional equipment to staff his customer service center. The cost is substantial and was not taken into consideration in the project budget. The project sponsor insists that the project must go forward as originally planned or the customer will suffer. Which of the following is true?

   A. The VP of customer service is correct. Since the cost was not taken into account at the beginning of the project, the project should not go forward as planned. Project initiation should be revisited to examine the project plan and determine how changes can be made to accommodate customer service.

   B. The conflict should be resolved in favor of the customer.

   C. The conflict should be resolved in favor of the project sponsor.

   D. The conflict should be resolved in favor of the VP of customer service.

7. Which of the following brings together a set of tools and techniques used to describe, organize, and monitor the work of project activities?

   A. Project managers

   B. *A Guide to the PMBOK*

   C. Project management

   D. Stakeholders

8. The Project Integration Management knowledge area is made up of which of the following processes?

   A. Initiation, Project Plan Development, and Integrated Change Control

   B. Project Plan Development, Project Plan Execution, and Integrated Change Control

   C. Project Plan Development, Initiation, and Scope Planning

   D. Initiation, Scope Planning, and Integrated Change Control

9. You are the project manager for Fun Days vacation packages. Your new project assignment is to head up the Fun Days resort opening in Austin, Texas. You are estimating the duration of the project plan activities, devising the project schedule, and monitoring and controlling deviations from the schedule. Which of the Project Management Knowledge Areas are you working in?

   A. Project Scope Management

   B. Project Quality Management

   C. Project Integration Management

   D. Project Time Management

10. You are the project manager for a large construction project. The project objective is to construct a set of outbuildings to house the Olympic support team that will be arriving in your city 18 months from the project start date. Resources are not readily available as they are currently assigned to other projects. Jack, an expert crane operator, is needed for this project two months from today. Which of the following skills will you use to get Jack assigned to your project?

   A. Negotiation and influencing skills

   B. Communication and organizational skills

   C. Communication skills

   D. Problem-solving skills

11. You've decided to try your hand at project management in the entertainment industry. You're working on a movie production and the team has just completed the storyboard phase of the project. Which of the following is true?

   A. The storyboard is a deliverable that marks the end of the phase. The deliverable must be approved before the next phase begins.

   B. The storyboard phase marks the end of the Initiating process group and the next phase of the project should begin.

   C. All of the phases of this project together make up a program.

   D. The division of phases and determining which processes to use in each phase is called tailoring.

12. You are managing a project to install a new postage software system that will automatically print labels and administer postage for certified mailings, overnight packages, and other special mailing needs. You've attempted to gain the cooperation of the business analyst working on this project and need some answers. She is elusive and tells you that this project is not her top priority. What should you do to avoid situations like this in the future?

   A. Establish the business analyst's duties well ahead of due dates and tell her you'll be reporting on her performance to her functional manager.

   B. Establish the business analyst's duties well ahead of due dates and tell her you are expecting her to meet these expectations because the customer is counting on the project meeting due dates to save significant costs on their annual mailings.

   C. Negotiate with the business analyst's functional manager during the planning process to establish expectations and request to participate in the business analyst's annual performance review.

   D. Negotiate with the business analyst's functional manager during the planning process to establish expectations and inform the functional manager of the requirements of the project. Agreement from the functional manager will assure the cooperation of the business analyst.

13. The amount of authority a project manager possesses can be related to _____.

   A. The project manager's communication skills

   B. The organizational structure

   C. The amount of authority the manager of the project manager possesses

   D. Key stakeholder's influence on the project

14. What is one of the advantages of a functional organization?

    A. All employees report to one manager and have a clear chain of command.

    B. All employees report to two or more managers, but project team members show loyalty to functional managers.

    C. The organization is focused on projects and project work.

    D. Teams are collocated.

15. You have been assigned to a project in which the objectives are to direct customer calls to an interactive voice response system before being connected to a live agent. You are in charge of the media communications for this project. You report to the project manager in charge of this project and the VP of marketing, who share responsibility for this project. Which organizational structure do you work in?

    A. Functional organization

    B. Weak matrix organization

    C. Projectized organization

    D. Balanced matrix organization

16. You have been assigned to a project in which the objectives are to expand three miles of the north-south highway through your city by two lanes in each direction. You are in charge of the demolition phase of this project, and you report to the project manager in charge of this project. You have been hired on contract and will be released at the completion of the demolition phase. What type of organizational structure does this represent?

    A. Functional organization

    B. Weak matrix organization

    C. Projectized organization

    D. Balanced matrix organization

17. What are the five project management process groups, in order?

    A. Initiating, Executing, Planning, Monitoring and Controlling, and Closing

    B. Initiating, Monitoring and Controlling, Planning, Executing, and Closing

    C. Initiating, Planning, Monitoring and Controlling, Executing, and Closing

    D. Initiating, Planning, Executing, Monitoring and Controlling, and Closing

18. You have been assigned to a project in which the objectives are to expand three miles of the north-south highway through your city by two lanes in each direction. You are interested in implementing a new project process called Design-Build in order to speed up the project schedule. The idea is that the construction team will work on the first mile of the highway reconstruction at the same time the design team is coming up with plans for the third mile of the reconstruction rather than completing all design before any construction begins. This is an example of _____.

    A. Managing the projects as a program

    B. Fast tracking

    C. Progressive elaboration

    D. Collocation

19. During which project management process are risk and stakeholder's ability to influence project outcomes the highest at the beginning of the process?

    A. Planning

    B. Executing

    C. Initiating

    D. Monitoring and Controlling

20. You are a project manager working on gathering requirements and establishing estimates for the project. Which process group are you in?

    A. Planning

    B. Executing

    C. Initiating

    D. Monitoring and Controlling

Answers to Review Questions

1. C. The Project Management Institute (PMI) is the industry-recognized standard for project management practices.

2. B. Projects exist to create a unique product or service. The logon screen in this question is not a unique product. A minor change has been requested, indicating this is an ongoing operation function. Some of the criteria for projects are that they are unique, temporary with definitive start and end dates, and considered complete when the project goals are achieved.

3. A. This is a project. The product line is new, which implies that this is a unique product—it hasn't been done before. We can discern a definite start and end date by the fact that the new appliances must be ready by the spring catalog release.

4. D. Progressive elaboration is the process of determining the characteristics and features of the product of the project. Progressive elaboration is carried out in steps in detailed fashion.

5. D. A project is considered successful when stakeholder needs and expectations are met or exceeded.

6. B. Conflicts between stakeholders should always be resolved in favor of the customer. This question emphasizes the importance of identifying your stakeholders and their needs as early as possible in the project. We'll discuss this more in later chapters.

7. C. Project management brings together a set of tools and techniques to organize project activities. Project managers are the ones responsible for managing the project processes.

8. B. Project Integration Management is made up of Project Plan Development, Project Plan Execution, and Integrated Change Control.

9. D. Project Time Management involves the following processes: Activity Definition, Activity Sequencing, Activity Duration Estimating, Schedule Development, and Schedule Control.

10. A. Negotiation and influencing skills are needed to convince Jack's boss and come to agreement concerning his assignment.

11. A. The storyboard is a deliverable. Phase endings are characterized by the completion, review, and approval of the deliverable. The next phase should not begin until the deliverable is approved.

12. C. Negotiate with the functional manager to participate in the business analyst's annual performance review.

13. B. The level of authority the project manager has is determined by the organizational structure. For instance, in a functional organization, the project manager has little to no authority, but in a projectized structure, the project manager has full authority.

14. A. An advantage for employees in a functional organization is that they have only one supervisor and a clear chain of command exists.

15. D. Employees in a balanced matrix often report to two or more managers. Functional managers and project managers share authority and responsibility for projects. There is a balance of power between the functional managers and project managers.

16. C. Projectized organizations are focused on the project itself. One issue with this type of structure is determining what to do with project team members when they are not actively involved on the project. One alternative is to release them when they are no longer needed.

17. D. Remember the acronym that sounds like syrup of ipecac: IPECC (Initiating, Planning, Executing, Monitoring and Controlling, and Closing).

18. B. Fast tracking is starting a new phase before the phase you're working on is completed. This compresses the project schedule, and as a result, the project is completed sooner.

19. C. The Initiating process is where stakeholders have the greatest ability to influence outcomes of the project. Risk is highest during this stage because of the high degree of unknown factors.

20. A. The Planning process is where requirements are fleshed out, stakeholders are identified, and estimates on project costs and time are made.

Creating the Project Charter and Preliminary Scope Statement

THE PMP EXAM CONTENT FROM THE INITIATING THE PROJECT PERFORMANCE DOMAIN COVERED IN THIS CHAPTER INCLUDES THE FOLLOWING:

- ✓ Conduct Project Selection Methods
- ✓ Define Scope
- ✓ Document Project Risks, Assumptions, and Constraints
- ✓ Identify and Perform Stakeholder Analysis
- ✓ Develop Project Charter
- ✓ Obtain Project Charter Approval

THE PMP EXAM CONTENT FROM THE PLANNING THE PROJECT PERFORMANCE DOMAIN COVERED IN THIS CHAPTER INCLUDES THE FOLLOWING:

- ✓ Conduct Kick-off Meeting

Now that you're fully armed with a detailed overview of project management, you can easily determine if your next assignment really is a project or an ongoing operation. You've also learned some of the basics of good project management techniques and the knowledge areas where you might need specific expertise. We're going to start putting those techniques into practice during the Initiating process group, which is where all projects start. And, as you've probably already guessed, we'll be using some of the general management skills outlined in Chapter 1, "What Is a Project?"

One of the first skills you will put to use will be your communication skills. Are you surprised? Of course you're not. It all starts with communication. You can't start defining the project until you've first talked to the project sponsor, key stakeholders, and management personnel. All good project managers have honed their communication skills to a nice sharp edge.

You'll remember from Chapter 1 that Initiating is the first process group in the five project management process groups. You can think of it as the official project kickoff. Initiating acknowledges that the project, or the next phase in an active project, should begin. This process group culminates in the publication of a project charter and a preliminary project scope statement. We'll cover each in this chapter.

At the end of this chapter, I'll introduce a case study that will illustrate the main points of the chapter. We'll take this case study with us from chapter to chapter and begin building a project using each of the skills we learn.

How Projects Come About

Your company's quarterly meeting is scheduled for today. You take your seat, and each of the department heads gets up and gives their usual "We can do it" rah-rah speech, one after the other. You sit up a little straighter when the CEO takes the stage. He starts out his part of the program pretty much the same way the other department heads did, and before long you find yourself drifting off. You are mentally reviewing the status of your current project when suddenly your daydreaming trance is shattered. You perk up as you hear the CEO say, "…and the new phone system will be installed by Thanksgiving."

Wait a minute. You work in the telecom department and haven't heard a word about this project until today. You also have a funny feeling that you've been elected to manage this project. It's amazing how good communication skills are so important for project managers but not…well, we won't go there.

Project *initiation* is the formal recognition that a project, or the next phase in an existing project, should begin and resources should be committed to the project. Unfortunately, many projects are initiated the way the CEO did in this example. Each of us, at one time or another, has experienced being handed a project with little to no information and told to "make it happen." The new phone system scenario is an excellent example of how *not* to initiate a project.

Taking one step back leads you to ask, "How do projects come about in the first place? Do CEOs just make them up as in this example?" Even though your CEO announced this new project at the company meeting with no forewarning, there is no doubt it came about as a result of a legitimate need. Believe it or not, CEOs don't just dream projects up to give you something to do. They're concerned about the future of the company and the needs of the business and its customers.

The business itself might drive the need for a project, customers might demand changes to products, or legal requirements may create the need for a new project. According to *A Guide to the PMBOK,* projects come about as a result of one of six needs or demands. Once those needs and demands are identified, the next logical step might include performing a feasibility study to determine the viability of the project. We'll look at these topics next.

Needs and Demands

Organizations exist to generate profits or serve the public. To stay competitive, organizations are always examining new ways of creating business, better ways of gaining efficiencies, or better ways to serve their customers. Sometimes laws are passed to force organizations to make their products safer or to less harmful to the environment. Projects result from all of these needs. Most projects will fit one of the six needs and demands described in the following list. It is those needs and demands that dictate the germination of a project. Needs and demands can also take the form of a business requirement, an opportunity, or a problem. Let's take a closer look at each of these areas:

Market demand   The demands of the marketplace can drive the need for a project. For example, a bank initiates a project to offer customers the ability to apply for mortgage loans over the Internet due to a drop in interest rates and an increase in demand for refinancing and new home loans.

Business need   The new phone system talked about earlier that was announced at the quarterly meeting came about as a result of a business need. The CEO, on advice from his staff, was advised that call volumes were maxed on the existing system. Without a new system, customer service response times would suffer, and that would eventually affect the bottom line.

Customer request   Customer requests run the gamut. Generally speaking, most companies have customers, and their requests can drive new projects. Customers can be internal or external to the organization. Government agencies don't have external customers per se (we're captive customers at any rate), but there are internal customers within departments and across agencies.

Perhaps you work for a company that sells remittance-processing equipment and you've just landed a contract with a local utility company. This project is driven by the need of the utility company to automate its process or upgrade its existing process. The utility company's request to purchase your equipment and consulting services is the project driver.

Technological advance   Do you happen to own one of those electronic personal digital assistants? They keep names and addresses handy and usually come with a calendar and a to-do list of some kind. I couldn't live without mine. However, there is always a newer, better version coming to market. The introduction of satellite communications now allows these little devices to connect to the Web or get e-mail almost anywhere in the world. The introduction of satellite communications is an example of a technological advance. Due to this introduction, electronics manufacturers revamped their products to take advantage of this new technology.

Legal requirement   Private industry and government agencies both generate new projects as a result of laws passed every legislative season. For example, new sales tax laws might require new programming to the existing sales tax system. The requirement that food labels appear on every package describing the ingredients and the recommended daily allowances is another example of a project driven by legal requirements.

Social need   The last need is a result of social demands. For example, perhaps a developing country is experiencing a fast-spreading disease that's infecting large portions of the population. Medical supplies and facilities are needed to vaccinate and cure those infected with the disease. Another example might include cleaning up waste products from the water supply of manufacturing plants prior to putting the water back into a local river or stream to prevent contamination.

Exam Spotlight

Understand each of the needs and demands that bring about a project for the exam.

All of these needs and demands represent opportunities, business requirements, or problems that need to be solved. Management must decide how to respond to these needs and demands, which will more often than not initiate new projects.

Feasibility Studies

After the opportunity for a project becomes evident, the next step might be to go ahead and initiate it, which means you're ready to jump right into creating a project charter for the project. But before you take that plunge, you should know that some organizations will require a feasibility study prior to making a final decision about starting the project.

Feasibility studies are undertaken for several reasons. One is to determine if the project is a viable project. A second reason is to determine the probability of the project succeeding. Feasibility studies can also examine the viability of the product of the project. For example, the study might ask, "Will the new lemon-flavored soda be a hit? Or is it marketable?" The study might also look at the technical issues related to the project and determine if the technology proposed is feasible, reliable, and easily assimilated into the organization's existing technology structure.

Feasibility studies may be conducted as separate projects, as subprojects, or as the first life cycle phase of the project. When you don't know the outcome of the study, it's best to treat it as a separate project. The group of people conducting the feasibility study should not be the same ones who will work on the project. Project team members may have built-in biases toward the project and will tend to influence the feasibility outcome toward those biases.

 Real World Scenario

The Interactive Voice Response Tax-Filing System

Jason, Sam, and Kate are web programmers working for the Department of Revenue in the State of Bliss. Ron, their manager, approaches them one day with an idea.

"Team, business unit managers are thinking it would be a great idea to offer taxpayers the ability to file their income tax returns over the telephone. We already offer them the ability to file on the Internet, thanks to all your efforts on that project last year. It's been a fabulous success. No other state has had the success that Bliss has had with our Internet system."

"Kate, I know you've had previous experience with IVR technology, but I'm not sure about you guys, so this is new territory for us. I'd like to hear what each of you thinks about this project."

Jason speaks up first. "I think it's a great idea. You know me, I'm always up for learning new things, especially when it comes to programming. When can we start?"

Sam echoes Jason's comments.

"This technology is pretty sophisticated," Kate says. "Jason and Sam are excellent coders and could work on the programming side of things, but I would have to pick up the telephony piece on my own. After we're up and running, we could go over the telephony portions step by step, so Jason and Sam can help me support it going forward. I'd really like to take on this project. It would be good for the team and good for the department."

Ron thinks for a minute. "Let's not jump right into this. I know you're anxious to get started, but I think a feasibility study is in order. The senior director of the tax business unit doesn't know if this project is cost justified and has some concerns about its life span. A feasibility study will tell us the answers to those questions. It should also help us determine if we're using the right technology to accomplish our goals, and it will outline alternative ways of performing the project that we haven't thought of. I don't want Kate going it alone without first examining all the issues and potential impacts to the organization."

Kicking Off the Project Charter

Our first stop in the Initiating group is a process called Develop the Project Charter. As the name of the process suggests, our purpose is to create a project charter. As we talked about in Chapter 1, the purpose for the Initiating group is to authorize a project, or the next phase of a project, to begin. It also gives the project manager the authority to apply resources to the project. These are also the purposes of a project charter: formally authorizing the project to begin and committing resources.

    The charter contains several elements which we'll discuss in the section "Formalizing and Publishing the Project Charter" later in this chapter.

Exam Spotlight

Understand the purposes of the project charter for the exam.

As you'll discover, every process has inputs, tools and techniques, and outputs and this one is no exception. We'll start with the inputs. Let's get to it.

Project Charter Inputs

Inputs to the project processes are typically informational in nature or they are outputs from previously completed processes. Inputs are used in combination with the tools and techniques to produce the outputs of each process. Process outputs are usually tangible, like a report or an update or a list, for example. In order to get to the output, we have to start with the inputs. Let's take a look at the Develop Project Charter process inputs:

- Contract (where applicable)
- Project statement of work
- Enterprise environmental factors
- Organizational process assets

The first input, a contract, is applicable only when the organization you are working for is performing a project for a customer external to the organization. The contract is used as an input to this process because it typically documents the conditions under which the project will be executed, the time frame, and a description of the work.

Project Statement of Work

The *project statement of work (SOW)* describes the product or service the project was undertaken to complete. This is usually a document written by either the project sponsor or the initiator of the project. When the project is external to the organization, the SOW is typically written by the buyer. For example, suppose you work for a consulting firm and have been assigned as the project manager for a project your company is performing on contract. The customer, the organization you'll be performing the project for, is the one who wrote the SOW.

According to *A Guide to the PMBOK,* a project SOW should contain or consider all of the following elements:

Business need   The business need for the project here relates to the needs of the organization itself. The need may be based on training, governmental standards, technological advances, market demands, or a legal requirement.

Product scope description   The product scope description describes the characteristics of the product or service of the project. The product scope description should be documented and should also include a description of the relationship between the business need or demand that's driving the project and the products being created.

Product descriptions contain less detail in the early phases of a project and more detail as the project progresses. Product scope descriptions, like the work of the project, are progressively elaborated. They will contain the greatest amount of detail in the project Executing processes.

When a project is performed under contract, typically the buyer of the product or service will provide the product description to the vendor or contractor. The product description can serve as a statement of work when the project is contracted to a vendor. A statement of work describes the product or service in enough detail so that the vendor can accurately price the contract and satisfactorily fulfill the requirements of the project.

Strategic plan   Part of the responsibility of a project manager during the Initiating processes is to take into consideration the company's strategic plan. Perhaps the strategic plan states that one of the company goals is to build 15 new stores by the end of the next fiscal year. If your project entails installing a new human resources software system, it would make sense to write the requirements for your project with the 15 new stores in mind. Your management team will refer to the strategic plan when choosing which new projects to initiate and which ones to drop, depending on their relationship to the strategic vision of the company.

Enterprise Environmental Factors

The enterprise environmental factors input shows up as an input to many of the other processes we'll discuss throughout the book. This input refers to the factors outside of the project itself that have (or may have) significant influence on the success of the project. According to *A Guide to the PMBOK,* the environmental factors include the following:

Organizational or company culture and structure   We talked about organizational structures and their influence on the organization in Chapter 1.

Governmental or industry standards   These include elements like regulatory standards and regulations (for instance, doctors must be licensed to practice medicine on people or pets), quality standards (International Standards Organization standards, for example), product standards, and workmanship standards.

Infrastructure   This refers to the organization's facilities and capital equipment. I would also include information technology in this category, even though PMI doesn't mention it.

Human resources   This refers to the existing staff's skills and knowledge.

Personnel administration   These are guidelines for hiring and firing, training, and employee performance reviews.

Organization's work authorization system   This defines how the work of the project is authorized.

Marketplace conditions   The old supply-and-demand theory applies here along with economic and financial factors.

Stakeholder risk tolerance   This is the level of risk stakeholders are willing to take on. We'll talk more about this in Chapter 5, "Risk Planning."

Commercial databases   These refer to industry-specific information, risk databases, and so on.

Project management information systems   This is typically a software product that allows you to schedule project activities and resources and collect and distribute project information.

These factors can influence the way you manage the project and, in some cases, the outcomes of the project. For example, perhaps the folks assigned to your project are junior level and don't have the skills, experience, or knowledge needed to complete the work of the project. It's up to the project manager to understand the organization's environmental factors and account for and consider how they can influence the management and outcomes of the project.

Organizational Process Assets

Organizational process assets refers to the organization's policies, guidelines, procedures, plans, approaches, or standards for conducting work, including project work. This includes a wide range of elements that may affect several aspects of the project, such as project management policies, safety policies, performance measurement criteria, templates, financial controls, communication requirements, issue and defect management procedures, change control procedures, risk control procedures, and the procedures used for authorizing work.

Organizational process assets also includes the information the organization has learned on previous projects (including how to store and retrieve that information). For example, previous project risks, performance measurements, earned value data, and schedules for past projects are valuable resources of knowledge for the current project. This information is also known as historical information. If you don't capture and store this information, however, it won't be available when starting a new project. You'll want to capture and store information such as project financial data (budgets, costs, overruns), historical information, lessons learned, project files, issues and defects, process measurements, and configuration management knowledge.

There are several elements included in the organizational process assets title, and I'll cover of each of them in later chapters of the book.

Organizational process assets and historical information should be reviewed and examined when starting a new project. Historical information can be very useful to project managers and to stakeholders. When you're evaluating new projects, historical information about previous projects of a similar nature can be very handy in determining if the new project should be accepted and initiated. Historical information gathered and documented during an active project is used to assist in determining whether the project should proceed to the next phase. Historical information will help you with the project charter, preliminary project scope statement, project scope statement, development of the project management plan, the process of defining and estimating activities, and more during the project-planning processes.

Understanding previous projects of a similar nature—their problems, successes, issues, and outcomes—will help you avoid repeating mistakes while reusing successful techniques to accomplish the goals of this project to the satisfaction of the stakeholders. Many of the processes in the project management process groups have organizational process assets as an input, implying that you should review the pertinent organizational assets that apply for the process you're about to start. For example, when performing the Cost Estimating process, you may find it helpful to review the activity estimates and budgets on past projects of similar size and scope before estimating the costs for the activities on the new project.

Exam Spotlight

Make certain you understand what the organizational process assets entail for the exam.

Using Tools and Techniques for Charter Development

The Develop Project Charter process has four tools and techniques you can use to help you produce the project charter. They are project selection methods, project management methodology, project management information system, and expert judgment. We'll look at each one next.

Selecting and Prioritizing Projects

Most organizations don't have the luxury of performing every project that's proposed. Even consulting organizations that sell their project management services must pick and choose which projects they want to work on. Selection methods help organizations decide among alternative projects. The project selection methods tool and technique calculates measurable differences between projects and determines the tangible benefits to the company of choosing or not choosing the project.

Project selection methods will vary depending on the company, the people serving on the selection committee, the criteria used, and the project. Sometimes selection methods will be purely financial, sometimes purely marketing, and sometimes they'll be based on public perception or political perception. In most cases, the decision is based on a combination of all of these and more.

Most organizations have a formal, or at least semiformal, process for selecting and prioritizing projects. In my organization, a steering committee is responsible for project review, selection, and prioritization. A *steering committee* is a group of folks comprising senior managers and sometimes midlevel managers who represent each of the functional areas in the organization.

Here's how our process works: The steering committee requests project ideas from the business staff prior to the beginning of the fiscal year. These project ideas are submitted in writing and contain a high-level overview of the project goals, a description of the deliverables, the business justification for the project, a desired implementation date, what the organization stands to gain from implementing the project, a list of the functional business areas affected by the project, and if applicable, a cost-benefit analysis (we'll talk about that in a bit).

A meeting is called to review the projects and a determination is made on each project as to whether it will be included on the upcoming list of projects for the new year. Once the no-go projects have been weeded out, the remaining projects are prioritized according to their importance and benefit to the organization. The projects are documented on an official project list, and progress is reported on the active projects at the regular monthly steering committee meetings.

In theory, it's a great idea. In practice, it works only moderately well. Priorities can and do change throughout the year. New projects come up that weren't originally submitted during the call for projects and they must be added to the list. Reprioritization begins anew, and resource alignment and assignments are shuffled. But again, we're getting ahead of ourselves. Just be aware that organizations usually have a process to recognize and screen project requests, accept or reject those requests based on some selection criteria, and prioritize the projects based on some criteria.

The project selection methods we'll talk about next are ones you should know and understand for the exam. However, keep in mind they are only one aspect of project selection in the real world. The individual opinion, and power, of selection committee members also plays a part in the projects the organization chooses to perform. Don't underestimate the importance of the authority, political standing, and individual aspirations of selection committee members. Those committee members who happen to carry a lot of weight in company circles, so to speak, are likely to get their projects approved just on the fact that they are who they are. This is sometimes how project selection works in my organization. How about yours?

Using Project Selection Methods

Project selection methods are concerned with the advantages or merits of the product of the project. In other words, selection methods measure the value of what the product or service of the project will produce and how it will benefit the organization. Selection methods involve the types of concerns executive managers are typically thinking about. This includes factors like market share, financial benefits, return on investment, customer retention and loyalty, and public perceptions. They are used to evaluate and choose between alternative ways of performing the project.

According to *A Guide to the PMBOK*, there are two categories of selection methods: *benefit measurement methods* and *mathematical models*. These selection methods are known as *decision models* and *calculation methods*. Decision models examine different criteria used in making decisions regarding project selection, while calculation methods provide a way to calculate the value of the project, which is then used in project selection decision making.

Exam Spotlight

Cross-reference your understanding of benefit measurement methods and mathematical models with the descriptions provided in *A Guide to the PMBOK*.

Mathematical Models

For the exam, all you need to understand about mathematical models is that they use linear, dynamic, integer, nonlinear, and/or multi-objective programming in the form of algorithms— or in other words, a specific set of steps to solve a particular problem. These are complicated mathematical formulas and algorithms that are beyond the scope of this book and require an engineering, statistical, or mathematical background to fully understand. Organizations considering undertaking projects of enormous complexity may use mathematical modeling techniques to make decisions regarding these projects. Mathematical models are also known as *constrained optimization methods*. The vast majority of project selection techniques will use the benefit measurement methods to make project selection decisions.

Benefit Measurement Methods

Benefit measurement methods employ various forms of analysis and comparative approaches to make project decisions. These methods include comparative approaches such as cost-benefit, scoring models, and benefit contribution methods that include various cash flow techniques and economic models. We'll examine several of these methods, starting with cost-benefit.

Cost-Benefit Analysis

One common benefit measurement method is the *cost-benefit* analysis. The name of this method implies what it does—it compares the cost to produce the product or service of the project to the benefit (usually financial in the form of savings or revenue generation) the organization will receive as a result of executing the project. Obviously, a sound project choice is one where the costs to implement or produce the product of the project are less than the financial benefits. How much less is the organization's decision. Some companies are comfortable with a small margin, while others are comfortable with a much larger margin between the two figures.

When examining costs for a cost-benefit analysis, include the costs to produce the product or service, the costs to take the product to market, and ongoing operational support costs. For example, let's say your company is considering writing and marketing a database software product that will allow banks to dissect their customer base, determine which types of customers buy which types of products, and then market more effectively to those customers. You will take into account some of the following costs:

- The costs to develop the software, such as programmer costs, hardware costs, testing, and testing costs.

- Marketing costs such as advertising, traveling costs to perform demos at potential customer sites, and so on.

- Ongoing costs such as having a customer support staff available during business hours to assist customers with product questions and problems.

Let's say the cost to produce this software plus the ongoing support costs total $5 million. Initial projections look like the demand for this product is high. Over a three-year period, the potential life of the software in its proposed form, projected revenues are $12 million. Taking only the financial information into account, the benefits outweigh the costs of this project. This project should receive a go recommendation.

Projects of significant cost or complexity usually involve more than one benefit measurement method when go or no-go decisions are being made or one project is being chosen over another. Keep in mind that selection methods can take subjective considerations into account as well—the project is a go because it's the new CEO's pet project; nothing else needs to be said.

Scoring Models

Another project selection technique in the benefit measurement category is a *scoring model,* or *weighted scoring model.* My organization uses weighted scoring models not only to choose between projects, but also as a method to choose between competing bids on out-sourced projects.

Weighted scoring models are quite simple. The project selection committee decides on the criteria that will be used on the scoring model—for example, profit potential, marketability of the product or service, the ability of the company to quickly and easily produce the product or service, and so on. Each of these criteria is assigned a weight depending on its importance to the project committee. More important criteria should carry a higher weight than less important criteria.

Then each project is rated on a scale from 1 to 5 (or some such assignment), with the higher number being the more desirable outcome to the company and the lower number having the opposite effect. This rating is then multiplied by the weight of the criteria factor and added to other weighted criteria scores for a total weighted score. Let's look at an example that brings this together (see Table 2.1).

TABLE 2.1   Weighted Scoring Model

Criteria	Weight	Project A Score*	Project B Score*	Project C Score*
Profit potential	5	5	5	3
Marketability	3	4	3	4
Ease to produce/support	1	4	3	2
Weighted score	—	41	37	29

*5 = highest

In this example, Project A is the obvious choice.

Cash Flow Analysis Techniques

The remaining benefit measurement methods involve a variety of cash flow analysis techniques, including payback period, discounted cash flows, net present value, and internal rate of return. We'll look at each of these techniques individually, and I'll provide you with a crash course on their meanings and calculations.

PAYBACK PERIOD

The *payback period* is the length of time it takes the company to recoup the initial costs of producing the product or service of the project. This method compares the initial investment to the cash inflows expected over the life of the product or service. For example, say the initial investment on a project is $200,000, with expected cash inflows of $25,000 per quarter every quarter for the first two years and $50,000 per quarter from then on. The payback period is two years and can be calculated as follows:

Initial investment = $200,000

Cash inflows = $25,000 × 4 (quarters in a year) = $100,000/year total inflow

Initial investment ($200,000) – year 1 inflows ($100,000) = $100,000 remaining balance

Year 1 inflows remaining balance – year 2 inflows = $0

Total cash flow year 1 and year 2 = $200,000

Payback is reached in two years.

The fact that inflows are $50,000 per quarter starting in year 3 makes no difference because payback is reached in two years.

Payback period is the least precise of all the cash flow calculations. That's because payback period does not consider the value of the cash inflows made in later years, commonly called the *time value of money*. For example, if you have a project with a five-year payback period, the cash inflows in year 5 are worth less than they are if you received them today. The next section will explain this idea more fully.

DISCOUNTED CASH FLOWS

As I just stated, money received in the future is worth less than money received today. The reason for that is the time value of money. If I borrowed $2,000 from you today and promised to pay it back in three years, you would expect me to pay interest in addition to the original amount borrowed. Okay, if you were a family member or a really close friend maybe you wouldn't, but ordinarily this is the way it works. You would have had the use of the $2,000 had you not lent it to me. If you had invested the money (does this bring back memories of your mom telling you to save your money?), you'd receive a return on it. Therefore, the future value of the $2,000 you lent me today is $2,315.25 in three years from now at 5 percent interest per year. Here's the formula for future value calculations:

$$FV = PV(1 + i)^n$$

In English, this formula says the future value (FV) of the investment equals the present value (PV) times (1 plus the interest rate) raised to the value of the number of time periods (n) the interest is paid. Let's plug in the numbers:

$$FV = 2,000(1.05)^3$$

$$FV = 2,000(1.157625)$$

$$FV = \$2,315.25$$

The *discounted cash flow* technique compares the value of the future cash flows of the project to today's dollars. In order to calculate discounted cash flows, you need to know the value of the investment in today's terms, or the present value (PV). PV is calculated as follows:

$$PV = FV \div (1 + i)^n$$

This is the reverse of the FV formula talked about earlier. So, if we ask the question, "What is $2,315.25 in three years from now worth today given a 5 percent interest rate?" we'd use the preceding formula. Let's try it:

$$PV = \$2,315.25 \div (1 + .05)^3$$

$$PV = \$2,315.25 \div 1.157625$$

$$PV = 2,000$$

$2,315.25 in three years from now is worth $2,000 today.

Discounted cash flow is calculated just like this for the projects you're comparing for selection purposes or when considering alternative ways of doing the project. Apply the PV formula to the projects you're considering and then compare the discounted cash flows of all the projects against each other to make a selection. Here is an example comparison of two projects using this technique:

Project A is expected to make $100,000 in two years.

Project B is expected to make $120,000 in three years.

If the cost of capital is 12 percent, which project should you choose?

Using the PV formula used previously, calculate each project's worth.

The PV of Project A = $79,719.

The PV of Project B = $85,414.

Project B is the project that will return the highest investment to the company and should be chosen over Project A.

NET PRESENT VALUE

Projects may begin with a company investing some amount of money into the project to complete and accomplish its goals. In return, the company expects to receive revenues, or cash inflows, from the resulting project. *Net present value (NPV)* allows you to calculate an accurate value for the project in today's dollars. The mathematical formula for NPV is complicated, and you do not need to memorize it in that form for the test. However, you do need to know how to calculate NPV for the exam, so I've given you some examples of a less-complicated way to perform this calculation in Tables 2.2 and 2.3 using the formulas you've already seen.

Net present value works like discounted cash flows in that you bring the value of future monies received into today's dollars. With NPV, you evaluate the cash inflows using the discounted cash flow technique applied to each period the inflows are expected instead of in one sum. The total present value of the cash flows is then deducted from your initial investment to determine NPV. NPV assumes that cash inflows are reinvested at the cost of capital.

Here's the rule: If the NPV calculation is greater than zero, accept the project. If the NPV calculation is less than zero, reject the project.

Look at the two project examples in Tables 2.2 and 2.3. Project A and Project B have total cash inflows that are the same at the end of the project, but the amount of inflows at each period differs for each project. We'll stick with a 12 percent cost of capital. Note that the PV calculations were rounded to two decimal places.

TABLE 2.2   Project A

Year	Inflows	PV
1	10,000	8,929
2	15,000	11,958
3	5,000	3,559

TABLE 2.2   Project A *(continued)*

Year	Inflows	PV
Total	30,000	24,446
Less investment	—	24,000
NPV	—	**446**

TABLE 2.3   Project B

Year	Inflows	PV
1	7,000	6,250
2	13,000	10,364
3	10,000	7,118
Total	30,000	23,732
Less investment	—	24,000
NPV	—	**<268>**

Project A has an NPV greater than zero and should be accepted. Project B has an NPV less than zero and should be rejected. When you get a positive value for NPV, it means that the project will earn a return at least equal to or greater than the cost of capital.

Another note on NPV calculations: Projects with high returns early in the project are better projects than projects with lower returns early in the project. In the preceding examples, Project A fits this criterion also.

INTERNAL RATE OF RETURN

The *internal rate of return (IRR)* is the most difficult equation to calculate of all the cash flow techniques that we've discussed. It is a complicated formula and should be performed on a financial calculator or computer. IRR can be figured manually, but it's a trial-and-error approach to get to the answer.

Technically speaking, IRR is the discount rate when the present value of the cash inflows equals the original investment. When choosing between projects or when choosing alternative methods of doing the project, projects with higher IRR values are generally considered better than projects with low IRR values.

Exam Spotlight

For the exam, you need to know three things concerning IRR:

- IRR is the discount rate when NPV equals zero.

- IRR assumes that cash inflows are reinvested at the IRR value.

- You should choose projects with the highest IRR value.

Exam Spotlight

Although *A Guide to the PMBOK* doesn't specifically address these cash flow techniques, you'll likely see exam questions on these topics. They are inferred in *A Guide to the PMBOK* under the heading "Benefit Measurement Methods."

Applying Project Selection Methods

Now that we've discussed some of the techniques used in the project selection methods tool and technique, let's look at how to apply them when choosing projects or project alternatives. One, two, or several of the benefit measurement methods can be used alone or in combination to come up with a selection decision. Remember that payback period is the least precise of all the cash flow techniques, NPV is the most conservative cash flow technique, and NPV and IRR will generally bring you to the same accept/reject conclusion.

Project selection methods, and particularly the benefit measurement methods, can be used to evaluate multiple projects or a single project. You might be weighing one project against another or simply considering if the project you're proposing is worth doing. Remember that project selection methods are a tool and technique of the Develop Project Charter process and this tool and technique covers two broad categories called mathematical methods (also known as constrained optimization methods) and benefit measurement methods. Both of these together are often called decision models.

Project Management Methodology and Information Systems

These two techniques are similar so I've put them together under the same heading. The project management methodology tool and technique refers to a methodology for managing projects much like *A Guide to the PMBOK* process groups and all of the processes contained within each of them. A project management methodology may be a formal, recognized project management standard like the one outlined in this book or an informal technique. Whether formal or informal, the methodology should help the project manager develop the project charter.

Real World Scenario

Fun Days Vacation Resorts

Jerry is a project manager for Fun Days Vacation Resorts. He is working on three different project proposals to present to the executive steering committee for review. As part of the information-gathering process, Jerry visits the various resorts pretending to be a guest. This gives him a feel for what Fun Days guests experience on their vacations, and it better prepares him to present project particulars and alternatives.

Jerry has prepared the project overviews for three projects and called upon the experts in marketing to help him out with the projected revenue figures. He works up the numbers and finds the following:

- Project A—payback period = 5 years; IRR = 8 percent

- Project B—payback period = 3.5 years; IRR = 3 percent

- Project C—payback period = 2 years; IRR = 3 percent

Funding exists for only one of the projects. Jerry recommends Project A and predicts this is the project the steering committee will choose since the projects are mutually exclusive.

Jerry's turn to present comes up at the steering committee. Let's listen in on the action.

"And, on top of all the benefits I've just described, Project A provides an IRR of 8 percent, a full 5 percent higher than the other two projects we discussed. I recommend the committee choose Project A."

"Thank you Jerry," Colleen says. "Good presentation." Colleen is the executive chairperson of the steering committee and has the authority to break ties or make final decisions when the committee can't seem to agree.

"However, here at Fun Days we like to have our fun sooner rather than later." Chuckles ensue from the steering committee. They've all heard this before. "I do agree that an 8 percent IRR is a terrific return, but the payback is just too far out into the future. There are too many risks and unknowns for us to take on a project with a payback period this long. As you know, our industry is directly impacted by the health of the economy. Anything can happen in five years' time. I think we're much better off going with Project C. I recommend we accept Project C. Committee members, do you have anything to add?"

Project management information system (PMIS) is listed in this process as a tool and technique. Notice that this is also noted as one of the enterprise environmental factors. A PMIS is a set of automated tools (generally a software program) that allows you to schedule project activities and resources and collect and distribute project information. As a tool and technique of the Develop Project Charter process, the PMIS facilitates the creation of the project charter, provides a way to capture feedback and changes to the charter, and publishes the finalized, approved charter.

Expert Judgment

Expert judgment is the last tool and technique in this process. The concept behind expert judgment is to rely on individuals, or groups of people, who have training, specialized knowledge, or skills in the areas you're assessing. These folks may be stakeholders, consultants, other experts in the organization, or technical or professional organizations. Expert judgment is a tool and technique used in other planning processes as well.

In the case of developing a project charter, expert judgment would be helpful in assessing the inputs of this process, the environmental factors, and organizational assets —that is, the project statement of work, product descriptions, strategic plan, project selection methods, and historical information. For example, as the project manager, you might rely on the expertise of your executive committee to help you understand how the proposed project gels with the strategic plan. Or you might rely on team members who have participated on similar projects in the past to make recommendations regarding the proposed project.

Formalizing and Publishing the Project Charter

The *project charter* is the official, written acknowledgment and recognition that a project exists. It ties the work of the project with the ongoing operations of the organization. It's usually issued by senior management and gives the project manager the authority to assign organizational resources to the work of the project.

The charter documents the business need or demand that the project was initiated to address and the project justification, and it includes a description of the product or service of the project. It is usually the first official document of the project once acceptance of the project has been granted. Project charters are often used as a means to introduce a project to the organization. Since this document outlines the high-level project description, the business opportunity or need, and the project's purpose, executive managers can get a "first glance" look at the benefits of the project. Good project charters that are well documented will address many of the questions your stakeholders are likely to have up front.

Let's take a brief look at the key stakeholders who may be involved with the project charter and the role they'll play in its development and on the project in the future.

Key Stakeholders

A Guide to the PMBOK states that the project sponsor or initiator is the one who provides the information for the project charter. It also says a manager who is external to the project should publish the charter. However, *A Guide to the PMBOK* and common project management practices don't always match up. In practice, my experience has been that the project charter is published under the name of the project sponsor. It also involves the input of key stakeholders. Often, the project sponsor or initiator won't have all the information needed to complete the charter and you'll be charged with digging out all the facts needed to create this document as well as the preliminary project scope statement. But remember, you're studying to pass the exam, so you should know that A *Guide to the PMBOK* states that the author of the project charter should be a manager external to the project and input comes from the initiator or sponsor.

Project Manager

The project manager is the person who assumes responsibility for the success of the project. The project charter identifies the project manager and describes the authority the project manager has in carrying out the project. The project manager's primary responsibilities are project planning and then executing and managing the work of the project. By overseeing the project charter and the project planning documents created later on in the project, the project manager is assured that everyone knows and understands what's expected of them and what constitutes a successful project.

Project managers are responsible for setting the standards and policies for the projects they work on. As a project manager, it is your job to establish and communicate the project procedures to the project team and stakeholders.

Project managers will identify activities and tasks, resource requirements, project costs, project requirements, performance measures, and more. Communication and documentation must become the project manager's best friends. Keeping stakeholders, the project sponsor, the project team, and all other interested parties informed is "job one," as the famous car manufacturer's ads say.

Project Sponsor

Have you ever attended a conference or event that was put on by a sponsor? In the information technology field, conferences and seminars are often sponsored by software development companies. The sponsor pays for the event, the facilities, and the goodies and provides an opportunity for vendors to display their wares. In return, the sponsor comes out looking like a winner. Because they are footing the bill for all this fun, the sponsor gets to call the shots on conference content and they get the prime spots for discussing their particular solutions. And last but not least, they usually provide the keynote speaker and get to present their information to a captive audience.

Project sponsors are similar to this in that they rally support from stakeholders and the executive management team for the project. The project sponsor is usually an executive in the organization who has the power and authority to make decisions and settle disputes or conflicts regarding the project. The sponsor takes the project into the limelight, so to speak, and gets to call the shots regarding project outcomes. The project sponsor is also the one with the big bucks who provides funds for your project. The project sponsor should be named in the project charter and identified as the final authority and decision maker for project issues.

Sponsors are actively involved in the Initiating and Planning phases of the project and tend to have less involvement during the Execution and Monitoring and Controlling phases. It's up to the project manager to keep the project sponsor informed of all project activities, project progress, and any conflicts or issues that arise. The sponsor is the one with the authority to resolve conflicts and set priorities when these things can't be dealt with any other way.

Project Champion

The project champion is another strong project supporter. Unlike the sponsor, the project champion doesn't necessarily have a lot of authority or executive powers. The champion helps focus attention on the project from a technical perspective. The project champion is usually someone with a great deal of technical expertise or industry knowledge regarding the project. They can lend credibility to the viability of the project and to the skills and abilities of the key project team members to carry out project activities. Sometimes, the project manager may act as project champion.

The project champion isn't necessarily identified in the project charter. But as a project manager, you'll want to know who this person is because they're a strong project advocate and you might need them later on to help rally support for project decisions.

Functional Managers

We covered functional managers briefly in Chapter 1. Project managers must work with and gain the support of functional managers in order to complete the project. Functional managers fulfill the administrative duties of the organization, provide and assign staff members to projects, and conduct performance reviews for their staff. It's a good idea to identify the functional managers who'll be working on project tasks or assigned project responsibilities in the charter.

It's also a good idea to identify the key project stakeholders in the project charter. While this isn't explicitly stated as part of this process, you'll see in the next section that stakeholder influences make up one of the components of the project charter. In order to identify stakeholder influences, I believe it's also necessary to identify the stakeholders and describe their role in high-level terms as I've done here.

Pulling the Project Charter Together

According to *A Guide to the PMBOK,* in order to create a useful and well-documented project charter, you should include at least these elements:

- Purpose or justification for the project

- Business need for the project

- Business justification for the project, including return on investment analysis

- High-level project description or product description

- Requirements that must be completed satisfactorily according to stakeholder, sponsor, and customer expectations

- Stakeholder influences

- Involvement of other departments (in the functional organization) and the level of participation needed

- Constraints

- Assumptions

- Summary milestone schedule (preliminary)

- Summary budget (preliminary)
- Name of the project manager and their authority levels

We've already discussed some of these elements. The purpose of the project, business need, and business justification were covered in earlier sections of this chapter. In the last section, we talked some about stakeholders and their roles. We'll cover this topic more thoroughly in the next chapter. The roles or involvement of other departments and their level of participation is a matter of defining the level of involvement and the types of actions required from the other departments to fulfill the purpose and requirements of the project.

A constraint is anything that restricts the actions of the project team. Perhaps the project has a hard end date. The date cannot move due to circumstances outside of the control of the project. Or perhaps the project has a set budget. Both of these things are examples of constraints. Assumptions are events or actions believed to be true. Both constraints and assumptions should be documented in the project charter. However, many of these elements are included in the processes related to creating a scope statement and become further refined as you get into the Planning process, so we'll talk more about these topics in Chapter 3, "Creating the Scope Statement."

The important thing to remember for the exam about the project charter is that it authorizes the project to begin, it authorizes the project manager to assign resources to the project, it documents the business need and justification, it describes the customer's requirements, and it ties the project to the ongoing work of the organization.

Exam Spotlight

In some organizations, the project charter might be written by the project manager. However, if you (as the project manager) are asked to write the charter, remember that your name should not appear as the author of the project charter document. Since the project charter authorizes the project and authorizes you as the project manager, it doesn't make sense for you to write a document authorizing yourself to manage the project. The author of the charter should be an executive manager in your organization (external to the project) with the power and authority to assign resources to this project. Remember for the exam that the charter is authorized external to the project organization.

Project Charter Sign-off

The project charter isn't complete until you've received sign-off from the project sponsor, senior management, and key stakeholders. Sign-off indicates that the document has been read by those signing it (let's hope so, anyway) and that they agree with its contents and are on board with the project. It also involves the major stakeholders right from the beginning and hopefully wins their continued participation in the project going forward. If someone has a problem with any of the elements in the charter, now is the time to raise the red flag.

One of the things I like to do prior to publishing the charter is to hold a kick-off meeting with the key stakeholders to discuss the charter and then obtain their sign-off. While *A Guide to the*

PMBOK doesn't bring stakeholders into the picture until the Planning processes, I think it's imperative that you identify your key stakeholders as soon as possible and involve them in the creation of the project charter and preliminary scope statement. Remember for the exam, however, that the initiator or sponsor provides the input for the charter and preliminary scope statement.

We'll talk more about key stakeholder roles in Chapter 3, "Developing the Project Scope Statement."

Signing the project charter document is the equivalent of agreeing to and endorsing the project. This doesn't mean that the project charter is set in stone, however. Project charters will change throughout the course of the project. As more details are uncovered and outlined and as the Planning processes begin, more project issues will come to light. This is part of the iterative process of project management and is to be expected. The charter will occasionally be revised to reflect these new details, project plans will be revised, and project execution will change to incorporate the new information or direction.

The last step in this process is publishing the charter. Publishing, in this case, simply means distributing a copy of the project charter to the key stakeholders, the customer, the management team, and others who may be involved with the project. Publication can take several forms, including printed format or electronic format distributed via the company e-mail system or on the company's intranet.

Next, I'll further describe the work of the project in a preliminary project scope statement.

Developing a Preliminary Project Scope Statement

The *preliminary scope statement* is the first blush, so to speak, of a definition of what the project entails. This preliminary document is a high-level look at the project objectives and deliverables. It serves the purpose of capturing the intended outcome of the project and its deliverables. It provides a brief background of the project and describes the business opportunity the company is attempting to benefit from. It also describes the business objectives the project should meet.

The preliminary scope statement is based on information provided by the project sponsor or initiator and lays the groundwork for future consensus on deliverables and project expectations and will be further elaborated in the Scope Definition process that we'll talk about in Chapter 3.

Preliminary Scope Statement Inputs and Techniques

The inputs for this process are as follows:

- Project charter
- Project SOW
- Enterprise environmental factors
- Organizational process assets

We've seen all of these previously in this chapter. Remember that many times, outputs from one process become inputs into the next process. That's the case here, where you'll examine the project charter, meet with the project sponsor or initiator, and develop the preliminary project scope statement. Before we get to what the scope statement contains, let's take a look at the tools and techniques of this process. These will look familiar too.

The tools and techniques for the Develop Preliminary Scope Statement process include project management methodology, project management information system, and expert judgment.

The Preliminary Scope Statement Document

The preliminary scope statement document contains several elements, most of which are repeated in the final scope statement created during the Planning process group. Creating a preliminary scope statement is a good thing for very large projects or projects with multiple phases. On large projects, each phase has its own preliminary scope statement document that can be reexamined, revised, and elaborated as the new phase begins. Small- to medium-sized projects probably will not need a preliminary scope statement. You could skip straight to the Planning processes from here, but I urge you, don't turn the page. You do need to know about this process for the exam even if you'll only use it a few times in the course of your project work. And remember, it's up to the project manager (that's you) to determine which processes should be completed for the project. My guess is the majority of the time you'll skip this one.

Exam Spotlight

For the exam, understand the purpose of the preliminary scope document, which is to describe the characteristics of the product of the project, what is and what is *not* included in project scope (*A Guide to the PMBOK* calls this "boundaries"), how the final product or service of the project will be accepted, and how scope will be controlled.

According to *A Guide to the PMBOK,* the preliminary scope statement should contain these elements:

- Project objectives
- Characteristics of the product or service of the project (i.e., a product description)
- Product objectives
- Project deliverables
- Requirements (both product and project)
- Exclusions from scope (project boundaries)
- Constraints
- Assumptions
- High-level risk list and definition

- Milestones
- Initial WBS
- Cost estimate (order of magnitude)
- Configuration management requirements
- Project acceptance criteria

I know you're dying to know more about some of these elements! I don't mean to keep you in suspense, but it makes a lot more sense to cover these elements when we talk about the scope statement in Chapter 3. You will *always* create a scope statement for your project, no matter how large or small. (You do this, right?) Besides, we've covered a lot of material in these first two chapters and you probably need a little breather to absorb what you've learned. Kick back, run through the end-of-chapter questions, and then you'll be ready to jump into these topics.

The Kitchen Heaven Project Case Study

This chapter introduces a case study that we'll follow throughout the remainder of the book. You'll find an updated case study closing out every chapter. They're designed to show you how a project manager might apply the material covered in the chapter to a real-life project. As happens in real life, not every detail of every process is followed during all projects. Remember that the processes from *A Guide to the PMBOK* that we'll cover in the remaining chapters are project management guidelines. You will often combine processes during your projects, which allows you to perform several steps at once. The case studies will present situations or processes that you might find during your projects and describe how one project manager resolves them.

Project Case Study: New Kitchen Heaven Retail Store

You are a project manager for Kitchen Heaven, a chain of retail stores specializing in kitchen utensils, cookware, dishes, small appliances, and some gourmet food stuffs such as bottled sauces and spices. You're fairly new to the position, having been hired to replace a PM who recently retired.

Kitchen Heaven currently owns 49 stores in 34 states and Canada. The world headquarters for Kitchen Heaven is in Denver, Colorado. Counting full-time and part-time employees, the company employs 1,500 people, 200 of whom work in the headquarters office.

The company's mission statement reads: "Great gadgets for people interested in great food."

Recently, the vice president of marketing came to pay you a visit. Dirk Perrier is a very nice man, well dressed, with the formal air that you would expect a person in his capacity might have. He shakes your hand and gives you a broad, friendly smile.

"We've decided to go forward with our 50th store opening! Sales are up, and our new line of ceramic cookware is a hot seller, no pun intended. I don't know if you're familiar with our store philosophy, so let me take a moment to explain it. We like to place our stores in neighborhoods that are somewhat affluent. The plain fact is that most of our shoppers have incomes of over $150,000 a year. So, we make an effort to place our stores in areas where those folks normally shop.

"We're interested in targeting the non-gourmet customer, one who's interested in cooking but won't be making Peking duck. So, the stores are upbeat and convey a little bit of a laid-back feel, if you will.

"Our next store is going to be right here in our home area—Colorado Springs. We have a store in Boulder and one in Denver, but none down south. Because this is going to be our 50th store, we plan on having a 50th grand-opening celebration, with the kind of surprises and activities you might expect for such a notable opening.

"Our stores generally occupy from 2,000 to 4,000 square feet of retail space, and we typically use local contractors for the build-out. A store build-out usually takes 120 days from the date the property has been procured until the doors open to the public. I can give you our last opening's project plan so you have a feel for what happens. Your job will be to procure the property, negotiate the lease, procure the shelving and associated store furnishings, get a contractor on the job, and prepare the 50th store festivities. My marketing folks will assist you with that last part.

"You have six months to complete the project. Any questions?"

You take in a deep breath and collect your thoughts. Dirk has just given you a lot of information with hardly a pause in between thoughts. A few initial ideas drift through your head while you're reaching for your notebook.

You work in a functional organization with a separate projectized department responsible for carrying out projects of this nature. You've been with the company long enough to know that Dirk is high up there in the executive ranks and carries the authority and the power to make things happen. Therefore, Dirk is the perfect candidate for project sponsor.

You grab your notebook and start documenting some of the things Dirk talked about, clarifying with him as you write:

- The project objective is to open a new store in Colorado Springs six months from today.

- The store should be located in an affluent area.

- The store will carry the full line of products from utensils to gourmet food items.

- The grand opening will be accompanied by lots of fanfare because this is the 50th store opening.

You have a question or two for Dirk.

"Is there a special reason we have to open…let's see…six months from now is February 1st?"

"Yes, we want the store open the first week in February. Early February is when the Garden and Home Show conference hits the Springs area. We'll have a trade show booth there. We know from experience in other areas that our stores generally see a surge in sales during this month as a result of the trade show. It's a great way to get a lot of advertising out there and let folks know where we're located."

"Another question, Dirk. Is there a budget set for this project yet?"

"We haven't set a hard figure," Dirk replies. "But again, from past experience we know it takes anywhere from $1.5 to $2 million to open a new store. And we don't want to forget the big bash for the grand opening."

"Thanks, Dirk. I'll get started writing the project charter right away. I'll be putting your name on the document since you're the project sponsor."

Dirk concludes with, "Feel free to come to me with questions or concerns at any time."

One week later.

You review your notes and reread the project charter you've prepared for the Kitchen Heaven retail store one last time before looking for Dirk. You finally run across Dirk in a hallway near the executive washroom.

"Dirk, I'm glad I caught you. I'd like to go over the project charter with you before the kickoff meeting tomorrow. Do you have a few minutes?"

"Sure," Dirk says to you. "Let's have it."

"The project charter states the purpose of the project, which of course is to open the 50th Kitchen Heaven store in Colorado Springs. I also documented some of the high-level requirements, many of which we talked about last time we met. I documented the assumptions and constraints you gave me with the understanding that we'll define these much more closely when I create the scope statement. I've included a section that outlines a preliminary milestone schedule and I've included some preliminary return on investment calculations. Using your estimate of $2 million as our initial budget request and based on the projected inflows you gave me last week, I've calculated a payback period of 16 months, with an IRR of 22 percent."

"That's impressive," replies Dirk. "Even better than our Phoenix store. If I recall, the payback period there was just over two years. Let's hope those numbers hold true."

"I think they're reliable figures. I researched our data based on recent store openings in similar-sized cities and factored in the economic conditions of the Colorado Springs area. Since they're on a growth pattern, we think the timing is perfect."

"As you know, the project kickoff is scheduled for tomorrow. What I'll need then is for you to talk about the project and the goals, talk about the commitment you'll need from the management team to support this project, and introduce me as the project manager. I've already forwarded a copy of the project charter to the meeting attendees so that they can review it before the meeting. And I included a list of the assumptions we've made so far as an appendix to the charter. Lastly, I'll need you to ask everyone present to sign a copy of the project charter."

"Sounds like you've covered everything," Dirk says. "I don't anticipate any problems tomorrow, as everyone is looking forward to this store opening."

Project Case Study Checklist

> **Project objective:** To open a new store in Colorado Springs six months from today.

> **Business need or demand for project:** Company data concludes that the Kitchen Heaven consumers have incomes of over $150,000 a year. The Colorado Springs area is home to a large number of people with that income. Currently, there is not a Kitchen Heaven there, but there appears to be a demand for one.

> **Project sponsor:** Dirk Perrier, VP of marketing.

> **Organizational structure:** Functional organization with a separate projectized department.

> **Project selection methods:** Payback period calculated at 16 months and IRR calculated at 22 percent.

> **Created project charter:** Project charter contains the following:

> - High-level overview of project
> - List of requirements that will satisfy sponsor expectations
> - Business case and justification for the project
> - High-level milestone schedule with initial completion date of February 1
> - Initial budget of $2 million
> - Definition of roles of project sponsor and project manager

> Kickoff meeting set up to discuss charter and obtain sign-off.

Summary

This chapter started with a discussion of how projects are initiated. Projects come about as a result of one of six needs or demands: market demand, business need, customer requests, technological advances, legal requirements, and social needs.

Then we talked about the Develop the Project Charter process. The project statement of work is an input to this process that describes the product or service the project was undertaken to complete. The SOW should include the business needs of the organization and a product scope description and should map to the organization's strategic plan.

Enterprise environmental factors are factors outside of the project that may have significant influence on the success of the project. Organizational process assets refer to policies, guidelines, and procedures for conducting the project work.

Project selection methods are a tool and technique of the Develop Project Charter process. Selection methods include decision models in the form of benefit measurement methods and mathematical models (also called constrained optimization methods). The mathematical methods utilize mathematical models. Benefit measurement methods come in the form of cost-benefit analyses, scoring models, and economic analyses. These are primarily comparative approaches. Besides cost-benefit analysis, the most commonly used form of benefit measurement methods is cash flow analysis.

Analysis of cash flows includes payback period, discounted cash flows, net present value (NPV), and internal rate of return (IRR). These last three methods are concerned with the time value of money—or in other words, converting future dollars into today's value. Generally, projects with a shorter payback period are desired over those with longer payback periods. Projects that have an NPV greater than zero should be accepted. Projects with the highest IRR value are considered a better benefit to the organization than projects with low IRR values.

Expert judgment is another tool and technique of this process. Experts usually have specialized knowledge or skills and can include staff from other departments in the company, external or internal consultants, and members of professional and technical associations or industry groups.

The output of this process is the project charter, which is the formal recognition that a project, or the next project phase, should begin. The charter authorizes the project to begin, it authorizes the project manager to assign resources to the project, it documents the business need and justification, it describes the customer's requirements, and it ties the project to the ongoing work of the organization.

The preliminary project scope statement is a high-level definition of what the project entails, including the project objectives and deliverables. It describes the business opportunity the company is attempting to benefit from and the business objectives the project intends to meet. Many of the elements included in the preliminary scope statement are also part of the project scope statement.

Exam Essentials

Be able to distinguish between the six needs or demands that bring about project creation. The six needs or demands that bring about project creation are market demand, business need, customer requests, technological advances, legal requirements, and social needs.

Be able to denote the Develop the Project Charter inputs. The inputs for Develop the Project Charter are contract (where applicable), project statement of work, enterprise environmental factors, and organizational process assets.

Be able to define decision models. Decision models are project selection methods that are a tool and technique of the Develop Project Charter process. Decision models include benefit measurement methods and mathematical models.

Be able to describe and calculate payback period. Payback period is the amount of time it will take the company to recoup its initial investment in the product of the project. It's calculated by adding up the expected cash inflows and comparing them to the initial investment to determine how many periods it takes for the cash inflows to equal the initial investment.

Be able to denote the decision criteria for NPV and IRR. Projects with an NPV greater than zero should be accepted, and those with an NPV less than zero should be rejected. Projects with high IRR values should be accepted over projects with lower IRR values. IRR is the discount rate when NPV is equal to zero, and IRR assumes reinvestment at the IRR rate.

Be able to describe the importance of the project charter. The project charter is the document that officially recognizes and acknowledges that a project exists. The charter authorizes the project to begin, it authorizes the project manager to assign resources to the project, it documents the business need and justification, it describes the customer's requirements, and it ties the project to the ongoing work of the organization.

Key Terms

You've learned a lot of new key words in this chapter. PMI has worked hard to develop and define standard project management terms that apply across industries. Here is a list of some of the terms you came across in this chapter:

benefit measurement methods	mathematical models
calculation methods	net present value (NPV)
constrained optimization methods	payback period
cost-benefit	preliminary scope statement
decision models	project charter
discounted cash flow	project statement of work (SOW)
expert judgment	scoring model
initiation	steering committee
internal rate of return (IRR)	weighted scoring model

Review Questions

1. When a project is being performed under contract, the SOW is provided by which of the following?

   A. The buyer

   B. The project sponsor

   C. The project manager

   D. The contractor

2. You've been hired as a manager for the Adjustments Department of a nationwide bank based in your city. The Adjustments Department is responsible for making corrections to customer accounts. This is a large department, with several smaller sections that deal with specific accounts; for example, personal checking or commercial checking. You've received your first set of management reports and can't make heads or tails of the information. Each section appears to use a different methodology to audit their work and record the data for the management report. You request a project manager from the PMO to come down and get started right away on a project to streamline this process and make the data and reports consistent. This project came about as a result of which of the following?

   A. Technological advance

   B. Business need

   C. Customer request

   D. Legal requirement

3. What are the inputs to the Develop Project Charter process?

   A. Contract, project SOW, enterprise environmental factors, organizational process assets

   B. Project SOW, project selection methods, organizational process assets

   C. Contract, project selection methods, enterprise environmental factors, organizational process assets

   D. Project SOW, project selection methods, enterprise environmental factors

4. You work for a large manufacturing plant. Your firm is thinking of initiating a new project to release an overseas product line. This is the company's first experience in the overseas market, and it hopes to make a big splash with the introduction of this product. The project entails producing your product in a concentrated formula and packaging it in smaller containers than the U.S. product uses. A new machine is needed in order to mix the first set of ingredients in the concentrated formula. Which of the following actions should the project manager take?

   A. The project manager should document the project's objectives and business justification in a project charter document and recommend that the project proceed.

   B. The project manager knows the project is a go and should document the project's objectives and known deliverables in a preliminary scope statement document.

   C. The project manager should document the business need for the project and recommend that a feasibility study be performed to determine viability of the project.

   D. The project manager should document the high-level product requirements and stakeholder expectations in a preliminary scope statement.

5. Which of the following lists the inputs and the tools and techniques that the two processes within the Initiating process group share?

A. Project SOW, enterprise environment factors, organizational process assets, project selection methods, expert judgment

B. Enterprise environment factors, organizational process assets, PMIS, expert judgment

C. Project SOW, enterprise environment factors, organizational process assets, project management methodology, PMIS, expert judgment

D. Project SOW, enterprise environment factors, organizational process assets

6. According to *A Guide to the PMBOK*, the project statement of work should contain or reference all of the following elements except for which one?

A. Strategic plan, product scope description, stakeholder influences, and business need

B. Business need, strategic plan, product scope description

C. Project purpose, business case, stakeholder influences, product scope description

D. Requirements, business need, stakeholder expectations

7. Your nonprofit organization is preparing to host its first annual 5K run/walk in City Park. You worked on a similar project for the organization two years ago when it cohosted the 10K run through Overland Pass. Which of the organizational process assets might be helpful to you on your new project?

A. The strategic plan, because you'll want to make sure the project reflects the overall strategic direction of the organization

B. Historical information on the 10K run project

C. The project SOW, which describes the high-level details of the run/walk program

D. The organization's PMIS system

8. Which of the following is true regarding product scope descriptions?

A. The product scope description is a component of the output of the Develop Project Charter process. It describes the characteristics of the product or service and contains a good deal of detail in the later phases of the project.

B. The product description is a component of the output of the Preliminary Scope Statement process. It describes the characteristics of the product or service and contains less detail in the early phases of the project.

C. The product description is a component of an input of the Preliminary Scope Statement process. It describes the characteristics of the product or service and contains a good deal of detail in the early phases of the project.

D. The product description is a component of an input of the Develop Project Charter process. It describes the characteristics of the product or service and contains less detail in the early phases of the project.

9. Comparative methods, scoring methods, and economic and cash flow analysis are all part of which of the following?

    A. Benefit measurement methods, which are a component of a tool and technique in the Develop Project Charter process

    B. Constrained optimization methods, which are a component of a tool and technique in the Preliminary Scope Statement process

    C. Benefit measurement methods, which are a component of an input to the Develop Project Charter process

    D. Mathematical modes, which are a component of an input to the Preliminary Scope Statement process

10. You are the project manager for the Late Night Smooth Jazz Club chain, with stores in 12 states. Smooth Jazz is considering opening a new club in Arizona or Nevada. You have derived the following information:

    Project Arizona: Payback period is 18 months, and the NPV is <250>.

    Project Nevada: Payback period is 24 months, and the NPV is 300.

    Which project would you recommend to the selection committee?

    A. Project Arizona, because the payback period is shorter than the payback period for Project Nevada.

    B. Project Nevada, because its NPV is a positive number.

    C. Project Arizona because its NPV is a negative number.

    D. Project Nevada, because its NPV is a higher number than Project Arizona's NPV.

11. You are the project manager for the Late Night Smooth Jazz Club chain, with stores in 12 states. Smooth Jazz is considering opening a new club in Kansas City or Spokane. You have derived the following information:

    Project Kansas City: The payback period is 27 months, and the IRR is 35 percent.

    Project Spokane: The payback period is 25 months, and the IRR is 32 percent.

    Which project should you recommend to the selection committee?

    A. Project Spokane, because the payback period is shortest.

    B. Project Kansas City, because the IRR is highest.

    C. Project Spokane, because the IRR is lowest.

    D. Project Kansas City, because the payback period is longest.

12. Which of the following is true regarding NPV?

    A. NPV assumes reinvestment at the cost of capital.

    B. NPV decisions should be made based on the highest value for all of the selections.

    C. NPV assumes reinvestment at the prevailing rate.

    D. NPV assumes reinvestment at the NPV rate.

13. You are the project manager for Insomniacs International. Since you don't sleep much, you get a lot of project work done. You're considering recommending a project that costs $575,000; expected inflows are $25,000 per quarter for the first two years and then $75,000 per quarter thereafter. What is the payback period?

    A. 40 months

    B. 38 months

    C. 39 months

    D. 41 months

14. Which of the following is true regarding IRR?

    A. IRR assumes reinvestment at the cost of capital.

    B. IRR is the discount rate when NPV is greater than zero.

    C. IRR is a constrained optimization method.

    D. IRR is the discount rate when NPV is equal to zero.

15. Mathematical models using linear, dynamic, integer, or algorithm models are considered _____.

    A. Project selection criteria

    B. A form of expert judgment

    C. Project selection methods

    D. A form of historical information

16. Your project selection committee used a weighted scoring model and found that Project B, with a score of 54, should be chosen over the other competing projects. Which of the following is true?

    A. Weighted scoring models are benefit measurement methods, which are used as a tool and technique during the Develop Project Charter process.

    B. Weighted scoring models are constrained optimization methods, which are used as a tool and technique in both Initiating process group processes.

    C. Weighted scoring models are benefit measurement methods and are the least efficient method of project selection.

    D. Weighted scoring models are a type of mathematical model that can be used both for project selection and vendor selection.

17. Your selection committee is debating between two projects. Project A has a payback period of 18 months. Project B has a cost of $125,000, with expected cash inflows of $50,000 the first year and $25,000 per quarter after that. Which project should you recommend?

    A. Either Project A or Project B, because the payback periods are equal.

    B. Project A, because Project B's payback period is 21 months.

    C. Project A, because Project B's payback period is 24 months.

    D. Project A, because Project B's payback period is 20 months.

18. Which of the following is true?

   A. Discounted cash flow analysis is the least precise of the cash flow techniques, because it does not consider the time value of money.

   B. NPV is the least precise of the cash flow analysis techniques, because it assumes reinvestment at the discount rate.

   C. Payback period is the least precise of the cash flow analysis techniques, because it does not consider the time value of money.

   D. IRR is the least precise of the cash flow analysis techniques, because it assumes reinvestment at the cost of capital.

19. You are a project manager for Zippy Tees. Your selection committee has just chosen a project you recommended for implementation. Your project is to manufacture a line of miniature stuffed bears that will be attached to your company's trendy T-shirts. The bears will be wearing the same T-shirt design as the shirt they're attached to. Your project sponsor thinks you've really impressed the big boss and wants you to skip to the manufacturing process right away. What is your response?

   A. Agree with the project sponsor because they are your boss, and they have a lot of authority and power in the company.

   B. Require that a preliminary budget be established and a resource list be put together to alert other managers of the requirements of this project. This should be published and signed by the other managers who are impacted by this project.

   C. Require a project charter be written and signed off on by all stakeholders before proceeding.

   D. Suggest that a preliminary scope statement be written as this will outline the objectives of the project and greatly assist in the development of the scope statement in the Planning processes

20. Which of the following is true regarding the project charter?

   A. The project charter should be published under the name of a manager external to the project.

   B. The project charter should be published under the project sponsor's name.

   C. The project charter should be published under the name of the project manager.

   D. The project charter should be published under the name of the project champion.

Answers to Review Questions

1. A. The buyer provides SOW when projects are performed under contract.

2. B. This came about due to a business need. Staff members were spending unproductive hours producing information for the management report that wasn't consistent or meaningful.

3. A. Develop Project Charter has four inputs and they are contract, project SOW, enterprise environmental factors, and organizational process assets.

4. C. The most correct answer is to perform a feasibility study. Since this project is taking the company into a new, unknown market, there's lots of potential for error and failure. A feasibility study would help the stakeholders determine if the project is viable and cost effective and whether it has a high potential for success.

5. C. The Develop Project Charter and Preliminary Scope Statement processes both have the following as inputs: project SOW, enterprise environment factors, and organizational process assets. Both processes share the following tools and techniques: project management methodology, PMIS, and expert judgment.

6. B. The project SOW should contain the business need for the project and the product scope description and should support the organization's strategic plan.

7. B. Historical information on projects of a similar nature can be very helpful when initiating new projects. They can help in formulating project deliverables and identifying constraints and assumptions and will be helpful further on in the project Planning processes as well.

8. D. The product description is a component of the project SOW, which is an input of both the Develop Project Charter and Preliminary Scope Statement processes. It describes the characteristics of the product or service and contains less detail in the early phases of the project and more detail as the project progresses.

9. A. Benefit measurement methods include comparative methods, scoring models, and cash flow analysis, which are all part of the project selection method tools and techniques in the Develop Project Charter process.

10. B. Projects with NPV greater than zero should be given an accept recommendation.

11. B. Projects with the highest IRR value are favored over projects with lower IRR values.

12. A. Net present value (NPV) assumes reinvestment is made at the cost of capital.

13. C. Year 1 and 2 inflows are each $100,000 for a total of $200,000. Year 3 inflows are an additional $300,000. Add one more quarter to this total and the $575,000 is reached in three years and three months, or 39 months.

14. D. IRR assumes reinvestment at the IRR rate and is the discount rate when NPV is equal to zero.

15. C. Mathematical models are one of the methods described in the project selection methods tool and technique of the Develop Project Charter process.

16. A. Benefit measurement methods include comparative methods and scoring models, among others, to make project selections during the Develop Project Charter process.

17. B. Project B has a payback period of 21 months. $50,000 is received in the first 12 months, with another $75,000 coming in over each of the next three quarters, or nine months.

18. C. Payback period does not consider the time value of money and is therefore the least precise of all the cash flow analysis techniques.

19. C. The project should be kicked off with a project charter that authorizes the project to begin, assigns the project manager, and describes the project objectives and business need for the project. This ensures that everyone is working with the same purposes in mind.

20. A. According to *A Guide to the PMBOK,* the project charter should be published by a manager external to the project but with sufficient power and authority to carry it off.

Chapter 3

Developing the Project Scope Statement

THE PMP EXAM CONTENT FROM THE PLANNING THE PROJECT PERFORMANCE DOMAIN COVERED IN THIS CHAPTER INCLUDES THE FOLLOWING:

- ✓ Define and Record Requirements, Constraints, and Assumptions
- ✓ Develop Change Management Plan

Great job! You've successfully completed the project Initiating processes and published the project charter and the preliminary scope statement. The project is officially under way. Stakeholders have been informed, there is management buy-in on the project, the project manager has been assigned, and the project objectives and description have been identified. A solid foundation for the Planning process is in place.

In this chapter, we will begin the Planning processes for the project. In fact, we will continue discussing the Planning processes through Chapter 7, "Creating the Project Schedule and Budget." Planning is a significant activity in any project and, if done correctly, will go a long way toward ensuring project success.

This chapter begins with the Develop Project Management Plan process. This process will describe the overall approach you'll use to manage the project. The result of this process is the project management plan document that describes how you'll execute and monitor and control the project outcomes as the project progresses and how to close out the project once it concludes.

Then we'll move on to the Scope Planning process. You'll use the project charter and preliminary scope statement you created in the last chapter—plus some other inputs—and then apply the tools and techniques of this process to come up with the project scope management plan. From there, you're off to the Scope Definition process, where you'll further elaborate the project objectives and deliverables. We'll talk in depth about project objectives, requirements, constraints, assumptions, and other elements of writing the project scope statement, which is an output of this process.

Developing the Project Management Plan

The first process in the Planning process group is the *Develop Project Management Plan* process. It's first for good reason. This process is a part of the Integration Management knowledge area and is concerned with defining, coordinating, and integrating all the various ancillary project plans. Remember when we talked about tailoring in Chapter 1?

This process involves defining and documenting the processes you're going to use to manage this project. For example, let's say you and the project team have determined you will use project management processes involving costs, human resources, risks, and a project schedule. (Warning: This is a demonstration only—don't try this at home. In reality, professionals perform many more processes than this on a typical project.) Each particular process may have a management plan that describes it. For instance, a cost management plan would describe how costs will be managed and controlled and how changes to costs will be approved and managed throughout the project. The Develop Project Management Plan process brings all these subsidiary plans together, along with the outputs of the Planning group processes, into one document called the *project management plan.*

In order to create and document the plan, we need to gather some inputs and build on the information we've already collected.

Developing Inputs

There are four inputs into the Develop Project Management Plan:

- Preliminary scope statement
- Project management processes
- Enterprise environmental factors
- Organizational process assets

Organizational process assets here are the same ones we considered when developing the project charter in Chapter 2, "Creating the Project Charter and Preliminary Scope Statement." There are some important elements to note in the remaining inputs, so let's take a look.

Preliminary scope statement   You'll recall that the preliminary scope statement describes the objectives of the project and the high-level requirements needed to satisfy stakeholder expectations. The reason it's an input into this process is because the content of the preliminary scope statement—including objectives, product requirements, schedule milestones, and so on—will help you and the team determine exactly which project management processes to use on the project.

 Remember, you're studying for the exam, so the correct input into this process is the preliminary scope statement. However, if you've skipped that process and only performed the project charter, you could use it as an input to this process.

Project management processes   The project management processes include all of the individual processes that make up the process groups we're talking about throughout this book. The Initiating group, for example, has two processes, Planning has a zillion (okay, not that many but it seems like it), and so on. Each of the processes you determine to use on the project will be documented in the project management plan.

Enterprise environmental factors   We've seen enterprise environmental factors before. Some of the key elements of the environmental factors you should consider when choosing the processes to perform for this project include standards and regulations (both industry and governmental), company culture, skills and knowledge of existing personnel, risk tolerances of stakeholders, and the project management information system (PMIS).

As we talked about in Chapter 1, the processes you choose to perform for the project will be based on the complexity of the project, the project scope, and the type of industry you work in. Your organization's standards, guidelines, and policies (a component of organizational process assets) or the project management office (PMO) may also dictate the types of processes you'll use for the project. You should also consider if your organization has existing change control processes in place, templates that you're required to use, or financial controls and processes. Don't forget to look for historical information and then use it to help you decide which processes to use for this project.

The tools and techniques for this process are also familiar. They include project management methodology, expert judgment, and PMIS. We covered expert judgment and project management methodology in Chapter 2, if you need a refresher.

Exam Spotlight

Be aware that *A Guide to the PMBOK* lists the PMIS as a tool and technique of some processes *and* as an input (it's part of the enterprise environmental factors) of others. The PMIS in the Develop Project Management Plan process includes a subsystem called the configuration management system (we'll cover this in Chapter 9, "Measuring and Controlling Project Performance") and the change control system, which is a subsystem of the configuration management system.

The PMIS in this case is an automated system used to document the subsidiary plans and the project management plan, facilitate the feedback process, and revise the documents. It incorporates the configuration management system and the change control system, both of which we'll cover in Chapter 9. Later in the project, the PMIS can be used to control changes to any of the plans. When you're thinking about the PMIS as an input (that is, as part of the enterprise environmental factors), think of it as a collection and distribution point for information as well as an easy way to revise and update documents. When you're thinking about the PMIS as a tool and technique, think of it just that way—as a tool to facilitate the automation of data collection and distribution and to automate and monitor processes like scheduling, resource leveling, budgeting, and web interfaces.

Documenting the Project Management Plan

The purpose of most every process is of course, to get to the output. Outputs are usually a report or document of some type or a deliverable. In this case, we end up with a document—the project management plan—that describes, integrates, and coordinates subsidiary plans for the processes you've determined to use for the project. The project management plan can be detailed or a high-level summary based on the needs of the project.

According to *A Guide to the PMBOK*, the project management plan defines how the project is executed, how it's monitored and controlled, and how it's closed. It also documents the outputs of the Planning group processes, which we'll cover over the next several chapters. The project management plan should include or discuss the following elements:

- Processes you'll use to perform the project
- Degrees of execution of each of the processes selected for the project

- Tools and techniques to use from each process
- Essential inputs and outputs from each of the processes and how they'll be used to manage the project
- Dependencies and interactions of the processes used to manage the project
- Methods for executing the work of the project to fulfill the objectives
- Methods for monitoring and controlling changes
- Methods to perform configuration management
- Methods for determining and maintaining the validity of performance baselines
- Communication needs of the stakeholders and techniques to fulfill those needs
- Project life cycle
- Project phases for multiphased projects
- Management reviews of issues and pending decisions

In addition to the elements just listed, the subsidiary plans that are associated with the processes you'll be using for this project should be documented in the project management plan. Each of these subsidiary management plans may contain the same elements as the overall project management plan does only it's specifically related to the topic at hand. For example, the cost management plan should define how changes to cost estimates will be reflected in the project budget and how changes or variances with a significant impact should be communicated to the project sponsor and stakeholders. The schedule management plan describes how changes to the schedule will be managed, and so on.

The subsidiary plans may be detailed or simply a synopsis, depending on the needs of the project. I've listed the subsidiary plans along with a brief description. We will cover each of these plans in more detail throughout the remainder of this book. According to *A Guide to the PMBOK,* the subsidiary plans are as follows:

Project scope management plan   Describes the process for determining project scope, facilitates creating the work breakdown structure (WBS), describes how the product or service of the project is verified and accepted, and documents how changes to scope will be handled.

Schedule management plan   Describes how the project schedule will be developed and controlled and how changes will be incorporated into the project schedule.

Cost management plan   Describes how costs will be managed and controlled and how changes to costs will be approved and managed.

Quality management plan   Describes how the organization's quality policy will be implemented. It must address and describe quality control procedures and measures, quality assurance procedures and measures, and continuous process improvement.

Process improvement plan   Describes how processes will be analyzed for the value they bring to the performance of project management. This analysis focuses on excluding or eliminating inefficiencies and waste.

Staffing management plan   Describes how human resource requirements for the project will be met, including how staff acquisition will occur and the time frames in which resources are needed.

Communications management plan   Describes the communication needs of the stakeholders, including timing, frequency, and methods of communications.

Risk management plan   Describes how risks will be managed and controlled during the project. This should include risk management methodology, roles and responsibilities, definitions of probability and impact, when project management will be performed, and the categories of risk, risk tolerances, and reporting and tracking formats.

Procurement management plan   Describes how the procurement processes will be managed throughout the project. This may include elements such as type of contract, procurement documents, lead times for purchases.

The project management plan is not limited to the subsidiary plans listed here. You may include other plans and documentation that help describe how the project will be executed or monitored and controlled. Perhaps you're working on a project that requires precise calculations and exact adherence to requirements. You could include a plan that describes these calculations, how they'll be monitored and measured, and the processes you'll use to make changes or corrections.

There's one more piece to this output. There are components of each of the processes associated with the subsidiary plans that should be considered when developing the plans. The components that *A Guide to the PMBOK* recommends you consider are as follows:

- Milestone list
- Resource calendar
- Schedule baseline
- Cost baseline
- Quality baseline
- Risk register

We'll talk about each of these in the remaining chapters as well.

WARNING   Be aware that I'm about to get on my soapbox. If you don't want to indulge me, skip the next few sentences and go to the next paragraph. I find it a little disconcerting that the 2004 version of *A Guide to the PMBOK* presents information that the reader has no knowledge of way in advance of learning the process. It's almost as if you need to be well versed in all the processes before you read the book! You're going to see several places throughout the remainder of this book where topics are introduced, as in the previous list, that you don't know anything about yet. Rest assured we will cover these topics in their proper place. If I began to tell you now about the risk management plan and risk register, for example, I'd first have to explain what risks are, the processes involved, and how the risk register is produced. I think it will make much more sense for you to see these elements in the processes they're produced in. Thanks…I feel better now.

Exam Spotlight

Understand that the purpose of the project management plan is to define how the project is executed, monitored and controlled, and closed, and to document the outputs of the Planning group processes you'll use during the project.

As the project progresses and more and more processes are performed, there may be changes to the subsidiary plans and to the project management plan itself. These changes should be reviewed and the project management plan should be updated to reflect the approved changes. Depending on the nature of the changes, the project manager, stakeholders, or sponsor (or some combination) should review and approve the changes.

Exam Spotlight

In practice, you'll find that you'll prepare the project management plan after you've progressed through several of the other Planning processes. It's difficult to create some of these subsidiary plans without performing the process they're associated with first. However, for the exam, remember that Develop Project Management Plan is the first process in the Planning group and it should be performed first.

Scoping Out the Project

Scope Planning is the first process in the Project Scope Management knowledge area and the second process in the Planning process group. You may recall from Chapter 1 that the purpose of the Project Scope Management knowledge area is to describe and control what is and what is *not* work of the project. *Scope* is collectively the product or service of the project and the results the project intends to produce.

The primary purpose of Scope Planning is to document the scope management plan. This is a planning tool that documents how the project team will go about defining project scope, how the work breakdown structure will be developed, how changes to scope will be controlled, and how project scope will be verified.

We'll talk more about this in the section "Documenting the Scope Management Plan" later in this chapter.

For now let's concentrate on the inputs to this process, which will help you get started documenting the decisions about the Scope Planning process for your project.

Scope Planning Inputs

I'm beginning to sound like a broken record...we've seen the inputs to the Scope Planning process before. They are as follows:

- Enterprise environmental factors
- Organizational process assets
- Project charter
- Preliminary project scope statement
- Project management plan

Even though we've talked about these before, there are some specific elements of some of these inputs we'll want to look at closely. Defining project scope and managing to that scope as you progress through the project has a direct relationship to the success of the project. It's difficult to document how you'll define project scope if you don't first understand the purpose behind the project, the product or service you're trying to produce, and the environmental factors and organizational process assets you're working under. The process of how you'll go about defining and managing scope is what the scope management plan (which is what we're ultimately getting to with this process) is about.

One of the environmental factors that may influence the way scope is managed is the human resources involved on the project. Their skills, knowledge, and ability to communicate and escalate issues appropriately may influence the way project scope is managed. Personnel policies governing those resources may also have an effect. For example, you may have a team member who has a close relationship with one of the stakeholders. Let's say the stakeholder wants a change to the project. The stakeholder and team member grab a cup of coffee together at the corner deli and the next thing you know, the team member is incorporating the change into the project. Scope can't be managed efficiently when it's being changed without the knowledge of the project manager or project team.

Other environmental factors that may affect scope management are the organization's culture, economic conditions, and physical and technological infrastructure.

Organizational process assets typically include things like policies and procedures, whether formal or informal. Your organization's policies or the policies and guidelines of your industry may have an effect on scope management, so make certain you're familiar with them. And don't forget historical information. You can review the scope management plan from previous projects of similar size and scope to help you craft the one for this project.

The project charter and preliminary scope statement describe the purpose and high-level requirements of the project. Analyzing the information in these documents will help you determine the appropriate tools and methodologies to use (as well as which processes to perform) for the project. The idea here is that you want to understand the size and complexity of the project so that you don't spend more time documenting how you're going to go about defining and managing scope than what's needed.

Scope Planning Tools and Techniques

There are two tools and techniques in Scope Planning:

Expert judgment   You'll rely on the expert judgment of people or groups with specific skills, knowledge, or training to help assess the process inputs. One expert you can count on in this process is the executive manager who wrote or contributed to the project charter. They can clarify questions you may have about the project objectives as well as the product description. Stakeholders or other project managers with previous experience on projects similar to yours can help you determine how scope management should work for this project.

Templates, forms, and standards   Your PMO may have scope management templates, forms, and standards that you can use to help define the scope management plan. Work breakdown structure templates and scope change control forms may also help because they outline how to break down work of the project and what elements are needed to describe changes.

Documenting the Scope Management Plan

The only output of the Scope Planning process is the *project scope management plan.* This plan describes how the project team will go about defining project scope, verifying the work of the project, and managing and controlling scope. According to *A Guide to the PMBOK*, the project scope management plan should contain the following:

- The process you'll use to prepare the project scope statement. The project scope statement (which we'll define later in this chapter) contains a detailed description of what the deliverables and requirements of the project are and is based on the information contained in the preliminary scope.

- A process for creating the work breakdown structure (WBS). The WBS (we'll cover that in the next chapter) further defines the work of the project (as defined in the project scope statement) by breaking down the deliverables into requirements.

- A definition of how the deliverables will be verified for accuracy and the process used for accepting deliverables.

- A description of the process for controlling scope change requests, including the procedure for requesting changes and how to obtain a change request form.

Exam Spotlight

The project scope management plan is a planning tool that documents how the project team will go about defining project scope, how the work breakdown structure will be developed, how changes to scope will be controlled, and how the work of the project will be verified and accepted. And don't forget, the scope management plan is a component of (or a subsidiary of) the project management plan.

Formulating Scope Definition

Now we're getting to the meat of the project Planning process group. The high-level objectives and deliverables and the initial constraints and assumptions of the project were defined in the preliminary scope statement. When we prepared the preliminary scope statement it was, well, preliminary. Now we're ready to further define these in the *Scope Definition* process and prepare a detailed project scope statement because more information is known now. The project scope statement (which we'll get to shortly) is what we'll use to further break down the work of the project into activities that we can assign to resources.

Exam Spotlight

You'll want to pay particular attention to the accuracy and completeness of this process. Defining project scope is critical to the success of the project since it spells out exactly what the product or service of the project looks like. Conversely, poor scope definition may lead to cost increases, rework, schedule delays, and poor morale.

First, we'll examine the inputs and tools and techniques of this process.

Defining the Scope Definition Inputs and Tools and Techniques

The inputs to the Scope Definition process are as follows:

- Organizational process assets
- Project charter
- Preliminary scope management plan
- Approved change requests

Some of the important information you'll want to key in on from these inputs are historical information, the product description, and the project objectives, assumptions, and constraints. (We'll cover each of these in the section "Writing the Project Scope Statement" later in this chapter.)

The approved change requests input will obviously impact the project scope. They may also impact quality, estimated costs, or the project schedule. As changes are approved, you'll have to modify the project scope statement (and other planning documents) to reflect them.

We're going to see some new tools and techniques in this process:

- Product analysis
- Alternatives identification
- Expert judgment
- Stakeholder analysis

We've covered expert judgment before. We'll cover product analysis, alternatives identification, and stakeholders in the following sections.

Exam Spotlight

In practice, you'll often find that you'll skip over the preliminary scope statement process and begin writing the project scope statement after the charter is documented. However, you're studying for the exam, so remember that the project scope statement is further elaborated based on the information contained in the preliminary scope statement. Most of the information found in the preliminary scope statement is also found in the project scope statement.

Also note that if the project charter and/or the preliminary project scope statement are missing or were not developed, you should use the product scope description as an input to this process.

Product Analysis

Product analysis goes hand in hand with the product scope description. Product analysis is a method for converting the product description and project objectives into deliverables and requirements. According to *A Guide to the PMBOK*, product analysis might include performing value analysis, functional analysis, systems-engineering techniques, systems analysis, or value-engineering techniques to further define the product or service.

Exam Spotlight

It's beyond the scope of this book to go into the various analysis techniques used in product analysis. For exam purposes, remember that product analysis is a tool and technique of the Scope Definition process and memorize the list of analysis techniques that might be performed in this process.

Alternatives Identification

Alternatives identification is a technique used for discovering different methods or ways of accomplishing the project. For example, brainstorming might be used to discover alternative ways of implementing one of the project objectives. Perhaps the project's budget doesn't allow for a portion of the project that the stakeholders really think needs to be included. Brainstorming might uncover an alternative that would allow the needed portion to be accomplished.

Lateral thinking is a form of alternatives identifications that can be used to help define scope. Edward de Bono created this term and has done extensive research and writing on the topic of lateral thinking. The simplest definition is that it's thinking outside the box. Lateral thinking is a process of separating the problem—or in our case the components of project scope (the deliverables and requirements)—looking at them from different angles than their obvious presentation, and encouraging team members to come up with ways to solve problems or look at scope that are not apparently obvious.

Stakeholder Analysis

During stakeholder analysis, you'll want to identify the influences stakeholders have in regard to the project and understand their expectations, needs, and desires. From there, you'll derive more specifics regarding the project goals and deliverables. Be warned that stakeholders are mostly concerned about their own interests and what they (or their organization) have to gain or lose from the project. In all fairness, we all fall into the stakeholder category, so we're all guilty of focusing on those things that impact us most.

> *A Guide to the PMBOK* doesn't heavily reference stakeholders prior to this process. You'll recall they state that the information for the project charter and preliminary scope statement comes from the project requestor or sponsor. In practice, you'll want to bring your stakeholders into the project as early in the process as you can, preferably when the project charter or preliminary scope statement is being written.

Your objective at this point is to begin defining exactly what the stakeholders' expectations are of project outcomes. This should include information like the project's objectives and how you'll recognize when the project is successfully completed. At the end of this identification and analysis process, you'll be able to describe and prioritize their expectations in terms of project requirements. But we're getting ahead of ourselves. We'll define objectives and requirements shortly. Let's discover who those stakeholders are first.

Identifying Stakeholders

Think of stakeholders and project participants as a highly polished orchestra. Each participant has a part to play. Some play more than others, and alas, some play their parts better than others. An integral part of project management is getting to know your stakeholders and the parts they play. You'll remember from Chapter 1 that stakeholders are those people or organizations who have a vested interest in the outcome of the project. They have something to either gain or lose as a result of the project and have the ability to influence project results. Stakeholders are officially identified in the Planning process. In practice, key stakeholders will have to be contacted early on to get their input for the project goals and deliverables.

Identifying key stakeholders seems as if it should be fairly easy, but once you get beyond the obvious stakeholders, the process can get difficult. Sometimes stakeholders, even key stakeholders, will change throughout the project's life. The key stakeholders on a project might include the project sponsor, the customer (who might be one and the same as the project sponsor), the project manager, project team members, management personnel, contractors, suppliers, and so on. Stakeholders can be internal or external to the organization. One way to uncover stakeholders whom you might not have thought about right at the start is to ask known stakeholders if they're aware of anyone else that might be impacted by this project. Ask team members if they're aware of stakeholders who haven't been identified. Stakeholders might also come to the forefront once you start uncovering some of the goals and deliverables of the project.

Don't forget important stakeholders. That could be a project killer. Leaving out an important stakeholder, or one whose business processes weren't considered during the Initiating and Planning processes, could spell disaster for your project.

Understanding Stakeholder Roles

It's important for the project manager to understand each stakeholder's role in the project and their role in the organization. Get to know them and their interests. Determine the relationship structure among the various stakeholders. Start cultivating partnerships with these stakeholders now, as it's going to get pretty cozy during the course of your project. If you establish good working relationships up front and learn a little about their business concerns and needs, it might be easier to negotiate or motivate them later on when you have a pressing issue that needs action. Knowing which stakeholders work well together and which don't can also help you in the future. One stakeholder may have the authority or influence to twist the arm of another, figuratively speaking, of course. Or conversely, you might know of two stakeholders who are like oil and water when put into the same room together. This can be valuable information to keep under your hat for future reference.

Stakeholders may have a significant amount of influence over the project and its outcomes. Understanding the organizational structure, and where the stakeholders fit in that structure, should be your first step in determining the level of influence they have. For example, if Melanie in accounting wields a significant amount of power and influence over the organization, when you need input or decisions from her regarding costs or budgets for the project you better believe that those decisions are not likely going to get overridden. Conversely, if stakeholders with little influence provide direction that you don't verify, that input could be overridden at a later date by a more powerful stakeholder, causing changes to the project.

Communicating with Stakeholders

Now those finely honed communication skills are going to come in handy. We're just about ready to start documenting the deliverables and requirements of the project. In order to determine the specifics of your project, you'll want to meet with each of the key stakeholders and document their needs, wants, and expectations. You may want to ask them what business process the project will likely change, enhance, or replace. Perhaps the existing business processes, and the systems that support them, are so old that little documentation exists for them. Determine if there is a critical business need for this project or if it's a "nice to have," as we say around our office. What will be the result of this project? Will customer service be improved or sales increased? Find out what prevents the stakeholders today from achieving the results they hope the project will accomplish. Ask about the deliverables and how they can be verified and measured. And always ask the stakeholders how they will know that the project was completed successfully.

One way to help identify project objectives (which we'll talk about in the next section) is to talk about what is not included in a project. For example, let's say you're working on a highway project to create a new on-ramp from a downtown city street. The goal of this project is to have a new on-ramp constructed and ready for traffic in 18 months from the project start date. Specifically excluded from this project is the demolition of a deteriorating bridge adjacent to the new on-ramp. Make sure you state this in the project scope statement.

Remember that the definition of a successful project is one that accomplishes the goals of the project and meets or exceeds stakeholders' expectations. Understand and document those expectations and you're off to a good start.

Writing the Project Scope Statement

The purpose of the *project scope statement* is to document the project objectives, deliverables, and requirements so that they can be used to direct the project team's work and as a basis for future project decisions. The scope statement is an agreement between the project and the project customer that states precisely what the work of the project will produce. Simply put, the scope statement tells everyone concerned with the project exactly what they're going to get when the work is finished.

Exam Spotlight

Understand that the purpose of the scope statement, according to *A Guide to the PMBOK*, is to provide all the stakeholders with a foundational understanding of project scope. Also remember that the scope statement defines and progressively elaborates the work of the project and guides the work of the project team during the Executing process and that all change requests will be evaluated against the scope statement. If the change request is outside the bounds of the project scope as documented here, it should be denied.

Since the scope statement serves as a baseline for the project, if questions arise or changes are proposed later in the project, they can be compared to what's documented in the scope statement. Making change decisions is easier when the original deliverables and requirements are well documented. You'll also know what is out of scope for the project simply because the work isn't documented here (or conversely, deliverables or elements are documented and noted as being specifically out of scope). The criteria outlined in the scope statement will also be used to determine if the project was completed successfully. Hopefully, you're already seeing the importance of documenting project scope.

Scope Statement Components

According to *A Guide to the PMBOK*, the project scope statement should include all of the following:

- Project objectives
- Product scope description
- Project deliverables
- Project requirements
- Project boundaries
- Product acceptance criteria
- Project constraints
- Project assumptions

- Initial project organization
- Initial defined risks
- Schedule milestones
- Fund limitations
- Cost estimates
- Project configuration management requirements
- Project specifications
- Approval requirements

If the details surrounding these are spelled out in other documents, you don't have to reenter all the information into the scope statement. Simply reference the other document in the scope statement so that readers know where to find it.

Are we there yet? Remember in Chapter 2 I promised you we'd get to the details of the preliminary scope statement when we got to this point? We're there! All of the elements in the preceding list are part of the preliminary scope statement as well as the project scope statement, and we're going to discuss each one of them. The explanations given here apply to these elements as they pertain to the preliminary *and* the project scope statements. The difference is that at this point in the project we know more then we did earlier on, so there'll be more detail here than in the preliminary scope statement. Are you ready? Here we go.

Several terms are tossed about when we start talking about project scope and sometimes they're used interchangeably. They are words such as *goals, objectives, requirements,* and *deliverables* (we'll get to these last two later in this section). I've referenced the term *objectives* several times throughout this chapter. Goals and objectives are the purpose for undertaking the project. These are the "what" it is you're trying to accomplish. They describe the final result of the project. "Increase warehouse space by 17 percent to house the new product line for distribution" and "Improve turnaround times by 25 percent on loan application services" are both examples of objectives. They state the purpose for the project and the desired end result. Some project managers in practice use the term *goals* to describe what *A Guide to the PMBOK* terms *objectives*. *A Guide to the PMBOK* doesn't use the word *goals* and you won't find it in its glossary. Be that as it may, we'll stick with the term it uses, *objective.* Just keep in mind that you can think of goals and objectives as interchangeable.

Project Objectives

Objectives are quantifiable criteria used to measure project success. They describe the *what* it is you're trying to do, accomplish, or produce. Quantifiable criteria should at least include schedule, cost, and quality measures. You may use business measures or quality targets as well.

In the case of project objectives, these elements are used as measurements to determine project satisfaction and successful completion. Costs are typically stated in monetary units (U.S. dollars, Euro dollars, and so on) and should be specific. Schedules are typically stated in time measurements, and I recommend sticking with a consistent measurement throughout your project. If you use hours, state all schedule-related topics in hours.

You've probably seen the acronym SMART regarding goals and objectives a dozen times, but it's worth repeating. If you follow these principles, you'll be certain that your objectives meet the "quantifiable criteria" needed to measure success. Objectives should follow the SMART rule:

S—Specific   Objectives should be specific and written in clear, concise, and understandable terms.

M—Measurable   Objectives should be measurable.

A—Accurate   Objectives should be accurate and should describe precisely what's required.

R—Realistic and tangible   Objectives that are impossible to accomplish are not realistic and not attainable. Objectives must be centered in reality. For example, it's not likely you and I will be sending up rocket ships full of chocolate candies to sell to tourists visiting the moon anytime soon.

T—Time bound   Objectives should have a time frame with an end date assigned to them.

Let's look at some examples of the tangible terms, or quantifiable criteria, we talked about earlier. If your objective is to increase warehouse space, it is better to say the objective is to build four new warehouses. Describing the number of new warehouses to be built is specific and tangible. For that reason, you'll know the project is completed when this objective is met. The objective of offering faster loan approvals might be better stated that the company will provide loan applications over the Internet to increase the speed of the application process by 25 percent by the end of the calendar year. In other words, the purpose for the project is to do something or accomplish something—an objective.

Let's say your company is going to produce a run of holiday beer. Your objective statement might be stated this way: "Beer Buddies, Inc. will produce two million cases of holiday beer to be shipped to our distributors by October 30 at a cost of $1.5 million or less." The objective criteria in this statement are clearly stated, and fulfillment of the project objective can be easily measured. Stakeholders will know the objective is met when the two million cases are produced and shipped by the due date within the budget stated.

Product Scope Description

The *product scope description* describes the characteristics of the product or service of the project. We talked about this in Chapter 2. If the product scope description is contained in the project charter, you can reference the project charter in the project scope statement. Chances are very good you'll be using a word processing system of some sort to write these documents. An even better idea is to copy and paste the information from the project charter into the scope statement. It won't hurt anything to have it in both places and will make reading the scope statement easier.

Project Deliverables

Deliverables are measurable outcomes, measurable results, or specific items that must be produced to consider the project or project phase completed. Deliverables, like objectives, must be specific and verifiable. For example, one of your deliverables might include widgets with a three-inch diameter that will in turn be assembled into the final product. This deliverable, a three-inch-diameter widget, is specific and measurable. However, if the deliverable was not documented or not communicated to the manager or vendor responsible for manufacturing the widgets, there could be a disaster waiting to happen. If they deliver two-inch widgets instead of the required three-inch version, it would throw the entire project off schedule or perhaps cause the project to fail. This could be a career-limiting move for the project manager, because it's the project manager's responsibility to document deliverables and monitor the progress of those deliverables throughout the project. Most projects have multiple deliverables. As in this example, if you are assembling a new product with many parts, each of the parts might be considered independent deliverables.

A *Guide to the PMBOK* describes a project deliverable as either a unique and verifiable product or result or a service that's performed. The product or service must be produced or performed in order to consider the project complete. The deliverables may also include supplementary outcomes like documentation or project management reports.

Critical Success Factors

Deliverables and objectives are sometimes referred to as *critical success factors.* Critical success factors are those elements that must be completed in order for the project to be considered complete. For example, if you're building a bridge, one of the deliverables might be to produce a specific number of trusses that will be used to help support the bridge. Without the trusses, the bridge can't be completed; in fact, the bridge might not stand without them. The trusses, in this case, are a critical success factor. Not all deliverables are necessarily critical success factors, but many of them will fall into this category and should be documented as such.

The bottom line is this: No matter how well you apply your project skills, if the wrong deliverables are produced or the project is managed to the wrong objectives, you will have an unsuccessful project on your hands.

Project Requirements

After all the deliverables are identified, the project manager needs to discover and document all of the requirements of the project. *Requirements* describe the characteristics of the deliverable. They may also describe functionality that the deliverable must have or specific conditions the deliverable must meet in order to satisfy the objective of the project. According to *A Guide to the PMBOK,* requirements are conditions that must be met or criteria that the product or service of the project must possess in order to satisfy the project documents, a contract, a standard, or a specification. Requirements quantify and prioritize the wants, needs, and expectations of the project sponsor and stakeholders.

Requirements may include things like dimensions, ease of use, color, specific ingredients, and so on. If we go back to our holiday beer example, you'll recall that the project objective was to produce a new bottle of beer for the holidays. One of the major deliverables is the cartons to hold the bottles. The requirements for that deliverable may include carton design, photographs that will appear on the carton, color choices, and so on.

Documenting *All* of the Deliverables and Requirements

One of the project manager's primary functions is to accurately document the deliverables and requirements of the project and then manage the project so that they are produced according to the agreed-upon criteria. Deliverables describe the components of the goals and objectives in a quantifiable way. Requirements are the specifications of the deliverables.

The project manager should use the project charter and preliminary scope statement as a starting point for identifying and progressively elaborating project deliverables, but it's possible that only some of the deliverables will be documented there. Remember that the charter was written by a manager external to the project, and it was the first take at defining the project objectives and deliverables. As the project manager, it's your job to make certain *all* the deliverables are identified and documented in the project scope statement. That's because the scope statement (not the project charter) serves as the agreement among stakeholders—including the customer of the project—regarding what project objectives and deliverables will be produced in order to meet and satisfy the requirements of the project.

Interview the stakeholders, other project managers, project team members, customers, management staff, industry experts, and any other experts who can help you identify all the deliverables of the project. Depending on the size of the project, you might be able to accomplish this in a group setting using simple brainstorming techniques, but large complex projects may have scope statements for each deliverable of the project. Remember that the project scope statement is progressively elaborated into finer detail and is used later on to help decompose the work of the project into smaller tasks and activities.

Again, the project manager needs to pull those communications skills out of her tool bag and use them to interview stakeholders, customers, project team members, and business process owners about the project requirements. While the project manager is responsible for making certain the requirements are documented, it doesn't mean this task must be performed by the project manager. The project manager can enlist the help of stakeholders, business analysts, requirements analysts, business process owners, and other team members to conduct the interviews and document the requirements. The project manager then reviews the requirements and incorporates them into the project documentation and project plan.

Business process owners are those people who are experts in their particular area of the business. They are invaluable resources to the project manager. They are usually the midlevel managers and line managers who still have their fingers in the day-to-day portion of the business. For example, it takes many experts in various areas to produce and market a great bottle of beer. There are machinists whose specialty is regulating and keeping the stainless steel and copper drums in top working order. There are chemists who daily check and adjust the secret formulas brewing in the vats. Graphic artists must develop colorful and interesting labels and cartons to attract the attention of those thirsty patrons. And of course, those great TV commercials advertising the tasty brew are produced by yet another set of business experts. These are the kinds of people you'll interview and ask to assist you in identifying requirements.

You can use the same techniques to determine requirements as you did to determine deliverables. There are several techniques discussed in Chapter 5, "Risk Planning," that you can use during the Scope Definition process as well to identify deliverables and requirements.

Getting the business process owners and stakeholders (who could be one and the same, depending on the project) together in a meeting room and brainstorming the requirements can produce terrific results. Depending on the size of the project, this isn't always possible, but the idea holds true. Interview your stakeholders and business experts to get at the requirements and then document them in the project scope statement. Remember that, according to *A Guide to the PMBOK*, the stakeholder analysis (a tool and technique of the Scope Definition process—yes we're still talking about that process) you performed ultimately turns their needs and expectations into prioritized requirements that are documented here in the project scope statement.

Project Boundaries

Project boundaries define what is and what is not included in the work of the project. In this section of the scope statement, you'll state what is excluded from scope. The following statement may seem obvious, but I'll note it anyway: objectives, deliverables, and requirements not specifically included in the project scope statement are explicitly excluded from the project. Stakeholders cannot become confused later and expect that a specific product or deliverable was going to be included in the project when it's stated here that it will not be produced.

Product Acceptance Criteria

Product *acceptance criteria* includes the process and the criteria that will be used to determine if the deliverables, and the final product or service of the project, are acceptable and satisfactory. Acceptance criteria may include any number of elements, such as quality criteria, fitness for use, and performance criteria.

Project Constraints

Constraints are anything that either restricts the actions of the project team or dictates the actions of the project team. Constraints put you in a box. (I hope you're not claustrophobic.) As a project manager, you have to manage *to* the project constraints, which sometimes requires creativity.

In my organization, and I'm sure the same is true in yours, there are far more project requests than we have resources to work on them. In this case, resources are a constraint. You'll find that a similar phenomenon occurs on individual projects as well. Almost every project you'll encounter must work within the triple constraint combination of scope, time, and cost. The quality of the project (or the outcomes of the project) is affected by how well these three constraints are managed. Usually one or two of the triple constraints, sometimes all three, apply, which restricts the actions of the project team. You might work on projects where you have an almost unlimited budget (don't we wish!), but time is the limitation. For example, if the president mandated that NASA put a man on Mars by the end of 2008, you'd have a time-constrained project on your hands.

Other projects might present the opposite scenario. You have all the time you need to complete the project, but the budget is fixed. Still other projects may incorporate two or three of the constraints. Government agencies are notorious for starting projects that have at least two and sometimes all three constraints. For example, new tax laws are passed that impact the computer programs, requiring new programs to calculate and track the tax changes. Typically, a due date is given when the tax law takes effect, and the organization responsible is required to implement the changes with no additions to budget or staff. In other words, they are told to use existing resources to accomplish the objectives of the project, and the specific requirements, or scope, of the project are such that they cannot be changed to try to meet the time deadline.

As a project manager, one of your biggest jobs is to balance the project constraints while meeting or exceeding the expectations of your stakeholders. In most projects, you will usually be faced with balancing only one or two of the triple constraints. For example, if one of the project objectives is to complete the project by the end of the year, the saying goes, "I can give it to you fast or I can give to you cheap, but I can't give it to you fast and cheap."

Constraints can take on many forms and aren't limited to time, cost, and scope. Anything that impedes your project team's ability to perform the work of the project or specifically dictates the way the project should be performed is considered a constraint. Governments are a good example here. Let's say in order to fulfill some of the deliverables of your project you'll have to purchase a large amount of materials and equipment. Procurement processes can be so cumbersome that ordering supplies for a project may literally add months to the project schedule. The procurement process itself becomes a constraint because of the methods and procedures you're required to use to get the materials in house.

Let's take a brief look at some of the common constraints you'll likely encounter on your future projects.

Time constraint   As I said, time can be a project constraint. This usually comes in the form of an enforced deadline, commonly known as the "make it happen now" scenario. If you are in charge of the company's holiday bash scheduled for December 10, your project is time constrained. Once the invitations are out and the hall has been rented, you can't move the date. All activities on this project are driven by the due date.

Budget constraints   Budgets are another one of the triple constraints. Budgets limit the project team's ability to obtain resources and might potentially limit the scope of the project. For example, component X cannot be part of this project because the budget doesn't support it.

Quality constraints   While *A Guide to the PMBOK* doesn't list quality as a constraint, you'll find in practice that quality can often be a constraint. Quality constraints typically are restricted by the specifications of the product or service. The specifications for those three-inch widgets talked about earlier could be considered a quality constraint. Most of the time, if quality is a constraint, one of the other constraints—time or budget—has to have some give. You can't produce high quality on a restricted budget and within a tightly restricted time schedule. Of course, there are exceptions, but only in the movies.

Schedule constraints   Schedule constraints can cause interesting dilemmas for the project manager. For example, say you're the project manager in charge of building a new football stadium in your city. The construction of the stadium will require the use of cranes—and crane operators—at certain times during the project. If crane operators are not available when your project plan calls for them, you'll have to make schedule adjustments so that the crane operators can come in at the right time.

Technology constraints   Technology is a marvelous thing. In fact, how did humans survive prior to the invention of computers and cell phones? Technology certainly can be marvelous, but it can also be a project constraint. For example, your project might require the use of brand-new technology that is still so new it hasn't been released on a wide-scale basis. One impact might be that the project will take an additional six months because the new technology isn't ready or hasn't been tested yet.

Directive constraints   Directives from management can be constraints as well. Your department may have specific policies that management requires for the type of work you're about to undertake. This may add time to the project, so you must consider those policies when identifying project constraints. And when you're performing work on contract, the provisions of the contract can be constraints.

Constraints, particularly the triple constraints, can be used to help drive out the objectives and requirements of the project. If it's difficult to discern which constraint is the primary constraint, ask the project sponsor something like this, "Ms. Sponsor, if you could only have one of these two alternatives, which would you choose? The project is delivered on the date you've stated, or the quality is manufactured to the exact specifications you've given." If Ms. Sponsor replies with the date response, you know your primary constraint is time. If push comes to shove during the project Planning processes, time might have to give because quality cannot.

You'll want to understand what the primary constraint is on the project. If you assume the primary constraint is budget when in actuality the primary constraint is time, in the immortal words of two-year-olds worldwide, "Uh-oh." Understanding the constraints and which one carries the most importance will help you out later on in the project Planning process group with things like scope planning, scheduling, estimating, and project plan development. That's assuming your project gets to the project Planning processes, which brings us to the next topic: project assumptions.

Project Assumptions

You've probably heard the old saying about the word *assume*, something about what it makes out of "u" and "me." In the case of project management, however, throw this old saying out the window, because it's not true.

Assumptions, for the purposes of project management, are things you believe to be true. For example, if you're working on a large construction project, you might make assumptions about the availability of materials. You may assume that concrete, lumber, drywall, and so on are widely available and reasonably priced. You may also assume that finding contract labor is either easy or difficult, depending on the economic times and the availability of labor in your locale. Each project will have its own set of assumptions, and they should be identified, documented, and updated throughout the project.

It's essential to understand and document the assumptions you're making, and the assumptions your stakeholders are making, about the project. It's also important to find out as many of the assumptions as you can up front. Projects can fail, sometimes after lots of progress has been made, because an important assumption was forgotten or the assumption was incorrect. You will have more assumptions at this point in the project then you did when creating the project charter because more is known about the goals and deliverables of the project. Defining new assumptions and refining old ones are another form of progressive elaboration.

Let's say you make plans to meet your buddy for lunch on Friday at 11:30 at your favorite spot. When Friday rolls around, you assume he's going to show up, barring any catastrophes between the office and the restaurant. Project assumptions work the same way. For planning purposes, you presume the event or thing you've made the assumptions about is true, real, or certain. For example, you might assume that key resources will be available when needed on the project. Document that assumption. If Nancy is the one and only resource who can perform a specific task at a certain point in the project, document your assumption that Nancy will be available and run it by her manager. If Nancy happens to be on a plane for Helsinki at the time you thought she was going to be working on the project, you could have a real problem on your hands.

Other assumptions could be factors such as vendor delivery times, product availability, contractor availability, the accuracy of the project plan, the assumption that key project members will perform adequately, contract signing dates, project start dates, and project phase start dates. This is not an exhaustive list but should get you thinking in the right direction. As you interview your stakeholders, ask them about their assumptions and add them to your list. Use brainstorming exercises with your team and other project participants to come up with additional assumptions.

Think about some of the factors you normally take for granted when you're trying to identify assumptions. Many times they're the elements everyone expects will be available or will behave in a specific way. Think about factors such as key team members' availability, access to information, access to equipment, management support, and vendor reliability.

Try to validate your assumptions whenever possible. When discussing assumptions with vendors, make them put it in writing. In fact, if the services or goods you're expecting to be delivered by your suppliers are critical to the project, include a clause in the contract to assure a contingency plan in case your suppliers fail to perform. For example, if you're expecting 200 PCs to be delivered, configured, and installed by a certain date, require the vendor to pay the cost of rental equipment in the event they can't deliver on the promised due date.

Remember, when assumptions are incorrect or not documented, it could cause problems halfway through the project and might even be a project killer.

Initial Project Organization

In the initial project organization section, you'll document who the stakeholders are on the project. We talked about stakeholders earlier in this chapter. You should also document the team members and the way the project will be organized here.

Initial Defined Risks

Risks pose threats and opportunities to the project. This section should contain a list of all known risks.

    We'll cover risks in much more detail in Chapter 5.

Schedule Milestones

Milestones are typically points in the project where something significant is achieved or completed. List the major milestones that you know about now in this section of the project scope statement.

    We'll talk more about milestones in Chapter 7.

Fund Limitations

Fund limitations really refer to the cost constraint. If there are fund limitations (and I've never worked on a project where there wasn't), document them here. Also document any time frames associated with the funding limitations. For example, I often work on projects where funding runs out at the end of the fiscal year. If you haven't spent the money by then, you'll no longer have access to it.

Cost Estimates

Cost estimates is the section where you list the cost estimates for the project. This should include overall costs for the project and some level of confidence in that estimate.

Project Configuration Management Requirements

Configuration management describes the characteristics of the product of the project and ensures that the description is accurate and complete.

    We'll talk more about configuration management in Chapter 9.

Project Specifications

If there are specification documents that the project should comply with, for example, industry specifications or technology specifications—note that in the project specifications section.

Approval Requirements

Approval requirements refer to how the objectives, deliverables, project management documents, and other outcomes and results of the project will be approved. This is different than product acceptance criteria—that element describes how the product itself will be approved, whereas this element describes the requirements that must be met in order to approve the objectives and so on. An example product acceptance criteria might be "all widgets must measure three inches." A deliverable approval requirement might be that the director of sales must approve a prototype before the project can proceed. This section may also contain the process and approval requirements of the project scope statement.

Approving and Publishing the Project Scope Statement

Just like the project charter, the project scope statement should be approved, agreed upon, published, and distributed to the stakeholders, key management personnel, and project team members. You can accomplish this with a formal sign-off procedure that's documented as part of the "approval requirements" section of the scope statement. When stakeholders sign off and agree to the scope statement, they're agreeing to the deliverables and requirements of the project. And, as with the project charter, their agreement and endorsement of the project requirements and deliverables will likely sustain their participation and cooperation throughout the rest of the project. That doesn't mean they'll agree to everything as the project progresses, but it does mean the stakeholders are informed and will likely remain active project participants.

Updating the Project Scope Management Plan

Two outputs of the Scope Definition process remain. Those outputs are requested changes and project scope management plan updates. When you're in the midst of defining deliverables and requirements, you'll often find that changes to the original objectives and requirements will occur. These requested changes, once reviewed and approved, will change the scope of the project. If the project scope statement has been approved and published, you'll need to make changes to it and notify stakeholders that changes have been made.

 We'll talk more about change control and change request processes in Chapter 9.

Approved changes may also impact the project scope management plan or some of the subsidiary plans that make up this plan. Make certain you update this plan as a result of the changes made during the Scope Definition process.

Real World Scenario

Mountain Streams Services

Maria Sanchez is the CEO of Mountain Streams Services. She recently accepted a prestigious industry award on behalf of the company. Maria knows that without the dedication and support of her employees, Mountain Streams Services wouldn't have achieved this great milestone.

Maria wants to host a reception for the employees and their guests in recognition of all their hard work and contributions to the company. Maria has appointed you to arrange the reception.

The reception is scheduled for April 12, and Maria has given you a budget of $125 per person. The company employs 200 people. The reception should be semiformal.

You've documented the deliverables as follows:

- Location selection

- Food and beverage menu

- Invitations

- Entertainment

- Insurance coverage

- Decorations

- Photographer

- Agenda

In addition to the deliverables, you want to go over the following requirements with Maria to be certain you both are in agreement:

- The location should be somewhere in the downtown area.

- Employees are encouraged to bring one guest but no children.

- There will be an open bar paid for by Maria.

- The agenda will include a speech by Maria, followed by the distribution of bonus checks to every employee. This is to be kept secret until the reception.

- The decorations should include gold-trimmed fountain pens with the company logo at every place setting for the attendees to keep.

Once you've documented all the particulars, you ask to speak with Maria to go over this project scope statement and get her approval before proceeding with the project.

Project Case Study: New Kitchen Heaven Retail Store

The project charter kickoff meeting was held and well attended. You're ready to start writing the project scope statement and have a question or two for Dirk. You knock on his door and he invites you in.

"Shoot."

"I'm ready to define the deliverables and requirements for this project. I want to make sure I get the right folks involved in the meeting. Who are key stakeholders you recommend I speak with?"

"There are a few people I can think of right off that you don't want to miss. There's Jake Peterson over in Facilities. He's in charge of store furnishings, shelving, things like that—any supplies for the stores that aren't retail products. He can help out with store build-outs, too. He supervised our last eight stores and did a terrific job."

"Anyone else?" you ask.

"You should also talk to Jill Overstreet, the director in charge of retail products. She can help with the initial store stocking, and once the store is open, her group will take over the ongoing operations. All the district managers report to Jill."

You thank Dirk and tell him you're going to contact Jake and Jill and set up a brainstorming session to determine requirements.

A few days later.

You review your notes and reread the first draft of the project scope statement you've prepared for the Kitchen Heaven retail store before looking for Dirk. After your meetings with the stakeholders, you were better able to refine the project objectives and deliverables.

"Dirk, I'm glad I caught you. I'd like to go over the project scope statement with you before I give it to the stakeholders. Do you have a few minutes?"

"Sure," Dirk says to you. "Let's have it."

"The project objective is to open the 50th Kitchen Heaven store in Colorado Springs by February 1. When I met with Jake, he confirmed it takes 120 days to do the store build-out. That includes having the shelves set up and in place, ready to stock with inventory."

Dirk asks if Jake told you about his store location idea.

"Yes, Jake gave me a contact name of the leasing agent, and I've left her a voice mail. The sooner we can get that lease signed, the better. It takes Jake 120 days to do the build-out, and Jill said she needs 2 weeks lead time to order the initial inventory and stock the shelves. That puts us pretty close to our February 1st deadline, counting the time to get the lease papers signed."

"Sounds good so far," Dirk replies. "What else?"

"I've included an updated description of the products and services the new store will offer, based on the documentation that was written from the last store opening. Jill reviewed the updates to the description, so we should be in the clear there. The store will include some new lines that we've decided to take on—cookware from famous chefs, that kind of thing.

"Jake has already made contact with a general contractor in Colorado Springs, and he is ready to roll once we've signed the lease.

"One more thing, Dirk. Since we're including the big bash at grand opening as part of the deliverables, I talked to some of your folks in marketing to get some ideas. They are thinking we should have some great giveaways as door prizes and that we will want to cater in the food. They also thought having some live cooking demonstrations with some local chefs would be a good attraction."

"Sounds like you're on the right track. So what's next?" Dirk asks.

"Once you approve the scope statement, I'd like to send a copy to the stakeholders. My next step is to break down the deliverables and requirements I've documented here into activities so we can get rolling on the work of the project."

Project Case Study Checklist

> **Stakeholder analysis:** Jake Peterson and Jill Overstreet interviewed. Needs, wants, and expectations recorded and requirements prioritized.

> **Organizational structure:** Functional organization with a separate projectized department.

> **Constraints:** February 1 date to coincide with home and garden show.

> **Assumptions:**

- A store build-out usually takes 120 days.

- Jill Overstreet will help with the initial store stocking.

- Jake Peterson will provide supplies for the stores that aren't retail products, such as store furnishings, shelving, etc., and can help with the store build-out as well.

- The budget for the project will be anywhere from $1.5 to $2 million.

Created project scope statement, which includes the following:

- **Project objectives:** Open 50th store by February 1 in Colorado Springs.

- **Project deliverables:**

  - Build out storefront, including shelving.

  - Retail product line delivered two weeks prior to grand opening.

  - Grand opening party with cooking demos.

- **Project requirements:**

  - Sign lease within 14 days.

  - New line of gourmet food products.

  - Classroom space needed in back of store for cooking demos and classes.

- **Constraints:** February 1 date to coincide with home and garden show.

- **Fund limitations:** No more than $2 million for the project.

- **Assumptions:** (The same as listed earlier).

Summary

This chapter started you on the road to project Planning via the Develop Project Management Plan process, the Scope Planning process, and the Scope Definition process.

The output of the Develop Project Management Plan process is the project management plan, which is concerned with defining, coordinating and integrating all the ancillary project plans. The purpose of this plan is to define how the project is executed, how it's monitored and controlled, and how it's closed

Scope Planning is where you produce the scope management plan, which is a planning tool that documents how the project team will go about defining project scope, how the work breakdown structure will be developed, how changes to scope will be controlled, and how project scope will be verified

The scope statement is produced during the Scope Definition process. It describes the project objectives, deliverables, and requirements. The scope statement forms a baseline you'll use to weigh future project decisions, most particularly change requests. The scope statement contains a list of project deliverables that will be used in future Planning processes. Measurement criteria for project objectives are agreed upon by the stakeholders and project manager. These criteria are associated with the deliverables and documented in the scope statement to track project progress.

The deliverables, requirements, and measurement criteria should be spelled out clearly and concisely in the scope statement to avoid any misunderstandings later in the project. Formal acceptance of the scope statement is required by the stakeholders and project manager. Acceptance is usually accompanied by sign-offs on the document indicating that it has been read and that the signing party agrees with the deliverables and requirements of the project.

The project scope statement contains many elements, including objectives, deliverables, requirements, boundary descriptions (exclusions from scope), constraints, assumptions, product acceptance criteria, project organization, initial risks, schedule milestones, fund limitations, configuration management requirements, cost estimates, project specifications, and approval requirements.

Constraints restrict or dictate the actions of the project team. Constraints usually involve time, cost, and scope but can also include schedules, technology, and more.

Assumptions are things believed to be true. You'll want to document project assumptions and validate them as the project progresses.

Exam Essentials

Be able to state the purpose of the Develop Project Management Plan process.   It defines, coordinates, and integrates all subsidiary project plans.

Be able to explain the purpose of the project management plan.   This plan defines how the project is executed, how it's monitored and controlled, and how it's closed, and also documents the outputs of the Planning group processes. The size and complexity of the project will determine the level of detail contained in this plan.

Be able to describe the purpose of the scope management plan.   The scope management plan has a direct influence on the project's success and describes the process for determining project scope, facilitates creating the WBS, describes how the product or service of the project is verified and accepted, and documents how changes to scope will be handled. The scope management plan is a subsidiary plan of the project management plan.

Be able to name the Scope Definition tools and techniques and outputs.   The tools and techniques from the Scope Definition process are product analysis, alternatives identification, expert judgment, and stakeholder analysis. The outputs are the project scope statement, requested changes, and project scope management plan updates.

Understand the purpose of the project scope statement.   The scope statement serves as a common understanding of project scope among the stakeholders. The project objectives and deliverables and their quantifiable criteria are documented in the scope statement and are used by the project manager and the stakeholders to determine if the project was completed successfully. It also serves as a basis for future project decisions.

Be able to define project constraints and assumptions.   Project constraints limit the options of the project team and restrict their actions. Sometimes constraints dictate actions. Time, budget, and quality are the most common constraints. Assumptions are conditions that are presumed to be true or real.

Key Terms

Before you take the exam, be certain you are familiar with the following terms:

acceptance criteria	product analysis
alternatives identification	project boundaries
approval requirements	project management plan
assumptions	project scope management plan
constraints	project scope statement
critical success factors	requirements
deliverables	scope
Develop Project Management Plan	scope definition
objectives	scope planning

Review Questions

1. You are a project manager for Laredo Pioneer's Traveling Rodeo Show. You're heading up a project to promote a new line of souvenirs to be sold at the shows. You are getting ready to write the project management plan and know that all of the following are true regarding the PMIS, except for which one?

    A. The PMIS is a tool and technique of the Scope Planning process.

    B. The configuration management system is a subsystem of the PMIS.

    C. The PMIS includes a change control system.

    D. The PMIS is an automated system.

2. You are a project manager for Laredo Pioneer's Traveling Rodeo Show. You're heading up a project to promote a new line of souvenirs to be sold at the shows. You're ready to document the processes you'll use to perform the project as well as define how the project will be executed, controlled, and closed. Which of the following is true?

    A. You are working on the project scope management plan.

    B. You are working on the product scope statement.

    C. You are working on the project management plan.

    D. You are working on the project scope statement.

3. You are a project manager responsible for the construction of a new office complex. You are taking over for a project manager who recently left the company. The prior project manager completed the scope statement and scope management plan for this project. In your interviews with some key team members, you conclude which of the following?

    A. They understand that the scope statement assesses the stability of the project scope and outlines how scope will be verified and used to control changes.

    B. They understand that the scope management plan describes how project scope will be defined and verified and used to control project scope.

    C. They understand that the scope management plan is deliverables-oriented and includes cost estimates and stakeholder needs and expectations.

    D. They understand that the scope statement describes how the high-level deliverables and requirements will be defined and verified.

4. Some of the functions of this process include describing the methods for executing the work of the project to fulfill the project objectives, documenting dependencies and interactions among the processes, determining the validity of and maintaining the performance baselines, and determining key management reviews for pending decisions. Which of the following does this describe? Choose the best answer.

    A. This process belongs to the Project Scope Management knowledge area.

    B. The output of the process is the project scope management plan.

    C. The project charter is an input of the process.

    D. The project scope management plan and quality management plan are two examples of the subsidiary plans contained in the output of the process.

5. Which of the following is true regarding the project scope statement?

   A. The project scope statement includes a change control system that describes how to make changes to the project scope.

   B. The project scope further elaborates the Initiating processes and serves as a basis for future project decisions.

   C. The project scope statement describes how the team will define and develop the work breakdown structure.

   D. The project scope statement assesses the reliability of the project scope and describes the process for verifying and accepting completed deliverables.

6. You are a project manager for an agricultural supply company. You have just completed and obtained sign-off on the project scope statement for your new Natural Bug Busters project. A key stakeholder has informed you that a deliverable is missing from the project scope statement. This deliverable is a critical success factor. Which of the following actions should you take?

   A. Inform the stakeholder that work not stated in the scope statement is excluded from the project.

   B. Modify the scope statement to reflect the new deliverable.

   C. Inform the stakeholder that this deliverable must be included in phase two of this project since sign-off has already been obtained.

   D. Modify the scope statement after an approved change request has been received from the stakeholder.

7. Your company has asked you to be the project manager for the product introduction of its new DeskTop Rock media system. You recently published a document that establishes the detailed project deliverables. Which of the following is true?

   A. This is the project scope statement, which is an output of the Scope Definition process.

   B. This is the scope management plan, which is an output of the Scope Planning process.

   C. This is the project scope statement, which is an output of the Scope Planning process.

   D. This is the scope management plan, which is an output of the Scope Definition process.

8. Which of the following statements is true regarding brainstorming and lateral thinking?

   A. They are forms of expert judgment that's used to help define and develop the project scope statement.

   B. They are used to elaborate the product scope description, which is an element of the output of the Scope Planning process.

   C. They are organizational process assets that are used to help define and develop the project management plan.

   D. They are an alternatives identification technique, which is a tool and technique of the Scope Definition process.

9. Your company has asked you to be the project manager for the product introduction of its new DeskTop Rock media system. You recently published the project scope statement. Which of the following is not contained in the project scope statement?

    A. Constraints

    B. Project specifications

    C. Requested changes

    D. Project configuration management requirements

10. You are a project manager for Giraffe Enterprises. You've recently taken over for a project manager who lied about his PMI certification and was subsequently fired. Unfortunately, he did a poor job of scope definition. Which of the following could happen if you don't correct this?

    A. The stakeholders will require overtime from the project team to keep the project on schedule.

    B. The poor scope definition will adversely affect the creation of the work breakdown structure, and costs will increase.

    C. The project management plan's process for verification and acceptance of the deliverables needs updated as a result of the poor scope definition.

    D. The project costs could increase, there might be rework, and schedule delays may result.

11. You work for a large manufacturing plant. You're working on a new project for an overseas product release. This is the company's first experience in the overseas market, and it hopes to make a big splash with the introduction of this product. The project entails producing your product in a concentrated formula and packaging it in smaller containers than the U.S. product uses. A new machine is needed in order to mix the first set of ingredients in the concentrated formula. Which of the following is true?

    A. The new machine, the concentrated formula, and the smaller package are all project constraints.

    B. The new machine, the concentrated formula, and the smaller package description must be incorporated into the product description document.

    C. The new machine, the concentrated formula, and the smaller package are all project assumptions.

    D. The new machine, the concentrated formula, and the smaller package are all considered deliverables.

12. Objectives can be described as all of the following except for which one? Choose the least correct answer.

    A. The purpose for undertaking the project

    B. The functionality and specific conditions that must be met in order to satisfy the project, contract, standard, or specification

    C. The monetary units used to express the cost criteria for the project

    D. The quantifiable results used to measure project success that should include schedule, cost, and quality criteria

13. You are a project manager working on a new software product your company plans to market to businesses. The project sponsor told you that the project must be completed by September 1. The company plans to demo the new software product at a trade show in late September and therefore needs the project completed in time for the trade show. However, the sponsor has also told you that the budget is fixed at $85,000 and it would take an act of Congress to get it increased. You must complete the project within the given time frame and budget. Which of the following is the primary constraint for this project?

    A. Budget

    B. Scope

    C. Time

    D. Schedule

14. All of the following are true regarding stakeholder analysis except for which one?

    A. It's a tool and technique of the Scope Definition process.

    B. It determines communication needs and methods for updating stakeholders.

    C. It documents the needs, wants, and expectations of the stakeholders

    D. It prioritizes and quantifies needs and wants to create project requirements.

15. You are in the process of translating project objectives into tangible deliverables and require-ments. All of the following are techniques used in the product analysis tool and technique of the Scope Definition process, except for which one?

    A. Value engineering and value analysis

    B. Product configuration and specification analysis

    C. Systems analysis and systems engineering

    D. Product breakdown and functional analysis

16. You are a project manager for a documentary film company. In light of a recent regional tragedy, the company president wants to get a new documentary on the rescue efforts of the heroic rescue teams to air as soon as possible. She's looking to you to make this documentary the best that's ever been produced in the history of this company. She guarantees you free rein to use whatever resources you need to get this project done quickly. However, the best photographer in the company is currently working on another assignment. Which of the following is true?

    A. The primary constraint is time because the president wants the film done quickly. She told you to get it to air as soon as possible.

    B. Resources are the primary constraint. Even though the president has given you free rein on resource use, you assume she didn't mean those actively assigned to projects.

    C. The schedule is the primary constraint. Even though the president has given you free rein on resource use, you assume she didn't mean those actively assigned to projects. The photog-rapher won't be finished for another three weeks on his current assignment, so schedule adjustments will have to be made.

    D. The primary constraint is quality because the president wants this to be the best film ever produced by this company. She's given you free rein to use whatever resources needed to get the job done.

17. Your project depends on a key deliverable from a vendor you've used several times before with great success. You're counting on the delivery to arrive on June 1. This is an example of a/an _____.

    A. Constraint

    B. Objective

    C. Assumption

    D. Requirement

18. What limits the options of the project team?

    A. Technology

    B. Constraints

    C. Deliverables

    D. Assumptions

19. Your company provides answering services for several major catalog retailers. The number of calls coming into the service center per month has continued to increase over the past 18 months. The phone system is approaching the maximum load limits and needs to be upgraded. You've been assigned to head up the upgrade project. Based on the company's experience with the vendor who worked on the last phone upgrade project, you're confident they'll be able to assist you with this project as well. Which of the following is true?

    A. You've made an assumption about vendor availability and expertise. The project came about due to a business need.

    B. Vendor availability and expertise are constraints. The project came about due to a business need.

    C. You've made an assumption about vendor availability and expertise. The project came about due to a market demand.

    D. Vendor availability and expertise are constraints. The project came about due to a market demand.

20. You are a project manager for Giraffe Enterprises. You've recently taken over for a project manager who lied about his PMI certification and was subsequently fired. Unfortunately, he didn't create a project charter or a preliminary scope statement. You are ready to elaborate the deliverables and requirements of the project and know that you can use one of the following in place of the charter or preliminary scope statement. Which one can you use?

    A. Business justification

    B. Product scope description

    C. Strategic plan

    D. Expert judgment

Answers to Review Questions

1. A. The PMIS is a tool and technique of the Develop Project Management Plan process. It's one of the elements of the enterprise environmental factors, which is an input to the Scope Planning process.

2. C. The project management plan describes the processes you'll use to perform the project and describes how the project will be executed, monitored, controlled, and closed.

3. B. The scope management plan describes how project scope will be defined and verified, how the scope statement will be developed, how the WBS will be developed, and how project scope will be controlled.

4. D. The Develop Project Management Plan involves describing the methods for executing the work of the project, documenting dependencies and interactions among the processes, determining the validity of and maintaining the performance baselines, and determining key management reviews for pending decisions, among other elements. The project scope management plan and quality management plans are examples of the subsidiary plans contained within the project management plan, which is the output of this process.

5. B. The scope statement further elaborates the project objectives, deliverables, requirements, and constraints and assumptions defined in the preliminary scope statement. It serves as a basis for future project decisions.

6. D. The project scope statement will change throughout the project as change requests are received and approved. Project managers must be certain to discover all deliverables before publishing the project scope statement to prevent situations like the one described in this question.

7. A. The project scope statement documents the detailed project deliverables and is an output of the Scope Definition process.

8. D. Alternatives identification is a tool and technique of the Scope Definition process that includes brainstorming and lateral thinking techniques.

9. C. Requested changes are an output of the Scope Definition process. They are not part of the project scope statement.

10. D. Option A might seem like a correct answer, but option D is more correct. There isn't enough information to determine if stakeholders will require overtime. We do know that poor scope definition may lead to cost increases, rework, schedule delays, and poor morale.

11. D. Deliverables are tangible, verifiable outcomes or items that must be produced in order to complete the project or project phase. These items wouldn't be considered objectives, because the objective of the project is to break into the overseas market with a successful product revamped for that audience.

12. B. According to *A Guide to the PMBOK*, functionality and specific conditions that must be met in order to satisfy the project, contract, standard, or specification describe the criteria for requirements, not objectives.

13. C. The primary constraint is time. Since the trade show demos depend on project completion and the trade show is in late September, the date cannot be moved. The budget is the secondary constraint in this example.

14. B. Stakeholder analysis is a tool and technique of Scope Definition used to determine and document the needs, wants, and expectations of stakeholders and prioritize and quantify those needs into project requirements.

15. B. Product analysis includes techniques like value engineering, value analysis, systems analysis, systems engineering, product breakdown, and functional analysis.

16. D. The primary constraint is quality. If you made the assumption as stated in option B, you assumed incorrectly. Clarify these assumptions with your stakeholders and project sponsors. This applies to option C as well.

17. C. This is an example of an assumption. You've used this vendor before and not had any problems. You're assuming there will be no problems with this delivery based on your past experience.

18. B. Constraints restrict the actions of the project team.

19. A. The project came about due to a business need. The phones have to be answered because that's the core business. Upgrading the system to handle more volume is a business need. An assumption has been made regarding vendor availability. Always validate your assumptions.

20. B. The product scope description can be used as an input to the Scope Definition process when the project charter and/or preliminary project scope statement are missing.

Creating the WBS and Communicating the Plan

THE PMP EXAM CONTENT FROM THE
PLANNING THE PROJECT PERFORMANCE
DOMAIN COVERED IN THIS CHAPTER
INCLUDES THE FOLLOWING:

✓ Create the WBS

Now that we have the deliverables and requirements well defined, we'll begin the process of breaking down the work of the project via a work breakdown structure (WBS). We'll accomplish this task in the Create WBS process. The WBS defines the scope of the project and breaks the work down into components that can be scheduled and estimated and easily monitored and controlled.

Next we'll talk about how project information is documented and communicated. We've talked a lot about documentation so far, and we will discuss it more in this chapter. Documentation is something you will do throughout the remainder of the project, and the Communications Planning process details how to collect information, how to store it, and when and how to distribute it to stakeholders.

We'll end this chapter by defining the quality plan in the Quality Planning process. This process focuses on determining the quality standards that are necessary for the project and documenting how we'll go about meeting them.

Creating the Work Breakdown Structure

Have you ever mapped out a family tree? In the Create WBS process, we'll construct something like it called a *work breakdown structure (WBS)*. It maps out the deliverables of the project with subdeliverables and other components stemming from each major deliverable in a tree or chart format. *A Guide to the PMBOK* describes a WBS as "a deliverable-oriented hierarchical decomposition of the work to be executed by the project team, to accomplish the project objectives and create the required deliverables. The WBS defines the total scope of the project." Simply put, a WBS is a deliverable-oriented hierarchy that defines the work of the project and only the work of the project. Like the scope statement, the WBS serves as a foundational agreement among the stakeholders and project team members regarding project scope.

Exam Spotlight

The subdividing of deliverables into smaller components is the purpose of the Create WBS process. *A Guide to the PMBOK* calls this decomposition, which is also a tool and technique of this process.

The WBS will be used throughout many of the remaining Planning processes and is an important part of project planning. As you probably have concluded, everything we've done so far builds on the previous step. The project charter and preliminary scope statement outline the project goals and major deliverables. The project scope statement further refines these deliverables into an exhaustive list and documents the requirements of the deliverables. Now that comprehensive list of deliverables produced in the project scope statement is going to be used to build the framework of the WBS.

 The importance and accuracy of the work you've done up to this point can't be stressed enough. Your WBS will only be as accurate as your list of deliverables. The deliverables will become the groupings that will form the higher levels of the WBS from which activities will be derived later in the Planning processes.

The WBS should detail the full scope of work needed to complete the project. This breakdown will smooth the way for estimating project cost and time, scheduling resources, and determining quality controls later in the Planning processes. Project progress will be based on the estimates and measurements assigned to the WBS segments. So again, accuracy and completeness are required when composing your WBS.

Before we begin constructing the WBS, we'll need to gather and review some important project documents. We'll look at those next.

Gathering the WBS Inputs

The inputs to the Create WBS process aren't new. They are as follows:

- Organizational process assets
- Project scope statement
- Project scope management plan
- Approved change requests

The important thing to note about the inputs to this process is that the approved project scope statement is the document you will use to define and organize the work of the project in the WBS. Make certain you're using the most current version of the scope statement. And note also that the WBS, just like the project scope statement, contains the work of the project and only the work of the project.

Decomposing the Deliverables

There are two tools and techniques for the Create WBS process. The first is the work breakdown structure templates. Many organizations and application areas (industries) have WBS templates they use for their projects. Keep in mind that you may use a WBS from a previous project as a template for your current project also. If you work in the same organization, and the same department within the organization, you'll often find yourself working on the same types of projects. WBS templates lend themselves well to this situation because even though a project is unique, it's similar to projects you've worked on in the past and probably has similar life cycle phases. Check with your PMO as they may also have WBS templates.

The next tool and technique is called *decomposition*. This technique involves breaking down the deliverables into smaller, more manageable components of work. The idea here is to break down the deliverables to a point where you can easily plan, execute, monitor and control, and close out the project deliverables. Decomposition typically pertains to breaking deliverables down into smaller deliverables, or component deliverables, where each level of the WBS (or each level of decomposition) is a more detailed definition of the level above it.

This breaking-down or decomposing process will accomplish several things for you, one of which is improving estimates. It's easier to estimate the costs, time, and resources needed for individual work components than it is to estimate them for a whole body of work or deliverable. Using smaller components also makes it easier to assign performance measures and controls. These give you a baseline to compare against throughout the project or phase. And finally, assigning resources and responsibility for the components of work makes better sense because several resources with different skills might be needed to complete one deliverable. Breaking them down assures that an assignment, and the responsibility for that assignment, goes to the proper parties.

According to *A Guide to the PMBOK*, decomposition is a five-step process:

1. Step one involves identifying all the major project deliverables and related work. *A Guide to the PMBOK* makes a point of noting that the major deliverables are identified by using the expert judgment technique to analyze the project scope statement.

2. Step two involves organizing the work of the project and determining the WBS structure.

 We'll talk more about this in the next section, "Constructing the WBS."

3. Step three involves decomposing the WBS levels into lower-level *components*. WBS components, like the deliverables and requirements, should be defined in tangible, verifiable terms so that performance and successful completion (or delivery) are easily measured and verified. Each component must clearly describe the product, service, or result in verifiable terms, and it must be assigned to a unit in the organization that will take responsibility for completing the work and making certain of its accuracy.

4. Step four is a process where you assign identification codes or numbers to each of the WBS components.

5. Step five is a verification step. Examine the decomposition to determine if all the components are clear and complete. Determine if each component listed is absolutely necessary to fulfill the requirements of the deliverable and verify that the decomposition is sufficient enough to describe the work.

We'll talk more about the process in step 4 in the section titled "Unique WBS Identifiers" later in this chapter.

The components you've identified can now be plugged into the WBS. This all sounds like a lot of work. I won't kid you—it is, but it's essential to project success. If you don't perform the WBS process adequately and accurately, you might end up setting yourself up for a failed project at worst or for lots of project changes, delayed schedules, and increased costs at best, not to mention all those team members who'll throw up their hands when you go back to them for the third or fourth time to ask that they redo work they've already completed. I know you won't let this happen, so let's move on to constructing the WBS.

There are several outputs of the Create WBS process, one of which is the WBS itself. We'll look at the specifics of how to create the WBS next.

Constructing the WBS

There is no "right" way to construct a WBS. In practice, the chart structure is used quite often. (This structure resembles an organization chart with different levels of detail.) But a WBS could be composed in outline form as well. The choice is yours. We'll look at both ways shortly, along with some figures that depict the different levels of a WBS.

According the *A Guide to the PMBOK,* there are also several ways you can organize the WBS:

Major deliverables and subprojects   The major deliverables of the project are used as the first level of decomposition in this structure. If you're opening a new store, for example, the deliverables might include determining location, store build-out, furnishings, product, and so on. We'll talk about subprojects under the next heading.

Subproject executed outside the project team   Another way to organize the work is by subprojects. Perhaps you're building out an existing highway and there are several subprojects involved. Some of your first level of decomposition may include these subprojects: demolition, design, bridgework, and paving. Each of the subprojects managers will develop a WBS for their subproject that details the work required for that deliverable. When subproject work is involved, often times the subproject work is contracted out. In our example, if we contracted out the bridgework deliverable, this subproject requires its own WBS, which the seller (the bridgework subcontractor) is responsible for creating as part of the contract and contract work.

Project phases   Many projects are structured or organized by project phases. For example, let's say you work in the construction industry. The project phases used in your industry might include project initiation, planning, design, build, inspection, and turnover. A feasibility study might be a deliverable under the project initiation phase, blueprints might be a deliverable under the planning phase, and so on. Each phase listed here would be the first level of decomposition (that is, the first level of the WBS) and their deliverables would be the next level and so on.

Combination approach   This approach combines some or all of the methods we've talked about. You may use project phases and major deliverables together as the first level of decomposition. Or you could have subprojects listed with major deliverables. You can use this approach in other levels of the WBS structure as well, not just the first level.

Let's take a look at some example WBS structures next.

Understanding the Various WBS Levels

Although the project manager is free to determine the number of levels in the WBS based on the complexity of the project, all WBS structures start out with the project itself. Some WBS structures show the project as level one. Others show the level under the project, or the first level of decomposition, as level one. *A Guide to the PMBOK* notes that level one is the first level of decomposition, so we'll follow that example here.

The first level of decomposition may be the deliverables, phases, or subprojects as we talked about earlier. The levels that follow show more and more detail and may include more deliverables, followed by requirements, and so on. Each of these breakouts is called a *level* in the WBS. The lowest level of any WBS is called the work package level. (We'll talk more about this in "Defining Work Packages" later in this chapter). The goal is to construct the WBS to the work package level where we can easily and reliably estimate cost and schedule dates.

Exam Spotlight

Remember that each descending level of the WBS is a more detailed description of the project deliverables than the level above it. Each component of the WBS should be defined clearly and completely and should describe how the work of the project will be performed and controlled.

There is some controversy among project managers over whether activities should be listed on the WBS. There isn't a rule in *A Guide to the PMBOK* regarding this; it's up to the project manager to determine how far to break the deliverables down and whether to include activities. In practice, I often include activities on my work breakdown structure for small projects as it facilitates other Planning processes later on. In this case, the activities are the work package level. However, you should realize that large, complex projects will not likely list activities on the WBS. And for the exam, remember that you will decompose activities during the Activity Definition process that we'll talk about in Chapter 6, "Resource Planning," and that activities are *not* part of the WBS.

The easiest way to describe the steps for creating a WBS is with an example. Let's suppose you work for a software company that publishes children's games. You're the project manager for the new Billy Bob's Bassoon game, which teaches children about music, musical rhythm, and beginning sight reading. The first box on the WBS is the project name; it appears at the top of the WBS, as shown in Figure 4.1.

The next level is the first level of decomposition and should describe the major deliverables for the project. In this example, some of the deliverables might be requirements definition, design specifications, and programming. This isn't an exhaustive list of deliverables; in practice, you would go on to place all of your major deliverables into the WBS as level one content. For illustration purposes, just look at a slice of the WBS for this project. Figure 4.1 shows the WBS with level one detail added.

FIGURE 4.1   WBS level one

Level two content might be the component deliverables that are further broken out from the major deliverables of level one, or it might be requirements or activities that contribute to the deliverable. The Billy Bob's Bassoon example shows further deliverables as level two content. See Figure 4.2 for an illustration of the WBS so far.

FIGURE 4.2   WBS levels one and two

The goal here is to eventually break the work out to the point where responsibility and accountability for each work package can be assigned to an organizational unit or a team of people. I've decomposed this WBS to the activity level because it's a small project. An easy way to differentiate between deliverables and activities in the WBS is to use nouns as the deliverable descriptors and verbs as activity descriptors. Reaching way back to my grade school English, I recall that a noun is a person, place, or thing. In this example, the deliverables in level one and level two are described using nouns. The activity level, level three in the example in Figure 4.3, is described using verbs, or action words. Some of the verbs used in level three are *define, design,* and *determine.* There are many more activities that would go with these deliverables, but for the sake of illustration, we've listed just a few for each deliverable to give you an idea of how the WBS is constructed.

FIGURE 4.3   WBS levels one, two, and three

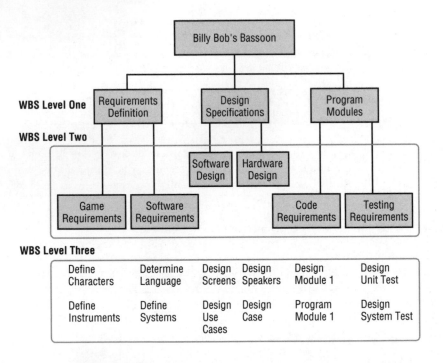

You can see from these illustrations how a poor scope definition or inadequate list of deliverables will lead to a poorly constructed WBS. Not only will this make the WBS look sickly, but the project itself will suffer and might even succumb to the dreaded premature project demise. The final cost of the project will be higher than estimated, and lots of rework (translate as late nights and weekends) will be needed to account for the missing work not listed on the WBS. You can construct a good WBS and maintain a healthy project by taking the time to document all the deliverables during the Scope Definition process.

WBS Templates

Don't forget that work breakdown structures can be constructed using WBS templates or the WBS from a similar completed project. A bit earlier, we mentioned that WBS templates are a tool and technique of the Create WBS process. While every project is unique, many companies and industries perform the same kind of projects over and over. The deliverables are similar from project to project, and they generally follow a consistent path. The WBS templates can be used in a case like this as a tool to simplify the WBS process, saving the project manager time.

Large, complex projects are often composed of several subprojects that collectively make up the main project. The WBS for a project such as this would show the subprojects as level one detail. These subprojects' major deliverables would then be listed as level two content, perhaps more deliverables as level three, and so on.

Don't get too carried away when creating a WBS. The object is to define the work of the project so you can easily plan, manage, and monitor and control the work. But, you don't want to take this too far. If you decompose the work to the point that you're showing every minute detail, you've ventured into inefficiency and will find it more difficult to plan and manage. In addition, you're potentially stifling the creativity of the people working on the project because everything is so narrowly defined.

Sometimes, particularly when working on large projects that consist of several subprojects, some of the subprojects may not be scheduled to be worked on until a future date. Obviously, it makes sense to develop the WBS in detail at that future date when the deliverables and subprojects are better known and more details are available. This technique is called *rolling wave planning*. The idea behind this technique is that you elaborate the work of the project to the level of detail you know about at the time. If a subproject or deliverable is scheduled sometime in the future, the only component that may appear on the WBS today is the subproject itself. As you get closer to the subproject, you'll elaborate the details of the subproject and record them on the WBS.

Exam Spotlight

Understand that rolling wave planning is a process of elaborating deliverables, project phases, or subprojects in the WBS to differing levels of decomposition depending on the expected date of the work. Work in the near term is elaborated in more detail than work to performed in the future.

Unique WBS Identifiers

Each element at each level of the WBS is generally assigned a unique identifier according to *A Guide to the PMBOK*. This unique identifier is typically a number, and it's used to sum and track the costs, schedule, and resources associated with the WBS elements. These numbers are usually associated with the corporation's chart of accounts, which is used to track costs by category. Collectively, these numeric identifiers are known as the *code of accounts*. The unique identifiers for the requirements definition branch of the WBS might look something like this:

10 Requirements Definition

10-1 Game Requirements

    10-1-1 Define Characters

    10-1-2 Define Instruments

10-2 Software Requirements

    10-2-1 Determine Language

    10-2-2 Define Systems

Defining Work Packages

As mentioned earlier, the project manager is free to determine the number of levels in the WBS based on the complexity of the project. You need to include enough levels to accurately estimate project time and costs but not so many levels that it's difficult to distinguish between the components. Regardless of the number of levels in a WBS, the lowest level in a WBS is called a *work package*.

Work packages are the components that can be easily assigned to one person, or team of people, with clear accountability and responsibility for completing the assignment. Assignments are easily made at the work package level; however, assignments can be made at any level in the WBS, as in the Lincoln Street office building scenario. The work package level is where time estimates, cost estimates, and resource estimates are determined.

Work package levels on large projects can represent subprojects that are further decomposed into their own work breakdown structures. They may also consist of project work that will be completed by a vendor, another organization, or another department in your organization. If you're giving project work to another department in your organization, you'll assign the work packages to individual managers, who will in turn break them down into activities during the Activity Definition process later in the Planning process group.

Work packages may be assigned to vendors or others external to the organization. For example, perhaps one of the deliverables in your project is special packaging and a vendor is responsible for completing this work. The vendor will likely treat this deliverable as a project within their own organization and construct their own WBS with several levels of decomposition. However, for your project, it's a deliverable listed at the work package level of the WBS.

NOTE   This may seem self-evident, but work elements not shown on the WBS are not included in the project. The same holds true for the project scope statement— if the deliverable isn't noted there, it isn't part of the project.

Real World Scenario

The Lincoln Street Office Building

Flagship International has just purchased a new building to house its growing staff. The folks at Flagship consider themselves very lucky to have won the bid on the property located in a prime section of the downtown area. The building is a historic building and is in need of some repairs and upgrades to make it suitable for office space. Constructing the renovations will require special handling and care as outlined in the *Historical Society Building Revisions Guide.*

Alfredo Martini is the project manager assigned to the renovation project. Alfredo has already gathered the deliverables for this project. In so doing, he's discovered that he will not be able to manage all the work himself. He will need several subproject managers working on individual deliverables, all reporting to him. Alfredo calls a meeting with the other project managers to deliver the WBS. Let's eavesdrop on the meeting.

"As you all know, we're planning to move into the Lincoln Street building by November 1st. There is quite a bit of work to do between now and then, and I'm enlisting each of you to manage a segment of this project. Take a look at this WBS."

A portion of the WBS Alfredo constructed looks like this:

Lincoln Street Building Renovation

    1.0 Facility Safety

        1.1 Sprinkler System

        1.2 Elevators

        1.3 Emergency Evacuation Plans

    2.0 Asbestos Abatement

        2.1 Inspection and Identification

        2.2 Plans for Removal

    3.0 Office Space

        3.1 Building Floor Plans

        3.2 Plans for Office Space Allocation

        3.3 Plans for Break Room Facilities

        3.4 Plans for Employee Workout Room

Alfredo continues, "I'm going to manage the Facility Safety project. Adrian, I'd like you to take the Asbestos Abatement project, and Orlando, you're responsible for the Office Space project."

"Alfredo," Adrian says. "Asbestos abatement is going to take contractors and specialized equipment. We don't have staff to do these tasks."

"I understand. You'll need to take charge of securing the contractor to handle this. Your responsibility will be to manage the contractor and keep them on schedule," Alfredo answers.

Orlando reminds Alfredo that he's missed a deliverable on the WBS. "Part of the Office Space project needs to include the network communications and telecommunications equipment rooms. I don't see that on here."

"Good point, Orlando," Alfredo says. "The level two and three elements of this WBS are not complete. Each of you has been assigned to the subproject level, level one. Your first assignment is to meet back here in two weeks with a WBS for your subproject. And I'd like to see some ideas about the staff assignments you'd make at the work package level and how long you think these components will take. We'll refine those after we meet next."

Other Breakdown Structures

One point that *A Guide to the PMBOK* makes that I want you to be aware of is that you should not confuse the WBS with other types of breakdown structures. I'm not sure why you would confuse them, but the team who wrote the guide makes a point of telling you about it, so you should be aware of it for the exam. Here are the other structures they point out that we'll see as we proceed through the remaining project processes:

Organization breakdown structure (OBS)   This is an organization chart that describes the hierarchical nature of the organization, what departments exist, and who reports to whom. It can be used to identify the organizational units responsible for the work package levels of the WBS.

Bill of materials (BOM)   BOMs are typically used in the manufacturing industry and identify the components needed to produce the product.

Risk breakdown structure (RBS)   This is a hierarchical picture of the risks identified on the project arranged by risk category.

Resource breakdown structure (RBS)   This is a hierarchical description of the resources, arranged by type, that will work on the project.

Now we'll move on to the remaining outputs of the Create WBS process.

Create WBS Process Outputs

There are six outputs of the Create WBS process:

- Project scope statement updates
- Work breakdown structure

- WBS dictionary
- Scope baseline
- Project scope management plan updates
- Requested changes

We've covered the WBS in detail already. Updates to the scope statement and scope management plan may come about as a result of approved changes that occur when you're creating the WBS. You can see from the examples we've walked through in this chapter how new deliverables or requirements may surface as a result of working on the WBS. These requested changes (the last output here) should be reviewed and either approved or denied using your change control processes. (We'll talk about that in Chapter 9, "Measuring and Controlling Project Performance.") The approved changes should be noted in the project scope statement and the project management plan should be updated to reflect the new approved project scope statement.

We'll look at the remaining outputs next.

WBS Dictionary

The *WBS dictionary* is where work component descriptions are documented. According to *A Guide to the PMBOK*, the WBS dictionary should include the following elements for each component of the WBS:

- Code of accounts identifier
- Statement of work, which describes the work of the component
- Organization responsible for completing the component
- List of schedule milestones

Here are some other elements that you may include in the WBS dictionary for each component:

- Contract information
- Quality requirements for the component
- Technical references that assist the responsible party with defining performance of the work

Let's look at an example of what a WBS dictionary entry might look like. We'll use the work package level defined in the sidebar "The Lincoln Street Office Building" earlier called Inspection and Identification. The WBS dictionary entry for this might look like the following:

2.1 Inspection and Identification

Statement of work: Inspect the building for asbestos and identify all areas where it's found. Update the plan for removal (WBS 2.2) with each location identified.

Responsible organization: Adrian in Facilities will hire and oversee a contractor to perform this work.

Schedule milestones: Inspection and identification to start after contractor is identified and hired (no later than July 1.) Work to be completed no later than Sep 15.

Contract information: Two contractors have been identified as qualified and experienced in this type of work. Contract process to close no later than June 12.

Scope Baseline

Remember how I said that everything we've done so far has built upon itself? This is an important concept you should know for this output. The *scope baseline* for the project is the approved project scope statement, the WBS, and the WBS dictionary. (You'll recall from Chapter 3 that the project scope statement serves as a baseline for future project decisions because it helps the team determine whether requested changes are inside or outside of scope.) In other words, these documents together describe in detail all of the work of the project. From these documents, you'll document schedules, assign resources, and monitor and control the work of the project according to what's described here.

Exam Spotlight

The scope baseline is defined as the detailed project scope statement, the WBS, and the WBS dictionary. Understand this concept for the exam.

If the WBS is constructed well, you've given yourself a huge helping hand with the remaining Planning processes. The completion of many of the remaining processes depend on the project scope statement and WBS to be accurate and complete. In Chapter 6, for example, we'll use the work packages created here to further elaborate the work into activities. From there, costs can be estimated, schedules can be developed, and so on. Before we get there though, we're going to take a little breather and look at some of the other Planning processes important to your project. Don't forget about the WBS! We're going to come back to this in the later planning chapters of this book.

Communicating the Plan

We've talked a good deal about documentation so far, and this topic will continue to come up throughout the remainder of the book. Keeping good documentation should become the motto of all good project managers. "Is that documented?" should be an ever-present question on the mind of the project manager. Documentation can save your bacon, so to speak, later in the project. Documentation is only one side of the equation though—communication is the other. You and your stakeholders need to know who gets what information and when.

The *Communications Planning* process involves determining the communication needs of the stakeholders by defining the types of information needed, the format for communicating the information, how often it's distributed, and who prepares it. All of this is documented in the communications management plan, which is the only output of this process.

Pop quiz: Do you remember where else the communications management plan belongs? I'll give you the answer later in the section "Communications Management Plan."

Communications Planning Inputs

The inputs to the Communications Planning process will look very familiar to you. They are as follows:

- Enterprise environmental factors
- Organizational process assets
- Project scope statement
- Constraints and assumptions elements of the project management plan

A Guide to the PMBOK notes that all the elements described in the enterprise environmental factors and in the organizational process assets are inputs to this process. However, special note is made of the lessons learned and historical information elements of the organizational process assets input. Information you learn as you're progressing through the project is documented as lessons learned. This information is helpful for future projects of similar scope and complexity. Historical information is also useful to review when starting the Communications Planning process. Either of these documents may contain information about communication decisions on past projects and their results. Why reinvent the wheel? If something didn't work well on a past project, you'd want to know that before implementing that procedure on this project, so review past project documentation.

The project scope management plan (we talked about this in Chapter 3) provides a common understanding of project scope among the stakeholders and serves a basis for future project decisions. (I'm sure you have this definition memorized by now—that's good.) Since you performed stakeholder analysis as part of the Scope Definition process (which produced the project scope statement as an output that became an input to this process), you should review the stakeholder analysis and refresh your memory on their communication needs.

The project management plan defines how the subsidiary plans will be defined and integrated into the overall project management plan. As such, it's rich with constraints and assumptions that you should review as they pertain to stakeholder communication needs.

Tools and Techniques for Communications Planning

The Communications Planning process concerns defining the types of information you're going to deliver, to whom, and when and then documenting this. There are two tools and techniques in this process to help determine these elements. They are communications requirements analysis and communications technology. We'll look at both of these next.

Requirements Analysis

Communications requirements analysis involves analyzing and determining the communication needs of the project stakeholders. According to *A Guide to the PMBOK,* there are several sources of information you can examine to help determine these needs, including the following:

- Company and departmental organizational charts
- Stakeholder relationships
- Other departments and business units involved on the project
- The number of resources involved on the project and where they're located in relation to project activities
- External needs that organizations like the media, government, or industry groups may have that require communication updates
- Communication needs that are internal to the organization
- Stakeholder information (a lot of this was documented during stakeholder analysis)

This tool and technique requires an analysis of the items in the preceding list to make certain you're communicating information that's valuable to the stakeholders. Communicating valuable information doesn't mean you always paint a rosy picture. Communications to stakeholders may consist of either good or bad news—the point is that you don't want to bury stakeholders in too much information but give them enough so that they're informed and can make appropriate decisions.

Project communication will always involve more than one person, even on the tiniest of projects. As such, communication network models have been devised to try to explain the relationships between people and the number or type of interactions needed between project participants. What you need to remember for the exam is that network models consist of nodes with lines connecting the nodes that indicate the number of communication channels, also known as lines of communication. Figure 4.4 shows an example of a network communication model with six channels of communication.

The nodes are the participants, and the lines show the connection between them all. You'll need to know how to calculate the number of communication channels when you take the exam. You could draw them out as in this example and count up the lines, but there's an easier way. The formula for calculating the lines of communication is as follows:

(number of participants × (number of participants less one)) divided by two

Here's the calculation in mathematical terms:

$n (n - 1) \div 2$

Figure 4.4 shows six participants, so let's plug that into the formula to determine the lines of communication:

$6 (6 - 1) \div 2 = 15$

Exam Spotlight

I recommend you memorize the communications channel formula before taking the exam.

FIGURE 4.4   Network communication model

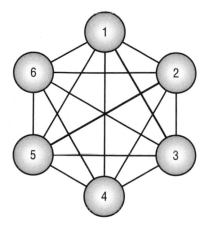

Nodes = participants
Lines = lines of communication between participants

Communications Technology

The second tool and technique of this process is communications technology. This examines the methods (or technology) used to communicate the information to, from, and among the stakeholders. Methods of communicating can take many forms, such as written, spoken, e-mail, formal status reports, meetings, online databases, online schedules, and so on. This tool and technique examines the technology elements that may affect project communications. You should consider several factors before deciding what methods you'll choose to transfer information. The timing of the information exchange or need for updates is the first factor. The availability of the technology you're planning on using to communicate project information is important as well. Do you need to procure new technology or systems, or are there systems already in place that will work? Staff experience with the technology is another factor. Are the project team members and stakeholders experienced at using this technology, or will you need to train them? Finally, consider the duration of the project and the project environment. Will the technology you're choosing work throughout the life of the project or will it have to be upgraded or updated at some point? And how does the project team function? Are they all located together or spread out across several campuses or locations?

The answers to these questions should be documented in the communications management plan. We'll cover that next.

Communications Management Plan

All projects require sound communication plans, but not all projects will have the same types of communication or the same methods for distributing the information. The *communications management plan,* which is the only output of the Communications Planning process, documents the types of information needs the stakeholders have, when the information should be distributed, and how the information will be delivered. The answer to the pop quiz I opened this section with is the communications management plan, which is a subsidiary plan of the project management plan we talked about in Chapter 3.

The type of information you will typically communicate includes project status, project scope statements and scope statement updates, project baseline information, risks, action items, performance measures, project acceptance, and so on. We'll cover all of these topics in greater detail in the remaining chapters of this book. What's important to know now is that the information needs of the stakeholders should be determined as early in the Planning process group as possible so that as you and your team develop project planning documents, you already know who should receive copies of them and how they should be delivered.

According to *A Guide to the PMBOK*, the communications management plan typically describes the following elements:

- Name of the item to be communicated

- Purpose for communication

- Frequency of communications

- Time frame for distribution, including starting and ending dates

- Format of the communication and method of transmission

- Person responsible for distributing the information

The information that will be shared with stakeholders and the distribution methods are based on the needs of the stakeholders, the project complexity, and the organizational policies. Some communications may be informal—a chat by the water cooler, for instance—while other communications are written and a copy is filed with the project files.

Exam Spotlight

The communications management plan documents how the communication needs of the stakeholders will be met, including the types of information that will be communicated, who will communicate it, who receives the communication, the methods used to communicate, the timing and frequency, the method for updating this plan as the project progresses, escalation process, and a glossary of common terms.

You might consider setting up an intranet site for your project and posting the appropriate project documentation there for the stakeholders to access any time they wish. If you use this method, make sure to document it in the communications management plan and notify your stakeholders when updates or new communication is posted.

Chapter 8, "Developing the Project Team," discusses communication methods in more depth.

Identifying Quality Standards

Quality is affected by the triple constraints (project scope, schedule, and cost), and quality concerns are found in all projects. Quality typically defines whether stakeholder expectations were met. Being on time and on budget is one thing; if you deliver the wrong product or an inferior product, on time and on budget suddenly don't mean much.

The *Quality Planning* process is concerned with targeting quality standards that are relevant to the project at hand and devising a plan to meet and satisfy those standards. The quality management plan is an output of this process that describes how the quality policy will be implemented by the project management team during the course of the project. Another key output of this process is the process improvement plan, which documents the actions for analyzing processes to ultimately increase customer value. Everything discussed in this section, including the inputs and tools and techniques of this process, will be used to help develop these two primary outputs.

Exam Spotlight

Quality Planning is a key process performed during the Planning processes and when developing the project management plan. It should be performed in conjunction with other Planning processes. According to *A Guide to the PMBOK,* "...quality is planned, designed, and built in— not inspected in."

Quality Inputs

The Quality Planning process has several inputs:

- Enterprise environmental factors
- Organizational process assets
- Project scope statement
- Project management plan

The two key elements we'll cover regarding inputs are standards and regulations (which are part of the enterprise environmental factors input) and the quality policy (which is part of the organizational process assets input).

Standards and Regulations

The project manager should consider any standards, regulations, guidelines, or rules that exist concerning the work of the project when writing the quality plan. A *standard* is something that's approved by a recognized body and that employs rules, guidelines, or characteristics that should be followed. For example, the Americans with Disabilities Act (ADA) has established standards for web page designers that outline alternative viewing options of web pages for people with disabilities. PMI guidelines regarding project management are another example of standards.

Standards aren't mandatory, but it's a good idea to follow them. For example, if you're creating a new software product that ignores standard protocols, your customers won't be able to use it.

Standards can be set by the organization, by independent bodies or organizations such as the International Organization for Standardization (ISO), and so on.

A *regulation* is mandatory. Regulations are almost always imposed by governments or institutions like the American Medical Association. However, organizations may have their own self-imposed regulations that you should be aware of as well. Regulations require strict adherence, particularly in the case of government-imposed regulations, or stiff penalties and fines could result—maybe even jail time if the offense is serious enough. Hmm, might be tough to practice project management from behind bars—not a recommended career move.

If possible, it's a good idea to include information from the quality policy (we'll cover this in the next section) and any standards, regulations, or guidelines that affect the project in the quality management plan. If it's not possible to include this information in the quality management plan, then at least make reference to the information and where it can be found. It's the project management team's responsibility to be certain all stakeholders are aware of and understand the policy issues and standards or regulations that might impact the project.

Contracts might have certain provisions for quality requirements that you should account for in the quality management plan. These provisions will also be discussed during the Procurement Planning processes. If the quality management plan has already been written by the time these processes are performed, you should update the quality plan to reflect it.

Quality Policy

The quality policy is part of the organizational process assets input. It's a guideline published by executive management that describes what quality policies should be adopted for projects the company undertakes. It's up to the project manager to understand this policy and incorporate any predetermined company guidelines into the quality plan. If a quality policy does not exist, it's up to the project management team to create one for the project.

Quality Planning Tools and Techniques

The Quality Planning process has five tools and techniques used to help construct the quality management plan:

- Cost-benefit analysis
- Benchmarking
- Design of experiments
- Cost of quality
- Additional quality planning tools

Make sure you understand each of these tools and techniques and its purpose for the exam. Let's take a look them now.

Cost-Benefit Analysis

You've seen the cost-benefit analysis technique before in the Initiating process group. In the case of quality management, you'll want to consider the trade-offs of the cost of quality. It's cheaper and more efficient to prevent defects in the first place than to have to spend time and money fixing them later. The benefits of meeting quality requirements are as follows:

- Stakeholder satisfaction is increased.

- Costs are lower.

- Productivity is higher.

- There is less rework.

A Guide to the PMBOK notes that the primary cost of meeting quality requirements for a project are the expenses incurred while performing project quality management activities.

Benchmarking

Benchmarking is a process of comparing previous similar activities to the current project activities to provide a standard to measure performance against. This comparison will also help you derive ideas for quality improvements on the current project. For example, if your current printer can produce 8 pages per minute and you're considering a new printer that produces 14 pages per minute, the benchmark is 8 pages per minute.

Design of Experiments

Design of experiments (DOE) is a statistical technique that identifies the elements—or variables—that will have the greatest effect on overall project outcomes. It is used most often concerning the product of the project but can also be applied to project management processes to examine trade-offs. DOE designs and sets up experiments to determine the ideal solution for a problem using a limited number of sample cases. It analyzes several variables at once, allowing you to change all (or some of) the variables at the same time and determine which combination will produce the best result at a reasonable cost.

Exam Spotlight

For the exam, remember that the key to DOE is that it equips you with a statistical framework that allows you to change all the important variables at once instead of changing one variable at a time.

Cost of Quality

The *cost of quality (COQ)* is the total cost to produce the product or service of the project according to the quality standards. These costs include all the work necessary to meet the product requirements whether the work was planned or unplanned. It also includes the costs of work performed due to nonconforming quality requirements.

There are three costs associated with the cost of quality:

Prevention costs   Prevention means keeping defects out of the hands of customers. *Prevention costs* are the costs associated with satisfying customer requirements by producing a product without defects. These costs are manifested early on in the process and include things like quality planning, training, design review, and contractor and supplier costs.

Appraisal costs   *Appraisal costs* are the costs expended to examine the product or process and make certain the requirements are being met. Appraisal costs might include costs associated with things like inspections and testing. Prevention and appraisal costs are often passed on to the acquiring organization due to the limited duration of the project.

Failure costs   *Failure costs* are what it costs when things don't go according to plan. Failure costs are also known as cost of poor quality. There are two types of failure costs:

Internal failure costs   These result when customer requirements are not satisfied while the product is still in the control of the organization. Internal failure costs may include corrective action, rework, scrapping, and downtime.

External failure costs   These occur when the product has reached the customer and they determine that their requirements have not been met. Costs associated with external failure costs may include inspections at the customer site, returns, and customer service costs.

The cost of quality can be affected by project decisions. Let's say you're producing a new product. Unfortunately, the product scope description and/or project scope statement were inadequate to describe the functionality of the product. And, the project team produced the product exactly as specified in the project scope statement, WBS, and other planning documents. Once the product hit the store shelves, the organization was bombarded with returns and warranty claims because of the poor quality. Therefore, your project decisions impacted the cost of quality. Recall of products can also impact the cost of quality.

Cost of quality is a topic you'll likely encounter on the exam. This section will discuss some of the pioneers in this field. Quality must be planned into the project, not inspected in after the fact to make certain the product or service meets stakeholders' expectations.

Three people in particular are responsible for the rise of the quality management movement and the theories behind the cost of quality: Philip B. Crosby, Joseph M. Juran, and W. Edwards Deming. Each of these men developed steps or points that led to commonly accepted quality processes that we use today and either developed or were the foundation for the development of quality processes such as Total Quality Management, Six Sigma, Cost of Quality, and Continuous Improvement. We'll also look at a quality technique called the Kaizen approach that originated in Japan.

Philip B. Crosby

Philip B. Crosby devised the *zero defects* practice, which means, basically, do it right the first time. (Didn't your dad use to tell you this?) Crosby says that costs will increase when quality planning isn't performed up front, which means you'll have to engage in rework, thus affecting productivity. Prevention is the key to Crosby's theory. If you prevent the defect from occurring in the first place, costs are lower, conformance to requirements is easily met, and the cost measurement for quality becomes the cost of nonconformance rather than the cost of rework.

Joseph M. Juran

Joseph M. Juran is noted for his *fitness for use* premise. Simply put, this means the stakeholders' and customers' expectations are met or exceeded. This says that conformance to specifications—meaning the product of the project that was produced is what the project set out to produce—is met or exceeded. Fitness for use specifically reflects the customers' or stakeholders' view of quality and answers the following questions:

"Did the product or service produced meet the quality expectation?"

"Did it satisfy a real need?"

"Is it reliable and safe?"

Juran also proposed that there could be grades of quality. However, you should not confuse grade with quality. Grade is a category for products or services that are of the same type but have differing technical characteristics. Quality describes how well the product or service (or characteristics of the product or service) fulfills the requirements. Low quality is usually not an acceptable condition; however, low grade might be. For example, your new Dad's Dollars Credit Card software tracking system might be of high quality, meaning there are no bugs and the product performs as advertised, but of low grade, meaning there are few features. You'll almost always want to strive for high quality, regardless of the acceptable grade level.

Exam Spotlight

Understand the difference between quality and grade for the exam.

W. Edwards Deming

W. Edwards Deming suggested that as much as 85 percent of the cost of quality is a management problem. Once the quality issue has hit the floor, or the worker level, the workers have little control. For example, if you're constructing a new highway and the management team that bid on the project proposed using inferior-grade asphalt, the workers laying the asphalt have little control over its quality. They're at the mercy of the management team that purchased the supplies.

Deming also proposed that workers cannot figure out quality on their own and thus cannot perform at their best. He believed that workers need to be shown what acceptable quality is and that they need to be made to understand that quality and continuous improvement are necessary elements of any organization—or project in your case.

Many consider Deming to be the founder (or major contributor) of *Total Quality Management (TQM)*. TQM, like Deming, says that the process is the problem, not people. Every person and all activities the company undertakes are involved with quality. TQM stipulates that quality must be managed in and that quality improvement should be a continuous way of doing business, not a one-time performance of a specific task or process.

Six Sigma is a quality management approach that is similar to TQM and is typically used in manufacturing and service-related industries. Six Sigma is a measurement-based strategy that focuses on process improvement and variation reduction by applying Six Sigma methodologies to the project. There are two Six Sigma methodologies. The first is known as DMADV (define, measure, analyze, design, and verify) and is used to develop new processes or products at the Six Sigma level. The second is called DMAIC (define, measure, analyze, improve, and control) and is used to improve existing processes or products. Another tidbit you should understand about Six Sigma is that it aims to eliminate defects and stipulates that no more than 3.4 defects per million are produced.

Kaizen Approach

The Kaizen approach is a quality technique from Japan. In fact, *Kaizen* means *continuous improvement* in Japanese. With this technique, all project team members and managers should be constantly watching for quality improvement opportunities. The Kaizen approach states that you should improve the quality of the people first, then the quality of the products or service.

Continuous improvement involves everyone in the organization watching for ways to improve quality, whether incrementally or by incorporating new ideas into the process. This involves taking measurements, improving processes by making them repeatable and systemized, reducing variations in production or performance, reducing defects, and improving cycle times. TQM and Six Sigma are examples of continuous improvement.

Exam Spotlight

Understand each of these men's theories on the cost of quality for the exam. Here's a key to help you remember:

- Crosby = zero defects and prevention or rework results.

- Juran = fitness for use, conformance.

- Deming = quality is a management problem.

- TQM = quality must be managed in and must be a continuous process.

- Six Sigma = Six Sigma is a measurement based strategy; no more than 3.4 defects per million.

- Kaizen = continuous improvement, improve quality of people first.

- Continuous improvement = watch continuously for ways to improve quality.

Additional Quality Planning Tools

The last tool and technique of the Quality Planning process is additional quality planning tools. *A Guide to the PMBOK* lists these additional tools as follows:

- Brainstorming and nominal group techniques (We'll cover both of these in Chapter 5, "Risk Planning.")
- Flowcharts (We'll cover this one in Chapter 10, "Measuring and Reporting Project Objectives.")
- Affinity diagrams
- Force field analysis
- Matrix diagram
- Prioritization matrices

I would memorize the names of these additional quality planning tools for the exam, but more importantly, you should understand both the names and concepts of the other tools and techniques we've already talked about in this section.

Quality Planning Outputs

Quality Planning uses many techniques to determine the areas of quality improvement that can be implemented, controlled, and measured throughout the rest of the project, as you've seen. These are recorded in the primary output of this process, which is called the quality management plan. The following list includes other outputs of this process:

- Quality metrics
- Quality checklists
- Process improvement plan
- Quality baseline
- Project management plan updates

Project management plan updates may come about as a result of changes to the quality management plan, which in turn may come about as result of changes or corrections resulting from the Perform Quality Assurance process. We'll talk about Perform Quality Assurance in Chapter 9. We'll look at the remaining outputs of Quality Planning next.

Quality Management Plan

The *quality management plan* describes how the project management team will enact the quality policy. It should document the resources needed to carry out the quality plan, the responsibilities of the project team in implementing quality, and all the processes and procedures the project team and organization should use to satisfy quality requirements, including quality control, quality assurance techniques, and continuous improvement processes.

The quality management plan is written by the project manager in cooperation with the project staff. You can assign quality actions to the activities listed on the work breakdown structure (WBS) based on the quality plan requirements. Isn't that WBS a handy thing? Later in the

Perform Quality Control process, measurements will be taken to determine if the quality to date is on track with the quality standards outlined in the quality management plan.

Exam Spotlight

The Quality Management knowledge area, which includes the Quality Planning, Perform Quality Assurance, and Perform Quality Control processes, involves the quality management of the project as well as the quality aspects of the product or service the project was undertaken to produce. We'll discuss Quality Assurance and Quality Control in later chapters.

Quality Metrics

A *quality metric,* also known as *operational definition,* describes what is being measured and how it will be measured by the Perform Quality Control process. For example, let's say you're managing the opening of a new restaurant in July of next year. Perhaps one of the deliverables is the procurement of flatware for 500 place settings. The operational definition in this case might include the date the flatware must be delivered and a counting or inventory process to ensure you received the number of place settings you ordered. Measurements consist of actual values, not yes or no results. In our example, receiving the flatware is a yes or no result (you have it or you don't), but the date it was delivered and the number of pieces delivered are actual values. Failure rates are another type of quality metric that is measurable, as are reliability, availability, test coverage, and defect density measurements.

Quality Checklists

If you're like me, you start your day at the office with a big to-do list that has so many items on it you won't be able to finish them all. Nevertheless, you faithfully write the list every day and check off the things that you accomplish throughout the day. *Checklists* are like this in that they provide a means to determine if the required steps in a process have been followed. As each step is completed, it's checked off the list. Checklists can be activity specific or industry specific and might be very complex or easy to follow. Sometimes, organizations may have standard checklists they use for projects. You might also be able to obtain checklists from professional associations.

Exam Spotlight

Be aware that checklist shows up as both a process output and tool and technique. Quality checklists are an output of the Quality Planning process and checklist analysis is a tool and technique of the Risk Identification process.

Real World Scenario

Candy Works

Juliette Walters is a contract project manager for Candy Works. It has introduced a new line of hard candy drops in various exotic flavors: caffe latte, hot buttered popcorn, and jalapeno spice, just to name a few.

Juliette is writing the quality management plan for this project. After interviewing stakeholders and key team members, she's found several quality factors of importance to the organization. Quality will be measured by the following criteria:

Candy size   Each piece should measure 3 mm.

Appearance   No visible cracks or breaks should appear in the candy.

Flavor   Flavor must be distinguishable when taste-tested.

Number produced   The production target is 9,000 pieces per week. The current machine has been benchmarked at 9,200 candies per week.

Intensity of color   There should be no opaqueness in the darker colors.

Wrappers   Properly fitting wrappers cover the candies, folding over twice in back and twisted on each side. There is a different wrapper for each flavor of candy, and they must be matched exactly.

The candy is cooked and then pulled into a long cylinder shape roughly 6 feet long and 2 feet in diameter. This cylinder is fed into the machine that molds and cuts the candy into drops. The cylinders vary a little in size, because they're hand-stretched by expert candy makers prior to feeding them into the drop maker machine. As a result, the end of one flavor batch—the caffe latte flavor—and the beginning of the next batch—the hot buttered popcorn flavor—merge. This means the drops that fall into the collection bins are intermingled during the last run of the first flavor batch. In other words, the last bin of the caffe latte flavor run has some hot buttered popcorn drops mixed in. And, there isn't a way to separate the drops once they've hit the bin. From here, the drops go on to the candy-wrapping machine, where brightly colored wrappers are matched to the candy flavor. According to the quality plan, hot buttered popcorn drops cannot be wrapped as caffe latte drops. Juliette ponders what to do.

As she tosses and turns that night thinking about the problem, it occurs to her to present this problem as an opportunity to the company rather than as a problem. In order to keep production in the 9,000 candies per week category, the machines can't be stopped every time a new batch is introduced. So Juliette comes up with the idea to wrap candies from the intermixed bins with wrappers that say "Mystery Flavor." This way, production keeps pace with the plan, and the wrapper/flavor quality problem is mitigated.

Process Improvement Plan

The *process improvement plan* focuses on finding inefficiencies in a process or activity and eliminating them. The idea here is that if you're doing activities or performing processes that don't add any value, you'll want to either stop doing what you're doing or modify the process so that you are adding value. You should note that the process improvement plan is a subsidiary plan of the project management plan. Some of the elements you should consider when thinking about process improvement are the process boundaries, which describes the purpose for the process and its expected start and end dates; the process configuration so that you know what processes are performed when and how they interact; the process metrics; and any specific elements you want to target for improvement.

Quality Baseline

Almost everything you've done throughout this process culminates in the quality baseline. The *quality baseline* is the quality objective of the project. It's what you'll use to measure and report quality against as you perform the remaining Quality processes.

> One of the results of the Quality Planning process is that your product or process may require adjustments to conform to the quality policy and standards. These changes may result in cost changes and schedule changes. You may also discover that you'll need to perform risk analysis techniques for problems you uncover or when making adjustments as a result of this process.

Project Case Study: New Kitchen Heaven Retail Store

You're just finishing a phone conversation with Jill, and you see Dirk headed toward your office.

Dirk walks in, crosses his arms over his chest, and stands next to your desk with an "I'm here for answers" look.

"I thought I'd drop by and see if you have signed a lease and gotten Jake started on that build-out yet," says Dirk.

"I just got off the phone with Jill," you reply. "The realtor found a great location and we've set up a tour at the end of this week."

"What's been the holdup?" Dirk asks. "I thought we'd be ready to start the build-out about now."

"I've been working on the project plans."

"Project plans," Dirk interrupts. "We already have a plan. That scope thing you drew up last week spelled things out pretty clearly."

"The charter was the project kickoff, and the project scope statement listed all the deliverables and requirements. From there I had to break the work of the project down into manageable units of work. So, I've drawn up a work breakdown structure with all the deliverables shown in a tree structure that I'd like to go over with you before showing it to the project team."

"We aren't building trees; we're building a new store. I don't understand why you're wasting all this time planning. We all know what the objectives are."

"Dirk," you reply, "if we put the right amount of effort and time into planning, the actual work of the project should go pretty smoothly. Planning is probably one of the most important things we can do on this project. If we don't plan correctly, we might miss something very important that could delay the store opening. That date is pretty firm, I thought."

"Yes, the date is firm. But I don't see how we could miss anything. You and I have met several times, and I know you've met with Jill and Jake. They're the other key players on this."

"You're right. I have met with Jill and Jake. And that's a perfect example of why we need to plan. When I met with Jill, she told me how all the store's data is communicated via a satellite network connection on a nightly basis. That means we need to involve the IT group."

You glance down at your notes. "Ricardo Ramirez heads up IT. I spoke with him last week about his deliverables, and I've included his group as a subproject on the work breakdown structure."

"Oh," Dirk replies. "I forgot about IT. You're right, that's an important part of the project, and we can't leave them out. Don't tell Ricardo I said this, but I'm not very technical myself and don't really know what you're going to need from him. I do know he also takes care of wiring and installing the point-of-sale terminals, but you'll have to work all that out with him. Okay, I'm beginning to see why you're taking planning seriously. Let's have a look at this work breakdown structure."

You hand Dirk a copy of the WBS. A partial version is shown here.

"Looks good to me."

"Great. Two more items, Dirk. After meeting with Jake, Ricardo, and Jill, I've also drafted a communication plan and a quality management plan. The communication plan describes the kind of information they need to receive, when, and how. And the quality management plan...well you know the old saying, 'Do it right the first time.' It describes the plan for implementing our quality policy. I also took the time to write down the specific quality metrics we're looking for, including the lease signing date (this one must start and finish on time) and the IT equipment specifications, and Jill's documented the gourmet products and the cookware line specifications.

Decomposed deliverables into a WBS

WBS includes:

- Level one is subprojects or deliverables.

- Level two is deliverables or activities.

- Remaining levels are activities.

- Last level of WBS is the work package level, where time and cost estimates can be defined in the next process.

Documented the communications management plan, including:

- Stakeholder communication needs

- Types of project communication and their format

- Frequency and method of communication

- Person responsible for producing communication

Documented the quality management plan and quality metrics, including:

- Lease signing start and end dates

- IT equipment specifications

- Gourmet products—availability rates and defects

- Cookware products—availability rates

Summary

A WBS is a deliverable-oriented group of project essentials. The highest levels of the WBS are described using nouns, and the lowest levels are described with verbs. Each element in the WBS has its own set of objectives and deliverables that must be met in order to fulfill the deliverables of the next highest level and ultimately the project itself. In this way, the WBS validates the completeness of the work.

The lowest level of the WBS is known as work packages. This breakdown allows the project manager to determine cost estimates, time estimates, resource assignments, and quality controls.

The purpose of the communications management plan is determining the communication needs of the stakeholders by defining the types of information needed, the format for communicating the information, how often it's distributed, and who prepares it. This plan is a subsidiary plan of the project management plan.

Quality Planning targets the quality standards that are relevant to your project. The quality management plan outlines how the project team will enact the quality policy.

You need to consider the cost of quality when considering stakeholder needs. Three men led to the rise of the cost of quality theories. Crosby is known for his zero defects theory, Juran for the fitness for use theory, and Deming for contributing 85 percent of cost of quality to the management team. The Kaizen approach says that the project team should continuously be on the lookout for ways to improve the process and that people should be improved first, then the quality of the products or services. TQM and Six Sigma are examples of continuous improvement techniques.

Cost-benefit analysis considers trade-offs in the Quality Planning process. Benchmarking compares previous similar activities to the current project activities to provide a standard to measure performance against. Design of experiments is an analytical technique that determines what variables have the greatest effect on the project outcomes. This technique equips you with a statistical framework, allowing you to change all the important variables at once instead of changing one variable at a time.

Cost of quality involves three types of costs: prevention, appraisal, and failure costs; the latter is also known as the cost of poor quality. Failure costs include both internal and external costs.

The process improvement plan is a subsidiary plan of the project management plan and targets inefficiencies in a process or activity. The quality baseline is used to document the quality objectives of the project and is used as a basis for future Quality processes.

Exam Essentials

Be able to define a WBS and its components. The WBS is a deliverable-oriented hierarchy. It uses the deliverables from the project scope statement or similar documents and decomposes them into logical, manageable units of work. Level one is the major deliverable level or subproject level, level two is a further elaboration of the deliverables, and so on. The lowest level of any WBS is called a work package.

Be able to describe the purpose of the communications management plan.   The communications management plan determines the communication needs of the stakeholders. It documents what information will be distributed, how it will be distributed, to whom, and the timing of the distribution.

Be able to identify the benefits of meeting quality requirements   The benefits of meeting quality requirements include increased stakeholder satisfaction, lower costs, higher productivity, and less rework and are discovered during the Quality Planning process.

Be able to define the cost of quality   The COQ is the total cost to produce the product or service of the project according to the quality standards. These costs include all the work necessary to meet the product requirements. The three costs associated with cost of quality are prevention, appraisal, and failure costs (also known as cost of poor quality).

Be able to name three people associated with COQ and some of the techniques they helped establish   Crosby, Juran, and Deming. Some of the techniques they helped to establish are TQM, Six Sigma, cost of quality, and continuous improvement. The Kaizen approach concerns continuous improvement and says people should be improved first.

Be able to name the tools and techniques of the Quality Planning process   Cost benefit analysis, benchmarking, design of experiments, cost of quality, additional quality planning tools.

Key Terms

You've learned a lot of new key words in this chapter. PMI has worked hard to develop and define standard project management terms that apply across industries. Here is a list of some of the terms you came across in this chapter:

appraisal costs

benchmarking

checklists

code of accounts

communications management plan

Communications Planning

components

continuous improvement

cost of quality (COQ)

decomposition

design of experiments (DOE)

failure costs

fitness for use

Kaizen

operational definition

prevention costs

process improvement plan

quality baseline

quality management plan

quality metric

Quality Planning

regulation

rolling wave planning

scope baseline

Six Sigma

standard

Total Quality Management (TQM)

WBS dictionary

work breakdown structure (WBS)

work package

zero defects

Review Questions

1. Which of the following makes up the project scope baseline?

   A. The project scope statement

   B. The scope management plan and WBS

   C. The WBS, project scope statement, and WBS dictionary

   D. The scope management plan, the WBS, and the WBS dictionary

2. You are working on a project that is similar in scope to a project performed last year by your company. You might consider which of the following?

   A. Using the previous project's alternatives identification as a template

   B. Reusing the previous project's cost-benefit analysis as justification for this project

   C. Using the previous project's WBS as a template

   D. Reusing the previous project's product description when writing the scope statement

3. Your company, Kick That Ball Sports, has appointed you project manager for its new Cricket product line introduction. This is a national effort, and all the retail stores across the country need to have the new products on the shelves before the media advertising blitz begins. The product line involves three new products, two of which will be introduced together and a third one that will follow within two years. You are ready to create the WBS. All of the following are true expect for which one?

   A. Each of the three products should be elaborated to the same number of levels. This is known as rolling wave planning.

   B. The WBS should be elaborated to a level where costs and schedule are easily estimated. This is known as the work package level.

   C. The WBS can be structured using each product as a level one entry.

   D. Each level of the WBS represents verifiable products or results.

4. Your company, Kick That Ball Sports, has appointed you project manager for its new Cricket product line introduction. This is a national effort, and all the retail stores across the country need to have the new products on the shelves before the media advertising blitz begins. The product line involves three new products, two of which will be introduced together and a third one that will follow within two years. Product number three will be elaborated in more detail closer to the product's release date, while the first two products will be elaborated in great detail now. The scope management plan has just been completed. Which of the following is true? (Choose the best response.)

    A. Only the deliverables associated with the work of the project should be listed on the WBS. Since product number three isn't being released until a later date it should not yet be included on the WBS.

    B. The WBS template from a previous project, a tool and technique of the Create WBS process, was used to create the WBS for this project. The WBS encompasses the major deliverables for the project.

    C. The WBS should be created next, and it encompasses the full scope of work for the project. Only the work of the project is listed on the WBS.

    D. The WBS encompasses the full scope of work for the project and the technique in the question is called rolling wave planning.

5. You work for a large manufacturing plant. You are working on a new project to release an overseas product line. This is the company's first experience in the overseas market, and it hopes to make a big splash with the introduction of this product. The project entails producing your product in a concentrated formula and packaging it in smaller containers than the U.S. product uses. A new machine is needed in order to mix the ingredients into a concentrated formula. In order to complete the Create WBS process sufficiently, you decide to do which of the following?

    A. Use the organizational breakdown structure and the WBS together and present this scope baseline to stakeholders.

    B. Record the code of account identifier, an SOW, responsible organization, and milestone schedule in the WBS dictionary for the components of the WBS.

    C. Elaborate the WBS to the point where the new machine specifications are clear and highly detailed.

    D. Record the approved change requests as one of the outputs of this process.

6. You are the project manager for Lucky Stars nightclubs. They specialize in live country and western band performances. Your newest project is in the Planning process group. You've published the scope statement and scope management plan. The document that describes who will receive copies of this information as well as future project information, how it should be distributed, and who will prepare it is which of the following?

    A. Scope management plan

    B. Communications management plan

    C. Information distribution plan

    D. Project charter

7. You are the project manager for Lucky Stars nightclubs. They specialize in live country and western band performances. Your newest project is in the Planning processes group. You are working on the WBS. The finance manager has given you a numbering system to assign to the WBS. Which of the following is true?

   A. The numbering system is a unique identifier known as the code of accounts, which is used to track the costs of the WBS elements.

   B. The numbering system is a unique identifier known as the WBS dictionary, which is used to track the descriptions of individual work elements.

   C. The numbering system is a unique identifier known as the code of accounts, which is used to track time and resource assignments for individual work elements.

   D. The numbering system is a unique identifier known as the WBS dictionary, which is used to assign quality control codes to the individual work elements.

8. You've constructed the WBS for your recent project. You've requested that the subproject managers report back to you in three weeks with each of their individual WBSs constructed. Which statement is not true regarding the subproject managers' WBS?

   A. The work package level facilitates resource assignments.

   B. The work package level is the lowest level in the WBS.

   C. The work package level defines the agreed-upon deliverables.

   D. The work package level facilitates cost and time estimates.

9. Which of the following statements about decomposition is the least true?

   A. Decomposition involves structuring and organizing the WBS so that deliverables are always listed at level one.

   B. Decomposition requires a degree of expert judgment and also requires close analysis of the project scope statement.

   C. Decomposition is a tool and technique used to create a WBS.

   D. Decomposition subdivides the major deliverables into smaller components until the work package level is reached.

10. Which of the following is not a major step of decomposition?

   A. Identify major deliverables.

   B. Identify components.

   C. Determine adequate cost and schedule estimates.

   D. Verify correctness of decomposition.

11. You have eight key stakeholders to communicate with on your project. Which of the following is true?

A. There are 36 channels of communication and this should be a consideration when using the communications technology tool and technique.

B. There are 28 channels of communication and this should be a consideration when using the communications requirements analysis tool and technique.

C. There are 28 channels of communication and this should be a consideration when using the communications technology tool and technique.

D. There are 36 channels of communication and this should be a consideration when using the communications requirements analysis tool and technique.

12. All of the following are true regarding Communications Planning except for which one?

A. It's the only output of the Communications Planning process.

B. It should be completed as early in the project phases as possible.

C. It's tightly linked with enterprise environmental factors and organizational influences, and lessons learned and historical information are two inputs that should get a lot of attention during this process.

D. Communications requirements analysis, communications technology, and PMIS are tools and techniques of this process.

13. All of the following are true regarding the Quality Planning process except for which one?

A. DOE is a tool and technique of this process that provides statistical analysis for changing product or process elements one at a time to optimize the process.

B. This is one of the key processes performed during the Planning process group and during the development of the project management plan.

C. Changes to the product as a result of meeting quality standards may require cost or schedule adjustments.

D. The tools and techniques of this process are cost-benefit analysis, benchmarking, DOE, COQ, and additional quality planning tools.

14. Three people are responsible for establishing cost of quality theories. Crosby and Juran are two them, and their theories respectively are _____.

A. Grades of quality, fitness for use

B. Fitness for use, zero defects

C. Zero defects, fitness for use

D. Cost of quality, zero defects

15. The theory that 85 percent of the cost of quality is a management problem is attributed to which of the following?

A. Deming

B. Kaizen

C. Juran

D. Crosby

16. All of the following are benefits of meeting quality requirements except which one?

    A. An increase in stakeholder satisfaction

    B. Less rework

    C. Low turnover

    D. Higher productivity

17. Which of the following describes the cost of quality associated with scrapping, rework, and downtime?

    A. Internal failure costs

    B. External failure costs

    C. Prevention costs

    D. Appraisal costs

18. The quality management plan documents how the project team will implement the quality policy. It must address all of the following except which one?

    A. Quality control

    B. Quality checklists

    C. Quality assurance

    D. Continuous process improvement

19. You work for a furniture manufacturer. You're project is going to design and produce a new office chair. The chair will have the ability to function as a normal chair and also the ability to transform its occupant into an upright, kneeling position. The design team is trying to determine the combination of comfort and ease of transformation to the new position that will give the chair the best characteristics while keeping the costs reasonable. Several different combinations have been tested. This is an example of which of the following tools and techniques of Quality Planning?

    A. Benchmarking

    B. Quality metrics

    C. COQ

    D. DOE

20. Which of the following best characterizes Six Sigma?

    A. Stipulates that quality must be managed in

    B. Focuses on process improvement and variation reduction by using a measurement-based strategy

    C. Asserts that quality must be a continuous way of doing business

    D. Focuses on improving the quality of the people first, then improving the quality of the process or project

Answers to Review Questions

1. C. The scope baseline consists of the project scope statement, the WBS, and the WBS dictionary.

2. C. WBSs from previous projects can be used as templates on projects that are producing similar products or services. Some companies write WBS templates to be used for projects of similar scope.

3. A. Each of the three products may have different amounts of elaboration and levels. The question said the third product would not be introduced until two years after the first two. This WBS entry may contain only one level stating the product name.

4. D. There isn't enough information in the question to know if option B is correct, although it could be. Option C is not correct because the next process after the scope management plan is created is the Scope Definition process. The WBS details the entire scope of the project and includes all deliverables. It is an output of the Create WBS process and the technique of elaborating some deliverables at a later date is called rolling wave planning.

5. B. The WBS dictionary should be documented with the code of account identifier, an SOW, the responsible organization, and a milestone schedule for the WBS components. Option C is not correct because the amount of elaboration and detail the question describes would make the WBS inefficient. You need only enough detail to make it easier for the project team to plan, manage, and control the work. Approved change requests are inputs to this process. Requested changes are the output.

6. B. The communications management plan documents what information will be distributed, how it will be distributed, to whom, by whom, and the timing of the distribution.

7. A. Each element in the WBS is assigned a unique identifier. These are collectively known as the code of accounts. Typically, these codes are associated with a corporate chart of accounts and are used to track the costs of the individual work elements in the WBS.

8. C. The work package level is the lowest level in the WBS and facilitates resource assignment and cost and time estimates. The agreed-upon deliverables in option C would consist of the higher levels in the WBS.

9. A. Decomposition subdivides the major deliverables into smaller components. It is a tool and technique of the Create WBS process, along with WBS templates, and is used to create a WBS. Level two components may be deliverables, phases, subprojects, or some combination.

10. C. The steps of decomposition include identify major deliverables, organize and determine the structure, identify lower-level components, assign identification codes, and verify correctness of decomposition.

11. B. There are 28 channels of communication, which is considered when using the communications requirements analysis tool and technique.

12. D. Communications requirements analysis and communications technology are the tools and techniques of the Communications Planning process.

13. A. Design of experiments is a tool and technique of the Quality Planning process that provides statistical analysis for changing key product or process elements all at once (not one at a time) to optimize the process.

14. C. Philip Crosby devised the zero defects theory, meaning do it right the first time. Proper Quality Planning leads to less rework and higher productivity. Joseph Juran's fitness for use says that stakeholders' and customers' expectations are met or exceeded.

15. A. W. Edwards Deming conjectured that the cost of quality is a management problem 85 percent of the time and that once the problem trickles down to the workers, it is outside their control.

16. C. The benefits of meeting quality requirements are increased stakeholder satisfaction, lower costs, higher productivity, and less rework.

17. A. Internal failure costs are costs associated with not meeting the customer's expectations while you still had control over the product. This results in rework, scrapping, and downtime.

18. B. Quality checklists are an output of the Quality Planning process.

19. D. This is an example of design of experiments.

20. B. Six Sigma is a measurement-based strategy that focuses on process improvement and variation reduction by applying Six Sigma methodologies to the project.

Risk Planning

THE PMP EXAM CONTENT FROM THE PLANNING THE PROJECT PERFORMANCE DOMAIN COVERED IN THIS CHAPTER INCLUDES THE FOLLOWING:

✓ Identify Risks and Define Risk Strategies

We're going to take breather from defining scope and breaking down the work of the project to look at the potential for threats or opportunities on your project, otherwise known as risk. The processes we're going to discuss here have outputs that become inputs to the Planning processes we'll discuss in the coming chapters.

Risk is evident in everything we do. When it comes to project management, understanding risk and knowing how to minimize its impacts (or take full advantage of its opportunities) on your project is essential for success. This entire chapter is dedicated to project risk. Five of the six risk processes (all contained in the Risk Management knowledge area) fall in the Planning process group. We'll cover Risk Management Planning, Risk Identification, Qualitative Risk Analysis, Quantitative Risk Analysis, and Risk Response Planning in this chapter. We'll follow up with the last risk process, Risk Monitoring and Control, in Chapter 9, "Monitoring and Controlling Project Performance."

Hold on to your hats! We're going to cover a lot of material in this chapter, but it will go fast, I promise.

Planning for Risks

Every one of us takes risks on a daily basis. Just getting out of bed in the morning is a risk. You might stub your toe in the dark on the way to the light switch or trip over the dog and break a leg. These things don't usually happen, but the possibility exists. The same is true for your project. Risk exists on all projects, and the potential that a particular risk will occur depends on the nature of the risk.

Risk, like most of the elements of the other Planning processes, changes as the project progresses and should be monitored throughout the project. As you get close to a risk event, that's the time to reassess your original assumptions about the risk and your plans to deal with the risk and to make any adjustments as required.

Not all risks are bad. Risks can present opportunities as well as threats to a project. All risks have causes, and if the risk event occurs during a project, there are consequences as a result of that risk. Those consequences will likely impact one or more of the project objectives, and you'll need to know if the consequences have positive or negative impacts.

Risk is, after all, uncertainty. The more you know about risks and their impacts, the better equipped you are to handle a risk when it occurs. The processes that involve risk, probably more than any other project Planning process, concerns balance. You want to find that point where you and the stakeholders are comfortable taking the risk based on the benefits you can potentially gain. In a nutshell, you're balancing the action of taking a risk against avoiding the consequences or impacts of a risk. The rest of this chapter will deal with finding out what risks may occur (and how to deal with those risks that are unknown), determining an organization's tolerance for risk taking, and developing action plans for those risks we've determined have hefty impacts. The first step is performing the Risk Management Planning process. Here, you determine the approach you'll use for risk management activities and document your plans for them in a risk management plan. Let's look at that process now.

Risk Management Planning

Risks come about for many reasons. Some are internal to the project, and some are external. The project environment, the planning process, the project management process, inadequate resources, and so on can all contribute to risk. Some risks you'll know about in advance and plan for during this process; others will occur unannounced during the project. The *Risk Management Planning* process determines how you'll plan for risks on your project.

Exam Spotlight

A Guide to the PMBOK states that the Risk Management Planning process is an important foundation for all the risk processes that follow "...to ensure that the level, type, and visibility of risk management are commensurate with both the risk and importance of the project to the organization, to provide sufficient resources and time for risk management activities, and to establish an *agreed-upon basis for evaluating risk* [emphasis mine]." Understand this concept, particularly that you're developing an agreed-upon basis for risk evaluation, for the exam.

In order to document the risk management plan, we need to gather some inputs that will help us determine our organizations risk policies and tolerance for risk. We'll look at those inputs next.

Inputs of Risk Management Planning

Risks associated with a project generally concern the project objectives, which in turn impact time, cost, scope, or quality or any combination of the four. As you might have guessed, the project scope statement is an input to this process since it spells out your project objectives. The inputs of this process are as follows:

- Enterprise environmental factors
- Organizational process assets
- Project scope statement
- Project management plan

One of the key elements of the enterprise environmental factors to consider as in input in this process is the *risk tolerance* levels of the organization and the stakeholders. Risk tolerance is that balance we talked about earlier where stakeholders are comfortable taking a risk because the benefits to be gained outweigh what could be lost—or just the opposite. They will avoid taking a risk because the cost or impact is too great given the amount of benefit that can be derived. Here's an example to describe risk tolerance: Suppose you're a 275-pound brute who's surrounded by three body guards of equal proportion everywhere you go. Chances are, walking down a dark alley in the middle of the night doesn't faze you in the least. That means your risk tolerance for this activity is high. However, if you're a petite 90-pounder without benefit of body guards or karate lessons, performing this same activity might give you cause for concern. Your risk tolerance is low, meaning you wouldn't likely do this activity. The higher your tolerance for risk, the more you're willing to take on risk and their consequences.

Organizations and stakeholders, as well as individuals, all have different tolerances for risk. One organization might believe that the risk of a potential 17 percent cost overrun is high, while another might think it's low. However, either one of these organizations may decide to accept the risk if they believe it's in balance with the potential rewards. It's important for the project manager to understand the tolerance level the organization and the stakeholders have for risk before evaluating and ranking risk.

Remember that organizational process assets include policies and guidelines that may already exist in the organization. Your organization's risk management policies are any policies it might have that you should consider when planning for risks. Defined roles and responsibilities that outline what authority levels the stakeholders and/or project manager have for making decisions regarding risk planning may exist in these policies. (Do consider that these decisions can affect other planning processes.) Your organization may also have preexisting templates that you can use during this process. These templates should be updated on a regular basis and examined for their appropriateness on this project.

The project scope statement, as mentioned earlier, contains the project objectives and deliverables. This is the first place you'll start looking when identifying risks and should be considered when determining the process you'll use to evaluate risks. The risk management plan (the only output of this process) will become part of the project management plan, so obviously, other project management processes and guidelines should be considered when performing this process so that the risk management plan is in line with the overall direction and management of the project.

Tools and Techniques for Risk Management Planning

There is only one tool and technique of the Risk Management Planning process: planning meetings and analysis. The purpose of these meetings, which are held with project team members, stakeholders, functional managers, and others who may have involvement in the risk management process, is to contribute to the risk management plan. During these meetings, the fundamental plans for performing risk management activities will be discussed and determined and then documented in the risk management plan.

The key outcomes of performing these planning meetings are as follows:

- Risk cost elements are developed for inclusion in the project budget.
- Schedule activities are developed for inclusion in the project schedule.
- Risk responsibilities are assigned.
- Templates for risk categories are defined or modified for this project.
- Definitions of terms (*probability, impact, risk types, risk levels,* and so on) are developed and documented.
- The probability and impact matrix is defined or modified for this project.

 We'll discuss risk responsibilities, define the terms in the preceding list, and construct our own probability and impact matrix in the remaining sections of this chapter.

Ultimately, our goal for this process concerns documenting the risk management plan (the output of this process). This document contains the basis for understanding the remaining risk processes. Since the risk management plan encompasses a wealth of information, I've given this topic its own section. Let's get to it.

Creating the Risk Management Plan

The purpose of the Risk Management Planning process is to create a *risk management plan,* which describes how you will define, monitor, and control risks throughout the project. The risk management plan is a subsidiary of the project management plan and it's the only output of this process.

The risk management plan details how risk management processes (including Risk Identification, Qualitative Risk Analysis, Quantitative Risk Analysis, Risk Response Planning, and Risk Monitoring and Control) will be implemented, monitored, and controlled throughout the life of the project. It details how you will manage risks but does not attempt to define responses to individual risks.

 We'll talk about how to develop those response plans in the section "Developing a Risk Response Plan" later in this chapter.

According to *A Guide to the PMBOK,* the risk management plan should include the following elements:

- Methodology
- Roles and responsibilities

- Budgeting
- Timing
- Risk categories
- Definitions of risk probability and impact
- Probability and impact matrix
- Revised stakeholder tolerances
- Reporting formats
- Tracking

Exam Spotlight

It's very important to spend time developing the risk management plan because it's an input to every other risk-planning process and enhances the probability of risk management success.

We'll take a look at most of these elements next. However, risk categories, probability and impact, and probability and impact matrix are pretty meaty topics, so we'll cover those in their own sections following this one.

Methodology   Methodology is a description of how you'll perform risk management, including elements like methods, tools, and where you might find risk data that you can use in the later processes.

Roles and responsibilities   Roles and responsibilities describe the team of people who are responsible for managing the identified risks and their responses and for each type of activity identified in the risk management plan. These risk teams might not be the same as the project team. Risk analysis should be unbiased, which may not be possible when project team members are involved.

Budgeting   The budget for risk management is included in the plan as well. In this section, you'll assign resources and estimate the costs of risk management and its methods. These costs will then be included in the project cost baseline. (We'll talk about that in Chapter 7, "Creating the Project Schedule and Budget.")

Timing   Timing documents the timing of the risk management processes (including when and how often they'll be performed on the project) and includes the activities associated with risk management in the project schedule.

Revised stakeholder tolerances   This is just as it implies. As you proceed through the risk management processes, you may find that risk tolerances will change. Document those new tolerance levels in the risk management plan.

Reporting formats   Reporting formats describe the content of the risk register and the format of this document. (We'll talk more about the risk register later in this chapter.) Reporting formats also detail how risk management information will be maintained, updated, analyzed, and reported to project participants.

Tracking   This includes a description of how you'll document the history of the risk activities for the current project and how the risk processes will be audited. You can reference this information when you're performing risk-planning processes later in the current project or on future projects. This information is also helpful for lessons learned, which we'll cover in Chapter 11, "Closing Out the Project."

Risk Categories

Risk categories are a way to systematically identify risks and provide a foundation for understanding. When determining and identifying risks, the use of risk categories helps improve the process by giving everyone involved a common language or basis for describing risk.

Risk categories should be identified during this process and documented in the risk management plan. You will use these categories during the next process, Risk Identification, to help identify risks. The following list includes some of the categories you might identify during this process (or modify based on previous project information):

- Technical, quality, or performance risks

- Project management risks

- Organizational risks

- External risks

There are a couple of ways you can go about describing categories of risk. One way is simply listing them. You could, and should, review prior projects for risk categories and then tailor them for this project.

You could also construct a *risk breakdown structure (RBS)*, which lists the categories and subcategories. A sample of an RBS is shown in Figure 5.1.

> Remember that the organizational process assets input may include an RBS that you can reference for this project. And don't forget your PMO. They may have templates or an RBS already developed.

Risk categories may reflect the type of industry or application area in which the project exists. For example, Information Technology projects will likely have many risks that fall into the technical category, whereas construction projects may be more subject to risks that fall into the external risks category. The categories do not have to be industry specific, however. Keep in mind that project management, for example, is a risk on every project in every industry. A description of each of the categories is shown next:

Technical/quality/performance risks   Technical, quality, or performance risks include risks associated with unproven technology, complex technology, or changes to technology anticipated during the course of the project. Performance risks may include unrealistic performance goals. Perhaps one of the project deliverables concerns a component manufactured to specific performance standards that have never been achieved. That's a performance risk.

Project management risks   The project management risk category includes improper schedule and resource planning, poor project planning, and improper or poor project management disciplines or methodologies.

FIGURE 5.1   Risk breakdown structure

Organizational risks   The organizational risk category can include resource conflicts due to multiple projects occurring at the same time in the organization; scope, time, and cost objectives that are unrealistic given the organization's resources or structure; and lack of funding for the project or diverting funds from this project to other projects.

External risks   The external risk category includes those things external to the project, such as new laws or regulations, labor issues, weather, changes in ownership, and foreign policy for projects performed in other countries. Catastrophic risks—known as *force majeure*—are usually outside the scope of risk management planning and instead require disaster recovery techniques. Force majeure includes events like earthquakes, meteorites, volcanoes, floods, civil unrest, terrorism, and so on.

Defining Probability and Impact

When you're writing the risk management plan, you'll want to document how probability and impact will be defined on the project. Probability describes the potential for the risk event occurring, while impact describes the impact, or consequences, the project will experience if the risk event occurs. This definition can be very sophisticated or simple. For example, you may use numeric values to define probability and impact or simply assign a high-medium-low rating to each risk. What's important to note now is that you don't use these probability and impact definitions here. You use these definitions later in the Qualitative Risk Analysis process. (We'll talk in depth about probability and impact in the section "Analyzing Risk Using Qualitative Techniques" later in this chapter.) But you should define and document them here in the risk management plan.

Probability and Impact Matrix

A *probability and impact matrix* defines the combination of probability and impact that helps you determine which risks need detailed risk response plans. For example, a risk with a high probability of occurring and a high impact will likely need a response plan. This matrix is typically defined by the organization, but if you don't have one, you'll need to develop this now—during your planning meeting and analysis (the tool and technique of this process). You'll use this matrix in the Qualitative Risk Analysis process, and we'll talk more in depth in the section about this technique. Again, you want to define (or modify) the probability and impact matrix in the risk management plan

The key thing to note about this process is that you'll define what the probability and impact tools look like now during Risk Management Planning so that the team has an agreed-upon basis for evaluating the identified risks later during the Qualitative Risk Analysis process.

To recap, the steps associated with these last few elements of the risk management plan are as follows:

- Define the risk categories (to be used in the Risk Identification process).

- Determine how probability and impact will be defined (to be used in the Qualitative Risk Analysis process).

- Define or modify the probability and impact matrix (to be used in the Qualitative Risk Analysis process).

All these things, together with the other elements of the risk management plan, give you and the risk management team a common understanding for evaluating risks throughout the remainder of the project.

Identifying Potential Risk

The *Risk Identification* process involves identifying all the risks that might impact the project, documenting them, and documenting their characteristics. Risk Identification is an iterative process that continually builds on itself. As you progress through the project, more risks may present themselves (those you didn't identify early on in the Planning process). Once you've identified or discovered a potential new risk, you should analyze it to determine if a response plan is needed. You can see that the risk management cycle starts again with Risk Identification and progresses through the remaining risk processes to determine what to do about them.

You can include several groups of folks to help identify risks, including project team members, stakeholders, subject matter experts, users, and anyone else who you think may help in the process. Perhaps in the first round of Risk Identification, you include just the project team and subject matter experts, and then you bring in the stakeholders or risk management team to further flesh out risks during the second round of identification.

 We'll talk more about the techniques you can use to identify risks in the section titled "Tools and Techniques Used to Identify Risk."

Risks may or may not adversely affect the project. Some risks have positive consequences, while others have negative consequences. However, all risk events and their consequences should be identified. Here's a partial list to get you thinking about where risk may be found:

- Budgets/funding
- Schedules
- Scope or requirements changes
- Project plan
- Project management processes
- Technical issues
- Personnel issues
- Hardware
- Contracts
- Political concerns
- Business risk
- Legal risk
- Environmental risk

This is by no means an exhaustive list. Remember that risk is uncertainty and realize that risk (uncertainty) is lurking almost anywhere on your project. It's your job to discover as many of the potential risks as possible using the tools and techniques of this process and to document these risks.

Risk Identification Inputs

The inputs to the Risk Identification process are as follows:

- Enterprise environmental factors
- Organizational process assets
- Project scope statement
- Risk management plan
- Project management plan

As usual, the enterprise environmental factors input concerns things from outside the project that may help you determine or influence project outcomes. Be certain to check for industry information (commercial databases, checklists, benchmarking studies, and so on) or academic research that might exist for your application areas regarding risk information.

As always, don't forget about historical information like previous project experiences via the project files. Project team knowledge is another form of historical information.

The project scope statement contains a list of project assumptions. Assumptions are things believed to be true. It's imperative during the risk-planning stages of your project and throughout the work of the project to revisit and revalidate your project assumptions. At the time you recorded an assumption about vendor deliveries, for example, the vendor had a great track record and never missed a date. Months later on the project, that vendor merges with one of its competitors. Now you'll need to reexamine your assumptions about delivery times and determine if the assumption is still valid or whether you have a risk on your hands.

You should pay particular attention to the roles and responsibilities section of the risk management plan and the budget and schedule for risk activities, and don't forget to examine the categories of risks. This is a great place to start when you get the team together and begin brainstorming your list of risks.

The project management plan contains several other management plans (like schedule, quality, and cost) that can be helpful sources also when identifying risks.

Although *A Guide to the PMBOK* doesn't mention it, I've found that other elements of your project are helpful when identifying risk, such as the work breakdown structure (WBS), cost and schedule estimates, the staffing management plan, project staff assignments, and resource availability. You should really examine the outputs of most of the processes.

Tools and Techniques Used to Identify Risk

The Risk Identification process is undertaken using five tools and techniques:

- Documentation reviews
- Information-gathering techniques
- Checklist analysis
- Assumptions analysis
- Diagramming techniques

Documentation reviews involve reviewing project plans, assumptions, and historical information from a total project perspective as well as at the individual deliverables or activities level. This review helps the project team identify risks associated with the project objectives. Pay attention to the quality of the plans (is the content complete or does it seem to be lacking detail?) and the consistency between plans. An exceptionally documented schedule is great, but if the budget isn't as well documented, you may have some potential risks. Let's look at the remaining tools and techniques of this process, starting with information gathering.

Information Gathering

Information gathering encompasses several techniques, including brainstorming, the Delphi technique, interviewing, root cause identification, and strength and weakness analysis. The goal of these techniques is to end up with a comprehensive list of risks at the end of the meeting. Let's take a quick look at each of these techniques.

Brainstorming

Brainstorming is probably the most often used technique of the Risk Identification process. You've probably used this technique many times for many purposes. Brainstorming involves getting subject matter experts, team members, risk management team members, and anyone else who might benefit the process in a room and asking them to start identifying possible risk events. The trick here is that one person's idea might spawn another idea and so on, so that by the end of the session you've identified all the possible risks. The facilitator could start the group off by going through the categories of risks to get everyone thinking in the right direction.

Delphi Technique

The *Delphi technique* is a lot like brainstorming, only the people participating in the meeting don't necessarily know each other. In fact, the people participating in this technique don't all have to be located in the same place and can participate anonymously. You can use e-mail to facilitate the Delphi technique very easily.

What you do is assemble your experts, from both inside and outside the company, and ask them via a questionnaire to identify potential risks. They in turn send their responses back to you (or to the facilitator of this process). All the responses are organized by content and sent back to the Delphi members for further input, additions, or comments. The participants then send their comments back one more time, and a final list of risks is compiled by the facilitator.

The Delphi technique is a great tool that allows consensus to be reached very quickly. It also helps prevent one person from unduly influencing the others in the group and thus prevents bias in the outcome because the participants are usually anonymous and don't necessarily know how others in the group responded.

Nominal Group Technique

Another technique that is similar to the Delphi technique is the *nominal group technique*. It isn't a named tool and technique of this process, but it is a technique you might find useful and that you may find on the exam.

This technique requires the participants to be together in the same room. Each participant has paper and pencil in front of them, and they are asked to write down what risks they think the project faces. Using sticky-backed notes is a good way to do this. Each piece of paper should contain only one risk. The papers are given to the facilitator, who sticks them up to the wall or a white board. The panel is then asked to review all the risks posted on the board; rank them and prioritize them, in writing; and submit the ranking to the facilitator. Once this is done, you should have a complete list of risks.

Interviewing

Interviews are question-and-answer sessions held with others, including other project managers, subject matter experts, stakeholders, customers, the management team, project team members, and users. These folks provide you with possible risks based on their past experiences with similar projects.

This technique involves interviewing those folks with previous experience on projects similar to yours or those with specialized knowledge or industry expertise. Ask them to tell you about any risks that they've experienced or that they think may happen on your project. Show them the WBS and your list of assumptions to help get them started thinking in the right direction.

Root Cause Identification

Did you ever hear someone say you're looking at the symptoms and not at the problem? That's the idea here. Root cause identification involves digging deeper than the risk itself and looking at what the cause of the risk is. This helps define the risk more clearly and it also helps you later when it's time to develop the response plan for the risk.

Strengths, Weaknesses, Opportunities, and Threats (SWOT)

Strengths, weaknesses, opportunities, and threats (also known as SWOT analysis) is an analysis technique that examines through each of these viewpoints (SWOT) the project itself, project management processes, resources, the organization, and so on. It also helps broaden your perspective of where to look for risks.

Exam Spotlight

Not all of the techniques listed here are detailed in *A Guide to the PMBOK*. Be aware that there might be questions on any of the techniques I've shown here. Understand the difference between the various information-gathering techniques for the exam.

Checklist Analysis

Checklists used during the Risk Identification process are usually developed based on historical information and previous project team experience. If you typically work on projects that are similar in nature, begin to compile a list of risks. You can then convert this to a checklist that will allow you to identify risks on future projects quickly and easily. You can also use the lowest level of the RBS as a checklist. However, don't rely solely on checklists for Risk Identification because you might miss important risks. It isn't possible for a single checklist to be an exhaustive source for all projects. You can improve your checklists at the end of the project by adding the new risks that were identified.

Assumptions Analysis

Assumptions analysis is a matter of validating the assumptions you identified and documented during the course of the project Planning processes. Assumptions should be accurate, complete, and consistent. Examine all your assumptions for these qualities. Assumptions are also used as a jumping-off point to further identify risks.

The important thing to note about the project assumptions is that all assumptions are tested against two factors:

- The strength of the assumption or the validity of the assumption

- The consequences that may impact the project if the assumption turns out to be false

All assumptions that turn out to be false should be evaluated and scored just as risks.

Diagramming Techniques

There are three types of diagramming techniques used in Risk Identification: cause-and-effect, system or process flowcharts, and influence diagrams. *Cause-and-effect diagrams* show the relationship between the effects of problems and their causes. This diagram depicts every potential cause and subcause of a problem and the effect that each proposed solution will have on the problem. This diagram is also called a fishbone diagram, or Ishikawa diagram after its developer, Kaoru Ishikawa. Figure 5.2 shows an example cause-and-effect diagram.

The system or process flowchart shows the logical steps needed to accomplish an objective, how the elements of a system relate to each other, and what actions cause what responses. This flowchart is probably the one you're most familiar with. It's usually constructed with rectangles and parallelograms that step through a logical sequence and allow for "yes" and "no" branches (or some similar type of decision). Figure 5.3 shows a flowchart to help determine if risk response plans should be developed for the risk (we'll talk about response plans in the Developing a Risk Response Plan section later in this chapter).

FIGURE 5.2 Cause-and-effect diagram

FIGURE 5.3   Flowchart diagram

Cause-and-effect diagrams and system or process flowcharts are used in the Risk Identification process as well as in the Perform Quality Control process.

A third diagramming technique used during Risk Identification is called *influence diagrams*. According to *A Guide to the PMBOK*, influence diagrams typically show the casual influences among project variables, the timing or time ordering of events, and the relationships among other project variables and their outcomes. Simply put, they visually depict risks (or decisions), uncertainties or impacts, and how they influence each other. Figure 5.4 shows an influence diagram for a product introduction decision. The weather is a variable that could impact delivery time and delivery time is a variable that can impact when revenues will occur.

FIGURE 5.4   Influence diagram

Each of these techniques provides a way for you to help identify project risks. It's important that you identify all the risks early on. The better job you do of identifying the project's risks at the Planning stage, the more comprehensive the risk response plan will be. Risk Identification is not an area of project Planning that you should skip.

Risk Identification Outputs

The output of the Risk Identification process is the *risk register*. Everything you've done in this process up to this point will get documented here. The risk register contains the following elements:

- List of identified risks
- List of potential responses
- Root causes of risks
- Updated risk categories

We'll take a look at each one next. Understand that all risks should be documented, tracked, reviewed, and managed throughout the project.

List of Identified Risks

Risks are all the potential events and their subsequent consequences that could occur as identified by you and others during this process. You might want to consider logging your risks in a risk database or tracking system to organize them and keep a close eye on their status. This can easily be done in spreadsheet format or whatever method you choose. List the risks and assign each risk a tracking number. This gives you a means to track the risks, their occurrence, and the responses implemented.

List of Potential Responses

Potential responses to risk may be identified at the same time you're identifying the risks. Sometimes just identifying the risk will tell you the appropriate response. Document those responses here. You'll refer to them again in the Risk Response Planning process a little later in this chapter.

Root Causes of Risk

We talked about this one before. When you're identifying risks, be sure you go further than that and try to identify the cause. Document those causes you've identified here in the risk register.

Updated Risk Categories

As a result of identifying and documenting your risks, you may well discover some categories of risk need changed or updated to reflect the risks for the current project. This might also include updating the RBS. It's a good practice to update those categories now, while you're in the midst of the process. Your next project will be all the better for it.

Triggers

If you've ever suffered from a hay fever attack, you can't mistake the itchy, runny nose and scratchy throat that can come on suddenly and send you into a sneezing frenzy. Signals like this are known as *triggers* and work the same way when determining if a risk event is about to occur. For example, if you're planning an outdoor gathering and rain clouds start rolling in from the north on the morning of the activity, you probably have a risk event waiting to happen. A key team member hinting about job hunting is a warning sign that they may be thinking of leaving, which in turn can cause schedule delays, increased costs, and so on. This is another example of a trigger.

Triggers are *not* listed as one of the risk register elements, but in practice, this is an appropriate place to list them. You will likely encounter questions on the exam about triggers, so don't say I didn't warn you. Also, throughout the remainder of the project, be on the alert for triggers that might signal that a risk event is about to occur.

Analyzing Risks Using Qualitative Techniques

The *Qualitative Risk Analysis* process involves determining what impact the identified risks will have on the project objectives and the probability they'll occur. It also ranks the risks in priority order according to their effect on the project objectives. This helps the team determine if Quantitative Risk Analysis should be performed or if you can skip right to developing response plans. The Qualitative Risk Analysis process also considers risk tolerance levels, especially as they relate to the project constraints (scope, time, cost, and quality) and the time frames of the potential risk events.

The Qualitative Risk Analysis process should be performed throughout the project. This process is the one you'll find you'll use most often when prioritizing project risk because it's fast, relatively easy to perform, and cost effective. *A Guide to the PMBOK* mentions two techniques you can use during this process to help correct biases that can occur in the data you've gathered: definitions of probability and impact (this is part of the risk management plan we discussed earlier in this chapter) and expert interviewing (we talked about this in the Risk Identification section of this chapter).

Qualitative Risk Analysis Inputs

The Qualitative Risk Analysis process has four inputs:

- Organizational process assets
- Project scope statement
- Risk management plan
- The risk register

As with the Risk Identification process, you should examine historical information and lessons learned from past projects as a guide for prioritizing the risks for this project. As we've discussed before, these are part of the organizational process assets input. The project scope statement describes the deliverables of the project, and from there you should be able to determine if you're dealing with a high level of uncertainty or a project that's similar in size and scope to one you've performed before. Projects with high levels of uncertainty or that are more complex than what the team has undertaken before require more diligence during the Qualitative Risk Analysis process.

The risk management plan documented the roles and responsibilities of risk team members, budget and schedule factors for risk activities, the stakeholder risk tolerances, the definitions for probability and impact, and the probability and impact matrix, all of which should be considered when prioritizing risks. We'll examine probability and impact more closely in the next section, "Using the Tools and Techniques of Qualitative Risk Analysis."

The critical element in this process, as with most of the processes you'll find where risk register is an input, is the list of risks.

The real key to this process lies in the tools and techniques you'll use to prioritize risks. Hold on tight because we're going in the deep end.

Using the Tools and Techniques of Qualitative Risk Analysis

The Qualitative Risk Analysis process's tools and techniques are primarily concerned with discovering the probability of a risk event and determining the impact (or consequences) the risk will have if it does occur. The output of this process is a risk register update where you'll document the prioritized risks you've scored using these tools and techniques. All of the information you gather regarding risks and probability needs to be as accurate as possible. It's also important that you gather unbiased information so that you don't unintentionally overlook risks with great potential or consequences.

The purpose of this process is to determine risk event probability and risk impact. You'll use the tools and techniques of this process to establish risk scores, which is a way of categorizing the probability and risk impact. The Qualitative Risk Analysis process includes the following tools and techniques:

- Risk probability and impact assessment
- Probability and impact matrix
- Risk data quality assessment
- Risk categorization
- Risk urgency assessment

We'll look at each of these tools and techniques next.

Risk Probability and Impact Assessment

This tool and technique assess the probability that the risk events you've identified will occur and it determines the effect their impacts have on the project objectives, including time, scope, quality, and cost. Analyzing risks in this way allows you to determine which risks require the most aggressive management. When determining probabilities and impacts, you'll refer back to the risk management plan element called "definitions of risk probability and impact."

Probability

Probability is the likelihood that an event will occur. The classic example is flipping a coin. There is a .50 probability of getting heads and a .50 probability of getting tails on the flip. One thing to note is that the probability that an event will occur plus the probability that the event will not occur always equals 1.0. In this coin-flipping example, there is a .50 chance that you'll get heads on the flip. There is also, therefore, a .50 chance you will not get heads on the flip. The two responses added together equal 1.0. Probability is expressed as a number from 0.0—which means there is no probability of the event occurring—to 1.0—which means there is 100 percent certainty the risk will occur.

Determining risk probability can be difficult because it's most commonly accomplished using expert judgment. In non-PMP terms, this means you're guessing (or asking other experts to guess) at the probability a risk event will occur. Granted, you're basing your guess on past experiences with similar projects or risk events, but no two risk events (or projects) are ever the same. It's best to fully develop the criteria for determining probability and get as many experts involved as you can. Carefully weigh their responses to come up with the best probability values possible.

Impact

Impact is the amount of pain (or the amount of gain) the risk event poses to the project. The risk *impact scale* can be a relative scale that assigns values such as high-medium-low (or some combination of these) or a numeric scale known as a *cardinal scale*. Cardinal scale values are actual numeric values assigned to the risk impact. Cardinal scales are expressed as values from 0.0 to 1.0 and may be stated in equal (linear) or unequal (nonlinear) increments.

Table 5.1 shows a typical risk impact scale for cost, time, and quality objectives based on a high-high to low-low scale. You'll notice that each of the "high-medium-low" value combinations on this impact scale have been assigned a cardinal value. We'll use these in the next section when we talk about the probability and impact matrix.

TABLE 5.1 Risk Impacts Scale

Objectives	Low-Low	Low	Medium	High	High-High
	0.05	0.20	0.40	0.60	0.80
Cost	No significant impact	Less than 6% increase	7–12% increase	13–18% increase	More than 18% increase
Time	No significant impact	Less than 6% increase	7–12% increase	13–18% increase	More than 18% increase
Quality	No significant impact	Few components impacted	Significant impact requiring customer approval to proceed	Unacceptable quality	Product not usable

When you're using a high-medium-low scale it's important that your risk team understands what criteria was used to determine a high score versus a medium or low score and how these should be applied to the project objectives.

Assessing Probability and Impact

The idea behind both probability and impact values is to develop predefined measurements that describe what value to place on a risk event.

Exam Spotlight

For the exam, don't forget that you defined probability and impact values during the Risk Management Planning process.

If these scales have not yet been determined, develop them as early on in the project as possible. You can use any of the techniques we talked about earlier in the section "Tools and Techniques Used to Identify Risk," such as brainstorming or the Delphi technique, to come up with the values for probability and impact.

During the Qualitative Risk Analysis process, you'll determine and assess probability and impact for every risk identified during the Risk Identification process. You could interview or hold meetings with project team members, subject matter experts, stakeholder or others to help assess these factors. During this process, you should document not only the probability and impact but also the assumptions your team members used to arrive at these determinations. The next technique—probability and impact matrix—take the probability and impact values one step further by assigning an overall risk score.

Probability and Impact Matrix

A probability and impact matrix assigns an overall risk rating to each of the project's identified risks. The combination of probability and impact results in a classification usually expressed as high, medium, or low. According to *A Guide to the PMBOK*, high risks are considered a red condition, medium risks are considered a yellow condition, and low risks are considered a green condition. This type of ranking is known as an *ordinal scale* because the values are rank-ordered from high to low. (In practice, ordinal values may also include ranking by position. In other words, the risks are listed in rank order as the first, the second, the third, and so on.)

Exam Spotlight

A Guide to the PMBOK notes that the probability and impact matrix values are usually set by the organization and are a part of the organizational process assets.

Now let's look at an example. You have identified a risk event that could impact project costs, and your experts believe costs could increase by as much as 9 percent. According to the risk impact rating matrix in Table 5.1, this risk carries a medium impact, with a value of 0.40. Hold onto that number because you're going to plug it into the probability impact matrix— along with the probability value—to determine an overall risk value next.

You'll remember from our discussion previously that probability values should be assigned numbers from 0.0 to 1.0. In this example, the team has determined that there is a 0.2 probability of this risk event occurring. The risk impact scale shows a medium or 0.4 impact should the event occur.

Now, to determine whether the combination of the probability and impact of this risk is high, medium, or low, you'll need to check the probability impact matrix. Table 5.2 shows a sample probability and impact matrix.

First look at the probability column. Your risk event has a probability of .2. Now follow that row until you find the impact score of .04. According to your probability and impact matrix values, this risk carries a score of 0.08 and falls in the low threshold, so this risk is assigned a low (or green condition) value.

The values assigned to the risks determine how Risk Response Planning is carried out for the risks later during the risk-planning processes. Obviously, risks with high probability and high impact are going to need further analysis and formal responses. Remember that the values for this matrix (and the probability and impact scales discussed earlier) are determined prior to the start of this process and documented in the Risk Management Plan. Also keep in mind that probability and impact do not have to be assigned the same values as I've done here. You may use 0.8, 0.6, 0.4, and 0.2 for probability, for example, and assign .05, 0.1, .03, 0.5, and 0.7 for impact scales.

TABLE 5.2   Sample Probability and Impact Matrix

Probability	Impact Values* .05	.20	.40	.60	.80
.8	.04	.16	*.32*	**.48**	*.64*
.6	.03	.12	**.24**	*.36*	*.48*
.4	.02	**.08**	.16	.24	*.32*
.2	.01	.04	.08	.12	.16

*The legend for the PI matrix is as follows: no formatting = low assignment or green condition; **bold** = medium assignment or yellow condition; ***bold italic*** = high assignment or red condition.

TABLE 5.3   PI Matrix for Screen Scrapers, Inc.

Probability	Impact Scores* .05	.20	.40	.60	.80
.8	.04	.16	*.32*	**.48**	*.64*
.6	.03	.12	**.24**	*.36*	*.48*
.4	.02	**.08**	.16	.24	*.32*
.2	.01	.04	.08	.12	.16

*The legend for the PI matrix is as follows: no formatting = low assignment or green condition; **bold** = medium assignment or yellow condition; ***bold italic*** = high assignment or red condition.

Real World Scenario

Screen Scrapers, Inc.

Screen Scrapers is a software-manufacturing company that produces a software product that looks at your mainframe screens, commonly called *green screens,* and converts them to browser-based screens. The browser-based screens look like any other Windows-compatible screens with buttons, scroll bars, and drop-down lists.

Screen Scrapers devised this product for companies that use mainframe programs to update and store data because many of the entry-level workers beginning their careers today are not familiar with green screens. They're cumbersome and difficult to learn, and no consistency exists from screen to screen or program to program. An F5 key in one program might mean go back one page, while an F5 key in another program might mean clear the screen. New users are easily confused, make a lot of mistakes, and have to write tablets full of notes on how to navigate all the screens.

Your company has purchased the Screen Scraper product and has appointed you the project manager over the installation. There are lots of issues to address on this project, and you've made great headway. You're now at the risk identification and qualitative risk analysis stage. You decide to use the Delphi technique to assist you in identifying risk and assigning probability and impact rankings. There are some experts available in your company who can serve on the Delphi panel, as well as some folks in industry organizations you belong to outside the company.

You assemble the group, and set up a summary of the project and send it out via e-mail, requesting responses to your questions about risk. After the first pass, you compile the list of risks as follows (this list is an example and isn't exhaustive because your list will be project specific):

- Vendor viability—will the software company stay in business?

- Vendor responsiveness with problems after implementation

- Software compatibility risks with existing systems

- Hardware compatibility risk

- Connection to the mainframe risk

- Training IT staff members to maintain the product

You send this list back to the Delphi members and ask them to assign a probability of 0.0–1.0 and an impact of high-high, high, medium, low, or low-low to each risk. The Delphi members assign probability and impact based on a probability scale and an impact scale designed by the risk management team. The values of the impact scale are as follows:

- High-high = 0.8

- High = 0.6

- Medium = 0.4

- Low = 0.2

- Low-low = 0.05

The team sends you back the following probability and impact values:

- Vendor viability = .6 probability, high impact

- Vendor responsiveness = .4 probability, medium impact

- Software compatibility = .4 probability, medium impact

- Hardware compatibility = .6 probability, high-high impact

- Mainframe connection = .2 probability, high-high impact

- Training = .2 probability, low-low impact

The probability and impact matrix you used to assign the overall risk scores were derived from the probability and impact matrix shown in Table 5.3.

Based on the probability and impact matrix thresholds, the project risks are assigned the following overall probabilities:

- Vendor viability = high

- Vendor responsiveness = medium

- Software compatibility = medium

- Hardware compatibility = high

- Mainframe connection = high

- Training = low

Risk Data Quality Assessment

The data quality assessment involves determining the usefulness of the data gathered to evaluate risk. Most importantly, the data must be unbiased and accurate. You will want to examine elements like the following when performing this tool and technique:

- The quality of the data used

- The availability of data regarding the risks

- How well the risk is understood

- The reliability and integrity of the data

- The accuracy of the data

Low-quality data will render the Qualitative Risk Analysis process's findings almost useless. Spend the time to validate and verify the information you've collected about risks so that your prioritization and analysis is as accurate as it can be. If you find that the quality of the data is questionable, you guessed it, go back and get better data.

Risk Categorizations

This tool and technique is used to determine the effects risk has on the project. You can examine not only the categories of risk determined during the Risk Management Planning process (and described in the RBS) but also the project phase and the WBS to determine the elements of the project that are affected by risk.

Risk Urgency Assessment

Using this tool you'll determine how soon the potential risks may occur and quickly determine responses for those risks that could occur soon. You should consider the risk triggers, the time to develop and implement a response, and the overall risk rating when determining how quickly responses are needed.

Ranking Risks in the Risk Register

The goal of the Qualitative Risk Analysis process is to rank the risks and determine which ones need further analysis and, eventually, risk response plans. The output of this process is risk register updates. As you can probably guess, you'll update the register with the following information:

- Risk ranking (or priority) for the identified risks
- Risks grouped by categories
- List of risks requiring near-term responses
- List of risks for additional analysis and response
- Watch list of low-priority risks
- Trends in Qualitative Risk Analysis results

Each of these elements become new entries in the risk register. For example, risk ranking assigns the risk score or priority you determined using the probability and impact matrix to the list of identified risks previously recorded in the risk register. We've discussed the categories and the list of risks requiring near-term responses earlier. Note these in the risk register.

You'll also note those risks that require further analysis (including using the Quantitative Risk Analysis process), you'll create a list of risks that have low risk scores to review periodically, and you should note any trends in qualitative risk analysis that become evident as you perform this process.

Quantifying Risk

The *Quantitative Risk Analysis* process evaluates the impacts of risk prioritized during the Qualitative Risk Analysis process and quantifies risk exposure for the project by assigning numeric probabilities to each risk and their impacts on project objectives. This quantitative approach is accomplished using techniques like Monte Carlo simulation and decision tree analysis. To paraphrase *A Guide to the PMBOK*, the purpose of this process is to perform the following:

- Quantify the project's possible outcomes and probabilities.
- Determine the probability of achieving the project objectives.
- Identify risks that need the most attention by quantifying their contribution to overall project risk.
- Identify realistic and achievable schedule, cost, or scope targets.
- Determine the best project management decisions possible when outcomes are uncertain.

Quantitative Risk Analysis—like Qualitative Risk Analysis—examines each risk and its potential impact on the project objectives. You may choose to use both of these processes to assess risk or only one of them, depending on the complexity of the project and the organizational policy regarding risk planning. The Quantitative Risk Analysis process can follow either the Risk Identification process or the Qualitative Risk Analysis process. If you do use this process, be certain to repeat it every time the Risk Response Planning process is performed and as part of the Risk Monitoring and Control process.

We have already covered many of the inputs to the Quantitative Risk Analysis process in previous sections of this chapter. They are as follows:

- Organizational process assets
- Project scope statement
- Risk management plan
- Risk register
- Project management plan

The elements of the project management plan you'll want to pay close attention to as an input to this process are the project schedule management plan and the project cost management plan.

Quantitative Risk Analysis Tools and Techniques

There are two sets of tools and techniques for the Quantitative Risk Analysis process: data gathering and representation techniques, and quantitative risk analysis and modeling techniques. Each of these sets of techniques include three techniques that we'll examine next.

Data Gathering and Representation Techniques

The data gathering techniques includes interviewing techniques, probability distributions, and expert judgment. Let's look at each of them.

Interviewing

This technique is like the interviewing technique discussed earlier in the section "Identifying Potential Risk." Project team members, stakeholders, and subject matter experts are prime candidates for risk interviews. Ask them about their experiences on past projects and about working with the types of technology or processes you'll use during this project.

For the exam, remember that interviewing is a tool and technique of the Quantitative Risk Analysis process. Although you can use this technique in the Risk Identification process, it isn't an "official" tool and technique of that process.

When using this technique, you should first determine what methods of probability distribution (described next) you'll use to analyze your information. The technique you chose will dictate the type of information you need to gather. For example, you might use a three-point scale that assess the optimistic, pessimistic, and most likely risk scenarios or take it a step further and use standard deviations calculations. We'll talk more about three-point estimates in Chapter 7.

Make certain you document how the interviewees decided upon the risk ranges, the criteria they used to place risks in certain categories, and the results of the interview. This will help you later in developing risk responses as well.

Exam Spotlight

For the exam, you should know that there are several types of probability distributions that are useful in determining and displaying risk information. The type of distribution you use determines the type of information you should gather during the interviewing process.

Probability Distributions

It's beyond the scope of this book to delve into probability distributions and calculations, so I'll point out a few things you should remember for the exam regarding them.

Continuous probability distributions (particularly beta and triangular distributions) are commonly used in Quantitative Risk Analysis. According to *A Guide to the PMBOK,* continuous probability distributions include normal, lognormal, triangular, beta, and uniform distributions. Distributions are graphically displayed and represent both the probability and time or cost elements.

Triangular distributions use estimates based on the three-point estimate (the pessimistic, most likely, and optimistic values). This means that during your interviews, you'll gather these pieces of information from your experts. Then you'll use them to quantify risk for each WBS element.

Normal and lognormal distributions use mean and standard deviations to quantify risk, which also require gathering the optimistic, most likely, and pessimistic estimates.

Expert Judgment

We've talked about this tool and technique before. Experts can come from inside or outside the organization and should have experience that's applicable to your project. For example, if your project involves manufacturing a new product or part, you might want to consider experts like engineers or statisticians. If you're dealing with sensitive data in an information technology project, consider bringing on a security expert.

Quantitative Risk Analysis and Modeling Techniques

There are four techniques encompassed in this tool and technique: sensitivity analysis, expected monetary value analysis, decision tree analysis, and modeling and simulation. Let's take a brief look at each of them.

Sensitivity Analysis

Sensitivity analysis is a quantitative method of analyzing the potential impact of risk events on the project and determining which risk event (or events) has the greatest potential for impact by examining all the uncertain elements at their baseline values. One of the ways sensitivity analysis data is displayed is a *tornado diagram*. Figure 5.5 shows a sample tornado diagram.

FIGURE 5.5   Tornado diagram

You can see by the arrangement of horizontal bars (each representing a sensitivity variable) how the diagram gets its name. The idea is that each sensitivity bar displays the low and high value possible for that element. (It's beyond the scope of this book to explain how these values are determined. The questions you may encounter on the exam are focused on the context of this type of analysis.) The variables with the greatest effect on the project are displayed at the top of the graph and decrease in impact as you progress down through the graph. This gives you a quick overview of how much the project can be affected by uncertainty in the various elements. It also allows you to see at a glance which risks may have the biggest impacts on the project and will require carefully crafted, detailed response plans. You can use tornado diagrams to determine sensitivity in cost, time, and quality objectives or for risks you've identified during this process.

Sensitivity analysis can also be used to determine stakeholder risk tolerance levels.

Expected Monetary Value (EMV) Analysis

Expected monetary value (EMV) analysis is a statistical technique that calculates the average, anticipated impact of the decision. EMV is calculated by multiplying the probability of the risk times its impact and then adding them together. EMV is used in conjunction with the decision tree analysis technique, which is covered next. I'll give you an example of the EMV formula in the next section. Positive results generally mean the risks you're assessing pose opportunities to the project while negative results generally indicate a threat to the project.

Decision Tree Analysis

Unfortunately, this isn't a tree outside your office door that produces "Yes" and "No" leaves that you can pick to help you make a decision. *Decision trees* are diagrams that show the sequence of interrelated decisions and the expected results of choosing one alternative over the other. Typically, more than one choice or option is available when you're faced with a decision or, in this case, potential outcomes from a risk event. The available choices are depicted in a tree form starting at the left with the risk decision branching out to the right with possible outcomes. Decision trees are usually used for risk events associated with time or cost.

Figure 5.6 shows a sample decision tree using expected monetary value (EMV) as one of its inputs.

The expected monetary value of the decision is a result of the probability of the risk event multiplied by the impact and then adding their results. The squares in this figure represent decisions to be made, and the circles represent the points where risk events may occur.

FIGURE 5.6   Decision tree

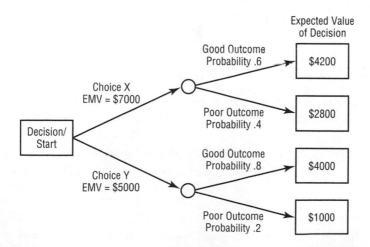

The decision with an expected value of $7,000 is the correct decision to make because the resulting outcome has the greatest value.

Modeling and Simulation

Modeling and simulation techniques are often used for schedule risk analysis and cost analysis. For example, modeling allows you to translate the potential risks at specific points in the project into their impacts so you can determine how the project objectives are affected. Simulation techniques compute the project model using various inputs such as cost or schedule duration, to determine a probability distribution for the variable chosen. (Cost risks typically use either a work breakdown structure or cost breakdown structure as the input variable. Schedule risks always use the precedence diagramming method as the input variable. We we'll cover schedule diagramming methods in Chapter 7.) If you used simulation techniques to determine project cost and use the cost of the project elements as the input variable, a probability distribution for the total cost of the project would be produced after running the simulation numerous times. Modeling and simulation techniques examine the identified risks and their potential impacts to the project objectives from the perspective of the whole project.

Monte Carlo analysis is an example of a simulation technique. Monte Carlo analysis is performed many times, typically using cost or schedule variables. Every time the analysis is performed, the values for the variable are changed using a probability distribution for each variable. Monte Carlo analysis can also be used during the Schedule Development process.

Exam Spotlight

According to *A Guide to the PMBOK,* simulation techniques are recommended for predicting schedule or cost risks because they're more powerful then EMV and less likely to be misused. For the exam, remember that simulation techniques are used to predict schedule or cost risks. Schedule simulations are usually performed using the precedence diagramming method, while cost simulation typically uses the WBS as its basis.

Quantitative Risk Analysis Outputs

The output of the Quantitative Risk Analysis process is—I'll bet you can guess—risk register updates. As with the Qualitative Risk Analysis process, there are new elements you'll record in the risk register:

Probabilistic analysis of the project   Probabilistic analysis of the project is the forecasted results of the project schedule and costs as determined by the outcomes of risk analysis. These results include projected completion dates and costs, along with a confidence level associated with each. According to *A Guide to the PMBOK,* this output is often expressed as a cumulative distribution and you'll use these results along with stakeholder risk tolerances to quantify the time and cost contingency reserves. (We'll talk about contingency reserves in the section "Developing a Risk Response Plan" later in this chapter.)

Confidence levels can also be used to describe the level of confidence placed on the outcome of the forecasted results. For example, suppose the projected schedule completion date is July 12 and the confidence level is .85. This says that you believe the project will finish on or before July 12 and that you have an 85 percent level of confidence that this date is accurate.

Probability of achieving the cost and time objectives   Using the tools and techniques of Quantitative Risk Analysis allows you to assign a probability of achieving the cost and time objectives of the project. This output documents those probabilities and as such requires a thorough understanding of the current project objectives and knowledge of the risks.

Prioritized lists of quantified risks   The prioritized list in this process is similar to the list produced during the Qualitative Risk Analysis process. The list of risks includes those that present the greatest risk or threat to the project and their impacts. It also lists those risks that present the greatest opportunities to the project. This list should also indicate which risks are most likely to impact the critical path and those that have the largest cost contingency.

Trends in Quantitative Risk Analysis results   Trends in Quantitative Risk Analysis will likely appear as you repeat the risk analysis processes. This information is useful as you progress, making those risks with the greatest threat to the project more evident, which allows you the opportunity to perform further analysis or go on to develop risk response plans.

Exam Spotlight

Understand the differences between the Qualitative Risk Analysis and Quantitative Risk Analysis processes for the exam.

Developing a Risk Response Plan

The *Risk Response Planning* process is the last process covered in this chapter. (I hear you cheering out there!) Risk Response Planning is a process of deciding what actions to take to reduce threats and take advantage of the opportunities discovered during the risk analysis processes. This process also includes assigning departments or individual staff members the responsibility of carrying out the risk response plans you'll outline in this process. These folks are known as risk owners.

The more effective your risk response plans are, the better your chances for a successful project. Well-developed and well-written risk response plans will decrease overall project risk.

Generally, you'll want to develop risk response plans for those risks with a combination of high probability of occurrence and significant impact to the project. Developing risk response plans for risks of low severity or insignificant impact is not efficient or a good use of the project team's time. Spend your time planning responses that are appropriate given the impact the risk itself poses (or the opportunity the risk presents) and don't spend more time, money, or energy to produce a response than the risk event itself would produce if it occurred.

Several strategies are used in this process to reduce or control risk. It's important that you choose the right strategy for each risk so that the risk and its impacts are dealt with effectively. After deciding on which strategy to use, you'll develop an action plan to put this strategy into play should the risk event occur. You may also choose to designate a secondary or backup strategy.

Exam Spotlight

The severity of the risk will dictate the level of risk response planning that should be performed. For example, a risk with low severity wouldn't warrant the time it takes to develop a detailed risk response plan. Risk responses should be cost effective—if the cost of the response is more than the consequences of the risk, you might want to examine a different risk response. Risk responses should also be timely, agreed to by all the project stakeholders, and assigned to an individual (risk owner) who is responsible for monitoring and carrying out the risk response plan if needed.

Risk Response Planning Tools and Techniques

There are four tools and techniques for the Risk Response Planning process and each one of them involves a strategy. The tools and techniques are as follows:

- Strategies for negative risks or threats
- Strategies for positive risks or opportunities
- Strategies for both threats and opportunities
- Contingence response strategy

We'll take a look at each.

Strategies for Negative Risks or Threats

There are three strategies to deal with negative risks or threats to the project objectives. They are avoid, transfer, and mitigate.

Avoid

To *avoid* a risk means you'll evade it altogether, eliminate the cause of the risk event, or change the project plan to protect the project objectives from the risk event. Let's say you're going to take a car trip from your home to a point 800 miles away. You know—because your friends who just took the same trip told you—that there is a long stretch of construction on one of the highways you're planning on using. To avoid the risk of delay, you plan the trip around the construction work and use another highway for that stretch of driving. In this way, you change your plans, avoid the risk of getting held up in construction traffic, and arrive at your destination on time.

With risk avoidance, you essentially eradicate the risk by eliminating its cause. Here's another example: Suppose your project was kicked off without adequate scope definition and requirements gathering. You run a high probability of experiencing scope creep—ever-changing requirements—as the project progresses, thus impacting the project schedule. You can avoid this risk by adequately documenting the project scope and requirements during the Planning processes and taking steps to monitor and control changes to scope so it doesn't get out of hand.

Risks that occur early in the project might easily be avoided by improving communications, refining requirements, assigning additional resources to project activities, refining the project scope to avoid risk events, and so on.

Transfer

The idea behind a risk *transfer* is to transfer the risk and the consequences of that risk to a third party. The risk hasn't gone away, but the responsibility for the management of that risk now rests with another party. Most companies aren't willing to take on someone else's risk without a little cash thrown in for good measure. This strategy will impact the project budget and should be included in the cost estimate exercises if you know you're going to use it.

Transfer of risk can occur in many forms but is most effective when dealing with financial risks. Insurance is one form of risk transfer. You are probably familiar with how insurance works. Car insurance is a good example. You purchase car insurance so that if you come upon an obstacle in the road and there is no way to avoid hitting it, the cost to repair the damage to the car is paid by the insurance company. Okay, minus the deductible and all the calculations for the age of the car, the mileage, the color and make of the car, the weather conditions the day you were driving—but I digress.

Another method of risk transfer is contracting. Contracting transfers specific risks to the vendor, depending on the work required by the contract. The vendor accepts the responsibility for the cost of failure. Again, this doesn't come without a price. Contractors charge for their services, and depending on the type of contract you negotiate, the cost might be quite high. For example, in a fixed-price contract, which we'll talk more about in the Procurement Planning section, the vendor (or seller) increases the cost of the contract to compensate for the level of risk they're accepting. A cost reimbursable contract, however, leaves the majority of the risk with you, the buyer. This type of contract may reduce costs if there are project changes midway through the project.

Keep in mind that contracting isn't a cure-all. You might just be swapping one risk for another. For example, say you hire a driver to go with you on your road trip and their job is to do all the driving. If the driver becomes ill or in some way can't fulfill their obligation, you aren't going to get to your destination on time. You've placed the risks associated with the drive on the contract driver; however, you've taken on a risk of delay due to nonperformance, which means you've just swapped one risk for another. You'll have to weigh your options in cases like this and determine which side of the risk coin your organization can more readily accept.

Other forms of transference include warranties, guarantees, and performance bonds.

Mitigate

When you *mitigate* a risk, you attempt to reduce the probability of a risk event and its impacts to an acceptable level. This strategy is a lot like defensive driving. You see an obstacle in the road ahead, survey your options, and take the necessary steps to avoid the obstacle and proceed safely on your journey. Seeing the obstacle ahead (identifying risk) allows you to reduce the threat by planning ways around it or planning ways to reduce its impact if the risk does occur (mitigation strategies).

According to *A Guide to the PMBOK,* the purpose of mitigation is to reduce the probability that a risk will occur and reduce the impact of the risk to a level where you can accept the risk and its outcomes. It's easier to take actions early on that will reduce the probability of a risk or its consequences than it is to fix the damage once it's occurred. Some examples of risk mitigation include performing more tests, using less-complicated processes, creating prototypes, and choosing more reliable vendors.

Exam Spotlight

Understand all of the strategies and their characteristics in each tool and technique for the exam.

Strategies for Positive Risk or Opportunities

There are three strategies for dealing with opportunities or positive risks that may present themselves on the project: exploit, share, and enhance.

Exploit

When you *exploit* a risk event, you're looking for opportunities for positive impacts. This is the strategy of choice when you've identified positive risks that you want to make certain will occur on the project. Examples of exploiting a risk include reducing the amount of time to complete the project by bringing on more qualified resources or by providing even better quality than originally planned.

Share

The *share* strategy is similar to transferring because you'll assign the risk to a third-party owner who is best able to bring about the opportunity the risk event presents. For example, perhaps what your organization does best is investing. However, it isn't so good at marketing. Forming a joint venture with a marketing firm to capitalize on a positive risk will make the most of the opportunities.

Enhance

The enhance strategy closely watches the probability and or impact of the risk event to assure that the organization realizes the benefits. This entails watching for and emphasizing risk triggers and identifying the root causes of the risk to help enhance impacts or probability.

Strategies for Both Threats and Opportunities

The third tool and technique of the Risk Response Planning process, strategies for both threats and opportunities, is called the acceptance strategy. *Acceptance* of a risk event is a strategy that can be used for risks that pose either threats or opportunities to the project. *Passive acceptance* is a strategy that means that you won't make any plans to try to avoid or mitigate the risk. You're willing to accept the consequences of the risk should it occur. Acceptance may also mean the project team was unable to come up with an adequate response strategy and must accept the risk and its consequences. Active acceptance may include developing contingency reserves to deal with risks should they occur. (We'll look at contingency reserves in the next section.)

Let's revisit the road trip example. You could plan the trip using the original route and just accept the risk of running into construction. If you get to that point and you're delayed, you'll just accept it. This is passive acceptance. You could also go ahead and make plans to take an alternate route but not enact those plans until you actually reach the construction and know for certain that it is going to impede your progress. This is active acceptance and may involve developing a contingency plan.

Contingency Planning

The last tool and technique of the Risk Response Planning process is called the contingent response strategy, better known as contingency planning. *Contingency planning* involves planning alternatives to deal with the risks should they occur. This is different than mitigation planning in that mitigation looks to reduce the probability of the risk and its impact whereas contingency planning doesn't necessarily attempt to reduce the probability of a risk event or its impacts. Contingency planning says the risk may very well occur and we better have plans in place to deal with it.

Contingency comes into play when the risk event occurs. This implies you need to plan for your contingencies well in advance of the threat. After the risks have been identified and quantified, contingency plans should be developed and kept at the ready.

Contingency allowances or reserves are a common contingency response. *Contingency reserves* include project funds that are held in reserve to offset any unavoidable threats that might occur to project scope, schedule, cost, or quality. It also includes reserving time and resources to account for risks. You should consider stakeholder risk tolerances when determining the amount of contingency reserves.

Fallback plans should be developed for risks with high impact or for risks with identified strategies that may not be the most effective.

In practice, you'll find that identifying, prioritizing, quantifying, and developing responses for potential threats may happen simultaneously. In any case, you don't want to be taken by surprise, and that's the point of the risk processes. If you know about potential risks early on, you can very often mitigate them or prepare appropriate response plans or contingency plans to deal with them.

Risk Response Planning Outputs

As you've no doubt concluded, the purpose of the Risk Response Planning process is to develop risk responses for those risks with the highest probability and impact on the project objectives. There are three outputs of the Risk Response Planning process: risk register updates, project management plan updates, and risk-related contractual agreements.

Remember that you might need to revisit other Planning processes after performing Risk Response Planning to modify project plans as a result of risk responses.

Risk Register Updates

Again, the risk register is updated at the end of this process with the information you've discovered during this process. The response plans are recorded in the risk register. You'll recall that the risk register lists the risk in order of priority (those with the highest potential for threat or opportunity first), so it makes sense that the response plans you have for these risks will be more detailed than the remaining lists. Some risks may not require response plans at all, but you should put them on a watch list and monitor them throughout the project.

Let's take a look at what the risk register should contain at this point. According to *A Guide to the PMBOK*, after Risk Identification, Qualitative Risk Analysis, and Quantitative Risk Analysis are preformed, the following elements should appear in the risk register:

- List of identified risks, including their descriptions, what WBS element they impact (or area of the project), categories (RBS), root causes, and how the risk impacts the project objectives
- Risk owners and their responsibility
- Risk triggers
- Response plans and strategies, including the steps to take to implement the strategy
- Cost and schedule activities needed to implement risk responses
- Contingency reserves for cost and time
- Contingency plans
- Fallback plans
- List of residual and secondary risks
- Probabilistic analysis of the project and other outputs of the Qualitative and Quantitative Risk Analysis processes

The only elements in the preceding list we haven't talked about so far are residual and secondary risks. A *residual risk* is a leftover risk so to speak. After you've implemented a risk response strategy—say mitigation, for example—some minor risk may still remain. The contingency reserve is set up to handle situations like this.

Secondary risks are risks that come about as a result of implementing a risk response. The example given previously where you transferred risk by hiring a driver to take you to your destination but they became ill along the way is an example of a secondary risk. Their illness delayed your arrival time, which is risk directly caused by hiring the driver or implementing a risk response. When planning for risk, identify and plan responses for secondary risks that could occur as well.

Risk-Related Contractual Agreements

If you're planning on using strategies such as transference or sharing, for example, you may need to purchase services or items from third parties. The contracts for those services can be prepared now and discussed with the appropriate parties.

Risks exist on all projects, and risk planning is an important part of the project Planning processes. Just the act of identifying risks and planning responses can decrease their impact if they occur. Don't take the "What I don't know won't hurt me" approach to risk planning. This is definitely a case where not knowing something can be devastating. Risks that are easily identified and have planned responses aren't likely to kill projects or your career. Risks that you should have known about but ignored could end up costing the organization thousands or millions of dollars, causing schedule delays, or ultimately killing the project. There could be a personal cost as well, as cost and schedule overruns due to poor planning on your part are not easily explained.

Project Case Study: New Kitchen Heaven Retail Store

Ricardo knocks on your office door and asks if you have a few minutes to talk. "Of course," you reply, and he takes a seat on one of the comfy chairs at the conference table. You have a feeling this might take a while.

"I think you should know that I'm concerned about the availability of the T1 line. I've already put in the call to get us on the list because, as I said last week, there's a 30- to 45-day lead time on these orders."

"We're only midway through the Planning processes. Do you need to order the T1 so soon? We don't even know the store location yet," you say.

"Even though they say lead time is 30 to 45 days, I've waited as much as five or six months to get a T1 installed in the past. I know we're really pushing for the early February store opening, so I thought I'd get the ball rolling now. What I need from you is the location address, and I'll need that pretty quick."

"We're narrowing down the choices between a couple of properties, so I should have that for you within the next couple of weeks. Is that soon enough?"

"The sooner the better," Ricardo replies.

"Great. I'm glad you stopped by, Ricardo. I wanted to talk with you about risk anyway, and you led us right into the discussion. Let me ask you, what probability would you assign to the T1 line installation happening six months from now?"

"I'd say the probability for six months is low. It's more likely that if there is a delay, it would be within a three- to four-month time frame."

"If they didn't get to it for six months, would it be a showstopper? In other words, is there some other way we could transfer Jill's data until the T1 did get installed?"

"Sure, there are other methods we could use. Jill won't want to do that for very long, but there are workarounds available."

"Good. Now, what about the risk for contractor availability and hardware availability and delivery schedules?" you ask.

You and Ricardo go on to discuss the risks associated with the IT tasks. Later, you ask Jill and Jake the same kinds of questions and compile a list of risks. In addition, you review the project information for the Atlanta store opening, as it's very similar in size and scope to this store. You add those risks to your list as well. You divide some of the risks into the following categories: IT, Facilities, and Retail. A sample portion of your list appears as follows, with overall assignments made based on Qualitative Risk Analysis and the probability and impact matrix:

Category: IT

- T1 line availability and installation. Risk score: Low

- Contractor availability for Ethernet installation. Risk score: Medium

- POS and server hardware availability. Risk score: Medium

Category: Facilities

- Desirable location in the right price range. Risk score: High

- Contractor availability for build-out. Risk score: Low

- Availability of fixtures and shelving. Risk score: Low

Category: Retail

- Product availability. Risk score: Medium

- Shipment dates for product. Risk score: Medium

After examining the risks, you decide that response plans should be developed for the last two items listed under the IT source, the first item under Facilities, and both of the risks listed under Retail.

Ricardo has already mitigated the T1 connection and installation risk by signing up several months ahead of when the installation is needed. The contractor availability can be handled with a contingency plan that specifies a backup contractor should the first choice not be available. For the POS terminals and hardware, you decide to use the transfer strategy. As part of the contract, you'll require these vendors to deliver on time, and if they cannot, they'll be required to provide and pay for rental equipment until they can get your gear delivered.

The Facilities risk and Retail risks will be handled with a combination of acceptance, contingency plans, and mitigation.

You've calculated the expected monetary value for several potential risk events. Two of them are detailed here.

Desirable location has an expected monetary value of $780,000. The probability of choosing an incorrect or less-than-desirable location is 60 percent. The potential loss in sales is the difference between $2.5 million in sales per year a high-producing store generates versus $1.2 million in sales per year an average store generates.

The expected monetary value of the product availability event is $50,000. The probability of the event occurring is 40 percent. The potential loss in sales is $125,000 for not opening the store in conjunction with the Garden and Home Show.

Project Case Study Checklist

Risk Management Planning

Risk Identification

- Documentation reviews

- Information-gathering techniques

Qualitative Risk Analysis

- Risk probability and impact

- Probability and impact rating

- List of prioritized risks

Quantitative Risk Analysis

- Interviewing

- Expected monetary value

Risk Response Planning

- Avoidance, transference, mitigation, and acceptance strategies

- Risk response plans documented

Summary

Congratulations! You've completed another fun-filled, action-packed chapter and all of it on a single topic—risk. Risk is inherent in all projects and risks pose both threats and opportunities to the project. Understanding the risks facing the project better equips you to determine the appropriate strategies to deal with those risks and helps you determine the response plans for the risks (and the level of effort you should put into preparing those plans).

The Risk Management Planning process determines how you will plan for risks on your project. Its only output is the risk management plan, which details how you'll define, monitor, and control risks throughout the project. The risk management plan is a subsidiary of the project management plan.

The Risk Identification process seeks to identify and document the project risks using brainstorming, the Delphi technique, interviewing, root cause identification, and SWOT. This list of risks gets recorded in the risk register, the only output of this process.

Qualitative Risk Analysis and Quantitative Risk Analysis involve evaluating risks and assigning probability and impact values to the risks. Many tools and techniques are used during these processes, including risk probability and impact, probability and impact matrix, interviewing, probability distributions, expert judgment, sensitivity analysis, decision tree analysis, and simulation.

A probability and impact matrix uses the probability multiplied by the impact value to determine the risk score. The threshold of risk based on high, medium, and low tolerances is determined by comparing the risk score based on the probability level to the probability and impact matrix.

Monte Carlo simulation is a technique used to quantify schedule or cost risks. Decision trees graphically display decisions and their various choices and outcomes and is typically used in combination with earned monetary value.

The Risk Response Planning process is the last Planning process and culminates with an update to the risk register documenting the risk response plans. The risk response plans detail the strategies you'll use to respond to risk and assign individuals to manage each risk response. Risk response strategies for negative risks include avoidance, mitigation, and transference. Risk strategies for positive risks include exploit, share, and enhance. Acceptance is a strategy for both negative and positive risks.

Contingency planning involves planning alternatives to deal with risk events should they occur. Contingency reserves are set aside to deal with risks associated with cost and time according to the stakeholder tolerance levels.

Exam Essentials

Be able to define the purpose of the risk management plan   The risk management plan describes how you will define, monitor, and control risks throughout the project. It details how risk management processes (including Risk Identification, Qualitative Risk Analysis, Quantitative Risk Analysis, Risk Response Planning, and Risk Monitoring and Control) will be implemented, monitored, and controlled throughout the life of the project. It describes how you will manage risks but does not attempt to define responses to individual risks. The risk management plan is a subsidiary of the project management plan and it's the only output of the Risk Management Planning process.

Be able to name the purpose of Risk Identification.   The purpose of the Risk Identification process is to identify all risks that may impact the project, document them, and identify their characteristics.

Be able to define the purpose of Qualitative Risk Analysis.   Qualitative Risk Analysis determines the impact the identified risks will have on the project and the probability they'll occur and puts the risks in priority order according to their effect on the project objectives.

Be able to define the purpose of Quantitative Risk Analysis.   Quantitative Risk Analysis evaluates the impacts of risk prioritized during the Qualitative Risk Analysis process and quantifies risk exposure for the project by assigning numeric probabilities to each risk and their impacts on project objectives.

Be able to define the purpose of the Risk Response Planning process.   Risk Response planning is the process where risk response plans are developed using strategies such as avoid, transfer, mitigate, exploit, share, and enhance. The risk response plan describes the actions to take should the identified risks occur. It should include all the identified risks, a description of the risks, how they'll impact the project objectives, and the people assigned to manage the risk responses.

Be able to define the risk register and some of its primary elements.   The risk register is an output of the Risk Identification process, and updates to the risk register occur as an output of every risk process that follows this one. By the end of the Risk Response Planning process, the risk register contains these primary elements: identified list of risks, risk owners, risk triggers, risk strategies, contingency plans, and contingency reserves.

Key Terms

You've learned a lot of new key words in this chapter. PMI has worked hard to develop and define standard project management terms that apply across industries. Here is a list of some of the terms you came across in this chapter:

acceptance	passive acceptance
avoid	probability
brainstorming	probability and impact matrix
cardinal scale	Qualitative Risk Analysis
cause-and-effect diagrams	Quantitative Risk Analysis
contingency planning	residual risk
contingency reserves	risk breakdown structure (RBS)
decision trees	risk categories
Delphi technique	Risk Identification
Enhance	risk management plan
expected monetary value (EMV)	Risk Management Planning
Exploit	risk register
force majeure	Risk Response Planning
impact	risk tolerance
impact scale	secondary risks
influence diagrams	sensitivity analysis
interviews	share
mitigate	tornado diagram
Monte Carlo analysis	transfer
nominal group technique	Triggers
ordinal scale	

Review Questions

1. You are a project manager for Fountain of Youth Spring Water bottlers. Your project involves installing a new accounting system and you're performing the risk-planning processes. You have identified several problems along with the causes of those problems. Which of the following diagrams will you use to show the problem and its causes and effects?

    A. Decision tree diagram

    B. Fishbone diagram

    C. Benchmark diagram

    D. Simulation tree diagram

2. The process of assessing the probability and consequences of identified risks to the project objectives, assigning a risk score to each risk, and creating a list of prioritized risks describes which of the following processes?

    A. Quantitative Risk Analysis

    B. Risk Identification

    C. Qualitative Risk Analysis

    D. Risk Management Planning

3. Each of the following statements is true regarding the risk management plan except for which one?

    A. The risk management plan is an output of the Risk Management Planning process.

    B. The risk management plan includes a description of the responses to risks and triggers.

    C. The risk management plan includes thresholds, scoring and interpretation methods, responsible parties, and budgets.

    D. The risk management plan is an input to all the remaining risk-planning processes.

4. You are using the interviewing technique of the Quantitative Risk Analysis process. You intend to use normal and lognormal distributions. All of the following statements are true regarding this question except which one?

    A. Interviewing techniques are used to quantify the probability and impact of the risks on project objectives.

    B. Normal and lognormal distributions use mean and standard deviation to quantify risks.

    C. Distributions graphically display the impacts of risk to the project objectives.

    D. Triangular distributions rely on optimistic, pessimistic, and most likely estimates to quantify risks.

5. The information-gathering techniques used in the Risk Identification process include all of the following except _____.

   A. Root cause identification

   B. Delphi technique

   C. SWOT analysis

   D. Checklist analysis

6. Which of the following processes assesses the likelihood of risk occurrences and their consequences using a numerical rating?

   A. Qualitative Risk Analysis

   B. Risk Identification

   C. Quantitative Risk Analysis

   D. Risk Response Planning

7. You are the project manager for a new website for the local zoo. You need to perform Qualitative Risk Analysis. When you've completed this process, you'll produce all of the following as part of the risk register update output except which one?

   A. Priority list of risks

   B. Watch list of low-priority risks

   C. Probability of achieving time and cost estimates

   D. Risks grouped by categories

8. You've identified a risk event on your current project that could save $100,000 in project costs if it occurs. Which of the following is true based on this statement? (Choose the best answer.)

   A. This is a risk event that should be accepted, because the rewards outweigh the threat to the project.

   B. This risk event is an opportunity to the project and should be exploited.

   C. This risk event should be mitigated to take advantage of the savings.

   D. This a risk event that should be shared to take full advantage of the potential savings.

9. You've identified a risk event on your current project that could save $500,000 in project costs if it occurs. Your organization is considering hiring a consulting firm to help establish proper project management techniques in order to assure it realizes these savings. Which of the following is true based on this statement? (Choose the best answer.)

   A. This is a risk event that should be accepted, because the rewards outweigh the threat to the project.

   B. This risk event is an opportunity to the project and should be exploited.

   C. This risk event should be mitigated to take advantage of the savings.

   D. This a risk event that should be shared to take full advantage of the potential savings.

10. Your hardware vendor left you a voicemail saying that a snowstorm in the Midwest might prevent your equipment from arriving on time. She wanted to give you a heads-up and asked that you return the call. Which of the following statements is true? (Choose the best answer.)

   A. This is a trigger.

   B. This is a contingency plan.

   C. This is a residual risk.

   D. This is a secondary risk.

11. You are constructing a probability and impact matrix for your project. Which of the following statements is true?

   A. The probability and impact matrix multiplies the risk's probability by the cost of the impact to determine an expected value of the risk event.

   B. The probability and impact matrix multiplies the risk's probability—which fall from 0.0 to 1.0—and the risk's impact and then adds them together to determine a risk score.

   C. The probability and impact matrix multiplies the risk's probability by the expected value of the risk event to determine a risk score based on a predetermined threshold.

   D. The probability and impact matrix multiplies the risk's probability by the risk impact—which both fall from 0.0 to 1.0—to determine a risk score.

12. Your stakeholders have asked for an analysis of the cost risk. All of the following are true except for which one?

   A. Monte Carlo analysis is the preferred method to use to determine the cost risk

   B. Monte Carlo analysis is a modeling technique

   C. A traditional work breakdown structure can be used as an input variable for the cost analysis

   D. A cost breakdown structure can be used as an input variable for the cost analysis

13. Your hardware vendor left you voicemail saying that a snowstorm in the Midwest will prevent your equipment from arriving on time. You identified a risk response strategy for this risk and have arranged for a local company to lease you the needed equipment until yours arrives. This is an example of which risk response strategy?

   A. Transfer

   B. Acceptance

   C. Mitigate

   D. Avoid

14. All of the following are elements of inputs of the Risk Identification process that you should evaluate except for which one?

   A. Assumptions analysis

   B. Historical information

   C. Roles and responsibilities

   D. Industry information

15. You work for a large manufacturing plant. You are working on a new project to release an over-seas product line. This is the company's first experience in the overseas market, and it hopes to make a big splash with the introduction of this product. The stakeholders are a bit nervous about the project and historically proceed cautiously and take a considerable amount of time to examine information before making a final decision. The project entails producing your product in a concentrated formula and packaging it in smaller containers than the U.S. product uses. A new machine is needed in order to mix the ingredients into a concentrated formula. After speaking with one of your stakeholders, you discover this will be the first machine your organization has purchased from your new supplier. Which of the following statements is true given the information in this question?

  A. The question describes risk tolerance levels of the stakeholders, which should be considered as an input to the Risk Management Planning process.

  B. This question describes the interviewing tool and technique used during the Risk Identification process.

  C. This question describes risk triggers that are derived using interviewing techniques and recorded in the risk register during the Qualitative Risk Analysis process.

  D. This question describes a risk that requires a response strategy from the positive risk category.

16. Your project team has identified several potential risks on your current project that could have a significant impact if they occurred. They examined the impact of the risks by keeping all the uncertain elements at their baseline values. What type of diagram will the team use to display this information?

  A. Fishbone diagram

  B. Tornado diagram

  C. Influence diagram

  D. Process flowchart

17. Your project team is in the process of identifying project risks on your current project. They have the option to use all of the following tools and techniques to diagram some of these potential risks except for which one?

  A. Ishikawa diagram

  B. Decision tree diagram

  C. Process flowchart

  D. Influence diagram

18. All of the following statements are true regarding the RBS except for which one?

  A. The RBS is contained in the risk management plan.

  B. It describes risk categories, which are a systematic way to identify risks and provide a foundation for understanding for everyone involved on the project.

  C. The lowest level of the RBS can be used as a checklist, which is a tool and technique of the Risk Identification process.

  D. The RBS is similar to the WBS in that the lowest level of both are easily assigned to a responsible party or owner.

19. Your team has identified the risks on the project and determined their risk score. They're in the midst of determining what strategies to put in place should the risks occur. After some discussion, they've determined that the risk of losing their network administrator is a risk they'll just deal with if and when it occurs. While they think it's a possibility and the impact would be significant, they've decided to simply deal with it after the fact. Which of the following is true regarding this question?

A. This is a negative response strategy.

B. This is a positive response strategy.

C. This is a response strategy for either positive or negative risk known as contingency planning.

D. This is a response strategy for either positive or negative risks known as passive acceptance.

20. All of the following are true regarding the Qualitative Risk Analysis process except which one?

A. Probability and impact and expert interview are used to help correct biases that occur in the data you've gathered during this process.

B. The probability and impact matrix is used during this process to assign red, yellow, and green conditions to risks.

C. Qualitative Risk Analysis is an easy method of determining risk probability and impact that usually takes a good deal of time to perform.

D. Risk urgency assessment is a tool and technique of this process used to determine which risks need near-term response plans.

Answers to Review Questions

1. B. The cause-and-effect flowcharts—also called fishbone diagrams or Ishikawa diagrams— show the relationship between the causes and effects of problems.

2. C. The purpose of Qualitative Risk Analysis is to determine what impact the identified risks will have on the project and the probability they'll occur. It also puts risks in priority order according to their effect on the project objectives and assigns a risk score for the project.

3. B. The risk management plan details how risk management processes will be implemented, monitored, and controlled throughout the life of the project. The risk management plan does not include responses to risks or triggers. Responses to risks are detailed in the Risk Response Planning process.

4. C. Distributions graphically display the probability of risk to the project objectives as well as the time and or cost elements.

5. D. The information-gathering techniques in the Risk Identification process are brainstorming, Delphi technique, interviewing, root cause identification, and SWOT analysis.

6. C. Quantitative Risk Analysis analyzes the probability of risks and their consequences using a numerical rating. Qualitative Risk Analysis may use numeric ratings but can use a high-medium-low scale as well.

7. C. Probability of achieving time and cost estimates is an update that is produced from the Quantitative Risk Analysis process.

8. B. This risk event has the potential to save money on project costs so it's an opportunity and the appropriate strategy to use in this case is the exploit strategy.

9. D. This risk event has the potential to save money on project costs. Sharing involves using a third party to help assure that the opportunity comes about.

10. A. The best answer is A. Triggers are warning signs of an impending risk.

11. C. The probability and impact matrix multiplies the probability, which falls from 0.0 to 1.0, and impact to determine a risk score. A high, medium, or low designation is assigned to the risk based on a predetermined threshold.

12. B. Monte Carlo analysis is a simulation technique.

13. C. Mitigation attempts to reduce the impact of a risk event should it occur. Making plans to arrange for the leased equipment reduces the consequences of the risk.

14. A. Assumptions analysis is a tool and technique of the Risk Identification process.

15. A. This question describes risk tolerance levels of the stakeholders. Risk triggers are recorded in the risk register during the Risk Response Planning process. The risk of buying a machine from a new supplier would pose a threat to the project, not an opportunity. Interviewing may have been used but this question wasn't describing the Risk Identification process.

16. B. The question describes sensitivity analysis, which is a tool and technique of the Quantitative Risk Analysis process. Tornado diagrams are often used to display sensitivity analysis data.

17. B. Decision tree diagrams are used during the Quantitative Risk Analysis process. All the other options are diagramming techniques of the Risk Identification process.

18. D. The RBS describes risk categories and the lowest level can be used as a checklist to help identify risks. Risk owners are not assigned from the RBS; they're assigned during the Risk Response Planning process.

19. D. This is a response strategy known as passive acceptance because the team has decided to take no action and make no plans for the risk. This is a strategy that can be used for either positive or negative risks.

20. C. Qualitative Risk Analysis is a fast and easy method of determining probability and impact.

Chapter
6

Resource Planning

THE PMP EXAM CONTENT FROM THE PLANNING THE PROJECT PERFORMANCE DOMAIN COVERED IN THIS CHAPTER INCLUDES THE FOLLOWING:

✓ Identify Project Team and Define Roles and Responsibilities

We're closing in on finishing up the Planning group processes. We're at a place where we need to talk about some processes that aren't necessarily related to each other but need to be completed before we can construct the project schedule and budget. So we'll start out this chapter with two procurement processes—Plan Purchases and Acquisitions and Plan Contracting—and then move on to Human Resource Planning, where we will develop the staffing management plan. This plan will help guide us later on in acquiring our project team members.

Then we'll get back on track with a theme by finishing up the chapter with two processes that will start us off on the right foot toward estimating and scheduling activities. They are the Activity Definition process and the Activity Sequencing process.

All of the processes we'll talk about in this chapter are used to develop both the project schedule and budget, which are two of the most important documents in our project plan (we'll discuss those in the next chapter). Let's get going.

Understanding Purchases and Acquisitions

Plan Purchases and Acquisitions is a process of identifying what goods or services you're going to purchase from outside of the organization and which project needs can be met by the project team. Part of what you'll accomplish in this process is determining whether you should purchase the goods or services and, if so, how much and when. Keep in mind that we're discussing the procurement from the buyer's perspective, as this is the approach used in *A Guide to the PMBOK*.

The Plan Purchases and Acquisitions process can influence the project schedule and the project schedule can influence this process. For example, availability of a contractor or special order materials may have a significant impact on the schedule. And conversely, your organization's business cycle may have an impact on the Plan Purchases and Acquisitions process if the organization is dependent on seasonal activity. The Activity Resource Estimating process, which we'll cover in Chapter 7, also can be influenced by this process, as will make-or-buy decisions (we'll get to those shortly).

You need to perform each process in the Project Procurement Management knowledge area (beginning with Plan Purchases and Acquisitions and ending with Contract Closure) for each product or service that you're buying outside of the organization. Obviously, if you're procuring all your resources from within the organization, the only process you'll perform in this knowledge area is the Plan Purchases and Acquisitions process.

Sometimes, your entire project will be procured from a vendor. In cases like these, the vendor will have a project manager assigned to the project. Your organization may choose to have an internal project manager assigned as well to act as the conduit between your company and the vendor and to provide information and monitor your organization's deliverables. When this happens, the vendor or contracting company is responsible for fulfilling all of the project management processes as part of the contract. In the case of an outsourced project, the seller—also known as the vendor, supplier, or contractor—manages the project and the buyer becomes the stakeholder. If you're hiring a vendor, don't forget to consider permits or professional licenses that may be required for the type of work you need them to perform.

Several inputs are needed when planning for purchases. We'll look at them next.

Plan Purchases and Acquisitions Inputs

The Plan Purchases and Acquisitions process has six inputs:

- Enterprise environmental factors
- Organizational process assets
- Project scope statement
- Work breakdown structure
- WBS dictionary
- Project management plan

The project management plan can include risk register, risk-related contractual agreements, resource requirements, project schedule, activity cost estimates, and cost baseline.

Marketplace conditions are the key element of enterprise environmental factors you should consider for this process. The organization's guidelines, policies, and organizational policies (including any procurement policies) are the elements of the organizational process assets you should pay attention to here.

Many organizations have procurement departments that are responsible for procuring goods and services and writing and managing contracts. Some organizations also require all contracts be reviewed by their legal department prior to signing. These are organizational process assets that you should consider when procuring goods and services is necessary.

It's important for the project manager to understand organizational policies because they may impact many of the Planning processes, including the Procurement Planning processes. For example, the organization may have purchasing approval processes that must be followed. Perhaps orders for goods or services that exceed certain dollar amounts need different levels of approval. As the project manager, you need to be aware of policies like this so you're certain you can execute the project smoothly. It's very frustrating to find out after the fact that you should have followed a certain process or policy and now, because you didn't, you've got schedule delays or worse. You could consider using the "Sin now, ask forgiveness later" technique in extreme emergencies, but you didn't hear that from me. By the way, that's not a technique that's authorized by *A Guide to the PMBOK*.

The project manager and the project team will be responsible for coordinating all the organizational interfaces for the project, including technical, human resource, purchasing, and finance. It will serve you well to understand the policies and politics involved in each of these areas in your organization.

My organization is steeped in policy. (A government organization steeped in policy? Go figure!) It's so steeped in policy we have to request the funds for large projects at least two years in advance. There are mounds and mounds of request forms, justification forms, approval forms, routing forms—you get the idea. But my point is if you miss one of the forms or don't fill out the information correctly, you can set your project back by a minimum of a year, if not two. Then once the money is awarded, there are more forms to fill out and policies to follow. Again, if you don't follow the policies correctly, you can jeopardize future project funds. Many organizations have a practice of not giving you all the project money up front in one lump sum. In other words, you must meet major milestones or complete a project phase before they'll fund your next phase. Know what your organizational policies are well ahead of time. Talk to the people that can walk you through the process and ask them to check your work to avoid surprises.

The project scope statement lists the deliverables and the acceptance criteria for the product or service of the project. Obviously, you'll want to consider these when thinking about procuring goods and services. You'll also want to consider the constraints (things like availability and timing of funds, availability of resources, delivery dates, vendor availability) and assumptions (things such as reliability of the vendor, assuming availability of key resources, adequate stakeholder involvement). The product scope description is included in the project scope statement as well and may alert you to special considerations (services, technical requirements, skills) needed to produce the product of the project.

The WBS and WBS dictionary identify the deliverables and describe the work required for each element of the WBS. The project management plan will provide you with guidance for procuring goods and services. For example, the risk-related contractual agreements component of this plan describes the types of services of goods needed for risk management. The transference strategy may require the purchase of insurance. Each of these elements should be reviewed when determining which goods and services will be performed within the project and which will be purchased.

Tools and Techniques for Plan Purchases and Acquisitions

There are three tools and techniques of the Plan Purchases and Acquisitions process. They are make-or-buy analysis, expert judgment, and contract types. We've already covered expert judgment, so we'll look at make-or-buy analysis next and then cover contract types after that.

Make-or-Buy Analysis

The main decision you're trying to get to in *make-or-buy analysis* is whether it's more cost effective to buy the products and services or more cost effective for the organization to produce the goods and services needed for the project. Costs should include both direct costs—in other words, the actual cost to purchase the product or service—and indirect costs, such as the salary of the manager overseeing the purchase process or ongoing maintenance costs. Costs don't necessarily mean the cost to purchase. In make-or-buy analysis, you might weigh the cost of leasing items versus buying them. For example, perhaps your project requires the use of a specialized piece of hardware that you know will be outdated by the end of the project. In a case like this, leasing may be a better option so that when the project is ready to be implemented, a newer version of the hardware can be tested and put into production during rollout.

Other considerations in make-or-buy analysis might include things like capacity issues, skills, availability, and trade secrets. Strict control might be needed for a certain process, and thus the process cannot be outsourced. Perhaps your organization has the skills in-house to complete the project but your current project list is so backlogged that you can't get to the new project for months, so you need to bring in a vendor.

Make-or-buy analysis is considered a general management technique and concludes with the decision to do one or the other.

Contract Types

A *contract* is a compulsory agreement between two or more parties and is used to acquire products or services from outside the organization. Typically, money is exchanged for the goods or services. Contracts are enforceable by law and require an offer and an acceptance.

There are different types of contracts for different purposes. *A Guide to the PMBOK* divides contracts into three categories:

- Fixed price or lump sum
- Cost reimbursable
- Time and materials (T&M)

Within the fixed price and cost reimbursable categories there are different types of contracts. We'll look at each in the following sections. Keep in mind that several things will impact the type of contract you should use. The product requirements (or service criteria) may drive the contract type. The market conditions may drive availability and price—remember back in the Year 2000 when there wasn't a programmer to be found for under $200 an hour? And the amount of risk, for the seller, the buyer, and the project itself, will help determine contract type.

> **Exam Spotlight**
>
> There may be an exam question or two regarding contract types, so spend some time getting familiar with them.

Fixed Price or Lump Sum Contracts

Fixed price contracts (also referred to as *lump sum contracts*) set a specific, firm price for the goods or services rendered. The buyer and seller agree on a well-defined deliverable for a set price. In this kind of contract, the biggest risk is borne by the seller. The seller—or contractor—must take great strides to assure they've covered their costs and will make a comfortable profit on the transaction. The seller assumes the risks of increasing costs, nonperformance, or other problems. However, to counter these unforeseen risks, the seller builds in the cost of the risk to the contract price.

Fixed price contracts can be disastrous for both the buyer and the seller if the scope of the project is not well defined or the scope changes dramatically. It's important to have accurate, well-defined deliverables when you're using this type of contract. Conversely, fixed price contracts are relatively safe for both buyer and seller when the original scope is well defined and remains unchanged. They typically reap only small profits for the seller and force the contractor to work productively and efficiently. This type of contract also minimizes cost and quality uncertainty.

Fixed price plus incentive contracts are another type of fixed price contract. The difference here is that the contract includes an incentive—or bonus—for early completion or for some other agreed-upon performance criterion that's exceeded according to contract specifications. The criteria for early completion, or other performance enhancements, must be spelled out in the contract so both parties understand the terms and conditions.

Another thing to note with fixed price plus incentive contracts is that some of the risk is borne by the buyer as opposed to the firm fixed price contract, where most all of the risk is borne by the seller. The buyer takes some risk, albeit minimal, by offering the incentive to, for example, get the work done earlier. Suppose the buyer really would like the product delivered 30 days prior to when the seller thinks they can deliver. In this case, the buyer assumes the risk for the early delivery via the incentive.

Cost Reimbursable Contracts

Cost reimbursable contracts are as the name implies. The allowable costs—allowable is defined by the contract—associated with producing the goods or services are charged to the buyer. All the costs the seller takes on during the project are charged back to the buyer; thus the seller is reimbursed.

Cost reimbursable contracts carry the highest risk to the buyer because the total costs are uncertain. As problems arise, the buyer has to shell out even more money to correct the problems. However, the advantage to the buyer with this type of contract is that scope changes are easy to make and can be made as often as you wish—but it will cost you.

Cost reimbursable contracts have a lot of uncertainty associated with them. There is little incentive for the contractor to work efficiently or be productive. This type of contract protects the contractor's profit because increasing costs are passed back to the buyer rather than taken out of profits as would be the case with a fixed price contract. Be certain to audit your statements when using a contract like this so that charges from some other project the vendor is working on don't accidentally end up on your bill.

Cost reimbursable contracts are used most often when there is a lot of uncertainty regarding the project scope, such as for cutting-edge projects and research and development. They are also used for projects that have large investments early in the project life. Let's discuss the three kinds of cost reimbursable contracts:

Cost plus fee (CPF) or cost plus percentage of cost (CPPC)   In the *cost plus fee (CPF)* contract, also called *cost plus percentage of cost (CPPC)*, the seller is reimbursed for allowable costs plus a fee that's calculated as a percentage of the costs. The percentage is agreed upon beforehand and documented in the contract. Since the fee is based on costs, the fee is variable. The lower the costs, the lower the fee, so the seller doesn't have a lot of motivation to keep costs low.

Cost plus fixed fee (CPFF)   *Cost plus fixed fee (CPFF)* contracts charge back all allowable project costs to the seller and include a fixed fee upon completion of the contract. This is how the seller makes money on the deal; the fixed fee portion is the seller's profit. The fee is always firm in this kind of contract, but the costs are variable. The seller doesn't necessarily have a lot of motivation to control costs with this type of contract, as you can imagine. And the only motivation to complete the project is driven by the fixed fee portion of the contract.

Cost plus incentive fee (CPIF)   The next category of cost reimbursable contract is *cost plus incentive fee (CPIF)*. This is the type of contract in which the buyer reimburses the seller for the seller's allowable costs and includes an incentive for exceeding the performance criteria laid out in the contract. An incentive fee actually encourages better cost performance by the seller, and there is a possibility of shared savings between the seller and buyer if performance criteria are exceeded. The qualification for exceeded performance must be written into the contract and agreed to by both parties, as should the definition of allowable costs; the seller can possibly lose the incentive fee if agreed-upon targets are not reached.

There is moderate risk for the buyer under the cost plus incentive fee contract, and if well-written, it can be more beneficial for both the seller and buyer than a cost reimbursable contract.

Time and Materials (T&M) Contracts

Time and materials (T&M) contracts are a cross between the fixed price and cost reimbursable contracts. The full amount of the material costs is not known at the time the contract is awarded. This resembles a cost reimbursable contract because the costs will continue to grow during the contract's life and are reimbursable to the contractor.

T&M contracts can resemble fixed price contracts when unit rates are used, for example. Unit rates may be used to preset the rates of certain elements or portions of the project. For example, a contracting agency might charge you $135 per hour for a Java programmer, or a leasing company may charge you $2,000 per month for the hardware you're renting during the testing phase of your project. These rates are preset and agreed upon by the buyer and seller ahead of time.

Exam Spotlight

Understand the difference between a fixed price contract and a cost reimbursable contract for the exam. Also know when each type of contract should be used and which party bears the most risk under each type of contract.

Plan Purchases and Acquisitions Outputs

There are four outputs of the Plan Purchases and Acquisitions process. The first is the *procurement management plan*. We've seen a lot of other outputs whose names end with the words *management plan*, so you're probably already ahead of me on this one. But hold the phone— let's make sure we touch on the important points. The other outputs are the contract statement of work, make-or-buy decisions, and requested changes.

Procurement Management Plan

The procurement management plan details how the procurement process will be managed. It includes the following information:

- The types of contract to use
- The authority of the project team
- How the procurement process will be integrated with other project processes
- Where to find standard procurement documents (provided your organization uses standard documents)
- How many vendors or contractors are involved and how they'll be managed
- How the procurement process will be coordinated with other project processes, such as performance reporting and scheduling
- How the constraints and assumptions may be impacted by purchasing
- How multiple vendors or contractors will be managed
- Coordination of purchasing lead times with the development of the project schedule
- The schedule dates that are determined in each contract
- Identification of prequalified sellers (if known)

The procurement management plan, like all the other management plans, becomes a subsidiary of the project management plan.

Contract Statement of Work

A *contract statement of work (SOW)* contains the details of the procurement item in clear, concise terms. It includes the following elements:

- The project objectives
- A description of the work of the project and any postproject operational support needed
- Concise specifications of the product or services required
- The project schedule, time period of services, and work location

The contract SOW may be prepared by either the buyer or the seller. Buyers might prepare the contract SOW and give it to the sellers, who in turn rewrite it so that they can price the work out properly. If the buyer does not know how to prepare a contract SOW or the seller would be better at creating the SOW due to their expertise about the product or service, the seller may prepare it and then give it to the buyer to review. In either case, the contract statement of work is developed from the project scope statement and the WBS and WBS dictionary.

The seller uses the contract SOW to determine whether they are able to produce the goods or services as specified. In addition, it wouldn't hurt to include a copy of the WBS with the contract SOW. Any information the seller can use to properly price the goods or services helps both sides understand what's needed and how it will be provided.

Projects may require some or all of the work of the project to be provided by a vendor. The Plan Purchases and Acquisitions process determines if goods or services should be produced within the organization or procured from outside, and if goods or services are procured from outside, it describes what will be outsourced and what kind of contract to use and then documents the information in the contract SOW and procurement management plan.

> You prepared a SOW during the Develop Project Charter process. You can use that SOW as the contract SOW during this process if you're contracting out the entire project. Otherwise, you can use just those portions of the SOW that describe the work you're contracting for.

Make-or-Buy Decisions

The make-or-buy decision is a document that outlines the decisions made during the process regarding which goods and or services will be produced by the organization and which will be purchased. This can include any number of items, including services, products, insurance policies, performance, and performance bonds.

Requested Changes

Like many of the other processes we've discussed so far, requested changes may come about as a result of the Plan Purchases and Acquisitions process. Those changes, like all the others, should be processed through the Integrated Change Control process.

Once we've determine which goods and services we're going to procure and decided on the best type of contract to use for our situation, we'll move into the Plan Contracting processes to prepare the information needed for choosing a vendor.

Plan Contracting

The purpose of *Plan Contracting* is to prepare the documents you'll use in the Request Seller Responses and Select Sellers processes. We'll discuss these processes in Chapter 9, "Measuring and Controlling Project Performance." The inputs to this process are the procurement management plan, contract statement of work, make-or-buy decisions, and the project management plan (with special attention to the risk register, risk-related contractual agreements, resource requirements, project schedule, activity cost estimates, and cost baseline). We've covered all these inputs previously.

The tools and techniques of Plan Contracting are standard forms and expert judgment. Standard forms are used to facilitate the procurement process. These are forms that are standardized for your organization and for the types of goods or services typically procured by the organization. Your organization may or may not have standard forms. They are usually found in organizations that write a lot of contracts and procure a significant number of goods and services. They may include standard contract forms, nondisclosure agreements, proposal evaluation criteria, and so on.

Plan Contracting Outputs

The three outputs of the Plan Contracting process are procurement documents, evaluation criteria, and contract statement of work updates. Let's take a quick look at each.

Procurement Documents

Procurement documents are used to solicit vendors and suppliers to bid on your procurement needs. You're probably familiar with some of the titles of procurement documents. They might be called request for proposal (RFP), request for information (RFI), invitation for bid (IFB), request for quotation (RFQ), and so on.

Procurement documents should clearly state the description of the work requested, they should include the contract SOW, and they should explain how sellers should format and submit their responses. These documents are prepared by the buyer to assure as accurate and complete a response as possible from all potential bidders. Any special provisions or contractual needs should be spelled out as well. For example, many organizations have data concerning their marketing policies, new products introductions planned for the next few years, trade secrets, and so on. The vendor will have access to this private information, and in order to ensure they maintain confidentiality, you should require that they sign a nondisclosure agreement.

A few terms are used during this process—usually interchangeably—that you should be aware of. When your decision is going to be made primarily on price, the terms *bid* and *quotation* are used, as in IFB or RFQ. When considerations other than price (such as technology or specific approaches to the project) are the deciding factor, the term *proposal* is used, as in RFP. These terms are used interchangeably in practice, even though they have specific meanings in *A Guide to the PMBOK*.

In my organization, all solicitation requests are submitted as RFPs, even though our primary deciding factor is price.

Exam Spotlight

Understand the differences in procurement document terms for the exam.

Procurement documents are posted or advertised according to your organizational policies. This may include ads in newspapers and magazines or Internet posting.

Evaluation Criteria

Evaluation criteria refers to the method your organization will use to choose a vendor from among the proposals you receive. The criteria may be subjective or objective. In some cases, price may be the only criteria, and that means the vendor that submits the lowest bid will win the contract. You should only use purchase price (which should include costs associated with purchase price, like delivery and setup charges) as the sole criteria when there are multiple qualified sellers to choose from.

Other projects may require more extensive criteria than price alone. In this case, scoring models might be used as well as rating models, or purely subjective methods of selection might be utilized. An example weighted scoring method was described in Chapter 2, "Creating the Project Charter and Preliminary Scope Statement," in the section "Benefit Measurement Methods." This method can easily be used to score vendor proposals.

Sometimes, the evaluation criteria are made public in the procurement process so that vendors know exactly what you're looking for. There are pros and cons to this approach. If the organization typically makes known the evaluation criteria, you'll find that almost all the vendors that bid on the project meet every criteria you've outlined (in writing that is). When it comes time to perform the contract, however, you may encounter some surprises. The vendor might have done a great job of writing up the bid based on your criteria, but in reality they don't know how to put the criteria into practice. On the other hand, having all the criteria publicly known beforehand gives ground to great discussion points and discovery later on in the procurement processes.

The following list includes some of the criteria you can consider using for evaluating proposals and bids:

Comprehension and understanding of the needs of the project as documented in the contract SOW

Technical ability of vendor and their proposed team

Experience on projects of similar size and scope, including references

Project management approach

Management approach

Financial stability and capacity

Intellectual and proprietary rights

You could include these in a weighted scoring model and rate each vendor on how well they responded to these issues.

Contract SOW Updates

You may find that changes to the contract statement of work are needed as a result of developing the procurement documents. These updates are usually made at the end of the Plan Contracting process.

Let's switch gears now and take a look at how we plan for the types of resources we'll need on the project in the Human Resource Planning process.

The Customer Relationship Management System Response

Ryan Hunter is preparing the evaluation criteria for an RFP for a customer relationship management (CRM) software system. After meeting with key stakeholders and other project managers in the company who've had experience working on projects of this size and scope, he devised the first draft of the evaluation criteria. A partial list is shown here.

- Successful bidder's response must detail how business processes (as documented in the RFP page 24) will be addressed with their solution.

- Successful bidder must document their project management approach, which must follow PMI's *A Guide to the PMBOK* project practices. Must provide an example project management plan based on a previous project experience of similar size and scope to the one documented in the RFP.

- Successful bidder must document previous successful implementations, including integration with existing organization's PBX and network operating system, and must provide references.

- Successful bidder must provide financial statements for the previous three years.

Human Resource Planning

All projects require human resources, from the smallest project to the largest. The *Human Resource Planning* process documents the roles and responsibilities of individuals or groups for various project elements and then documents the reporting relationships for each. Reporting relationships can be assigned to groups as well as to individuals, and the groups or individuals may be internal or external to the organization or a combination of both. Communications Planning goes hand in hand with Human Resource Planning, because the organizational structure affects the way communications are carried out among project participants and the project interfaces.

The three outputs of this process include documenting roles and responsibilities, creating and documenting the staffing management plan, and creating the organization chart.

Human Resource Planning Inputs

Human Resource Planning has three inputs: enterprise environmental factors, organizational process assets, and project management plan (particularly the activity resource requirements). We'll take a look at the key elements of each of these next.

Key Environmental Factors for Human Resource Planning

Enterprise environmental factors play a key role in determining human resource roles and responsibilities. The type of organization you work in, the reporting relationships, and the technical skills needed to complete the project work are a few of the factors you should consider when developing the staffing management plan. Let's briefly look at the factors *A Guide to the PMBOK* details:

Organizational factors   Consider what departments or organization units will have a role on the project, the interactions between and among departments, and the level of formality in these working relationships.

Technical factors   Consider the types of specialized skills needed to complete the work of the project (for example, programming languages, engineering skills, knowledge of pharmaceuticals) and any technical considerations during hand-off from phase to phase or from project completion to production.

Interpersonal factors   Interpersonal factors have to do with potential project team members. You should consider their experience, skills, current reporting relationships, cultural considerations, and perceptions regarding their levels of trust and respect for coworkers and superiors.

Location and logistics   Consider where the project team is physically located and whether they are all located together or at separate facilities (or cities or countries).

Political factors   Political factors involve your stakeholders. Consider the amount of influence the stakeholders have, their interactions and influence with each other, and the power they can exert over the project.

In addition to these factors, you should also consider project constraints. The topic of constraints seems to come up a lot, so you probably remember that constraints are things that limit the options available to the project team. These typically involve time, costs, scope, and quality. However, there are a few new constraints regarding project teams that you should know about:

Organizational structures   Organizational structures can be constraints. For example, a strong matrix organization provides the project manager with much more authority and power than the weak matrix organization does. Functional organizations typically do not empower their project managers with the proper authority to carry out a project. If you work in a functional organization as I do, it's important to be aware that you'll likely face power struggles with other managers and, in some cases, a flat-out lack of cooperation. Don't tell them I said this, but functional managers tend to be territorial and aren't likely to give up control easily. The best advice I have for you in this case is as follows:

- Establish open communications early on in the project.
- Include all the functional managers with key roles in important decisions.
- Get the support of your project sponsor to empower you (as the project manager) with as much authority as possible. It's important that the sponsor makes it clear to the other managers that their cooperation on project activities is expected.

Collective bargaining agreements   Collective bargaining agreements are actually contractual obligations of the organization. Collective bargaining is typically associated with unions and organized employee associations. Other organized employee associations or groups may require specialized reporting relationships as well—especially if they involve contractual obligations. You will not likely be involved in the negotiations of collective bargaining agreements, but if you have an opportunity to voice opinions regarding employee duties or agreements that would be helpful to your project or future projects, by all means take it.

Economic conditions   These conditions refer to the availability of funds for the project team to perform training, hire staff, and travel. If funds are severely limited and your project requires frequent trips to other locations, you have an economic constraint on your hands.

Exam Spotlight

Understand the key environmental factors and the three constraints that can impact the Human Resource Planning process for the exam.

Organizational Process Assets in Human Resource Planning

There are two primary elements of the organizational process assets input you should consider during this process. They are templates and checklists.

Templates, in this case, refers to documentation like project descriptions, organizational charts, performance appraisals, the organization's conflict management process, and so on.

Checklists may include elements like training requirements, project roles and responsibilities, skills and competency levels, safety issues, and so on.

Exam Spotlight

According to *A Guide to the PMBOK,* using templates and checklists is one way to ensure that you don't miss any key responsibilities when planning the project and will help reduce the amount of time spent on project planning.

Project Management Plan

We've examined the project management plan as an input to other Planning processes. In the Human Resource Planning process, you'll want to pay particular attention to the activity resource requirements because they outline the types and quantities of resources needed for project activities. (Activity resource requirements are an output of the Activity Resource Estimating process, which we'll talk about in Chapter 7, "Creating the Project Schedule and Budget.")

Human Resource Planning Tools and Techniques

There are three tools and techniques in the Human Resource Planning process. Remember that our goal is to produce the organizational chart, roles and responsibilities, and staffing management plan outputs at the end of this process. You'll see that the tools and techniques directly contribute to these outputs. They are organization charts and position descriptions, networking, and organizational theory. We'll look at each of these in the following sections.

Organization Charts and Position Descriptions

We've all seen an organization chart. It usually documents your name, your position, your boss, your boss's boss, your boss's boss's boss, and so on. The important thing to note in this tool and technique is that there are three ways this information may be presented: hierarchical (which describes most organization charts), matrix, and text.

Hierarchical Charts

Hierarchical charts, like a WBS, are designed in a top-down format. The head boss is at the top, the directors that report to the head boss are shown next, and so on descending down the structure. An *organization breakdown structure (OBS)* is a form of organization chart that shows how the WBS elements relate to the organization's departments, work units, or teams rather than individuals.

A *resource breakdown structure (RBS)* is another type of hierarchical chart that breaks down the work of the project according to the types of resources needed. (RBS also stands for risk breakdown structure as we learned in the last chapter.) For example, you may have programmers, database analysts, and network analysts as resource types on the RBS. However, they won't all necessarily work on the project team. You may have programmers reporting to the project team, the finance department, and the customer service department, for example. An RBS can help track project costs because it ties to the organization's accounting system. Let's suppose you have programming resources in the RBS at the junior, advanced, and senior levels. Each of these levels of programmer has an average hourly salary recorded in the accounting system that makes it easy for you to track project costs. Ten senior programmers, 14 advanced, and 25 junior-level programmers are easy to calculate and track.

Matrix-Based Charts

Matrix-based charts are used to show the type of resource and the responsibility they have on the project. Many times a project manager will use a *Responsibility Assignment Matrix (RAM)* to graphically display this information. A RAM is usually depicted as a chart with resource names listed in each row (for example, programmers, testers and trainers) and project phases or WBS elements listed as the columns. (It can also be constructed using team member names.) Indicators in the intersections show where the resources are needed. However, the level of detail is up to you. One RAM might be developed showing only project phases. Another RAM may show level 2 WBS elements for a complex project, with more RAMs subsequently produced for the additional WBS levels. Or a RAM might be constructed with level 3 elements only.

Exam Spotlight

According to *A Guide to the PMBOK*, the RAM relates the OBS to the WBS to assure that every component of the work of the project is assigned to an individual.

Table 6.1 shows a sample portion of a type of RAM called a *RACI chart* for a software development team. In this example, the RACI chart shows the level of accountability each of the participants has on the project. The letters in the acronym RACI are the designations shown in the chart:

R = Responsible for performing the work

A = Accountable, the one who approves or signs off on the work

C = Consult, someone who has input to the work or decisions

I = Inform, someone who must be informed of the decisions or results

TABLE 6.1   Sample RAM

	Karen	Rae	Melinee	JoJo
Design	R	A	C	C
Test	I	R	C	A
Implement	C	I	R	A

Legend: R = Responsible, A = Accountable, C = Consult, I = Inform

In this example, Karen is responsible for design, meaning she does the work, but Rae is accountable and the one who must approve design. This a great tool because it shows at a glance not only where a resource is working but what that resource's responsibility level is on the project.

Text-Oriented Formats

Text-oriented formats are used when you have a significant amount of detail to record. These are also called position descriptions or role-responsibility-authority forms. These forms detail (as the name implies) the role, responsibility, and authority of the resource and they make great templates to use for future projects.

Don't forget that other subsidiary plans of the project management plan may also describe roles and responsibilities. For example, you'll recall from Chapter 5 that the risk register lists the risk owners and their responsibility, so be certain to check these documents when outlining roles and responsibilities as well.

Networking

Networking in this process doesn't refer to the technical kind of networking with servers, switches, and fiber. It means human resource networking; that is, you know someone who knows someone who knows someone. According to *A Guide to the PMBOK*, there are several types of networking activities: proactive communication, lunch meetings (my personal favorite), informal conversations (ah...the information you learn by hanging out at the water cooler), and trade conferences (another favorite because they get you out of the office).

Organizational Theory

Organizational theory refers to all the theories that attempt to explain what makes people, teams, and work units perform the way they do. We'll talk more about motivation techniques (which are a type of organizational theory) in Chapter 8, "Developing the Project Team." Organizational theory improves the probability that planning will be effective and helps shorten the amount of time it takes to produce the Human Resource Planning outputs.

Human Resource Planning Outputs

The Human Resource Planning process has three outputs: roles and responsibilities, project organizational charts, and the staffing management plan. We've already covered organization charts in detail, so we'll take a look at the other two outputs now.

Roles and Responsibilities

This output is the list of roles and responsibilities for the project team. It can take the form of the RAM or RACI chart we talked about earlier or the roles and responsibilities can be recorded in text format. The key elements you should include in the roles and responsibilities documentation are the following:

Roles   Describes what part of the project the individuals or teams are accountable for. This should also include a description of authority levels, responsibilities, and what work is not included as part of the role.

Authority   Describes the amount of authority the resource has to make decisions, dictate direction, and approve the work.

Responsibility   Describes the work required to complete the project activities.

Competency   Describes the skills and ability needed to perform the project activities.

Staffing Management Plan

The staffing management plan documents how and when human resources are introduced to the project and the criteria for releasing them. As with the other management plans we've discussed, the level and amount of detail contained in this plan are up to you. It can be formal or informal, and it can contain lots of detail or only high-level detail.

The staffing management plan is a subsidiary plan to the project management plan and should be updated throughout the project. There are several elements that should be considered for inclusion in the staffing management plan, including the following:

Staff acquisition   This describes how team members are acquired (from inside or outside the organization), where they're located, and the costs for specific skills and expertise. We'll talk more about staff acquisition in Chapter 8.

Timetable   This describes the time frames in which the resources will be needed on the project and when the recruitment process should begin. The resources can be described individually, by teams, or by function (programmers, testers, etc.). Many staffing management plans make use of a resource histogram. This is usually drawn in chart form, with project time along the horizontal axis and hours needed along the vertical axis. The following example histogram shows the hours needed for an asphalt crew on a construction project:

Resource Histogram for Asphalt Crew

Release criteria   Attention should be given to how you'll release project team members at the end of their assignment. You should have reassignment procedures in place to move folks on to other projects or back to assignments they had before the project. This reduces overall project costs because you pay them only for the time they work and then release them. You won't have a tendency to simply keep them busy between assignments or until the end of their scheduled end date if they complete their activities early. Having these procedures in place will also improve morale because everyone will be clear about how reassignment will occur. This should reduce anxiety about their opportunity for employment at the conclusion of the project or their assignment.

Training needs   This describes any training plans needed for team members who don't have the required skills or abilities to perform project tasks.

Recognition and rewards   This describe the systems you'll use to reward and reinforce desired behavior. We'll talk more about recognition and rewards in Chapter 8.

Compliance   If your project involves regulations that must be met or contractual obligations (such as union contracts), the staffing management plan should detail these and any human resource policies the organization has in place that deal with compliance issues.

Safety   Any safety policies and procedures that are applicable to the project or industry you work in should be included in the staffing management plan.

Exam Spotlight

Make certain you understand the roles and responsibilities and the staffing management output and what each of these entails for the exam.

Defining Activity Definition

Now we're off and running toward the development of our project schedule. In order to develop the schedule, we first need to define the activities, sequence them in the right order, estimate resources, and estimate the time it will take to complete the tasks. We'll cover the Activity Definition here, cover Activity Sequencing processes next, and pick up with the estimating processes in the next chapter.

 Activity Definition, Activity Sequencing, Activity Resource Estimating, Activity Duration Estimating, and Schedule Development are separate processes, each with inputs, tools and techniques, and outputs. In practice, especially for small- to medium-sized projects, these processes can be combined into one process or step. We'll take a look at the first two activity-related processes now. Chapter 7 describes the Activity Resource Estimating, Activity Duration Estimating, and Schedule Development processes.

The *Activity Definition* process is a further breakdown of the work package elements of the WBS. It documents the specific activities needed to fulfill the deliverables detailed on the WBS. This process may be performed by the project manager, or when the WBS is broken down to the subproject level, this process (and all the "Activity" processes that follow) might be assigned to a subproject manager.

Activity Definition Process Inputs

The inputs to the Activity Definition process and the key elements you should consider as inputs to this process are shown in the following list:

- Enterprise environmental factors (project management information systems and scheduling software tools)
- Organizational process assets (existing guidelines and policies)
- Project scope statement (deliverables, constraints, and assumptions)
- WBS (this is the primary input to this process)
- WBS dictionary
- Project management plan (schedule management plan)

Tools and Techniques for Defining Activities

The tools and techniques of the Activity Definition process are as follows:

- Decomposition
- Templates
- Rolling wave planning
- Expert judgment
- Planning component

Decomposition is the process of breaking the work packages into smaller, more manageable units of work called schedule activities. These are not deliverables but the individual units of work that must be completed to fulfill the deliverables. Activity lists (which are one of the outputs of this process) from prior projects can be used as templates in this process. Rolling wave planning involves planning near-term work in more detail than future-term work. Expert judgment, in the form of project team members with prior experience developing project scope statements and WBSs, can help you define activities.

The planning component is a new tool and technique we haven't seen before. Two of the planning components discussed in *A Guide to the PMBOK* are the control account and the planning package. The idea with this tool and technique is that you may have WBS elements that really can't be broken down much further. In that case, the work package level in those branches of the WBS can be used to develop high-level schedules and plan future work at higher levels of the WBS. You can use a control account within the WBS to assign a management control point anywhere above the work package level to use as a basis for planning when the work package level hasn't been planned. The planning package is any element on the WBS that's below the control account but still above the work package level used for planning purposes.

Exam Spotlight

The purpose of the Activity Definition process is to decompose the work packages into schedule activities where the basis for estimating, scheduling, executing, and monitoring and controlling the work of the project are easily supported and accomplished.

Activity Definition Outputs

Activity Definition has four outputs:

- Activity list
- Activity attributes
- Milestone list
- Requested changes

You'll be happy to know that we aren't going to create an Activity Definition management plan at the end of this process. We've looked at requested changes before. We'll examine the rest of the outputs here.

Activity List

One primary output of the Activity Definition process is called an *activity list*. The activity list should contain all the schedule activities that will be performed for the project, with a scope of work description of each activity and an identifier (such as a code or number) so that team members understand what the work is and how it is to be completed. The schedule activities are individual elements of the project schedule, and the activity list is a subsidiary of the project management plan.

NOTE In practice, when you're working on a small project or projects that aren't that complex, Activity Definition might be accomplished during the construction of the WBS and the activities themselves become the work package level. However, for the exam, remember that activities are elements of the project schedule but they are *not* a part of the WBS.

Activity Attributes

Activity attributes describe the characteristics of the activities and are an extension of the activity list. Activity attributes may describe information such as the activity identifier or code, descriptions, constraints and assumptions associated with the activity, activities that come before this activity (predecessor activities) and after this activity (successor activities), resource requirements, the individual responsible for completing the work, and so on. The activity attributes are used in the schedule model tool and technique of the Schedule Development process (we'll talk about this in the next chapter).

Milestone Lists

Milestones are typically major accomplishments of the project and mark the completion of major deliverables or some other key event in the project. For example, approval and sign-off on project deliverables might be considered milestones. Other examples might be completion of a prototype, system testing, contract approval, and so on. The milestone list records these accomplishments and documents whether the milestone is mandatory or optional. The milestone list is part of the project management plan and is also used to help develop the project schedule.

Understanding the Activity Sequencing Process

Now that you've identified the schedule activities, you need to sequence them in a logical order and find out if dependencies exist among the activities. The interactivity of logical relationships must be sequenced correctly in order to facilitate the development of a realistic, achievable project schedule in a later process.

Consider a classic example. Let's say you're going to paint your house but, unfortunately, it's fallen into a little disrepair. The old paint is peeling and chipping and will need to be scraped before a coat of primer can be sprayed on the house. After the primer dries, the painting can commence. In this example, the primer activity depends on the scraping. You can't—okay, *you shouldn't*—prime the house before scraping off the peeling paint. The painting activity depends on the primer activity in the same way. You really shouldn't start painting until the primer has dried.

During *Activity Sequencing*, you will use a host of inputs and tools and techniques to produce the primary output, project schedule network diagrams. We've already seen all of the inputs. They are project scope statement, activity list, activity attributes, milestone list, and approved change requests. These were discussed in this and other chapters. There are several new tools and techniques that we'll look at now.

Activity Sequencing Tools and Techniques

Activity Sequencing has five tools and techniques, all of which are new to us:

- Precedence diagramming method (PDM)

- Arrow diagramming method (ADM)

- Schedule network templates

- Dependency determination

- Applying leads and lags

I'm going to switch the order of these and look at dependency determination first. In practice, you'll define dependencies either before or while you're using the PDM or ADM methods to draw your network templates, so to make sure we're all on the same page with *A Guide to the PMBOK* terminology regarding dependencies, we'll cover them first and then move on to the other tools and techniques.

Dependency Determination

Dependencies are relationships between the activities in which one activity is dependent on another to complete an action or perhaps an activity is dependent on another to start an action before it can proceed. Dependency determination is a matter of determining where those dependencies exist. Thinking back to the house-painting example, we couldn't paint until the scraping and priming activities were completed. There are three types of dependencies you'll want to know about for the exam:

- Mandatory dependencies

- Discretionary dependencies

- External dependencies

As you've probably guessed, *A Guide to the PMBOK* defines dependencies differently depending on their characteristics.

Let's look at each of these in more detail.

Mandatory dependencies   *Mandatory dependencies*, also known as *hard logic* or *hard dependencies,* are defined by the type of work being performed. The scraping, primer, painting sequences are examples of mandatory dependencies. The nature of the work itself dictates the order in which the activities should be performed. Activities with physical limitations are a telltale sign that you have a mandatory dependency on your hands.

Discretionary dependencies   *Discretionary dependencies* are defined by the project management team. Discretionary dependencies are also known as *preferred logic, soft logic,* or *preferential logic.* These are usually process or procedure driven or "best practices" techniques based on past experience. For example, both past experience and best practices on house-painting projects has shown that all trim work should be hand-painted while the bulk of the main painting work should be done with a sprayer.

External dependencies   *External dependencies* are, well, external to the project. This may seem obvious, but *A Guide to the PMBOK* points out that even though the dependency is external to the project (and therefore a non-project activity), it impacts project activities. For example, perhaps your project is researching and marketing a new drug. The FDA must approve the drug before your company can market it. This is not a project activity, but the project cannot move forward until approval occurs. That means FDA approval is an external dependency.

Once you've identified the dependencies and assembled all the other inputs for the Activity Sequencing process, you'll take this information and produce a diagram—or schematic display—of the project activities. The project schedule network diagram shows the dependencies—or logical relationships—that exist among the activities. You can use one of the other tools and techniques of this process to produce this output. Let's examine each in detail.

Precedence Diagramming Method (PDM)

The *precedence diagramming method (PDM)* is what most project management software programs use to do activity sequencing today. Precedence diagrams use boxes or rectangles to represent the activities (called nodes). The nodes are connected with arrows showing the dependencies between the activities. This method is also called *activity on node (AON).*

The minimum information that should be displayed on the node is the activity name, but you may put as much information about the activity on the node as you'd like. Sometimes the nodes are displayed with activity name, activity number, start and stop dates, due dates, slack time, and so on. (We'll cover slack time in Chapter 7. For the exam, remember that the PDM uses only one time estimate to determine duration.)

The following graphic shows a PDM—or AON—of the house-painting example.

The PDM is further defined by four types of *logical relationships* (also known as dependencies; *precedence relationships* is another term used to describe these relationships). You may already be familiar with these if you've used Microsoft Project or similar project management software program. The four dependencies, or logical relationships, are as follows:

Finish-to-start (FS)   The finish-to-start relationship is the most frequently used relationship. This relationship says that the independent—or *from* activity—must finish before the dependent—or *to* activity—can start. In PDM diagrams, this is the most often used logical relationship.

Start-to-finish (SF)   The start-to-finish relationship says that the independent activity must start before the dependent activity can finish. This logical relationship is seldom used.

Finish-to-finish (FF)   The finish-to-finish relationship says that the independent activity must finish before the dependent activity finishes.

Start-to-start (SS)   I think you're getting the hang of this. The start-to-start relationship says that the independent activity must start before the dependent activity can start.

Keep these logical relationships (or dependencies) in mind when constructing your project schedule network diagram. Remember that finish-to-start is the most commonly used dependency in the PDM method. This is also the dependency type you should employ when you're using project management software to diagram your activities. Using the other dependencies in most project management software programs will likely produce unpredictable results.

Arrow Diagramming Method (ADM)

The *arrow diagramming method (ADM)* is visually the opposite of the PDM. The arrow diagramming method places activities on the arrows, which are connected to dependent activities with nodes. This method is also called *activity on arrow (AOA)*. This technique isn't used nearly as often as PDM, but there are some industries that prefer the ADM to the PDM. For the record, note that ADM allows for more than one time estimate to determine duration and uses only the finish-to-start dependency. And there's one more unique note about ADM to tuck away: Sometimes dummy activities must be plugged into the diagram to accurately display the dependencies.

The following example shows the ADM method applied to the house-painting example:

Schedule Network Templates

Schedule network templates are like the templates we've talked about in other processes. Perhaps the project you're working on is similar to a project that's been completed in the past. You can use a previous project schedule network diagram as a template for the current project. Or you may be working on a project with several deliverables that are fairly identical. You can use the first network diagram as a template and then modify it for each of the other deliverables.

Applying Leads and Lags

Leads and lags should be considered when determining dependencies. *Lags* delay *successor activities* (those that follow a predecessor activity) and require time added either to the start date or to the finish date of the activity you're scheduling. *Leads,* conversely, speed up the successor activities and require time to be subtracted from the start date or the finish date of the activity you're scheduling.

Exam Spotlight

I recommend you memorize the following graphic to help you remember the tools and techniques of the Activity Sequencing process and their characteristics for the exam. This may look a little strange, but I think it will work for you now that you understand what each of these diagramming methods is about. This is information you need to know for the exam. If this graphic isn't useful for you, come up with your own mnemonic or sample that will help you remember which of these is which. Don't say I didn't warn you.

Let's revisit the house-painting example to put all this in perspective. In order to paint, you first need to scrape the peeling paint and then prime. However, you can't begin painting until the primer has dried, so you shouldn't schedule priming for Monday and painting for Tuesday if you need the primer to dry on Tuesday. Therefore, the priming activity requires lag time, so you need to add time to the end of this activity to allow for the drying time needed before you can start painting.

Lead time works just the opposite. Suppose, for this example, you could start priming before the scraping is finished. Maybe there are areas on the house that don't require scraping, so you don't really need to wait until the scraping activity finishes to begin the priming activity. Priming in this example has lead time subtracted from the beginning of the activity so that this activity begins prior to the previous activity finishing.

Activity Sequencing Outputs

Here are the outputs of the Activity Sequencing process:

- Project schedule network diagrams
- Activity list updates
- Activity attributes updates
- Requested changes

We've just spent a good deal of time describing the different types of project schedule network diagrams you can construct using PDM or ADM techniques. Project schedule network diagrams can be generated on a computer, or you can draw them out by hand. Like the WBS, these diagrams may contain all the project details or may contain only summary-level details, depending on the complexity of the project. Summary-level activities are a collection of related activities also known as *hammocks*. Think of hammocks as a group of related activities rolled up into a summary heading that describes the activities likely to be contained in that grouping.

Keep in mind that the construction of these project schedule network diagrams might bring activities to light that you missed when defining your activity list, or it might make you break an activity down into two activities in places where you thought one activity might work. If this is the case, you will produce both activity list updates based on this new information as well as activity attributes updates.

After the activities are sequenced, the next steps involve estimating the resources and estimating the durations of the activities so that they can be plugged into the project schedule. We'll look at these topics in the next chapter.

Project Case Study: New Kitchen Heaven Retail Store

"Thanks everyone for your timely responses. I'll look over your list of roles and responsibilities, skills needed for the activities, and your activity lists." The meeting adjourns, and you head back to your office to review the documents. You'd like to get the project schedule constructed soon and go over it with Dirk.

Ricardo Ramirez from the IT department has outlined his resource needs and activity list. He reminds you that data is sent from each store over a T1 connection, not over satellite as Jill told you originally. Ricardo's activities are as follows. He's also taken the trouble to write them in sequential order:

1. Procure the T1 connection. This can be done concurrently with the other activities listed here. Ricardo will work on the procurement documents for this activity.

2. Run Ethernet cable throughout the building. This activity depends on the lease being signed and must finish before the build-out can start. Ricardo has one person on staff who can complete this specialized activity. His first available date is October 5.

3. Purchase the router, switch, server, and rack for the equipment room and four point-of-service terminals. Delivery time is two weeks. Ricardo will prepare the procurement documents for these items.

4. Install the router and test the connection. Testing depends on the T1 installation at demarcation. Ricardo's staff will do this activity.

5. Install the switch. Ricardo's staff will do this activity.

6. Install the server and test. The testing depends on the T1 connection installation. Ricardo's staff will do this activity.

7.   The web team will add the new store location and phone number to the lookup function on the Internet site. Ricardo will assign his applications-programming manager to this activity. This activity depends on the lease being signed.

Jake and Jill give you similar activity lists with human resource needs. You use a project management software tool to create a first draft of the project schedule network diagram. As you're staring at the screen, Dirk walks into your office.

"You look worried," Dirk says.

"Yes, I think we may have a problem. Jill mentioned she needs some lead time to stock shelves and that might interfere with the store build-out activity assigned to Jake's team. I don't have enough information yet to finish this. I need to get some time and cost estimates from everyone before I know for sure if there's a problem."

"I'd rather know sooner than later if there's a problem, so get right on those estimates."

You toggle over to the calendaring system and see all three stakeholders are free Thursday morning. You set up a meeting time so you can explain to each of them what information you need next.

Project Case Study Checklist

   Procurement

- Make-or-buy analysis

- Expert judgment

- Procurement documents prepared

   Human Resource Planning

- Roles and responsibilities documented

   Activity Definition

- Decomposition

- Expert judgment

- Activity list created

   Activity Sequencing

- Dependencies determined

- Leads and lags determined

- Project schedule network diagram drafted

Exam Spotlight

You may find that the Activity Sequencing process gets a lot of coverage on the exam. Be certain you understand its inputs and tools and techniques well. Then again, remember the exam is randomly generated from a pool of questions, so don't ever concentrate all your memorization efforts on only one or two processes.

Summary

This chapter's focus was on planning for project resources. There are several aspects involved in these planning activities, including procurement of goods and services, human resource planning, and defining the activities human resources will be involved in.

We started out with the Plan Purchases and Acquisitions process. This process identifies the goods or services you're going to purchase from outside of the organization and determines which project needs can be met by the project team. This involves tools and techniques like make-or-buy decisions, expert judgment, and contract types. The procurement management plan is one of the outputs of this process and describes how procurement services will be managed throughout the project. The contract statement of work (another output of this process) describes the work that will be contracted out.

Plan Contracting creates the documents you'll use to procure the goods and services needed from outside the organization.

The Human Resource Planning process identifies and assigns roles and responsibilities and reporting relationships. Many times the roles and responsibilities assignments are depicted in a Responsibility Assignment Matrix (RAM) or a RACI chart. The staffing management plan describes how and when project team members will be acquired is an output of the Human Resource Planning process.

The Activity Definition process involves decomposing the work packages into individual units of work called schedule activities that can be easily assigned and estimated. The output of this process is the activity list, activity attributes, milestone list, and requested changes.

The Activity Sequencing process takes the activities and puts them in a logical, sequential order based on dependencies. Dependencies exist when the current activity is reliant on some action from a predecessor activity or it impacts a successor activity. There are three types of dependencies: mandatory, discretionary, and external. PDM (also known as AON) and ADM (also known as AOA) are two methods for displaying project schedule network diagrams. PDM has four logical relationships, or dependencies: finish-to-start, start-to-finish, finish-to-finish, and start-to-start.

Exam Essentials

Be able to name the purpose for the Plan Purchases and Acquisitions process.   The purpose of the Plan Purchases and Acquisitions process is to identify which project needs should be obtained from outside the organization. Make–or-buy analysis is used as a tool and technique to help determine this.

Be able to identify the contract types and their usage.   Contract types are a tool and technique of the Plan Purchases and Acquisitions process and include fixed price and cost reimbursable contracts. Use fixed price contracts for well-defined projects with a high value to the company, and use cost reimbursable contracts for projects with uncertainty and large investments early in the project life. The three types of cost reimbursable contracts are CPF (or CPPC), CPFF, and CPIF. Time and materials contracts are a cross between fixed and cost reimbursable contracts.

Be able to name the outputs of the Plan Contracting process.   The outputs of Plan Contracting are procurement documents, evaluation criteria, and contract statement of work updates.

Be able to name the purpose of the Human Resource Planning process.   Human Resource Planning involves determining roles and responsibilities, reporting relationships for the project, and creating the staffing management plan, which describes how team members are acquired and the criteria for their release.

Be able to name the purpose of the Activity Definition process.   The Activity Definition process decomposes the work packages into schedule activities and creates an activity list, activity attributes, a milestone list, and requested changes as its outputs.

Be able to identify the tools and techniques of Activity Sequencing.   The tools and techniques of Activity Sequencing are the precedence diagramming method (PDM), the arrow diagramming method (ADM), schedule network templates, dependency determination, and applying leads and lags.

Be able to discuss the difference between PDM and ADM.   PDM (also known as AON) displays activity on nodes with connecting arrows showing dependencies. PDM has four logical relationships and uses the finish-to-start relationship most often. ADM (also known as AOA) displays activities on arrows with connecting nodes showing dependencies and uses only the finish-to-start relationship.

Key Terms

You've learned a lot of new key words in this chapter. PMI has worked hard to develop and define standard project management terms that apply across industries. Here is a list of some of the terms you came across in this chapter:

Activity Definition	lags
activity list	leads
activity on arrow (AOA)	logical relationships
activity on node (AON)	lump sum contracts
Activity Sequencing	make-or–buy analysis
arrow diagramming method (ADM)	mandatory dependencies
contract	milestones
contract statement of work (SOW)	organization breakdown structure (OBS)
cost plus fee (CPF)	Plan Contracting
cost plus fixed fee (CPFF)	Plan Purchases and Acquisitions
cost plus incentive fee (CPIF)	precedence diagramming method (PDM)
cost plus percentage of cost (CPCC)	precedence relationships
cost reimbursable contracts	preferential logic
dependencies	preferred logic
discretionary dependencies	procurement documents
external dependencies	procurement management plan
fixed price contracts	RACI chart
fixed price plus incentive contracts	resource breakdown structure (RBS)
hammocks	Responsibility Assignment Matrix (RAM)
hard dependencies	soft logic
hard logic	successor activities
Human Resource Planning	time and materials (T&M) contracts

Review Questions

1. You are the project manager for an upcoming outdoor concert event. You're working on the procurement plan for the computer software program that will control the lighting and screen projections during the concert. You're comparing the cost of purchasing a software product to the cost of your company programmers writing a custom software program. You are engaged in which of the following?

   A. Procurement planning

   B. Using expert judgment

   C. Creating the procurement management plan

   D. Make-or-buy analysis

2. You are the project manager for an outdoor concert event scheduled for one year from today. You're working on the procurement plan for the computer software program that will control the lighting and screen projections during the concert. You've decided to contract with a professional services company that specializes in writing custom software programs. You want to minimize the risk to the organization, so you'll opt for which contract type?

   A. Fixed price plus incentive

   B. Cost plus fixed fee

   C. Fixed price

   D. Cost plus incentive

3. You are the project manager for Heart of Texas casual clothing company. It's introducing a new line of clothing called Black Sheep Ranch Wear. You will outsource the production of this clothing line to a vendor. The vendor has requested a contract SOW. All of the following statements are true except for which one?

   A. The SOW contains a description of the new clothing line.

   B. As the purchaser, you are required to write the SOW.

   C. The SOW contains the objectives of the project.

   D. The vendor requires a SOW to determine if they can produce the clothing line given the very detailed specifications of this product.

4. You are the project manager for Heart of Texas casual clothing company. It's introducing a new line of clothing called Black Sheep Ranch Wear. You will outsource the production of this clothing line to a vendor. Your legal department has recommended you use a contract that reimburses the seller's allowable costs and builds in a bonus based on performance criteria they've outlined in their memo. Which of the following contract types will you use?

   A. CPIF

   B. CPFF

   C. CPF

   D. CPPC

5. All of the following statements are true regarding the Human Resource Planning process except for which one?

    A. Human Resource Planning involves determining roles and responsibilities.

    B. One of the Human Resource Planning outputs includes project organization charts that show the project's reporting relationships.

    C. The staffing management plan created in this process describes how and when resources will be acquired and released.

    D. A RAM (or RACI chart) is an output of this process that allows you to see all of the people assigned to an activity.

6. Sally is a project manager working on a project that will require a specially engineered machine. There are only three manufactures who can make the machine to the specifications Sally needs. The price of this machine is particularly critical to this project. The budget is limited and there's not a chance of securing additional funds if the bids for the machine come in higher than budgeted. She's developing the evaluation criteria for the bidders' responses and knows all of the following are true except for which one?

    A. Sally will use standard contract forms provided by her procurement department to write the contract for this machine.

    B. Sally will review the project management plan, including the risk register, as inputs to this process.

    C. Sally will base the evaluation criteria on price alone since the budget is a constraint.

    D. Sally will update the contract statement of work with any new information.

7. Which of the following are constraints that you might find during the Human Resource Planning process?

    A. Organizational structures, collective bargaining agreements, and economic conditions

    B. Organizational structures, technical interfaces, and interpersonal interfaces

    C. Organizational interfaces, collective bargaining agreements, and economic conditions

    D. Organizational interfaces, technical interfaces, and interpersonal interfaces

8. You are the project manager for a scheduled version release of your company's software tracking product. You have identified resources according to their activities. You might want to display this information in which of the following?

    A. AON

    B. PDM

    C. AOA

    D. RAM

9. All of the following statements describe the activity list except which one?

    A. The activity list is an output of the Activity Definition process.

    B. The activity list includes all activities of the project.

    C. The activity list is an extension of and a component of the WBS.

    D. The activity list includes an identifier and description of the activity.

10. You are the project manager for Design Your Web Site, Inc. Your company is designing the website for a national grocery store chain. You have your activity list in hand and are ready to diagram the activity dependencies using the PDM technique. Which of the following statements is true?

A. PDM is also the AON diagramming method.

B. PDM is also the AOA diagramming method.

C. PDM is also the ADM diagramming method.

D. PDM is also the AND diagramming method.

11. You are the project manager for Design Your Web Site, Inc. Your company is designing the website for a national grocery store chain. You have your activity list in hand and several time estimates for each activity and are ready to diagram the activity dependencies. You should use which of the following?

A. PDM techniques

B. PDM or ADM techniques

C. AON techniques

D. ADM techniques

12. You are the project manager for Changing Tides video games. You have produced a project schedule network diagram and have updated the activity list. Which process have you just finished?

A. The Activity Sequencing process, which identifies all the specific activities of the project

B. The Activity Sequencing process, which identifies all the activity dependencies

C. The Activity Definition process, which diagrams project network time estimates

D. The Activity Definition process, which identifies all the activity attributes

13. You are working on a project that requires resources with expertise in the areas of hospitality management and entertainment. You are preparing your project schedule network diagram and know that you will use only finish-to-start dependencies. Which of the following diagramming methods does this describe?

A. PDM

B. ADM

C. AON

D. Network template

14. You have been hired as a contract project manager for Grapevine Vineyards. Grapevine wants you to design an Internet wine club for its customers. Customers must register before being allowed to order wine over the Internet so that legal age can be established. You know that the module to verify registration must be written and tested using data from Grapevine's existing database. This new module cannot be tested until the data from the existing system is loaded. This is an example of which of the following?

A. Preferential logic

B. Soft logic

C. Discretionary dependency

D. Hard logic

15. Which logical relationship does the PDM use most often?

A. Start-to-finish

B. Start-to-start

C. Finish-to-finish

D. Finish-to-start

16. You have been hired as a contract project manager for Grapevine Vineyards. Grapevine wants you to design an Internet wine club for its customers. Customers must register before being allowed to order wine over the Internet so that legal age can be established. You know that the module to verify registration must be written and tested using data from Grapevine's existing database. This new module cannot be tested until the data from the existing system is loaded. You are going to hire a vendor to perform the programming and testing tasks for this module to help speed up the project schedule. Since they'll have access to your customer list and potentially other trade secrets, you'll asked them to sign a nondisclosure agreement. This is an example of which of the following?

A. Standard form

B. Organizational process asset

C. Fixed cost contract

D. Procurement documents

17. You are the project manager for BB Tops, a nationwide toy store chain. Your new project involves a creating a prototype display at several stores across the country. You are using a RACI chart to display individuals and activities. What does RACI stand for?

A. Responsible, accountable, consult, inform

B. Responsible, assignment, control, inform

C. Resource, activity, control, identify

D. Resource, accountable, consult, identify

18. This process can directly influence the project schedule.

A. Human Resource Planning

B. Plan Purchases and Acquisitions

C. Activity Sequencing

D. Plan Contracting

19. You are the project manager for BB Tops, a nationwide toy store chain. Your new project involves a creating a prototype display at several stores across the country. You are hiring a contractor for portions of the project. The contact stipulates that you'll pay all allowable costs and an 8 percent fee over and above the allowable costs at the end of the contract. All of the following describe this type of contract except for which one?

A. CPPC

B. CPIF

C. CPF

D. Cost reimbursable contract

20. This process uses tools like decomposition and rolling wave planning to produce the activity list and other outputs. Due to the purpose of this process, which of the following is considered its primary input?

A. WBS

B. Project management plan

C. PMIS (as part of enterprise environmental factors)

D. Constraints and assumptions

Answers to Review Questions

1. D. Make-or-buy analysis is determining whether it's more cost effective to purchase the goods or services needed for the project or more cost effective for the organization to produce them internally.

2. C. Fixed price contracts have the highest risk to the seller and the least amount of risk to the buyer. However, the price the vendor charges for the product or service will compensate for the amount of risk they're taking on.

3. B. The SOW can be written by either the buyer or the seller. Sometimes the buyer will write the SOW and the seller may modify it and send it back to the buyer for verification and approval.

4. A. The cost plus incentive fee contract is one that the buyer reimburses the seller for the seller's allowable costs and includes an incentive or bonus for exceeding the performance criteria laid out in the contract.

5. D. The RAM and RACI charts are tools and techniques of this process.

6. C. Evaluation criteria can be based on price alone when there are several vendors who can readily supply the good or services. The question states that only three vendors make the machine, which means evaluation criteria should be based on more than price.

7. A. Constraints can be anything that limits the option of the project team. Organizational structures, collective bargaining agreements, and economic conditions are all constraints that might be encountered during this process.

8. D. The Responsibility Assignment Matrix (RAM) links project resources with project activities.

9. C. The activity list is a component of the project schedule, not the WBS. The activity list includes all the project activities, an identifier, and a description of the activity. The activity list is an output of the Activity Definition process.

10. A. The precedence diagramming method is also known as the activity on node (AON) diagramming method.

11. D. PDM uses one time estimate to determine duration, while ADM can use more than one time estimate.

12. B. The Activity Sequencing process produces project schedule network diagrams, updates to the activity list, updates to the activity attributes, and requested changes. The purpose of this process is to identify all activity dependencies.

13. B. The arrow diagramming method uses only finish-to-start dependencies.

14. D. This is an example of a mandatory dependency, also known as hard logic. Mandatory dependencies are inherent in the nature of the work. Discretionary dependencies, also called preferred logic, preferential logic, and soft logic, are defined by the project management team.

15. D. Finish-to-start (FS) is the most commonly used logical relationship in PDM and most project management software packages.

16. A. Standard forms are a tool and technique of the Plan Contracting process. Standard forms can be nondisclosure agreements, standardized contracts, and so on.

17. A. RACI stands for responsible, accountable, consult, and inform.

18. B. Plan Purchases and Acquisitions can directly influence the project schedule and the project schedule can directly influence this process.

19. B. This is a cost reimbursable contract that includes a fee as a percentage of allowable costs. This type of contract is known as a cost plus fee (CPF) or a cost plus percentage of cost (CPPC) contract. A CPIF is a cost plus incentive fee contract that reimburses allowable costs and adds an incentive for exceeding the performance criteria laid out in the contract.

20. A. This question is describing the Activity Definition process. The purpose of this project is to decompose the work package elements of the WBS into activities. The WBS is the primary input of this process.

Creating the Project Schedule and Budget

THE PMP EXAM CONTENT FROM THE PLANNING THE PROJECT PERFORMANCE DOMAIN COVERED IN THIS CHAPTER INCLUDES THE FOLLOWING:

✓ **Obtain Plan Approval**

The Planning process group has more processes than any other process group. As a result, a lot of time and effort goes into the Planning processes of any project. You'll find on some projects that you may spend almost as much time planning the project as you do executing and controlling it. This isn't a bad thing. The better planning you do up front, the more likely you'll have a successful project. Speaking of planning…the Planning, Executing, and Monitoring and Controlling process groups together account for almost 70 percent of the PMP exam questions, so *plan* on spending about the same percentage of your study time on these areas.

We have another fun-filled, action-packed chapter. We're going to pick up from where we left off last chapter and create estimates for our project activities and then wrap up the remaining Planning processes. We'll spend a good deal of time on developing the project schedule and discussing the project budget. These two documents are two of your most important planning documents. Everything we've done up to this point will help us create an accurate schedule and budget. You'll use these documents throughout the Executing and Monitoring and Controlling processes (along with several other documents we've created along the way) to help measure the progress of the project.

We'll start the Executing process group in the next chapter. But before we do that, let's get a good grasp of the project schedule and budget.

Activity Resource Estimating

All projects, from the smallest to the largest, require resources. The term *resources* in this case does not mean just people; it means all the physical resources required to complete the project. *A Guide to the PMBOK* defines resources as people, equipment, and materials. In reality, this includes people, equipment, supplies, materials, software, hardware—the list goes on depending on the project you're working on. *Activity Resource Estimating* is concerned with determining the types of resources needed (both human and materials) and in what quantities for each schedule activity within a work package. You might be asking, "Didn't we already do the people part in the Human Activity Resource Estimating process?" The answer is…no. Remember that Human Activity Resource Estimating determines roles and responsibilities and describes reporting relationships. Activity Resource Estimating determines what types or resources are needed and how many.

Remember, the activity resource output from this process is an input into the Human Activity Resource Estimating process.

A *Guide to the PMBOK* notes that Activity Resource Estimating should be closely coordinated with the Cost Estimating process (we'll talk about Cost Estimating later in this chapter). That's because resources—whether people or material or both—are typically the largest expense you'll have on any project. Identifying the resources becomes a critical component of the project planning process so estimates—and ultimately the project budget—can be accurately derived. We'll look at the inputs and tools and techniques that will help you document these requirements next.

Activity Resource Estimating Inputs

The Activity Resource Estimating process has several inputs you are already familiar with:

- Enterprise environmental factors
- Organizational process assets
- Activity list
- Activity attributes
- Resource availability
- Project management plan

The only one we haven't seen before is resource availability.

Resource availability is an output of the Acquire Project Team process. The Acquire Project Team process isn't performed until the Executing process group, so we're a little out of order. In practice, you'll likely perform both Human Resource Planning and Acquire Project Team during the Planning stages of the project. For the exam, remember that resource availability isn't determined until the Executing stage and becomes an input to the Activity Resource Estimating process.

The resource availability output describes, believe it or not, the time frames in which resources (both human and material) are available. This will help you estimate the types of resources you may need for the project. For example, if you are working on a project that requires the use of specialized equipment during one of the project phases and the resource availability document shows that this equipment isn't available until sometime after the time frame in which you need it, you know you'll need to either make schedule adjustments or find another supplier who can provide the equipment when you need it. The same is true for human resources.

Tools and Techniques for Estimating Activities

Our goal with the Activity Resource Estimating process is to determine the activity resource requirements, including quantity and availability. This process has five tools and techniques to help accomplish this output: expert judgment, alternatives analysis, published estimating data, project management software, and bottom-up estimating. We already know what expert judgment entails, so let's take a look at the remaining tools:

Alternatives analysis   Alternatives analysis is used when thinking about the methods you might use to accomplish the activities your resources have been assigned. Many times, there's more than one way to accomplish an activity, and alternatives analysis helps decide among the possibilities. For example, a subcompact car drives on the same roads a six-figure sports car travels. The sports car has a lot more features than the subcompact, it's faster, it's probably more comfortable, and it has a visual appeal that the subcompact doesn't. The sports car may be the valid resource choice for the project, but there are alternatives you should consider. The same idea applies to human resources in that you might apply senior-level resources versus junior-level or you could add resources to speed up the schedule. You can also consider make-or-buy analysis when determining alternatives.

Published estimating data   Estimating data may include organizational guidelines, industry rates or estimates, production rates, and so on. For example, your organization may have established price agreements with vendors that outline rates by resource type, or there may be industry estimates for production rates for your particular activity.

Project management software   Here we see project management software named as a tool and technique rather than as an organizational asset input. Project management software can help estimate resource needs and document resource availability. It may also produce an RBS, resource rates, calendars, and availability.

Bottom-up estimating   Bottom-up estimating is a process of estimating individual activities or costs and then adding these up together to come up with a total estimate. Here you estimate every schedule activity individually and then roll up that estimate, or add them all together, to come up with a total. This is a very accurate means of estimating provided the estimates at the schedule activity level are accurate. However, it takes a considerable amount of time to perform bottom-up estimating because every activity must be assessed and estimated accurately to be included in the bottom-up calculation. The smaller and more detailed the activity, the greater the accuracy and cost of this technique.

Activity Resource Estimating Outputs

As mentioned, the purpose of the Activity Resource Estimating process is to develop the activity resource requirements output that describes the types of resources and the quantity needed for each schedule activity. Work package estimates are derived from the cumulative total of each schedule activity within the work package. You should also prepare a narrative description for this output that describes how you determined the estimate and the assumptions you made about the resources and their availability.

We'll use the information from this output in the next process (Activity Duration Estimates) to determine the length of time each activity will take to complete. That, of course, depends on the quantity and skill level of the resources assigned, which is the reason we estimate resources before we try to determine duration.

The remaining outputs of this process are activity attribute updates, resource breakdown structure, resource calendar updates, and requested changes. We've covered each of these outputs previously with the exception of resource calendar updates.

Resource calendars look at a particular resource or groups of resources and their skills, abilities, quantity, and availability. Perhaps your project calls for a marketing resource and the person assigned to the marketing activities is on an extended vacation in October. The resource calendar would show this person's vacation schedule. It also shows holidays the company recognizes. Resource calendars also examine the quantity, capability, and availability of equipment and material resources that have a potential to impact the project schedule. For example, suppose your project calls for a hydraulic drill and your organization owns only one. The resource calendar will tell you if it's scheduled for another job at the same time it's needed for your project. The updates portion of this output refer to updating the resource calendar with changes to any of the elements you've recorded here.

You can see how these "Activity" processes have built upon each other. First we defined the activities, then we determined dependencies and sequenced them in the correct order, and next we determined what types and quantities of resources are required to complete the activities. Now we're ready to begin estimating the duration of these activities so that we can plug them into the project schedule.

Estimating Activity Durations

The *Activity Duration Estimating* process attempts to estimate the work effort, resources, and number of work periods needed to complete each schedule activity. The primary output of this process is the *activity duration estimates*. These are quantifiable estimates expressed as the number of work periods needed to complete a schedule activity. Work periods are usually expressed in hours or days. However, larger projects might express duration in weeks or months. Work periods are the activity duration estimates, and they become inputs to the project schedule in a later process.

When you're estimating activity duration, you are estimating the length of time the activity will take to complete, including any elapsed time needed from the beginning to the ending of the activity. For example, let's look at the house-painting project. You estimate that it will take three days, including drying time, to prime the house. Now, let's say priming is scheduled to begin on Saturday, but your crew doesn't work on Sunday. The activity duration in this case is four days, which includes the three days to prime and dry plus the Sunday the crew doesn't work. Most project management software programs will handle this kind of situation automatically.

Progressive elaboration comes into play during this process also. Estimates typically start out at a fairly high level, and as more and more details are known about the deliverables and their associated activities, the estimates become more accurate. You should rely on those folks who have the most knowledge of the activities you're trying to estimate to help you with this process.

Activity Duration Estimating Inputs

The inputs to this process include enterprise environmental factors, organization process assets, project scope statement, activity list, activity attributes, activity resource requirements, resource calendars, and the project management plan including the risk register and activity cost estimates.

A few of the important elements regarding these inputs apply here as we've seen in past processes, including databases, historical information, constraints, and assumptions. The project calendars (considered a part of the organizational process assets) and activity resource requirements are especially useful during this process.

Activity Duration Estimating Tools and Techniques

There are several new tools and techniques in the Activity Duration Estimating process:

- Expert judgment
- Analogous estimating
- Parametric estimating
- Three-point estimates
- Reserve analysis

We'll take a look at each of these tools and techniques next.

Expert Judgment

Activities are most accurately estimated by the staff members who will perform them. In this case, expert judgment is used by team members because of their experience with similar activities in the past. You should be careful with these estimates, though, as they are subject to bias and aren't based on any scientific means. Your experts should consider that resource levels, resource productivity, resource capability, risks, and other factors can impact estimates. It's good practice to combine expert judgment with historical information and use as many experts as you can.

Analogous Estimating aka Top-down Estimating

Analogous estimating, also called *top-down estimating,* is a form of expert judgment. With this technique, you will use the actual duration of a similar activity completed on a previous project to determine the duration of the current activity—provided the information was documented and stored with the project information on the previous project. This technique is most useful when the previous activities you're comparing are similar to the activity you're estimating and don't just appear to be similar. And you want the folks who are working on the estimate to have experience with these activities so they can provide reasonable estimates. This technique is especially helpful when detailed information about the project is not available, such as in the early phases of the project.

Top-down estimating techniques are also used to estimate total project duration, particularly when you have a limited amount of information about the project. The best way to think about top-down techniques is to look at the estimate as a whole. Think about being on a mountaintop where you can see the whole picture as one rather than all the individual items that make up the picture.

For instance, let's go back to the house-painting example. You would compare a previous house-painting project to the current house-painting project, where the houses are of similar size and the paint you're using is the same quality. The first house-painting project can be used to estimate the project duration for the second house-painting project because of the similarities in the project.

Top-down techniques are useful when you're early on in the project Planning processes and are only just beginning to flesh out all the details of the project. Sometimes during the project selection process, the selection committee may want an idea of the project's duration. You can derive a project estimate at this stage by using top-down techniques.

Exam Spotlight

A Guide to the PMBOK states that you can also use analogous estimating to determine overall project duration. *However* (this is the key word), calculating overall project duration is performed during the Schedule Development process, not the Activity Duration Estimating process.

Parametric Estimating

Parametric estimating is a quantitatively based estimating method that multiplies the quantity of work by the rate. The best way to describe it with is with an example. Suppose you are working on a companywide network upgrade project. This requires you to run new cable to the switches on every floor in the building. Parametric estimates can be used to determine activity duration estimates by taking a known element—in this case, the amount of cable needed—and multiplying it by the amount of time it takes to install a unit of cable to come up with an estimate. In other words, suppose you have 10,000 meters of new cable to run. You know from past experience it takes one hour to install 100 meters. Using this measurement, you can determine an estimate for this activity of 100 hours to run the new cable. Therefore, the cable activity duration estimate is 100 hours.

Three-Point Estimates

Three-point estimates, as you can probably guess, use three estimates that are averaged to come up with a final estimate. The three estimates are the most likely, optimistic, and pessimistic. You'll want to rely on experienced folks to give you these estimates. The most likely estimate assumes there are no disasters and the activity can be completed as planned. The optimistic estimate is the fastest time frame in which your resource can complete the activity. And the pessimistic estimate assumes the worst happens and it takes much longer than planned to get the activity completed. These three estimates are averaged to come up with an overall estimate.

 We'll look more closely at this tool and technique later in this chapter in the section "Schedule Development Tools and Techniques."

Reserve Analysis

Reserve time—also called *buffer* or *contingency time* in *A Guide to the PMBOK*— means adding a portion of time to the activity to account for schedule risk. You might choose to add a percentage of time or a set number of work periods to the activity or the overall schedule. For example, you know it will take 100 hours to run new cable based on the quantitative estimate you came up with earlier. You also know that sometimes you hit problem areas when running the cable. To make sure you don't impact the project schedule, you build in a reserve time of 10 percent of your original estimate to account for the problems you might encounter. This brings your activity duration estimate to 110 hours for this activity.

 Real World Scenario

Desert State University (DSU)

DSU has hired a contract agency to create its new registration website. The website will allow students in good academic standing to register for classes over the Internet. You have been appointed the project manager for the DSU side of this project. You'll be working with Henry Lu from Web Sites International to complete this project.

Henry has given you an activity list and asked for time estimates that he can plug into the project plan.

Your first stop is Mike Walter's desk. He's the expert on the mainframe registration system and will be writing the interface programs to accept registration data from the new website. Mike will also create the download that the Internet program will use to verify students' academic standing. Mike has created other programs just like this in the past. His expertise and judgment are very reliable.

The next stop is Kate Langdon. She's the new team leader over the testing group. Kate has been with DSU for only one month. Since she has no experience working with DSU data and staff members, she tells you she'll get back to you within a week with estimates for the testing activities. She plans to read through the project binders of some similar projects and base her estimates against the historical information on similar projects. She'll run the estimates by her lead tester before giving them to you.

You've asked both of your resources to provide you with three-point estimates. Mike Walter's estimates are an example of using the tool and technique of expert judgment to derive activity duration estimates. The estimates expected from Kate Langdon will be derived using historical information (implied by the research she's going to do into past similar projects) and expert judgment because she's involving her lead tester to verify the estimates.

Activity Duration Estimating Outputs

Everything we've talked about up to this point has brought us to the primary output of this process: the activity duration estimates. The inputs and tools and techniques are used to establish these estimates. As mentioned in the opening of this section, activity duration estimates are an estimate of the required work periods needed to complete the activity. This is a quantitative measure usually expressed in hours, weeks, days, or months.

One thing to note about your final estimates as an output to this process is that they should contain a range of possible results. In the cable-running example, you would state the activity duration estimates as "100 hours ± 10 hours" to show that the actual duration will take at least 90 hours and may go as long as 110 hours. Or you could use percentages to express this range.

The other output of Activity Duration Estimating is activity attribute updates. You will update the activity attributes with the duration estimate and the assumptions you used when deriving the estimates.

Now that we have all the activity information in hand, along with a host of other inputs, we're ready to develop the project schedule.

Developing the Project Schedule

The *Schedule Development* process is the heart of the Planning process group. This is where you lay out the schedule for your project activities, determine their start and finish dates, and finalize activity sequences and durations. This process, along with Activity Resource Estimating and Activity Duration Estimating, is repeated several times before you actually come up with the project schedule. The project schedule, once it's approved, serves as the *schedule baseline* for the project that you can track against in later processes.

You'll learn later in this section that project management software comes in very handy during this process. In fact, it is one of the tools and techniques of this process.

Although there are no exam questions regarding the order in which the processes are performed, it might help to understand that Schedule Development cannot be performed until all of the following processes of project Planning are completed: Scope Planning, Scope Definition, Create WBS, Risk Identification, Risk Response Planning, Plan Purchases and Acquisitions, Activity Resource Estimating, Activity Definition, Activity Sequencing, and Activity Duration Estimating.

It's interesting to note that there is a schedule management plan but it isn't created during this process, nor is it an output of this process as other management plans have been. *A Guide to the PMBOK* notes that the schedule management plan (a subsidiary of the project management plan) is produced as part of the Develop Project Management Plan process and contains the criteria for formatting, developing, and controlling the project schedule.

We've got a lot of material to cover in this process. We'll start out with the inputs to the Schedule Development process and then follow up with an in-depth discussion of the tools and techniques of the process. These techniques will help you get to the primary output of this process, which is the project schedule.

Schedule Development Inputs

Schedule Development has nine inputs, seven of which are outputs from other Planning processes. The inputs are as follows:

- Organizational process assets
- Project scope statement
- Activity list
- Activity attributes
- Project schedule network diagrams
- Activity resource requirements
- Resource calendars
- Activity duration estimates
- Project management plan (risk register)

You can see how important it is to perform all of the Planning processes accurately because the information you derive from almost every process in the Planning group is used somewhere else in Planning, many of them here. Your project schedule will reflect the information you know at this point in time. If you have incorrectly estimated activity durations or didn't identify the right dependencies, for example, the inputs to this process will be distorted and your project schedule will not be correct. It's definitely worth the investment of time to correctly plan your project and come up with accurate outputs for each of the Planning processes.

As with several other processes, constraints and assumptions are highlighted as the elements of the project scope statement to pay particular attention to. Constraints are with you throughout the life of the project. The most important constraints to consider in the Schedule Development process are time constraints. According to *A Guide to the PMBOK*, the time constraints in this process fall into two categories: imposed dates and key events or major milestones.

Imposed dates are used to restrict the start or finish date of activities. The two most common constraints used to restrict dates are enforced by most computerized project management software programs. They are "start no earlier than" and "finish no later than" constraints. For example, let's go back to Chapter 6's house-painting example. The painting activity cannot start until the primer has dried. If the primer takes 24 hours to dry and is scheduled to be completed on Wednesday, this implies the painting activity can *start no earlier than* Thursday. This is an example of an imposed date.

Key events or milestones refer to the completion of specific deliverables by a specific date. Stakeholders, customers, or management staff may request that certain deliverables be completed or delivered by specific dates. Once you've agreed to those dates (even if the agreement is only verbal), it's often cast in stone and very difficult to change. These dates, therefore, become constraints.

Be careful of the delivery dates you commit to your stakeholders or customers. You may think you're simply discussing the matter or throwing out ideas, while the stakeholder may take what you've said as fact. Once the stakeholder believes the deliverable or activity will be completed by a specific date, there's almost no convincing them that the date needs changing.

Schedule Development Tools and Techniques

The primary output of Schedule Development is the project schedule. You can employ several tools and techniques in order to produce this output. The tools and techniques you choose will depend on the complexity of the project. For the exam, however, you'll need to know them all.

There are 10 tools and techniques used in Schedule Development:

- Schedule network analysis
- Critical path method
- Schedule compression
- What-if scenario analysis
- Resource leveling
- Critical chain method
- Project management software
- Applying calendars
- Adjusting leads and lags
- Schedule model

A lot of information is packed into some of these tools and techniques, and you should dedicate study time to each of them for the exam. A few of these inputs were discussed earlier but they have new twists in the Schedule Development process so we'll take a look at each of them next.

Schedule Network Analysis

Schedule network analysis produces the project schedule. It involves calculating early and late start dates and early and late finish dates for project activities (as does the critical path method). It uses a schedule model and other analytical techniques such as critical path and critical chain method, what-if analysis, and resource leveling (all of which are other tools and techniques in this process) to help calculate these dates and create the schedule. These calculations are performed without taking resource limitations into consideration, so the dates you end up with are theoretical. What you're attempting to establish at this point is the time periods within which the activities can be scheduled. Resource limitations and other constraints will be taken into consideration when you get to the outputs of this process.

Critical Path Method

Critical path method (CPM) is a schedule network analysis technique. It determines the amount of float, or schedule flexibility, for each of the network paths by calculating the earliest start date, earliest finish date, latest start date, and latest finish date for each activity. This is a schedule network analysis technique that relies on sequential networks (one activity occurs before the next, or a series of activities occurring concurrently are completed before the next series of activities, and so on) and on a single duration estimate for each activity. Keep in mind that CPM is a method to determine schedule durations without regard to resource availability.

The *critical path (CP)* is generally the longest full path on the project. Any project activity with a float time that equals zero is considered a critical path task. The critical path can end under a few conditions. When activities with float time use up all their float, they can become critical path tasks. Or you may have a milestone midway through the project with a finish-no-later-than constraint that can change the critical path if it isn't met.

Float time is also called *slack time,* and you'll see these terms used interchangeably. There are two types of float: total float and free float. *Total float (TF)* is the amount of time you can delay the earliest start of a task without delaying the ending of the project. *Free float (FF)* is the amount of time you can delay the start of a task without delaying the early start of a successor task.

In the following section, you'll calculate the CP for a sample project and illustrate how all the dates, the CP, and the float times are derived.

Gathering Activity and Dependency Information

Let's say you are the project manager for a new software project. The company you are working for is venturing into the movie rental business over the Web. You need to devise a software system that tracks all the information related to rentals and also supplies the management team with reports that will help them make good business decisions. For purposes of illustration, I'm showing only a limited portion of the tasks that you would have on a project like this.

You'll start this example by plugging information from the processes you've already completed into a table (a complete example is shown later in Table 7.1 in the section "Calculating the Critical Path"). The list of activities comes from the Activity Definition process. The durations for each activity are listed in the Duration column and were derived during the Activity Duration Estimating process. The duration times are listed in days.

The Dependency column lists the activities that require a previous activity to finish before the current activity can start. You're using only finish-to-start relationships. For example, you'll see that activity number 2 and activity number 4 each depend on activity 1 to finish before they can begin. The dependency information came from the Activity Sequencing process. Now, you'll proceed to calculating the dates.

Calculating the Forward and Backward Pass

Project Deliverables is the first activity and, obviously, where the project starts. This activity begins on April 1. Project Deliverables has a 12-day duration. So take April 1 and add 12 days to this to come up with an early finish date of April 12. Watch out, because you need to count day one, or April 1, as a full work day. The simplest way to do this calculation is to take the early start date, add the duration, and subtract one. Therefore, the early finish date for the first activity is April 12. By the way, we are ignoring weekends and holidays for this example. Activity 2 depends on activity 1, so it cannot start until activity 1 has finished. Its earliest start date is April 13. Add the duration to this date minus one to come up with the finish date.

You'll notice that activity 4 depends on activity 1 finishing, so its earliest start date is also April 13. Continue to calculate the remaining early start and early finish dates in the same manner. This calculation is called a *forward pass*.

To calculate the late start and late finish dates, you begin with the last activity. The late finish for activity 9 is July 10. Since the duration is only one day, July 10 is also the late start date. You know that activity 8 must finish before activity 9 can begin, so activity 8's late finish date, July 9, is one day prior to activity 9's late start date, July 10. Subtract the duration of activity 8 (three days) from July 9 and add one to get the late start date of July 7. You're performing the opposite calculation that you did for the forward pass. This calculation is called a *backward pass,* as you might have guessed. Continue calculating the late start and late finish through activity 4.

Activity 3 adds a new twist. Here's how it works. Activity 7 cannot begin until activity 3 and activity 6 are completed. No other activity depends on the completion of activity 3. If activity 7's late start date is June 29, activity 3's late finish date must be June 28. June 28 minus eight days plus one gives you a late start date of June 21. Activity 3 depends on activity 2, so activity 2 must be completed prior to beginning activity 3. Calculate these dates just as you did for activities 9 through 4.

Activity 1 still remains. Activity 4 cannot start until activity 1 is completed. If activity 4's late start date is April 13, the late finish date for activity 1 must be April 12. Subtract the duration of activity 1 and add one to come up with a late start date of April 1. Alternatively, the forward pass and backward pass can be calculated by saying the first task starts on day zero and then adding the duration to this. For example, activity number 1's early start date is April 1, which is day zero. Add 12 days to day zero and you come up with an early finish date of April 12.

The calculation for float/slack time is determined by subtracting the early start date from the late start date. If the float time equals zero, the activity is on the critical path.

Calculating the Critical Path

To determine the CP duration of the project, add up the duration of every activity with zero float. You should come up with 101 days because you're adding the duration for all activities except for activity 2 and activity 3. A critical path task is any task that cannot be changed without impacting the project end date. By definition, these are all tasks with zero float.

Another way to determine the critical path is by looking at the network diagram. If the duration is included with the information on the node, or if start and end dates are given, you simply calculate the duration and then add up the duration of the longest path in the diagram to determine the CP. However, this method is not as accurate as what's shown in Table 7.1. Figure 7.1 shows the same project in diagram form. Duration is printed in the top-right corner of each node. Add up the duration of each path to determine which one is the critical path.

Remember that CP is usually the path with the longest duration. In Figure 7.1, path 1-2-3-7-8-9 equals 34 days. Path 1-4-5-6-7-8-9 equals 101 days; therefore, this path is the critical path.

TABLE 7.1 CPM Calculation

Activity Number	Activity Description	Dependency	Duration	Early Start	Early Finish	Late Start	Late Finish	Float/ Slack
1	Project Deliverables	—	12	4/1	4/12	4/1	4/12	0
2	Procure Hardware	1	2	4/13	4/14	6/19	6/20	68
3	Test Hardware	2	8	4/15	4/22	6/21	6/28	68
4	Procure Software Tools	1	10	4/13	4/22	4/13	4/22	0
5	Write Programs	4	45	4/23	6/6	4/23	6/6	0
6	Test and Debug	5	22	6/7	6/28	6/7	6/28	0
7	Install	3, 6	8	6/29	7/6	6/29	7/6	0
8	Training	7	3	7/7	7/9	7/7	7/9	0
9	Acceptance	8	1	7/10	7/10	7/10	7/10	0

Expected Value Using PERT

Program Evaluation and Review Technique (PERT) is a method that isn't discussed in *A Guide to the PMBOK* but you may encounter on the exam. The PERT was developed in the 1950s by the United States Navy. They were working on one of the most complex engineering projects in history at the time—the Polaris Missile Program—and needed a way to manage the project and forecast the project schedule with a high degree of reliability. PERT was developed to do just that.

PERT and CPM are similar techniques. The difference is that CPM uses the most likely duration to determine project duration, while PERT uses what's called expected value (or the weighted average). *Expected value* is calculated using the three-point estimates for activity duration (we talked about three-point estimates earlier in this chapter) and then finding the weighted average of those estimates. If you take this one step further and determine the standard deviation of each activity, you can assign a confidence factor to your project estimates. Without getting too heavily involved in the mathematics of probability, understand that for data that fits a bell curve, which is what you're about to calculate with the PERT technique, the following is true:

- Work will finish within plus or minus three standard deviations 99.73 percent of the time.

- Work will finish within plus or minus two standard deviations 95.44 percent of the time.

- Work will finish within plus or minus one standard deviation 68.26 percent of the time.

FIGURE 7.1   Critical path diagram

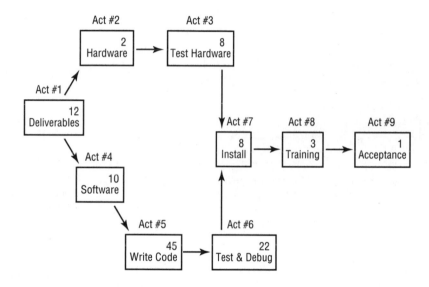

Calculating Expected Value

The three-point estimates used to calculate expected value are the optimistic estimate, the pessimistic estimate, and the most likely estimate. Going back to the software example, let's find out what these three time estimates might look like for the activity called Write Programs. You get these estimates by asking the lead programmer, or key team member, to estimate the optimistic, pessimistic, and most likely duration for the activity based on their past experience. Other historical information could be used to determine these estimates as well. Say in this case that you're given 38 days for the optimistic time, 57 days for the pessimistic, and 45 days for the most likely. (45 days was derived from the Activity Duration Estimating process and is the estimate you used to calculate CPM.)

The formula to calculate expected value is as follows:

(optimistic + pessimistic + (4 × most likely)) ÷ 6

The expected value for the Write Programs activity is as follows:

(38 + 57 + (4 × 45)) ÷ 6 = 45.83

The formula for standard deviation, which helps you determine confidence level, is as follows:

(pessimistic − optimistic) ÷ 6

The standard deviation for your activity is as follows:

(57 − 38) ÷ 6 = 3.17

You could say the following given the information you now have:

- There is a 68.26 percent chance that the Write Programs activity will be completed in 42.66 days to 49 days.

- There is a 95.44 percent chance that the Write Programs activity will be completed in 39.49 days to 52.17 days.

You calculated the range of dates for the 68.26 percent chance by adding and subtracting one standard deviation, 3.17, from the expected value, 45.83. The 95.44 percent chance was calculated by multiplying the standard deviation times 2, which equals 6.34, and adding and subtracting that result from the expected value to come up with the least number of days and the most number of days it will take to finish the activity. Generally speaking, two standard deviations, or 95.44 percent, is a close enough estimate for most purposes.

 The higher the standard deviation is for an activity, the higher the risk. Since standard deviation measures the difference between the pessimistic and the optimistic times, a greater spread between the two, which results in a higher number, indicates a greater risk. Conversely, a low standard deviation means less risk.

Determining Date Ranges for Project Duration

Let's bring your table of activities back and plug in the expected values and the standard deviation for each (please see Table 7.2).

Now let's look at the total project duration using PERT and the standard deviation to determine a range of dates for project duration. You should add only the tasks that are on the critical path. Remember from the CPM example that tasks 2 and 3 are not on the critical path, so their expected value and standard deviation calculations have been left blank in this table. When you add all the remaining tasks, the total expected value duration is 102.99 days, or 103 days rounded to the nearest day.

Your next logical conclusion might be to add the Standard Deviation column to get the standard deviation for the project. Unfortunately, you cannot add up the standard deviations because you will come out with a number that is much too high. Totaling the standard deviations assumes that all of the tasks will run over schedule, and that's not likely. It is likely that a few tasks will run over, but not every one of them. So now you're probably wondering how to calculate the magic number.

You might have noticed an extra column at the right called SD Squared. This is the standard deviation squared—or for those of you with math phobias out there, the standard deviation multiplied by itself.

TABLE 7.2   PERT Calculation

Activity Number	Activity Description	Optimistic	Pessimistic	Most Likely	Expected Value	Standard Deviation	SD Squared
1	Project Deliverables	10	14	12	12.00	0.67	0.45
2	Procure Hardware	—	—	—	—	—	—
3	Test Hardware	—	—	—	—	—	—
4	Procure Software Tools	8	14	10	10.33	1.00	1.0
5	Write Programs	38	57	45	45.83	3.17	10.05
6	Test and Debug	20	30	22	23.00	1.67	2.79
7	Install	5	10	8	7.83	0.83	0.69
8	Training	3	3	3	3.00	0	0
9	Acceptance	1	1	1	1.00	0	0
Totals for CP tasks					**102.99**		**14.98**

Once you have calculated the standard deviation squared for each activity, add up the squares, for a total of 14.98. There's one more step and you're done. Take the square root of 14.98 (you'll need a calculator) to come up with 3.87. This is the standard deviation you will use to determine your range of projected completion dates. Here's a recap of these last few calculations:

Total expected value = 103.00

Sum of SD Squared = 14.98

Square root of SD Squared = 3.87

You can now make the following predictions regarding your project:

- There is a 68.26 percent chance that the project will be completed in 99.13 days to 106.87 days.
- There is a 95.44 percent chance that the project will be completed in 95.26 days to 110.74 days.

Exam Spotlight

For the exam, I recommend that you know that one standard deviation gives you a 68 percent (rounded) probability and two standard deviations gives you a 95 percent (rounded) probability. Also know how to calculate the range of project duration dates based on the expected value and standard deviation calculation. You probably don't need to memorize how to calculate the standard deviation, because I believe most of the questions give you this information. You should, however, memorize the PERT formula and know how it works. It wouldn't hurt to go ahead and memorize the standard deviation formula as well—you never know what might show up on the exam.

PERT is not used very often today. When it is, it's used for very large, highly complex projects. However, PERT is a useful technique to determine project duration when your activity durations are uncertain. It's also useful for calculating the duration for individual tasks in your schedule that may be very complex or risky. You might decide to use PERT for a handful of the activities, those with the highest amount of risk for example, and use other techniques to determine duration for the remaining activities.

Schedule Compression

Schedule compression is a form of mathematical analysis that's used to shorten the project schedule without changing the project scope. Compression is simply shortening the project schedule to accomplish all the activities sooner than estimated.

Schedule compression might happen when the project end date has been predetermined or if after performing the CPM or PERT techniques, you discover that the project is going to take longer than the original promised date. In the CPM example, you calculated the end date to be July 10. What if the project was undertaken and a July 2 date was promised? That's when you'll need to employ one of two duration compression techniques called crashing and fast tracking.

Crashing

Crashing is a compression technique that looks at cost and schedule trade-offs. One of the things you might do to crash the schedule is add resources—from either inside or outside the organization—to the critical path tasks. It wouldn't help you to add resources to noncritical path tasks, as these tasks don't impact the schedule end date anyway because they have float time. You might also limit or reduce the project requirements. Ask stakeholders if the features or functions are "nice to have" or necessary. You might also try changing the sequence of tasks. This sometimes shortens the schedule but isn't always possible.

Fast Tracking

We talked about fast tracking in Chapter 1, "What Is a Project?" *Fast tracking* is starting at the same time two tasks that were previously scheduled to start sequentially. Fast tracking can increase project risk and might cause the project team to have to rework tasks. For example, fast tracking is often performed in object-oriented programming. The programmers might begin writing code on several modules at once, out of sequential order and prior to the completion of the design phase.

Be certain to check the critical path when you've used the crashing technique because crashing might have changed the critical path. Also consider that crashing doesn't always come up with a reasonable result. It often increases the costs of the project as well. The idea with crashing is to try to gain the greatest amount of schedule compression with the least amount of cost.

What-If Scenario Analysis

What-if scenario analysis uses different sets of activity assumptions to produce multiple project durations. For example, what would happen if a major deliverable was delayed or the weather prevents you from completing a deliverable on time? What-if analysis weighs these questions and their assumptions and determines the feasibility of the project schedule under these conditions. Simulation techniques such as Monte Carlo analysis use a range of probable activity durations for each activity, and those ranges are then used to calculate a range of probable duration results for the project itself. Monte Carlo runs the possible activity durations and schedule projections many, many times to come up with the schedule projections and their probability, critical path duration estimates, and float time.

Exam Spotlight

For the exam, remember that Monte Carlo is a simulation technique that shows the probability of all the possible project completion dates.

Exam Spotlight

Resource leveling can cause the original critical path to change.

Resource Leveling

Earlier, I said that CPM and PERT do not consider resource availability. Now that you have a schedule of activities and have determined the critical path, it's time to plug in resources for those activities and adjust the schedule according to any resource constraints you discover.

Resource leveling—also called the *resource-based method*—is used when resources are limited or time constrained (especially those assigned to critical path activities) and when specific schedule dates need to be met.

Remember that you identified resources and resource estimates during the Human Resource Planning and Activity Resource Estimating processes. Now during Schedule Development, resources are assigned to specific activities. Usually, you'll find that your initial schedule has periods of time with more activities than you have resources to work on them. You will also find that it isn't always possible to assign 100 percent of your team members' time to tasks. Sometimes your schedule will show a team member who is overallocated, meaning they're assigned to more work than they can physically perform in the given time period. Other times, they might not be assigned enough work to keep them busy during the time period. This problem is easy to fix. You can assign underallocated resources to multiple tasks to keep them busy.

Resource Assignments

Having overallocated resources is a little more difficult problem to resolve. Resource leveling attempts to smooth out the resource assignments to get tasks completed without overloading the individual while trying to keep the project on schedule. This typically takes the form of allocating resources to critical path tasks first.

There are several ways the project manager can accomplish resource leveling. You might delay the start of a task to match the availability of a key team member. Or you might adjust the resource assignments so that more tasks are given to team members who are underallocated. You could require the resources to work mandatory overtime—that one always goes over well! Perhaps you can split some tasks so that the team member with the pertinent knowledge or skill performs the critical part of the task and the noncritical part of the task is given to a less-skilled team member. All of these methods are forms of resource leveling.

Generally speaking, resource leveling of overallocated team members extends the project end date. If you're under a date constraint, you'll have to go back and rework the schedule after assigning resources to keep the project on track with the committed completion date. This might include moving key resources off of noncritical tasks and assigning them to critical path tasks or adjusting assignments as previously mentioned. Reallocating those team members with slack time to critical path tasks to keep them on schedule is another option. Don't forget, fast tracking is an option to keep the project on schedule also.

Reverse Resource Allocation Scheduling

Reverse resource allocation scheduling is a technique used when key resources—like a thermodynamic expert, for example—are required at a specific point in the project and they are the only resource, or resources, available to perform these activities. This technique requires the resources to be scheduled in reverse order (that is, from the end date of the project rather than the beginning) in order to assign this key resource at the correct time.

Critical Chain Method

Critical chain method is a schedule network analysis technique that accounts for limited or restricted resources when modifying the project schedule. This method typically schedules high risk tasks early in the project so that problems can be identified and addressed right away. It allows for combining several tasks into one task when one resource is assigned to all the tasks.

Critical chain uses both deterministic (step-by-step) and probabilistic approaches. There are a few steps involved in the critical chain process:

- Construct the schedule network diagram using activity duration estimates (you'll use non-conservative estimates in this method).

- Define dependencies.
- Define constraints.
- Calculate critical path.
- Enter resource availability into the schedule.

Often, the critical path will change once you've entered the resource availability. That's because the critical chain method adds non-work activities where needed as duration buffers to help manage the planned activity durations. After the buffers are added, the planned activities are then scheduled at their latest start and finish dates.

Exam Spotlight

CPM manages the total float of schedule networks paths, whereas critical chain manages buffer activity durations and resources.

Project Management Software

Given the examples you've worked through on Schedule Development and resource leveling, you probably already have concluded how much project management software might help you with these processes. Project management software automates the mathematical calculations (like forward and backward pass) and performs resource-leveling functions for you. Obviously, you can then print the schedule that's been produced for final approval and ongoing updates. It's common practice to e-mail updated schedules with project notes so that stakeholders know what activities are completed and which ones remain to be done.

It's beyond the scope of this book to go into all the various software programs available to project managers. Suffice it to say that project management software ranges from the very simple to the very complex. The level of sophistication and the types of project management techniques that you're involved with will determine which software product you should choose. Many project managers that I know have had great success with Microsoft Project software and use it exclusively. It contains a robust set of features and reporting tools that will serve most projects well.

Don't forget that you are the project manager, and your good judgment should never be usurped by the recommendation of a software product. Your finely tuned skills and experience will tell you if relationship issues between team members might cause bigger problems than what the resource-leveling function indicates. Constraints and stakeholder expectations are difficult for a software package to factor in. Rely on your expertise when in doubt. If you don't have the experience yet to make knowledge-based decisions, seek out another project manager or a senior stakeholder, manager, or team member and ask them to confirm if you're on the right track. And a word of caution: don't become so involved with the software that you're managing the software instead of managing the project. Project management software is a wonderful tool, but it is not a substitute for sound project management practices or experience.

🌐 Real World Scenario

Sunny Surgeons, Inc.

Kate Newman is a project manager for Sunny Surgeons, Inc. Sunny Surgeons is a software company that produces software for handheld display devices for the medical profession. The software allows surgeons to keep notes regarding patients, upcoming surgeries, and ideas about new medicines and techniques to research. Kate's latest project is to write an enhanced version of the patient-tracking program with system integration capabilities to a well-known desktop software product used by the medical industry.

There has been some recent turnover in the programming department. Fortunately, Stephen, the senior programmer who led the development effort on the original version of the patient tracker, still works for Sunny. His expertise with handheld technologies as well as his knowledge of the desktop software product make him an invaluable resource for this project.

Kate discovered a problem during the development of the project schedule. Stephen is overallocated for three key activities. Kate decides to see what his take is on the situation before deciding what to do.

Stephen, the eternal optimist programmer who loves his job and does all but sleep in his office at night, says he can easily complete all the activities and that Kate shouldn't give it a second thought. He also suggests to Kate that Karen Wong, a junior programmer on his team who worked on the last project with him, might be able to handle the noncritical path task on her own, with a little direction from Stephen.

Kate thinks better of the idea of overallocating her key project resource, even if he does think he can do the entire thing single-handed. She decides to try some resource leveling to see what that turns up.

Kate discovers that rearranging the order of activities, along with assigning Karen to handle the noncritical path activity, might be a possible solution. However, this scenario lengthens the project by a total of eight days. Since Kate knows the primary constraint on this project is quality, she's fairly sure she can get buy-off from the project sponsor and stakeholders on the later schedule date. She can also sell the resource-leveled schedule as a low-risk option as opposed to assigning Stephen to all the activities and keeping the project end date the same. Overallocating resources can cause burnout and stress-related illnesses, which will ultimately have a negative impact on the project schedule.

Applying Calendars

Calendars are divided into two types: project calendars and resource calendars. *Project calendars* concern all the resources involved in the project and specify the working periods for those resources. For example, if your project work will be completed during normal working hours, the project calendar shows work periods from Monday through Friday between the hours of 8 AM and 5 PM. Project calendars are also a part of the organizational process input for this process.

Resource calendars look at a particular resource or groups of resources and their availability, which were discussed earlier in this chapter. Perhaps your project calls for a marketing resource and the person assigned to the marketing activities is on an extended vacation in October. The resource calendar would show this person's vacation schedule.

Exam Spotlight

Know the difference between project calendars and resource calendars for the exam.

Adjusting Leads and Lags

We talked about leads and lags in Chapter 6. You'll recall that lags delay successor activities and require time added either to the start date or to the finish date of the activity you're scheduling. Leads require time to be subtracted from the start date or the finish date of the activity. Keep in mind that as you go about creating your project schedule, you may need to adjust lead and lag time to come up with a workable schedule.

Schedule Model

Schedule model is a tool that you use to create your project schedule. You can think of this as a template. After you've determined activities, estimates, durations, dependencies, and resources, you use the schedule model in combination with your project management software to create the schedule.

Schedule Development Process Outputs

The Schedule Development process has eight outputs:

- Project schedule
- Schedule model data
- Schedule baseline
- Resource requirement updates
- Activity attributes updates
- Project calendar updates
- Requested changes
- Project management plan updates (updates to the schedule management plan)

We'll take a look at the first three outputs of this process. We've covered all the other outputs previously. Take note that the two primary outputs from this process that will carry forward throughout the rest of the project are the project schedule and the schedule baseline.

Project Schedule

The purpose of the Schedule Development process is to determine the start and finish dates for each of the project activities. One of the primary outputs of this process is the *project schedule*, which details this information as well as the resource assignments. However, depending on the size and complexity of your project or your organization's culture, the resource assignments and start and finish dates may not be completed yet. If that's the case, the project schedule is considered preliminary until the resources are assigned to the activities.

WARNING   In *A Guide to the PMBOK* terms, the project schedule is considered preliminary until resources are assigned. In reality, beware that once you've published the project schedule (even though it's in a preliminary state), some stakeholders may regard this as the actual schedule and expect you to manage to the dates shown. Use caution when publishing schedules in their preliminary form.

The project schedule should be approved and signed off by stakeholders and functional managers. This assures you that they have read the schedule, understand the dates and resource commitments, and will likely cooperate. You'll also need to obtain confirmation that resources will be available as outlined in the schedule when you're working in a functional organization. The schedule cannot be finalized until you receive approval and commitment for the resource assignments outlined in it.

Once the schedule is approved, it will become your baseline for the remainder of the project. Project progress and task completion will be monitored and tracked against the project schedule to determine if the project is on course as planned.

The schedule can be displayed in a variety of ways, some of which are variations on what you've already seen. Project schedule network diagrams, like the ones discussed in Chapter 6, will work as schedule diagrams when you add the start and finish dates to each activity. These diagrams usually show the activity dependencies and critical path. Figure 7.2 shows a sample portion of a project schedule network diagram highlighting the programming activities.

Gantt charts are easy to read and commonly used to display schedule activities. Depending on the software you're using to produce the Gantt chart, it might also show activity sequences, activity start and end dates, resource assignments, activity dependencies, and the critical path. Figure 7.3 is a simple example that plots various activities against time. These activities do not relate to the activities in the tables or other figures shown so far. Gantt charts are also known as *bar charts*.

Milestone charts are another way to depict schedule information. Milestones mark the completion of major deliverables or some other key event in the project. For example, approval and sign-off on project deliverables might be considered a milestone. Other examples might be completion of a prototype, system testing, contract approval, and so on.

Milestone charts might show the key events and their start or completion dates in a bar chart form similar to a Gantt chart. Or they can be written in a simple table format with milestones listed in the rows and expected schedule dates in one column and actual completion dates in another, as in the following example. As the milestones are met, the Actual Date column is filled in. This information can be included with the project status reports.

FIGURE 7.2   Project schedule network diagram with activity dates

FIGURE 7.3   Gantt chart

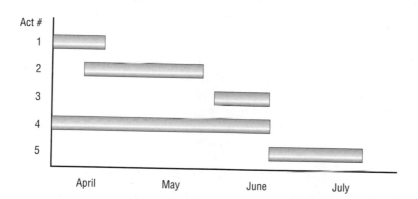

Milestone	Scheduled Date	Actual Date
Sign-off on deliverables	4/12	4/12
Sign-off on hardware test	4/22	4/25
Programming completed	6/06	
Testing completed	6/28	
Acceptance and sign-off	7/10	
Project closeout	7/10	

Schedule Model Data

The schedule model data refers to documenting the supporting data for the schedule. The minimum amount of information in this output includes the milestones, schedule activities and activity attributes, and documenting the assumptions and constraints regarding the schedule. Other information that should be documented but doesn't necessarily fit into the other categories would get documented here. Always err on the side of too much documentation rather than not enough.

You will have to be the judge of what other information to include here, as it will depend on the nature of the project. *A Guide to the PMBOK* suggests that you might include resource histograms. There is an example resource histogram in Chapter 6 if you need to review. Resource histograms typically display hours needed on one axis and period of time (days, weeks, months, years) on the other axis. You might also include alternative schedules or contingency schedule reserves in this section.

Schedule Baseline

I think of the schedule baseline as the final, approved version of the project schedule with baseline start and baseline finish dates and resource assignments. *A Guide to the PMBOK* notes that you derive this baseline from a schedule network analysis of the schedule model.

As I've noted during discussions of some of the other Planning processes, project planning and project management are an iterative process. Rarely is anything cast in cement. You will continue to revisit processes throughout the project to refine and adjust. Eventually, processes do get put to bed. You wouldn't want to come back to the Planning process at the conclusion of the project, for example, but keep in mind that the Planning, Executing, and Monitoring and Controlling process groups are iterative, and it's not unusual to have to revise processes within these process groups as you progress on the project.

In practice for small to medium-sized projects, Activity Definition, Activity Sequencing, Activity Resource Estimating, Activity Duration Estimating, and Schedule Development are easily completed at the same time with the aid of good project management software. Gantt charts, critical path, resource allocation, activity dependencies, what-if analysis, and various reports are easily produced after plugging your scheduling information in to most project management software tools. Regardless of your methods, be certain to obtain sign-off of the project schedule and provide your stakeholders and project sponsor with regular updates. And keep your schedule handy—there will likely be changes and modifications as you go. While you're at it, make certain to save a schedule baseline for comparative purposes. Once you get into the Executing and Monitoring and Controlling processes you'll be able to compare what you planned to do against what actually happened.

Now we're ready to prepare our last planning document, the project budget. First, we'll look at some cost estimating techniques, and then we'll plug those estimates into the project budget.

Cost Estimating

You now have an exhaustive breakdown of project activities, and you have some pretty good duration estimates. Now the question that's forever on the mind of the executive management staff: How much is it going to cost? The purpose of the Cost Estimating process is to answer that question.

Every project has a budget, and part of completing a project successfully is completing it within the approved budget. Sometimes project managers are not responsible for the budget portion of the project. This function is assigned instead to a functional manager who is responsible for tracking and reporting all the project costs. I believe project mangers will have more and more responsibility in this area as the project management discipline evolves. Keep in mind that if you, as the project manager, don't have responsibility for the project budget, your performance evaluation for the project should not include budget or cost measurements.

Before we dive into the Cost Estimating and Cost Budgeting process particulars, you should know that these processes are governed by a cost management plan that is created when you perform the Project Management Plan process. Just like the schedule management plan, the cost management plan isn't developed during these processes and it isn't an output of any of the Cost processes. There are a couple of things you should know about this plan for the exam. Like all the other management plans, it's a subsidiary of the project management plan. According to *A Guide to the PMBOK,* some of the elements of this plan include, but aren't limited to, the following:

- Precision levels, or the rounding you'll use for project costs (hundreds, thousands, and so on)

- Units of measure for resources such has hours for staff resources and hourly rates for contractor staff

- Control account links so that cost estimates for WBS elements can be linked directly to the accounting system

- Variance thresholds for costs

- Earned value rules (We'll talk about this in the tools and techniques section.)

- Reporting formats

- Process descriptions

As with time estimates, the work breakdown structure (WBS) is the key to determining accurate cost estimates. The *Cost Estimating* process develops a cost estimate for the resources (human and material) required for each schedule activity. This includes weighing alternative options and examining trade-offs.

Let's look at an example. Many times software development projects take on a life of their own. The requested project completion dates are unrealistic; however, the project team commits to completing the project on time and on budget anyway. How do they do this? By cutting things like design, analysis, and documentation. In the end, the project might get completed on time and on budget, but was it really? The costs associated with the extended support period due to a lack of design and documentation and the hours needed by the software programmers to fix the reported bugs aren't included in the original cost of the project (but they should have been). Therefore, the costs actually exceed what was budgeted. You should examine trade-offs such as these when determining cost estimates.

When you are determining cost estimates, be certain to include all the costs of the project over its entire life cycle. As in the preceding example, software projects often have warranty periods that guarantee bug fixes or problem resolution within a certain time frame. This is a legitimate cost that should be included in your estimates.

Don't confuse pricing with Cost Estimating. If you are working for a company that performs consulting services on contract, for example, the price you will charge for your services is not the same thing as the costs to perform the project. The costs are centered on the resources needed to produce the product or service of the project. The price your company might charge for the service includes not only these costs, but a profit margin as well.

Cost Estimating Inputs

You are already familiar with all of the Cost Estimating inputs. They are as follows:

- Enterprise environmental factors
- Organizational process assets
- Project scope statement
- WBS
- WBS dictionary
- Project management plan (including the schedule management plan, staffing management plan, and risk register)

As with several other processes we've covered, keep in mind organizational policies (such as cost estimating policies or templates), historical information, previous project files, constraints, and assumptions when deriving your cost estimates.

Cost Estimating Tools and Techniques

Cost Estimating has eight tools and techniques used to derive estimates:

- Analogous estimating
- Determine resource cost rates
- Bottom-up estimating
- Parametric estimating
- Project management software
- Vendor bid analysis

- Reserve analysis
- Cost of quality

We covered analogous, parametric estimating, and reserve analysis techniques in the Activity Duration Estimating section. All of the information talked about there applies here as well, except we're using the tools and techniques to derive cost estimates. And, in the case of reserve analysis, we're adding cost reserves (or contingencies) during this process, not schedule reserves. You could aggregate these cost contingencies and assign them to a schedule activity or work package level. The Project management software is a tool that can help you establish project cost estimates and helps you quickly determine estimates given different variables and alternatives. We talked about cost of quality way back in Chapter 4. We'll look at the remaining techniques next.

Determine Resource Rates

Resource rates are determined a number of ways. Your organization may have a vendor list with published rates that you'll use. These are usually updated once or twice a year. You could request quotes from vendors or do some Internet searching to find rates. Don't forget to include the resource rates of the folks who work within the organization as well. These rates apply to both human resources and materials.

Bottom-Up Estimating

We discussed this technique in the Activity Resource Estimating process. This technique estimates costs associated with every activity individually and then rolls them up to derive a total project estimate. You wouldn't choose this technique to provide a cost estimate for the project during Initiating if one were requested because you don't have enough information at that stage to use the bottom-up technique. Instead, use the top-down estimation technique (analogous estimating) when a project cost estimate is needed early on in the project selection stage.

Vendor Bid Analysis

As the name implies, this is a process of gathering information from vendors to help you establish cost estimates. You can accomplish this by requesting bids or quotes or working with some of your trusted vendor sources for estimates. You should compare vendor bids when using this tool and technique and not rely solely on one vendor to provide you with estimates.

Exam Spotlight

For the exam, make sure you're familiar with all the cost estimating tools and techniques, their benefits, and under what conditions you use them.

Cost Estimating Process Outputs

Obviously, one of the outputs of the Cost Estimating process is the activity cost estimates. These are quantitative amounts—usually stated in monetary units—that reflect the cost of the resources needed to complete the project activities. The tools and techniques we just described help you derive these estimates. Resources in this case include human resources, material, equipment, information technology needs, and so on as well as any contingency reserve amounts and inflation factors (if you're using them).

Activity Cost Estimating supporting detail, requested changes, and cost management plan updates are the remaining Cost Estimating outputs. Supporting detail is just as you've seen in other processes. Any information that supports how the estimates were developed, what assumptions were made during the Cost Estimating process, and any other details you think need to be documented go here. According to *A Guide to the PMBOK*, the supporting detail should include the following:

- A description of the work that was estimated.
- A description of how the estimate was developed or the basis for the estimate.
- A description of the assumptions made about the estimates or the method used to determine them.
- A description of the constraints.
- A range of possible results. Like the time estimates, the cost estimates should be stated within ranges such as "$500 ± $75."

Cost variances will occur and estimates will be refined as you get further into your project. As a result, you'll update cost estimates and ultimately the project budget to reflect these changes.

Cost Estimating uses several techniques to make an accurate assessment of the project costs. In practice, using a combination of techniques is your best bet to come up with the most reliable cost estimates. The activity cost estimates will become an input to the Cost Budgeting process, which allows you to establish a baseline for project costs to track against.

Establishing the Cost Budget Baseline

Our next process concerns determining the cost baseline, which is the primary output of the Cost Budgeting process. The *Cost Budgeting* process aggregates the cost estimates of activities and establishes a cost baseline for the project that is used to measure performance of the project throughout the remaining process groups. Only the costs associated with the project become part of the project budget. For example, future period operating costs are not project costs and therefore aren't included in the project budget.

The *cost baseline* is the expected cost for the project. Remember that costs are tied to the financial system through the chart of accounts—or code of accounts—and are assigned to project activities at the work package level of the WBS.

The budget will be used as a plan for allocating costs to project activities.

Cost Budgeting Inputs

The Schedule Development and Cost Estimating processes must be completed prior to working on Cost Budgeting because some of their outputs become the inputs to this process. The inputs for Cost Budgeting are as follows:

- Project scope statement
- Work breakdown structure
- WBS dictionary
- Activity cost estimates
- Activity cost estimate supporting detail
- Project schedule
- Resource calendars
- Contract
- Cost management plan

We've covered all these inputs before. As usual, don't forget to look at project constraints, particularly funding limitations in this case.

Cost Budgeting Tools and Techniques

There are four tools and techniques in the Cost Budgeting process, including two that we haven't seen before:

- Cost aggregation
- Reserve analysis
- Parametric estimating
- Funding limit reconciliation

Reserve analysis and parametric estimating have been covered previously. Note that reserve analysis in this process also takes into consideration management contingency reserves for unplanned changes to project scope and project costs.

Cost aggregation   Cost aggregation is the process of tallying the schedule activity cost estimates at the work package level and then totaling the work package levels to higher-level WBS component levels (such as the control accounts).

Funding limit reconciliation   Funding limit reconciliation involves reconciling the amount of funds spent with the amount of funds budgeted for the project. These limits are set by the organization or by the customer. Reconciling the project expenses will require adjusting the schedule so that the expenses can be smoothed. This is done by placing imposed date constraints (we talked about these in the Schedule Development process) on work packages or other WBS components in the project schedule.

Cost Budgeting Process Outputs

The goal of Cost Budgeting is to develop a cost baseline (an output of this process) for the project that you can use in the Executing and Monitoring and Controlling processes to measure performance. We now have all of the information we need to create the cost baseline. In addition, we'll establish the project funding requirements.

The following are all of the outputs of the Cost Budgeting process:

- Cost baseline
- Project funding requirements
- Cost management plan updates
- Requested changes

The cost management plan updates and requested changes outputs have been covered previously. We'll look at the cost baseline in the following sections.

Documenting the Cost Baseline

The cost baseline, the first output of Cost Budgeting, is developed by adding up the costs of the WBS elements (remember, these costs were aggregated with the cost aggregation tool and technique) according to time periods. Most projects span some length of time and most organizations time the funding with the project. In other words, you won't get all the funds for the project at the beginning of the project; they'll likely be disbursed over time. The cost baseline provides the basis for measurement, over time, of the expected cash flows (or funding disbursements) against the requirements.

Cost baselines can be displayed graphically, with time increments on one axis and dollars expended on the other axis, as shown in Figure 7.4. The costs shown on this graph are cumulative costs, meaning that what you spent this period is added to what was spent last period and then charted. Many variations of this graph exist showing dollars budgeted against dollars expended to date and so on. Cost budgets can be displayed using this type of graph as well, by plotting the sum of the estimated costs excepted per period.

FIGURE 7.4   Cost baseline

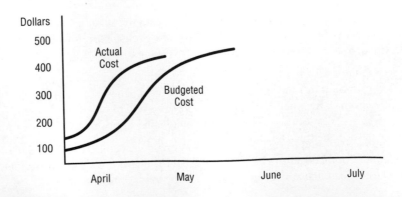

The cost baseline should contain the costs for all of the expected work on the project. You would have identified most of these costs in the Cost Estimating process. You'll find most projects' largest expense is resource costs (as in labor costs). In the case of projects where you're purchasing the final product, the purchase price is the largest cost.

Schedule Development might have uncovered additional activities that need to be added to the budget as well, so don't forget to add them to your budget.

Large projects may have more than one cost baseline. For example, you may be required to track human resource costs, material costs, and contractor costs separately.

The cost baseline should also contain appropriations for risk response. We covered several categories and tools of Risk Response Planning in Chapter 5, "Risk Planning," including avoidance, mitigation, insurance, and contingency plans. Some of the budget should be allocated to each of the techniques that you identified in your risk management plan. Additionally, you'll want to set aside money for contingency reserves. This is for the unforeseen, unplanned risks that may occur. Even with all of the time and effort you spend on planning, unexpected things do crop up. Better to have the money set aside and not need it than to need it and not have it.

We'll revisit the cost baseline when we talk about the Cost Control process and examine different ways to measure costs.

Project Funding Requirements

Project funding requirements (which are also known as the project budget) are the total amount of money spent on the project. They are determined from the cost baseline and may include a management contingency reserve that's used to manage cost overruns, particularly early on in the project. As I said earlier, spending usually starts out slowly on the project and picks up speed as you progress. Sometimes, the expected cash flows don't match the pace of spending. Project funding requirements accounts for this by using a management reserve contingency (usually a margin or percentage of the cost baseline) that's released in increments with the project budget. Figure 7.5 shows the cost baseline, the funding requirements, and the expected cash flows plotted on the S curve. This example shows a negative amount of management reserve because the difference between the funding requirements and the cost baseline at the end of project is the management reserve.

FIGURE 7.5   Cost baseline, funding requirements, and cash flow

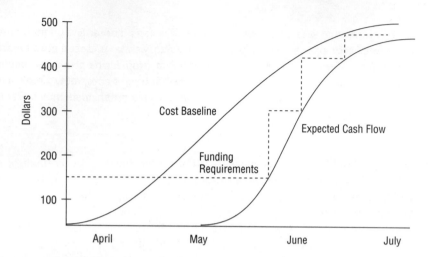

Bringing It All Together

Believe it or not, we have officially completed the Planning process group. Along the way, I've mentioned gaining approvals for portions of the project plan like the schedule and budget.

The *project plan* is the approved, formal, documented plan that's used to guide you throughout the project Executing process group. The plan is made up of all the outputs of the Planning process groups, including the Project Management Plan. It's the map that tells you where you're going and how to perform the activities of the project plan during the Project Plan Execution process. It serves several purposes, the most important of which is tracking and measuring project performance through the Executing and Monitoring and Controlling processes and making future project decisions. The project plan is critical in all communications you'll have from here forward with the stakeholders, management, and customers. The project plan also documents all project planning assumptions, all project planning decisions, and important management reviews needed.

The project plan encompasses everything we've talked about up to now and is represented in a formal document, or collection of documents. This document contains the project scope statement, deliverables, assumptions, risks, WBS, milestones, project schedule, resources, and more. It becomes the baseline you'll use to measure and track progress against. It's also used to help you control the components that tend to stray from the original plan so you can get them back in line.

The project plan is used as a communication and information tool for stakeholders, team members, and the management team. They will use the project plan to review and gauge progress as well.

Exam Spotlight

Performance measurement baselines are management controls that should change only infrequently. Examples of the performance measurement baselines we've looked at so far are Cost Budgeting baselines and schedule baselines. However, the project plan itself also becomes a baseline. If changes in scope or schedule do occur after Planning is complete, there's a formalized process that you should go through to implement the changes, which we'll cover in a Chapter 10, "Monitoring and Controlling Change."

Don't forget that sign-off is an important part of this process. Your last step in the Planning process group is obtaining sign-off of the project plan from stakeholders, the sponsor, and the management team. If they've been an integral part of the Planning processes all along (and I know you know how important this is), obtaining sign-off of the project plan should simply be a formality.

The important thing to note here is that all the management plans we discussed during the Planning processes—the project management plan and its subsidiary plans, including the scope management plan, the schedule management plan and so on, plus the cost budgeting baseline and the schedule baseline—are used throughout the Executing process group to manage the project and keep the performance of the project on track with the project objectives. If you don't have a project plan, you'll have no way of managing the process. You'll find that even with a project plan, project scope has a way of changing. Stakeholders and others tend to sneak in a few of the "Oh, I didn't understand that before" statements and hope that they slide right by you. With that signed, approved project plan in your files, you are allowed to gently remind them that they read and agreed to the project plan and you're sticking to it.

Project Case Study: New Kitchen Heaven Retail Store

The stakeholders provided you with an activity list the last time you met. After creating a complete activity list and the first draft of the project schedule network diagram, you went back to each of them to ask for time and cost estimates for each of the activities. Ricardo's estimates are shown below with the activities he gave you last time:

1. Procure the T1 connection. This takes 30 to 45 days and will have ongoing costs of $300 per month. This can be done concurrently with the other activities listed here. Ricardo will handle this activity.

2. Run Ethernet cable throughout the building. This activity depends on the lease being signed and must finish before the build-out can start. The estimated time to complete is 16 hours, which was figured using parametric estimating techniques. Ricardo has one person on staff who can complete this specialized activity. His first available date is October 5.

3. Purchase the router, switch, server, and rack for the equipment room and four point-of-service terminals. The estimated costs are $17,000. Delivery time is two weeks. Ricardo will do this activity.

4. Install the router and test the connection. Testing depends on the T1 installation at demarcation. The time estimate to install is eight hours. Ricardo's staff will do this activity.

5. Install the switch. Based on past experience, the time estimate to install is two hours. Ricardo's staff will do this activity.

6. Install the server and test. The testing depends on the T1 connection installation. Based on past experience, the time estimate to install is six hours. Ricardo's staff will do this activity.

7. The web team will add the new store location and phone number to the lookup function on the Internet site. The time estimate is eight hours. Ricardo will assign his applications-programming manager to this activity. This activity depends on the lease being signed.

Jake and Jill have each written similar lists with estimates and resource assignments. You begin to align all the activities in sequential order and discover a problem. Jill needs 14 days to hire personnel and stock shelves, meaning that the build-out must be finished by January 16. Build-out takes approximately 120 days and can't start before September 20 due to the contractor's availability. This is a problem because Ricardo's Ethernet cable expert isn't available until October 5, and he needs 2 days to complete the cabling. This pushes out the build-out start date by almost 2 weeks, which means the project completion date, or store-opening date, is delayed by 2 weeks.

After gathering more information from Ricardo, you head to Dirk's office.

"So, Dirk," you conclude after filling him in on all the details, "We have two options. Hire a contractor to perform the cable run since Ricardo's person isn't available, or push the store opening out by two weeks."

Dirk asks, "How much will the contractor charge to run the cable, and are they available within the time frame you need?"

"Yes, they are available, and I've already requested Ricardo book the week of September 18 to hold this option open for us. They've quoted a price of $10,000."

"Okay, let's bring in the contractor. At this point, $10,000 isn't going to break the budget. How is that planning coming anyway? Signed a lease yet?"

"Yes, we've signed the lease. Jake has been meeting with Gomez construction on the build-out. We've used Gomez on three out of the last five new stores and have had good luck with them."

You spend the next couple of days working on the project schedule in Microsoft Project, clarifying tasks and activities with Jake, Ricardo, and Jill. You decide that a Gantt chart will work excellently for reporting status for this project. A portion of your first draft of the Gantt chart shows the following at the end of the project:

You stare intensely at the problem you see on the screen. The Grand Opening task (number 18) is scheduled to occur 13 days later than when you need it! Grand opening must happen February 1 and 2, not February 14 and 15 as the schedule shows. You trace the problem back and see that Grand Opening depends on Train Store Personnel, which itself depends on several other tasks, including Hire Store Personnel and Install and Test Hardware. Digging deeper, build-out can't begin until the Ethernet cable is run throughout the building. Ricardo already set up the time with the contractor to run the cable September 18. This date cannot move, which means build-out cannot start any sooner than September 20, which works with Gomez's availability.

You pick up the phone and dial Jake's number. "Jake," you say into the receiver, "I'm working on the project schedule, and I have some issues with the Gomez activity."

"Shoot," Jake says.

"Gomez Construction can't start work until the Ethernet cable is run. I've already confirmed with Ricardo that there is no negotiation on this. Ricardo is hiring a contractor for this activity, and the earliest they can start is September 18. It takes them two days to run the cable, which puts the start date for build-out at September 20."

"What's the problem with the September 20th date?" Jake asks.

"Jill wants to have the build-out finished prior to hiring the store personnel. During the last store opening, those activities overlapped, and she said it was unmanageable. She wants to hire folks and have them stock the shelves in preparation for store opening but doesn't want contractors in there while they're doing it. A September 20 start date for Gomez puts us at a finish date of January 26, which is too late to give Jill time to hire and stock shelves. My question is this, is 120 days to finish a build-out a firm estimate?"

"Always—I've got this down to a science. Gomez has worked with me on enough of these build-outs that we can come within just a couple of days of this estimate either way," Jake says.

You pick up your schedule detail and continue, "I've scheduled Gomez's resource calendar as you told me originally. Gomez doesn't work Sundays and neither do we. Their holidays are Labor Day, a couple of days at Thanksgiving, Christmas, and New Year's, but this puts us too far out on the schedule. We must have our February 1 opening coincide with the Garden and Home Show dates."

"I can't change the 120 days. Sounds like you have a problem."

"I need to crash the schedule," you say. "What would the chances be of Gomez agreeing to split the build-out tasks? We could hire a second contractor to come in and work alongside Gomez's crew to speed up this task. That would shorten the duration to 100 days, which means we could meet the February 1 date."

"Won't happen. I know Gomez. They're a big outfit and have all their own crews. We typically work with them exclusively. If I brought another contractor into the picture, I might have a hard time negotiating any kind of favors with them later if we get into a bind."

"All right," you say. "How about this? I'm making some changes to the resource calendar while we're talking. What if we authorize Gomez's crew to work six 10-hour days, which still leaves them with Sundays off, and we ask them to work Labor Day and take only one day at Thanksgiving instead of two?"

The detail showing these changes is as follows:

"I think Gomez would go for that. You realize it's going to cost you?"

"Project management is all about trade-offs. We can't move the start date, so chances are the budget might take a hit to accommodate schedule changes or risk. Fortunately, I'm just now wrapping up the final funding requirements, or the cost budget, so if you can get me the increased cost from Gomez soon, I'd appreciate it. This change will keep us on track and resolve Jill's issues too."

"I don't think Gomez's crew will mind the overtime during the holiday season. Everyone can use a little extra cash at that time of year, it seems. I'll have the figures for you in a day or two."

Project Case Study Checklist

Activity Duration Estimating

Activity Resource Estimating

Developing project schedule

- Calendars

- Lead and lag time

- Critical path

Duration compression

- Crashing

Utilizing project management software

Producing project schedule

- Milestones

- Gantt chart

- Resource leveling

Cost estimates

Cost baseline

Finalized project plan

Summary

Great job, you've made it through the entire Planning process group. We covered several processes in this chapter, including Activity Resource Estimating, Activity Duration Estimating, Schedule Development, Cost Estimating, and Cost Budgeting.

The Activity Resource Estimating process considers all the resources needed and the quantity of resources needed to perform project activities. This information is determined for each schedule activity and is documented in the activity resource requirements output.

Duration estimates are produced as a result of the Activity Duration Estimating process. Activity duration estimates document the number of work periods needed for each activity, including their elapsed time. Analogous estimating—also called top-down estimating—is one way to determine activity duration estimates. Top-down techniques can also be used to estimate project durations and total project costs. Parametric estimating techniques multiply a known element—like the quantity of materials needed—by the time it takes to install or complete one unit of materials. The result is a total estimate for the activity. Three-point estimates average the most likely estimate, a pessimistic estimate, and an optimistic estimate. Reserve analysis takes schedule risk into consideration by adding an additional percentage of time or another work period to the estimate just in case you run into trouble.

Schedule Development is the process in which you assign beginning and ending dates to activities and determine their duration. You might use CPM to accomplish this. CPM calculates early start, early finish, late start, and late finish dates. It also determines float time. All tasks with zero float are critical path tasks. The critical path is usually the longest path in the project.

PERT calculates a weighted average estimate for each activity by using the optimistic, pessimistic, and most likely times and then determines variances, or standard deviations, to come up with a total project duration within a given confidence range. Work will finish within plus or minus one standard deviation 68.26 percent of the time. Work will finish within plus or minus two standard deviations 95.44 percent of the time.

Schedules sometimes need to be compressed to meet promised dates or to shorten the schedule times. Crashing looks at cost and schedule trade-offs. Adding resources to critical path tasks and limiting or reducing the project requirements or scope are ways to crash the schedule. Fast tracking involves beginning at the same time two tasks that were originally scheduled to start one after the other. Fast tracking increases project risk.

Monte Carlo analysis can be used in the Schedule Development process to determine multiple, probable project durations.

Resource leveling attempts to smooth out the schedule and properly allocate resources to critical path tasks. This may require updates to the resource management plan.

The project schedule details the activities in graphical form through the use of project schedule network diagrams with dates, Gantt charts, milestone charts, or project schedule network diagrams.

The Cost Estimating process determines how much the project resources will cost and these costs are usually stated in monetary amounts. Analogous estimating is one technique that can be used to determine cost estimates. Another technique is parametric estimating. Bottom-up estimating can be used for project cost estimates. This involves estimating the cost of each schedule activity and then rolling these up to come up with a total work package cost.

The Cost Budgeting baseline will be used throughout the project to measure project expenditures, variance, and project performance. The cost baseline is graphically displayed as an S curve.

Exam Essentials

Be able to name the purpose of the Activity Resource Estimating process.   The purpose of Activity Resource Estimating is to determine the types of resources needed (human, equipment, and materials) and in what quantities for each schedule activity within a work package.

Be able to name the tools and techniques of Activity Duration Estimating.   The tools and techniques of Activity Duration Estimating are expert judgment, analogous estimating, parametric estimating, three-point estimates, and reserve analysis.

Be able to define the difference between analogous estimating and bottom-up estimating.   Analogous estimating is a top-down technique that uses expert judgment and historical information. Bottom-up estimating performs estimates for each work item and rolls them up to a total.

Be able to calculate the critical path.   The critical path includes the activities whose durations add up to the longest full path of the project schedule network diagram. Critical path is calculated using the forward pass, backward pass, and float calculations.

Be able to define a critical path task.   A critical path task is a project activity with zero float.

Be able to describe and calculate PERT duration estimates.   This is a weighted average technique that uses three estimates: optimistic, pessimistic, and most likely. The formula is as follows: (optimistic + pessimistic + (4 × most likely)) ÷ 6.

Be able to name the duration compression techniques.   The duration compression techniques are crashing and fast tracking.

Be able to identify and describe the primary output of the Cost Estimating process.   The primary output of Cost Estimating is activity cost estimates. These estimates are quantitative amounts—usually stated in monetary units—that reflect the cost of the resources needed to complete the project activities.

Be able to describe the cost baseline.   The cost baseline is the expected cost of the project and is used to measure performance. It's displayed as an S curve.

Key Terms

You've learned a lot of new key words in this chapter. PMI has worked hard to develop and define standard project management terms that apply across industries. Here is a list of some of the terms you came across in this chapter:

activity duration estimates	milestone charts
Activity Duration Estimating	parametric estimating
Activity Resource Estimating	Program Evaluation and Review Technique (PERT)
analogous estimating	project calendars
backward pass	project plan
bar charts	project schedule
buffer	reserve time
contingency time	resource calendars
cost baseline	resource leveling
Cost Budgeting	resource-based method
Cost Estimating	resources
Crashing	reverse resource allocation scheduling
critical chain method	schedule baseline
critical path (CP)	schedule compression
critical path method (CPM)	Schedule Development
fast tracking	schedule network analysis
float time	slack time
forward pass	three-point estimates
Gantt charts	top-down estimating

Review Questions

1. You are the project manager for Changing Tides video games. You have gathered the inputs for the Activity Duration Estimating process. Which of the following tools and techniques will you employ to produce the outputs for this process?

   A. Activity list, expert judgment, alternatives analysis, project management software, bottom-up estimating

   B. Activity list, expert judgment, published estimating data, project management software

   C. Expert judgment, alternatives analysis, published estimating data, project management software, bottom-up estimating

   D. Expert judgment, alternatives analysis, published estimating data, bottom-up estimating

2. Your project sponsor has requested a cost estimate for the project you're working on. This project is similar in scope to a project you worked on last year. She would like to get the cost estimates as soon as possible. Accuracy is not her primary concern right now. She needs a ballpark figure by tomorrow. You decide to use _____ .

   A. Analogous estimating techniques

   B. Bottom-up estimating techniques

   C. Parametric modeling techniques

   D. Computerized modeling techniques

3. Your project's primary constraint is quality. In order to make certain the project team members don't feel too pressed for time and to avoid schedule risk, you decide to use which of the following activity estimating tools?

   A. Expert judgment

   B. Quantitatively based durations

   C. Reserve analysis

   D. Analogous estimating

4. You have been hired as a contract project manger for Grapevine Vineyards. Grapevine wants you to design an Internet wine club for their customers. One of the activities for this project is the installation and testing of several new servers. You know from past experience it takes about 16 hours per server to accomplish this task. Since you're installing 10 new servers, you estimate this activity to take 160 hours. Which of the estimating techniques have you used?

   A. Analogous estimating

   B. Bottom-up estimating

   C. Parametric estimating

   D. Reserve analysis

5. Your project sponsor has requested a cost estimate for the project. She would like the cost estimate to be as accurate as possible because this might be her one and only chance to secure the budget for this project due to recent cuts in special projects. You decide to use _____.

   A. Analogous estimating techniques

   B. Bottom-up estimating techniques

   C. Top-down estimating techniques

   D. Expert judgment techniques

6. The project schedule is used to determine all of the following except which one?

   A. Cost estimates

   B. Activity start dates

   C. Float times

   D. Activity end dates

7. You are a project manager for Picture Shades, Inc. It manufactures window shades that have replicas of Renaissance-era paintings on the inside for hotel chains. Picture Shades is taking its product to the home market, and you're managing the new project. It will offer its products at retail stores as well as on its website. You're developing the project schedule for this undertaking and have determined the critical path. Which of the following statements is true?

   A. You calculated the most likely start date and most likely finish dates, float time, and weighted average estimates.

   B. You calculated the activity dependency and the optimistic and pessimistic activity duration estimates.

   C. You calculated the early and late start dates, the early and late finish dates, and float times for all activities.

   D. You calculated the optimistic, pessimistic, and most likely duration times and the float times for all activities.

8. You are a project manager for Picture Shades, Inc. It manufactures window shades that have replicas of Renaissance-era paintings on the inside for hotel chains. Picture Shades is taking its product to the home market, and you're managing the new project. It will offer its products at retail stores as well as on its website. You're developing the project schedule for this undertaking. Looking at the following graph, which path is the critical path?

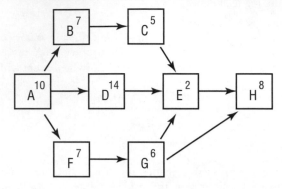

A. A-B-C-E-H

B. A-D-E-H

C. A-F-G-H

D. A-F-G-E-H

9. Use the following graphic to answer this question. If the duration of activity B was changed to 10 days and the duration of activity G was changed to 9 days, which path is the critical path?

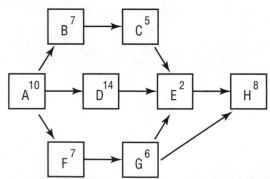

A. A-B-C-E-H

B. A-D-E-H

C. A-F-G-H

D. A-F-G-E-H

10. Which of the following statements is true regarding the critical path?

    A. It should never be compressed.

    B. It allows for looping and branching.

    C. The critical path technique is the same as PERT.

    D. It's the duration of all tasks with zero float.

11. You are a project manager for Move It Now trucking company. Your company specializes in moving household goods across the city or across the country. Your project involves upgrading the nationwide computer network for the company. Your lead engineer has given you the following estimates for a critical path activity: 60 days most likely, 72 days pessimistic, 48 days optimistic. What is the weighted average or expected value?

    A. 54

    B. 66

    C. 60

    D. 30

12. You are a project manager for Move It Now trucking company. Your company specializes in moving household goods across the city or across the country. Your project involves upgrading the nationwide computer network for the company. Your lead engineer has given you the following estimates for a critical path activity: 60 days most likely, 72 days pessimistic, 48 days optimistic. What is the standard deviation?

    A. 22

    B. 20

    C. 2

    D. 4

13. If you know expected value is 500 and the standard deviation is 12, you can say with approximately a 95 percent confidence rating which of the following?

    A. The activity will take from 488 to 512 days.

    B. The activity will take from 464 to 536 days.

    C. The activity will take from 494 to 506 days.

    D. The activity will take from 476 to 524 days.

14. If your expected value is 110 and the standard deviation is 12, which of the following is true?

    A. There is approximately a 99 percent chance of completing this activity in 86 to 134 days.

    B. There is approximately a 68 percent chance of completing this activity in 98 to 122 days.

    C. There is approximately a 95 percent chance of completing this activity in 98 to 122 days.

    D. There is approximately a 75 percent chance of completing this activity in 86 to 134 days.

15. You are the project manager working on a research project for a new drug treatment. Your preliminary project schedule runs past the due date for a federal grant application. The manager of the R&D department has agreed to release two resources to work on your project in order to meet the federal grant application date. This is an example of _____ .

   A. Crashing

   B. Fast tracking

   C. Resource leveling

   D. Adjusting the resource calendar

16. You are the project manager for Rivera Gourmet Adventure Vacations. Rivera combines the wonderful tastes of great gourmet food with outdoor adventure activities. Your project involves installing a new human resources software system. Jason, the database analyst working on this project, is overallocated. Which of the following statements is true?

   A. You should use resource requirements updates to determine availability and smooth out resource overallocation.

   B. You should use crashing to resource-level the critical path tasks.

   C. You should use resource leveling to smooth out resource assignments.

   D. You should use fast tracking to resource-level the critical path tasks.

17. What is one of the problems with project management software?

   A. The project manager manages the software instead of the project.

   B. Project duration calculations are sometimes approximate.

   C. You cannot override the project management software decisions regarding schedules.

   D. It's expensive and difficult to use.

18. Obtaining formal project plan approval and sign-off is important for all of the following reasons except which one?

   A. Stakeholders are able to recommend a project Planning methodology to follow throughout the remaining process groups.

   B. Stakeholders are aware of the project details, which makes them more likely to participate in future project decisions.

   C. Stakeholders will be more likely to cooperate.

   D. Stakeholders are aware of the specific details regarding project schedules, budgets, and risks.

19. You are the project manager for a custom home-building construction company. You are working on the model home project for the upcoming Show Homes Tour. The model home includes Internet connections in every room and talking appliances. You are working on the cost budget for this project. All of the following statements are true except which one?

A. This process assigns cost estimates to project activities, including risks and contingency plans.

B. The cost baseline will be used to measure variances and future project performance.

C. This process assigns cost estimates for expected future period operating costs.

D. The cost baseline is the expected cost for the project.

20. Which of the following is displayed as an S curve?

A. Gantt

B. Cost baseline

C. Critical path

D. Schedule baseline

Answers to Review Questions

1. C. The tools and techniques for Activity Duration Estimating are expert judgment, alternatives analysis, published estimating data, project management software, bottom-up estimating.

2. A. Analogous—or top-down—estimating techniques are a form of expert judgment. Since this project is similar to another recent project, you can use the cost estimates from the previous project to help you quickly determine estimates for the current project.

3. C. Reserve analysis takes schedule risk into consideration and adds a percentage of time or additional work periods to the estimate to prevent schedule delays.

4. C. Parametric estimating multiplies a known element—like the quantity of materials needed—by the time it takes to install or complete one unit of materials. The result is a total estimate for the activity. In this case, 10 servers multiplied by 16 hours per server gives you a 160-hour total duration estimate.

5. B. Bottom-up techniques are the most time-consuming and the most accurate estimates you can use. With bottom-up estimating, each work item is estimated and rolled up to a project total.

6. A. The project schedule determines the start and ending dates of activities, determines float times, generally shows resource assignments, and details the activity sequences and durations.

7. C. The CPM calculates a single early and late start date and a single early and late finish date for each activity. Once these dates are known, float time is calculated for each activity to determine the critical path. The other answers contain elements of PERT calculations.

8. B. The only information you have for this example is activity duration, therefore the critical path is the path with the longest duration. Path A-D-E-H with a duration of 34 days is the critical path.

9. D. The only information you have for this example is activity duration, so you must calculate the critical path based on the durations given. The duration of A-B-C-E-H increased by 3 days for a total of 35 days. The duration of A-F-G-H and A-F-G-E-H each increased by 3 days. A-F-G-E-H totals 36 days and becomes the new critical path.

10. D. The critical path is calculated by adding together the durations of all the tasks with zero float. The critical path can be compressed using crashing techniques.

11. C. The calculation for PERT is the sum of optimistic time plus pessimistic time plus four times the most likely time divided by 6. The calculation for this example is as follows: $(48 + 72 + (4 \times 60)) \div 6 = 60$.

12. D. The standard deviation is calculated by subtracting the optimistic time from the pessimistic time and dividing the result by 6. The calculation for this example is as follows: $(72 - 48) \div 6 = 4$.

13. D. There is a 95 percent probability that the work will finish within plus or minus two standard deviations. The expected value is 500, and the standard deviation times 2 is 24, so the activity will take from 476 to 524 days.

14. B. A 68 percent probability is calculated using plus or minus one standard deviation, a 95 percent probability uses plus or minus two standard deviations, and a 99 percent probability uses plus or minus three standard deviations.

15. A. Crashing the schedule includes things like adding resources to the critical path tasks or limiting project requirements.

16. C. Resource leveling attempts to smooth out resource assignments by splitting tasks, assigning underallocated team members to more tasks, or delaying the start of tasks to match team members' availability.

17. A. Project management software is a very useful tool for the project manager, and it automates project scheduling, allowing for what-if analysis and easy changes. But if you focus too much on the tool and ignore the project, the tool becomes a hindrance.

18. A. Stakeholders ordinarily will not have much say in the project Planning methodology used by the project manager. The methodology employed is usually determined by the organization, the project office, or the project manager.

19. C. Future period operating costs are considered ongoing costs and are not part of project costs.

20. B. The cost baseline is displayed as an S curve because of the way project spending occurs. Spending begins slowly, picks up speed until the spending peak is reached, and then tapers off as the project winds down.

Developing the Project Team

THE PMP EXAM CONTENT FROM THE EXECUTING THE PROJECT PERFORMANCE DOMAIN COVERED IN THIS CHAPTER INCLUDES THE FOLLOWING:

- ✓ **Execute Tasks Defined in Project Plan**
- ✓ **Ensure Common Understanding and Set Expectations**
- ✓ **Implement the Procurement of Project Resources**
- ✓ **Manage Resource Allocation**
- ✓ **Improve Team Performance**

This chapter begins the project Executing process group. We'll cover four of the processes in this chapter: Direct and Manage Project Execution, Acquire Project Team, Develop Project Team, and Distributing Information. We'll jump around a bit in this chapter as you can tell from the processes we'll cover. Many of these processes are extensions, so to speak, of the Planning processes leading up to them. We'll cover the remaining Executing processes in the next chapter.

Direct and Manage Project Execution is the action process. This is where you'll put the plans into action and begin working on the project activities. Execution also involves keeping the project in line with the original project plan and bringing wayward activities back into alignment.

Several things happen during the Executing processes. The majority of the project budget will be spent during this process group, and often the majority of the project time is expended here as well. The greatest conflicts you'll see during the project Executing processes are schedule conflicts. In addition, the product description will be finalized here and contain more detail than it did in the Planning processes.

Hang with me during this chapter, because there are several references to the next process—the Monitoring and Controlling process group—that are inputs to the Executing process group. These are the only two process groups that serve as inputs to each other. Since we can't discuss both of them at the same time, we'll tell you when there's something specific from the Monitoring and Controlling process group that will be discussed in a later chapter.

There might be several exam questions from every process within the Executing process group. You'll find the majority of questions are about the Direct and Manage Project Execution, the Acquire Project Team, and Develop Project Team processes. Don't skip studying the other processes, however, as roughly a quarter of the exam questions concern the entire Executing process group. Are you ready to dive into Executing? Let's go.

Executing the Project Plan

The purpose of the *Direct and Manage Project Execution* process is to carry out the project plan. This is where your project comes to life and the work of the project happens. The work is authorized to begin and activities are performed. Resources are committed and carry out their assigned activities to create the product or service of the project. Funds are spent to accomplish project objectives. Performing project activities, training, selecting sellers, collecting project data, utilizing resources, and so on are all integrated with or a part of this process.

Direct and Manage Project Execution is where the rubber meets the road. If you've done a good job planning the project, things should go relatively smoothly for you during this process.

The deliverables and requirements are agreed to, the resources have been identified and are ready to go, and the stakeholders know exactly where you're headed because you had them review, agree to, and approve the project plan.

Some project managers think this is the time for them to kick back and put their feet up. After all, the project plan is done, everyone knows what to do and what's expected of them, and the work of the project should almost carry itself out because your project plan is a work of genius, right? Wrong! You must stay involved. Your job now is a matter of overseeing the actual work, staying on top of issues and problems, and keeping the work lined up with the project plan.

Exam Spotlight

The project plan serves as the project baseline. During the Executing processes, you should continually compare and monitor project performance against the baseline so that corrective actions can be taken and implemented at the right time to prevent disaster. This information will also be fed into the Monitoring and Controlling processes for further analysis.

One of the most difficult aspects of this process is coordinating and integrating all the elements of the project. While you do have the project plan as your guide, there are still a lot of balls in the air. You'll find yourself coordinating and monitoring many project elements—occasionally all at the same time—during the course of the Direct and Manage Project Execution process. You may be negotiating for team members at the same time you're negotiating with vendors at the same time you're working with another manager to get a project component completed so your deliverable stays on schedule. Risks and risk triggers should be monitored closely. The Plan Purchases and Acquisitions process may need intervention or cause you delays. The organizational, technical, and interpersonal interfaces may require intense coordination and oversight. And of course, you should always be concerned about the pulse of your stakeholders. Are they actively involved in the project? Are they throwing up roadblocks now that the work has started?

According to *A Guide to the PMBOK,* this process also requires implementing corrective actions to bring the work of the project back into alignment with the project plan, preventive actions to reduce the probability of negative consequences, and defect repairs to correct product defects discovered during the quality processes.

As you can see, your work as project manager is not done yet. There are many elements to the project that require your attention, so let's get to work.

 Later in this chapter we'll also talk about Develop Project Team because this is an integral part of the Direct and Manage Project Execution process as well. You'll want to monitor the team's performance, the status of their work, and their interactions with you and other team members as you execute the project plan.

Executing Inputs

Direct and Manage Project Execution has seven inputs:

- Project management plan
- Approved corrective actions
- Approved preventive actions
- Approved change requests
- Approved defect repair
- Validated defect repair
- Administrative closure procedure

The project management plan documents the collection of outputs of the Planning processes and describes and defines how the project should be executed, monitored, controlled, and closed. We'll take a brief look at each of the other inputs next.

Approved Corrective Actions

In my organization, a corrective action means an employee has big trouble coming. Fortunately, this isn't what's meant here. *Corrective actions* are taken to get the anticipated future project outcomes to align with the project plan. Maybe you've discovered that one of your programmers is adding an unplanned feature to the software project because he's friends with the user. You'll have to redirect him to the activities assigned to him originally to avoid schedule delays. Perhaps your vendor isn't able to deliver the laboratory equipment needed for the next project phase. You'll want to exercise your contract options (hopefully there's a clause in the contract that says they must provide rental equipment until they can deliver your order), put your contingency plan into place, and get the lab the equipment that's needed to keep the project on schedule.

Corrective actions are outputs of processes in the Monitoring and Controlling process group, but they serve as inputs to the Direct and Manage Project Execution process. We'll talk more about corrective actions in Chapter 10, "Monitoring and Controlling Change."

Approved Preventive Action

Preventive action involves anything that will reduce the potential impacts of risk events should they occur. Contingency plans and risk responses are examples of preventive action. These and other risk responses are described in the Risk Response Planning process discussed in Chapter 5, "Risk Planning." You should be aware of contingency plans and risk responses so that you're ready to implement them at the first sign of trouble. Approved preventive actions are an output of processes in the Monitoring and Controlling process group.

Approved Change Requests

Approved change requests, another output of the Monitoring and Controlling process group, are changes that either expand or reduce project scope. Approved changes may also cause revisions to project budgets, schedules, procedures, project management plans, and so on. Change requests can be internal or external to the project or organization. For example, a new law that's passed that affects your project may require changes.

Approved Defect Repairs

Okay, it's your turn to figure it out: Defect repairs are an output of what process? Approved defect repairs authorize corrections to product defects that are discovered during the Perform Quality Assurance process (primarily during product inspection or during quality audits). Approved defect repairs are an output of the Integrated Change Control process.

Validated Defect Repair

The difference between a validated defect repair and a defect repair is that the validated defect repair is the result of a reinspection of the original defect repair. In other words, you found a problem with the product during the Quality processes, you corrected the problem (defect repair), and now you're reinspecting that repair (validated defect repair) to make certain the fix is accurate, correct, and fixed the problem.

Administrative Closure Procedure

The *administrative closure procedure* is a document that outlines how administrative closure will occur on the project, the activities needed to perform this procedure, and the essential roles and responsibilities.

Exam Spotlight

For the exam, remember that the outputs of the Executing and Monitoring and Controlling process groups are also inputs to each other.

Tools and Techniques of Direct and Manage Project Execution

The tools and techniques of the Direct and Manage Project Execution process are project management methodology and project management information system. We've looked at both of these before. Remember that in the Executing processes, you'll be actively using both of these tools (employing the methodology you've developed in Planning and referring to the PMIS to update and track progress).

A curious thing happens here. While *A Guide to the PMBOK* no longer lists work authorization systems as a tool and technique of the Direct and Manage Project Execution process, it's still listed in its glossary as a tool. That's curious because it's also part of the enterprise environmental factors input. Even though this isn't listed in *A Guide to the PMBOK,* I recommend understanding what a work authorization system is for the exam and how you use it. And for the record, you'll use these during the Executing processes.

Work authorization systems clarify and initiate the work of each work package or activity. This is a formal procedure that authorizes work to begin in the correct sequence and at the right time. Work authorization systems are usually written procedures defined by the organization. They might include e-mail, intranet-based, or paper-based systems. Verbal instructions may work well with small projects. Understand the complexity of the project and balance the cost of instituting a work authorization system against the benefit you'll receive from it. This may be overkill on small projects, and as stated earlier, verbal instructions might work just as well.

Work is usually authorized using a form that describes the task, the responsible party, anticipated start and end dates, special instructions, and whatever else is particular to the activity or project. Depending on the organizational structure, the work is assigned and authorized by either the project manager or the functional manager.

Some of the outputs of this process are going to look familiar. Let's examine them next.

Outputs of Direct and Manage Project Execution

Most of the outputs of the Planning process group, and some of the outputs of the Monitoring and Controlling process group, are utilized by the Direct and Manage Project Execution process. The outputs of the Direct and Manage Project Execution process are as follows:

- Deliverables
- Requested changes
- Implemented change requests
- Implemented corrective actions
- Implemented preventive actions
- Implemented defect repairs
- Work performance information

The two primary outputs are deliverables, meaning actually accomplishing the activities leading to completion of the product or service you set out to produce, and work performance information. Without having completed the prior processes, you wouldn't know what the work of the project should look like.

The outputs starting with *implemented* were covered in the tools and techniques section. The only difference between the tools and techniques and the output is that during the output, the action or request is implemented. Because I haven't mentioned it in a while, now's a good time for a documentation reminder—it's not a bad idea to record all of the approved and implemented actions for future reference. Let's take a look at the other three outputs.

Deliverables

During Direct and Manage Project Execution, you'll gather and record information regarding the outcomes of the work, including activity completion dates, milestone completions, the status of the deliverables, the quality of the deliverables, costs, schedule progress and updates, and so on. Deliverables aren't always tangible. For example, perhaps your team members require training on a piece of specialized equipment. Completion of the training is recorded as a work result. Capabilities required to perform a service that's described in the project management plan are also considered a deliverable. All of this information gets used during the Performance Reporting process, which we'll discuss during the Monitoring and Controlling processes.

Executing and Monitoring and Controlling are two process groups that work hand in hand. As you gather the information from work results, you'll measure the outputs and take corrective actions where necessary. This means you'll loop back through the Executing processes to put the corrections into place. *A Guide to the PMBOK* breaks these processes up for ease of explanation, but in practice, you'll work through several of the Executing and Monitoring and Controlling processes together.

Requested Changes

As a result of working through activities and producing your product or service, you will inevitably come upon things that need to be changed. This might encompass schedule changes, scope changes, or requirements or resource changes. The list really could go on. Your job as project manager, if you choose to accept it, is to collect the change requests and make determinations about their impact to the project.

We'll discuss change requests in the coming chapters. Requested changes are an output of several process, including the Direct and Manage Project Execution process and the Performance Reporting process in the Monitoring and Controlling process group. Remember that Executing and Monitoring and Controlling outputs feed each other as inputs.

Exam Spotlight

Direct and Manage Project Execution is where the work of the project is performed and the project plan is put into action and carried out. In this process, the project manager is like an orchestra conductor signaling the instruments to begin their activities, monitoring what should be winding down, and keeping that smile going to remind everyone that they should be enjoying themselves. I recommend that you know the outputs of the Direct and Manage Project Execution process for the exam.

Work Performance Information

Work performance information concerns gathering, documenting, and recording the status of project activities. According to *A Guide to the PMBOK,* these are the types of information you might gather during this process:

- Schedule status and progress

- Status of deliverable completion

- Progress and status of schedule activities

- Adherence to quality standards

- Status of costs (those authorized and costs incurred to date)

- Schedule activity completion estimates for those activities started

- Schedule activities percent complete

- Lessons learned

- Resource consumption and utilization

Work performance information becomes an input to a few of the Monitoring and Controlling processes where you'll perform further analysis on the data. It's important that you document this information so that when you get to the Monitoring and Controlling processes, you don't have to backtrack.

We're going to switch topics now. I told you the Executing process group is about performing the work of the project, and in order to do that, we need resources. We'll look at two processes, Acquire the Project Team and Develop the Project Team, in the next few sections.

Acquiring the Project Team

The *Acquire Project Team* process involves attaining and assigning human resources to the project. Project staff may come from inside the company or from outside the company in the form of full-time employees hired specifically for the project or as contract help. In any case, it's your job as the project manager to ensure that resources are available and skilled in the project activities they're assigned to. However, in practice you may find that you don't always have control over the selection of team members. Someone else, the big boss for example, may hand-pick the folks they want working on the project and it's up to you to assess their skills and decide where they best fit on the project.

The Acquire Project Team process inputs are as follows: enterprise environmental factors, organizational process assets, roles and responsibilities, project organization charts, and staffing management plan.

Some project activities may require special skills or knowledge in order to be completed. The enterprise environmental factors input involves taking this information into account as well as considering personal interests, characteristics, and availability of potential team members before making assignments. For example, consider the previous experience of the staff member you're thinking of assigning to a specific activity. Have they performed this function before? Do they have the experience necessary for the level of complexity this project activity calls for? Are they competent and proficient at these skills?

Personal interests and personal characteristics play a big role as well. If the person you're thinking of just isn't interested in the project, they aren't likely to perform at their best. If you can, think about assigning someone else in a case like this. Unfortunately, some people just don't play well with others. When you're assigning staff, if at all possible, don't put the only two people in the whole company who can't get along together on the same project. If the staff member you need has a skill no one else has or they can perform a function like no one else can, you might not have a choice. In this case, you'll have to employ other techniques to keep the team cohesive and working well together despite the not-so-friendly characteristics of the vital team member.

One final consideration: Check on the availability of key team members. If the team member you must have for the activity scheduled in February is on their honeymoon, you probably aren't going to win the toss.

Exam Spotlight

Even though the availability, experience levels, interests, cost, and abilities of your resources are considered part of the enterprise environmental factors input, you should understand these inputs and their importance to the Acquire Project Team process for the exam.

Recruitment practices are an example of the organizational process assets to watch for in this process. This is a matter of making certain you consult any organizational procedures or policies currently in place when hiring and assigning staff. Organizational policies that dictate recruitment practices are constraints.

We've looked at the other inputs in previous processes, so we'll move on to the tools and techniques of this process.

Tools and Techniques of Acquire Project Team

Preassignment, negotiation, acquisitions, and virtual teams are tools and techniques of the Acquire Project Team process. As the project manager, you will use the negotiation technique a lot. You'll have to negotiate with functional managers and other organizational department managers—and sometimes with the vendor to get some of their best people—for resources for your project and for the timing of those resources.

Preassignment can happen when the project is put out for bid and specific team members are promised as part of the proposal or when internal project team members are promised and assigned as a condition of the project. When staff members are promised as part of the project proposal—particularly on internal projects—they should be identified in the project charter.

Availability is one part of the negotiating equation. You'll have to work with the functional manager or other project managers to ensure that the staff member you're requesting is available when the schedule says they're needed.

The second part of the equation is the competency level of the staff member they're assigning to your project. I remember hearing someone say once that availability is not a skill set. Be wary of functional managers who are willing to offer up certain individuals "anytime" while others are "never available." Be certain your negotiations include discussions about the skills and personal characteristics of the team members you're asking for.

Acquisition is another tool and technique of the Acquire Project Team process. It involves hiring individuals or teams of people for certain project activities, either as full-time employees or as contract help during the course of the project or project phase or for specific project activities. Procurement is usually required when the organization does not have employees with the required skills and competencies available to work on the project.

Chapter 6, "Resource Planning," covers the Plan Purchases and Acquisitions process in more detail.

Virtual teams are teams that don't necessarily work in the same location but all share the goals of the project and have a role on the project. This type of team allows you to include folks from different geographic locations, those who work different hours or shifts than the other team members, those with mobility limitations, and so on. According to *A Guide to the PMBOK*, "Virtual teams can be defined as groups of people with a shared goal, who fulfill their roles with little or no time spent meeting face to face." In today's wonderful world of technology, team members can use the Internet, e-mail, videoconferencing, and teleconferencing to meet and communicate on a regular basis. This of course brings to light the importance of communication. Make certain all team members are aware of the protocols for communicating in a virtual team environment, understand the expectations, and are clear regarding decision making processes. It's vital in this type of team structure that you as the project manager give credit to the appropriate team members for their performance and actions on the project.

Outputs of Acquire Project Team

The resulting outputs of the Acquire Project Team process are project staff assignment, resource availability, and staffing management plan updates.

Your ability to influence the selection of resources (using the negotiating technique) will impact the project staff assignment output. After determining elements like the roles and responsibilities, reviewing recruitment practices, and negotiating for staff, you assign project team members to project activities. Along with this output, a project team directory is published listing the names of all project team members and stakeholders. Don't forget to also include team member names in project organization charts, RAM charts, and other planning documents if their assignments or names weren't known when you created those documents.

🌐 Real World Scenario

The Only Candidate

"Hey, did you hear?" your friend Story asks. "Roger has been assigned to the project team."

"Over my dead body," you reply, pushing away from your computer screen. You head straight for the project manager's office and don't wait for a response from Story.

Ann seats the phone into the cradle just as you walk through the door. Fortunately for you, Ann's door is always open and she welcomes drop-ins.

"Seems like something is on your mind," Ann says. "What can I help with?"

"Story just told me that Roger has been assigned to the project team. I can't work with Roger. He's arrogant and doesn't respect anyone's work but his own. He belittles me in front of others, and I don't deserve that. I write good code copy, and I don't need Roger looking over my shoulder. I want to be on this team, but not if Roger is part of it."

Ann thinks for a minute and replies, "I want you to have the opportunity to work on this project; it's a great opportunity for you. But there isn't anyone else who can work on the analysis phase of this project except Roger. He's the only one left who has a solid understanding of the mainframe legacy code. Unfortunately, those old programs were never documented well, and they've evolved over the years into programs on top of programs. Without Roger's knowledge of the existing system, we'd blow the budget and time estimates already established for this project. What would you say to a meeting with you and Roger and me to talk about these issues and see if we can't work this out?"

The time periods your project staff are available are documented in the resource availability output. This document comes in handy when you're creating the final schedule and assigning resources to activities.

The *staffing management plan* may require updates to document the project roles and responsibilities of the staff assigned to the project. This document may require updates throughout the project if you have staff members leave due to promotion or, heaven forbid, if they leave for employment in another company (unless you want them to leave—that's another story).

Now we have the team, what do we do with them? We'll look at topics like motivation, rewards, and recognition in the next process, Develop Project Team.

Developing the Project Team

Projects exist to create a unique product or service within a limited time frame. Projects are performed by people, and most projects require more than one person to perform all of the activities.

If you've got more than one person working on your project, you've got a team. And if you've got a team, you've got a wide assortment of personalities, skills, needs, and issues in the mix. Couple this with part-time team members, teams based in functional organizations whose loyalty lies with the functional manager, or teams based in matrix organizations that report to you for project-related activities and another manager for their functional duties and you could have some real challenges on your hands. Good luck—okay, I won't leave you hanging like that.

The *Develop Project Team* process is about creating an open, encouraging environment for your team and developing it into an effective, functioning, coordinated group. Projects are performed by individuals, and the better they work together, the smoother and the more efficient the execution of the project will be. I'm sure you all have had the experience of working with a team that pitched in and shared workloads when the work became unbalanced. I'm also sure you all have worked with teams that didn't do this, teams whose members took on a "me first" attitude and could care less about the plight of their fellow team members. I'd much rather work with a team like the first example.

Proper development of the team is critical to a successful project. Since teams are made up of individuals, individual development becomes a critical factor to project success. Individual team members need the proper development and training to perform the activities of the project or to enhance their existing knowledge and skills. The development needed will depend on the project. Perhaps you have a team member who's ready to make the jump into a lead role but they don't have any experience at lead work. Give them some exposure by assigning them a limited amount of activities in a lead capacity, provide them with some training if needed, and be available to coach and mentor where needed. The best option is to work with the management team to provide this person with the development they need prior to the start of the project (if you're lucky enough to know that early on who your resources might be and what their existing skills are).

Develop Project Team inputs include project staff assignments, staffing management plan, and resource availability. Funny thing, these inputs are all outputs that we discussed in the Acquire Project Team process, so we'll move on.

Tools and Techniques for Develop Project Team

The tools and techniques of Develop Project Team are as follows:

- General management skills
- Training
- Team building activities
- Ground rules
- Collocation
- Recognition and rewards

We'll cover all these tools and techniques next.

General Management Skills

You learned about general management skills back in Chapter 1, "What Is a Project?" These include skills like general business knowledge, budgeting, organizational skills, problem solving skills, and so on. What's important to note here is that the general management skills of leadership, influence negotiation, communications, empathy, and creativity are especially useful during this process and others in the Executing process group.

One other thing to consider regarding this tool and technique is that you'll have resources from other departments who have assignments on the project that you're responsible for overseeing. For example, the finance department and the marketing department may have assigned project activities, and as the project manager, you'll manage their progress. This implies that you'll need general knowledge management skills to understand what the assignments entail and strong leadership skills to influence the departments to stay on schedule.

Training

Training is a matter of assessing your team's skills and abilities, assessing the project needs, and providing the training necessary for the team members to carry out their assigned activities. Training can sometimes be a reward as well. In the software industry, programmers seek out positions that offer training on the latest and greatest technologies, and they consider it a benefit or bonus to attend training on the company dollar and time. If you know early in the Planning processes that training is necessary, include the details of this in the staffing management plan. During the course of the project, you might observe team members that need training or they may ask for training. Update the staffing management plan with this information.

Team-Building Activities

Many times, project teams are made up of folks who don't know each other. They aren't necessarily aware of the project objectives and may not even want to be a part of the team. The project manager may not have worked with the people assigned to the project team before either. Sound like a recipe for disaster? It's not. Thousands of projects are started with team members and project managers who don't know each other and come to a successful completion. How is that done? It's a result of the project manager's team-building and communication skills.

The project manager's job is to bring the team together, get its members all headed in the right direction, and provide motivation, reward, and recognition to keep the team in tip-top shape. This is done using a variety of team-building techniques and exercises. *Team building* is simply getting a diverse group of people to work together in the most efficient and effective manner possible. This may involve management events as well as individual actions designed to improve team performance. There are entire volumes on this subject, and it's beyond the scope of this book to go into all the team-building possibilities. The exam tends to focus more on the theories behind team building and the characteristics of effective teams, so that's what we'll spend our time looking at.

All newly formed teams go through four stages of development:

- Forming
- Storming

- Norming
- Performing

You've probably seen this elsewhere, but since these stages may show up on the exam, you'll want to memorize them. Let's take a brief look at each of them.

Forming   This one's easy. Forming is the beginning stage of team formation, when all the members are brought together, introduced, and told the objectives of the project. This is where team members learn why they're working together. During this stage, team members tend to be formal and reserved and take on an "all-business" approach.

Storming   Storming is where the action begins. Team members become confrontational with each other as they're vying for position and control during this stage. They're working through who is going to be the top dog and jockeying for status.

Norming   Now things begin to calm down. Team members know each other fairly well by now. They're comfortable with their positions in the team, and they begin to deal with project problems instead of people problems. In the norming stage, they confront the project concerns and problems instead of each other. Decisions are made jointly at this stage, and team members exhibit affection and familiarity with one another.

Performing   Ahh, perfection. Well, almost, anyway. This is where great teams end up. This stage is where the team is productive and effective. The level of trust among team members is high, and great things are achieved. This is the mature development stage.

Exam Spotlight

Different teams progress through the stages of development at different rates. When new team members are brought onto the team, the development stages start all over again. It doesn't matter where the team is in the forming process—a new member will start the cycle all over again.

Let's take a closer look at focusing your team members throughout these stages of development, along with some of the characteristics of effective teams.

Team Focus

Have you ever watched any of those old pirate movies on late-night TV? Remember the scenes where the captain goes down into the bowels of the ship to check on the teams of rowers? He scrutinizes the crew and literally whips the rowers who aren't pulling their weight into shape. I don't recommend this as a team-building technique, but imagine for a minute that your project team members are like those rowing teams. If the members on the left are rowing one way and the members on the right are rowing another, you're creating a lot of energy and looking very busy, but in the end you aren't making any progress.

It's paramount that the team members know and understand the goals and objectives of the project. They should all understand the direction you're headed and work toward that end. After all, that's the reason they've been brought together in the first place. Keep in mind that people see and hear things from their own perspective. A room full of people attending a speech will each come away with something a little different because what was said speaks to their particular situation in life at the time. In other words, their own perceptions filter what they hear. It's your job as project manager to make certain the team members understand the project goals and their own assignments correctly. The whip was effective for the captain in the old movies, but I suggest you use solid communication skills to get your point across. Ask your team members to tell you in their own words what they believe the project goals are. This is a great way to know if you've got everyone on board and a great opportunity for you to clarify any misunderstandings regarding the project goals.

Effective Team Characteristics

Effective teams are typically very energetic teams. Their enthusiasm is contagious, and it feeds on itself. They generate a lot of creativity and become good problem solvers. Teams like this are every project manager's dream. Investing yourself in team building as well as relationship building—especially when you don't think you have the time to do so—will bring many benefits. Here's a sample of the benefits:

- Better conflict resolution
- Commitment to the project
- Commitment to the project team members and project manager
- High job satisfaction
- Enhanced communication
- A sense of belonging and purpose
- A successful project

Dysfunctional teams will typically produce the opposite results of the benefits just listed. Dysfunctional teams don't just happen by themselves any more than great teams do. Sure, sometimes you're lucky enough to get the right combination of folks together right off the bat. But usually, team building takes work and dedication on the part of the project manager. Even in the situations where you do get that dynamite combination of people, they will benefit from team-building exercises and feedback.

Unfortunately, sour attitudes are just as contagious as enthusiasm. Watch for these symptoms among your team members and take action to correct the situation before the entire team is affected:

- Lack of motivation or "don't care" attitudes
- Project work that isn't satisfying
- Status meetings that turn into whining sessions
- Poor communication
- Lack of respect and lack of trust for the project manager

No amount of team building will make up for poor project planning or ineffective project management techniques. Neglecting these things and fooling yourself into thinking that your project team is good enough to make up for the poor planning or poor techniques could spell doom for your project. And besides that, it's not fair to your project team to put them in that position.

Ground Rules

Ground rules are the expectations you as the project manager set describing acceptable behavior from the team. For example, one of my pet peeves is team members who interrupt each other. In this case, one of the ground rules is one person speaks at a time during a meeting. Another ground rule might be reporting potential issues as soon as the team member becomes aware of them. Outlining ground rules like this helps the team understand your expectations and increases productivity.

Collocation

Team members are often in the same physical location—for example, the same office building or office complex. This tool and technique is called collocation. *Collocation* enables teams to function more effectively than if they're spread out among different localities. Many times on large projects, the project manager will make provisions in the project budget to bring the team together at the same location. (It's difficult, but not impossible, to manage project team members who are not physically located together.) One way to achieve collocation might be to set aside a common meeting room, sometimes called a war room, for team members who are located in different buildings or across town to meet and exchange information.

Multiple locations can also be a big time waster for you as the project manager and for your team members. If some team members are located in one part of town and another set of team members are located across town, you'll find yourself in the car (or the bus) driving back and forth to make face-to-face contact and get status updates. Conducting team meetings also becomes a hassle as one set of team members or the other must drive to another location (or both to a central location) to have a meeting.

There is a lot of value in face-to-face contact with your team members and stakeholders. I'm a huge e-mail fan—it's one of my favorite forms of communication—but e-mail cannot reveal tone of voice, facial expressions, and body language. Whenever possible, practice the technique of collocation and get your team together.

In reality, it's often difficult to get your team together physically. A good solution in lieu of having people relocate is conference calling. Team members scattered across the country all have access to the telephone and it's relatively easy to find a time everyone can meet over the phone.

Recognition and Rewards

We have quite a bit of ground to cover with recognition and rewards. As I said earlier, there could be several exam questions regarding team building, so dig out all your favorite memorization techniques and put them to use.

Team building starts with project planning and doesn't stop until the project is completed. It involves employing techniques to improve your team's performance and keeping team members motivated. Motivation helps people work more efficiently and produce better results. If clear expectations, clear procedures, and the right motivational tools are used, project teams will excel.

Motivation can be extrinsic or intrinsic. Extrinsic motivators are material rewards and might include bonuses, the use of a company car, stock options, gift certificates, training opportunities, extra time off, and so on.

Intrinsic motivators are specific to the individual. Some people are just naturally driven to achieve—it's part of their nature. (I suspect this is a motivator for you since you're reading this book.) Cultural and religious influences are forms of intrinsic motivators as well. Reward and recognition—a tool and technique of the Develop Project Team process—are examples of extrinsic motivators. We'll look at them next.

Recognition and rewards are an important part of team motivation. They are formal ways of recognizing and promoting desirable behavior and are most effective when carried out by the management team and the project manager.

Recognition and rewards should be proportional to the achievement. In other words, appropriately link the reward to the performance. For example, a project manager who has responsibility for the project budget and the procurement process and keeps the costs in line with the budget should get rewarded for this achievement. However, if these functions are assigned to a functional manager in the organization, it wouldn't be appropriate to reward the project manager because they were not the one responsible for keeping the costs in line.

Team members should be rewarded for going above and beyond the call of duty. Perhaps they put in a significant amount of overtime to meet a project goal or spent nights round-the-clock babysitting ill-performing equipment. These types of behaviors should get rewarded and formally recognized by the project manager and the management team. On the other hand, if the ill-performing equipment was a direct result of mistakes made or if it happened because of poor planning, rewards would not be appropriate, obviously.

Consider individual preferences and cultural differences when using rewards and recognitions. Some people don't like to be recognized in front of a group; others thrive on it. Some people appreciate an honest thank-you with minimal fanfare, and others just won't accept individual rewards as their culture doesn't allow it. Keep this in mind when devising your reward system.

There are many theories on motivation. As a project manager, it's important to understand them so that you can tailor your recognition and rewards programs to take into account the reasons people do what they do. You may encounter questions on these theories on the exam, so I'll discuss their primary points in the following sections.

Real World Scenario

Baker's Gift Baskets

You're a contract project manager for Baker's Gift Baskets. This company assembles gift baskets of all styles and shapes with every edible treat imaginable. The company has recently experienced explosive growth, and you've been brought on board to manage its new project. The owners of the company want to offer "pick-your-own" baskets that allow customers to pick the individual items they want included in the basket. In addition, they're introducing a new line of containers to choose from, including things like miniature golf bags, flowerpots, serving bowls, and the like. This means changes to the catalog and the website to accommodate the new offerings.

The deadline for this project is the driving constraint. The website changes won't cause any problems with the deadline. However, the catalog must go to press quickly to meet holiday mailing deadlines, which in turn are driving the project deadline.

Your team members put their heads together and came up with an ingenious plan to meet the catalog deadline. It required lots of overtime and some weekend work on their part to pull it off, but they met the date.

You decide this is a perfect opportunity to recognize and reward the team for their outstanding efforts. You've arranged a slot on the agenda at the next all-company meeting to bring your team up front and praise them for their cooperation and efforts to get the catalog to the printers on time. You'll also present each of them with two days of paid time off and a gift certificate for a dinner with their family at an exclusive restaurant in the city.

Motivational Theories

Motivational theories came about during the modern age. Prior to today's information and service type jobs and yesterday's factory work, the majority of people worked the land and barely kept enough food on the table to feed their family. No one was concerned about motivation at work. You worked because you wouldn't have anything to eat if you didn't. Fortunately, that isn't the case today.

Today we have a new set of problems in the workplace. Workers in the service and knowledge-based industries aren't concerned with starvation—that need has been replaced with other needs like job satisfaction, a sense of belonging and commitment to the project, good working conditions, and so on. Motivational theories present ideas on why people act the way they do, and how we can influence them to act in certain ways to get the results we want. Again, there are libraries full of books on this topic. We'll cover four of them here.

MASLOW'S HIERARCHY OF NEEDS

You have probably seen this classic example of motivational theory. Abraham Maslow hypothesized that humans have five basic needs arranged in hierarchical order. The first needs are physical needs, like the need for food, clothing, and shelter. The idea is that these needs must be met before the person can move to the next level of needs in the hierarchy, which includes safety and security needs. Here, the concern is for the person's physical welfare and the security of their belongings. Once that need is met, they progress to the next level, and so on.

Maslow's hierarchy of needs theory suggests that once a lower-level need has been met, it no longer serves as a motivator and the next higher level becomes the driving motivator in a person's life. Maslow conjectures that humans are always in one state of need or another. Here is a recap of each of the needs, starting with the highest level and ending with the lowest:

Self-actualization   Performing at your peak potential

Self-esteem needs   Accomplishment, respect for self, capability

Social needs   A sense of belonging, love, acceptance, friendship

Safety and security needs   Your physical welfare and the security of your belongings

Basic physical needs   Food, clothing, shelter

The highest level of motivation in this theory is the state of self-actualization. The United States Army had a slogan a few years ago that I think encapsulates self-actualization very well: "Be all that you can be." When all the physical, safety, social, and self-esteem needs have been met, a person reaches a state of independence where they're able to express themselves and perform at their peak. They'll do good work just for the sake of doing good work. Recognition and self-esteem is the motivator at lower levels; now the need for being the best they can be is reached.

HYGIENE THEORY

Frederick Herzberg came up with the *Hygiene Theory*, also known as the *Motivation-Hygiene Theory*. He postulates that there are two factors that contribute to motivation: hygiene factors and motivators. Hygiene factors deal with work environment issues. The thing to remember about hygiene factors is that they prevent dissatisfaction. Examples of hygiene factors are pay, benefits, the conditions of the work environment, and relationships with peers and managers. Pay is considered a hygiene factor because Herzberg believed that over the long term, pay is not a motivator. Being paid for the work prevents dissatisfaction but doesn't necessarily bring satisfaction in and of itself. He believed this to be true as long as the pay system is equitable. If two workers performing the same functions have large disparities in pay, then pay can become a motivator.

Motivators deal with the substance of the work itself and the satisfaction one derives from performing the functions of the job. Motivators lead to satisfaction. The ability to advance, the opportunity to learn new skills, and the challenges involved in the work are all motivators according to Herzberg.

Exam Spotlight

For the exam, remember that Herzberg was the inventor of the Hygiene Theory and that this theory claims that hygiene factors prevent dissatisfaction while motivators lead to satisfaction.

EXPECTANCY THEORY

The *Expectancy Theory* says that the expectation of a positive outcome drives motivation. People will behave in certain ways if they think there will be good rewards for doing so. Also note that this theory says the strength of the expectancy drives the behavior. This means the expectation or likelihood of the reward is linked to the behavior. For example, if you tell your two-year-old to put the toys back in the toy box and you'll give her a cookie, chances are she'll put the toys away. This is a reasonable reward for a reasonable action. However, if you promise your project team members vacations in Hawaii if they get the project done early and they know there is no way you can deliver that reward, there is little motivation to work toward it.

This theory also says that people become what you expect of them. If you openly praise your project team members and treat them like valuable contributors, you'll likely have a high-performing team on your hands. Conversely, when you publicly criticize people or let them know that you have low expectations regarding their performance, they'll likely live up (or down as the case may be) to that expectation as well.

ACHIEVEMENT THEORY

Achievement Theory says that people are motivated by the need for three things: achievement, power, and affiliation. The achievement motivation is obviously the need to achieve or succeed. The power motivation involves a desire for influencing the behavior of others. And the need for affiliation is relationship oriented. Workers want to have friendships with their coworkers and a sense of camaraderie with their fellow team members. The strength of your team members' desire for each of these will drive their performance on various activities.

Exam Spotlight

Understand the theories of motivation and their premises for the exam.

We'll cover two more theories in the leadership section, which is next. These deal specifically with how leaders interact with their project team members.

Leadership versus Management

Chapter 1 talked about leaders versus managers. There's a bit more information to add here regarding leadership theories and the types of power leaders possess. Let's recap leadership and management first before we talk about those theories.

Recall that leadership is about imparting vision and rallying people around that vision. Leaders motivate and inspire and are concerned with strategic vision. Leaders have a knack for getting others to do what needs done.

Two of the techniques they use to do this are power and politics. *Power* is the ability to get people to do what they wouldn't do ordinarily. It's also the ability to influence behavior. *Politics* imparts pressure to conform regardless of whether people agree with the decision. Leaders understand the difference between power and politics and when to employ each technique. We'll talk more about power shortly.

Good leaders have committed team members who believe in the vision of the leader. Leaders set direction and time frames and have the ability to attract good talent to work for them. Leaders inspire a vision and get things done through others by earning loyalty, respect, and cooperation from team members. They set the course and lead the way. Good leaders are directive in their approach but allow for plenty of feedback and input. Good leaders commonly have strong interpersonal skills and are well respected.

Managers are generally task oriented and concerned with things like plans, controls, budgets, policies, and procedures. They're generalists with a broad base of planning and organizational skills, and their primary goal is satisfying stakeholder needs. They also possess motivational skills and the ability to recognize and reward behavior.

Project managers need to use the traits of both leaders and managers at different times during a project. On very large projects, a project manager will act more like a leader inspiring the sub–project managers to get on board with the objectives. On small projects, project managers will act more like managers because they're responsible for all the planning and coordinating functions.

There are three theories that we'll discuss regarding leadership and management. They are Douglas McGregor's Theory X and Theory Y and the Contingency Theory. Then we'll end this section with a discussion of the types of power leaders use and the outputs of Develop Project Team.

THEORY X AND THEORY Y

Douglas McGregor defined two models of worker behavior, Theory X and Theory Y, that attempt to explain how different managers deal with their team members. *Theory X* managers believe most people do not like work and will try to steer clear of it; they believe people have little to no ambition, need constant supervision, and won't actually perform the duties of their job unless threatened. As a result, Theory X managers are like dictators and impose very rigid controls over their people. They believe people are motivated only by punishment, money, or position. Unfortunately for the team members, Theory X managers unknowingly also subscribe to the Expectancy Theory. If they expect people to be lazy and unproductive and treat them as such, their team members probably will be lazy and unproductive.

Theory Y managers believe people are interested in performing their best given the right motivation and proper expectations. These managers provide support to their teams, are concerned about their team members, and are good listeners. Theory Y managers believe people are creative and committed to the project goals, that they like responsibility and seek it out, and that they are able to perform the functions of their positions with limited supervision.

CONTINGENCY THEORY

The Contingency Theory builds on a combination of Theory Y behaviors and the Hygiene Theory. The Contingency Theory, in a nutshell, says that people are motivated to achieve levels of competency and will continue to be motivated by this need even after competency is reached.

The Power of Leaders

As stated earlier, power is the ability to influence others to do what you want them to do. This can be used in a positive manner or a negative one. But that old saying of your grandmother's about attracting more flies with honey than vinegar still holds true today.

Leaders, managers, and project managers use power to convince others to do things a specific way. The kind of power they use to accomplish this depends on their personality, their personal values, and the company culture.

There are several forms of power that a project manager might use. We've already talked about reward power, which is the ability to grant bonuses or incentive awards for a job well done. Let's look at a few more:

Punishment power   Punishment, also known as coercive or penalty power, is just the opposite of reward power. The employee is threatened with consequences if expectations are not met.

Expert power   Expert power occurs when the person being influenced believes the manager, or the person doing the influencing, is knowledgeable about the subject or has special abilities that make them an expert. The person goes along just because they think the influencer knows what they're doing and it's the best thing for the situation.

Legitimate power   Legitimate, or formal, power comes about as a result of the influencer's position. Because that person is the project manager, or executive vice president, or CEO, they have the power to call the shots and make decisions.

Referent power   Referent power is inferred to the influencer by their subordinates. Project team members who have a great deal of respect and high regard for their project managers willingly go along with decisions made by the project manager because of referent power.

Punishment power should be used as a last resort. There are times when you'll have to use this method, but hopefully much less often than the other three forms of power. Sometimes, you'll have team members who won't live up to expectations and their performance suffers as a result. This is a case where punishment power is enacted to get the employee to correct their behavior.

Exam Spotlight

Know the Theory of X and Y, the Contingency Theory, and types of power for the PMP exam. Understand the circumstances when each type of power might be used.

Outputs of Develop Project Team

We're now ready to close out the Develop Project Team process. There is only one output of this process: team performance assessment. As a result of positive team-building experiences, you'll see individuals improving their skills, team behaviors and relationships improving, conflict resolutions going smoothly, and team members recommending ways to improve the work of the project. We talked about effective team characteristics in an earlier section of this chapter. Assessing these characteristics will help you determine where (or if) the project team needs improvements.

Project managers wear a lot of hats. This is one of the things that make this job so interesting. You need organization and planning skills to plan the project. You need motivation and sometimes disciplinary skills to execute the project plans. You need to exercise leadership and power where appropriate. And all the while, you have a host of relationships to manage, involving team members, stakeholders, managers, and customers. It's a great job and brings terrific satisfaction.

Distributing Project Information

The *Information Distribution* process is concerned with getting stakeholders information about the project in a timely manner. This can come about in several ways: status reports, project meetings, review meetings, and so on. Status reports are actually a part of the work performance information we saw in the output of the Direct and Manage Project Execution process. Status reports inform stakeholders about where the project is today in regard to project schedule and budget, for example. They also describe what the project team has accomplished to date. This might include milestones completed to date, the percentage of schedule completion, and what remains to be completed. The Information Distribution process describes how this report is distributed and to whom.

In the Information Distribution process, the communications management plan that was defined during the Communications Planning process is put into action and it's the only input to this process. Communication and Information Distribution work together to report the progress of the project team.

There are several tools and techniques of Information Distribution and we'll look at each of them next.

Information Distribution Tools and Techniques

The tools and techniques of this process are as follows:

- Communication skills
- Information gathering and retrieval systems
- Information distribution methods
- Lessons learned process

Communication skills are probably the single most important skill in your project management toolbox. We'll start with this tool and technique.

Developing Great Communication Skills

Every aspect of your job as a project manager will involve communications. It's been estimated that project managers spend as much as 90 percent of their time communicating in one form or another. Therefore, communication skills are arguably one of the most important skills a project manager can have. They are even more important than technical skills. Good communication skills foster an open, trusting environment. The ability to communicate well is a project manager's best asset.

Exam Spotlight

According to *A Guide to the PMBOK,* communications skills are not the same as project management communications. They're related, but not the same thing.

Chapter 1 talked about how important good communication skills are. This section discusses the act of communication, listening behaviors, and conflict resolution. You'll employ each of these techniques with your project team, stakeholders, customers, and management team.

Information Exchange

Communication is the process of exchanging information. There are three elements to all communication:

Sender   The sender is the person responsible for putting the information together in a clear and concise manner. The information should be complete and presented in a way that the receiver will be able to correctly understand it. Make your messages relevant to the receiver. Junk mail is annoying, and information that doesn't pertain in any way whatsoever to the receiver is nothing more than that.

Message   The message is the information being sent and received. It might be written, verbal, nonverbal, formal, informal, internal, external, horizontal, or vertical. Horizontal communications are messages sent and received to peers. Vertical communications are messages sent and received down to subordinates and up to executive management.

Make your messages as simple as you can to get your point across. Don't complicate the message with unnecessary detail and technical jargon that others may not understand. A simple trick that helps clarify your messages, especially verbal messages, is to repeat the key information periodically. Public speakers are taught that the best way to organize a speech is to first tell the audience what you're going to tell them; second, tell them; and third, tell them what you just told them.

Receiver   The receiver is the person the message is intended for. They are responsible for understanding the information correctly and making sure they've received all of the information.

Keep in mind that receivers filter the information they receive through their knowledge of the subject, culture influences, language, emotions, attitudes, and geographic locations. The sender should take these filters into consideration when sending messages so that the receiver will clearly understand the message that was sent.

This book is an example of the sender-message-receiver model. I'm the sender of the information. The message concerns topics you need to know to pass the PMP exam (and if I've done my job correctly, is written in a clear and easily understood format). You, the reader, are the receiver.

METHODS OF INFORMATION EXCHANGE

Senders, receivers, and messages are the elements of communication. The way the sender packages or encodes the information and transmits it and the way the receiver unpacks or decodes the message are the methods of communication exchange.

Senders encode messages. Encoding is a method of putting the information into a format the receiver will understand. Language, pictures, and symbols are used to encode messages. Encoding formats the message for transmitting.

Transmitting is the way the information gets from the sender to the receiver. Spoken words, written documentation, memos, e-mail, voicemail, and so on are all transmitting methods.

Decoding is what the receiver does with the information when they get it. They convert it into an understandable format. Usually, this means they read the memo, listen to the speaker, read the book, and so on.

FORMS OF COMMUNICATION

Communication occurs primarily in written or verbal form. Granted, you can point to something or indicate what you need with motions, but usually you use the spoken or written word to get your message across.

Verbal communication is easier and less complicated than written communication, and it's usually a fast method of communication. Written communication, on the other hand, is an excellent way to get across complex, detailed messages. Detailed instructions are better provided in written form because it gives the reader the ability to go back over information they're not quite sure about.

Both verbal and written communications might take a formal or an informal approach. Speeches or lectures are an example of formal verbal communications. Most project status meetings take more of a formal approach, as do most written project status reports. Generally speaking, the project manager should take an informal approach when communicating with stakeholders and project team members outside of the status meetings. This makes you appear more open and friendly and easier to approach with questions and issues.

Effective Listening Skills

What did you say? Often we think we're listening when we really aren't. In all fairness, we can take in only so much information at one time. But it's important to perform active listening when someone else is speaking. As a project manager, you will spend the majority of your time communicating with team members, stakeholders, customers, vendors, and others. This means you should be as good a listener as you are a communicator.

There are several techniques you can use to improve your listening skills. There are books devoted to this topic, so we'll try to highlight some of the most common techniques here:

- Appear interested in what the speaker is saying. This will make the speaker feel at ease and will benefit you as well. By acting interested, you become interested and thereby retain more of the information being presented.

- Making eye contact with the speaker is another effective listening tool. This lets the speaker know you are paying attention to what they're saying and are interested.

- Put your speaker at ease by letting them know beforehand that you're interested in what they're going to talk about and that you're looking forward to hearing what they have to say. While they're speaking, nod your head, smile, or make comments when and if appropriate to let the speaker know you understand the message. If you don't understand something and are in the proper setting, ask clarifying questions.

- Another great trick that works well in lots of situations is to recap what the speaker said in your own words and tell it back to them. Start with something like this, "Let me make sure I understand you correctly, you're saying…," and ask the speaker to confirm that you did understand them correctly.

- Just as your mother always said, it's impolite to interrupt. Interrupting is a way of telling the speaker that you aren't really listening and you're more interested in telling them what you have to say than listening to them. Interrupting gets the other person off track, they might forget their point, and it may even make them angry.

Not to disagree with Mom, but there probably are some occasions where interrupting is appropriate. For example, if you're in a project status meeting and someone wants to take the meeting off course, sometimes the only way to get the meeting back on track is to interrupt them. You can do this politely. Start first by saying the person's name to get their attention. Then let them know that you'd be happy to talk with them about their topic outside of the meeting or add it to the agenda for the next status meeting if it's something everyone needs to hear. Sorry, Mom.

Resolving Conflicts

I said earlier in this chapter that if you have more than one person working on your project, you have a team. Here's another fact: If you have more than one person working on your project, you'll have conflict. I put conflict resolution in the communication section because conflict resolution involves communication, as you'll see in a moment.

Everyone has desires, needs, and goals. Conflict comes into the picture when the desires, needs, or goals of one party are incompatible with the desires, needs, or goals of another party (or parties). *Conflict,* simply put, is the incompatibility of goals, which often leads to one party resisting or blocking the other party from attaining their goals. Wait—this doesn't sound like a party!

There are five ways of resolving conflict that may show up on the exam:

Forcing   *Forcing* is just as it sounds. One person forces a solution on the other parties. This is where the boss puts on the "Because I'm the boss and I said so" hat. While this is a permanent solution, it isn't necessarily the best solution. People will go along with it because, well, they're forced to go along with it. It doesn't mean they agree with the solution. This isn't the best technique to use when you're trying to build a team. This is an example of a win-lose conflict resolution technique. The forcing party wins, and the losers are those who are forced to go along with the decision.

Smoothing   *Smoothing* does not lead to a permanent solution. It's a temporary way to resolve conflict where someone attempts to make the conflict appear less important than it is. Everyone looks at each other and scratches their head and wonders why they thought the conflict was such a big deal anyway. As a result, a compromise is reached and everyone feels good about the solution until they get back to their desk and start thinking about the issue again. When they realize that the conflict was smoothed over and really is more important than they were led to believe, they'll be back at it and the conflict will resurface. This is an example of a lose-lose conflict resolution technique because neither side wins.

Compromise   *Compromise* is achieved when each of the parties involved in the conflict gives up something to reach a solution. Everyone involved decides what they will give on and what they won't give on, and eventually through all the give and take, a solution is reached. Neither side wins or loses in this situation. As a result, neither side is really gung ho about the decision that was reached. They will drag their feet and reluctantly trudge along. If, however, firm commitments are made by both parties to the resolution, then the solution becomes a permanent one.

Confrontation   *Confrontation* is also called problem solving and is the best way to resolve conflict. One of the key actions you'll perform with this technique is a fact-finding mission. The thinking here is that one right solution to a problem exists and the facts will bear out the solution. Once the facts are uncovered, they're presented to the parties and the decision will be clear. Thus the solution becomes a permanent one and the conflict expires. This is the conflict resolution approach project mangers use most often and is an example of a win-win conflict resolution technique.

Withdrawal   *Withdrawal* never results in resolution. This occurs when one of the parties gets up and leaves and refuses to discuss the conflict. It is probably the worst of all the techniques because nothing gets resolved. This is an example of a lose-lose conflict resolution technique.

Exam Spotlight

Know each of the conflict resolution techniques for the exam. Also remember that these techniques will not necessarily yield long-term results. The smoothing and withdrawal techniques have temporary results and aren't always good techniques to use to resolve problems. Forcing, compromise, and confrontation techniques tend to have longer-lasting results.

Keep in mind that group size makes a difference when you're trying to resolve conflict or make decisions. Remember the channels of communication you learned about in Chapter 4? The larger the group, the more lines of communication and the more difficult it will be to reach a decision. Groups of 5 to 11 people have been shown to make the most accurate decisions.

Use communication, listening, and conflict resolution skills wisely. As a project manager, you'll find that your day-to-day activities encompass these three areas the majority of the time. Project managers with excellent communication skills can work wonders. Communication won't take the place of proper planning and management techniques, but a project manager who communicates well with their team and the stakeholders can make up for a lack of technical skills any day, hands down. If your team and your stakeholders trust you and you can communicate the vision and the project goals and report on project status accurately and honestly, the world is your oyster.

Information Gathering and Retrieval Systems

The *Information gathering and retrieval systems* tool and technique of the Information Distribution process includes ways that project information is stored and shared among project team members. You've probably used one or more of these gathering and retrieval systems such as project management software, manual filing systems, intranet project sites, and electronic databases.

Information Distribution Methods

Information distribution methods are ways of getting the project information to the project team or stakeholders. As the name implies, these are ways to distribute the information and might include e-mail, hard copy, voicemail, videoconferencing, and so on.

Exam Spotlight

Don't confuse information gathering and retrieval systems with information distribution methods. Remember that retrieval systems are ways for the project team to get at project information, while distribution methods are ways of getting the information into the hands of the stakeholders or team members.

Lessons Learned Process

Lessons learned is information that you gather and document throughout the course of the project that can be used to benefit the current project, future projects, or other projects currently being performed by the organization. Lessons learned may include positive as well as negative lessons.

During the Information Distribution process, you'll begin conducting lessons learned meetings focusing on many different areas depending on the nature of your project. These areas might include project management processes, product development, technical processes, project team performance, stakeholder involvement, and so on.

Lessons learned meetings should always be conducted at the end of project phases and at the end of the project at minimum. Team members, stakeholders, vendors, and others involved on the project should participate in these meetings. It's important to understand, and to make your team members understand, that this is not a finger pointing meeting. The purpose of lessons learned is to understand what went well and why—so you can repeat it on future projects—and what didn't go so well and why—so you can perform differently on future projects. These meetings make good team-building sessions because there is an atmosphere of trust and sharing and building on each other's strengths to improve performance.

Some of the updates that may occur as a result of lessons learned meetings are updates to the lessons learned knowledge base, and to policies, procedures, processes, and business skills and updates to the risk management plan.

Exam Spotlight

According to *A Guide to the PMBOK,* it's a project manager's professional obligation to hold lessons learned meetings.

We'll talk more about lessons learned in Chapter 11, "Closing Out the Project."

Outputs of Information Distribution

The first output of the Information Distribution process is organizational process assets updates. The updates here consist of six elements:

Lessons learned documentation   You'll document the lessons learned we talked about earlier as this output. You should document the reasons or causes for the issues, the corrective action taken and why, and any other information that future projects may benefit from.

Project records   *Project records* include, as you might guess, memos, correspondence, and other documents concerning the project. The best place to keep information like this is in a project notebook or in a set of project notebooks, depending on the size of the project. The project notebooks are ordinary three-ring binders where project information gets filed. They are maintained by the project manager or project office and contain all information regarding the project. You could also keep the information on a project website, the company intranet, or CDs. If you're keeping the information electronically, make certain it's backed up periodically. Individual team members may keep their own project records as well in notebooks or electronically. These records serve as historical information once the project is closed.

Project reports   *Project reports* include the project status reports and minutes from project meetings. If you're keeping an issues log, they would be included with the project reports as well.

Project presentations   *Project presentations* involve presenting project information to the stakeholders and other appropriate parties when necessary. The presentations might be formal or informal and depend on the audience and the information being communicated.

Feedback from stakeholders   This one ties into lessons learned. Feedback you receive from the stakeholders that can improve future performance on this project or future projects should be captured and documented. If the information has an impact on the current project, distribute it to the appropriate team members so that future project performance can be modified to improve results.

Stakeholder notifications   Remember that the focus of this process is distributing information so this elements fits because you'll want to notify them when you have implemented solutions and approved changes. This also involves informing them of project status. We'll cover project status review meetings in the section "Establishing Performance Measurements" in Chapter 9.

The only other output of this process is requested changes, which we've talked about before.

In the next chapter, we'll examine the processes associated with finding and selecting vendors, administering contracts, managing stakeholders and team members, quality assurance, and reporting on performance.

Project Case Study: New Kitchen Heaven Retail Store

Dirk Perrier logs on and finds the following e-mail addressed to all the stakeholders and project team members from you:

Project Progress Report

Project Name   Kitchen Heaven Retail Store

Project Number   081501-1910

Prepared by   Project Manager

Date   September 20, 2006

Section 1: Action Items

- Action Item 1: Call Cable Vendor—Responsible Party: Ricardo; Resolution Date: 9/14

- Action Item 2: T1 Connection Status—Responsible Party: Ricardo; Resolution Date: Pending

- Action Item 3: Build-Out Begins—Responsible Party: Jake; Resolution Date: Pending

Section 2: Scheduled and Actual Completion Dates

- Sign Lease—Scheduled: 8/21/06; Completed: 8/21/06

- Gomez Contract Signed—Scheduled: 9/12/06; Completed: 9/12/06

- Ethernet Cable Run—Scheduled: 9/18/06; Completed: 9/19/06

- Build-Out Started—Scheduled: 9/20/06; Completed: Open

Section 3: Activity That Occurred in the Project This Week

The Ethernet cable run was completed without a problem.

Gomez construction started the build-out process. This task was fast-tracked with the Ethernet cable run as planned.

Jill made initial calls regarding retail products order.

Section 4: Progress Expected This Reporting Period Not Completed

None. Project is on track to date.

Section 5: Progress Expected Next Reporting Period

Build-out will continue. Jake reports that Gomez expects to have electrical lines run and drywall started prior to the end of the next reporting period.

Ricardo should have a T1 update. There's a slim possibility that the T1 connection will have occurred by next reporting period.

Section 6: Issues

We had to start the build-out on the last day of the cable run (this is called fast-tracking) to keep the project on schedule. Jake and Ricardo reported only minor problems with this arrangement in that the contractors got into each other's way a time or two. This did not impact the completion of the cable run as most of day two this team was in the back room and Gomez's crew was in the storefront area.

A key member of the Gomez construction crew was out last week due to a family emergency. Gomez assures us that it will not impact the build-out schedule. They replaced the team member with someone from another project, so it appears so far that build-out is on schedule.

Ricardo is somewhat concerned about the T1 connection because the phone company won't return his calls inquiring about status. We're still ahead of the curve on this one because hardware isn't scheduled to begin testing until January 21. Hardware testing depends on the T1 connection. This is a heads-up at this point, and we'll carry this as an issue in the status report going forward until it's resolved.

One of the gourmet food item suppliers Jill uses regularly went out of business. She is in the process of tracking down a new supplier to pick up the slack for the existing stores and supply the gourmet food products for the new store.

"Good job on the status," Dirk says as you pick up the phone. "I was beginning to wonder when we'd see some action on the project, but it looks like things are underway."

"A lot has happened in just the past two weeks, as you can see. I'll publish these project status updates twice a month in conjunction with the regular project status meetings. Starting in January, I'll publish them once a week until project completion."

"Keep me posted on that T1 line. That isn't going to be a showstopper, is it?"

"We have a contingency plan in place," you reply. "We talked about that last week."

"Okay. I'll see you at the project meeting Friday."

"See you then," you say.

Project Case Study Checklist

Communication (reporting on work performance information)

- Sender makes it clear and concise.

- There's no unnecessary technical jargon.

- Formal written communication is provided.

- It's the receiver's responsibility to understand information.

- The status report is a vertical and horizontal communication method.

Direct and Manage Project Execution

- Deliverables

- Work results

- Work performance information

Develop Project Team

Information Distribution

- Project information is delivered to stakeholders in a timely manner.

- The information distribution method is status reports via e-mail and project meetings.

- The status report is part of the project reports filed in the project notebook or filed for future reference as historical information.

Summary

This chapter described four processes from the Executing process group: Direct and Manage Project Execution, Acquire Project Team, Develop Project Team, and Information Distribution.

In Direct and Manage Project Execution, the project plans come to life. Activities are authorized to begin and the product or service of the project is produced. Status review meetings are held to inform stakeholders of project progress and updates.

Acquire Project Team involves negotiation with other functional managers, project managers, and organizational personnel to obtain human resources to complete the work of the project. The project manager may not have control over who will be a part of the team. Availability, ability, experience, interests, and costs are all enterprise environmental factors that should be considered when you are able to choose team members.

Develop Project Team involves creating an open, inviting atmosphere where project team members will become efficient and cooperative, increasing productivity during the course of the project. It's the project manager's job to bring the team together into a functioning, productive group.

There are four stages of team development: forming, storming, norming, and performing. All groups proceed through these stages, and the introduction of a new team member will always start the process over again.

Collocation is physically placing team members together in the same location. This might also include a common meeting room or gathering area where team members can meet and collaborate on the project.

Several motivational theories exist, including reward and recognition, Maslow's hierarchy of needs, the Hygiene Theory, the Expectancy Theory, and the Achievement Theory. These theories conjecture that motivation is driven by several desires including needs, anticipation of expected outcomes, or needs for achievement, power, or affiliation. The Hygiene Theory proposes that hygiene factors prevent dissatisfaction.

Leaders inspire vision and rally people around common goals. Theory X leaders think most people are motivated only through punishment, money, or position. Theory Y leaders think most people want to perform the best job they can. The Contingency Theory says that people naturally want to achieve levels of competency and will continue to be motivated by the desire for competency even after competency is reached.

Leaders exhibit five types of power: reward, punishment, expert, legitimate, and referent power.

Communication skills are the most important skills a project manager exercises. People who send messages are responsible for making sure the messages are clear, concise, and complete. Receivers are responsible for understanding the messages correctly and making sure they've received all of the information.

Listening skills put speakers at ease. Several techniques tell your speaker you're listening attentively, including making eye contact, nodding, asking clarifying questions, and limiting interruptions.

Information Distribution is a matter of getting project information out to the stakeholders. Information retrieval systems generally store project information and include project management software, filing cabinets, and electronic databases. Information distribution methods are ways to get the information to the stakeholders and include e-mail, paper, voicemail, or videoconferencing.

Exam Essentials

Be able to identify the distinguishing characteristics of Direct and Manage Project Execution.
Direct and Manage Project Execution is where the work of the project is performed, and the majority of the project budget is spent during this process.

Be able to name the four stages of group formation.   The four stages of group formation are forming, storming, norming, and performing.

Be able to define Maslow's highest level of motivation.   Self-actualization occurs when a person performs at their peak and all lower-level needs have been met.

Be able to name the five levels of power.   The five levels of power are reward, punishment, expert, legitimate, and referent.

Be able to differentiate between senders and receivers of information.   Senders are responsible for clear, concise, complete messages, while receivers are responsible for understanding the message correctly.

Be able to identify the five styles of conflict resolution.   The five styles of conflict resolution are forcing, smoothing, compromise, confrontation, and withdrawal.

Key Terms

You've learned a lot of new key words in this chapter. PMI has worked hard to develop and define standard project management terms that apply across industries. Here is a list of some of the terms you came across in this chapter:

Achievement Theory

Acquire Project Team

administrative closure procedure

collocation

communication

conflict

confrontation

corrective actions

Develop Project Team

Direct and Manage Project Execution

Expectancy Theory

Hygiene Theory

Information Distribution

information distribution methods

information gathering and retrieval systems

lessons learned

Maslow's hierarchy of needs

Motivation-Hygiene Theory

politics

power

preassignment

project presentations

project records

project reports

recognition and rewards

team building

Theory X

Theory Y

virtual teams

Review Questions

1. You are a project manager for an international marketing firm. You are ready to assign resources to your new project using a work authorization system. Which of the following statements is not true?

    A. Work authorization systems clarify and initiate the work for each work package.

    B. Work authorization systems are written procedures defined by the organization.

    C. Work authorization systems are used throughout the project Execution processes.

    D. Work authorization systems are used throughout the Execution processes and are a tool and technique of the Direct and Manage Project Execution process.

2. You are a project manager for a growing dairy farm. It offers its organic dairy products regionally and is expanding its operations to the West Coast. It is in the process of purchasing and leasing dairy farms to get operations under way. You are in charge of the network operations part of this project. An important deadline is approaching that depends on the successful completion of the testing phase. You've detected some problems with your hardware in the testing phase and discover that the hardware is not compatible with other network equipment. You take corrective action and exchange the hardware for more compatible equipment. Which of the following statements is true?

    A. This is not a corrective action because corrective action involves human resources, not project resources.

    B. Corrective action is taken here to make sure the future project outcomes are aligned with the project management plan.

    C. Corrective action is not necessary in this case because the future project outcomes aren't affected.

    D. Corrective action serves as the change request to authorize exchanging the equipment.

3. You are a project manager for a growing dairy farm. It offers its organic dairy products regionally and is expanding its operations to the West Coast. It's in the process of purchasing and leasing dairy farms to get operations under way. The subproject manager in charge of network operations has reported some hardware problems to you. You're also having some other problems coordinating and integrating other elements of the project. Which of the following statements is true?

    A. You are in the Direct and Manage Project Execution process.

    B. Your project team doesn't appear to have the right skills and knowledge needed to perform this project.

    C. You are in the Information Distribution process.

    D. Your project team could benefit from some team-building exercises.

4. Which of the following processes serve as inputs to each other?

    A. Executing, and Monitoring and Controlling

    B. Executing and Closing

    C. Planning, and Monitoring and Controlling

    D. Executing and Initiation

5. Your team members have just completed training on specialized equipment. This is one of the work results you've gathered and recorded. Which of the following outputs of the Direct and Manage Project Execution process does this describe?

    A. Corrective action

    B. Deliverable

    C. Preventive action

    D. Work performance information

6. You are reporting on project elements such as schedule status, deliverables completion, lessons learned, and resource utilization. Which of the following outputs of the Direct and Manage Project Execution does this describe?

    A. Corrective action

    B. Deliverable

    C. Preventive action

    D. Work performance information

7. You are in the process of making project staff assignments. You've got several candidates for a position on the project team that requires specific qualifications. All the candidates seem to meet the qualifications. You also consider personal interests, characteristics, and availability of these potential candidates. Which of the following is true?

    A. You are considering the organizational process assets input of the Develop Project Team process.

    B. You are considering the staffing management plan input of the Develop Project Team process.

    C. You are considering the enterprise environmental factors input of the Acquire Project Team process.

    D. You are considering the roles and responsibilities input of the Acquire Project Team process.

8. Your project team consists of 12 people in the same building you're located in, 4 people from the West Coast office, 2 people from the Kansas City office, and 6 people from the London office. Your office works different hours than all the other offices. Additionally, not all of the resources in your building are available at the same times during the day. Three of the 12 team members work swing shift hours. You use tools like web conferencing and e-mail to distribute information to the team. Which of the following is true?

    A. This question describes the staffing management plan from the Acquire Project Team process and communication skills from the Information Distribution process.

    B. This question describes resource availability from the Develop Project Team process and information distribution methods from the Information Distribution process.

    C. This question describes virtual teams from the Acquire Project Team process and information distribution methods from the Information Distribution process.

    D. This question describes project staff assignments from the Develop Project Team process and communication skills from the Information Distribution process.

9. You are the project manager for a cable service provider. Your team members are amiable with each other and are careful to make project decisions jointly. Which of the following statements is true?

    A. They are in the smoothing stage of Develop Project Team.

    B. They are in the norming stage of Develop Project Team.

    C. They are in the forming stage of Develop Project Team.

    D. They are in the forcing stage of Develop Project Team.

10. You are the project manager for a cable service provider. Your project team is researching a new service offering. They have been working together for quite some time and are in the performing stage of team development. A new member has been introduced to the team. Which of the following statements is true?

    A. The team will start all over again with the storming stage.

    B. The team will continue in the performing stage.

    C. The team will start all over again with the forming stage.

    D. The team will start all over again at the storming stage but quickly progress to the performing stage.

11. You are the project manager for a cable service provider. Your project team is researching a new service offering. They have been working together for quite some time and are in the performing stage of Develop Project Team. This stage of Develop Project Team is similar to which of the following?

    A. Smoothing

    B. Achievement Theory

    C. Hygiene Theory

    D. Self-actualization

12. Receivers in the communication model filter their information through all of the following except _____ .

A. Culture

B. Knowledge of subject

C. Conflict

D. Language

13. You've promised your team two days of paid time off plus a week's training in the latest technology of their choice if they complete their project ahead of schedule. This is an example of which of the following?

A. Achievement Theory

B. Expectancy Theory

C. Maslow's Theory

D. Contingency Theory

14. Your team is split between two buildings on either side of town. As a result, the team isn't very cohesive because the members don't know each other very well. The team is still in the storming stage because of the separation issues. Which of the following should you consider?

A. Corrective action

B. Collocation

C. Training

D. Conflict resolution

15. Which conflict resolution technique do project managers use most often?

A. Smoothing

B. Norming

C. Confronting

D. Forcing

16. You are a fabulous project manager, and your team thinks highly of you. You are well respected by the stakeholders, management team, and project team. When you make decisions, others follow your lead as a result of which of the following?

A. Referent power

B. Expert power

C. Legitimate power

D. Punishment power

17. Theory Y managers believe which of the following?

   A. People are motivated only by money, power, or position.

   B. People will perform their best if they're given proper motivation and expectations.

   C. People are motivated to achieve a high level of competency.

   D. People are motivated by expectation of good outcomes.

18. You have accumulated project information throughout the project and need to distribute some important information you just received. Which of the following is not an information distribution methods?

   A. Electronic databases

   B. Videoconferencing

   C. Electronic mail

   D. Voicemail

19. You know that the next status meeting will require some discussion and a decision for a problem that has surfaced on the project. In order to make the most accurate decision, you know that the number of participants in the meeting should be limited to _____ .

   A. 1 to 5

   B. 5 to 11

   C. 7 to 16

   D. 10 to 18

20. You are holding end-of-phase meetings with your team members and key stakeholders to learn what has hindered and helped the project team's performance of the work. All of the following are true regarding this situation except for which one?

   A. The information learned from these meetings concerns processes and activities that have already occurred, so it should be documented because the information is only useful for future projects.

   B. These meetings are called lessons learned meetings and they're a tool and technique of the Information Distribution process. They're also a good team-building activity.

   C. Project reports, part of the organizational process output of the Information Distribution process, include status meetings and lessons learned (which this question describes).

   D. These meetings should be documented as part of the lessons learned documentation, which is an element of the organizational process assets updates output of the Information Distribution process.

Answers to Review Questions

1.   D. Work authorization systems are a tool used during Project Execution processes but are not a specific tool and technique listed in the Direct and Manage Project Execution process. They formally initiate the work of each work package and clarify the assignments.

2.   B. Corrective action brings anticipated future project outcomes back into alignment with the project management plan. Since there is an important deadline looming that depends on a positive outcome of this test, the equipment is exchanged so that the project plan and project schedule are not impacted.

3.   A. The most difficult aspect of the Direct and Manage Project Execution process is coordinating and integrating all the project elements. The clue to this question is in the next-to-last sentence.

4.   A. The Executing process group and Monitoring and Controlling process group serve as inputs to each other.

5.   B. This question describes the deliverable output. Deliverables can be intangibles, such as the completion of training.

6.   D. Work performance information includes elements like schedule status, the status of deliverables completion, lessons learned, and resource utilization.

7.   C. The enterprise environmental factors input of the Acquire Project Team process considers elements like personal interests, characteristics, and availability of potential team members.

8.   C. Virtual teams are teams that don't necessarily work in the same location or have the same hours but all share the goals of the project and have a role on the project. The web conferencing and e-mail references describe the information distribution methods tool and technique of the Information Distribution process.

9.   B. Teams in the norming stage of Develop Project Team exhibit affection and familiarity with one another and make joint decisions. Smoothing and forcing are conflict resolution techniques, not Develop Project Team stages.

10.   C. The introduction of a new team member will start the formation and development of the team all over again with the forming stage.

11.   D. The performing stage is similar to Maslow's self-actualization. Both involve team members at the peak of performance, concerned with doing good and being the best.

12.   C. Receivers filter information through cultural considerations, knowledge of the subject matter, language abilities, geographic location, emotions, and attitudes.

13.   B. The Expectancy Theory says that people are motivated by the expectation of good outcomes. The outcome must be reasonable and attainable.

14.   B. Collocation would bring your team members together in the same location and allow them to function more efficiently as a team. At a minimum, team members meeting in a common room, such as a war room, for all team meetings would bring the team closer together.

15. C. Confronting is a problem-solving technique that seeks to determine the facts and find solutions based on the facts. That results in a win-win resolution for all parties.

16. A. Referent power is power that is inferred on a leader by their subordinates as a result of the high level of respect for the leader.

17. B. Theory Y managers believe that people will perform their best if they're provided with the proper motivation and the right expectations.

18. A. Electronic databases are a type of information gathering and retrieval system, not a distribution method.

19. B. Group sizes of 5 to 11 participants make the most accurate decisions.

20. A. Lessons learned (which is what this question describes) are useful for future processes and activities for the current project as well as future projects.

Chapter

9

Measuring and Controlling Project Performance

THE PMP EXAM CONTENT FROM THE EXECUTING THE PROJECT PERFORMANCE DOMAIN COVERED IN THIS CHAPTER INCLUDES THE FOLLOWING:

- ✓ Ensure Common Understanding and Set Expectations
- ✓ Implement Quality Management Plan
- ✓ Implement Approved Changes
- ✓ Implement Approved Actions and Workarounds

This chapter will wrap up the Executing process group and introduce the Monitoring and Controlling process group. The Executing processes covered in this chapter are Request Seller Responses, Select Sellers, and Perform Quality Assurance. Then we'll move into the Monitoring and Controlling process group and examine several processes, including Monitor and Control Project Work, Contract Administration, Manage Project Team, Manage Stakeholders, and Performance Reporting.

Request Seller Responses and Select Sellers are both Executing processes. They are usually performed in conjunction with the Contract Administration process, which belongs to the Monitoring and Controlling process group. In order to keep the dividing line even, we'll talk about Request Seller Responses and Select Sellers together and then finish up the Executing process group with Perform Quality Assurance. Then we'll introduce the Monitor and Control Project work process because it provides the framework for the Monitoring and Controlling process. *Then* we'll cover the Contract Administration process.

The Monitoring and Controlling process group involves taking measurements and performing inspections to find out if there are variances in the plan. If variances are discovered, corrective action is taken to get the project back on track and the affected project Planning processes are repeated to make adjustments to the plan as a result of the variances.

During the Manage Team Project process, you'll monitor the performance of the team, provide feedback to team members, resolve issues, and take actions (when needed) to realign the project team's performance with the goals of the project. The Manage Stakeholders process involves communicating project status and issues and resolving stakeholder issues and concerns. Performance Reporting also concerns communicating information about the project's progress to the stakeholders.

Once again we have a lot of ground to cover. Grab your favorite beverage and dig in.

Requesting Seller Responses

Many times project managers must purchase goods or services to complete some or all of the work of the project. Sometimes the entire project is completed on contract. The *Request Seller Responses* process is concerned with obtaining responses to bids and proposals from potential vendors.

There are three inputs to this process:

- Organizational process assets
- Procurement management plan
- Procurement documents

We've talked about these in previous chapters. Organizational process assets were discussed in several of the Planning processes we've covered in previous chapters. The procurement documents and procurement management plan were prepared during the Plan Contracting process. We talked about them in Chapter 6, "Resource Planning." Procurement documents include requests for proposals (RFPs), requests for information (RFIs), requests for quotations (RFQs), and so on. The vendors—or potential sellers—bear the majority of work in the Request Seller Responses process by preparing responses to the RFPs. Depending on the RFP and the effort needed to respond, costs to the vendor can become quite substantial.

The Request Seller Responses process is only used if you're obtaining goods or services from outside your own organization. If you have all the resources you need to perform the work of the project within the organization, you won't use this process.

In the following sections we'll examine some new tools and techniques that will help vendors give you a better idea of their responses and then we'll move on to the outputs of this process, one of which is the vendor proposal.

Requesting Seller Responses Tools and Techniques

Remember that the purpose of the Request Seller Responses process is to obtain responses to your RFP (or similar procurement document). The three tools and techniques of this process are actually designed to assist the vendors in getting their proposals to you:

Bidder conferences   *Bidder conferences* are meetings with prospective vendors or sellers that occur prior to the completion of their response proposal. A bidder conference is prearranged by you or someone from your procurement department. The purpose is to allow all prospective vendors to meet with the buyers to ask questions and clarify issues they have regarding the project and the RFP. The meeting is held once, and all vendors attend at the same time. The bidder conference is held before the vendor prepares their responses so that they are sure their RFP response will address the project requirements.

Advertising   *Advertising* is letting potential vendors know that an RFP is available. The company's Internet site, professional journals, or newspapers are examples of where advertising might appear.

Develop qualified sellers lists   *Develop qualified seller lists* is part of the organizational process asset input if they already exist in the organization. If the lists don't exist, you'll have to create them. They are lists of prospective sellers who have been preapproved or prequalified to provide contract services (or provide supplies and materials) for the organization. For example, your organization might require vendors to register and maintain information regarding their experience, offerings, and current prices on a qualified seller list. Vendors must usually go through the procurement department to get placed on the list. Project managers are then required to choose their vendors from the qualified seller list published by the procurement department. However, not all organizations have qualified seller lists. If a list isn't available, you'll have to work with the project team to come up with your own requirements for selecting vendors.

Request Seller Responses Outputs

There are three outputs to the Request Seller Responses process: qualified sellers list, procurement document package, and proposals. We talked about developing qualifying seller lists in the last section. The output here can be the qualified seller lists you used as inputs (as part of the organizational process asset input) if they exist. If they don't exist, you'll need to develop them as an input and use them as an output.

The procurement document package is prepared by the buyer. This is the formal request that's posted, advertised, or otherwise sent to each of the sellers and is the basis for the seller's bid. These might be an RFP, RFQ, IFB, and so on.

Proposals are the seller-prepared documents that describe how the vendor intends to meet the needs of your project. And if they've done their job correctly, the proposal should detail responses to each of the items as they were outlined in your RFP. These proposals become the input to the next process, Select Sellers. After proposals are prepared and submitted, often vendors are invited to an oral presentation where they provide additional information about their product or service and buyers may ask questions about the seller's proposal.

Exam Spotlight

A Guide to the PMBOK makes a distinction between the Request Seller Responses process and the Select Sellers process that you should know: Request Seller Responses *obtains* bids and proposals; Select Sellers is the *receipt* of bids and proposals and evaluating each in order to award a winner.

Selecting Sellers

In the *Select Sellers* process you evaluate the proposals you've received against your predefined evaluation criteria. Evaluation criteria was defined in the Plan Contracting process.

Select Sellers has several inputs:

- Organizational process assets
- Procurement management plan
- Evaluation criteria
- Procurement document package
- Proposals
- Qualified sellers list
- Project management plan (risk register and risk-related contractual agreements)

We've covered all of these inputs previously but there a few points you should be aware of. Proposals, as mentioned, are obtained in the Request Seller Responses process and used as an input to the Select Sellers process. Proposals may be divided into sections, including a management section, technical approach, and pricing section. Remember that while cost might be the primary driver behind your decision, the low-cost provider may not end up being low cost in the end if they are unable to deliver the products or services as described and on time. Take the time to evaluate the proposals on more than cost alone.

Evaluation criteria is what you'll use to compare proposals. You developed evaluation criteria as part of the Plan Contracting process in Chapter 6. However, let's take a little closer look at this topic now since you'll actually be using the criteria during this process.

In practice, you will probably perform Plan Contracting, Request Seller Responses, and Select Sellers all as one process.

Evaluation Criteria

Evaluation criteria is one method of rating and scoring proposals. Keep in mind this is an input to the Select Sellers process, not a tool and technique, even though you'll be using it as you would a tool and technique.

The types of goods and services you're trying to procure will dictate how detailed your evaluation criteria is. (Of course, if your organization has policies in place for evaluating proposals, then you'll use the format or criteria already established.) The selection of some goods and services may be price driven only. In other words, the bidder with the lowest price will win the bid. This is typical when the items you're buying are widely available.

When you're purchasing goods, you might request a sample from each vendor in order to compare quality (or some other criteria) against your need. For example, perhaps you need a special kind of paper stock for a project you're working on at a bank. This stock must have a watermark, it must have security threads embedded through the paper, and when the paper is used for printing, the ink must not be erasable. You can request samples of stock from the vendors with these qualities and then test them out to see if they'll work for your project.

It's always appropriate to ask the vendor for references, especially when you're hiring contract services. It's difficult to assess the quality of services because it's not a tangible product. References can tell you if the vendor delivered on time, if they had the technical capability to perform the work, and if their management approach was appropriate when troubles surfaced. Create a list of questions to ask the references before you call.

Financial records may be requested to assure you—the buyer—that the vendor has the fiscal ability to perform the services they're proposing and that they can purchase whatever equipment is needed to perform the services. If you examine the records of the company and find they're two steps away from bankruptcy, they may not be a likely candidate for your project. (Remember those general management skills? Here's another example where they come into play.)

One of the most important criteria is the evaluation of the response itself to determine if the vendor has a clear understanding of what you're asking them to do or provide. If they missed the mark (remember, they had an opportunity at the bidder conferences to ask clarifying questions) and didn't understand what you were asking them to provide, you'll probably want to rank them very low.

Now you can compare each proposal against the criteria and rate or score each proposal for its ability to meet or fulfill these criteria. This can serve as your first step in eliminating vendors that don't match your criteria. Let's say you received 18 responses to an RFP. After evaluating each one, you discover that 6 of them don't match all the evaluation criteria. Those 6 vendors are eliminated in this round. The next step is to apply the tools and techniques of this process to further evaluate the remaining 12 potential vendors.

Tools and Techniques of Select Sellers

The following tools and techniques of Select Sellers are used to further evaluate vendors:

- Weighting systems
- Independent estimates
- Screening systems
- Contract negotiation
- Seller rating systems
- Expert judgment
- Proposal evaluation techniques

Let's look at each one.

Weighting Systems

Weighting systems assign numerical weights to evaluation criteria and then multiply them by the weights of each criteria factor to come up with total scores for each vendor. According to *A Guide to the PMBOK*, this tool and technique quantifies the qualitative data to keep personal biases to a minimum. Weighting systems are useful when you have multiple vendors to choose from because they allow you to rank-order the proposals to determine the sequence of negotiations.

There is an example of a weighted scoring system in Chapter 2, "Creating the Project Charter and Preliminary Scope Statement." These systems are commonly used to evaluate vendor proposals.

Independent Estimates

Your procurement department might conduct *independent estimates* (also known as *should cost estimates*) of the costs of the proposal and use these to compare to the vendor prices. If there are large differences between the independent estimate and the proposed vendor cost, one of two things is happening: The statement of work (SOW), or the terms of the contract, was not detailed enough to allow the vendor to come up with an accurate cost, or the vendor simply failed to respond to all the requirements laid out in the contract or SOW.

Screening Systems

Screening systems use predefined performance criteria to screen out vendors. Perhaps your project requires board-certified engineers. One of the screening criteria would be that vendors propose project team members who have this qualification. If they don't, they're eliminated from the selection process.

Weighting systems and screening systems are often used in combination to come up with a selection.

Contract Negotiation

In *contract negotiation,* both parties come to an agreement regarding the contract terms. Negotiation skills are put into practice here as the details of the contract are ironed out between the parties. At a minimum, contract language should include price, responsibilities, regulations or laws that apply, and the overall approach to the project.

You might see the term *fait accompli* show up on the exam. Fait accompli tactics are used during contract negotiation when one party tries to convince the other party discussing a particular contract item that it is no longer an issue. It's a distraction technique, as the party practicing fait accompli tactics is purposely trying to keep from negotiating an issue and claims the issue cannot be changed. For example, during negotiations the vendor tells you that the key resource they're assigning to your project must start immediately or you'll lose that resource and they'll get assigned work elsewhere. However, you don't know—because the vendor didn't tell you—that they can reserve this resource for your project and hold them until the start date. They used fait accompli tactics to push you into starting the project, or hiring this resource, sooner than you would have otherwise.

Seller Rating Systems

Seller rating systems use information about the sellers—such as past performance, delivery, contract compliance, and quality ratings—to determine seller performance. Your organization may have seller rating systems in place and you should check with your procurement department to see if they exist for the bidders on your project. Part of the Contract Administration process (we'll talk about this one later in this chapter) concerns gathering and recording this type of information. Don't use seller rating systems as your sole criteria for evaluating vendors.

Expert Judgment

Expert judgment applies here as it has on many of the other processes we've discussed. Include experts from all areas of the organization when evaluating proposals and selecting vendors. Don't forget your legal and financial folks, marketing, sales, engineering, and so on.

Proposal Evaluation Techniques

Proposal evaluation techniques are a combination of all the techniques we've just talked about. All techniques use some form of expert judgment and evaluation criteria—whether it's objective or subjective criteria. The evaluation criteria are usually weighted, much like a weighted scoring system, and those participating as reviewers provide their ratings (usually to the project manager) to compile into a weighted proposal to determine an overall score.

After all the RFPs are examined and scored, we move to the outputs of this process, where sellers are selected and contracts awarded.

 Real World Scenario

Vendor Selection for Fitness Counts HR System

Amanda Jacobson is the project manager for Fitness Counts, a nationwide chain of gyms containing all the latest and greatest fitness equipment, aerobics classes, swimming pools, and such.

Fitness Counts is converting its human resources system. There are several requirements that were specifically addressed in the RFP, including the following:

- The new system must run on a platform that's compatible with the company's current operating system.

- Hardware must be compatible with company standards.

- Data conversion of existing HR data must be included in the price of the bid.

- Fitness Counts wants to have the ability to add its own custom modules using internal programmers.

- Training of Fitness Counts programmers must be included in the bid.

The project team is in the Select Sellers process and has received bids based on the RFP published earlier this month. Fitness Counts is using a combination of selection criteria and weighted scoring model to choose a vendor.

One of the evaluation criteria said that the vendor must have prior experience with a project like this. Four vendors met that criteria and proceeded to the weighted scoring selection process.

Amanda is one of the members of the selection committee. She and four other members on the committee rated the four vendors who met the initial selection criteria. The results are shown in Tables 9.1 and 9.2 (following this sidebar).

Vendor C is the clear winner of this bid. Based on the weighted scoring model, their responses to the RFP came out ahead of the other bidders. Amanda calls them with the good news and also calls the other vendors to thank them for participating in the bid. Vendor C is awarded the contract, and Amanda moves on to the Contract Administration process.

TABLE 9.1   Example Weighted Scoring Model

Criteria	Weight*	Vendor A Weighting Factor	Vendor A Score	Vendor B Weighting Factor	Vendor B Score
Platform	5	3	15	2	10
Hardware	4	3	12	3	12
Data Conversion	5	3	15	4	20
Custom Modules/Training	4	4	16	3	12
Totals	—		58		54

*1–5; 5 highest

TABLE 9.2   Example Weighted Scoring Model

Criteria	Vendor C Weighting Factor	Vendor C Score	Vendor D Weighting Factor	Vendor D Score
Platform	4	20	3	15
Hardware	4	16	3	12
Data Conversion	4	20	2	10
Custom Modules/Training	3	12	4	16
Totals		68		53

*1–5; 5 highest

Select Sellers Outputs

The Select Sellers process has six outputs:

- Selected sellers
- Contract
- Contract management plan

- Resource availability
- Project management plan updates
- Requested changes

Selected sellers is obvious; you choose the seller or sellers that you'll award the project to. We'll talk more about the contract and the contract management plan next. The other outputs have been discussed previously.

Elements of a Contract

You may recall that a contract is a legally binding agreement between two or more parties, typically used to acquire goods or services. Contracts have several names, including agreements, memorandums of understanding (MOUs), subcontracts, and purchase orders.

The type of contract you'll award will depend on the product or services you're procuring and your organizational policies. We talked about the types of contracts—fixed price, cost reimbursable, and so on—in Chapter 6 if you need a refresher. If your project has multiple sellers, you'll award contracts for each of them.

The contract should clearly address the elements of the SOW, time period of performance, pricing and payment plan, acceptance criteria, warranty periods, dispute resolution procedures, and so on.

Since contracts are legally binding and obligate your organization to fulfill the terms, they'll likely be subject to some intensive review, and often by several different people. Be certain you understand your organization's policies on contract review and approval before proceeding.

Contracts, like projects, have a life cycle of their own. You might encounter questions on the exam regarding the stages of the contract life cycles, so let's look at this topic next.

Contract Life Cycles

The contract life cycle consists of four stages:

- Requirement
- Requisition
- Solicitation
- Award

These stages are closely related to the following Project Procurement knowledge areas processes from *A Guide to the PMBOK*:

- Plan Purchases and Acquisitions
- Plan Contracting
- Request Seller Responses
- Select Sellers

A description of each of the contract life cycles follows.

Requirement

The requirement stage is the equivalent of *A Guide to the PMBOK*'s Plan Purchases and Acquisitions process, which was discussed in Chapter 6. The project and contract needs are established in this cycle, and the requirements of the project are defined. The SOW is used to define the work of the project, the objectives, and a high-level overview of the deliverables. A work breakdown structure (WBS) is developed, a make-or-buy analysis takes place, and cost estimates are determined.

The SOW is provided by the buyer when the project is performed under contract to describe the requirements of the project. The product description can serve as the SOW.

Requisition

The requisition stage is similar to *A Guide to the PMBOK*'s Plan Contracting process, discussed in Chapter 6.

In the requisition stage, the project objectives are refined and confirmed. Solicitation materials such as the request for proposals (RFP), request for information (RFI), and request for quotations (RFQ) are prepared during this phase. Generally, the project manager is the one responsible for preparing the RFP, RFI, and RFQ. A review of the potential qualified vendors takes place, including checking references and reviewing other projects the vendor has worked on that are similar to your proposed project.

Solicitation

The solicitation stage is where vendors are asked to compete for the contract and respond to the RFP. You will use the tools and techniques of *A Guide to the PMBOK*'s Request Seller Responses process during this contract stage. The resulting output is the proposals.

Award

Vendors are chosen, and contracts are awarded and signed during the award stage. The equivalent to the award stage in *A Guide to the PMBOK* is the Select Sellers process.

The project manager—or the selection committee, depending on the organizational policy—receives the bids and proposals during the award phase and applies evaluation criteria to each in order to score or rank the responses. After ranking each of the proposals, an award is made to the winning vendor and the contract is written.

Once you have a contract, someone has to administer it. In large organizations, this responsibility will fall to the procurement department. The project manager should still have a solid understanding of administering contracts because they'll work with the procurement department to determine the satisfactory fulfillment of the contract.

Contract Management Plan

The contract management plan describes the contract administrative activities of the project. The plan also outlines how the contract will be administered based on the SOW elements in the contract, delivery requirements, and performance requirements both the buyer and the seller must meet. The contract management plan is a subsidiary of the project management plan.

Laying Out Quality Assurance Procedures

The Quality Planning process laid out the quality standards for the project and determined how those standards are satisfied. The *Perform Quality Assurance* process involves performing systematic quality activities and uses quality audits to determine which processes should be used to achieve the project requirements and to assure they are performed efficiently and effectively.

Project team members, the project manager, and the stakeholders are responsible for the quality assurance of the project. It could be that a quality assurance department or organization is assigned to the project to oversee these processes. In that case, quality assurance may be provided to (rather than part of) the project team, the stakeholders (whether they are involved in the work of the project or not), the customer, the project sponsor, or the management team. The project manager will have the greatest impact on the quality of the project during this process.

We'll review the inputs to this process next and then spend some time exploring a few new tools and techniques for assuring a quality product and project.

Inputs to Perform Quality Assurance

The inputs to Perform Quality Assurance are what you use to measure the organizational project quality management processes against. The quality management processes were defined during Quality Planning. The inputs to the Perform Quality Assurance process are as follows:

- Quality management plan
- Quality metrics
- Process improvement plan
- Work performance information
- Approved change requests
- Quality control measurements
- Implemented change requests
- Implemented corrective actions
- Implemented defect repair
- Implemented preventive action

You've heard about the inputs to Perform Quality Assurance before so we'll move right into the tools and techniques of this section.

Perform Quality Assurance Tools and Techniques

There are four tools and techniques of the Perform Quality Assurance process: quality planning tools and techniques, quality audits, process analysis, and quality control tools and techniques.

We discussed quality planning tools and techniques along with the Quality Planning process in Chapter 6. You'll recall that the tools and techniques are cost benefit analysis, benchmarking, design of experiments, and cost of quality. These tools can be used during this process as well to measure project performance.

The quality control tools and techniques listed in this process are the same tools and techniques discussed in the Perform Quality Control process we'll talk about in Chapter 11, "Controlling Work Results and Closing Out the Project." We'll look at the remaining tools and techniques in the following sections.

Quality Audits

Quality audits are independent reviews performed by trained auditors or third-party reviewers. The purpose of a quality audit is the same as the purpose of the Perform Quality Assurance process, to identify ineffective and inefficient processes used on the project. These audits may examine and uncover inefficient processes and procedures as well.

Quality audits may be performed on a regular schedule or at random depending on the organizational policies. Quality audits performed correctly will provide the following benefits:

- The product of the project is fit for use and meets safety standards.
- Applicable laws and standards are adhered to.
- Corrective action is recommended and implemented where necessary.
- The quality plan for the project is adhered to.
- Quality improvements are identified.
- The implementation of approved change requests, corrective actions, preventive actions, and defect repairs are confirmed.

Quality improvements come about as a result of the quality audits. During the course of the audit, you may discover ways of improving the efficiency or effectiveness of the project, thereby increasing the value of the project and more than likely exceeding stakeholder expectations.

Quality improvements are implemented by submitting change requests or taking corrective action (two of the outputs of this process). Quality improvements interface with the Monitoring and Controlling processes because of the need to file change requests.

We'll look at change requests and change request procedures in Chapter 10, "Measuring and Reporting Project Objectives."

Quality audits are generally performed by experienced specialists. The specialist's job is to produce an independent evaluation of the quality process. Some organizations are large enough to have their own quality assurance departments or quality assurance teams; others may have to hire contract personnel to perform this function. Internal quality assurance teams report results to the project team and management team of the organization. External quality assurance teams report results to the customer.

Process Analysis

Process analysis looks at process improvement from an organizational and technical perspective. According to *A Guide to the PMBOK,* process analysis follows the steps in the process improvement plan and examines the following:

- Problems experienced while conducting the project
- Constraints of the project
- Inefficient and ineffective processes identified during process operation

One of the techniques of process analysis includes performing root cause analysis. (We talked about root cause analysis in the Risk Identification process in Chapter 4.) While you're examining problems and constraints, for example, you should look for what's causing the problem. The result of this exercise will allow you to develop preventive actions for problems that are similar to the problem you're examining or that have the similar root causes.

Perform Quality Assurance Outputs

There are four outputs of the Perform Quality Assurance process:

- Requested changes
- Recommended corrective actions
- Organizational process assets updates
- Project management plan updates

None of these are new, but there is one new idea embedded in the recommended corrective actions output. During this process, the recommended corrective actions, whether they are a result of a quality audit or process analysis, should be acted upon immediately. Let's say you're manufacturing parts for one of the deliverables of your project. Obviously, the moment you discover that the parts are not correct, you'd correct the process by calibrating the machine perhaps, or using different raw materials, to make certain the parts are produced accurately.

We've completed the Executing process group with the Perform Quality Assurance process. Remember that the Executing processes and Monitoring and Controlling processes serve as inputs to each other and that Executing and Monitoring and Controlling are both iterative process groups. As your project progresses and it becomes evident controls need to be exercised to get the project back on track, you'll come back through the Executing process group and then proceed back through the Monitoring and Controlling processes again. Let's move on to the Monitoring and Controlling process group now and find out what it's all about.

Quality Improvements

While it isn't stated as an output, one of the overarching goals of the Perform Quality Assurance process is to provide a foundation for continuous process improvements. As the name implies, continuous improvements are iterative. This process of continuous improvements sets the stage, so to speak, for improving the quality of all the project processes. This can mean project management processes, but it also means the processes involved in accomplishing the work of the project, or the organizational business processes.

We talked about continuous improvement in Chapter 4; however, there a few more things you need to know about it. The advantage of continuous process improvement is that it reduces the time the project team spends on ineffective or inefficient processes. If the activities don't help you meet the goals of the project or, worse yet, hinder your progress, it's time to look at ways to improve them. *A Guide to the PMBOK* states that the organizational business processes are the objective for process improvement identification and review.

Monitor and Control Project Work

The processes in the Monitoring and Controlling process group concentrate on monitoring and measuring project performance to identify variances from the project plan and get it back on track.

The *Monitor and Control Project Work* process is concerned with monitoring all the processes in the Initiating, Planning, Executing, and Closing process groups. Collecting data, measuring results, and reporting on performance information are some of the activities you'll perform during this process.

According to *A Guide to the PMBOK*, the Monitor and Control Project Work process involves the following:

- Reporting and comparing actual project results against the project management plan
- Analyzing performance data and determining if corrective or preventive action should be recommended
- Monitoring the project for risks to make certain they're identified and reported, their status is documented, and the appropriate risk response plans have been put into action
- Documenting all appropriate product information throughout the life of the project
- Gathering, recording, and documenting project information that provides project status, measurements of progress, and forecasting to update cost and schedule information that is reported to stakeholders, project team members, management, and others
- Monitoring approved change requests

Monitor and Control Project Work Inputs

The inputs of this process include project management plan, work performance information, and rejected change requests. We've covered project management plan and work performance information in previous chapters. Rejected change requests should be documented so that if a request to perform the change comes up in the future, or there's a question about the disposition of the request, there's a record of what the change request was about and why it was rejected.

Tools and Techniques of Monitor and Control Project Work

We've seen most all of the tools and techniques of the Monitor and Control Project Work process:

- Project management methodology
- Project management information system
- Earned value technique
- Expert judgment

We'll look more closely at the earned value technique during the discussion of the Cost Control process, which we'll cover in Chapter 10.

Monitor and Control Project Work Outputs

The outputs of the Monitor and Control Project Work process will also look familiar. They are as follows:

- Recommended corrective actions
- Recommended preventive actions
- Forecasts
- Recommended defect repair
- Requested changes

The forecasts output includes information that has been gathered concerning project performance and used to predict future project outcomes. For example, the amount of time it's taken to complete the project activities to date might be used to help predict how much longer the project will take to complete.

 We'll examine several formulas that will help us do this in the next chapter.

Administering the Contract

Let's shift our focus back to the procurement arena. We talked about Request Seller Responses and Select Sellers earlier in this chapter. Now that the contract has been awarded, we need to administer it.

The *Contract Administration* process concerns monitoring the vendor's performance and ensuring that all the requirements of the contract are met. When there are multiple vendors providing goods and services to the project, Contract Administration entails coordinating the interfaces among all the vendors as well as administering each of the contracts. If vendor A has a due date that will impact whether or not vendor B can perform their service, the management and coordination of the two vendors become important. Vendor A's contract and due dates must be monitored closely because failure to perform could impact other vendor's ability to perform, not to mention the project schedule. You can see how this situation could multiply quickly when you have six or seven or more vendors involved.

It's imperative that the project manager and project team are aware of any contract agreements that may impact the project so the team does not inadvertently take action that violates the terms of the contract.

Depending on the size of the organization, administering the contract might fall to someone in the procurement department. This doesn't mean that you're off the hook as the project manager. It's still your responsibility to oversee the process and make sure the project objectives are being met, regardless of whether a vendor is performing the activities or your project team members are performing the activities. You'll be the one monitoring the performance of the vendor and informing them when and if performance is lacking. You'll also monitor the contract's financial conditions. For example, the seller should be paid in a timely manner when they've satisfactorily met the conditions of the contract and it will be up to you to let the procurement department know it's okay to pay the vendor. If administering the contract is your responsibility, you may have to terminate the contract when the vendor violates the terms or doesn't meet the agreed-upon deliverables. If the procurement department has this responsibility, you'll have to document the situation and provide this to the procurement department so that they can enforce or terminate the contract.

Administering the contract is closely linked with project management processes. You'll monitor the progress of the contract, execute plans, track costs, measure outputs, approve changes, take corrective action, and report on status, just as you do for the project itself. According to *A Guide to the PMBOK*, integration and coordination of the Direct and Manage Project Plan Execution, Performance Reporting, Perform Quality Control, Integrated Change Control, and Risk Monitoring and Control processes must be applied during Contract Administration.

Exam Spotlight

You might find several questions on the exam that involve the Request Seller Responses, Select Sellers, and Contract Administration processes. While Contract Administration belongs to the Monitoring and Controlling group, these processes are usually performed in the order stated here.

Contracting Inputs

There are six inputs to Contract Administration:

- Contract
- Contract management plan
- Selected sellers
- Performance reports
- Approved change requests
- Work performance information

The contract, contract management plan, and selected sellers are outputs from the Select Sellers process. We'll cover performance reports in more depth in Chapter 11, "Closing Out the Project." Performance reports for the Contract Administration process includes information related to the seller (or vendor).

Approved Change Requests

Sometimes as you get into the work of the project, you'll discover changes need to be made. This could entail changes to the contract as well. Approved change requests are used to process the project or contract changes and might include things like modifications to deliverables, changes to the product or service of the project, changes in contract terms, or termination for poor performance. Contracts can be amended at any time prior to contract completion provided the changes are agreed to by all parties and conform to the change control processes outlined in the contract.

Exam Spotlight

Work performance information is an output of the Direct and Manage Project Execution process. The results you gather in the Contract Administration process are actually collected as part of the Direct and Manage Project Execution work result output.

Work Performance Information

Work performance information concerns monitoring work results and examining the vendor's deliverables. This includes monitoring their work results against the project management plan and making certain activities are performed correctly and in sequence. You'll need to determine which deliverables are complete and which ones have not been completed to date. You'll also need to consider the quality of the deliverables and the costs that have been incurred to date.

Vendors request payment for the goods or services delivered in the form of *seller invoices*. Seller invoices should describe the work that was completed or the materials that were delivered and should include any supporting documentation necessary to describe what was delivered. The contract should state what type of supporting documentation is needed with the invoice.

Remember that seller invoices are an element of the work performance information input to the Contract Administration process, not an output. Also, don't confuse seller invoices with the payment system, which is a tool and technique of this process.

Administering Contracts with Tools and Techniques

Administering the contract requires several tools and techniques:

- Contract change control system
- Buyer conducted performance review
- Inspections and audits
- Performance reporting
- Payment system
- Claims administration
- Records management system
- Information technology

We will look at each of these in the following sections.

Contract Change Control System

Much like the management plans found in the Planning processes, the *contract change control system* describes the processes needed to make contract changes. Since the contract is a legal document, changes to it require the agreement of all parties. A formal process must be established to process and authorize (or deny) changes. (Authorization levels are defined in the organizational policies.)

The purpose of the contract change control system is to establish a formal process for submitting change requests. It documents how to submit changes, establishes the approval process, and outlines authority levels. It includes a tracking system to number the change requests and record their status. The procedures for dispute resolution are spelled out in the change control system as well.

The change control system, along with all the management plan outputs, becomes part of the Integrated Change Control process that we'll discuss later in this chapter.

Buyer Conducted Performance Reviews

Buyer conducted performance reviews examine the seller's performance on the contract to date. These reviews may be conducted at the end of the contract or at intervals during the contract period. Buyer reviews examine the contract terms and seller performance for elements such as these:

- Meeting project scope
- Meeting project quality
- Staying within project budgets
- Meeting the project schedule

The performance reviews themselves may take the form of quality audits or inspections of documents as well as the work of the product itself. The point of the review is to determine where the seller is succeeding at meeting scope, quality, cost, and schedule issues, for example, or where they're not measuring up. If the seller is not in compliance, action must be taken to either get them back into compliance or terminate the contract. The yardstick you're using to measure their performance against is the contract SOW and the terms of the contract itself. When the RFP is included as part of the contract (which it usually is), you may also use it to determine contract compliance.

Inspections and Audits

We talked about quality audits as part of the Perform Quality Assurance process. The idea is the same here. The buyer, or some designated third party, will physically inspect the work of the seller and perform audits to determine if there are any deficiencies in the seller's product or service.

Performance Reporting

Performance reporting is a large part of project management. This tool and technique entails providing your managers and stakeholders with information about the vendor's progress meeting the contract objectives. This information is also part of the Performance Reporting process that we'll discuss in depth later in this chapter.

Payment Systems

Vendors submit seller invoices as an input to this process, and the *payment system* is the tool and technique used to issue payment. The organization may have a dedicated department, such as accounts payable, that handles vendor payments, or it might fall to the project manager. In either case, follow the policies and procedures the organization established regarding vendor payments.

Claims Administration

Claims administration involves documenting, monitoring, and managing changes to the contract. Changes that cannot be agreed upon are called *contested changes*. Contested changes usually involve a disagreement about the compensation to the vendor for implementing the change. You might believe the change is not significant enough to justify additional compensation, whereas the vendor believes they'll lose money by implementing the change free of charge. Contested changes are also known as *disputes, claims,* or *appeals.* These can be settled directly between the parties themselves, through the court system, or by a process called arbitration. *Arbitration* involves bringing all parties to the table with a third, disinterested party who is not a participant in the contract to try to reach an agreement. The purpose of arbitration is to reach an agreement without having to go to court.

Records Management System

I think it's been a while since we've talked about documentation, but discussing *records management systems* reminds us of the importance of having an organized system for contract documentation. A records management system involves not just documentation, but policies, control functions, and automated tools as part of the project management information system (which is both a part of the enterprise environmental factors and a tool and technique of several processes) used to manage project documents as well as contract documents. Records management systems typically index documents for easy filing and retrieval.

Information Technology

Information technology, in this process, refers to the automated ways you can put some of the tools and techniques, outputs, processes, and so on to use. I don't know about you, but I've reached a point where I can't live without information technology. Having my e-mail, contacts, project documents, to-do lists, policy documents, and so on at my fingertips wherever I go is invaluable.

As mentioned earlier, using a project management software tool to help build the project schedule and allocate resources is much easier than developing all this by hand. Contract information and general project information and processes can be much more efficient when you use information technology to help you out.

Managing Contract Outputs

The outputs to the Contract Administration process are as follows:

- Contract documentation
- Requested changes
- Recommended corrective actions
- Organizational process asset updates
- Project management plan updates

These outputs relate to the tools and techniques just talked about and, in practice, work hand in hand with them. We've talked about recommended corrective actions and project management plan updates before and there's nothing new to add here. The remaining outputs are either new or involve additional information you need to know.

Contract Documentation

Here's our favorite topic again. This output includes (but isn't limited to) all of the following:

- Contract
- Performance information
- Warranties
- Financial information (like invoices and payment records)
- Inspection and audit results
- Supporting schedules
- Approved and unapproved changes

The records management system we talked about earlier is the perfect place to keep all these documents.

Requested Changes

Requested contract changes are coordinated with the Direct and Manage Project Execution and Integrated Change Control processes so that any changes impacting the project itself are communicated to the project team and appropriate actions are put into place to realign the objectives. This might also mean the project management plan itself will require changes. That requires you to jump back to the Planning process group to bring the project management plan up-to-date. Once the plan is up-to-date, the Direct and Manage Project Execution process may require changes as well to get the work of the project in line with the new plan. Remember that project management is an iterative process and it's not unusual to revisit the Planning or Executing processes, particularly as changes are made or corrective actions are put into place.

Contract changes will not always impact the project management plan, however. For example, late delivery of key equipment probably would impact the project management plan, but changes in the vendor payment schedule probably would not. It's important that you are kept abreast of any changes to the contract so that you can evaluate whether the project management plan needs adjusting.

Organizational Process Asset Updates

Organizational process assets consist of organizational policies, procedures, and so on. There are three elements of this output that relate to contracts:

Correspondence   Correspondence is information that needs to be communicated in writing to either the seller or the buyer. Examples might be changes to the contract, clarification of contract terms, and notification of performance issues. You would also use correspondence to notify a vendor that you're terminating the contract because performance is below expectations and is not satisfying the requirements of the contract.

Payment schedules and requests   Many times, contracts are written such that payment is made based on a predefined performance schedule. For example, perhaps the first payment is made after 25 percent of the product or service is completed. Or maybe the payment schedule is based on milestone completion. In any case, as the project manager, you will verify that the vendor's work (or delivery) meets expectations before the payment is authorized. It's almost always your responsibility as the project manager to verify that the terms of the contract to date have or have not been satisfied. Depending on your organizational policies, someone from the accounting or procurement department may request written notification from you that the vendor has completed a milestone or made a delivery. Monitoring the work of the vendor is as important as monitoring the work of your team members.

A Guide to the PMBOK states that the payment schedules and requests element pertains to payment systems that are external to the project. For example, if the procurement department is responsible for paying the contractor, the payment schedule (which is one of the terms of the contract) is managed by them. The seller submits a payment request, an inspection or review of their performance is conducted to make certain the terms of the contract were fulfilled, and the payment is made. If the contract payments are being managed by the project team, this output is called payments.

Seller performance evaluation   Seller performance evaluation is a written record of the seller's performance on the contract. It should include information about whether the seller successfully met contract dates, fulfilled the requirements of the contract and/or contract statement of work, whether the work was satisfactory and so on. Seller performance evaluations can be used as a basis for terminating the existing contract if performance is not satisfactory. They should also indicate whether this vendor should be allowed to bid on future work. Seller performance evaluations can also be included as part of the qualified sellers lists.

Don't confuse payment systems (a tool and technique of Contract Administration) with payment schedules and requests (an output of Contract Administration). Payment systems include reviews and authorization to issue the check. The payment schedules and request output is where the check gets sent to the seller.

Exam Spotlight

I recommend remembering the inputs, tools and techniques, and outputs of the contracting processes, including Request Seller Responses, Select Sellers, and Contract Administration. Be certain you understand the purposes of these processes and don't simply memorize their components.

Managing Project Teams

The *Manage Project Team* process is concerned with tracking and reporting on the performance of individual team members. During this process, performance appraisals are prepared and conducted, issues are identified and resolved, and feedback is given to the team members. Some team behavior is also observed during this process, but the main focus here is on individuals and their performance.

Exam Spotlight

Take note that *A Guide to the PMBOK* states that one of the outcomes or results of the Manage Project Team process is an update to the staffing management plan. However, staffing management plan updates are not listed as an output of this process.

We've seen all of the inputs to this process before:

- Organizational process assets
- Project staff assignments
- Roles and responsibilities
- Project organization charts
- Staffing management plan
- Team performance assessment
- Work performance information
- Performance reports

Tools and Techniques for Managing Teams

Most of the tools and techniques for this process are new

- Observation and conversation
- Project performance appraisal
- Conflict management
- Issue log

We'll take a closer look at each of these tools.

Observation and Conversation

Observation and conversation is another one of those obvious tools and techniques. In order to assess team member performance, you have to observe it. Hopefully, you've also learned how important communication is to the success of the project. This includes communicating with your team members. I know project managers who are reticent to engage their teams in conversation unless it's official project business. I've even known project managers who instructed their administrative assistant to give a specific direction to another team member. Surely you don't engage in these activities. It's difficult to understand a team member's attitude or viewpoint toward the project if you're communicating through someone else. Establish an open door policy with your team members and live up to it. The benefits are so great that it's worth a few minutes a day of chitchat to establish that feeling of trust and camaraderie.

Project Performance Appraisal

Project performance appraisals are typically annual or semiannual affairs where managers let their employees know what they think of their performance over the past year and rate them accordingly. These are usually manager-to-employee exchanges but can incorporate a *360-degree review,* which takes in feedback from just about everyone the team member interacts with, including stakeholders, customers, project manager, peers, subordinates, and the delivery person if they have a significant amount of project interaction. I'm not a fan of 360-degree reviews because it makes most non-manager types uncomfortable. "I don't want to rate my peer," is a typical response. I also find 360-degree reviews are biased. At best you'll get a response like, "Oh, Ken is great, just great. No problems, good guy," or exactly the opposite if the person you're speaking with doesn't like the team member you're asking about. Performance appraisal should be a bit more constructive than this. Nonetheless, understand the 360-degree concept for the exam.

No matter what type of appraisal is conducted, project managers should contribute to the performance appraisals of all project team members. You should be aware of potential loyalty issues when you're working in a matrix organizational structure. The team member in this structure reports to both you (as the project manager) and a functional manager. If the project manager does not have an equal say, or at least some say, in the employee's performance, it will cause the team member to be loyal to the functional manager and show little loyalty to the project or project manager. Managing these dual reporting relationships is often a critical success factor for the project and it is the project manager's responsibility to assure that these relationships are managed effectively.

Performance appraisal time is also a good time to explore training needs, to clarify roles and responsibilities, to set goals for the future, and so on.

Conflict Management

We talked about conflict management in the last chapter. Here it's important to note that, as in any situation, you'll want to deal with conflict as soon as it arises. During the Manage Project Team process, most conflicts come about as a result of schedule issues, availability of resources (usually the lack of availability), or personal work habits. When project team members are having a conflict, address them first in private with the person who has the issue. Work in a direct and collaborative manner but be prepared to escalate the issue into a more formalized procedure (potentially even disciplinary action) if needed.

If conflicts exist between two of the team members, encourage resolution between them without intervention on your part. The best conflict resolution will come about when they can work out the issues between them. When that isn't possible, you'll have to step in and help resolve the matter.

Remember that solid ground rules and established policies and procedures will help mitigate conflict before it arises.

Issue Log

The issue log is a place to document the issues that keep the project team from meeting project goals. These can range from differences of opinion to newly surfaced responsibilities that need assigned to a project team member. Each issue should be recorded in the log along with the person responsible for resolving it. You should also note the date the resolution is needed.

Managing Project Team Outputs

The outputs of the Manage Project Team process are the result of the conversations, performance appraisals, and conflict resolution we've talked about previously. There are five outputs of this process:

- Requested changes
- Recommended corrective actions
- Recommended preventive actions
- Organizational process asset updates
- Project management plan updates

Remember that the elements of these outputs pertain to human resources. For example, requested changes may come about as a result of a change in staffing, corrective actions may come about because of disciplinary actions or training needs, and preventive actions may be needed to reduce the impact of potential human resource issues. Any of these actions may cause changes to the staffing management plan which means the project management plan should also be updated.

The organizational process asset updates output has two components: input to organizational performance appraisals and lessons learned documentation. Input to organizational performance appraisals comes from team members with significant interactions with the project and each other.

Lessons learned encompasses everything you've learned about the human resources aspect during this project, including documentation that can be used as templates on future projects (such as org charts and position descriptions), techniques used to resolve conflict, the types of conflict that came up during the project, ground rules, when and how virtual teams were used on the project and the procedures associated with them, special skills needed during the project that weren't known about during the Planning processes, and the issues log.

Managing Stakeholders

In my experience, managing stakeholders is much more difficult than managing project team members. Stakeholders are often managers or directors in the organization who may be higher in the food chain than the project manager and aren't afraid to let you know it. Having said that, you *can* manage stakeholders and it's done using communication.

 NOTE If you need a refresher or on the definition and role of stakeholders, please see Chapter 1, "What Is a Project?"

The *Manage Stakeholders* process is about satisfying the needs of the stakeholders by managing communications with them, resolving issues, and improving project performance by implementing requested changes.

Stakeholders need lots of communication in every form you can provide. If you are actively engaged with your stakeholders and interacting with them, providing project status, and resolving issues, your chances of a successful project are much greater than if you don't do these things.

The inputs of this process are the communications management plan and organizational process assets. We've seen both of these before. The tools and techniques include communication methods and issue logs. Keep in mind that face-to-face communications are the most effective with stakeholders. The issue log in this process is more like an action item log where you record the actions needed to resolve stakeholder concerns and project issues they raise. As with the issue log in the Manage Project Team process, you'll assign a responsible party and a due date for resolution.

The outputs of the Manage Stakeholder process are resolved issues, approved change requests, approved corrective actions, organizational process assets updates, and project management plan updates. Resolved issues are logged in the issues log.

Establishing Performance Measurements

As mentioned, the Monitoring and Controlling process group concentrates on monitoring and measuring project performance to identify variances from the project plan. *Performance Reporting* is the process where the collection of baseline data occurs and is documented and reported. Performance Reporting is part of the Communications Management knowledge area, as is the Manage Stakeholders process. Thus, it involves collecting information regarding project progress and project accomplishments and reporting it to the stakeholders. This information may also be reported to project team members, the management team, and other interested parties. Reporting might include information concerning project quality, costs, scope, project schedules, procurement, and risk.

Performance Reporting Inputs

We've examined all the inputs to the Performance Reporting process. They are listed here:

- Work performance information
- Performance measurements
- Forecasted completion
- Quality control measurements
- Project management plan
- Approved change requests
- Deliverables

One thing I should note about these inputs is that the project management plan contains the project management baseline data (typically cost, schedule, and scope factors), which you'll use to monitor and compare results. Deviations from this data are reported to management. Performance measures are taken primarily during the Cost Control, Schedule Control, and Perform Quality Control processes, which we'll look at in the next chapter.

Performance Reporting Tools and Techniques

The tools and techniques of this process are as follows:

- Information presentation tools
- Performance information gathering and compilation
- Status review meetings
- Time reporting systems
- Cost reporting systems

Information Presentation Tools

Information presentation tools include automated tools like spreadsheet and presentation software that help you create presentable reports and information regarding the progress and status of the project for stakeholder review.

Performance Information Gathering and Compilation

If you and your team members have been diligently documenting your project's performance, you need to gather all that information and keep it in one place. Performance information gathering and compilation can occur manually, as in everyone turns in hard copy reports to the project manager or other designated person, or you can gather information automatically from project management software systems, databases, or other systems. The important thing is the documentation should be kept in one place and be easily accessible to anyone who needs it.

Status Review Meetings

Status review meetings are important functions during the course of the project. (We introduced status review meetings with the Information Distribution Process in the last chapter.) The purpose of the status meeting is to provide updated information regarding the progress of the project. These are not show-and-tell meetings. If you have a prototype to demo, set up a different time to do that. Status meetings are meant to exchange information and provide project updates. They are a way to formally exchange project information. I've worked on projects where it's not unusual to have three or four status meetings conducted for different audiences. They can occur between the project team and project manager, the project manager and stakeholders, the project manager and users or customers, the project manager and the management team, and so on.

Notice that the project manager is always included in status review meetings. Take care that you don't overburden yourself with meetings that aren't necessary or could be combined with other meetings. Any more than three or four status meetings is unwieldy.

> Regular, timely status meetings prevent surprises down the road because you are keeping stakeholders and customers informed of what's happening. Team status meetings alert the project manager to potential risk events and provide the opportunity to discover and manage problems before they get to the uncontrollable stage.

The project manager is usually the expediter of the status meeting. As such, it's your job to use status meetings wisely. Don't waste your team's time or stakeholders' time either. Notify attendees in writing of the meeting time and place. Publish an agenda prior to the meeting and stick to the agenda during the meeting. Every so often, summarize what's been discussed during the meeting. Don't let side discussions lead you down rabbit trails, and keep irrelevant conversations to a minimum. It's also good to publish status meeting notes at the conclusion of the meeting, especially if any action items resulted from the meeting. This will give you a document trail and serves as a reminder to the meeting participants of what actions need to be resolved and who is responsible for the action item.

It's important that project team members are honest with the project manager and that the project manager is in turn honest about what they report. A few years ago, a department in my agency took on a project of gargantuan proportions and unfortunately didn't employ good project management techniques. One of the biggest problems with this project was that the project manager did not listen to their highly skilled project team members. The team members warned of problems and setbacks, but the project manager didn't want to hear of it. The project manager took their reports to be of the "Chicken Little" ilk and refused to believe the sky was falling. Unfortunately, the sky *was* falling! The project manager, because they didn't believe it, refused to report the true status of the project to the stakeholders and oversight committees. Millions of dollars were wasted on a project that was doomed for failure, while the project manager continued to report that the project was on time and activities were completed when in fact they were not.

There are hundreds of project stories like this, and I'll bet you've got one or two from your experiences as well. Don't let your project become the next bad example. Above all, be honest in your reporting. No one likes bad news, but bad news delivered too late along with millions of dollars wasted is a guaranteed career showstopper.

Time and Cost Reporting Systems

Time and cost reporting systems are used to, obviously, record time and cost information about the project. Most specifically, these systems will report the time and cost that's been expended on the project to date.

Performance Reporting Outputs

There are several outputs to the Performance Reporting process:

- Performance reports
- Forecasts
- Requested changes
- Organizational process assets updates

Performance reports is the primary output of this process. It's here that performance information is gathered, documented, and reported to the stakeholders as outlined in the communication management plan. These reports might take many forms, including S curves (cost baselines are recorded this way), bar charts, tables, and histograms. Earned value information is often reported during this process as well. We'll examine this topic in the next chapter during the discussion of the Cost Control process.

In the next chapter we'll explore the main change control processes and the measurement tools you'll use to provide the variance measurements that are gathered and reported to the stakeholder during the Performance Reporting process.

Project Case Study: New Kitchen Heaven Retail Store

Your regularly scheduled status meeting is coming up. Let's see how it's progressing.

"Thank you all for coming," you begin. You note those stakeholders who are present and pass out the agendas. "First, we have a contract update. Jake, would you give us the update please?"

"Gomez Construction has submitted a seller payment request for the work completed through November 30. Shelly in our contract management office manages the payment system and handles all payment requests. She'll get a check cut and out to Gomez by the end of this month. They are doing an outstanding job as always. As you know, I've also hired an independent inspector, aside from the city and county types, so that we make sure we're up to code before the city types get there. I don't want to get caught in that trap and end up delaying the project because we can't get the city inspector back out to reinspect quickly enough."

"Thank you, Jake. Any problems with those inspections so far?"

Jake clears his throat. "It turned out to be a good move because the contractor did find some things that we were able to correct before bringing out the official inspectors."

"Ricardo, do you have a contract update for us today?"

"Yes. The contract management office used a fixed price contract on the hardware and IT supplies order. That contract is just now making its way through the sign-off processes. My group will manage the quality control and testing once all this equipment arrives."

"Jill, can you give us the update on the store?" you ask.

"I've ordered all the retail products, the cookware line, and have lined up the chef demos. The costs for the new gourmet supplier we're using are higher than our original vendor. This impacts ongoing operations, but the hit to the project budget is minimal. I should also mention that a change request was submitted."

You point everyone's attention to the issues list. "Last meeting I reported that Gomez had an important crew member out on a family emergency. Gomez was able to replace the team member with no impact to the schedule. Next issue was the T1 connection—I reported that Ricardo was not receiving phone calls back. Good news—that issue has been cleared, the date has been set, and we can close this issue. Are there any new issues to be added this week?"

One of the stakeholders from the marketing department speaks up, "I need someone from the project team to work with me on the website announcement. I haven't heard anything and I don't want to cut this so close that we put up something sub-par on the website. The 50th anniversary deserves a little splash."

"Okay," you reply. "I'll set up a meeting with you to get more information and then we'll determine who is the best fit. I've noted we need to assign someone to this activity in the issues log. On another note, I have one more issue to report. Unfortunately, we lost a valuable team member last week. I don't want to go into all the details here but this employee violated our Internet acceptable use policy. This person was placed on disciplinary action on this very issue once before. This will cause an impact to the project schedule because his activities were on the critical path. I've already interviewed two internal candidates who've expressed interest in working on the project. I believe either one would work out nicely. However, there is some ramp-up time needed.

"What's the forecast?" Dirk asks. "Are we on track for meeting the grand opening date given all these issues?

"I'll have performance figures for you at the next status meeting and I have some ideas on how we can make up this time other ways so that we still meet the date."

You thank everyone for coming and remind them of the next meeting time.

Project Case Study Checklist

Contract Administration

- Contract documentation

- Seller invoices

- Payment systems

- Records management system

Perform Quality Assurance

- Quality audits

- Making certain the project will meet and satisfy the quality standards of the project

Manage Project Team

- Observation and conversation

- Recommended corrective actions

- Conflict management

- Issue log

Manage Stakeholders

- Communications methods

- Issue log

- Resolved issues

Performance Reporting

- Performance reports (status meetings)

- Forecasts

Summary

This chapter finished up the Executing process group and looked at the first process in the Monitoring and Controlling process group. We discussed Request Seller Responses, Select Sellers, Contract Administration, and Perform Quality Assurance from the Executing process group. We also covered several processes in the Monitoring and Controlling process group including Monitor and Control project Work, Contract Administration, Manage Project Team, Manage Stakeholders, and Performance Reporting. Request Seller Responses involves obtaining bids and responses from vendors. The tools and techniques of this process include bidder conferences, advertising, and develop qualified sellers list.

Select Sellers involves receiving bids or proposals. In this process, the selection committee will use evaluation criteria to prioritize the bids and proposals and the outcome is that a seller (or sellers) is selected and contracts awarded.

During the Perform Quality Assurance process, quality audits are performed to ensure that the project will meet and satisfy the project's quality standards set out in the quality plan.

The Monitor and Control Project Work project concerns monitoring all the project process groups, collecting data, measuring results, reporting on performance information, and taking corrective action to keep the project in scope and on schedule.

Contract Administration is the process where you'll monitor the vendor's performance and ensure that all the requirements of the contract are met. If there is more than one vendor working on the project, Contract Administration entails coordinating the interfaces among all the vendors as well as administering each of the contracts.

Contracts have cycles of their own, much like projects. Phases of the contracting life cycle include requirement, requisition, solicitation, and award. Changes to the contract are managed with change requests.

Changes that cannot be agreed upon are called contested changes. These take the form of disputes, claims, or appeals. They might be settled among the parties directly, through a court of law, or through arbitration.

Request Seller Responses and Select Sellers belong to the Executing process group and the Contract Administration belongs to the Monitoring and Controlling process group. In practice, you'll generally perform Request Seller Responses, Select Sellers, and Contract Administration in that order.

Manage Project Teams involves tracking and reporting on project team member performance. Performance appraisals are performed during this process and feedback is provided to the team members.

The Manage Stakeholders process concerns making certain communication needs of the stakeholders are met, managing any issues stakeholders might raise, and implementing change requests.

The last process in this chapter, Performance Reporting, is one of the ways stakeholders (and others) are kept informed of project progress. Performance Reporting includes tools and techniques like information presentation tools and status reports to report performance, requested changes, forecast future project performance, and update organizational process assets.

Exam Essentials

Be able to describe the difference between the Request Seller Responses process and the Select Sellers process. Request Seller Responses obtains bids and proposals from vendors. Select Sellers is the receipt of bids and proposals and the selection of a vendor.

Be able to name the tools and techniques of the Select Sellers process. The tools and techniques of the Select Sellers process are weighting systems, independent estimates, screening systems, contract negotiation, seller rating systems, expert judgment, and proposal evaluation techniques.

Be able to describe the purpose of the Perform Quality Assurance process. The Perform Quality Assurance process is concerned with making certain the project will meet and satisfy the quality standards of the project.

Be able to describe the purpose of the Monitor and Control Project Work process. Monitor and Control Project Work monitors the project process groups including Initiating, Planning, Executing, and Closing. This process reports and compares project results with the project management plan, monitors approved change requests, and analyzes, documents, and records project information.

Be able to name the contracting life cycle stages. Contracting life cycles include requirement, requisition, solicitation, and award.

Be able to name the tools and techniques of the Manage Project Team process. The tools and techniques of Manage Project Team are observation and conversation, project performance appraisal, conflict management, and issue log.

Be able to describe the purpose of the Manage Stakeholders process Manage Stakeholders concerns satisfying the needs of the stakeholders by managing communications with them.

Be able to define the purpose of the Performance Reporting process. The Performance Reporting process collects and reports information regarding project progress and project accomplishments. The technique used often to report on project performance is earned value analysis.

Key Terms

You've learned a lot of new key words in this chapter. PMI has worked hard to develop and define standard project management terms that apply across industries. Here is a list of some of the terms you came across in this chapter:

360-degree review	Manage Project Team
advertising	Manage Stakeholders
appeals	Monitor and Control Project Work
arbitration	payment system
bidder conferences	Perform Quality Assurance process
claims	Performance Reporting
claims administration	process analysis
contested changes	quality audits
Contract Administration	Request Seller Responses
contract change control system	screening systems
contract negotiation	Select Sellers
develop qualified seller lists	seller invoices
disputes	seller rating systems
evaluation criteria	should cost estimates
fait accompli	status review meetings
independent estimates	work performance information

Review Questions

1. You are a project manager for Dakota Software Consulting Services. You're working with a major retailer that offers its products through mail-order catalogs. The company is interested in knowing customer characteristics, the amounts of first-time orders, and similar information. As a potential bidder for this project, you worked on the RFP response and submitted the proposal. When the selection committee received the RFP responses from all the vendors bidding on this project, they used a weighted system to make a selection. Which process did this occur in?

   A. Select Sellers

   B. Request Seller Responses

   C. Plan Contracting and Purchases

   D. Contract Administration

2. You have been asked to submit a proposal for a project that has been put out for bid. First, you attend the bidder conference to ask questions of the buyers and to hear the questions some of the other bidders will ask. Which of the following statements is true?

   A. Bidder conferences are a tool and technique of the Select Sellers process.

   B. Bidder conferences are an output of the Select Sellers process.

   C. Bidder conferences are an output of the Request Seller Responses process.

   D. Bidder conferences are a tool and technique of the Request Seller Responses process.

3. You have been asked to submit a proposal for a project that has been put out for bid. Prior to submitting the proposal, your company must register so that its firm is on the qualified seller list. Which of the following statements is true?

   A. The qualified seller list provides information about the sellers and is a tool and technique of the Request Seller Responses process.

   B. The qualified seller list provides information about the project and the company that wrote the RFP and is an output of the Select Sellers process.

   C. The qualified seller list provides information about the project and the company that wrote the RFP and is a tool and technique of the Select Sellers process.

   D. The qualified seller list provides information about the sellers and is an output to the Request Seller Responses.

4. Which of the following tools and techniques of the Select Sellers process is used to check proposed pricing?

   A. Screening systems

   B. Seller rating systems

   C. Independent estimates

   D. Proposal evaluation technique

5. During the opening rounds of contract negotiation, the other party uses a fait accompli tactic. Which of the following statements is true about fait accompli tactics?

   A. One party agrees to accept the offer of the other party but secretly knows they will bring the issue back up at a later time.

   B. One party claims the issue under discussion was documented and accepted as part of Scope Verification.

   C. One party claims the issue under discussion has already been decided and can't be changed.

   D. One party claims to accept the offer of the other party, provided a contract change request is submitted describing the offer in detail.

6. The tools and techniques of the Request Seller Responses process include all of the following except which one?

   A. Bidder conferences

   B. Information technology

   C. Advertising

   D. Develop qualified sellers list

7. All of the following are tools and techniques of the Contract Administration process except for which one?

   A. Contract change control system, buyer conducted performance review, inspections and audits

   B. Performance reporting, payment system, claims administration

   C. Records management system, information technology

   D. Contract performance information gathering, contract reporting systems

8. You are a project manager for an engineering company. Your company won the bid to add ramp-metering lights to several on-ramps along a stretch of highway at the south end of the city. You subcontracted a portion of the project to another company. The subcontractor's work involves digging the holes and setting the lamp poles in concrete. The subcontractor's performance is not meeting the contract requirements. Which of the following is not a valid option?

   A. You document the poor performance in written form and send the correspondence to the subcontractor.

   B. You terminate the contract for poor performance and submit a change request through Contract Administration.

   C. You submit a change request through Contract Administration demanding that the subcontractor comply with the terms of the contract.

   D. You agree to meet with the subcontractor to see if a satisfactory solution can be reached.

9. You are a project manager for an engineering company. Your company won the bid to add ramp-metering lights to several on-ramps along a stretch of highway at the south end of the city. You subcontracted a portion of the project to another company. The subcontractor's work involves digging the holes and setting the lamp poles in concrete. You discover, through an independent review, that the process the subcontractor uses to report their progress is inefficient. Which of the following is true?

   A. You are in the Perform Quality Assurance process and have performed a quality audit.

   B. You are in the Perform Quality Assurance process and have performed a process analysis.

   C. You are in the Contract Administration process and have completed a contract audit to ensure that the subcontractor's performance meets the contract requirements.

   D. You are in the Performance Reporting process and have completed a performance review of the contractor's work.

10. The purpose of a quality audit includes all of the following except which one?

    A. To determine which project processes are inefficient or ineffective

    B. To examine the work of the project and formally accept the work results

    C. To improve processes and reduce the cost of quality

    D. To improve processes and increase the percentage of product or service acceptance

11. You are a contract project manager for a wholesale flower distribution company. Your project involves developing a website for the company that allows retailers to place their flower orders online. You will also provide a separate link for individual purchases that are ordered, packaged, and mailed to the consumer directly from the grower's site. This project involves coordinating the parent company, growers, and distributors. You've discovered a problem with one of the technical processes needed to perform this project. You decide to perform root cause analysis to determine the cause of this problem and then recommended preventive actions. Which of the following is true?

    A. You are using the process analysis technique.

    B. You are using the quality audit technique.

    C. You are using the root cause identification technique.

    D. You are using a Quality Control tool and technique.

12. The tools and techniques of the Perform Quality Assurance process include all of the following except which one?

    A. Quality audits

    B. Process analysis

    C. Continuous process improvements

    D. Quality Control tools and techniques

13. When working in a matrixed environment, all of the following are true regarding the Manage Project Team process except for which one?

    A. Communication methods and issue logs are used to create performance appraisals, provide feedback, and track issues.

    B. Managing project teams in a matrix environment is often a critical success factor for the project.

    C. It's the project manager's responsibility to make certain this dual reporting relationship is managed effectively.

    D. Loyalty issues may arise when managing projects in a matrixed environment.

14. You are preparing project performance appraisals and have decided you'd like each team member to get feedback regarding their performance from several sources, including peers, superiors, and subordinates. Which of the following is true?

    A. This is called 360-degree feedback and is part of the input to the organizational project performance appraisals, which is part of the organizational process assets updates input of the Manage Project Team process.

    B. This is called 360-degree feedback and is considered part of the team performance assessment input of the Manage Project Team process.

    C. This is called 360-degree feedback and is considered part of the work performance information input of the Manage Project Team process.

    D. This is called 360-degree feedback and is part of the project performance appraisals tool and technique of the Manage Project Team process.

15. You are performing actions such as reporting and comparing actual project results against the project management plan, analyzing performance data and determining if corrective or preventive action should be recommended, documenting all appropriate product information throughout the life of the project, gathering and recording project information, and monitoring approved change requests. Which process are you performing?

    A. Performance Reporting

    B. Manage Stakeholders

    C. Monitor and Control Project Work

    D. Perform Quality Assurance

16. You are collecting information regarding project progress and project accomplishments and reporting it to the stakeholders. You will manage these communication needs and resolve issues using the communication management plan as your guideline. Which of the following is true?

   A. You are using the Performance Reporting process, which involves reporting project progress and accomplishments to the stakeholders. You are using the performance information gathering and compilation tool, which is used in conjunction with the communications management plan, to coordinate and report information.

   B. You are using both the Performance Reporting and Manage Stakeholders processes, which are both part of the Project Communications Management knowledge area.

   C. You are using the communications method (an input) and issue logs (a tool and technique) of the Manage Stakeholder process.

   D. You are creating performance reports and recommended corrective actions, which are both outputs of the Performance Reporting process.

17. You are working on a project and discover that one of the business users responsible for testing the product never completed this activity. She's written an e-mail requesting that one of your team members drop everything to assist her with a problem that could have been avoided if she would have performed the test. This employee reports to a stakeholder, not to the project team. All project team members and stakeholders are collocated. Since your team needs her to also participate in an upcoming test, you decide to do which of the following?

   A. You decide to record the issue in the issue log and bring it up at the next status meeting. Everyone can benefit from understanding the importance of stakeholders fulfilling their roles and responsibilities on the project.

   B. You decide to record the issue in the issue log and then phone the stakeholder to explain what happened. You know speaking with the stakeholder directly is the most effective means for resolving issues.

   C. You decide to have a face-to-face meeting with the stakeholder because this is the most effective means for resolving issues with them.

   D. You decide to e-mail the stakeholder and explain what happened in a professional manger because this is the most effective means for resolving issues with them.

18. You are working on a project and discover that one of the business users responsible for testing the product never completed this activity. She's written an e-mail requesting that one of your team members drop everything to assist her with a problem that could have been avoided if she would have performed the test. This employee reports to a stakeholder, not to the project team. You estimate that the project may not be completed on time as a result of this missed activity. All of the following are true except for which one?

   A. You should recommend a corrective action to bring the expected future project performance back into line with the project management plan because of this employee's failure to perform this activity.

   B. You should recommend a preventive action to reduce the possibility of future project performance veering off track because of this employee's failure to perform this activity.

   C. You've created a forecast, an output of the Monitor and Control Project Work process, using past performance to predict what the project's future condition may look like.

   D. You may have to request a change to the project schedule as a result of this missed activity.

19. All of the following are tools and techniques of the Performance Reporting process except which one?

   A. Performance measurements

   B. Cost reporting systems

   C. Information presentation tools

   D. Time reporting systems

20. Your project is progressing as planned. The project team has come up with a demo that the sales team will use when making presentations to prospective clients. You will do which of the following at your next stakeholder project status meeting?

   A. Preview the demo for stakeholders and obtain their approval and sign-off.

   B. Report on the progress of the demo and note that it's a completed task.

   C. Review the technical documentation of the demo and obtain approval and sign-off.

   D. Report that the demo has been noted as a completed task in the information retrieval system.

Answers to Review Questions

1. A. Select Sellers involves the receipt of bids and proposals. Weighted systems are one of the tools and techniques of this process used to evaluate vendors based on selection criteria defined by the organization.

2. D. Bidder conferences are a tool and technique of the Request Seller Responses. Solicitation is where proposals are submitted by vendors and obtained by the organization.

3. D. Qualified seller lists are an output of the Request Seller Responses. Their purpose is to provide information about the sellers.

4. C. Independent estimates, also called should cost estimates, are a way to check proposed pricing.

5. C. Fait accompli is a tactic used during contract negotiations where one party convinces the other that the particular issue is no longer relevant or cannot be changed. Option B is not correct because Scope Verification does not generally occur during contract negotiations since the work of the project has not yet been performed.

6. B. Information technology is a tool and technique of the Contract Administration process.

7. D. The tools and techniques of the Contract Administration process are contract change control system, buyer conducted performance review, inspections and audits, performance reporting, payment system, claims administration, records management system, and information technology.

8. C. The contract change control system describes the processes you'll use to make changes to the contract, not as a means of communication. The changes might include contract term changes, date changes, and termination of a contract.

9. A. You have performed a quality audit, which is a structured, independent review of the either the organizational or project processes, policies, or procedures. Process analysis examines the root causes and follows steps in the process improvement plan.

10. B. The acceptance of work results happens later during the Scope Verification process, not during Perform Quality Assurance.

11. A. The process analysis technique in the Perform Quality Assurance process includes root cause analysis to analyze a problem and solution and to create preventive actions.

12. C. Continuous process improvements are a result of the Perform Quality Assurance process but not a tool and technique.

13. A. Communication methods are not a tool and technique of the Manage Project Team process.

14. D. This technique is called 360-degree feedback. It's part of the performance appraisals tool and technique of the Manage Project Team process.

15. C. The Monitor and Control Project Work process involves reporting and comparing project results, gathering and recording data, recommending actions, and monitoring approved change requests.

16. B. This question describes the Performance Reporting process (concerned with collecting and reporting information regarding project progress and project accomplishments to the stakeholders) and the Manage Stakeholders process (of which communications methods and issue logs are tools and techniques).

17. C. Face-to-face meetings are the most effective means for resolving stakeholder issues provided these meetings are practical.

18. B. You are in the Monitor and Control Project Work process. Preventive actions reduce the possibility of negative impacts from risk events and does not apply to this situation.

19. A. The tools and techniques of the Performance Reporting process are information presentation tools, performance information gathering and compilation, status review meetings, time reporting systems, and cost reporting systems.

20. B. Status meetings are to report on the progress of the project. They are not for demos or show-and-tell. Option C is not correct because stakeholders are not concerned about the content of the technical documentation; they need to know that the technical documentation has been reviewed by a qualified technician and that the documentation task is accurate and complete.

Monitoring and Controlling Change

THE PMP EXAM CONTENT FROM THE MONITORING AND CONTROLLING THE PROJECT PERFORMANCE DOMAIN COVERED IN THIS CHAPTER INCLUDES THE FOLLOWING:

✓ Measure Project Performance

✓ Verify and Manage Changes to the Project

✓ Monitor all Risks

We started examining the Monitoring and Controlling processes in the last chapter. This chapter will finish up the remaining processes in the Monitoring and Controlling process group.

Performance reports, which are an output of the Performance Reporting process, serve as an input to some of the Monitoring and Controlling processes we'll talk about in this chapter. Performance reports are used during the Monitoring and Controlling processes, along with tools and techniques, to measure project performance. These measurements and control tools allow the project manager to take corrective action during the Monitoring and Controlling processes to remedy wayward project results and realign future project results with the project management plan.

We'll cover several processes in this chapter, including Integrated Change Control, Cost Control, Schedule Control, and Risk Monitoring and Control.

Integrated Change Control lays the foundation for all of the change control processes. We'll spend time during this process to explain how change control works. The Cost Control and Schedule Control processes are very similar to Integrated Change Control. Remember when you're reading these sections that the information from the Integrated Change Control process applies to these areas as well. Risk Monitoring and Control monitors the project for risks and monitors the risk response plans that have been put into action or may need to be put into action.

You've learned a lot about project management by this point and have just a few more things to add to your study list. Keep up the good work. You're getting closer to exam day.

Managing Integrated Change Control

The *Integrated Change Control* process serves as an overseer, so to speak, of the Monitoring and Controlling processes. This is where the project's change control process is established. Changes, updates, and corrective actions are common outputs across all the Monitoring and Controlling processes. (And don't forget that requested change requests are also an output of the Direct and Manage Project Plan Execution process, which is an Executing process.) These outputs often generate change requests that are managed through this process.

We've seen all of the inputs, tools and techniques, and outputs of this process before. There isn't any new information to add to these. However, there are likely exam questions on several topics that involve change and the Integrated Change Control process. Configuration management, for example, isn't listed as a tool and technique of this process, but you really can't perform Integrated Change Control without it. We'll discuss this shortly. First, let's look at change, what it is, and how it comes about.

Changes come about on projects for many reasons. It's the project manager's responsibility to manage these changes and see to it that organizational policies regarding changes are implemented. Changes don't necessarily mean negative consequences. Changes can produce positive results as well. It's important that you manage this process carefully, because too many changes—even one significant change—will impact cost, schedule, scope, and/or quality. Once a change request has been submitted, you've got some decisions to make. Ask yourself questions such as, Should the change be implemented? If so, what's the cost to the project in terms of project constraints: cost, time, scope, and quality? Will the benefits gained by making the change increase or decrease the chances of project completion?

Just because a change is requested doesn't mean you have to implement it. You'll always want to discover the reasons for the change and determine if they're justifiable, and you'll want to know the cost of the change. Remember that cost can take the form of increased time. Let's say the change you're considering increases the schedule completion date. That means you'll need human resources longer than expected. If you've leased equipment or project resources for the team members to use during the course of the project, a later completion date means your team needs the leased equipment for a longer period of time. All this translates to increased costs. Time equals money, as the saying goes, so manage time changes wisely and dig deep to find the impacts that time changes might make on the budget.

How Change Occurs

As the project progresses, the stakeholders or customers may request a change directly. Team members might also recommend changes as the project progresses. For example, once the project is under way, they may discover more efficient ways of performing tasks or producing the product of the project and recommend changes to accommodate the new efficiencies. Changes may also come about as a result of mistakes that were made earlier in the project (in the Planning or in the Executing processes. Hopefully, you've applied all the great practices and techniques we've talked about to date and didn't experience many of these.

Changes to the project may occur indirectly as a result of contingency plans, other changes, or team members performing favors for the stakeholders by making that one little change without telling anyone about it. Many times, the project manager is the last to know about changes like this one. There's a fine line here because you don't want to discourage good working relationships between team members and stakeholders, yet at the same time, you want to ensure that all changes come through the change control process. If a dozen little changes slip through like this, your project scope suddenly exits stage left.

Change Control Concerns

Integrated Change Control, according to *A Guide to the PMBOK,* is primarily concerned with the following:

- Influencing the factors that cause change and reaching agreement on their resulting change requests
- Determining that change is needed or has happened

- Managing approved changes
- Updating the requirements that impact scope, quality, schedule, and budgets based on approved changes
- Documenting requested changes and their impacts

Factors that may cause change include project constraints, stakeholder requests, team member recommendations, vendor issues, and many others. You'll want to understand the factors that are influencing or bringing about change and how a proposed change may impact the project if implemented. Performance measures and corrective actions may dictate that a project change is needed as well.

 Modifications to the project are submitted in the form of change requests and managed through the change control process. Obviously, you'll want to implement those changes that are most beneficial to the project. We'll talk more about change requests later in this chapter.

Managing changes may involve making changes to the project scope, schedule, or cost baseline, also known as the *performance measurement baseline*. This baseline may also involve quality or technical elements. The performance measurement baseline is the approved project management plan that describes the work of the project. This is used through Executing and Monitoring and Controlling to measure project performance and determine deviations from the plan. It's your responsibility to maintain the reliability of the performance measurement baselines. If changes are not appropriately reflected in the baselines, they become meaningless. Changes that impact a previous project management process will require updates to those processes, which might mean additional passes through the appropriate Planning and Executing processes.

The management plans created during the Planning process group should reflect the changes as well, which may require updates to the project management plan or the project scope statement. This requires a close eye on coordination among all the processes that are impacted. For example, changes may require updates to risk response alternatives, schedule, cost, resource requirements, or other elements. Changes that impact product scope always require an update to the project scope.

Exam Spotlight

Managing changes involves maintaining accurate and reliable performance measurement baselines, coordinating all processes impacted as a result of the change, including revisiting Planning and Executing processes where needed and updating project scope to reflect any changes in product scope.

I caution you to not change baselines at the drop of a hat. Examine the changes, their justification, and their impacts thoroughly before making changes to the baselines.

Configuration Management

Configuration management is generally a subset of the project management information system. It describes the process for submitting change requests and includes processes for tracking the changes and their disposition, processes for defining the approval levels for approving and denying changes, and a process for authorizing the changes. We'll talk about each of these topics later.

Let's take a look at what *A Guide to the PMBOK* notes are the activities associated with configuration change management in the Integrated Change Control process:

Configuration identification   Configuration identification describes the characteristics of the product of the project and makes sure the description is accurate and complete. This description is the basis that's used to verify when changes are made and how they're managed.

Configuration status accounting   This activity doesn't really have to do with financials as you might guess from its title. It's about accounting for the status of the changes by documenting and storing the configuration information needed to effectively manage the product information.

Configuration verification and auditing   Verification and audits are performed as part of configuration management to determine if the performance and functional requirements have been met.

Exam Spotlight

Understand for the exam that configuration management involves identifying the physical characteristics of the product of the project (or of the individual components of the product), controlling changes to those characteristics, and documenting changes to verify that requirements are met. It also includes the change management system and documents the process for requesting, tracking, and determining if change requests should be approved or denied.

Change Control System

If you were to allow changes to occur to the project whenever requested, you would probably never complete the project. Stakeholders, the customer, and end users would continually change the project requirements if given the opportunity to do so. That's why careful planning and scope definition are important in the beginning of the project. It's your job as project manager to drive out all the compelling needs and requirements of the project during the Planning process so that important requirements aren't suddenly "remembered" halfway through the project. However, we're all human, and sometimes things are not known, weren't thought about, or simply weren't discovered until a certain point during the project. Stakeholders will probably start thinking in a direction they weren't considering during the Planning process, and new requirements will come to light. This is where the *change control system* comes into play.

The Purpose of the Change Control System

Change control systems are documented procedures that describe how to submit change requests, how to manage change requests, and the management impacts of the changes as they pertain to project performance. They are usually subsystems of the configuration management system. They can include preprinted change request forms that provide a place to record general project information such as the name and project number, the date, and the details regarding the change request.

The change control system also tracks the status of change requests, including their approval status. Not all change requests will receive approval to be implemented. Those changes that are not approved are also tracked and filed in the project notebook for future reference.

The change control system may define the level of authority needed to approve changes if it wasn't previously defined in the configuration management system. Some change requests could receive approval based on the project manager's decision; others may need more formal approval or more levels of approval such as the project sponsor, executive management, and so on.

Procedures should be defined that detail how emergency changes are approved as well. For example, you and your team might be putting in some weekend hours and are close to the completion of a deliverable when you discover that thing one will not talk to thing two no matter what you do. The team brainstorms and comes up with a brilliant solution that requires a change request. Do you stop work right then and wait until the change control board or committee can meet sometime next week and make a decision, or do you—the project manager—make the decision to go forward with this solution and explain the change to the appropriate parties later? That answer depends on the change procedures you have in place to handle situations like this and the authority you have to make emergency changes as outlined in the change control system.

Many organizations have formal change control or change request systems in place. If that's the case, you can easily adopt those procedures and use the existing system to manage project change. But if no procedures exist, you'll have to define them.

Exam Spotlight

The change control system and configuration management system together identify, document, and control the changes to the performance baseline.

Requirements for Change

There are two things you should require at the beginning of all projects regarding change. First, require that all change requests be submitted in writing. This is to clarify the change and make sure no confusion exists regarding what's requested. It also allows the project team to accurately estimate the time it will take to incorporate the change. Keep in mind that you will get verbal change requests as well.

Change requests may be verbal or written, but it's good practice to require them in writing.

Second, all change requests must come through the formal change control system. Make sure no one is allowed to go directly to team members and request changes without the project manager knowing about it. Also make certain your stakeholders understand that this can cause schedule delays, cost overruns, and sacrifices to quality and isn't good change management practice. Encourage them from the beginning of the project to use the formal procedures laid out in the change control system to request changes.

Change Control Board

In some organizations, a *configuration control board (CCB)* is established to review all change requests. The board is given the authority to approve or deny change requests as defined by the organization. It's important that its authority is clearly defined and that separate procedures exist for emergency changes. The CCB may meet only once a week, once every other week, or even once a month, depending on the project. When emergencies arise, the preestablished procedures allow the project manager to implement the change on the spot. This will always require a follow-up with the CCB and the completion of a formal change request even though it's after the fact.

CCB members may include stakeholders, managers, project team members, and others who may not have any connection to the project at hand. Some organizations have permanent CCBs that are staffed by full-time employees dedicated to managing change for the entire organization, not just project change. You may want to consider establishing a CCB for your project if the organization does not have one.

Some organizations use other types of review boards that have the same responsibilities as the CCB. Some other names you might see are technical assessment board (TAB), technical review board (TRB), engineering review board (ERB), and change control board (CCB).

Integrated Change Control Inputs

The inputs to the Integrated Change Control process are similar to its outputs. The inputs are "requested" or "recommended," while the outputs are "approved." For example, requested changes are inputs and approved or rejected change requests are outputs; recommended corrective actions are inputs and approved corrective actions are outputs. The inputs for the Integrated Change Control process are as follows:

- Project management plan
- Requested changes
- Recommended preventive actions
- Recommended corrective actions
- Recommended defect repair
- Deliverables

Remember that the project management plan includes all the documents together that make up that plan—the project schedule, budget, scope statement, and so on.

Integrated Change Control Tools and Techniques

We've seen all the tools and techniques for Integrated Change Control in previous processes:

- Project management methodology
- Project management information system
- Expert judgment

The project management methodology tool and technique really comes in handy with this process because part of this methodology defines how you'll perform change control. The project management information system is used to document and track change information and expert judgment helps determine the disposition of change requests.

Integrated Change Control Outputs

The outputs of the Integrated Change Control process are as follows:

- Approved change requests
- Rejected change requests
- Project management plan updates
- Project scope management plan updates
- Approved corrective actions
- Approved preventive actions
- Approved defect repair
- Validated defect repair
- Deliverables

Project management plan updates are typically required as a result of an approved change or corrective action. These changes are noted in the change control system or the configuration management system and stakeholders are informed at the status meetings of the changes that have occurred, their impacts, and where the description of the changes can be found.

All of the actions taken in the Integrated Change Control process (whether implemented or not) should be documented. You should also record the reason for the variance. In other words, how did this particular change request come about? How did it change the original project management plan? Is this something you could or should have known about in the Planning processes? The corrective action taken and the justification for choosing that particular corrective action should be noted as part of lessons learned also. You can use the information you capture here in your configuration management system as lessons learned for future projects. When you take on a new project, it's a good idea to review the lessons learned of similar projects so that you can plan appropriately and avoid, where possible, the variances that occurred in the first project.

Exam Spotlight

"Recommended" corrective action is an output of several of the change control processes, including Scope Change Control, Schedule Control, Cost Control, Risk Monitoring and Control, and Perform Quality Control. "Approved" corrective action is an output of the Integrated Change Control process. Remember that Integrated Change Control is where all change requests are processed and either approved or denied. Also note that corrective action is an output of the Monitoring and Controlling processes and an input to the Executing processes.

Managing Cost Changes

The *Cost Control* process manages changes to project costs as outlined in the cost management plan. It's concerned with monitoring project costs to prevent unauthorized or incorrect costs from getting included in the cost baseline. This means you're also using Cost Control to assure that the project budget isn't exceeded (resulting in cost overruns) and that changes to the budget are managed and agreed to, to assure that unapproved changes are not made, to inform stakeholders of changes, and to actively manage expected cost overruns so they stay within acceptable limits.

Cost Control Inputs

The Cost Control process includes the following inputs:

- Cost baseline
- Project funding requirements
- Performance reports
- Work performance information
- Approved change requests
- Project management plan

These inputs are examined using the tools and techniques of this process to determine if revised cost estimates or budget updates are required. We've covered each of these inputs in previous chapters.

Cost Control Tools and Techniques

The tools and techniques of the Cost Control process are as follows:

- Cost change control system
- Performance measurement analysis
- Forecasting
- Project performance reviews
- Project management software
- Variance management

Real World Scenario

Mustang Enterprises's New Accounting System

You are a stakeholder of the New Accounting System project for Mustang Enterprises. The existing accounting system lives on a mainframe, and some of the programs used to process data on this system are over 15 years old. Your company decided to hire a contract software services firm to write a thin-client, browser-based version of the accounting system so that the mainframe programs could be retired.

The project is in the Monitoring and Controlling process group and the contract project manager keeps reporting that everything is okay and on schedule. When you asked him detailed questions and requested performance data, the project manager patted you on the back and said, "Don't worry, I've got everything under control."

You are a little worried because some of the key project team members have come to you confidentially to inform you of the progress of the project.

After further investigation, you discover that the project manager changed the database from SQL to Oracle midway through the project and didn't tell anyone except the project team. The project scope stated specifically that project development required a SQL database. The change in database products changed the project scope and product scope without letting the stakeholders know.

This change has caused schedule delays because the project team members have told you they need training in the new database development tools before they can proceed. Additionally, many of the programs have already been written to interface with SQL, not Oracle, and will have to be modified. To add insult to injury, the database switch will impact the project budget in two ways. First, purchasing the Oracle database involves substantially more money than the SQL database and it requires the purchase of new development tools for the programming team. Second, several members of the programming staff will have to attend multiple training sessions on the new database product to fully integrate the programs and system. Training is currently running $2,200 per session per person.

Since you're a key stakeholder, you decide to bring the information you've discovered out into the open at the next project status meeting. Additionally, you plan to meet with the project sponsor and the procurement department to determine what alternatives you have to request that the contracting firm replace the current project manager with a new project manager. This may cause further setback to the project, but the project management plan and project schedule will require updates anyway as a result of the existing project manager's decisions. You also determine to document all that's happened as a lesson learned and to set up a change control process to prevent this from happening in the future.

Cost Change Control System

The cost change control system describes how changes are submitted, approved, and tracked and is closely linked with the integrated change control system. Cost variances (both positive and negative) are calculated using the performance measurement analysis tool (specifically earned value techniques). We'll look at this next.

Performance Measurement Analysis

Performance measurement analysis is accomplished using a technique called *earned value technique (EVT)*. Simply stated, EVT compares what you got to what you spent.

The EVT continuously monitors the planned value, earned value, and actual costs expended to produce the work of the project (we'll cover the definition of these terms shortly). When variances that result in cost changes are discovered (including schedule variances and cost variances), those changes are managed using the cost change control system. The primary function of this analysis technique is to determine and document the cause of the variance, to determine the impact of the variance (we'll do this with the EVT formulas shortly), and to determine if a corrective action should be implemented as a result.

EVT looks at schedule, cost, and scope project measurements together and compares them to the actual work completed to date. It is the most often used performance measurement method. To perform the EVT calculations, you need to first gather the three measurements we mentioned earlier: the planned value (PV), actual cost (AC), and earned value (EV).

Let's look at a definition of each of these before we dive into the actual calculations.

 If you do any research on your own regarding these values, you may come across acronyms that are different than what you see here. I've included their alternate names and acronyms at the end of each description. I recommend you memorize planned value (PV), actual cost (AC), and earned value (EV) and make certain you understand the meaning of each before progressing.

Planned value The *planned value (PV)* is the cost of work that's been budgeted for a schedule activity or WBS component to be completed during a given time period. These budgets are established during the Planning processes. PV is also called budgeted cost of work scheduled (BCWS).

Exam Spotlight

Remember to read exam questions carefully. PV might mean present value (like we talked about in Chapter 2) or planned value as defined here.

Actual cost *Actual cost (AC)* is the cost of completing the work (a schedule activity or WBS component) in a given time period. Actual costs may include direct and indirect costs but must correspond to what was budgeted for the activity. If the budgeted amount did not include indirect costs, do not include them here. Later you'll see how to compare this to PV to come up with variance calculation results. AC is also called actual cost of work performed (ACWP)

Earned value   *Earned value (EV)* is the value of the work (schedule activity or WBS component) completed to date as it compares to the budgeted amount assigned to the work component. EV is also called budgeted cost of work performed (BCWP)

Exam Spotlight

PV, AC, and EV are really easy to mix up. In their simplest forms, here's what each means:

- PV = The approved budget assigned to work to be completed during a given time period

- AC = Money that's actually been expended to date (or during a given time period) for completed work

- EV = The value of the work completed to date compared to the budget

---

According to our earlier definition, EV is the sum of the cumulative budgeted costs for completed work for all activities that have been accomplished as of the measurement date. For example, if your total budget is $1,000 and 50 percent of the work has been completed as of the measurement date, your EV would equal $500. The PV, AC, and EV measurements can be plotted graphically to show the variances between them. If there are no variances in the measurements, all the lines on the graph remain the same, which means the project is progressing as planned. Figure 10.1 shows an example that plots these three measurements.

FIGURE 10.1   Earned value

All of these measurements include a cost component. Costs are displayed in an S curve because spending is minimal in the beginning of the project, picks up steam toward the middle, and then tapers off at the end of the project. This means your earned value measurements will also take on the S curve shape.

Now you can calculate whether the project is progressing as planned using a variety of formulas discussed in the following sections. Use Figure 10.1 as your example for the formulas that follow. Figure 10.1 totals are as follows: PV = 400; EV = 375; AC = 325.

Cost Variance

Cost variance is one of the most popular variances that project managers use, and it tells you if costs are higher than budgeted (with a resulting negative number) or lower than budgeted (with a resulting positive number).

The *cost variance (CV)* is calculated as follows:

CV = EV – AC

Let's calculate the CV using the numbers from Figure 10.1:

50 = 375 – 325

The CV is positive, which means you're spending less than what you planned as of July 1 (which Figure 10.1 shows because AC is below EV).

If you come up with a negative number as the answer to this formula, it means that costs are higher than what you'd planned as of July 1.

Schedule Variance

Schedule variance, also a popular variance, tells you if the schedule is ahead or behind what was planned for this period in time. The *schedule variance (SV)* is calculated as follows:

SV = EV – PV

Let's plug in the numbers:

–25 = 375 – 400

The resulting schedule variance is negative, which means you are behind schedule, or behind where you planned to be as of July 1.

Together, the CV and SV are known as efficiency indicators for the project.

Performance Indexes

Cost and schedule performance indexes are primarily used to calculate performance efficiencies. They're often used in trend analysis to predict future performance. You'll need to know the calculations and what the results mean. If your result in either formula is greater than 1, you've got better than expected performance. If the result is less than 1, you've got poor performance. If it equals 1, you're right on target.

The *cost performance index (CPI)* is calculated this way:

CPI = EV ÷ AC

Let's plug in the numbers and see where you stand.

1.15 = 375 ÷ 325

This means cost performance is better than expected. You get an A+ on this assignment!

Cumulative CPI (CPI^C) is a commonly used calculation to predict project costs at the completion of the project. It also represents the cumulative CPI of the project at the point the measurement is taken. First, you need to sum the earned value calculations taken to date (EV^C) and the actual costs to date (AC^C). The formula looks just like the CPI formula only it uses the sums as follows:

$$CPI^C = EV^C \div AC^C$$

The difference between this and the CPI formula earlier is that the CPI formula is used for a single work component whereas the CPI^C is calculated using the sum of all the costs of all the work components. Additionally, you may also use CPI to calculate the total cost of a work component like a deliverable for example. Let's say you have a deliverable with 75 schedule activities that need to be completed. You would total the EV and AC at the measurement date for all 75 schedule activities to determine the cost performance index for the deliverable.

The *schedule performance index (SPI)* is calculated this way:

$$SPI = EV \div PV$$

Again, let's see where you stand with this example:

$$.94 = 375 \div 400$$

Uh oh, not so good. Schedule performance is not what you expected. Let's not grade this one.

Forecasting

Forecasting uses the information you've gathered to date and estimates the future conditions or performance of the project based on what you know when the calculation is performed. Forecasts are based on work performance information (an output from the Executing process group). There are two types of forecasting techniques: estimate to complete and estimate at completion. Each has three variations. Both of these formulas use a new parameter we haven't seen yet called *budget at completion (BAC)*. BAC is the sum of all the budget values established for all the work of the project.

Let's look at each of the techniques.

Estimate to Complete

Estimate to complete (ETC) tells you how much it will cost to complete all the work remaining for a schedule activity or WBS component or the project. There is one variation of ETC that doesn't require a formula. It's called ETC based on a new estimate. This is simply a revised estimate based on the performance of the resources to date. By examining how quickly or how productively the resources have been utilized so far, the project team can determine a noncalculated ETC by looking at the remaining work and determining a new estimate based on the comparison to past work. This ETC, according to *A Guide to the PMBOK,* is the most accurate and comprehensive ETC calculation.

The two remaining ETC calculations use earned value data. These are quick to perform but not as accurate as the project team manually examining the remaining work and making a new estimate based on past performance.

When you believe that future cost variances will be similar to the types of variances you've seen to date, you'll use this formula to calculate ETC:

$$ETC = (BAC - EV^C) \div CPI^C$$

Assuming our EV^C value is 725, CPI^C value is 1.12, and BAC is 1000, let's plug in the numbers:

245.5 = (1000 − 725) ÷ 1.12

Therefore, at the measurement date (July 1), we need $245.50 to complete all the remaining work of this work component (or project if you're using project totals) assuming variances in the future will be the same as they have been to date.

When you believe that future cost variances will *not* be similar to the types of variances you've seen to date, you'll use this formula to calculate ETC:

ETC = (BAC − EV^C)

Let's calculate our value:

275 = (1000 − 725)

In this case, we need $275 to complete all the remaining work of this work component assuming variances in the future are different than they have been to date.

Estimate at Completion

There are only a few calculations remaining that will help you finish up your analysis of project progress. *Estimate at completion (EAC)* estimates (or forecasts) the expected total cost of a work component, schedule activity, or the project at its completion. This is the probable final value for the work component (or project).

There are three ways to calculate EAC. The first one is EAC using a new estimate. This assumes that the original assumptions used when estimating were flawed or that changes have occurred that have changed the original estimates. ETC in this calculation is provided by the performing organization (the ETC based on a new estimate figure.) The formula looks like this:

EAC = AC^C + ETC

Assuming our AC^C is 650 and ETC is 275, we get this:

925 = 650 + 275

This means the expected total value of the project $925.

The last two methods for calculating EAC are the most common. The first EAC uses CPI^C and the second calculates EAC using remaining budget. Let's look at EAC using CPI^C first.

EAC using CPI^C is the second way to perform an ETC calculation. This formula is the AC^C plus ETC (when variances are typical). It looks like this:

EAC = AC^C + ((BAC − EV) ÷ CPI^C)

Our numbers look like this:

1096.43 = 650 + ((1000 − 500) ÷ 1.12)

When using the CPI^C efficiency indicator and ETC with typical variances, our expected final value for this work component (or project) is $1,096.43.

EAC using remaining budget is the AC^C plus the budget needed to finish the remaining work. This calculation is used when you expect variances to be atypical. The formula looks like this:

EAC = AC^C + BAC − EV

Our example project estimates looks like this using an EV value of 500:

$1150 = 650 + 1000 - 500$

Based on our remaining budget, the expected final value for this work component assuming variances are atypical is $1,150.

For study purposes, the three EAC calculations are shown together next:

$EAC = AC^C + ETC$ (Use when you have a new estimate or when original assumptions were flawed.)

$EAC = AC^C + ((BAC - EV) \div CPI^C)$ (Use when variances are typical.)

$EAC = AC^C + BAC - EV$ (Use when variances are atypical.)

Project Performance Reviews

Project performance reviews are similar to status reviews. They examine milestones due and those that have been met. They also look at the costs associated with performance and schedule activities that are over and under budget. Typically, performance reviews take place as meetings and their purpose is to examine schedule activities, work packages, or cost account status and their progress to date. There are three types of analyses associated with performance reviews: variance analysis, trend analysis, and earned value technique. We've already covered the earned value technique, so let's look at the other two.

Variance at Completion

Variance at completion (VAC) calculates the difference between the budget at completion and the estimate at completion. It looks like this:

$VAC = BAC - EAC$

Use the most optimistic EAC number:

$-171.43 = 925 - 1096.43$

The negative number means you're not doing as well with costs as you anticipated and that variance exists. As the project progresses, variances will become smaller.

Remember that variance analysis is a tool and technique of both Schedule Control and Scope Control and this formula can be used in conjunction with the variance analysis tool and technique of these processes.

Trend Analysis

According to *A Guide to the PMBOK*, trend analysis determines if project performance is improving or worsening over time by periodically analyzing project results. These results are measured with mathematical formulas that attempt to forecast project outcomes based on historical information and results. There are several formulas you can use to predict project trends, but it's outside the scope of this book to go into them. For the exam, you're expected to understand the concept behind trend analysis, not the formulas used to calculate it. You'll want to remember that the results you've analyzed using trend analysis formulas can be used to predict future project behavior or trends.

NOTE You'll be given some scratch paper when you go into the exam. I recommend that you write these formulas down on a piece of your scratch paper before you start the exam and keep it handy. That way, the formulas are off your mind and you've got them in front of you to reference when you get to the portion of the exam where these questions appear. You might want to use this tip for other items you've memorized as well. If you write them down before you begin, you don't have to jog your memory on every question. If you forget something, leave a blank space where it goes and as soon as you remember it or see a question that reminds you what it is, fill in the blank.

Project Management Software and Variance Management

I know you thought we were done, but there a couple of remaining tools and techniques of this process you should know: project management software and variance management.

We've discussed project management software before. Obviously, many of these calculations can be performed and monitored using project management software.

Variance management includes the processes for managing cost variances and appropriate responses based on the impact and level of variance. The cost management plan should describe the variance management.

Cost Control Outputs

There are eight outputs to the Cost Control process:

- Cost estimate updates
- Cost baseline updates
- Performance measurements
- Forecasted completion
- Requested changes
- Recommended corrective actions
- Organizational process asset updates (lessons learned)
- Project management plan updates

We've discussed most of these before or they are self-explanatory. However, I'll point out a few things you should be aware of for the exam.

Updated cost estimates include updating original cost estimates and other areas of the project management plan that these estimates may impact. As an example, perhaps the cost estimate for new hardware required for your project was recently revised. Suppose the cost estimate was needed because the equipment originally planned for in the project is no longer available and new equipment is ordered in its place. This may require revisions to other project activities, which will require you to revisit the project Planning and Executing processes.

Recap of Formulas

There are a lot of formulas to memorize. Keep in mind that you'll be given a calculator when you take the exam, so you don't have to do the math manually. Remember that EVT is used with both the performance analysis measurement tool and technique and the project performance reviews tool and technique. Variance and trend analysis are part of the project performance reviews tool and technique. Here are the formulas we've covered in this chapter:

Performance measurements   Cost variance: $CV = EV - AC$
Schedule variance: $SV = EV - PV$

Performance indexes   Cost performance index: $CPI = EV \div AC$
Cumulative cost performance index: $CPI^c = EV^c \div AC^c$
Schedule performance index: $SPI = EV \div PV$

Forecasting   Estimate to complete (cost to complete remaining work)

- Based on new estimate: manual calculation by project team

- ETC with typical variances: $ETC = (BAC - EV^c) \div CPI^c$

- ETC with atypical variances: $ETC = (BAC - EV^c)$

  Estimate at completion (expected total cost at completion)

- Using new estimate when assumptions are flawed: $EAC = AC^c + ETC$

- EAC using CPI^c (typical variances): $EAC = AC^c + ((BAC - EV) \div CPI^c)$

- EAC using remaining budget (atypical variances): $EAC = AC^c + BAC - EV$

Variance Analysis   Variance analysis: $VAC = BAC - EAC$

Remember that there are 12 formulas total (one is simply a manual calculation by the project team). You might want to devise an acronym or some other mnemonic to help you memorize them. For example, the earned value and performance index formulas are (based on the first letter of each formula): C-S-C-C-S. The forecasting formulas are: ETC new; ETC typical, ETC atypical; EAC new, EAC atypical, EAC typical.

Cost Control problems come about for many reasons, including incorrect estimating techniques, predetermined or fixed budgets with no flexibility, schedule overruns, inadequate WBS development, and so on. Good project management planning techniques during the Planning processes may prevent cost problems later in the project. At a minimum, proper planning will reduce the impact of these problems if they do occur.

Always inform appropriate stakeholders of revised cost estimates and any changes of significant impact to the project. Keep them updated on changes, status, and risk conditions during regularly scheduled project meetings.

Monitoring and Controlling Schedule Changes

The *Schedule Control* process involves determining the status of the project schedule, determining if changes have occurred or should, and influencing and managing schedule changes. In the following sections, we will look at this process's inputs, tools and techniques, and outputs.

Schedule Control Inputs

Schedule Control inputs include the following:

- Schedule management plan
- Schedule baseline
- Performance reports
- Approved change requests

We've covered each of these inputs previously. Keep in mind that the Schedule Control process works hand in hand with the Integrated Change Control process covered earlier (as all the change control processes do).

Schedule and Control Tools and Techniques

The tools and techniques of the Schedule Control process are as follows:

- Progress reporting
- Schedule change control system
- Performance measurement
- Variance analysis
- Project management software
- Schedule comparison bar charts

Progress Reporting

Progress reporting examines elements like actual start and end dates for schedule activities and the remaining time to finish uncompleted activities. If you've taken earned value measurements, that information is included in the progress report. All of this information should be documented.

Schedule Change Control System

As you've probably already guessed, the *schedule change control system* works just like the cost change control system, except that it defines how changes to the schedule are made and managed. It tracks and records change requests, describes the procedures to follow to implement schedule changes, and details the authorization levels needed to approve the schedule changes.

Schedule changes may be potential hot buttons with certain stakeholders and can burn you if you don't handle them correctly. No one likes to hear that the project is going to take longer than originally planned. That doesn't mean you should withhold this information, however. Always report the truth. If you've been keeping your stakeholders abreast of project status, they should already know that the potential for schedule changes exists. Nevertheless, be prepared to justify the reason for the schedule change, or start dusting off your resume—one or the other.

Performance Measurement

Performance measurements for schedule control include the schedule variance and schedule performance index. Both of these should be used to determine if corrective action is needed to get the schedule back on track.

Variance Analysis

Variance analysis is a key factor in monitoring and controlling project time because this technique helps determine variances in schedule start and end dates. Comparing the estimated dates to the actual or forecasted dates will show you where variances have occurred—or may occur—and will allow you to implement corrective actions to keep the schedule on track.

Keeping the schedule on track means you're monitoring and controlling time—one of the triple constraints.

Make sure to examine the float variance of the critical path activities. Thinking back to the Schedule Development process, you'll recall that float is the amount of time you can delay starting an activity without increasing the amount of time it takes to complete the project. Because the activities with the least amount of float have the potential to cause the biggest schedule delay, examine float variance in ascending order of critical activities.

However, not all schedule variances will impact the schedule. For example, a delay to a noncritical path task will not delay the overall schedule and may not need corrective action. Use caution here though—if a delay occurs on a noncritical path task or its duration is increased for some reason, that task can actually become part of the critical path. Delays to critical path tasks will *always* cause delays to the project completion date and do require corrective action. Careful watch of the variances in schedule start and end dates helps you control the total time element of the project.

Project Management Software

Project management software is used to track the actual schedule dates against planned schedule dates. One particular use for project management software in the Schedule Control process is to forecast the impacts of schedule changes (both potential changes and actual changes) to the schedule.

Schedule Comparison Bar Charts

The last tool and technique is the schedule comparison bar charts. This is a standard bar chart that depicts two bars for each schedule activity—one bar for the approved schedule baseline and one bar for the actual status.

Schedule Control Outputs

The Schedule Control process has the following outputs:

- Schedule model data updates
- Schedule baseline updates
- Performance measurements
- Requested changes
- Recommended corrective action
- Organizational process asset updates (lessons learned)
- Activity list updates
- Activity attributes updates
- Project management plan updates

Schedule data model updates involve adjusting activities and dates to coincide with approved changes and/or corrective actions and updating any schedule model data used to manage the project.

Often, project schedule network diagrams require updates as a result of schedule model data updates. Don't forget to document these changes and inform your stakeholders.

Changes to approved schedule start and end dates (in the schedule baseline) are called *revisions*. These generally occur as a result of a project scope change or changes to activity estimates and may result in a schedule baseline update. Schedule baseline updates occur when significant changes to the project schedule are made like the changes just mentioned. This means a new schedule baseline is established that reflects the changed project activity dates. Once the new baseline is established, it is used as the basis for future performance measurements. Never rebaseline a schedule without first saving a copy of the original baseline and schedule.

Take care when rebaselining a project schedule because you may lose the original baseline information. Why do you care? Because the original baseline serves as historical information to reference for future projects. Make a backup copy of the original schedule so that you have a record of the original baseline as a reference. Even though some project management software allows you to save several baselines plus the original, it's still good practice to make a backup copy of the original.

The performance measurements for Schedule Control are the schedule variance and schedule performance index. I know this sounds like a broken record, but make certain to document this information and communicate it to the stakeholders.

Changes to the project schedule may or may not require updates to other elements of the project plan. For example, extending a schedule activity involving a contractor may impact the costs associated with that activity.

Recommended corrective actions, as with other processes we've looked at, require root cause analysis. In the Schedule Control process, because you're dealing with time issues, it's imperative that you act as quickly as possible to implement corrective actions so that the schedule is brought back in line with the plan and the least amount of schedule delay as possible is experienced. The remaining Schedule Control outputs have been discussed previously.

Monitoring and Controlling Risk

Now we'll shift our attention to risk. The *Risk Monitoring and Control* process primarily involves identifying and responding to new risks as they occur. The other functions of this process are as follows:

- Tracking and monitoring identified risks
- Evaluating risk response plans that are put into action as a result of risk events
- Monitoring the project for risk triggers
- Reexamining existing risks
- Monitoring residual risks
- Ensuring that policies and procedures are followed
- Ensuring that risk response plans and contingency plans are put into action appropriately and are effective
- Contingency reserves (for schedule and cost) are updated

Risk Monitoring and Control is a busy process. During the course of the project, risk responses (developed during the Planning process group) have been implemented and hopefully reduced or averted the impact of risk events.

Risk Monitoring and Control Inputs

There are five inputs to this process:

- Risk management plan
- Risk register
- Approved change requests
- Work performance information
- Performance reports

You'll recall that the risk management plan details how risk is managed and the risk response plan describes how you will implement plans and strategies in the event of an actual risk event. Keep in mind that some risk events identified in risk planning will happen and some will not. You will have to stay alert for risk event occurrences and be prepared to respond to them when they do occur. This means you should monitor the risk register regularly.

Approved change requests can introduce new risks to the project. It's good practice to review all approved change requests for the potential for new threats or opportunities or in light of previously identified risks and opportunities. They may also alter previously identified risks, which can mean action is needed during this process to bring response plans into alignment with the changes.

Work performance information gathered during the Performance Reporting process, cost changes, schedule changes, and/or scope changes may identify new risks.

Performance reports include information such as status reports, performance measurements, and forecasts. These should also be examined from the perspective of risks or risk response plans that may need close monitoring or changes to the response plans to coincide with the performance reports data.

Additional risk response planning may be needed to deal with the new risks or with expected risks whose impact was greater than expected. This may require repeating the Risk Response Planning process to create new contingency plans or alternative plans to deal with the risk, or it may require modification to existing plans.

Risk Monitoring and Control Tools and Techniques

The tools and techniques of Risk Monitoring and Control are used to monitor risks throughout the life of the project. Periodic reviews, audits, and new earned value analyses should be performed to check the pulse of risk activity and to make certain risk management is enacted effectively.

The tools and techniques of this process are as follows:

- Risk reassessment
- Risk audits
- Variance and trend analysis
- Technical performance measurement
- Reserve analysis
- Status meetings

Let's look at risk reassessment, risk audits, and technical performance measurements next. We've examined all the other tools and techniques of this process in discussions of previous processes.

Risk Reassessment

Periodic, scheduled reviews of identified risks, risk responses, and risk priorities should occur during the project. The idea here is to monitor risks and their status and determine if their consequences still have the same impact on the project objectives as when they were originally planned. Every status meeting (another output of this process) should have a time set aside to discuss and review risks and response plans.

Risk identification and monitoring is an ongoing process throughout the life of the project. Risks can change, and previously identified risks may have greater impacts than originally thought as more facts are discovered. Reassessment of risks should be a regular activity performed by everyone involved on the project. Monitor the risk register, including those risks that have low scores, and risk triggers. You should also monitor the risk responses that have been implemented for their effectiveness in dealing with risk. You may have to revisit the Qualitative and Quantitative Risk Analysis processes when new risk consequences are discovered or risk impacts are found to be greater than what was originally planned.

Risk Audits

Risk audits are carried out during the entire life of the project by risk auditors. Risk auditors are not typically project team members and are expertly trained in audit techniques and risk assessment. These audits are specifically interested in looking at the implementation and the effective use of risk strategies.

Technical Performance Measurements

This tool and technique compares the technical accomplishments of project milestones completed during the Executing processes to the technical milestones defined in the project Planning processes. Variances may indicate that a project risk is looming, and you'll want to analyze and prepare a response to it if appropriate. For example, a technical milestone for a new computer software project might require that the forms printed from a particular module include a bar code at the bottom of the page. If the bar code functionality does not work once the module is coded, a technical deviation exists, which means you should reexamine project risks. In this particular example, project scope is likely at risk.

Risk Monitoring and Control Outputs

Risk Monitoring and Control should occur throughout the life of the project. Identified risks are monitored and plans are reexamined to determine if they will adequately resolve the risk as it approaches during this process. Several outputs may come about as a result of monitoring risks:

- Risk register updates
- Requested changes
- Recommended corrective action
- Recommended preventive action
- Organizational process updates (lessons learned, risk templates)
- Project management plan updates

We've discussed many of these outputs before, so I'll just bring to your attention the new points you need to know here.

The risk register should be updated under two conditions. The first condition is when a risk audit or risk reassessment concludes that some element of the original risk information has changed. For example, the impact or probability scores are updated to reflect new conditions, or the priority of the risk has changed, or the response plan has been updated, and so on. The second condition for updating the risk register is when the risk needs to be closed. If you have a risk event occur, you'll record that in the risk register along with the effectiveness of the response plan. This information becomes an input to the Close Project Process, which we'll cover in the next chapter.

Requested changes must be processed through the Integrated Change Control process. You may find a workaround is needed when implementing a requested change or recommended corrective action. A *workaround* is an unplanned response to a negative risk event. It attempts to deal with the risk in a productive, efficient manner. If no risk response plan exists (this might be the case when you accept a risk event during the Planning process), or an unplanned risk occurs, workarounds are implemented to deal with the consequences of the risk.

Project Case Study: New Kitchen Heaven Retail Store

Stakeholders have asked for an updated status on the project schedule as well as a remaining cost projection. You decide to provide several cost and schedule performance figures for the project on the status report.

"Build-out is behind schedule. They were scheduled to be completed by the 15th of January, but they aren't going to finish up until the 24th."

"What's that do to my schedule?" Jill asks. "I'm starting interviews for the store positions on the 16th. I hope to have that wrapped up by the 19th. As long as I have the majority of the staff hired by the 20th, we can have them stocking shelves starting the 22nd."

You tell Jill, "Let's finish up the status of the other items, and I'll come back to that.

You've calculated some performance measurements, including earned value measures, and you show them to Jill and Dirk (all figures are in millions of dollars):

BAC = 2; PV = 1.86; EV^c = 1.75; AC^c = 1.70

CPI^c is 1.03. (1.75 ÷ 1.70)

SPI is .94 (1.75 ÷ 1.86)

EAC is 1.94 (1.70 + ((2 − 1.75) ÷ 1.03)))

ETC is .24 (1.94 − 1.70)

"What is all this telling us?" Dirk asks.

"The cost performance index tells us we're getting a good return for the money spent on the project so far. In other words, we've experienced a $1.03 value for every dollar spent to date.

"The schedule performance index isn't as cheery, but it's not dreadful news either. This performance indicator says that work is progressing at 94 percent of what we anticipated by this point.

"The estimate at completion tells us that based on what we know today, the total project will cost $1.94 million. That's coming in under the original $2 million we had budgeted for completion, so we're on track with the project budget.

"The last figure is the estimated cost of the remaining work."

"It looks like we're a little behind schedule based on what you have figured here," Dirk says.

"Yes, that's correct," you reply. "That brings us back to Jill's question. I have two alternatives to propose. One, we overlap the schedule and allow Gomez's crew to complete their work while Jill's staff starts stocking shelves."

Jill says, "I don't like this option. We'll be tripping over each other, and I don't want merchandise damaged by workers who are still dragging equipment around inside the store. What's your other option?"

"We could ask Gomez to increase the crew size so that they complete on time according to the contract. We have a provision in the contract that stipulates they add crew members if it looks as though they'll miss the scheduled completion date. I will instruct the contract management department to inform Gomez that we're requiring additional crew members."

"That will do the trick," Jill says. "We need the storefront to ourselves when stocking and preparing for opening. I'm glad you had that stipulation in the contract."

Your next agenda item is change requests. Ricardo submitted a change request regarding the hardware installation at the new store site. A new, much anticipated operating system was just released, and Ricardo has plans to upgrade the entire company to the new operating system. Since he must purchase new equipment for this store anyway, he contends that it makes sense to go ahead and purchase the hardware with the newest operating system already loaded. His staff won't have to upgrade this store as part of the upgrade project because the store will already have the new operating system.

Ricardo's change request was submitted in writing through the change control system. A CCB was set up during the Planning stages of this project to handle change requests. At the CCB meeting, the following questions come up regarding Ricardo's request: Has the new operating system been tested with the existing system? Are there compatibility problems? If so, what risks are associated with getting the problems resolved and the equipment installed by opening day? Is the vendor ready to ship with the new operating system?

The CCB defers their decision for this request until Ricardo gives them answers to these questions.

During the next CCB meeting, the board reviews a change request from Jill Overstreet. The gourmet food supplier she used went out of business a month or so ago, and Jill contracted with a new vendor. She received a sample shipment from the new vendor and was very unhappy with the results. Upon inspecting the products, she found broken containers and damaged packaging. Meanwhile, Jill found another vendor, who has sent her a sample shipment. She is very pleased with the new vendor's products and service. However, this vendor's prices are even higher than the first replacement vendor she contracted with. Jill submitted a cost change request to the CCB because of the increased cost of the gourmet food product shipment. The change in cost does not have a significant impact on the budget because the new EAC with this change is $1.90 million. The original project budget estimate was $2 million, so the project is still coming in under budget.

You hold a seat on the CCB and are aware of the change requests and their impacts to the project. Ricardo satisfactorily answered all the questions the CCB had, so his request and Jill's request were both approved during the meeting.

Project Case Study Checklist

Integrated change management

- Identify that a change has occurred

- Review and approve changes

Configuration management systems

- Configuration identification

- Configuration status accounting

- Configuration verification and auditing

- Change control system

Formal change request procedures

Cost change

- Cost change control system

- Performance measurement analysis

- Forecasting

Summary

This chapter examined several change control processes starting with Integrated Change Control. Change control is an important part of the project process. It's your responsibility as project manager to manage change and implement corrective action where needed to keep the project on track with the plan.

Integrated Change Control concerns influencing the things that cause change and managing the change once it has occurred. One or more of the triple constraints are generally affected when change occurs. Managing change may involve changes to the project plan, the project schedule, or the project budget. Changes that impact processes you've already completed require updates to those processes. Corrective action is often a result of change and ensures that the future performance of the project lines up with the project management plan.

Configuration management systems typically include change control systems that document the procedures to manage change and how change requests are implemented. Change requests may come in written or verbal forms, but ideally you should ask for all your change requests in writing. Change requests are processed through a formal change control system, and configuration control boards have the authority to approve or deny change requests.

Lessons learned become part of the historical information used on future projects. They also are used to document the causes of the variances that occur on the project. Lessons learned are updated as part of the organizational process asset outputs of the change control processes.

Schedule Control involves determining the status of the project schedule, determining if changes have occurred or should, and influencing and managing schedule changes.

Cost Control involves managing changes to project costs. It's also concerned with monitoring project costs to prevent unauthorized or incorrect costs from getting included in the cost baseline. Cost Control uses tools and techniques like performance measurement analysis (such as CV, SV, CPI, SPI), forecasting (ETC and EAC), and project performance reviews (variance analysis, trend analysis, and EVT) to monitor costs.

Risk Monitoring and Control responds to risks as they occur and implements workarounds for unplanned risk events. Some risks planned for during the Risk Response Planning process will occur, and some will not. Perhaps risks that were previously identified do occur, and their impacts are much greater than anticipated during the Risk Response Planning process. These will require updates to the risk management plan or workarounds.

Exam Essentials

Name the purpose of the Integrated Change Control process.   Integrated Change Control is performed throughout the life of the project and involves reviewing all the project change requests, establishing a configuration management and change control process, and approving or denying changes.

Be able to define the purpose of a configuration management system.   Configuration management systems are documented procedures that describe the process for submitting change requests, the processes for tracking changes and their disposition, and processes for defining the approval levels for approving and denying changes, and it includes a process for authorizing the changes. Change control systems are generally a subset of the configuration management system. Configuration management also describes the characteristics of the product of the project and ensures accuracy and completeness of the description.

Be able to describe a CCB.   The configuration control board (CCB) has the authority to approve or deny change requests. Their authority is defined and outlined by the organization.

Name the purpose of the Cost Control process.   The Cost Control process is concerned with monitoring project costs to prevent unauthorized or incorrect costs from getting included in the cost baseline.

Be able to describe performance measurement techniques.   Performance measurement techniques use the earned value technique (EVT) to continuously monitor the planned value, earned value, and actual costs expended to produce the work of the project. There are performance measures, performance indexes, forecasting, and variance analysis techniques.

Describe the purpose of Risk Monitoring and Control   Risk Monitoring and Control involves identifying and responding to new risks as they occur. Risk monitoring and reassessment should occur throughout the life of the project.

Key Terms

You've learned a lot of new key words in this chapter. PMI has worked hard to develop and define standard project management terms that apply across industries. Here is a list of some of the terms you came across in this chapter:

actual cost (AC)	Integrated Change Control
budget at completion (BAC)	performance measurement baseline
change control system	planned value (PV)
configuration control board (CCB)	project performance review
configuration management	revisions
Cost Control	Risk Monitoring and Control
cost performance index CPI	schedule change control system
cost variance (CV)	Schedule Control
cumulative CPI (CPIᶜ)	schedule performance index (SPI)
earned value (EV)	schedule variance (SV)
earned value technique (EVT)	variance at completion (VAC)
estimate at completion	workaround
estimate to complete (ETC)	

Review Questions

1. You are a project manager for Bluebird Technologies. Bluebird writes custom billing applications for several industries. A schedule change has been requested. You know change is concerned with all of the following except which one?

   A. Managing change

   B. Verifying change

   C. Influencing causes of change

   D. Determining that a change occurred

2. You are a project manager for Bluebird Technologies. Bluebird writes custom billing applications for several industries. One of your users verbally requests changes to one of the screen displays. You explain to her that the change needs to go through the change control system, which is a subset of the configuration management system. You explain that a change control system does all of the following except for which one?

   A. Document procedures for change requests

   B. Track the status of change requests

   C. Describe the management impacts of change

   D. Determine if changes are approved or denied

3. You are a project manager for Star Light Strings. Star Light manufactures strings of lights for outdoor display. Its products range from simple light strings to elaborate lights with animal designs, bug designs, memorabilia, and so on. Your newest project requires a change. You have documented the characteristics of the product and its functionality using which of the following tools and techniques?

   A. Change control system

   B. Corrective action

   C. Configuration management

   D. Updates to the project management plan

4. You are a project manager for Star Light Strings. Star Light manufactures strings of lights for outdoor display. Its products range from simple light strings to elaborate lights with animal designs, bug designs, memorabilia, and so on. Your newest project requires a change. One of the business unit managers submitted a change through the change control system, which utilizes a CCB. Which of the following is true regarding the CCB?

   A. The CCB describes how change requests are managed.

   B. The CCB requires all change requests in writing.

   C. The CCB approves or denies change requests.

   D. The CCB requires updates to the appropriate management plan.

5. Which of the following statements is true regarding schedule variances?

   A. Schedule variances impact scope, which impacts the schedule.

   B. Schedule variances sometimes impact the schedule.

   C. Schedule variances always impact the schedule.

   D. Schedule variances never impact the schedule.

6. You are a project manager for Laurel's Theater Productions. Your new project is coming in over budget and requires a cost change through the cost change control system. You know all of the following statements are true regarding Cost Control except for which one?

   A. Performance is monitored to detect variances.

   B. Changes are reflected in the cost baseline.

   C. Changes are monitored and reflected in the project scope.

   D. Changes are monitored so that inappropriate changes do not get into the cost baseline.

7. Which of the following might require rebaselining of the cost baseline?

   A. Corrective action

   B. Revised cost estimates

   C. Updates to the cost management plan

   D. Budget updates

8. All of the following are activities of the configuration management system except for which one?

   A. Variance analysis

   B. Identification

   C. Status accounting

   D. Verification and auditing

9. Which of the following is not an activity of configuration management during the Integrated Change Control process?

   A. Verification

   B. Funding

   C. Status accounting

   D. Auditing

10. What are the performance measurements for the Schedule Control process?

   A. SV (EV − PV) and SPI (EV ÷ PV)

   B. SV (EV − AC) and SPI (EV ÷ AC)

   C. SV (EV − BAC) and SPI (EV ÷ BAC)

   D. SV (PV − EV) and SPI (PV ÷ EV)

11. This measurement is the value of the work that's been completed to date compared to the budget.

    A. PV

    B. AC

    C. EV

    D. EAC

12. You are a contract project manager for a wholesale flower distribution company. Your project is to develop a website for the company that allows retailers to place their flower orders online. You will also provide a separate link for individual purchases that are ordered, packaged, and mailed to the consumer directly from the grower's site. This project involves coordinating the parent company, growers, and distributors. You are preparing a performance review and have the following measurements at hand: PV = 300, AC = 200, and EV = 250. What do you know about this project?

    A. The EAC is a positive number, which means the project will finish under budget.

    B. You do not have enough information to calculate CPI.

    C. The CV is a negative number in this case, which means you've spent less than you planned to spend as of the measurement date.

    D. The CV is a positive number in this case, which means you're under budget as of the measurement date.

13. A negative result from an SV calculation means which of the following?

    A. PV is higher than EV.

    B. PV equals 1.

    C. EV is higher than PV.

    D. EV is higher than AC.

14. You are a contract project manager for a wholesale flower distribution company. Your project is to develop a website for the company that allows retailers to place their flower orders online. You will also provide a separate link for individual purchases that are ordered, packaged, and mailed to the consumer directly from the grower's site. This project involves coordinating the parent company, growers, and distributors. You are preparing a performance review and have the following measurements at hand: PV = 300, AC = 200, and EV = 250. What is the CPI of this project?

    A. 0.80

    B. 1.25

    C. 1.5

    D. 0.83

15. You do not expect the types of variances that have occurred on the project to date to continue. If BAC = 800, ETC = 275, PV = 300, AC^C = 200, EV = 250, and CPI^C = 1.25, what is the EAC?

 A. 640

 B. 750

 C. 600

 D. 550

16. You know that BAC = 375, PV = 300, AC = 200, and EV^C = 250. Variances that have occurred on the project to date are not expected to continue. What is the ETC?

 A. 75

 B. 50

 C. 125

 D. 150

17. You expect the types of variances that have occurred on the project to date to continue. If BAC = 800, ETC = 275, PV = 300, AC^C = 200, EV = 250, and CPI^C = 1.25, what is the EAC?

 A. 640

 B. 750

 C. 600

 D. 550

18. You know that BAC = 500, PV = 325, AC^C = 275, CPI = .9. and EV = 250 and that you are experiencing atypical variances. Variance at completion tells you which of the following?

 A. 25

 B. −52

 C. 52

 D. −25

19. You know that BAC = 500, PV = 325, AC^C = 275, and EV^C = 250 and that you are experiencing typical variances. What is ETC?

 A. 227.3

 B. 250

 C. 274.7

 D. 525

20. Your project progressed as planned up until yesterday. Suddenly, an unexpected risk event occurred. You quickly devised a response to deal with this negative risk event using which of the following outputs of Risk Monitoring and Control?

 A. Risk management plan updates

 B. Workarounds

 C. Corrective action

 D. Additional risk identification

Answers to Review Questions

1. B. Integrated Change Control, Schedule Control, and Cost Control are all concerned with three things: influencing the things that cause change, determining that change is needed or has happened, and managing the change.

2. D. Change control systems are documented procedures that describe how to submit change requests. They track the status of the change requests, document the management impacts of change, track the change approval status, and define the level of authority needed to approve changes. Change control systems do not approve or deny the changes—that's the responsibility of the configuration control board (CCB).

3. C. The key to this question was that the characteristics of the product were documented with this tool. Configuration management documents the physical characteristics and the functionality of the product of the project.

4. C. Configuration control boards (CCBs) review change requests and have the authority to approve or deny them. Their authority is defined by the organization.

5. B. Schedule variances will sometimes—but not always—impact the schedule. Changes to non-critical path tasks will not likely impact the schedule, but changes to critical path tasks will always impact the schedule.

6. C. Cost Control tracks project performance to detect variances and reflect them in the cost baseline. It's also used to prevent inappropriate changes from getting into the cost baseline.

7. D. Budget updates may require cost rebaselining.

8. A. The three activities associated with configuration management include configuration identification, configuration status accounting, and configuration verification and auditing.

9. B. Configuration identification involves identifying the products of the project, determining the status of changes to the configuration, and verifying and auditing the configuration to determine if the performance and functional requirements have been met.

10. Answer: A. Schedule variance is (EV – PV) and schedule performance index is (EV ÷ PV).

11. C. Earned value is referred to as the value of the work that's been completed to date compared to the budget.

12. D. The CV is a positive number and is calculated by subtracting AC from EV as follows: 250 – 200 = 50. A positive CV means the project is coming in under budget, meaning you've spent less than you planned as of the measurement date.

13. A. The SV calculation is EV – PV. If PV is a higher number than EV, you'll get a negative number as a result.

14. B. CPI is calculated as follows: EV ÷ AC. In this case, 250 ÷ 200 = 1.25.

15. B. When variances are not expected to continue, or are atypical in nature, EAC is calculated as follows: AC^c + BAC – EV. Therefore, the calculation for this question looks like this: (200 + 800) – 250 = 750.

16. C. The correct formula for ETC for this question is as follows: BAC – EV^c. Therefore, ETC is as follows: 375 – 250 = 125.

17. A. When variances are expected to continue, EAC is calculated as follows: AC^c + ((BAC – EV) ÷ CPI^c). Therefore, the calculation for this question looks like this: 200 + ((800 – 250) ÷ 1.25) = 640.

18. D. You first have to calculate EAC in order to calculate VAC. EAC for variances that are atypical is AC^c + BAC – EV. So our numbers are 275 + 500 – 250 = 525. VAC is calculated this way: BAC – EAC. Therefore, 500 – 525 = –25. Our costs are not doing as well as anticipated.

19. C. You must first calculate CPI^c in order to calculate ETC. CPI^c is EV^c ÷ AC^c. We have 250 ÷ 275 = .91. ETC with typical variances is (BAC – EV^c) ÷ CPI^c. Our numbers are (500 – 250) ÷ .91 = 274.7.

20. B. Workarounds are unplanned responses. Workarounds deal with negative risk events as they occur. As the name implies, workarounds were not previously known to the project team. The risk event was unplanned, so no contingency plan existed to deal with the risk event, and thus it required a workaround.

Controlling Work Results and Closing Out the Project

THE PMP EXAM CONTENT FROM THE MONITORING AND CONTROLLING THE PROJECT PERFORMANCE DOMAIN COVERED IN THIS CHAPTER INCLUDES THE FOLLOWING:

✓ Ensure Project Deliverables Conform to Quality Standards

THE PMP EXAM CONTENT FROM THE CLOSING THE PROJECT PERFORMANCE DOMAIN COVERED IN THIS CHAPTER INCLUDES THE FOLLOWING:

✓ Obtain Final Acceptance for the Project

✓ Obtain Financial, Legal, and Administrative Closure

✓ Release Project Resources

✓ Identify, Document, and Communicate Lessons Learned

✓ Create and Distribute Final Project Report

✓ Archive and Retain Project Records

✓ Measure Customer Satisfaction

You've made it to the homestretch. This chapter covers the last group of project processes. We'll close out the Monitoring and Controlling process group and also discuss the Closing process group. Most of the hard part is over, but you aren't quite done yet.

In the Monitoring and Controlling group, we'll cover Perform Quality Control, Scope Verification, and Scope Control. The Perform Quality Control process involves several new tools and techniques that may show up on the exam. Take some time here to understand the tools and techniques in the Perform Quality Control process and to differentiate them from the tools and techniques associated with the Quality Planning and Perform Quality Control processes. Remember that Perform Quality Control tools and techniques are listed as tools and techniques for the Perform Quality Assurance process. Scope Verification involves verifying and accepting work results. Scope Control is like the change control processes we discussed in Chapter 10 and is concerned with controlling changes to project scope.

The Closing process group has two processes: Close Project and Contract Closure. The Close Project process is concerned with verifying that the work of the project was completed correctly and to the stakeholders' satisfaction. Contract Closure supports the Close Project process and also verifies that the work of the project was completed correctly and the deliverables accepted.

Project closeout is the most often neglected process of all the project processes. Once the project is over, it's easy to pack things up, throw some files in a drawer, and start moving right into planning the next project. However, don't be so quick to chuck your project just yet. There are a few things to take care of during this process that might make life easier for you on the next project.

One of the most important functions of this process is obtaining formal acceptance of the product of the project from stakeholders and customers. You'll want to get an official sign-off from the stakeholders acknowledging acceptance of the product and then file this with the project documents.

Utilizing Perform Quality Control Techniques

Quality Planning, Perform Quality Assurance, and Perform Quality Control are part of the project Quality Management Knowledge Area. These processes work together to define and monitor the work of the project and to make certain the results meet the quality requirements laid out in the plan.

Perform Quality Control is specifically concerned with monitoring work results to see if they comply with the standards set out in the quality management plan. Perform Quality Control should be practiced and performed throughout the project to identify and remove the causes of unacceptable results. Remember that Perform Quality Control is concerned with project results both from a management perspective, such as schedule and cost performance, and from a product perspective. In other words, the end product should conform to the requirements and product description defined during the Planning processes.

Perform Quality Control Inputs

Perform Quality Control includes the following inputs:

- Quality management plan
- Quality metrics
- Quality checklists
- Organizational process assets
- Work performance information
- Approved change requests
- Deliverables

We've discussed each of these inputs previously, so let's move on to tools and techniques.

Perform Quality Control Tools and Techniques

This list of tools and techniques in the Perform Quality Control process includes several that haven't been discussed before:

- Cause-and-effect diagram
- Control charts
- Flowcharting
- Histogram
- Pareto chart
- Run chart
- Scatter diagram
- Statistical sampling
- Inspection
- Defect repair review

The primary purpose of each of these tools is to examine the product and/or the project processes for conformity to standards. If the results fall within the tolerance range specified, the results are acceptable. Alternatively, if the results fall within the control limits set for the product (as defined by the various tools and techniques we'll discuss in the following sections), the process is said to be in control. Spend time understanding these tools and techniques and their individual uses because there may be exam questions on each of them.

We talked about cause-and-effect diagrams as a diagramming technique in the Risk Identification process in Chapter 5, "Risk Planning." If you need a refresher, refer to Figure 5.2 in that chapter.

We also discussed flowcharts in the same section of Chapter 5. Flowcharts are diagrams that show the logical steps that must be performed in order to accomplish an objective. They can also show how the individual elements of a system interrelate. Flowcharting can help identify where quality problems might occur on the project and how problems happen. This is important because it allows the project team the opportunity to develop alternative approaches for dealing with anticipated quality problems identified with this tool and technique.

Histograms are typically bar charts that depict the distribution of variables over time. There is an example histogram in Chapter 6, "Resource Planning." In Perform Quality Control, the histogram usually depicts the attributes of the problem or situation. (We'll discuss attributes shortly.)

We will look at the other tools and techniques in more detail in the following sections.

Control Charts

Control charts measure the results of processes over time and display the results in graph form. Control charts are a way to measure variances to determine if process variances are in control or out of control.

A control chart is based on sample variance measurements. From the samples chosen and measured, the mean and standard deviation are determined. Perform Quality Control is usually maintained—or said to be in control—within plus or minus three standard deviations. In other words, Perform Quality Control says that if the process is in control (that is, the measurements fall within the control limits), you know that 99.73 percent of the parts going through the process will fall within an acceptable range of the mean. If you discover a part outside of this range, you should investigate and determine if corrective action is needed.

Figure 11.1 illustrates an example control chart.

FIGURE 11.1 Control chart

You've determined from your sample measurements that 5 mm is the mean in the example control chart. One standard deviation equals 0.02. Three standard deviations on either side of the mean become your upper and lower control points on this chart. Therefore, if all control points fall within plus or minus three standard deviations on either side of the mean, the process is in control. If points fall outside of the acceptable limits, the process is not in control and corrective action is needed.

Control charts are used most often in manufacturing settings where repetitive activities are easily monitored. For example, the process that produces widgets by the case lot must meet certain specifications and fall within certain variances to be considered in control. However, you aren't limited to using control charts only in the manufacturing industry. They can be used to monitor any output. You might consider using control charts to track and monitor project management processes. You could plot cost variances, schedule variances, frequency or number of scope changes, and so on to help monitor variances in the project management process.

Pareto Chart

You have probably heard of the 80/20 rule. Vilfredo Pareto is the person credited with discovering this rule. He observed that 80 percent of the wealth and land ownership in Italy was held by 20 percent of the population. Over the years, others have shown that the 80/20 rule applies across many disciplines and areas. As an example, generally speaking, 80 percent of the deposits of any given financial institution are held by 20 percent of its customer base. Let's hope that rule doesn't apply to project managers though, with 20 percent of the project managers out there doing 80 percent of the work!

According to Pareto, the 80/20 rule as it applies to quality says that a small number of causes (20 percent) create the majority of the problems (80 percent). Have you ever noticed that with your project or department staff? It always seems that just a few people cause the biggest headaches. But we're getting off track.

Pareto charts are displayed as histograms that rank-order the most important factors such as delays, costs, defects, or other factors by their frequency over time. His theory is that you get the most benefit if you spend the majority of your time fixing the most important problems. The information shown in Table 11.1 is plotted on an example Pareto chart shown in Figure 11.2.

TABLE 11.1 Frequency of Failures

Item	Defect Frequency	Percent of Defects	Cumulative Percent
A	800	.33	.33
B	700	.29	.62
C	400	.17	.79
D	300	.13	.92
E	200	.08	1.0

FIGURE 11.2   Pareto chart

The problems are rank-ordered according to their frequency and percentage of defects. The defect frequencies in this figure are shown as black bars, and the cumulative percentages of defects are plotted as circles. The rank-ordering of these problems shows you where corrective action should be taken first. You can see in Figure 11.2 that problem A should receive priority attention because the most benefit will come from fixing this problem.

Run Charts

Run charts are used to show variations in the process over time or to show trends (like improvements or lack of improvements) in the process. Differences in results will occur in processes because there is no such thing as a perfect process. When processes are considered in control, differences in results may occur due to common causes of variances or special cause variances.

Common causes of variances come about as a result of circumstances or situations that are relatively unique to the process you're using and are easily controlled at the operational level. Perhaps a machine needs calibration or procedures for the process need refinement. Perhaps your process is very detailed, with specific procedures that are carried out to produce the output. Not following these detailed procedures could result in variances known as special cause variances.

For the exam, you should understand the three types of variances that make up common causes of variances:

Random variances   Random variations may be normal, depending on the processes you're using to produce the product or service of the project, but they occur as the name implies, at random.

Known or predictable variances   Known or predictable variances are variances that you know exist in the process.

Variances that are always present in the process   The process itself will have inherent variability that is perhaps caused by human mistakes, machine variations or malfunctions, the environment, and so on, which are known as variances always present in the process.

Common cause variances that do not fall within the acceptable range are difficult to correct and usually require a reorganization of the process. This has the potential for significant impact, and decisions to change the process always require management approval.

Exam Spotlight

According to *A Guide to the PMBOK,* when a process is in control, it should not be adjusted. It's okay to change the process to bring about improvements, but it should not be adjusted.

Trend analysis is another technique that's carried out using run charts. Trend analysis in the Perform Quality Control process is a mathematical technique that uses historical results to predict future outcomes. Trend analysis often tracks variances in cost and schedule performance by monitoring the number of activities completed with significant variances within a certain time period. This information can then be used to forecast future performance. Trend analysis also tracks technical performance by determining the number of defects observed and the number of defects not corrected. *Technical performance measurements* compare the technical accomplishments of project milestones completed to the technical milestones defined in the project Planning process group.

Scatter Diagrams

Scatter diagrams use two variables, one called an independent variable, which is an input, and one called a dependent variable, which is an output. Scatter diagrams display the relationship between these two elements as points on a graph. As an example, maybe your scatter diagram plots the ability of your employees to perform a certain task. Their experience performing this task in months is plotted as the independent variable on the X axis, and their score—the dependent variable—is plotted on the Y axis.

The important thing to remember about scatter diagrams is that they plot the dependent and independent variables and the closer the points resemble a diagonal line, the closer these variables are related. A sample scatter diagram is shown in Figure 11.3.

Statistical Sampling

Statistical sampling involves taking a sample number of parts from the whole population and examining them to determine if they fall within the variances outlined by the Perform Quality Control plan. Perhaps you determine to statistically sample 25 parts out of a lot or run. The quality plan outlines that the lot will pass if four parts or fewer fall outside the allowable variance.

Statistical sampling may also involve determining the standard deviation for a process as discussed in the control chart tool and technique. The quality plan determines if plus or minus two standard deviations—95.44 percent of the population—is adequate or if plus or minus three standard deviations—99.73 percent—is adequate.

FIGURE 11.3   Scatter diagram

Inspection

Inspection involves physically looking at, measuring, or testing results to determine if they conform to the requirements or quality standards. It's a tool used to gather information and improve results. Inspections might occur after the final product is produced or at intervals during the development of the product to examine individual components. Acceptance decisions are made when the work is inspected and the work is either accepted or rejected. When work is rejected, it might have to go back through the process for rework.

Exam Spotlight

Don't confuse inspection with prevention; they're two different things. Inspection keeps errors in the product from reaching the customer. *Prevention* keeps errors from occurring in the process. It always costs less to prevent problems in the first place than it does to fix problems built into the product after the fact. Rework, labor costs, material costs, and potential loss of customers are all factors to consider when weighing prevention costs versus the cost of rework. Philip Crosby developed the theory of zero defects, which deals with prevention costs. Loosely translated, zero defects means doing it right the first time.

Inspection may take actual measurements of components to determine if they meet requirements. Maybe a component part for your product must be exactly 5 mm in length. In order to pass inspection, the parts are measured and must meet the 5 mm length requirement. If they measure 5 mm, they pass; if they do not, they fail.

Measurements can vary even if the variances are not noticeable. Machines wear down, people make mistakes, the environment may cause variances, and so on. Measurements that fall within a specified range are called *tolerable results*. So, instead of 5 mm exactly, maybe a range between 4.98 mm and 5.02 mm is an acceptable or tolerable measurement for our component. If the samples that are measured fall within the tolerable range, they pass; otherwise, they fail inspection.

One inspection technique uses measurements called *attributes*. The measurements taken during attribute sampling determine whether they meet one of two options, conforming or nonconforming. In other words, the measurements conform or meet the requirement, or they do not conform. This can also be considered a pass/fail or go/no-go decision.

Attribute conformity and inspections are not necessarily performed on every component part or every end product that's produced. That's time consuming and inefficient when you're producing numerous components. Inspection in cases like this is usually performed on a sampling of parts or products where every X number of parts is tested for conformity or measurement specifics.

Inspection will tell you where problems exist and give you the opportunity to correct them, thus leading to quality improvements. The other tools and techniques we'll talk about in these sections also lead to quality improvements in the product or process, or both. Quality improvements are an output of the Perform Quality Control process.

Defect Repair Review

In this tool and technique, the quality control department will review the repairs that were made (as a result of quality audits) to make certain the repairs were made correctly and that the deliverable, or product of the project, is in compliance. You'll remember that approved defect repairs are a result of a quality audit performed during the Perform Quality Assurance process or an inspection as part of the Perform Quality Control process. (Approved defect repairs are an input to the Direct and Manage Project Execution process.) Defect repairs correct problems you find with the product of the project. Now you'll examine those repairs to make certain they corrected the problem.

Perform Quality Control Outputs

Quality improvements, as mentioned in the Perform Quality Assurance process discussed Chapter 9, are a primary goal of the quality processes. Failure to meet quality requirements can have a significant impact on the project and the project team and may result in rework. *Rework* will cause a project to take longer than originally planned because the project team has to repeat processes already completed to correct the work. You should try to keep rework to a minimum so as not to impact the project schedule. Rework has the potential to cause morale issues as well, especially if the team members thought they were doing a good job all along. Rework may require the project team to put in extra long hours, which in turn may cause more errors or other negative consequences. Monitor quality periodically so that rework is kept to a minimum.

Perform Quality Assurance is concerned with assuring that the project is using the correct and most efficient processes to meet the project requirements while Perform Quality Control is concerned with the accuracy of the project results.

Real World Scenario

The Never-Ending Bridge Project

One of the main thoroughfares into your city requires a bridge replacement. You were appointed the project manager for the city and have managed this project since its initiation 15 months ago.

The project entailed hiring a contractor to build and construct the new bridge and then managing the contract and the work of the contracting agency to bring the project to a successful completion.

Approximately 28,000 vehicles travel across this bridge on a daily basis, carrying commuters and college students back and forth to the downtown area. One of the requirements was the closure of no more than three of the six lanes of traffic at one time during construction. Another requirement stated that two coats of paint were to be applied to the steel before bringing it on-site, and a third coat of paint was to be applied at the site after construction. The paint is guaranteed to last 25 to 30 years.

You assisted the Perform Quality Control department with a recent inspection. The inspection revealed that some of the paint was peeling. After further investigation, you discovered that the contractor did not allow the first coat of paint to cure properly, so when the second coat was applied, it didn't stick correctly and peeled and flaked in places.

You've instructed the contractor that according to the terms of the contract and the SOW specifications, they're required to apply three coats of paint to the bridge as part of the work of the project. Corrective action is needed to get this project back on track. As a result, the contract company decides to subcontract out the paint work to another company while they finish up their remaining tasks on the project.

Unfortunately, the subcontractor that was hired found they were in way over their heads and were not able to complete the paint job. Several months have passed, and the original project completion date was missed long ago. Obviously, revisions to the project schedule were required when it became clear that the subcontractor wasn't going to make the date. Now another revision to the project schedule is necessary due to the subcontractor's failure to complete the painting task.

The original contractor did some searching and found another subcontractor capable of completing the painting job. It's now the middle of winter. Because the temperatures are cold, the painting crew must hang insulated tarps between the bays on the bridge and use heaters to warm up small areas of steel to the proper temperature to apply the paint. This process has extended the completion date of this activity by over three times its original estimate and ultimately delayed the completion of the project by two years.

Corrective action was taken as a result of the inspection, and eventually the project was completed, but not without schedule delays, schedule changes, scope changes, and rework—not to mention the increased cost to the original contractor. Since the contract was a fixed-price contract, the contractor's profit was eaten away paying for the painting job. The cost to correct the quality issue did not impact the city, but it did impact the contractor. This is a case where an ounce of prevention would have been worth a pound of cure, as the old saying goes.

Perform Quality Control has several outputs:

- Quality control measurements
- Validated defect repair
- Quality baseline updates
- Recommended corrective actions
- Recommended preventive actions
- Requested changes
- Recommended defect repair
- Organizational process asset updates (checklists, lessons learned)
- Validated deliverables
- Project management plan updates

We've already discussed many of these outputs, but I'll add a few quick notes here.

Validated defect repairs are the results of defects that have been corrected and examined. Recommended corrective and preventive actions may result in quality improvements. Remember that processes that are in control can be changed to bring about improvements, but processes in control should not be adjusted. Processes out of control may require adjusting, but this should occur only as a result of a management decision.

Recommended defect repairs may also result from this process. The quality control department or team will identify the defects using the tools and techniques of this process and the defects should be logged in a database or some other tracking tool to keep track of status and resolution.

Completed checklists become part of the project's documentation and are included as part of the organizational process asset updates. Lessons learned should include the causes of variances found during this process and why the corrective actions were recommended.

Validated deliverables are the result of the work of the project. This output assures that the deliverables meet the quality standards outlined in the quality management plan.

Verifying Project Scope

Managing and reporting on project progress is the primary focus of the Monitoring and Controlling processes. One of the Monitoring and Controlling processes that helps manage and control project progress is the *Scope Verification* process.

The inputs of the Scope Verification are the project scope statement, WBS dictionary, project scope management plan, and deliverables. This process involves evaluating these inputs to determine if the work is complete and if it satisfies the project objectives. Evaluation is performed using inspection, which is the only tool and technique of this process. You should perform Scope Verification—even if the project is canceled—to document the degree to which the project was completed. This serves as historical information, and if the project is ever started up again, you've got documentation that tells you what was completed and how far the project progressed.

Exam Spotlight

The most important thing you should know about the Scope Verification process is that Scope Verification formalizes the acceptance of the project scope and is primarily concerned with the acceptance of work results. Don't confuse this process with the Perform Quality Control process that we just discussed.

You can remember the difference between Scope Verification and Perform Quality Control this way:

- Scope Verification = *accepting* work results

- Perform Quality Control = *checking* for correct work results (assuring that the quality requirements are met)

The outputs of Scope Verification are accepted deliverables, requested changes, and recommended corrective actions. Accepted deliverables concern the formal acceptance of the work by the stakeholders. Remember that stakeholders include customers, the project sponsor, the project team, the management team, and so on. Document their acceptance with formal sign-off and file it in your project notebook.

Controlling Scope Changes

The Scope Management Knowledge Area includes Scope Planning, Scope Definition, Create WBS, Scope Verification, and Scope Control. You'll recall that project scope describes the work required to produce the product or service of the project. This includes the requirements of the product, which describe the features and functionality of the product or service. Product scope, on the other hand, is the description of the product features. The product description is the document that defines the characteristics of the product or service of the project.

You can conclude from this that the *Scope Control* process involves changes to the project scope. Any modification to the agreed-upon WBS is considered a scope change. (It's been eons ago that we looked at this so remember that the WBS, or work breakdown structure, is a deliverables-oriented hierarchy that defines the total work of the project.) This means that the addition or deletion of activities or modifications to the existing activities on the WBS constitute a project scope change.

Changes in product scope will require changes to the project scope as well. Let's say one of your project deliverables is the design of a piece of specialized equipment that's integrated into your final product. Now let's say that due to engineering setbacks and some miscalculations, the specialized equipment requires design modifications. The redesign of this equipment impacts the end product, or product scope. Since changes to the product scope impact the project requirements, which are detailed in the scope document, changes to project scope are also required.

This change, along with recommended corrective actions, should be processed through the Integrated Change Control process.

Scope Control Inputs

There are seven inputs to the Scope Control process, all of which you've seen before:

- Project scope statement
- WBS
- WBS dictionary
- Project scope management plan
- Performance reports
- Approved change requests
- Work performance information

The first four inputs were covered in the Planning process group and the last three were discussed in the Monitoring and Controlling process group.

Scope Control Tools and Techniques

There are four tools and techniques of the Scope Control process:

- Change control system
- Variance analysis
- Replanning
- Configuration management system

The change control system here is just like the one described in the discussion of the Integrated Change Control process. It tracks and records change requests, describes the procedures to follow to implement scope change, and details the authorization levels needed to approve the changes. When your project is performed under contract, scope changes will also require conformance to the provisions of the contract and the contract change system.

Variance analysis includes reviewing project performance measurements to determine if there are variances in project scope. It's also important to determine the cause of variances and examine those against the scope baseline so that you can implement corrective actions if needed.

Replanning involves updating the WBS, WBS dictionary, project scope statement, and project management plan when a change in scope has occurred.

If you are using a configuration management system to control product scope, the change control system must also integrate with it. The configuration management system manages changes to product and project scope and assures that these changes are reasonable and make sense before they're processed through the Integrated Change Control process.

Scope Control Outputs

The outputs of the Scope Control process are as follows:

- Project scope statement updates
- WBS updates
- WBS dictionary updates
- Scope baseline updates
- Requested changes
- Recommended corrective action
- Organizational process assets update
- Project management plan updates

Let's take a look at project scope statement changes and scope baseline updates. The remaining outputs have all been discussed previously.

Changes to scope will likely require that you run back through the project Planning processes and make any needed adjustments. This also means you'll need to update the project scope statement so it accurately reflects the project work after the change.

Scope changes include any changes to the project scope as defined by the agreed-upon WBS. This in turn may require changes or updates to project objectives, costs, quality measures or controls, or time in the form of schedule revisions. Scope changes always require schedule revisions.

Schedule revisions are always needed as a result of scope changes. But not all scope changes will necessarily cause increases to the project schedule. Some scope changes may reduce the number of hours needed to complete the project, which in turn may reduce the project budget.

When scope changes are requested, all areas of the project should be investigated to determine what the changes will impact. The project team should perform estimates of the impact and of the amount of time needed to make the change. Sometimes, however, the change request is so extensive that even the time to perform an estimate should be evaluated before proceeding. In other words, if the project team is busy working on estimates, they aren't working on the project. That means extensive change requests could impact the existing schedule because of the time and effort needed just to evaluate the change. Cases like these require you to make a determination or ask the change control board (CCB) to decide if the change is important enough to allow the project team time to work on the estimates.

Changes in scope will require an update to the project scope baseline. They may also require updates to the schedule, cost, or performance measurement baselines established during the Planning processes. When change is necessary, adjustments to the performance measurement baselines are made, documented, and distributed to the stakeholders as needed.

Always remember to update your stakeholders regarding the changes you're implementing and their impacts. They'll want to know how the changes impact the performance baselines, including the project costs, project schedule, project scope, and quality.

This process concludes the Monitoring and Controlling process groups. We'll look at the Closing processes in the next section.

Formulating Project Closeout

All good projects must come to an end, as the saying goes. Hopefully, you've practiced all the things we've talked about that have led up to this point, and you've delivered a successful project to the stakeholders and customers. You've also put some of the vital tools of project management into play—planning, executing, controlling, and communicating—to help you reach that goal.

But how do you know when a project has ended successfully? Delivering the product or service of the project doesn't mean it's been completed satisfactorily. Remember back in the opening chapters that I said a project is completed successfully when it meets or exceeds stakeholders' expectations and satisfies the goals of the project. During the Closing processes—Close Project and Contract Closure—you'll document acceptance of the product of the project with a formal sign-off and file it with the project records for future reference. The formal sign-off is how the stakeholders will indicate that the goals have been met and that the project meets or exceeds their expectations so that the project ends.

Characteristics of Closing

There are a few characteristics common to all projects during the Closing processes. One is that the probability of completing the project is highest during this process and risk is lowest. You've already completed the majority of the work of the project—if not all of the work—so the probability of not finishing the project is very low.

Stakeholders have the least amount of influence during the Closing processes, while project managers have the greatest amount of influence. Costs are significantly lower during this process because the majority of the project work and spending has already occurred. Remember those cost S curves we talked about in the Cost Budgeting process? This is where they taper off as project spending comes to an end.

One last common characteristic of projects during closing is that weak matrix organizations tend to experience the least amount of stress during the Closing processes.

All projects do eventually come to an end. Let's examine a few of the reasons for project endings before getting into the Close Project and Contract Closure processes.

Project Endings

Projects come to an end for several reasons:

- They're completed successfully.
- They're canceled or killed prior to completion.
- They evolve into ongoing operations and no longer exist as projects.

There are four formal types of project endings you might need to know for the exam:

- Addition
- Starvation
- Integration
- Extinction

Let's look at each of these ending types in detail.

Addition

Projects that evolve into ongoing operations are considered projects that end due to *addition;* in other words, they become their own ongoing business unit. An example of this is the installation of an enterprise resource planning system. These systems are business management systems that integrate all areas of a business, including marketing, planning, manufacturing, sales, financials, and human resources. After the installation of the software, these systems can develop into their own business unit because ongoing operations, maintenance, and monitoring of the software require full-time staff. These systems usually evolve into an arm of the business reporting system that no one can live without once it's installed.

A project is considered a project when it meets these criteria: It is unique, has a definite beginning and ending date, and is temporary in nature. When a project becomes an ongoing operation, it is no longer a project.

Starvation

When resources are cut off from the project or are no longer provided to the project, it's starved prior to completing all the requirements and you're left with an unfinished project on your hands. *Starvation* can happen for any number of reasons:

- Other projects come about and take precedence over the current project, thereby cutting the funding or resources for your project.
- The customer curtails an order.
- The project budget is reduced.
- A key resource quits.

Resource starving can include cutting back or withholding human resources, equipment and supplies, or money. In any case, if you're not getting the people, equipment, or money you need to complete the project, it's going to starve and probably end abruptly.

This is one of those cases where documentation becomes your best friend. Organizations tend to have short memories. As you move on to bigger and better projects, your memory regarding the specifics of the project will fade. Six months from now when someone important wonders why that project was never completed and begins the finger-pointing routine, the project documents will clearly outline the reasons why the project ended early. That's one of the reasons why project documentation is such an important function. We'll talk more about documenting project details shortly.

Integration

Integration occurs when the resources of the project—people, equipment, property, and supplies—are distributed to other areas in the organization or are assigned to other projects. Perhaps your organization begins to focus on other areas or other projects and the next thing you know, functional managers come calling to retrieve their resources for other, more important things. Again, your project will come to an end due to lack of resources because they have been reassigned to other areas of the business or have been pulled from your project and assigned to another project.

The difference between starvation and integration is that starvation results in funding or resource cuts while integration results in reassignment or redeployment of the resources.

Again, good documentation describing the circumstances that brought about the ending of a project due to integration should be archived with the project records for future reference.

Extinction

This is the best kind of project end because *extinction* means the project has been completed and accepted by the stakeholders. As such, it no longer exists because it had a definite ending date, the goals of the project were achieved, and the project was closed out.

Real World Scenario

Pied Piper

Jerome Reed is the project manager for Pied Piper's newest software project. His team is working on a program that will integrate the organization's human resource information, including payroll records, leave time accruals, contact information, and so on. His top two programmers, Brett and Kathy, are heading up the coding team and are in charge of the programming and testing activities.

Pied Piper recently hired a new CIO who started working with the company just a few weeks ago. Jerome is concerned about his human resources project. It was the former CIO's pet project, but he's not sure where it falls on the new CIO's radar screen.

Jerome is in the computer room checking out the new hardware that just arrived for his project. Liz Horowitz, the director of network operations, approaches Jerome.

"That's a nice piece of hardware," Liz comments.

"It sure is. This baby is loaded. It's going to process and serve up data to the users so fast they'll be asking us to upgrade all the servers."

Liz replies, "You're right about that. I've asked Richard to burn it in and load the software."

"What software?" Jerome asks.

"You know, the new customer relationship management software. The CIO hired some vendor she's worked with before to come in and install their CRM system here. She said it was our top priority. I knew this new server was already on order, and it happens to be sized correctly for the new CRM system."

"I purchased this server for the human resources project. What am I supposed to use for that?"

Liz answers, "I've got a server over there on the bottom of the third rack that might work, or maybe you can order another one. But you should take this up with the CIO. All I know is she authorized me to use this server. She understood I was taking it from your project, so maybe she's thinking about going another direction with the human resources project.

"You probably should know I also asked to have Brett and Kathy assigned to the CRM project. Even though it's a vendor project, it still requires some of our coders. The CIO wanted the best, and they're the best we've got. It shouldn't take them long to make the changes I need, and then you can have them back for your project. In the meantime, they can give directions to your other programmers so they can keep working."

"I'm going to go see if the CIO is in," Jerome replies.

This is a case where Jerome's project ends by integration due to the reassignment of resources. The new CIO came on board and changed the direction and focus of the project priorities, making her new project a higher priority than the previous project. As a result, Jerome's hardware and his top two resources were reassigned to the new project. Had the CIO cut the resources and equipment on the original project altogether, it would have ended due to starvation.

Closing Out the Project

The key activity of the *Close Project* process is concerned with gathering project records and disseminating information to formalize acceptance of the product, service, or project as well as to perform project closure. You'll want to review the project documents to make certain they are up-to-date. For example, perhaps some scope change requests were implemented that changed some of the characteristics of the final product. The project information you're collecting during this process should reflect the characteristics and specifications of the final product. Don't forget to update your resource assignments as well. Some team members will have come and gone over the course of the project; you need to double-check that all the resources and their roles and responsibilities are noted.

Once the project outcomes are documented, you'll request formal acceptance from the stakeholders or the customer. (We'll look at formal acceptance later when we talk about the outputs.) They're also interested in knowing if the product or service of the project meets the goals the project set out to accomplish. If your documentation is up-to-date, you'll have the project results at hand to share with them.

The Close Project process is also concerned with analyzing the project management processes to determine their effectiveness and to document lessons learned concerning the project processes. And one of the other key functions of the Close Project process is the archiving of all project documents for historical reference. You can probably guess that Close Project belongs to the Project Integration Management knowledge area since this process touches so many areas of the project.

Every project requires closure. According to *A Guide to the PMBOK*, the completion of each project phase requires project closure as well.

Exam Spotlight

Project closure occurs at the end of each phase of the project in order to properly document project information and keep it safe for future reference. You shouldn't wait until project completion to perform the Close Project process but rather perform it at the end of every phase, no matter if the project phase was completed successfully or was ended for some other reason.

Close Project Inputs

The Close Project process gathers all the project records and verifies that they are up-to-date and accurate. The project records must correctly identify the final specifications of the product or service the project set out to produce. Close Project is the place to ensure that this information accurately reflects the true results of the project.

The six inputs to the Close Project process are as follows:

- Project management plan
- Contract documentation
- Enterprise environmental factors
- Organizational process assets
- Work performance information
- Deliverables

We've talked about all of these inputs with the exception of contract documentation. Contract documentation includes the contract and any other information, like contract changes, product descriptions, technical specifications, and so on.

Close Project Tools and Techniques

You've seen all of the tools and techniques of Close Project in other processes:

- Project management methodology
- Project management information system (PMIS)
- Expert judgment

The project management methodology should outline processes for both project and administrative closeout. The PMIS and expert judgment are used to perform these processes.

Close Project Outputs

Sometimes you'll work on projects where everything just clicks. Your project team functions at the performing stage, the customers and stakeholders are happy, and things just fall into place according to plan. I often find it difficult to close projects that have progressed particularly well, just because I don't want them to end. Believe it or not, the majority of your projects can fall into this category if you practice good project management techniques and exercise those great communication skills.

The Close Project process has the following outputs:

- Administrative closure procedure
- Contract closure procedure
- Final product, service, or result
- Organizational process assets updates

Let's take a brief look at each.

Administrative Closure Procedure

Administrative closure procedures involves collecting all the records associated with the project, analyzing the project success (or failure), documenting and gathering lessons learned, and archiving project records. Keep in mind that when projects are performed under contract, the archiving of financial records is especially important. These records may need to be accessed if there are payment disputes, so you need to know where they are and how they were filed. Projects with large financial expenditures also require particular attention to the archiving of financial records for the same reasons. Financial information is especially useful when estimating future projects, so again, make sure to archive the information so it's easily accessible.

All of these documents should be indexed for reference and filed in a safe place. Don't forget to include electronic databases and electronic documents as part of your project archives as well. These records can be stored on a network drive or copied onto a CD that's kept with the project binder.

Administrative closure procedures also document the project team members' and stakeholders' roles and responsibilities in performing this process. According to *A Guide to the PMBOK*, this should include the processes and methodologies for defining the following:

- Approval requirements of the stakeholders for project deliverables and changes to deliverables.

- Assuring and confirming that the project meets the requirements of the stakeholders, customers, and sponsor. Documenting necessary actions to verify that the deliverables have been accepted and exit criteria have been met.

- Assuring and confirming that the exit criteria for the project is satisfied.

Contract Closure Procedure

Contract closure procedures, like the administrative closure procedures, document the roles and responsibilities of the project team members and stakeholders in closing out the contract. This procedure details the methodology you use to assure that contract exit criteria and contract conditions have been satisfied. We'll talk more about contract closure in the section "Contract Closure."

Final Product, Service, or Result

The name of this output is somewhat misleading. This actually refers to the acceptance of the final product, service, or result and the turnover of the product to the organization. This usually requires a formal sign-off (we'll talk about that next) and, in the case of a project performed on contract, definitely requires a formal sign-off or receipt indicating acceptance of the project.

Formal acceptance includes distributing notice of the acceptance of the product or service of the project by the stakeholders, customer, or project sponsor to stakeholders and customers. You should require formal sign-off indicating that those signing accept the product of the project.

> The final product, service, or result is concerned with obtaining formal acceptance while organizational process assets involves documenting and archiving formal acceptance.

Organizational Process Assets Updates

The organizational process assets output is where the formal sign-off of the acceptance of the product is documented, collected, and archived for future reference. Documenting formal acceptance is important because it signals the official closure of the project and it is your proof that the project was completed satisfactorily.

Another function of sign-off is that it kicks off the beginning of the warranty period. Sometimes project managers or vendors will warranty their work for a certain time period after completing the project. Projects that produce software programs, for example, may be warranted from bugs for a 60- or 90-day time frame from the date of implementation or acceptance. Typically in the case of software projects, bugs are fixed for free during the warranty period. Watch out, because users will try to squeeze new requirements into the "bug" category mold. If you offer a warranty, it's critical that the warranty spells out exactly what is covered and what is not.

This is also where the other project records and files are collected and archived. This includes the project planning documents (project scope statement, budget, schedule, risk responses, quality plan and baselines, and so on), change records and logs, issue logs, and so on.

Project closure documents are included in this output. These include documentation showing the transfer of the product of the project to the organization (or department responsible for ongoing maintenance and support). If your project is canceled or ends prematurely, you should document the reasons for its premature end as well as the procedures for transferring the completed and uncompleted deliverables.

Lessons learned are used to document the successes and failures of the project. As an example, lessons learned document the reasons why specific corrective actions were taken, their outcomes, the causes of performance variances, unplanned risks that occurred, mistakes that were made and could have been avoided, and so on.

Unfortunately, sometimes projects do fail. There are things that can be learned from failed projects as well as from successful projects, and this information should be documented for future reference. Most project managers, however, do not document lessons learned. The reason for this is that employees don't want to admit to making mistakes or learning from mistakes made during the project. And they do not want their name associated with failed projects or even with mishaps on successful projects.

NOTE   Lessons learned can be some of the most valuable information you'll take away from a project. We can all learn from our experiences, and what better way to have even more success on your next project than to review a similar past project's lessons learned document? But lessons learned will only be there if you document them now. I strongly recommend you not skip this step.

You and your management team will have to work to create an atmosphere of trust and assurance that lessons learned are not reasons for dismissing employees but are learning opportunities that benefit all those associated with the project. Lessons learned allow you to carry knowledge gained on this project to other projects you'll work on going forward. They'll also prevent repeat mistakes in the future if you take the time to review the project documents and lessons learned prior to undertaking your new project.

Post-implementation audits aren't an official output, but they are a good idea. These go hand in hand with lessons learned because they examine the project from beginning to end and look at what went right and what went wrong. They evaluate the project goals and determine if the product or service of the project satisfies the objectives. Post-implementation audits also examine the activities and project processes to determine if improvements are possible on future projects.

Organizations that do not document lessons learned probably do conduct post-implementation audits. Documenting and gathering information during this procedure can serve the same function as lessons learned if you're honest and include all the good, the bad, and the ugly. Let's hope there's very little ugly.

Contract Closure

Contracts have life cycles of their own—just like projects. We talked about the contract life cycles in Chapter 9, "Measuring and Controlling Project Performance." As such, contracts come to a close just as projects come to a close. As you might guess, there is a process that deals with contract closings; it's called Contract Closure.

Real World Scenario

Cimarron Research Group

The Cimarron Research Group researches and develops organic pesticides for use on food crops. It is a medium-sized company and has established a project management office (PMO) to manage all aspects of project work. The PMO consists of project managers and administrative staff who assist with information handling, filing, and disbursement.

Terri Roberts is the project manager for a project that has just closed. Terri diligently filed all the pertinent project documents as the project progressed and has requested the research files and engineering notes from the director of engineering to include them with the project archives as well. All information regarding the research on this project is included with the project archives. The engineering department chooses to keep their own set of research records as well, but it's important to keep a copy of these notes with the project archives so that all the information about the project is located in one place.

Terri's assistant has indexed all the project documents and recently sent notice of formal acceptance and approval of this project to the stakeholders, project sponsor, and management team. This notice officially closes the project. The next step is to archive the files onto CDs and store them.

The *Contract Closure* process is concerned with completing and settling the terms of the contract. It supports the Close Project process because the Contract Closure process determines if the work described in the contract was completed accurately and satisfactorily. This is called *product verification*. Projects that have multiple deliverables may have contracts for some of the deliverables but not all. Obviously, this process applies only to those phases, deliverables, or portions of the project that were performed under contract.

Contract Closure updates records and archives the information for future reference. These records detail the final results of the work of the project. We'll look at the specifics of this when we examine the Contract Closure outputs.

Contracts may have specific terms or conditions for completion and closeout. You should be aware of these terms or conditions so that project closure isn't held up because you missed an important detail. If you are not administering the contract yourself, be certain to ask your procurement department if there are any special conditions that you should know about so that your project team doesn't inadvertently delay contract or project closure.

Close Project verifies and documents the project outcomes just like the Contract Closure process. Keep in mind that not all projects are performed under contract so not all projects require Contract Closure. However, all projects do require the Close Project process. Since verification and documentation of the project outcomes occur in both of these processes, projects that are performed under contract need to have project results verified only one time.

> **Exam Spotlight**
>
> For the exam, remember that product verification performed during the Closing processes determines if all of the work of the project was completed correctly according to the contract terms and satisfactorily according to stakeholder expectations whereas product documentation is verified and accepted during the Scope Verification process. One more note: When projects end prematurely, the Scope Verification process is where the level of detail concerning the amount of work completed gets documented.

Contract Closure Inputs

The Contract Closure process has four inputs:

- Procurement management plan
- Contract management plan
- Contract documentation
- Contract Closure procedures

We've discussed all these inputs before, but there's a few more things you should know about contract documentation for this process. Contract documentation includes the contract itself and all the supporting documents that go along with it. These might include things such as the WBS, the project schedule, change control documents, technical documents, financial and payment records, quality control inspection results, and so on. This information—along with all the other information gathered during the project—is filed once the project is closed out so that anyone considering a future project of similar scope can reference what was done.

 Contract documentation is an input to both the Close Project and Contract Closure processes.

Contract Closure Tools and Techniques

The Contract Closure process has two tools and techniques: procurement audits and records management system. The records management system here serves the same function as the records management system we talked about in the discussion of the Contract Administration process in Chapter 9. *Procurement audits* are reviews of procurement processes to determine if they are meeting the right needs and are being performed correctly and according to standards. *A Guide to the PMBOK* says procurement audits are concerned with reviewing the procurement process, starting with the Plan Purchases and Acquisitions process all the way through Contract Administration.

The primary purpose of the procurement audit is to identify lessons learned during the procurement process. Procurement audits examine the procurement process to determine areas of improvement and to identify flawed processes or procedures. This allows you to reuse the successful processes on other procurement items for this project, on future projects, or elsewhere in the organization. It also alerts you to problems in the process so that you don't repeat them.

Procurement audits may be used by either the buyer or the vendor, or by both, as an opportunity for improvement. Documenting the lessons learned—including the successes and failures that occurred—allows you to improve other procurement processes currently under way on this project or other projects. It also gives you the opportunity to improve the process for future projects.

Contract Closure Outputs

One of the purposes of the Contract Closure process is to provide formal notice to the seller—usually in written form—that the contract is complete. The output of Contract Closure that deals with this is called closed contracts. This is *formal acceptance and closure* of the contract. It's your responsibility as project manager to document the formal acceptance of the contract. Many times the provisions for formalizing acceptance and closing the contract are spelled out in the contract itself.

If you have a procurement department that handles contract administration, they will expect you to inform them when the contract is completed and will in turn follow the formal procedures to let the seller know the contract is complete. However, you'll still note the contract completion in your copy of the project records.

 Depending on the terms of the contract, early termination (whether by agreement, default, or for cause) may result in additional charges to the buyer. Be certain to note the reasons for early termination in your contract documentation.

The other output of Contract Closure is organizational process updates. This includes updating the contract file, deliverables acceptance, and lessons learned. The *contract file* is simply a file of all the contract records and supporting documents. These records should be indexed for easy reference and included as part of the project files in the Close Project process.

> ### Exam Spotlight
>
> *A Guide to the PMBOK* shows the Close Project process being performed before the Contract Closure process. In practice, you will likely close out the contract before closing the project and archiving project documents. Note that the contract file (part of the organizational process assets update) output of the Contract Closure process is an input to the Close Project process (called contract documentation).

This process is your organization's way of formally accepting the product of the project from the vendor and closing out the contract. The deliverable acceptance portion of the organizational process updates includes the formal written notice from the buyer that the deliverables are acceptable and satisfactory or have been rejected. If the product or service does not meet expectations, the vendor will need to correct the problems before you issue a formal acceptance notice. Hopefully, quality audits have been performed during the course of the project and the vendor was given the opportunity to make corrections earlier in the process than the Closing stage. It's not a good idea to wait until the very end of the project and then spring all the problems and issues on the vendor at once. It's much more efficient to discuss problems with your vendor as the project progresses because it provides the opportunity for correction when the problems occur.

Lessons learned include information and documentation about what worked well and what didn't work well regarding the procurement processes. This information can be used on future projects to improve performance and prevent inefficiencies.

Releasing Project Team Members

Releasing project team members is not an official process. However, it should be noted that at the conclusion of the project, you will release your project team members, and they will go back to their functional managers or get assigned to a new project if you're working in a matrix type organization.

You will want to keep the functional managers or other project managers informed as you get closer to project completion so that they have time to adequately plan for the return of their employees. Start letting them know a few months ahead of time what the schedule looks like and how soon they can plan on using their employees on new projects. This gives the other managers the ability to start planning activities and scheduling activity dates.

Celebrate!

I think it's a good idea to hold a celebration at the conclusion of a successfully completed project. The project team should celebrate their accomplishment, and you should officially recognize their efforts and thank them for their participation. Any number of ideas come to mind here—a party, a trip to a ball game, pizza and sodas at lunch time, and so on. This shouldn't be the only time you've recognized your team, as discussed during the Team Development process, but now is the time to officially close the project and thank your team members.

A celebration helps team members formally recognize the project end and brings closure to the work they've done. It also encourages them to remember what they've learned and to start thinking about how their experiences will benefit them and the organization during the next project.

Project Case Study: New Kitchen Heaven Retail Store

Dirk strolls into your office maintaining his formal and dignified manners as always and then sits down in the chair beside your desk.

"I just want to congratulate you on a job well done," he says. "The grand opening was a success, and the store had a better-than-expected week the first week. I'm impressed you were able to pull this off and get the store opened prior to the Garden and Home Show. That was the key to the great opening week."

"Thank you, Dirk. Lots of people put in a lot of hard work and extra hours to get this job done. I'm glad you're happy with the results."

"I thought the banner with our logo, 'Great Gadgets for People Interested in Great Food,' was a wonderful touch."

"That was Jill's idea. She had some great ideas that made the festivities successful. As you know, though," you continue, "we did have some problems on this project. Fortunately, they weren't insurmountable, but I think we learned a thing or two during this project that we can carry forward to other projects."

"Like what?" Dirk asks.

"We should have contracted with Gomez Construction sooner so that we didn't have to pay overtime. We had a very generous budget, so the overtime expense didn't impact this project, but it might impact the next one.

"And we came fairly close to having a hardware disaster on our hands. Next time, we should order the equipment sooner, test it here at headquarters first, and then ship it out to the site after we know everything is working correctly."

"Good ideas. But that's old news. Now that this project is over, I'd like to get you started on the next project. We're going to introduce cooking classes in all of our retail stores. The focus is the home chef, and we might just call the classes the Home Chef Pro series. We'll offer basic classes all the way to professional series classes if the project's a hit. We'll bring in guest chefs from the local areas to give demos and teach some of the classes as well."

"I'm very interested in taking on this project and can't wait to get started. I'm thrilled that you want me to head this up. But I do have a few things here to wrap up before I start work on the new project," you reply.

Dirk says, "The project's over. The grand opening was a success. It's time to move on. Let Jill take over now; the retail stores are her responsibility."

"Jill has taken over the day-to-day operations. However, I've got to finish collecting the project information, close out the contract with Gomez, and make the final payment. Jake verified that all the work was completed correctly and to his satisfaction. Then I need to publish the formal acceptance notice to all of the stakeholders via e-mail. I will also create a document that outlines those things I told you earlier about that we should remember and reference during the next project; that document is called lessons learned. Then after all those things are completed, all of the project records need to be indexed and archived. I can have all that done by the end of the week and will be free starting Monday to work on requirements gathering and the charter document for the new project."

"This is just like the planning process discussion we got into with the tree, the breakdown structure thing, and all the planning, I suspect. I do have to admit all the planning paid off. I'll give you until the end of the week to close out this project. Come see me Monday to get started on Home Chef Pro."

Project Case Study Checklist

Scope Verification

- Verified work results

Perform Quality Control

- Assured quality requirements were met

Close Project

- Product verification (work was correct and satisfactory)

- Collecting project documents

- Disseminating final acceptance notice

- Documenting lessons learned

- Archiving project records

Contract Closure

- Product verification (work was correct and satisfactory)

- Formal acceptance and closure

Summary

We closed out the Monitoring and Controlling process group with this chapter by covering the Perform Quality Control, Scope Verification, and Scope Control processes.

Perform Quality Control monitors work results to see if they fulfill the quality standards outlined in the quality management plan. Perform Quality Control should occur throughout the life of the project. It uses many tools and techniques. Inspection measures results to determine if the results conform to the quality standards. Attributes are measurements that either conform or do not conform. Control charts measure the results of processes over time, and Pareto charts are histograms that rank-order the most important quality factors by their frequency over time. You should not adjust processes that are in control; however, you can change these processes to realize improvements.

Scope Verification involves verifying and accepting work results, while Scope Control is concerned with controlling changes to project scope.

Project closure is the most often neglected process of all the project management processes. The two processes in the Closing process group are Close Project and Contract Closure. The four most important tasks of closure are as follows:

- Checking the work for completeness and accuracy

- Documenting formal acceptance

- Disseminating project closure information

- Archiving records and lessons learned

Close Project involves checking that the work of the project was completed correctly and to the satisfaction of the stakeholders. Documenting formal acceptance of the product of the project is an important aspect of project closure as well. This assures that the stakeholder or customer is satisfied with the work and that it meets their needs.

Projects come to an end in one of four ways: addition, starvation, integration, or extinction. Addition is when projects evolve into their own business unit. Starvation happens because the project is starved of its resources. Integration occurs when resources are taken from the existing project and dispersed back into the organization or assigned to other projects. And extinction is the best end because the project was completed, accepted, and closed.

Close Project is performed at the end of each phase of the project as well as at the end of the project. Close Project involves documenting formal acceptance and disseminating notice of acceptance to the stakeholders, customer, and others. All documentation gathered during the project and collected during this process is archived and saved for reference purposes on future projects.

Contract Closure is performed after Close Project and is concerned with settling the contract and completing the contract according to its terms. Its primary outputs include the contract file and formal acceptance and closure (both are components of the organizational process assets update).

Lessons learned document the successes and failures of the project and of the procurement processes. Many times lessons learned are not documented because staff members do not want to assign their names to project errors or failures. You and your management team need to work together to assure employees that lessons learned are not exercises used for disciplinary purposes but benefit both the employee and the organization. Documenting what you've learned from past experiences lets you carry this forward to new projects so that the same errors are not repeated. It also allows you to incorporate new methods of performing activities that you learned on past projects.

Exam Essentials

Be able to name the tools and techniques of Perform Quality Control.   The tools and techniques of the of Perform Quality Control process are cause-and-effect diagram, control charts, flowcharting, histogram, Pareto chart, run chart, scatter diagram, statistical sampling, inspection, and defect repair review.

Name the purpose of the Scope Verification process.   The purpose of Scope Verification is to determine if the work is complete and if it satisfies the project objectives.

Be able to name the purpose of the Closing processes.   The purpose of the Closing processes is to verify that the work was satisfactorily completed, to disseminate information, to document formal acceptance, to archive records, to close out the contract, and to document lessons learned.

Be able to describe product verification.   Product verification confirms that all the work of the project performed on contract was completed accurately and to the satisfaction of the stakeholder.

Be able to name the primary activity of the Closing processes.   The primary activity of the Closing processes is to distribute information that formalizes project completion.

Be able to describe when the Close Project process is performed.   Close Project is performed at the close of each project phase and at the close of the project.

Be able to define the purpose for lessons learned.   The purpose of lessons learned is to describe the project successes and failures and to use the information learned on future projects.

Key Terms

You've learned a lot of new key words in this chapter. PMI has worked hard to develop and define standard project management terms that apply across industries. Here is a list of some of the terms you came across in this chapter:

addition

attributes

Close Project

common causes of variances

Contract Closure

contract file

control charts

extinction

formal acceptance and closure

inspection

integration

Pareto charts

Perform Quality Control

prevention

procurement audits

product verification

rework

run charts

scatter diagrams

Scope Control

Scope Verification

starvation

statistical sampling

technical performance measurements

tolerable results

Review Questions

1. You are working on a project that was proceeding well until a manufacturing glitch occurred that requires corrective action. It turns out the glitch was an unintentional enhancement to the product, and the marketing people are absolutely crazy about its potential. The corrective action is canceled, and you continue to produce the product with the newly discovered enhancement. As the project manager, you know that a change has occurred to the product scope because the glitch changed the characteristics of the product. Which of the following statements is true?

   A. Changes to product scope are reflected in the project scope.

   B. Changes to product scope are reflected in the integrated change control plan.

   C. Changes to product scope are a result of changes to the product description.

   D. Changes to product scope are a result of corrective action.

2. You are working on a project that was proceeding well until a manufacturing glitch occurred that requires corrective action. It turns out the glitch was an unintentional enhancement to the product, and the marketing people are absolutely crazy about its potential. The corrective action is canceled, and you continue to produce the product with the newly discovered enhancement. As the project manager, you know that a change has occurred to the project scope. Which of the following statements is true?

   A. Project scope changes do not require CCB approval.

   B. Performance measurement baselines may be affected by scope changes.

   C. Project scope change uses inspection to determine if change has occurred.

   D. Project scope change uses workarounds to correct unexpected problems with scope change.

3. Your project has experienced some changes to the agreed-upon WBS elements. The changes were approved through the proper change control process. The WBS changes may in turn require which of the following?

   A. Scope changes

   B. Cost changes

   C. Schedule revisions

   D. Risk response changes

4. You are a project manager for Dakota Software Consulting Services. You're working with a major retailer that offers its products through mail-order catalogs. It is interested in knowing customer characteristics, the amounts of first-time orders, and similar information. The stakeholders have accepted the project scope. Work has begun on the project, and you're confirming some of the initial work results with the stakeholders. You've asked for acceptance of the work results. Which process are you in?

   A. Quality Assurance

   B. Quality Control

   C. Scope Verification

   D. Close Project

5. You are the project manager for a top secret software project for an agency of the United States government. Your mission—should you choose to accept it—is to complete the project using internal resources. The reason is that finding contractors with top secret clearances takes quite a bit of time and waiting for clearances would jeopardize the implementation date. Your programmers are 80 percent of the way through the programming and testing work when your agency appoints a new executive director. Slowly but surely your programmers are taken off this project and reassigned to the executive director's hot new project. Which of the following type of project ending is this?

   A. Starvation

   B. Extinction

   C. Addition

   D. Integration

6. You are the project manager for a top secret software project for an agency of the United States government. Your mission—should you choose to accept it—is to complete the project using internal resources. The reason is that getting top secret clearances for contractors takes quite a bit of time and waiting for clearances would jeopardize the implementation date. Your programmers are 80 percent of the way through the programming and testing work when your agency appoints a new executive director. Your programmers are siphoned off this project to work on the executive director's hot new project. Which of the following addresses the purpose of Scope Verification in this case?

   A. Scope Verification determines the correctness and completion of all the work.

   B. Scope Verification documents the level and degree of completion.

   C. Scope Verification determines if the project results comply with quality standards.

   D. Scope Verification documents the correctness of the work according to stakeholders' expectations.

7. You are a project manager for Cinema Snicker Productions. Your company specializes in producing comedy films for the big screen. Your latest project has just been canceled due to budget cuts. Which of the following statements is true?

   A. This project ended due to starvation because the funding was cut off.

   B. This project ended due to integration because the resources were distributed elsewhere.

   C. This project ended due to starvation because the resources were distributed elsewhere.

   D. This project ended due to integration because the funding was cut off.

8. You are a project manager for Cinema Snicker Productions. Your company specializes in producing comedy films for the big screen. Your latest project has just been completed and accepted. You've been given your next project, which starts right away. Which of the following statements is true?

   A. This project ended due to extinction because it was completed and accepted.

   B. This project ended due to integration because it was completed and accepted and the project manager moved on to a new project.

   C. This project ended due to addition because it was completed and accepted and archived into the company's catalog of available films.

   D. This project ended due to integration because it was completed and accepted.

9. Which of the following processes are performed in the Closing process group and in what order?

   A. Contract Closure, then Close Project

   B. Scope Verification, then Close Project

   C. Contract Closure, then Scope Verification

   D. Close Project, then Contract Closure

10. You are a project manager for Dutch Harbor Consulting. Your latest project involved the upgrade of an organization's operating system on 236 servers. You performed this project under contract. You are in the Contract Closure process and know that you should document which of the following? (Choose the best response.)

    A. Administrative closure procedures

    B. Contract closure procedures

    C. Formal acceptance

    D. Product verification

11. You are a project manager for Dutch Harbor Consulting. Your latest project involved the upgrade of an organization's operating system on 236 servers. You performed this project under contract. You are in the Closing process and know that product verification is for what purpose?

    A. To verify the goals of the project and ensure that the product of the project is complete

    B. To evaluate all the work of the project and compare the results to project scope

    C. To verify that all the work was completed correctly and satisfactorily

    D. To evaluate project goals and ensure that the product of the project meets the requirements

12. You are a project manager for Dutch Harbor Consulting. Your latest project involved the upgrade of an organization's operating system on 236 servers. You performed this project under contract. You are in the Contract Closure process and have reviewed the contracting process to identify lessons learned. What is the name of the tool and technique of you used to perform this function?

    A. Procurement audits

    B. Performance reviews

    C. Performance audits

    D. Procurement reviews

13. You are a project manager for Penguin Software. Your company creates custom software programs for hospitals and large dental offices. You have just completed a project and are gathering the documentation of the product of the project. This might include all of the following except _____.

    A. Technical specifications

    B. Electronic files

    C. Organizational process assets

    D. Enterprise environmental factors

14. The outputs of the Close Project process include all of the following except for which one?

   A. Administrative closure procedure

   B. Formal acceptance

   C. Lessons learned

   D. Closed contracts

15. You have collected the work performance information for your project to be included in the project archives. What is the purpose of the work performance information?

   A. The work performance information is used as part of the formal acceptance process to verify contract expenditures.

   B. The work performance information is used to determine the status of project activities and make certain the project goals and objectives are met.

   C. The work performance information is included in the project archive documentation after its accuracy is confirmed.

   D. The work performance information is used as historical information for future projects that are similar in scope to this project.

16. Your project was just completed. Due to some unfortunate circumstances, the project was delayed, causing cost overruns at the end of the project. Which of the following statements is true?

   A. You should document the circumstances as lessons learned.

   B. You should pay particular attention to archiving the financial records for this project.

   C. Your project ended due to starvation because of the cost overruns.

   D. You should document the circumstances surrounding the project completion during the Scope Verification process.

17. Your project was just completed. Due to some unfortunate circumstances, the project was delayed, causing cost overruns at the end of the project. This information might be useful on future projects in all of the following activities except for which one?

   A. Cost estimating

   B. Allocating resources

   C. Product verification

   D. Activity estimating

18. Your project was just completed, accepted, and closed. As is customary for your organization, you conduct a post-implementation audit. The purpose of this audit includes all of the following except for which one?

   A. Evaluating project goals and comparing them to the project's product

   B. Reviewing successes and failures

   C. Documenting the acceptance of the work results

   D. Documenting possible improvements for future projects

19. Contract documentation is an input to both the Close Project and Contract Closure processes. Contract documentation might include all of the following except for which one?

   A. Supporting documents

   B. Contract changes

   C. Financial documents

   D. Procurement audit documents

20. Procurement audits review which of the following?

   A. The procurement process from Procurement Planning through Contract Administration

   B. The contract administration process from Solicitation Planning through Contract Administration

   C. The procurement process from Procurement Planning through Contract Closure

   D. The contract administration process from Solicitation Planning through Contract Closure

Answers to Review Questions

1.   A. Changes to product scope should be reflected in the project scope.

2.   B. A project scope change affects the performance measurement baselines, which may include schedule baselines and cost baselines.

3.   C. WBS element changes are scope changes. Schedule revisions are often required as a result of scope changes.

4.   C. The Scope Verification process is concerned with the acceptance of work results. It also formalizes the acceptance of the project scope.

5.   D. Integration occurs when resources, equipment, or property are reassigned or redeployed back to the organization or to another project.

6.   B. Scope Verification should document the level and degree of completion of the project. If you come back at a later date and restart this project, Scope Verification will describe how far the project progressed and give you an idea of where to start.

7.   A. Starvation occurs because the project no longer receives the resources needed to continue. Resources could include people, equipment, money, and the like.

8.   A. Extinction is the best type of project end because it means the project was completed successfully and accepted by the sponsor or customer.

9.   D. Close Project and Contract Closure are the processes in the Closing process group and are performed in that order.

10. C. The project manager is responsible for documenting the formal acceptance of the work of the contract. This should be done during Contract Closure when projects are performed under contract or during Close Project if no work was performed under contract. In cases where part of the work was performed under contract and part with in-house staff, formal acceptance should occur in both of these processes.

11. C. Product verification examines all the work of the project and verifies that the work was completed correctly and satisfactorily.

12. A. Procurement audits are used to review the procurement process and identify and document any lessons learned during the procurement process for future reference.

13. D. Enterprise environmental factors is an input to the Close Project process and wouldn't be included in the documentation of the product of the project.

14. D. Closed contracts are an output of the Contract Closure process. Formal acceptance is part of the final product, service, or result output. Lessons learned are part of organizational process assets updates.

15. B. The work performance information is reviewed to determine the status of project activities and make certain the project goals and objectives are met. This is an input to the Close Project process.

16. A. Lessons learned document the experiences, successes, and failures that occurred during this project for future reference. There isn't enough information in the question to determine if option B or D is correct. Option C is not correct because the project was completed.

17. C. Product verification involves examining the work of the project for completeness and correctness. This process occurs on the existing project and isn't of much benefit to future projects because you'll perform product verification on future project work at the close of the project. By definition, a project is unique and creates a unique product or service.

18. C. Post-implementation audits are similar to lessons learned in that they review and document the project successes and failures, look for possible improvements for future projects, and evaluate the project goals and compare these to the end product.

19. D. Procurement audits are a tool and technique of Contract Closure and not an input. Contract documentation might include all of the other options shown as well as the contract itself, technical documentation, quality inspection reports related to the contract, and so on.

20. A. According to *A Guide to the PMBOK*, the procurement audit examines the procurement process from Procurement Planning through Contract Administration.

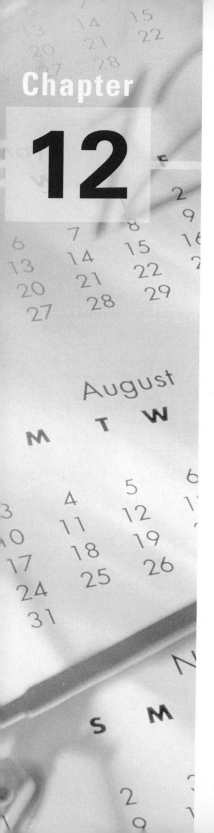

Professional Responsibility

**THE PMP EXAM CONTENT FROM THE PRO-
FESSIONAL AND SOCIAL RESPONSIBILITY
PERFORMANCE DOMAIN COVERED IN THIS
CHAPTER INCLUDES THE FOLLOWING:**

✓ Ensure Individual Integrity

✓ Contribute to the Project Management Knowledge Base

✓ Enhance Personal Professional Competence

✓ Promote Interaction Among Stakeholders

Congratulations! You've made terrific progress and are well equipped to take the Project Management Professional (PMP) exam. We've covered all of *A Guide to the PMBOK* process groups, so the good news is you don't have any more inputs, tools and techniques, outputs, or formulas to memorize. However, there is one final area that the PMP exam will include: professional responsibility.

Once you've obtained the PMP designation, you have an obligation to maintain integrity, apply your subject matter knowledge and project management knowledge, and maintain the code of conduct published by PMI. You'll also be required to balance the interests and needs of stakeholders with the organization's needs. The exam may include questions on any of these topics.

As a project manager, you'll find yourself in many unique situations, different organizations, and possibly even different countries. Even if you never get involved in international project management, you will still come in contact with people from different cultures and backgrounds than yours. If you work as a contract project manager, you'll be exposed to many different organizations that each has its own cultures and ways of doing things. You should always strive to act in a professional, nonoffensive manner in these situations.

We'll talk about each of these topics in this chapter.

Ensuring Integrity

As a project manager, one of your professional responsibilities is to ensure integrity of the project management process, the product, and your own personal conduct. We've spent the majority of this book discussing how to achieve project management integrity by following the project management processes. Now we'll turn our focus to accurately ensuring the integrity of the product.

A product that has integrity is one that is complete and sound, or fit for use.

The correct application of the project management processes you've learned will ensure the integrity of the product. The effective execution of the Planning, Executing, and Monitoring and Controlling processes, including documenting scope, performing quality inspections, measuring performance, and taking corrective actions, will ensure that a quality product is produced that satisfies the requirements of the stakeholders (and the project plan). And as you learned in the Chapter 11, you will seek acceptance of the product from the stakeholders and customer during the Closing process group.

There are several facets of integrity including personal integrity, avoiding conflict of interest situations, and professionalism. We'll look at each of these next.

Personal Integrity

Personal integrity means sticking to an ethical code. As a certified Project Management Professional, you are required to adhere to PMI's *Project Management Professional Code of Professional Conduct.* You can find a copy of this code at the PMI website: www.pmi.org.

You should read and understand this code because you will be agreeing to adhere to its terms as part of the certification process. One of the aspects of personal integrity includes your truthfulness about your PMP application and certification, your qualifications, and the continuing reports you provide to PMI to maintain your certification.

Exam Spotlight

I recommend reading the *PMP Code of Professional Conduct* as part of your project management studies.

Truthfulness and integrity involve not only information regarding your own background and experience, but information regarding the project circumstances as well. For example, let's say you're a project manager working on contract. Part of your compensation consists of a bonus based on total project billing. Now let's suppose your project is finishing sooner than anticipated, and this means your personal profit will decrease by $1,500. Should you stretch the work to meet the original contracted amount so that your personal bonus comes in at the full amount even though your project team is finished? I think you know the answer is of course not.

Your personal gain should never be a consideration when billing a customer or completing a project. Personal gain should never be a factor in any project decision. If the project finishes sooner than planned, you should bill the customer for the work completed, not for the full contracted amount. Compromising the project for the sake of your personal gain shows a lack of integrity, which could ultimately cost you your PMP status and even your job.

Conflict of Interest

Another area the *PMP Code of Professional Conduct* discusses is your responsibility to report to the stakeholders, customers, or others any actions or circumstances that could be construed as a *conflict of interest.*

A conflict of interest is when your personal interests are put above the interests of the project or when you use your influence to cause others to make decisions in your favor without regard for the project outcome. In other words, your personal interests take precedence over your professional obligations, and you make decisions that allow you to personally benefit regardless of the outcome of the project. Let's take a look at a few examples.

Associations and Affiliations

Conflicts of interest may include your associations or affiliations. For example, perhaps your brother-in-law owns his own construction company and you are the project manager for a construction project that's just published an RFP. Your brother-in-law bids on the project and ends up winning the bid.

If you sat on the decision committee and didn't tell anyone about your association with the winning bidder, that is clearly a conflict of interest. If you influenced the bid decision so that it went to your brother-in-law, he benefited from your position. Therefore, you put your personal interests, or in this case the interests of your associations, above the project outcome. Even if you did not influence the decision in any way, when others on the project discover the winning bidder is your brother-in-law, they will assume a conflict of interest occurred. This could jeopardize the awarding of the bid and your own position as well.

The correct thing to do in this case would be to, first, inform the project sponsor and the decision committee that your brother-in-law intends to bid on the project. Second, refrain from participating on the award decision committee so as not to unduly influence others in favor of your brother-in-law. And last, if you've done all these things and your brother-in-law still wins the bid, appoint someone else in your organization to administer the contract and make the payments for the work performed by him. Also, make certain you document the decisions you make regarding the activities performed by him and keep them with the project files. The more documentation you have, the less likely someone can make a conflict of interest accusation stick.

Vendor Gifts

Many professionals work in situations in which they are not allowed to accept gifts in excess of certain dollar amounts. This might be driven by company policy, the department manager's policy, and so on. In my organization, it's considered a conflict of interest to accept anything from a vendor, including gifts (no matter how small), meals, even a cup of coffee. Vendors and suppliers often provide their customers and potential customers with lunches, gifts, ballgame tickets, and the like. It's your responsibility to know if a policy exists that forbids you from accepting these gifts. It's also your responsibility to inform the vendor if they've gone over the limit and you are unable to accept the gift.

The same situation can occur here as with the brother-in-law example earlier. If you accept an expensive gift from a vendor and later award that vendor a contract or a piece of the project work, it looks like and probably is a conflict of interest. This violates PMI guidelines and doesn't look good for you personally either.

Using the "I didn't know there was a policy" reasoning probably won't save you when there's a question of conflict of interest. Make it your business to find out if the organization has a conflict of interest policy and understand exactly what it says. Get a copy and keep it with your files. Review it periodically. Put a note on your calendar every six months to reread the policy to keep it fresh in your mind. This is a case where not knowing what you don't know can hurt you.

Don't accept gifts that might be construed as a conflict of interest. If your organization does not have a policy regarding vendor gifts, set limits for yourself depending on the situation, the history of gift acceptance by the organization in the past, and the complexity of the project. It's always better to decline a gift you're unsure about than to accept it and later lose your credibility, your reputation, or your PMP status because of bad judgment.

Stakeholder Influence

Another potential area for conflict of interest comes from stakeholders. Stakeholders are usually folks with a good deal of authority and an important position in the company. Make certain you are not putting your own personal interests above the interests of the project when you're dealing with powerful stakeholders. They may have the ability to promote you or reward you in other ways. That's not a bad thing, but if you let that get in the way of the project or let a stakeholder twist your arm with promises like this, you're getting mighty close to a conflict of interest. Always weigh your decisions with the objectives of the project and the organization in mind—not your own personal gain.

Keep in mind that you may not always be on the receiving end of the spectrum. You should not offer inappropriate gifts or services or use confidential information you have at your disposal to assist others because this can also be considered a conflict of interest.

Professional Demeanor

Acting in a professional manner is required of most everyone who works in the business world. While you are not responsible for the actions of others, you are responsible for your own actions and reactions. Part of acting professionally involves controlling yourself and your reactions in questionable situations. For example, a stakeholder or customer may lash out at you but have no basis for their outburst. You can't control what they said or did, but you can control how you respond. As a professional, your concern for the project and the organization should take precedence over your concern for your own feelings. Therefore, lashing out in return would be unprofessional. Maintain your professional demeanor and don't succumb to shouting matches or ego competitions with others.

As project manager, you have a good deal of influence over your project team members. One of the items on the agenda at the project team kickoff meeting should be a discussion of where the team members can find a copy of organizational policies regarding conflict of interest, cultural diversity, standards and regulations, and customer service and standards of performance. Better yet, have copies with you that you can hand out at the meeting or have available the addresses of website where they can find these documents.

When you see project team members acting out of turn or with less-than-desirable customer service attitudes, coach and influence those team members to conform to the standards of conduct expected by you and your organization. Your team members represent you and the project. As such, they should act professionally. It's your job as the project leader to ensure that they do.

Real World Scenario

The Golf Trip

Amanda Lewis is a project manager for a network upgrade project for her organization. This project will be outsourced to a vendor. Amanda will manage the vendor's work. She also wrote the RFP and is a member of the selection committee.

The project consists of converting the organization's network from 100MB Ethernet to Gigabit Ethernet. This requires replacing all of the routers and switches. Some of the cabling in the buildings will need to be replaced as well. The RFP requires that the vendor who wins the bid install all the new equipment and replace the network interface cards in each of the servers with Gigabit Ethernet cards. The grand total for this project is estimated at $1.2 million.

Don James is a vendor with whom Amanda has worked in the past. Don is very interested in winning this bid. He drops in on Amanda one day shortly after the RFP is posted.

"Amanda, it's good to see you," Don says. "I was in the neighborhood and thought I'd stop in to see how things are going."

"Just great, Don," Amanda replies. "I'll bet you're here to talk to me about that RFP. You know I can't say anything until the whole process closes."

"You bet we bid on the project. I know you can't talk about the RFP, so I won't bring it up. I wanted to chat with you about something else. My company is sending 15 lucky contestants and one friend each to Scottsdale, Arizona, for a 'conference.' The conference includes the use of the Scottsdale Golf Club, green fees paid of course, and all hotel and meal expenses are on us for the length of the trip. I know Scottsdale is one of your favorite places to golf, so I thought of you. What do you say?"

Amanda sits forward in her chair and looks at Don for a minute. "That sounds fabulous, and I do love Scottsdale. But you and I both know this isn't a conference. I wouldn't feel right about accepting it."

"Come on, Amanda. Don't look a gift horse in the mouth. It is a conference. I'll be there and so will the top brass from the company. We have some presentations and demonstrations we'd like to show you while you're there, no obligation of course, and then you're free to spend the rest of the time however you'd like."

"I appreciate the offer. Thanks for thinking of me, but no thanks. I'm on the selection committee for the RFP, and it would be a conflict of interest if I attended this conference. Besides, the value of the conference is over the $100 limit our company sets for vendor gifts and meals," Amanda says.

"Okay. We'll miss you. Maybe next time."

You probably remember something your mother always told you: Actions speak louder than words. Always remember that you lead by example. Your team members are watching. If you are driven by high personal ethics and a strong desire to produce excellent customer service, those who work for you will likely follow your lead.

Applying Professional Knowledge

Professional knowledge involves the knowledge of project management practices as well as specific industry or technical knowledge required to complete an assignment.

As a PMP, you should apply project management knowledge to all your projects. Take the opportunity to educate others regarding project management practices by keeping others up-to-date on project management practices, training your team members to use the correct techniques, and informing stakeholders of the correct processes and then sticking to those processes throughout the course of the project. This isn't always easy, especially when the organization doesn't have any formal processes in place. But once the stakeholders see the benefits of good project management practices, they'll never go back to the "old" way of performing their projects.

One way to apply professional knowledge is to become and remain knowledgeable in project management best practices techniques. We'll look at this topic next along with a discussion of the *PMP Code of Professional Conduct,* becoming a PMI education provider, and the importance of having industry knowledge.

Project Management Knowledge

Project management is a growing field. Part of your responsibility as a PMP is to stay abreast of project management practices, theories, and techniques. There are many ways to do this, one of which includes joining a local PMI chapter. There are hundreds of local chapters in every state and in other countries as well. You can check the PMI website (www.pmi.org) to find a chapter near you.

Chapter meetings give you the opportunity to meet other project managers, find out what techniques they're using, and seek advice regarding your project. Usually guest speakers appear at each chapter meeting and share their experiences and tips. Their stories are always interesting, and they give you the opportunity to learn from someone else's experiences and avoid making wrong turns on your next project. You may have a few stories of your own worth sharing with your local chapter. Volunteer to be a speaker at an upcoming meeting and let others learn from your experiences.

One of the things you'll get when you join the PMI organization and pay your yearly dues is their monthly magazine. This publication details real-life projects and the techniques and issues project managers have to deal with on those projects. Reading the magazine is a great way to learn new project management techniques or reinforce the information you already know. You might discover how to apply some of the knowledge you've already learned in more efficient ways as well.

PMI offers educational courses through their local chapters and at the national level as well. These are yet another way for you to learn about project management and meet others in your field.

Next we'll look your responsibility for accurately and honestly reporting the level of knowledge and qualifications you possess, what an education provider is, and why industry knowledge is important.

Professional Conduct

We talked about honesty earlier in this chapter, but it's worth repeating: Don't mislead others regarding your experience in the project management field. The *PMP Code of Professional Conduct* requires that you honestly report your qualifications, your experience, and your past performance of services to potential employers, customers, PMI, and others.

Be honest about what you know and what you don't know. For example, the Quality Control processes as described in *A Guide to the PMBOK* are used extensively in the manufacturing industry. However, the information technology field looks at quality issues in different ways. If you're a project manager in the information technology field, you've probably never used control charts and cause-and-effect diagramming techniques. Don't lead others to believe that you have used techniques you haven't used or that you have experience you don't have.

Emphasize the knowledge you do have and how you've used it in your specific industry and don't try to fudge it with processes and techniques you've never used. Potential clients and employers would much rather work with you and provide training where you might need it than think they've got someone fully experienced with the project or industry techniques needed for a project when they don't.

If you're working on contract or you're self-employed, you have a responsibility to ensure that the estimates you provide potential customers are accurate and truthful. Make certain you clearly spell out what services you're providing and let the customer know the results they can expect at the end of the project. Accurately represent yourself, your qualifications, and your estimates in your advertising and in person.

Education Providers

PMI has a program that allows you or your organization to become a Registered Education Provider (R.E.P.). This allows you—once you're certified—to conduct PMI-sanctioned project management training, seminars, and conferences. The best part is that your attendees are awarded professional development units (PDUs) for attending the training or seminar. As a PMP, and especially as an R.E.P., you have a responsibility to the profession and to PMI to provide truthful information regarding the PMI certification process, the exam applications, PDU requirements, and so on. Keep up-to-date on PMI's certification process by periodically checking the website.

Industry Knowledge

Contributing and applying professional knowledge goes beyond project management experience. You likely have specific industry or technical experience as well. Part of applying your professional knowledge includes gaining knowledge of your particular industry and keeping others informed of advances in these areas.

Information technology has grown exponentially over the last several years. It used to be that if you specialized in network operations, for example, it was possible to learn and become proficient in all things related to networks. Today that is no longer the case. Each specialized area within information technology has grown to become a knowledge area in and of itself. Many other fields have either always had individual specialties or just recently experienced this phenomenon, including the medical field, bioengineering, manufacturing, pharmaceuticals, and so on. You need to stay up-to-date regarding your industry so that you can apply that knowledge effectively. Today's fast-paced advances can leave you behind fairly quickly if you don't stay on top of things.

I mentioned in the beginning of the book that as a project manager you are not required to be a technical expert, and that still holds true. But it doesn't hurt to stay abreast of industry trends and knowledge in your field and have a general understanding of the specifics of your business. Again, you can join industry associations and take educational classes to stay on top of breaking trends and technology in your industry.

Truthful Reporting

As a project manager, you are responsible for truthfully reporting all information in your possession to stakeholders, customers, the project sponsor, and the public. Always be up front regarding the project's progress.

> Nothing good will come of telling stakeholders or customers that the project is on track and everything looks great when in fact the project's behind schedule or several unplanned risks have occurred that have thrown the project team a curveball. I've personally witnessed the demise of the careers of project managers who chose this route.

Tell the truth regarding project status, even when things don't look good. Stakeholders will likely go to great lengths to help you solve problems or brainstorm solutions. Sometimes, though, the call needs to be made to kill the project. This decision is usually made by the project sponsor and/or the stakeholders based on your recommendation and predictions of future project activities. Don't skew the reporting to prevent stakeholders from making this decision when it is the best solution based on the circumstances.

Truthful reporting is required when working with the public as well. When working in situations where the public is at risk, truthfully report the facts of the situation and what steps you're taking to counteract or reduce the threats. I recommend you get approval from the organization regarding public announcements prior to reporting the facts. Many organizations have public relations departments that will handle this situation for you.

Laws and Regulations Compliance

This may seem obvious, but since it's part of the *PMP Code of Professional Conduct,* we'll mention it here. As a professional, you're required to follow all applicable laws and rules and regulations that apply to your industry, organization, or project. This includes PMI organizational rules and policies as well. You should also follow any ethical standards and principles that may govern your industry or the state or country you're working in. Remember that rules or regulations you're used to in the United States may or may not apply to other countries and vice versa.

As a PMP, one of the responsibilities that falls into this category is the responsibility to report violations of the PMP code of conduct. In order to maintain integrity of the profession, PMPs must adhere to the code of conduct that makes all of us accountable to each other.

When you know a violation has occurred and you've verified the facts, notify PMI. Part of this process—and a requirement of the code of conduct—is that you'll comply with ethics violations and will assist PMI in the investigation by supplying information, confirming facts and dates, and so on. Violations include anything listed in the *PMP Code of Professional Conduct,* such as conflicts of interest, untruthful advertising and reporting of PMP experience and credentials, and so on, as well as appearances of impropriety. This one calls for some judgment on your part, but it's mostly based on common sense. For example, a PMP in most situations should not have a family member working on the project team reporting to them (unless they own and run a family business).

Confidential Information

Many project managers work for consulting firms where their services are contracted out to organizations that need their expertise for particular projects. If you work in a situation like this, you will likely come across information that is sensitive or confidential. Again, this may seem obvious, but as part of the *PMP Code of Professional Conduct,* you agree not to disclose sensitive or confidential information or use it in any way for personal gain.

Often when you work under contract, you'll be required to sign a nondisclosure agreement. This agreement simply says that you will not share information regarding the project or the organization with anyone—including the organization's competitors—or use the information for your personal gain.

However, you don't have to work on contract to come into contact with sensitive or private information. You may work full-time for an organization or a government agency that deals with information regarding its customer base or citizens. For example, if you work for a bank, you may have access to personal account information. If you work for a government agency, you may have access to personal tax records or other sensitive material. It would be highly unethical and maybe even illegal to look up the account information of individuals not associated with the project at hand just to satisfy your own curiosity. In my organization, that is grounds for dismissal.

Don't compromise your ethics or your organization's reputation by sharing information that is confidential to the organization or would jeopardize an individual's privacy.

Company Data

While it may seem obvious that you should not use personal information or an organization's trade secrets for personal gain, sometimes the organization has a legitimate need to share information with vendors, governmental agencies, or others. You need to determine which vendors or organizations are allowed to see sensitive company data. In some cases, you may even need to determine which individuals can have access to the data. When in doubt, ask.

Here are some examples. Maybe the company you're working with has periodic mailings it sends to its customer base. If one of your project activities includes finding a new vendor to print the mailing labels, your organization may require the vendor to sign a nondisclosure agreement to guard the contents of the customer lists. Discovering just who should have access to this information might be tricky.

Another example involves data on citizens that is maintained by the government. You might think that because the data belongs to one agency of the government—say the Internal Revenue Service—any other agency of the government can have access to it. This isn't the case. Some agencies are refused access to the data even though they may have good reason to use it. Others may have restricted access, depending on the data and the agency policy regarding it. Don't assume that others should have access to data because it seems logical.

Most organizations require vendors or other organizations to sign nondisclosure agreements when the vendors or others will have access to sensitive company data. It's your responsibility to ensure that the proper nondisclosure agreements are signed prior to releasing the data. This function is often handled by the procurement department.

Intellectual Property

You are likely to come into contact with intellectual property during the course of your project management career. Intellectual property includes items developed by an organization that have commercial value but are not tangible and copyrighted material such as books, software, and artistic works. It may also include ideas or processes that are patented. Or it might involve an industrial process, business process, or manufacturing process that was developed by the organization for a specific purpose.

Intellectual property is owned by the business or person that created it. You may have to pay royalties or ask for written permission to use the property. Intellectual property should be treated just like sensitive or confidential data. It should not be used for personal gain or shared with others who should not have access to it.

Balancing Stakeholders' Interests

Projects are undertaken at the request of customers, project sponsors, executive managers, and others. Stakeholders are those who have something to gain or lose by implementing the project. As such, stakeholders have different interests and needs, and one of your jobs is to balance the needs of the stakeholders.

Customer satisfaction is probably the primary goal you're striving for in any project. If your customer is satisfied, it means you've met or exceeded their expectations and delivered the product or service they were expecting. You've got a winning combination when the customer is satisfied with the product, and you've also provided excellent customer service along the way. Satisfied customers tell others about your success and will most likely use your services in the future.

One of the key ways to assure that customer satisfaction is achieved is to apply appropriate project management techniques to your project. This includes taking the time to discover all the requirements of the project and documenting them in the scope statement. You will find that stakeholders who have a clear understanding of the requirements and have signed off on them won't suffer from faulty memory and pull the ever famous "I thought that *was* included" technique. Take the time to define your requirements and get stakeholder sign-off. You can't forget or fudge what's written down.

In the following sections we'll discuss juggling the competing needs of stakeholders, how to handle the issues and problems with stakeholders, and finally how to balance project constraints against stakeholder needs.

Competing Needs

Stakeholders come from all areas of the organization and include your customer as well. Because stakeholders do not all work in the same areas, they have competing needs and interests. One stakeholder's concern on a typical IT project might take the form of system security issues, while another stakeholder is concerned about ease of use. As the project manager, you will have situations in which stakeholder needs compete with each other, and you'll have to decide between them and set priorities. Sometimes you'll be able to accommodate their needs, and sometimes you'll have to choose. You need to examine the needs against the project objectives and then use your negotiation and communication skills to convince the stakeholders of priorities.

Individual stakeholders may or may not have good working relationships with other stakeholders. Because of this, office politics will come into play. I advise you to stay away from the politics game but get to know your stakeholders. You'll need to understand their business processes and needs in order to make decisions about stakeholder requirements.

Dealing with Issues and Problems

Problems will occur on your project—it's part of the process. We've talked throughout this book about how to deal with problems and risks and how to use conflict resolution techniques in handling problems. Balancing stakeholder needs comes into play here also.

You'll have to determine alternatives that will meet the key requirements of the project without jeopardizing the competing needs of stakeholders. Once you're into the Executing processes of the project and beyond, redefining scope becomes less and less of an option. So your responsibility is to resolve issues and determine alternative solutions to problems as they occur without changing the original objectives of the project. Enlist the help of your project team members and stakeholders during these times. Use some of the techniques we talked about in Chapter 5, "Risk Planning," like brainstorming and the Delphi technique, to find solutions.

You may also have difficulty trying to make stakeholders understand your decision or the technical nature of a problem. Again, this is where communication skills help you immensely. Take the case of a technical problem that's cropped up on your project. You should not expect your stakeholder to understand the technical aspects of rocket science if they work in the finance department, for example. It's up to you to keep the explanation at a level they can understand without loading them down with technical jargon and specifications. Keep your explanations simple, yet don't skip important details they'll need to make decisions.

Balancing Constraints

Your toughest issues will almost always center on the triple constraints: time, cost, and quality. Because of the very nature of the constraints, one of these is the primary driver and one is the least important. Keep a close eye on stakeholders who want to switch the priority of the constraints for their own purposes. Let's say the project sponsor already told you that time is the primary constraint. Another stakeholder tells you that a requirement of the project is being overlooked and quality is suffering. Be careful that the stakeholder isn't trying to divert the primary constraint from time to quality to suit their own objectives.

 Real World Scenario

The Geographic Information System

Ryan Loveland is a project manager for a multinational company. He's working on a complex software project that involves rewriting the organization's mainframe accounting system to become a browser-based system running on thin-client architecture. A major problem with the existing system occurs when new accounts are entered into the system or account information changes. The accounts are tied to geographic areas, which are assigned to individual sales associates. Sales commissions are paid based on where the account resides. To date, the process of determining which territory an account belongs to has been done manually by looking at a map.

The project sponsor, Victor, requested a geographic information system (GIS) as part of the requirements of this project. The hope is that errors will be eliminated and commissions will get processed correctly. The sponsor is hoping that Ryan's internal team can write the GIS system that will tie to the accounting system. Let's drop in on Ryan and Victor's conversation.

"I just don't understand," Victor says. "I can go onto that Internet site and plug in an address and get directions and a map detailing those directions from my house to anywhere in the country. It seems easy enough to me. Why can't your team write code like that?"

"It isn't that we can't write a program to do that. But there are several issues surrounding this request that I'd like to explain to you. I'd like you to understand why I'm asking to purchase a software product from an external vendor that will take care of these functions for us."

"Let's hear it," Victor says.

"One of the first problems is that our sales force is multinational. It would take us months just to obtain address information to populate the program. The second issue is that our sales districts are not divided by any known boundaries. Most GIS systems work off of latitude and longitude or geographic boundaries like county borders or zip code boundaries."

Victor interrupts, "Well, here's what we do. You give me a set of maps and I'll hand-draw in the sales districts and then you can scan it into the system."

"Unfortunately, it's not that easy. Our sales district boundaries are not consistent with known boundaries, and our existing address database is not standardized. For example, some addresses use the word *Street* spelled out; some use the abbreviation *St.* All of the addresses need to be standardized, and then we have to figure out which addresses belong to which territory.

"This process could take a great deal of time. There are vendors that specialize in GIS systems that could have us operational in a matter of weeks. I've already checked on a couple of the top vendors, and there aren't any problems interfacing with our new system. The time we'd save in the long run far outweighs the cost associated with purchasing this system from a vendor. And one last point: If I were to build this system internally, I'd have to take our top programming team off of existing project priorities to put them on this. GIS systems are extremely complicated. We're talking several months—if not a year or more delay—to get our programmers up to speed on GIS techniques and then write the programs."

Victor says, "If we're talking about a major delay in the schedule as you say, we can at least look at what these vendors have to offer. It's important that this system is accurate as well, and I think I hear you saying, 'Why reinvent the wheel.' Let's have a look at the costs."

Respecting Differences in Diverse Cultures

You have probably taken diversity or cultural differences training classes sometime during your career. Most organizations today require diversity training for all employees and contractors. Project managers who work on contract may find themselves taking these classes multiple times, as companies want to ensure that every employee and contractor has taken their own version of the class.

I won't attempt to repeat diversity training here, but I will point out some of the things you should know about working in other countries and about working with people who have backgrounds and belief systems that are different than yours. I'll also touch on training as a diversity awareness tool and discuss how people's perceptions influence their reactions.

Global Competition

More and more companies compete in the global marketplace. As a result, project managers with multinational experience are increasingly in demand. This requires a heightened awareness of cultural influences and customary practices of the country where you're temporarily residing.

If you are used to working in the U.S., for example, you know that our culture tends to value accomplishments and individualism. We tend to be informal and call each other by our first names, even if we've just met. Europeans tend to be more formal, using surnames instead of first names in a business setting, even when they know each other well. Their communication style is more formal than in the U.S., and while they tend to value individualism, they also value history, hierarchy, and loyalty. The Japanese, on the other hand, tend to communicate indirectly and consider themselves part of a group, not as individuals. The Japanese value hard work and success, as most of us do.

One thing I've witnessed when working in foreign countries is U.S. citizens who try to force their own culture or customs on those with whom they're visiting or working. That isn't recommended, and it generally offends those you're trying to impress. Don't expect others to conform to your way of doing things, especially when you're in their country. You know the saying "When in Rome, do as the Romans do"? While you may not want to take that literally, the intent is good. For example, a quick kiss on both cheeks is a customary greeting in many countries. If that is the case and it's how you're greeted, respond with the same.

Culture Shock

Working in a foreign country can bring about an experience called *culture shock*. When you've spent years acting certain ways and expecting normal, everyday events to follow a specific course of action, you might find yourself disoriented when things don't go as you expected. This is known as culture shock.

One of the ways you can avoid this is to read about the country you're going to work in before getting there. The Internet is a great resource for information like this. Your local library is another place to research customs and acceptable practices in foreign countries.

When in doubt about a custom or what you should do in a given situation, ask your hosts or a trusted contact from the company you'll be working with to help you out. People are people all over the world, and they love to talk about themselves and their culture. They're also generally helpful, and they will respect you more for asking what's expected rather than acting as though you know what to do when you clearly do not.

Respecting Your Neighbors

Americans tend to run their lives at high speed and get right down to business when working with vendors or customers. It isn't unusual for a business person to board a plane in the morning, show up at the client site and take care of business, and hop another flight to the next client site that night.

You'll find that this is not that common in many other countries. People in other countries will expect you to take time to get to know them first, building an atmosphere of trust and respect. Some cultures build relationships first and then proceed to business. And don't expect to do that relationship building in a few hours. It could take several days, depending on the culture. They may even want you to meet their family and spend time getting to know them. Resist the urge to get right down to business if that's not customary in the culture because you'll likely spoil the deal or damage relationships past the point of repair.

Spend time building relationships with others. Once an atmosphere of mutual trust and cooperation is established, all aspects of project planning and management—including negotiating and problem solving—are much easier to navigate.

Training

Sometimes you may find yourself working with teams of people from different countries or cultures. Some team members might be from one country and some from another. The best way to ensure that cultural or ethical differences do not hinder your project is to provide training for all team members.

Team-building activities are ways to build mutual trust and respect and bond team members with differing backgrounds. Choose activities that are nonoffensive and ones in which everyone can participate.

Diversity training makes people aware of differences between cultures and ethnic groups, and it helps them to gain respect and trust for those on their team. Provide training regarding the project objectives and the company culture as well.

Project objectives are why you are all together in the first place. Project objectives cut across cultural boundaries and keep everyone focused on the project and tasks at hand.

Perceiving Experiences

All of us see the world through our own experiences. Your experiences are not someone else's experiences, and therefore what you perceive about a situation might be very different from what others believe. Keep this in mind when it appears that a misunderstanding has occurred or that someone you're working with didn't respond as you expected. This is especially true when you're working with someone from another country. Always give others the benefit of the doubt and ask for clarification if you think there is a problem. Put your feelings in check temporarily and remember that what you think the other person means is not necessarily as it appears.

Project Case Study: New Kitchen Heaven Retail Store

Jill Overstreet thought you did such a great job of managing this project that she's offered to buy you lunch at one of those upscale, white tablecloth–type French restaurants. The iced teas have just been delivered, and you and Jill are chatting about business.

"I'm impressed with your project management skills. This store opening was the best on record. And you really kept Dirk in line—I admire that. He can be headstrong, but you had a way of convincing him what needed doing and then sticking to it."

"Thanks," you reply. "I've got a few years of project management experience, so many of those lessons learned on previous projects helped me out with this project. I enjoy project management and read books and articles on the subject whenever I get the chance. It's nice when you can learn from others' mistakes and avoid making them yourself."

Jill takes a long drink of tea. She glances at you over the top of her glass and pauses before setting it down. The look on her face implies she's sizing you up and deciding whether to tell you what's on her mind.

"You know," Jill starts, "we almost didn't hire anyone for your position. Dirk wanted to do away with the project management role altogether. He had a real distaste for project management after our last project."

"Why is that?"

Jill explains, "The last project manager got involved in a conflict of interest situation. She was working on a project that involved updating and remodeling all the existing stores. Things like new fixtures, signs, shelving, display cases, and such were up for bid. And it was a very sizable bid. Not only did she accept an all-expenses-paid weekend visit to a resort town from one of the vendors bidding on the contract, she also revealed company secrets to them, some of which leaked to our competitors."

Your mouth drops open. "I can't believe she would accept gifts like that from a vendor. And revealing company secrets is almost worse. Conflict of interest situations and not protecting intellectual property violate the code of professional conduct that certified PMPs agree to adhere to. I can understand why Dirk didn't want to hire another project manager. Behavior like that makes all project managers look bad."

"I'm glad you kept things above board and won Dirk back over. The project management role is important to Kitchen Heaven, and I know your skills in this discipline are what made this project such a success."

"Jill, not only would I never compromise my own integrity through a conflict of interest situation, I would report the situation and the vendor to the project sponsor and to PMI as an ethics violation. It's better to be honest and let the project sponsor or key stakeholders know what's happening than to hide the situation or, even worse, compromise your own integrity by getting involved in it in the first place. You have my word that I'll keep business interests above my own personal interests. I'll report anything that even looks like it would call my actions into question just to keep things honest and out in the open."

"That's good to hear," Jill replies. "Congratulations on your new assignment. Dirk and I were discussing the new Home Chef Pro project yesterday. We're venturing into new territory with this project, and I'm confident you'll do an excellent job heading it up. Dirk made a good choice."

Project Case Study Checklist

> Ensuring personal and professional integrity
>
> Adhering to the *PMP Code of Professional Conduct*
>
> Not placing personal gain above business needs
>
> Avoiding conflict of interest situations
>
> Truthfully reporting questionable situations and maintaining honesty
>
> Protecting intellectual property

Summary

Project Management Professionals are responsible for reporting truthful information about their PMP status and project management experience to prospective customers, clients, and employers and to PMI. As a project manager, you're responsible for the integrity of the project management process and the product. In all situations, you are responsible for your own personal integrity.

Personal integrity means adhering to an ethical standard. As a PMP, you'll be required to adhere to the *PMP Code of Professional Conduct* established by PMI. Part of this code involves avoiding putting your own personal gain above the project objectives.

As a professional, you should strive to maintain honesty in project reporting. You're required to abide by laws, rules, and regulations regarding your industry and project management practices. You should also report any instances that might appear to be a conflict of interest. It's always better to inform others of an apparent conflict than to have it discovered by others and have your methods called into question after the fact.

You will very likely come across confidential information or intellectual property during your project management experiences. Respect the use of this information and always verify who may have permission to access the information and when disclosures are required.

Stakeholders have competing needs and business issues and as such will sometimes cause conflict on your project. You will be required to balance the needs and interests of the stakeholders with the project objectives.

Many project managers today are working in a global environment. It's important to respect and understand the cultural differences that exist and not try to impose your cultural beliefs on others. Culture shock is an experience that occurs when you find yourself in a different cultural environment than you're familiar with. Training is a good way to provide project team members with relationship management techniques regarding cultural and ethnic differences.

Exam Essentials

Be able to define integrity.   Integrity means adhering to an ethical standard.

Be able to name the ethical standard PMPs are required to adhere to.   The ethical standard PMPs are required to adhere to is described in the *PMP Code of Professional Conduct*.

Describe the areas in which PMPs must apply professional knowledge.   PMPs must apply professional knowledge in the areas of project management practices, industry practices, and technical areas.

Know the key activity that ensures customer satisfaction.   The key activity that ensures customer satisfaction is documenting project requirements.

Define how multinational project managers must manage relationships.   Multinational project managers manage relationships by building relationships based on mutual trust and acceptance and recognizing and respecting diverse cultures and ethnic beliefs.

Key Terms

You've learned a lot of new key words in this chapter. PMI has worked hard to develop and define standard project management terms that apply across industries. Here is a list of some of the terms you came across in this chapter:

conflict of interest

culture shock

Project Management Professional Code of Professional Conduct

Review Questions

1. As a project manager, you're responsible for maintaining and ensuring integrity for all of the following except which one?

   A. Personal integrity of others

   B. Project management process

   C. Personal integrity

   D. Product integrity

2. You are a project manager working on contract. You've performed earned value analysis and discovered that the project will be completed on time and under the original estimated amount. This means the profit to your company will decrease as will your personal bonus. Which of the following should you do?

   A. Add activities to the project to increase the cost enough to meet the original estimated amount.

   B. Tell the customer you're adding requirements to the project that were originally cut because of cost constraints.

   C. Upon completion, inform the customer the project has come in under budget.

   D. Bill the customer for the full amount of the contract because this was the original agreed-upon price.

3. Integrity in the project management field is accomplished through all of the following except which one?

   A. Training to learn how to manage relationships with others from different cultures

   B. Adhering to an ethical code

   C. Applying established project management processes

   D. Following the *PMP Code of Professional Conduct*

4. You are a project manager for a manufacturing firm that produces Civil War–era replicas and memorabilia. You discover a design error during a test production run on your latest project. Which of the following is the most likely response to this problem?

   A. Reduce the technical requirements so that the error is no longer valid.

   B. Go forward with production and ignore the error.

   C. Go forward with production but inform the customer of the problem.

   D. Develop alternative solutions to address the error.

5. You are a project manager for a telecommunications firm. You're working on a project that entails upgrading technical hardware and equipment. The estimated cost of the hardware and equipment is $1,725,000. You are reviewing products from three different vendors. One of the vendors invites you to lunch. What is the most appropriate response?

   A. Thank them but let them know this could be a conflict of interest since you haven't made a decision about which vendor you're going to choose.

   B. Thank them and decline. You know this could be considered personal gain, which could call your integrity into question.

   C. Thank them and accept. You don't believe there is a conflict of interest or a personal integrity issue.

   D. Thank them and decline. You believe this could be a conflict of interest on the part of the vendor, and you don't want to encourage that behavior.

6. You are a project manager for a telecommunications firm. You're working on a project that entails upgrading technical hardware and equipment. The estimated cost of the hardware and equipment is $1,725,000. You are reviewing products from three different vendors. One of the vendors offers you and your family the use of the company yacht for the upcoming three-day weekend. What is the most appropriate response?

   A. Thank them and accept. You don't believe there is a conflict of interest or an integrity issue at stake.

   B. Thank them and decline. You know this could be considered personal gain, which could call your integrity into question.

   C. Thank them and accept. Immediately report your actions to the project sponsor so that your motives are not called into question after the fact.

   D. Thank them and decline. You know this could be considered an integrity issue on the part of the vendor.

7. You are a project manager working on contract with a company in a foreign country. At the project kickoff meeting, you are given an expensive-looking gift. The person who presented this to you said that it is customary in their country to give their business partners gifts. What is the most appropriate response?

   A. Thank them and decline. Explain that this is considered personal gain, which is unacceptable in your country.

   B. Thank them and accept. You don't believe there is a conflict of interest or an integrity issue at stake.

   C. Thank them and decline. Explain that this is considered a conflict of interest, which is unacceptable in your country.

   D. Thank them and accept since you know that it would be considered offensive to decline the gift in their culture. Immediately report the acceptance of the gift to the appropriate parties at your company so that your actions are not called into question later.

8. Life seems to be going very well for your close friend, a fellow PMP. She's taken a trip to France, bought a new car, and stocked her wine cellar with a half-dozen expensive bottles of wine, all within the last six months. After a few cocktails one evening, she tells you her secret. The vendor she's working with on the $4 billion project she's managing has given her all of these items as gifts. Which of the following should you do? (Choose the best answer.)

    A. You tell your friend these gifts probably aren't appropriate and leave it at that.

    B. You and your friend have a long conversation about the gifts and she decides to return them (with the exception of the trip) and not accept any more gifts in the future.

    C. You're happy for your friend and say nothing.

    D. Your friend doesn't see a problem with accepting these gifts at all. You know this is a conflict of interest situation and should be reported as a *PMP Code of Professional Conduct* violation.

9. As a project manager, you know that the most important activity to ensure customer and stakeholder satisfaction is which of the following?

    A. Documenting the requirements

    B. Documenting the performance measurements

    C. Reporting changes and updating the project plan and other project documents where appropriate

    D. Reporting project status regularly and in a timely manner

10. As a PMP, you will be required to comply with the *PMP Code of Professional Conduct*. This code refers to all of the following except which one?

    A. Reporting conflicts of interest

    B. Reporting experience and PMP status truthfully

    C. Complying with the stakeholder requirements

    D. Complying with the rules and standards of foreign countries

11. You are a contract project manager working with the State of Bliss. Your latest project involves rewriting the Department of Revenue's income tax system. One of the key stakeholders is a huge movie buff, and she has the power to promote you into a better position at the conclusion of this project. She's discovered that one of her favorite superstars lives in the State of Bliss and therefore must file income tax returns in that state. She asks you to look up the account of this movie star. What is the most appropriate response?

    A. Report her to the management team.

    B. Refuse to comply with the request, citing conflict of interest and violation of confidential company data.

    C. Look up the information she's requested. Since the data is considered part of the project, there is no conflict of interest.

    D. You believe that tax records are public information, so you comply with the request.

12. You are a contract project manager working with the State of Bliss. Your latest project involves rewriting the Department of Revenue's income tax system. As project manager, you have taken all the appropriate actions regarding confidentiality of data. One of the key stakeholders is a huge movie buff, and she has the power to promote you into a better position at the conclusion of this project. She's reviewing some report data that just happens to include confidential information regarding one of her favorite movie superstars. What is the most appropriate response?

A. Report her to the management team.

B. Request that she immediately return the information, citing conflict of interest and violation of confidential company data.

C. Do nothing, because she has the proper level of access rights to the data and this information showed up unintentionally.

D. Request that she immediately return the information until you can confirm that she has the proper level of access rights to the data.

13. As a PMP, you are required to comply with the *PMP Code of Professional Conduct*. Part of your responsibility concerns applying professional knowledge. All of the following are part of applying professional knowledge except for which one?

A. Developing relationships based on mutual respect

B. Staying abreast of project management practices

C. Keeping up with industry trends and new technology

D. Honestly reporting your project management experience

14. You are a project manager with several years of experience in project management. You've just accepted your first project in a foreign country. You've been in the country a week or two and are experiencing some disorientation. This is known as which of the following?

A. Collocation

B. Diversity shock

C. Global culturing

D. Culture shock

15. You are a project manager for a software manufacturing firm. The project you've just finished created a new software product that is expected to become a number-one seller. All prerelease of software is handled through the marketing department. A friend of yours is a certified software instructor. They have asked you for a copy of the software prior to the beta release so they can get familiar with it. What is the most appropriate response?

A. Since your friend is certified to teach your company's brand of software, provide them with a copy of the software.

B. Ask them to sign a nondisclosure agreement before releasing a copy of the software.

C. Decline the request since you stand to gain from this transaction by receiving free training.

D. Decline the request because the software is the intellectual property of the company.

16. Your upcoming project includes project team members from a foreign country. In order to make certain that cultural differences don't interfere with team performance, thereby affecting the success of the project, your first course of action is to do which of the following?

A. Provide diversity training to all the team members.

B. Collocate the project team.

C. Perform team-building exercises.

D. Inform the team members of the organization's rules and standards.

17. You are a project manager for Pizza Direct, which is a retail pizza delivery store. Your company is competing with another retail store for the option of opening two new stores in a foreign country. You have been invited to dinner with the prospective foreign business partners and their spouses upon your arrival. You know that all of the following statements are generally true except for which one?

A. You should spend time building relationships with your prospective foreign business partners before getting down to business.

B. You should explain your company's rules, standards, and operating policies at your first meeting with the prospective foreign business partners.

C. You should build an atmosphere of mutual trust and cooperation.

D. You should respect the cultural differences you'll encounter when working with your prospective foreign business partners.

18. You are a project manager for Pizza Direct, which is a retail pizza delivery store. Your company is competing with another retail store for the option of opening two new stores in a foreign country. You've been told that it is culturally unacceptable to eat certain foods in this country. You know that one of these foods happens to be a secret ingredient in the pizza sauce. What is the most appropriate response?

A. Inform the potential partners that your sauce recipe is secret but you're certain there are no forbidden ingredients in it.

B. Inform the potential partners that you suspect there might be a forbidden ingredient in the sauce and you'll request an investigation to determine if it exists in the sauce.

C. Inform the potential partners that a forbidden ingredient exists in the sauce and determine to work with them to come up with another ingredient to replace that one.

D. Don't tell the potential partners about the ingredient because the sauce they'll be using in the stores is shipped to them already prepared in cans. They won't know the ingredient is in the sauce.

19. You are a project manager for Pizza Direct, which is a retail pizza delivery store. Your company is competing with another retail store for the option of opening two new stores in a foreign country. You know, but have not yet informed your company, that you are going to go to work for the competitor, which happens to be bidding for this same opportunity. What is the most appropriate response?

A. You decline to participate in the initial meetings with the foreign business partners due to a conflict of interest.

B. You've not yet received an official offer from the competing company for your new job opportunity, so you choose to participate in the initial meetings with the foreign business partners.

C. You decide to participate in the initial meetings with the foreign business partners because any information you gain now will help you when you make the move to the new company.

D. You inform the foreign business partners that you're going to be working with a new company and that you know the deal they'll receive from the competing company is better than the one this company is proposing.

20. You are the project manager for a new construction project in your city. Your longtime personal friend is bidding on the project. They've asked you to give them an indication of the budget for this project so that they do not overbid and lose the deal. What is the most appropriate response?

A. Give the information to your friend. You know their character and can trust that they won't tell anyone.

B. Tell your friend that after all this time, they should know you better than to think you'd put your personal integrity on the line or compromise your job due to a conflict of interest. Decline to give them the information.

C. Tell your friend you'll give them the information if they'll promise not to tell anyone and if they'll agree to help you out with some materials on your basement-refinishing project.

D. Give the information to your friend and inform the project sponsor so that the information can be shared with the other bidders as well.

Answers to Review Questions

1. A. You are not responsible for the personal integrity of others, but as project manager you do have influence over others, such as your project team members.

2. C. Integrity means you'll honestly report project outcomes and status. Your personal gain should not be placed above the satisfaction of the customer.

3. A. Diversity training is used to help you manage project teams that are made up of people from other countries or cultures. Integrity is accomplished by following an ethical code and applying project management practices.

4. D. The best answer to this problem is to develop alternative solutions to address design error. Reducing technical requirements might be an alternative solution, but it's not one you'd implement without looking at all the alternatives. Ignoring the error and going forward with production will result in an unsatisfactory product for the customer.

5. A. A luncheon date could be considered a conflict of interest prior to awarding a contract to a vendor. Consider what a competitor of this vendor would think if they spotted you having lunch together.

6. B. The best response to this situation is to thank the vendor and decline based on the fact that this could be considered personal gain on your part. Answer D may seem correct, but remember, you're not responsible for the integrity of others. And it's often common business practice for vendors to offer gifts to potential customers.

7. D. The best response in this case is to accept the gift because it would cause great offense to the other party if you were to decline. Report the gift and the circumstances as soon as possible to the appropriate parties at your company.

8. D. This is a conflict of interest situation and should be reported as a violation of the *PMP Code of Professional Conduct.*

9. A. Documenting the requirements is one of the key things you can do to ensure customer satisfaction. The requirements describe what the customer is looking for, and the final product is compared against them to determine if all of the requirements were met.

10. C. Stakeholder requirements are needed to determine if the project is successful and are not a part of the professional code.

11. B. The situation presented here requires you to put the interest of the company and the confidentiality of the data above your own personal interests or those of your stakeholders. Option D is not the most correct response because it says you believe the information is public. This implies you haven't verified whether the data is private or public. Until you know, treat the data as confidential. In this case, the information is confidential and should be shared only with those who have a valid reason for using it.

12. C. As project manager, it's your responsibility to make sure the people you will be sharing data with have the proper permissions to see the data; this question indicated that you did that. In this case, option D is not correct because it implies that you did not verify ahead of time that the stakeholder had the proper level of approvals to use the data.

13. A. Applying professional knowledge involves staying abreast of project management practices, industry trends, and new technology and honestly reporting your experiences.

14. D. Culture shock is the disoriented feeling that people may experience when working in a foreign country.

15. D. The most appropriate response is to deny the request. Software is considered intellectual property and should not be used for personal gain or given to others without prior consent from the organization. This question states that the release of the beta software is handled through the marketing department, so you should not give your friend a copy of the software outside of this process.

16. A. The most correct response is to first provide training to your team members to teach them how to respect and work with others from different cultures. Collocation may not be possible when you're working with team members from two different countries. Team-building exercises are a good idea as well but are not your first course of action.

17. B. Your first meeting with foreign partners should be spent getting to know them on a personal basis. Many cultures like to spend time building relationships first and then talking business. Since you've been invited to dinner upon your arrival and the dinner includes the spouses of your prospective partners, chances are they want to spend some time getting to know you personally first. Discussion of the company's rules, standards, and operating policies should occur at the second or third meeting.

18. C. The most appropriate response is to inform the potential partners that an ingredient exists in the sauce that is not acceptable and determine to come up with a solution to the problem. As a professional, you're required to be honest in your reporting. Not telling them, or stalling by promising an investigation, is not an honest response.

19. A. The most appropriate response is to decline to participate due to a conflict of interest.

20. B. This situation is clearly a conflict of interest and should be avoided. Decline to provide your friend this information.

Workbook Exercises

We're glad you have purchased and started reading the *PMP Project Management Professional Study Guide*. It's a terrific way to study for the PMP exam, and you will want to read what it has to say about taking the exam and take all the practice tests in it. But maybe you are new to project management and some of the concepts you read about are unfamiliar, or some of the knowledge area tools and techniques or outputs are unclear. The workbook exercises support what you read in the *PMP Project Management Professional Study Guide*, as well as reiterate some of its most important aspects. They can also be used to support basic project management processes and outputs that you need to learn and use in your project management career.

If you are a teacher, you might find the workbook exercises useful to supplement classroom exercises or as homework assignments. You may want your students to complete all exercises from a chapter to help them build a good foundation for the concept you are teaching. You might use the exercises in the order they are presented, or pull some from one chapter, then use one from another chapter based on the order or way you teach your classes. You may also want to use some of the exercises to spark class discussions since some of the exercises might require critical thinking and ideas from real project management experiences.

The workbook exercises do not repeat everything from the *A Guide to the Project Management Body of Knowledge*. We tried to create exercises focusing on the most important inputs, tools and techniques, or outputs of the nine knowledge areas from the *Project Management Body of Knowledge Guide (PMBOK Guide)*, or those concepts that might be best learned through critical thinking and practice. Since we are both teachers of beginning project management, we selected many of the same concepts and kinds of exercises we teach in our own classes.

What the Workbook Exercises Cover

The workbook exercises are based on concepts from the process groups and knowledge areas in the *Project Management Body of Knowledge Guide*. The sections are organized the same as the rest of the *PMP Project Management Professional Study Guide* in order to facilitate your learning. This book is organized as follows:

Section 1   This section covers some fundamentals of the PMBOK Guide. In this chapter we cover the different types of organization structures, including matrixed organizations. We also look at the authority level of project managers in each of these structures.

Section 2   In this section we discuss the most important aspects of the Initiating process group, including developing the project charter. Two exercises are spent on project selection—how to select and justify a project based on a selection matrix and using financial return methods for project selection.

Section 3   The section begins the first of many chapters that cover the Planning process group. We start with creating a project management plan. We then examine creating a scope management plan and the project scope statement.

Section 4   This section reviews the beginning processes for the Planning process group. First we look at creating a work breakdown structure. Second we examine communicating with your stakeholders. Next we review the Quality Planning process and the quality planning tools. We end this section with inspecting the cost of quality, a very important concept to understand for the exam.

Section 5   This section is dedicated solely to risk management. In it we cover creating a risk management plan that is used to guide your activities through the rest of the risk processes. We then cover identifying risks. Next we move into risk analysis, both qualitative and quantitative. We finish up with exercises concerning risk response strategies and dealing with risk responses.

Section 6   This section continues with the Planning process group. In it we begin by covering two ways of acquiring resources. The first way to acquire resources is via the knowledge area of Procurement Management. Exercises include contract types, creating a procurement management plan, creating a contract statement of work, and evaluating and selecting the right vendor. The second way to acquire resources is through internal company policies. In this section we cover creating a staffing management plan and creating a responsibility assignment matrix. Once the resources are in place you can then determine what work should be done in what order. We examine this concept in an exercise concerning activity sequencing. Finally we discuss creating resource estimates.

Section 7   This section focuses on some important planning process exercises for time and cost management. For time management we examine estimating duration activity, calculating critical path, creating a PERT estimate, duration compression, and finally creating Gantt charts. For cost management we explore the ranges of cost estimates, cost estimating, and creating a budget and cost baseline.

Section 8   This section looks at the important aspects of the Executing Process Group. In this chapter we begin by looking at the integration management process of directing and managing project execution. We then discuss the acquisition and development of the project team as well as resolving conflicts while communicating to the team. Since we're on the subject of communication we finish up with an exercise on distributing information.

Section 9   In this section we continue looking at Executing group processes. We start with creating the contract and then move on to performing quality assurance. The last exercise in this chapter is a critical thinking exercise, understanding your stakeholders.

Section 10   This section covers some critical exercises regarding the Monitoring and Controlling process group. We start with a discussion concerning change control and follow up later in this chapter with more change control discussions that get specific on how to control changes to the cost and the schedule. The last exercise covers performance reporting and spends a lot of time on the earned value technique.

Section 11   In this section we complete our review of monitoring and controlling processes with a look at quality control and the tools and techniques used in the process. We then review closing a project, phase, or contract.

Section 12   We finish off with a discussion on professional responsibility. This exercise helps you understand why you need to include professional responsibility in your everyday project choices and management.

Making the Most of the Workbook Exercises

Each exercise has the same format: we provide background information about the particular topic. The background might contain terms, examples, and the general steps you might perform to create the deliverable for the exercise. We outline a brief scenario for each exercise. The scenario is set up to describe your role as a project management consultant who will help an organization apply the concepts to their particular situation. You will read the scenario, then answer the questions at the end. At the end of the exercises, you will find answers to the exercise questions. Some of the answers will be very specific, while others require interpretation and critical thinking, so the answers in the workbook may not be exactly the same as those you provide.

We sincerely hope that these exercises help you in extending your knowledge of project management techniques and concepts. Good luck in your project management career!

About the Authors

Claudia Baca has been active in the project management industry since 1984 and has experience in the information technology, telecommunications, and e-commerce industries. During her varied career, Claudia has managed many mission-critical projects for a major telecommunication company, and several Internet companies. Claudia currently is an independent consultant. She lectures and teaches for the Project Management Institute chapter in Denver as well as for Colorado State University. Claudia is currently a member of the leadership team that is producing the ANSI standard for Project Management Maturity, OPM3, Second Edition. She has a Masters Certificate in Program Management from Denver University. She earned her PMP in 1995 and has re-certified in 2001 and 2004. Claudia also has much experience writing and editing. She is a co-author of the paper "Organizational Project Management Maturity Model (OPM3)" presented at the PMI Global Congress Europe, 2003. She also co-authored the "The Past, the Present and the Future of OPM3" presented at the PMI Global Congress North America, 2004. In addition, she is the technical editor of the *PMP Project Management Professional Study Guide* and the *IT Project + Study Guide* and is the co-author of *PMP Project Management Professional Workbook,* all published by Sybex. Her new book, *Project Management Spotlight on Change Management,* is available May, 2005.

Patti Jansen is a project manager and trainer with QuantumPM and has over 18 years experience in the information technologies industry and 10 years in project and program management. She has managed multimillion-dollar, multisystem integration projects for telecommunication and Internet companies. She has a BA from Colorado State University, a Master's in Applied Communication and a certificate in Program Management from the University of Denver. She is a technical editor of the *PMP Project Management Professional Study Guide* and *Project Management JumpStart, Herding Chickens: Innovative Techniques for Project Management,* published by Sybex. She is teaching several project management classes at Colorado State University Denver Center.

What Is a Project?

The following exercises are presented in this section:

- Exercise 1.1: Organizational Structure
- Exercise 1.2: Project Management Office

Exercise 1.1: Organizational Structure

The objectives for Exercise 1.1 are as follows:

- Describe the three major types of organizational structures.
- Describe the authority level of project managers in each organization.
- Describe the three levels of matrix organizations.

Background

An area of potential conflict on projects is the way the organization is structured. Different structures create different challenges. This exercise will examine the types of organizational structures and their impact on a project manager's ability to execute the project.

There are three major types of organizational structures: projectized, functional, and matrix. Each type of structure will influence the project manager's authority, how resources are committed to the project, and the administrative help available to the project manager. A project manager may have more or less power depending on how the organization is structured.

Projectized organizations   A projectized organization is organized around project management. These organizations have realized that organizing around project management allows them to focus on their primary objective—delivery of projects to realize the corporation's goals. Projectized organizations provide from high levels of authority to complete authority to their project managers and usually provide administrative support. Personnel assigned to a project are usually committed on a full-time basis. There is very little dotted-line reporting in these types of organizations. The following depicts an organization chart for a projectized organization.

Functional organizations   A functional organization has been established to perform certain functions, such as sales, marketing, or accounting. A functional organization will perform projects but the projects are sometimes confined to a functional area. If projects cross functional boundaries, project managers are challenged to find and keep resources and executive support. Most people believe that a project manager has little or no authority in a functional organization. The following depicts a functional organization chart.

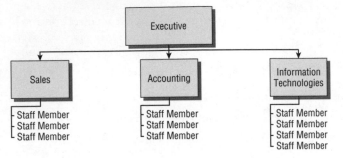

Matrix organizations   Matrix organizations use components of both functional and projectized organizations. There are three levels of progression in a matrix organization that correspond to how projectized or functional the organization is structured. These levels are a weak matrix, balanced matrix, and strong matrix, with strong matrix being very close to a projectized organization. The authority level of the project manager will also vary according to how weak or strong the matrix organization is. The following depicts a balanced matrix organization.

When you are assigned a new project, remember to analyze the organization structure in which you are working. This knowledge will assist you in acquiring resources and understanding the challenges you may face.

In Exercise 1.1, you will test your knowledge about organizational structures as you help the Sensational Advertisement Productions company.

Scenario

Your consulting company, Terrific Project Management Partners (TPMP), has brought project management processes to an advertising firm, Sensational Advertisement Productions (SAP), and the project managers at SAP are learning how to use the eight knowledge areas of scope, time, cost, quality, human resource, communications, risk, and procurement management. You want them to understand how organizational structures can impact their projects. You are working with Pam Rosenbaum, who has been assigned account management functions for a telecommunications client's important new product: a new cell phone that integrates normal service with PDA functions right on the phone, which will be sold at a competitive price with normal cell phone services. The account has several project managers for the various sales campaigns: Michael Harland for the print campaigns, Judy Arakawa for the TV campaigns, and Joseph Matumbo for the telemarketing campaigns. Each project manager is working with marketing managers within the telecommunications company to get direction and approval for the work they will produce. Pam is trying to act as the program manager on behalf of her product.

Organizational Structures

1. What are the three major types of organizational structures?
2. What are the three levels of progression in a matrixed organization?
3. What do the three levels in a matrixed organization correspond to?
4. Pam works for the vice president of account management, who in turn works for the CEO. The other vice presidents head departments such as Sales, Operations, Media, and Direct Mail. What type of an organization is this?
5. What is Pam's authority level in this organization?
6. If Pam worked directly for the CEO, what type of organizational structure would she be working in?

Exercise 1.2: Project Management Office

The objectives for Exercise 1.2 are as follows:

- Describe the continuum of project management offices.
- Describe the difference between the project manager's objectives and the project management office's objectives.

Background

A project management office (also known as a PMO) helps its organization manage and centralize its projects and programs, focusing on aligning the projects with the strategic objectives of the organization. As project managers need to balance the competing needs of their stakeholders while focusing on the project objectives, project management offices need to balance their organization's strategic needs while helping the project managers attain their specific project goals.

There is a continuum of the kind of PMOs that exist within organizations. The first and simplest PMO on the left side of the continuum may be organized to simply assist project managers in providing a central repository and guidance for the organization's tools, templates, policies, standards, and methodologies of project management. This would probably not be a large PMO, but project managers would have somewhere to go to help them use common project practices within the organization. Another type of PMO along the continuum would be a group that provides training, assistance, and mentoring. They may also manage and have authority over the entire project management system, which provides the tools, processes, methodology, and resources that project managers use for their projects. A PMO toward the far right end of the continuum may have a great deal of authority and responsibility to include directing project managers in the running and measurement of their projects to meet organizational objectives. They may provide project managers for projects and be responsible for the results of the project. In an organizational structure, they might report directly to a high-level executive or have a high-level executive as the manager of the PMO.

A PMO with a great deal of authority may help select what projects will be initiated, prioritize initiated projects to help with directing resources to the highest-priority projects, help in project planning and execution, and kill projects that no longer meet organizational business objectives. In such an organization, they would have to create excellent processes for project selection and measurements that help indicate when a project should be killed.

Many organizations do not have a project management office, yet they have many projects. In such organizations, you will often see projects being run using various methodologies, several scheduling tools, and often with little prioritization among projects. Other organizations may have one person who supports a PMO while also carrying out other duties. This kind of project management office usually has very little authority and can only chip away at trying to establish common standards and processes among projects. More organizations today are trying to establish robust PMOs that not only manage the project management system at the organizational level but also direct the reporting, prioritizing, and balancing of projects for the organization. Still, many organizations do not see value in a PMO because it is usually an overhead department. However, without a PMO, an organization will have a very difficult time reporting on projects on an overall enterprise level and the consistency and integrity of the data may be suspect, if it is collected at all. Without a PMO, it is doubtful any organization can do true enterprise reporting on its projects. No matter what kind of PMO an organization has, it's important that the role of the PMO is clearly defined and upper management sponsors and supports its activities.

This list includes some of the activities or deliverables a PMO might provide:

- A central repository for the templates, standards, processes, tools, methodologies, and policies that project managers must use for the organization. You might want to enter "project management office" in your browser search engine. You will find some examples of organizations that provide project management templates and processes online.

- Training options, training, mentoring, and/or project managers for projects.

- Status reports on project schedules and budgets, project interdependencies, reporting measures including variances, and communication expectations for all projects.

- The lessons learned, overall organization project risks, and archived project information to help improve current and future project management.

In Exercise 1.2, you will think about the kind of PMO that could help the Sensational Advertisement Productions company as it introduces the project management discipline to the organization.

Scenario

TPMP has brought project management processes to an advertising firm, Sensational Advertisement Productions (SAP). SAP has over 100 projects, many of which are complex and with large budgets. The project managers at SAP are learning how to use the project management methodology to guide their projects. You recently met Randy Bobier. Everyone at SAP calls him the PMO. They say he has a PMO website and that there are some templates they are supposed to use for their projects; some project managers have admitted they don't particularly like the templates and don't use them. No one else works in the department, and Randy is currently running three projects. He lets you know that he has created a website and where he has placed some project management templates he found on the Internet, and a SAP project manager's process handbook, which was written two years ago when the company hired a consultant to help organize the PMO. He says he has let the project managers know the templates and handbook are on the website. He also lets you know several of the project managers at SAP meet about once a month to discuss common problems and issues. You try to set up several meetings with him to get more information about the PMO, but he lets you know that one of his projects is very high priority and he doesn't have a lot of time to talk about the PMO.

Project Management Office

1. Describe where you think SAP's PMO is on the continuum of PMOs. Why?

2. What is Randy focused on as a project manager versus what he would be focused on as the PMO in the SAP organization?

3. If SAP's PMO were at the highest level of the PMO continuum, what might its PMO look like?

4. What would you suggest that SAP do with its PMO?

5. What would be the best kind of PMO for any organization to have?

Answers to Section 1 Exercises

Answers to Exercise 1.1

Your answers may be somewhat different, but the following answers provide a guide.

1. The three major types of organizational structures are projectized, matrix, and functional.

2. The levels of progression in matrixed organizations are weak matrix, balanced matrix, and strong matrix.

3. The three levels of progression in a matrix organization correspond to how projectized or functional the organization has been structured.

4. Pam works in a functional organization.

5. Pam has little or no authority in a functional organization.

6. If Pam worked directly for the CEO, she would be working in a projectized organization.

Answers to Exercise 1.2

Your answers may be somewhat different, but the following answers provide a guide.

1. SAP's PMO is probably toward the left of the PMO continuum. Although it has a PMO, and Randy has provided some templates and processes, it does not appear that the project managers are required to use them. Randy seems to have very little time to take an active role in providing guidance or training to the project managers. He does not direct the other project managers on what to do, and he does not seem to have any authority in directing the project managers to use what standards they do have on the website.

2. As a project manager, Randy is focused on his project's goals and objectives. He wants to meet the needs of his project and stakeholders and make sure it successfully finishes on time and meets its budget. As a PMO, Randy would be focused on bringing standardization in the project management discipline to his organization. He would keep an enterprise-wide focus on activities and deliverables of the PMO. If the PMO were to move toward the right of the continuum, he would want to ensure that all projects are prioritized, planned, executed, and measured with the organization's strategies in mind.

3. If SAP's PMO were toward the highest level of the PMO continuum, Randy would probably be an executive in charge of the PMO staff. The project managers might even report to him and be provided to the other departments to lead their projects. He would have a fully realized project selection, prioritization, and reporting process to ensure that management receives enterprise projects and program status. His organization would manage the project management system, which would ensure that all the project managers use the same methodology, processes, templates, and tools to manage their projects. He might report to the chief executive officer of his organization.

4. Since some project managers are meeting regularly to discuss common issues, they may signal the need for a much stronger PMO. You might suggest that the PMO become a full-time job. You might suggest that the first activity of the department is to create a plan that would ensure that the PMO provides the standard templates, processes, tools, and methodology that project managers will be required to use. The plan should also include how the PMO would become the enterprise-wide project and program-reporting clearinghouse at SAP. SAP might consider having several people within the organization to help implement this plan. You should also suggest that the new organization report to the CEO or a very high-level executive who sponsors and helps ensure that the PMO starts exerting some authority required to bring discipline and consistency to the projects at SAP.

5. There is no one best kind of PMO. What is best depends on the size, complexity, and needs of the business. In some organizations, having a PMO that only provides tools, standards, templates, and other project management resources may be enough. The organization may be small enough and its projects may be managed well and efficiently enough that management has adequate understanding of the value of each project. In some organizations, numerous and complex projects and programs demand a central organization that can help management measure and understand project value.

Initiating and Creating the Project Charter

The following exercises are presented in this section:

- Exercise 2.1: Justifying a Project—Project Selection Matrix
- Exercise 2.2: Project Selection Methods—Financial Returns
- Exercise 2.3: Project Initiation and the Project Charter

Exercise 2.1: Justifying a Project— Project Selection Matrix

The objectives for Exercise 2.1 are as follows:

- Describe various project selection criteria.
- Select and justify a project based on a project selection matrix exercise.

Background

Organizations need to be selective about the projects they undertake. Otherwise, they would work on all proposed projects, which most organizations cannot afford. Projects need to align with the organization's strategy and provide some kind of return on investment, whether it is financial or based on some other criteria the organization finds important.

A well-defined method, such as using a project selection matrix (which could be based on a weighted scoring model), and predefined project selection criteria, helps an organization select projects. A project selection committee, a project management office, or some other organization authorized by an enterprise may use this matrix to make decisions. First, the organization sets up the criteria for selecting projects, and then, for each criterion, it decides what methods to use to measure the project's potential. (For instance, see Exercise 2.2 for an example of financial return methods.)

The matrix allows a project selection committee to make objective decisions (at least, as objective as possible) in deciding which projects to undertake. It also helps the organization prioritize the selected projects—allowing the organization to cut lower-ranked projects if budgets or resources become tight. An organization may have several criteria for selecting projects and may use several project selection methods. Sometimes, even though a project may look financially risky, it may be worth undertaking because it will provide a public perception boost the organization needs to regain or improve its market penetration. So, even after using the project selection matrix, a selection committee may choose to proceed with a project based on some other criteria that may not have been part of the initial selection process.

Using a Project Selection Matrix

When creating a project selection matrix, you must first decide on the project selection criteria and weight the criteria according to the organization's strategic goals and other objectives. This list includes some possible criteria:

- Financial return
- Effect on employees/alignment with corporate culture
- Technical advancement or innovation
- Market value/share
- Public perception
- Alignment with/advancement of corporate strategy

For each criterion in your matrix, complete each project's objective or subjective measurements. Table 2.1 provides some possible benefit measurements for sample criteria.

TABLE 2.1 Project Selection Criteria

Criteria	Possible Benefit Measurements
Financial return	• Net present value (NPV). • Cost/benefit analysis. • Internal rate of return (IRR).
Cost avoidance	• Cost/benefit analysis (calculate savings and all costs).
Technical advancement or innovation	• Will it apply only to the project or to the entire organization, or will what is developed during the project be marketable outside the organization? • Will it appear as innovative to others in the industry, thus creating prestige for the organization?
Market value/share	• Increase value/share according to set formula, research, or surveys.
Public perception	• Measure perceived increase/decrease in perception based on focus groups, surveys, or interviews. Estimate the awareness/perception that will be created. • Calculate the number of people affected/made aware.
Alignment with organization expertise	• Does the project team have the expertise to do the project? Can the organization acquire the expertise and does it want to? • Will the project efforts help develop some expertise or skill it wants developed?
Needed infrastructure improvement	• Improved productivity—show cost savings if possible. • Describe old system/processes that might collapse or decline and include impact. • Compare with other infrastructure projects.

Project Justification Criteria

When justifying a project, follow these steps:

1. Select five to seven main criteria to justify your organization's projects. If you select more, this exercise will become difficult to manage. Assign a weighting factor to each criterion according to what is most important to the organization.

2. For each criterion, select the benefit measurement or measurements you will use.

3. Create the list of all proposed projects. Note that most should have a written business case to provide more information for the project selection committee.

4. Put the projects in a matrix and rate each project according to the method selected. Then, multiply the weighting factor to each rating received.

5. Eliminate any projects based on any minimum standards or thresholds you have established prior to the ranking exercise (for instance, if the project would lose money and all other rankings are below a 5 average, it automatically is eliminated).

6. Rank the remaining projects.

7. Select the projects you want to proceed with from this ranking.

8. Make sure you document justifications for each project selected based on this process. You can use the justification in your project charter, scope statement, business case, or any other document supporting the project.

In this exercise, you are going to practice using a project selection matrix to justify a project. Then, using a scenario involving your company, Terrific Project Management Partners (TPMP), you will put those practices to use.

Scenario

Your consulting company, Terrific Project Management Partners (TPMP), has been asked to help an established investment company, Best Investments Company (BIC), create a project selection process. The company tends to take on all projects that are proposed, and it has become increasingly difficult to manage the company's project portfolio. You will help the company establish a semiannual review process using a project selection matrix based on the company's major project criteria.

BIC has a choice between the following three projects:

- Build investment kiosks and put them in major malls across the United States, known as the kiosk project.

- Create a program to recruit community financial advisors who provide services to investors within a particular territory based on per-capita income of various communities, known as the financial advisor project.

- Build franchises that work like fast food restaurants in strip malls, known as the franchise project.

BIC could choose all or one of these projects to increase its presence in the community. After much discussion with the project selection committee, TPMP got agreement that the following are the most important objectives for the company. They also created a weighting factor for each (presented in Table 2.2). These weighting factors will be multiplied by the benefit measurement ratings each of the projects received for the criteria. BIC project managers will meet to determine their rating or scoring system for each of the criteria.

This process will help rank projects so that those with good rating scores for higher-weighted projects will be selected prior to those that might have high ratings for less-important criteria.

TABLE 2.2   Best Investments Company Criteria and Weighting

Criteria	Weight Factor
Increase market share as the investment company of choice	5
Good financial return	4
Provide possible innovation in investment tools and techniques	3
Support the corporate culture of employee supporting employee	2
Increase public awareness	1

After BIC's business analysts researched each proposed project, they applied project measurement ratings for each of the criteria supplied in Table 2.2. The projects were given scores as shown in the following tables (with 10 being the highest possible mark). The kiosk project ratings are represented in Table 2.3.

TABLE 2.3   Kiosk Project Criteria Ratings

Criteria	Rating
Increase market share	5
Good financial return	6
Innovation	9
Support culture	1
Increase public awareness	8

For the financial advisor project, BIC came up with the ratings shown in Table 2.4.

TABLE 2.4   Financial Advisor Project Criteria Ratings

Criteria	Rating
Increase market share	7
Good financial return	3
Innovation	5
Support culture	5
Increase public awareness	5

Finally, for the franchise project, BIC created the ratings shown in Table 2.5.

TABLE 2.5   Franchise Project Criteria Ratings

Criteria	Rating
Increase market share	7
Good financial return	7
Innovation	4
Support culture	3
Increase public awareness	6

Justifying a Project—Project Selection Matrix

Complete the following matrix using the preceding information. Remember that the actual score for a criterion is the rating times the criteria weight factor.

1. Fill in the following Best Investment Company project selection matrix based on the preceding information.

Criteria	Kiosk	Financial Advisor	Franchise
Increase market share			
Good financial return			

Criteria	Kiosk	Financial Advisor	Franchise
Innovation			
Support culture			
Increase public awareness			
Total Score			
Project Rank			

2. If you could choose only one project after this process, which one would it be and why?
3. Does the project ranking determine which project will be selected over the other?
4. Is this a good method for selecting projects? Why or why not?
5. What other criteria might a company use for deciding on projects?
6. What are some potential problems using this method of selecting projects?

Exercise 2.2: Project Selection Methods— Financial Returns

The objectives for Exercise 2.2 are as follows:

- Describe the importance of having a measurement methodology for selecting projects for a particular criterion.
- Describe various cash flow analysis techniques.
- Use financial return methods to select a project.

Background

Project selection methods help an organization objectively decide what proposed projects to pursue. Project selection methods also help the organization prioritize projects based on the outcome of applying the selected method to the approved projects. The method used is based on the selection criteria an organization uses (as explored in the previous exercise). The more objective methods an organization uses, the better it can justify the selection and sustain the project over time. If your organization does not use selection criteria and project selection methods, projects might be selected according to the person who lobbies the loudest for their project or the organization may overload itself with projects. One of the best methods for selecting projects is analyzing cash flow to estimate financial return for the project. Some of the most common cash flow analysis techniques are payback period, net present value (NPV), return on investment (ROI), and internal rate of return (IRR).

In Exercise 2.2, you'll explore financial return methods for project selection. Then you'll help Terrific Project Management Partners (TPMP) provide project advice for one of its clients.

Before you begin the project selection process, you will have to make a few decisions regarding your approach.

First, decide on the project selection criteria that you want to measure. In Exercise 2.1, we listed several of those criteria. Next, decide on a consistent and standardized approach for measuring benefits for the criteria. For instance, for financial return you could use one or more of the following:

- Payback period
- Net present value (NPV)
- Internal rate of return (IRR)
- Other forms of cost/benefit analysis

Finally, apply the same method for each project using objective measurements.

NOTE Subjective measurements, based on expert judgment or some kind of methodology created by the organization or team, work as well as using objective measurements. For instance, how do you measure an increase in public perception? Using previous similar projects as a basis, you could use a focus survey or market research to measure success. These methods offer a way to measure criteria in a consistent and standard approach and have an outcome based on analysis to help you better justify your decision.

Scenario

Your consulting company, Terrific Project Management Partners (TPMP), has been asked to help an established investments company, Best Investments Company (BIC), use project selection methods. Best Investments Company tends to take on any project proposal, so it has become increasingly difficult to manage the company's project portfolio. Just as BIC helps its customers achieve the best return on their investment, it would like to ensure that its three projects have the best financial return; the selection team decided to use financial return as their major project selection method.

In order to select the best financial return method, you will take the executives at BIC through several exercises to help them decide which one they should use. They have decided that they want their project managers to be able to calculate these financial return methodologies; they do not want to make the work too complex, but they want the most accurate method possible.

You will take them through the following financial return methods:

Payback period   Payback period is the amount of time it takes a company to recoup its initial investment in the cost of producing a product or service. It is fairly simple to use but is not as accurate as other methods because it does not consider how the value of money is affected by interest over time. The decision is based on when the payback comes, not on how much the organization will make after that payback point.

Discounted cash flow/net present value (NPV)   Net present value (NPV) brings the value of future monies received into today's dollars minus the initial investment. It is a fairly accurate method because it takes into account the time value of money, but it uses more complicated formulas. You would choose projects with the highest NPV.

Internal rate of return (IRR)   IRR is the discount rate when the present value of the cash inflows equals the original investment. This is a complex but accurate calculation. You should choose projects with the highest IRR value.

When completing Exercise 2.2, you will use the following projects and financial projections to help the company see how these methods work:

Build an investment kiosk.   Initial cost is $5 million to install in targeted locations, and return is expected to be $750,000 the first year, $500,000 per quarter over the next two years, and $750,000 semiannually thereafter.

Create a program to recruit community financial advisors.   Initial cost is $8 million to recruit and train the advisors, and return is expected to be $1.5 million the first year, $400,000 per quarter over the next three years, and $750,000 semiannually thereafter.

Build franchises that work like fast food restaurants in strip malls.   Initial cost is $11 million to build or convert existing buildings in targeted locations and to hire employees, and return is expected to be $1 million the first six months, $2.5 million the second six months, $500,000 per quarter the second year, $600,000 per quarter the third year, $3 million annually thereafter.

Project Selection Methods—Financial Returns

Determine financial return for the three BIC projects. You might want to create tables for each project.

1. Based on the three projects, which one has the best payback? Rank them.
2. Will the project manager be able to calculate this information? Why?
3. For Best Investments Company, what are some of the advantages/disadvantages of the payback period method?

Based on the kiosk, financial advisor, and franchise projects, use the net present value (NPV) method to answer questions 4–6. You may use the same investment and expected financial projection information described in the project setup, but in this case, the time value of money (interest rate) is 5 percent and you will calculate NPV over five years for each project.

You will need to lay out the actual inflows for each year and apply the present value formula to each year and then subtract the initial investment. Also, round to the nearest dollar. To make this easier, use the following interest rate table.

Year 1: $(1 + .05)^1 = 1.0500$

Year 2: $(1 + .05)^2 = 1.1025$

Year 3: $(1 + .05)^3 = 1.1576$

Year 4: $(1 + .05)^4 = 1.2155$

Year 5: $(1 + .05)^5 = 1.2763$

4. Based on these three projects, which one will provide the best NPV? Rank them.
5. Will the project manager be able to calculate this information?
6. For Best Investment Company, what are some of the advantages/disadvantages of this method?

Finally, for questions 7–9, you will use IRR without actually calculating IRR. In the case of the three projects, the following shows the IRR value for each project:

- Build an investment kiosk. IRR = 5.5 percent
- Create a program to recruit community financial advisors. IRR = 3 percent
- Build franchises in strip malls that work like a fast food restaurant. IRR = 5 percent

7. Based on the kiosk, financial advisor, and franchise projects, which one will provide the best IRR? Rank them.

8. Will the project manager be able to calculate this information?

9. For BIC, what are some of the advantages/disadvantages of this method?

10. Which financial return method would you recommend for BIC and why?

Exercise 2.3: Project Initiation and the Project Charter

The objectives for Exercise 2.3 are as follows:

- Describe the need for a project charter.
- Describe the essential elements of a project charter.
- Create parts of a project charter.

Background

A project charter is the official written acknowledgment and recognition that a project exists. It's issued by an appropriate senior manager commensurate to the funding level of the project and gives the project manager authority to assign organizational resources to the work of the project. It is usually the result of applying project selection methods and the organization choosing to proceed working on a project. Previous feasibility analysis or justification should be included in the charter to ensure that it's linked to the organization's strategic initiatives. It's best if the project manager is selected for the project and assigned to help develop the project charter, although that doesn't always happen in reality. When writing a charter, you will capture and document information such as the following:

- In an introduction, a description of the stakeholder requirements for the product or service and an overview of the project. This may include a list of the project deliverables.
- Projection of purpose and goals/objectives.
- Stakeholders, including any participating functional organizations, and their needs and influences.
- The business case, justification, and business need for the project. This could include any feasibility study or business justification already developed.
- Preliminary high-level resource and cost estimates (budget).
- Preliminary high-level schedule, including milestones.
- Authorization for and responsibilities of the project manager.
- Initial assumptions and constraints.

You will use this charter to continue to ensure that the decisions you are making during planning and executing are valid, and you may use it to confirm that you should move to the next phase of the project.

In this exercise, you will learn the steps required for writing a project charter and lead BIC through the process as well.

A project charter describes the basic elements of the project and authorizes the project to continue. To write a project charter, follow these steps:

1. Interview the sponsor of the project, any product managers, and any other organizational leaders involved in the project to ensure that you understand the product and service and the purpose of the project. For each succeeding interview, as you listen to the information and take notes, confirm that all of the interviewees concur with the major points you progressively discover.

2. Ask your sponsor and other stakeholders what the main goals and objectives of the project are. Ask questions such as this: When you get to the end of this project, what is the product or service going to look like and what will it do? Have them attempt to define what success looks like for the project. Ask them what constraints and assumptions they have about the project.

3. Ask your sponsor and other stakeholders what tangible deliverables will be part of the project. Give them some examples based on the typical life cycle of your product or service. Ask what skills and functional organizations they think may be needed to help with the project.

4. Collect the business case for your project and attach it to the plan. If it has not been completed, then complete it yourself. Note that you may want to share the major points of the business case with your sponsor and other interviewees, and confirm that all the product justifications have been included and that your stakeholders agree with the business case.

5. Start an estimate of resource needs, costs, and schedules with milestones. Use previous projects as comparisons; ask your stakeholders for estimates, and based on size and complexity and the kind of industry you are in, start accumulating this information.

6. Write the project charter with all the information you have gathered.

7. Include a description of the authority the project manager will need (can you hire/fire, control budget, reward/punish performance?).

8. Ensure that all elements described in the introduction are documented.

9. Ask your sponsor or a senior leader to review and change the charter as needed, and have them sign it and distribute it to leadership and management affected by the project.

10. Have a meeting to ensure concurrence with the charter for all executives and identified team members.

Scenario

Your company, Terrific Project Management Partners (TPMP), has been asked to help the Best Investments Company (BIC) with its project initiation processes. BIC has selected a project and wants to understand how a project charter can help further define and authorize the project. The company has decided to build electronic kiosks in major malls throughout the United

States. Jim Thoroughgood has been assigned as project manager, and you will be mentoring him on the project. You will help Jim write a project charter.

BIC expects the kiosk project to deliver most of the standard items for a new investment program, but this one has a twist: BIC is an investment company, not a construction company, and the project involves the construction of kiosks. The project also involves electronic innovation—specifically, easy computerized menus for mall users. So, some of the things you might need are a software application with an easy user interface, a finished kiosk, the investment program you will try to sell, advertisements for this new investment program, and other items that will be part of a successful new product. Martha Pena, your sponsor, has asked that the first kiosk be in place within nine months and the budget for initial implementation of 25 kiosks should be no more than $5 million. She says the company doesn't expect anything glitzy—just something efficient and attractive to the average investor.

Project Initiation and the Project Charter

1.   Describe the product and service of the project. Do this in your own words, and don't hesitate to add some of your own thoughts to this description.

2.   What are the main goals and objectives of this project? Again, don't hesitate to add some things you know need to be included that may not be included in the exercise setup description. Include some assumptions and constraints that the project might have.

3.   What are the main, high-level project deliverables?

4.   List the responsibility and authority Jim Thoroughgood would require to succeed on this project.

5.   Is it a good idea to have the project manager's responsibility and authority written in the project charter? Why?

6.   What are the resource and cost estimates? Can you list some major milestones and when they might occur?

7.   Who signs the charter, and to whom is the charter given?

Answers to Section 2 Exercises

Answers to Exercise 2.1

Your answers should be similar to the following. Note that many of your answers do not need to match the answers provided. You may think of other information or justifications besides those given.

1. The following shows you how the Best Investments Company project selection matrix would be completed.

Criteria	Kiosk	Financial Advisor	Franchise
Increase market share	5 × 5 = 25	7 × 5 = 35	7 × 5 = 35
Good financial return	6 × 4 = 24	3 × 4 = 12	7 × 4 = 28
Innovation	9 × 3 = 27	5 × 3 = 15	4 × 3 = 12
Support culture	1 2 = 2	5 × 2 = 10	3 × 2 = 6
Increase public awareness	8 × 1 = 8	5 × 1 = 5	6 × 1 = 6
Total Score	86	77	87
Project Rank	2	3	1

2. The franchise project provides the greater increase in the market share and financial return, although the kiosk project is so close in overall ranking and may be considered. By looking at the details of what was rated so high, you can see that innovation is what made the kiosk project achieve a higher rating, which is a lower-weighted criterion.

3. The project ranking certainly provides a good way of ranking projects and is clearly demonstrated in this exercise. However, in this case, if the company found that the innovation of the kiosk project was important to its strategic advancement, it might choose the kiosk project over the franchise project. Or perhaps it would decide to undertake both projects because the innovation of the kiosk project is so compelling. At any rate, this process provides a consistent and objective method of selection, but it may not be the only factor in choosing one project over the other.

4. Yes, the project ranking is an excellent method. There may be other kinds of selection methods, but this provides a consistent approach to ranking projects. There may be some projects that could have the same ratings, and there would need to be a method for breaking ties as well.

5. Some other criteria a company might use are included in the following list:

    Cost avoidance. (Cost/benefit analysis—calculate savings and all costs.)

Alignment with company expertise. (Does the project team have the expertise to do the project? Can the company acquire the expertise and does it want to? Will the project efforts help develop some expertise it wants developed?)

Needed infrastructure improvement. (Improved productivity—show cost savings if possible. Describe old systems/processes that might collapse or slow down and include impact. Compare with other infrastructure projects.)

6. It is possible that each project would not be rated consistently. The project criterion measurement and the selection method and the way they are applied need to be consistent. Also, there may be times when a project may rate and rank low but there is some intrinsic value that might be ignored. The project selection committee must use good judgment and instinct to think about projects. It is also possible that the selection process can be overridden by leaders or politics in the company. This may be okay, or it may undermine the selection process so that no one takes it seriously.

Answers to Exercise 2.2

The best way to answer this exercise is by setting up a year-by-year expected cash flow matrix. It would look something like the following set of tables. You may think of other information or justification besides those in the answers provided.

The first table shows kiosk cash inflows with an initial investment of $5,000,000.

Year	Cash Inflow in Dollars
1	750,000
2	2,000,000
3	2,000,000
4	1,500,000
5	1,500,000
6	1,500,000

The next table shows financial advisor cash inflows with an initial investment of $8,000,000.

Year	Cash Inflow in Dollars
1	1,500,000
2	1,600,000
3	1,600,000
4	1,600,000
5	1,500,000
6	1,500,000

This last table shows franchise cash inflows with an initial investment of $11,000,000.

Year	Cash Inflow in Dollars
1	3,500,000
2	2,000,000
3	2,400,000
4	3,000,000
5	3,000,000
6	3,000,000

1. The Kiosk project has the best payback, which would be early in the fourth year. The original investment was $5 million, and by adding each year's totals incrementally, the payback of $5,500,000 would occur in the first half of the fourth year. This would rank number 1.

    The franchise project has the second best payback, which would be early in the fifth year. The original investment was $11 million, and by adding each year's totals incrementally, the payback of $13,900,000 would occur in the fifth year (it would be paid back early in that year). This would rank number 2.

    The financial advisor project has the third best payback, which would be in the sixth year. The original investment was $8 million, and by adding each year's totals incrementally, the payback of $9,300,000 would occur in the sixth year. This would rank number 3.

2. Yes, the project manager could do this calculation. It is one of the simplest financial return calculations. After the cash inflows are projected, the project manager can make this calculation with simple addition/subtraction.

3. Some advantages of the payback period method are that it is simple to calculate and easy to understand. A major disadvantage is that it does not take into account the time value of money (interest), and thus, it is not as accurate as the other methods. It also does not take into account how much profit is estimated after the payback is achieved.

4. The best NPV is the kiosk project, and the second is the franchise project. Since the financial advisor project has a negative NPV, it should not be considered for selection. The following tables describe how the NPV was calculated for each.

    The first table shows NPV for kiosk inflow based on the initial investment of $5,000,000.

Year	Cash Inflow in Dollars	Calculation	Totals
1	750,000	750,000 ÷ 1.0500 =	714,286
2	2,000,000	2,000,000 ÷ 1.1025 =	1,814,059
3	2,000,000	2,000,000 ÷ 1.1576 =	1,727,713
4	1,500,000	1,500,000 ÷ 1.2155 =	1,234,060

Year	Cash Inflow in Dollars	Calculation	Totals
5	1,500,000	1,500,000 ÷ 1.2763 =	1,175,272
Total			6,665,390
Less Investment			(5,000,000)
NPV			1,665,390

The next table shows NPV for the financial advisor project based on the initial investment of $8,000,000.

Year	Cash Inflow in Dollars	Calculation	Totals
1	1,500,000	1,500,000 ÷ 1.0500 =	1,428,571
2	1,600,000	1,600,000 ÷ 1.1025 =	1,451,247
3	1,600,000	1,600,000 ÷ 1.1576 =	1,382,170
4	1,600,000	1,600,000 ÷ 1.2155 =	1,316,331
5	1,500,000	1,500,000 ÷ 1.2763 =	1,175,272
Total			6,753,591
Less Investment			(8,000,000)
NPV			(1,246,409)

The last table shows the NPV for the franchise project based on the initial $11,000,000 investment.

Year	Cash Inflow in Dollars	Calculation	Totals
1	3,500,000	3,500,000 ÷ 1.0500 =	3,333,333
2	2,000,000	2,000,000 ÷ 1.1025 =	1,814,059
3	2,400,000	2,400,000 ÷ 1.1576 =	2,073,255
4	3,000,000	3,000,000 ÷ 1.2155 =	2,468,120
5	3,000,000	3,000,000 ÷ 1.2763 =	2,350,545
Total			12,039,312
Less Investment			(11,000,000)
NPV			1,039,312

5. No. NPV is not as simple to calculate as payback period, so it may be difficult for some project managers to calculate. It will require a certain amount of financial acumen.

6. An advantage of the NPV method is that it is more accurate because it includes the time value of money. A disadvantage is that it is more complex to calculate.

7. Since the kiosk project has the highest internal rate of return at 5.5 percent, it ranks number 1. The franchise project ranks second with 5 percent IRR. The financial advisor project ranks last at 3 percent IRR.

8. No, it's complex to calculate IRR in this situation. IRR requires a financial calculator and thus it may be difficult for the project manager to calculate.

9. An advantage of IRR is that it is more accurate. A disadvantage is that it is more complex to calculate.

10. Since the managers at Best Investments Company stated that they are interested in an accurate method that offers the best investments, which NPV provides, we recommend the NPV method.

Answers to Exercise 2.3

Your answers may be similar to the following:

1. A sample product description:

Create kiosks that provide investment solutions to new and returning customers shopping at America's major malls. This kiosk must be attractive and easy to use in order to bring in new customers to our investment portfolio. The kiosk must have an easy-to-use interface for customers to start their investment portfolios. The kiosk will include a new and innovative application that allows customers to analyze and create a portfolio using our current investment products. The main customers for this product are those people who do not have computers in their homes and those browsing the malls. The kiosk must be compelling enough to grab the customer's attention. The main reason for creating this kiosk is to increase our market by 10 percent.

Note that a product statement evolves as the project progresses, and the description may become far more detailed. Also, this description would need to be in greater detail if a vendor would be used to do the work (or portions of the work).

2. Some possible objectives:

(A) We will increase our total investment penetration based on this innovative product by 10 percent within two years. (B) With the innovation created by our new application and interface, we will increase our image within the industry within six months by having at least three independent articles printed in major industry magazines lauding our kiosks. (C) The application must be secure for the customer and must use basic information so that the customer does not have to have a lot of information to start their portfolio.

Some assumptions might be that Martha will continue to be your sponsor throughout the project, you will continue to have the budget approved for you throughout project execution, the technology created will work as expected, and the kiosk project will continue to be a strategic initiative. Some constraints might be that you have to stay within budget, you have to hire an outside company to build the kiosk, the kiosk should not be especially elaborate (glitzy), and the kiosk has to work without a person staffing it.

3. Some of the deliverables might be:

   Design, construction, and testing of the kiosk. Concept, design, and implementation (including testing) of the interface and new investment application.

   Marketing of the kiosk concept. Also, surveys and market research to ensure that market increase is achieved and that the designs will be innovative.

4. Jim's responsibilities will be to ensure that the project is properly planned, executed, and managed. Specifically his responsibilities should include the following:

   - Set standards and policies for the project's work and establish and communicate the project procedures to the project team and stakeholders and any contractors used on the project.

   - Identify activities and tasks, resource requirements, project costs, project requirements, and performance measures.

   - Ensure that all project information is documented.

   - Communicate status to management, stakeholders, and the team as needed.

   - As the project proceeds, ensure that the ongoing plan and schedule accurately reflect cost, time, and performance as the plan is executed and make any corrective steps as necessary.

   For authority, Jim could require the following:

   - Control over the budget.

   - The ability to choose, add, and remove members from the team.

   - Authority to negotiate and manage the contract terms and the contractor. Contract management might include requiring status and specific performance measurements from the contractor. Also, the project manager should have input into performance reviews for the work performed on the project.

   - Help from management to escalate and solve major project issues.

   - The opportunity to work on an equal basis with functional managers within the company to get issues solved.

   - The ability to create, change (with appropriate approval), and communicate the project plan and focus as needed.

5. Yes, it is an excellent idea to write the project manager's responsibility and authority into the charter (as well as other roles and responsibilities, if possible). It is better to have it in writing rather than just assumed. If issues come up in the project that require the project manager to assert authority, they will then be able to point to the charter to help support their actions.

6.   You have been given a budget estimate of $5 million, and you can start with that as your cost estimate, although you will need to state that one of your planning deliverables will be to create a more accurate cost estimate. For resources, you might initially list in the charter that you will need a market researcher, functional team members (from the investment portfolio department and IT groups), kiosk builders (you might consider a contractor with this experience), and marketing/sales people to sell the kiosks at the malls.

   Some major milestones may be complete plans and requirements for software and kiosk two months into the project, complete software five months into the project, complete test of software seven months into project, complete building of kiosk six months into the project, load and test software into the kiosk eight months into the project, market kiosk eight months into the project. Complete project at nine months.

7.   Martha Pena or a senior manager actually issues the project charter, although Jim Thoroughgood might write it. Jim, the project sponsor, key stakeholders, and other key major senior managers will sign the project charter as a sign of approval. All stakeholders should receive them.

Creating the Scope Statement

The following exercises are presented in this section:

- Exercise 3.1: Creating the Project Management Plan
- Exercise 3.2: Creating a Scope Management Plan and Managing Scope Change
- Exercise 3.3: Creating the Project Scope Statement

Exercise 3.1: Creating the Project Management Plan

The objectives for Exercise 3.1 are follows:

- Describe the project planning process.
- Understand when the project management plan is created.
- Describe typical components of a project management plan.

Background

There is a point in time on a project when you have completed the planning and are ready to start executing the plan. This point is when one of the project integration management processes—Develop Project Management Plan—is performed. Develop Project Management Plan takes all the information created in the previous planning processes and integrates it into one comprehensive document that will serve as a guide during project execution and monitoring and controlling processes. This document usually has the formal approval of the project stakeholders. Throughout this book we have described the planning processes performed in the other eight knowledge areas. The project management plan contains elements of all the project management planning processes. These are processes such as Scope Planning, Schedule Development, Cost Budgeting, Quality Planning, Acquire Project Team, Communications Planning, Risk Management Planning, and Plan Purchases and Acquisitions. There are 21 total planning processes that can be incorporated into the project management plan. Part of your job as project manager is deciding which processes will be used on your project. Your project management plan will cover the planning processes you will use.

If the project management plan is a comprehensive document that guides you in project execution and control, then what should it contain? In this exercise, we examine the most common components of a typical project management plan.

Components of a Project Management Plan

There are 14 common components of a typical project management plan.

Management plans   Through the course of this book, you have had many opportunities to explore management plans—for example, the scope management plan in Chapter 3 and quality management plan in Chapter 4. You need to include portions of your management plans in your project management plan. Remember that this project management plan serves as a guide for the project during the execution and monitoring and controlling processes. Therefore, you will need to determine which sections should be included to guarantee the objectives of the project. These management plans should correspond directly to the processes that you have selected for your project. The project management plan should include some portions of all of these:

- Project scope management plan

- Schedule management plan

- Cost management plan

- Quality management plan

- Process improvement plan

- Staffing management plan

- Communications management plan

- Risk management plan

- Procurement management plan

Other components   You may wish to also include other pertinent pieces of information in your project management plan. These components again should provide information and guidance as you execute the project. You might consider including the following information:

Milestone list   As you worked through the WBS and project schedule, you probably determined what deliverables will be created at what points of time. These deliverables create a milestone list. It would be advantageous to include these in the project schedule as a baseline of what you plan to deliver.

Schedule baseline   The project schedule is created during the Schedule Development process of the Planning phase of a project. It is created with tools and techniques like calculating critical path and duration compression. The original schedule is called the schedule baseline. The schedule baseline is documented in the project management plan so the project team understands the sequence of the work that must be done.

Resource calendar   Resource calendars need to be included in the project management plan so team members understand exactly what days they are active and what days they are idle.

Cost baseline   At the end of the Cost Planning process, you created a cost baseline. This baseline conveys what you plan on spending on the project. The cost baseline should be kept in the project management plan as a point of comparison as you execute the project.

Risk register   The risk register is created in the Risk Identification process and includes risks, potential responses and other pertinent information. It is kept in the project management plan as ongoing documentation that must be inspected and acted upon through the execution of the project.

Be sure to include in your project management plan any other documentation that will guide the project to successful completion. This document should act as a litmus test for project personnel when they are in doubt about what to do.

In this exercise, you will test your knowledge about creating a project management plan as you help the Sensational Advertisement Productions company create a project management plan for its advertising campaign for a new cell phone service.

Scenario

TPMP has brought project management processes to an advertising firm, Sensational Advertisement Productions (SAP), and the project managers at SAP are learning how to use the eight knowledge areas involving Project Scope Management, Project Time Management, Project Cost Management, Project Quality Management, Project Human Resource Management, Project Communications Management, Project Risk Management, and Project Procurement Management. However, you need to help them start using the processes and tools of what is probably their most important function: project integration management.

You are working with Pam Rosenbaum, who has been assigned account management functions for a telecommunications client's important new product: a new cell phone that integrates normal service with PDA functions right on the phone, which will be sold at a competitive price with normal cell phone services. The account has several project managers for the various sales campaigns: Michael Harland for the print campaigns, Judy Arakawa for the TV campaigns, and Joseph Matumbo for the telemarketing campaigns. Each project manager is working with marketing managers within the telecommunications company to get direction and approval for the work they will produce.

Because these projects must integrate and a change in one campaign could affect the other, Pam knows she must create an integrated project management plan. Even though the telecommunications company is putting a lot of money into the campaign, SAP still has a tight budget for all its advertising. You will help Pam put together an integrated project management plan that guides the work for both SAP and its client.

Creating the Project Management Plan

1. When is a project management plan created?
2. Describe the Project Management Planning process.
3. Pam is working on the cost portion of the project management plan. How should she organize the costs in the project management plan?
4. Name three sections that Pam could include in her project management plan.

Exercise 3.2: Creating a Scope Management Plan and Managing Scope Change

The objectives for Exercise 3.2 are as follows:

- Describe the need for a scope management plan.
- Describe the parts of a scope management plan.
- Be able to create a scope management plan.
- Learn how to manage scope change.

Background

Is the scope of your project well defined? If the scope changes for your project, what will you do? Do your stakeholders know what to do if they need to suggest a change to the scope of your project? When should you change the scope of your project versus not changing it? All of these questions (and many more) will be answered if you create a scope management plan, a component of the integrated project management plan. As with all PMI's knowledge areas, PMI suggests using documentation to manage the Scope Management knowledge area. If criteria for your project don't get written down early in the planning process, you will tend to make them up along the way. Documenting the methods for defining scope and the processes for managing changes prevents you from becoming disorganized and helps you manage the project consistently. It also means you and your team can more easily identify when scope change occurs and will not allow change that shouldn't occur on the project.

For the scope management plan, you and your team need to define what methods you will use to define scope (including the work breakdown structure) and identify the stability of the scope at the time you document it. You will need to decide how the work the scope describes will be verified and approved for accuracy and completeness, how often the scope could change, and the impact to your project if the scope does change. You also need to document how you will manage the scope and its change. For instance, will you have a form that must be completed, or can people just send e-mail? Whose approval will you need and when? Are there some scope changes the project can absorb without too much impact and informal change control processes? Also, after you have completed more of your scope definition, you may have found that you need to update the scope management plan. For instance, you may have found a new field you need to add to the scope change request form to help prioritize change more accurately.

In Exercise 3.2, you will learn the elements that make up a scope management plan, and the methods for creating one. Finally, you will continue to help the Best Investment Company (BIC) in its project management endeavors.

Scope Management Plan Elements

You will document the following elements for your scope management plan:

- How will you and your project team define the project's scope and work breakdown structure? What tools and techniques will you use to do so?

- How will you verify the accuracy of the work of the project, and what constitutes acceptance of the deliverables?

- Once it's defined, what is the stability of the project scope? Is it early in scope development and the scope is likely to change as you build more information about your project? Or is the scope simple and well defined or are you in the later stages of you planning process which would indicate a more stable scope?

- How often do you estimate the scope might change, and why?

- If the scope changes, what will the impact be to your project in terms of duration, cost, quality, or any other important areas of the project? Do some scope changes have more impact than others? Why?

For managing scope change you will want to ensure that you answer the following questions:

- What kind of information about the change needs to be captured?

- Are there specific processes you will use? How will you log and track change and ensure that it is incorporated into the project? How will you manage scope changes not accepted for this phase of the project?

- Who needs to approve change?

- How often will scope changes be reviewed?

Creating a Scope Management Plan

When creating a scope management plan, follow these steps:

Identify how your team and you will create the project scope statement and the work breakdown structure (WBS). Document how you will create the project scope statement and WBS and make sure you answer the following questions. In defining project scope and WBS, will you and your project team be using methods defined by your organization, methods defined by the project management office (PMO), or other methods? Do you have a template or some other format you must use to define project scope? Will you need to use a graphic WBS, or will an outline method be okay? Do you already have enterprise WBS templates you should use? What are the minimum required items (such as deliverables, objectives, requirements, assumptions and constraints, etc.) that must be included in the project scope statement? Don't forget to define how the project scope statement will be approved and who will approve it.

Describe how you and your team will assure that the deliverables defined in the project scope are verified for accuracy. Document the process for how you will accept deliverables. For instance, for each deliverable, you might identify who the designated reviewers and approvers are. (A Responsibility Assignment Matrix might work well for this). Then, describe the time frames for review and perhaps require a walk-through of critical deliverables, with a question and answer period, or multiple walk-throughs for each deliverable. Finally, you might require an e-mail or signature from each approver of the deliverable to verify that they believe the deliverable is accurate.

Document the scope change process. You will want to integrate the scope change process into your overall change control procedures that will be described in a later exercise. You will need to document general information about change, such as the date, a brief description, and who is requesting the change. You will also need to indicate whether it is business, technical, or other need for the change. You will also need to include a description of the resulting analysis of the change (a subject matter expert needs to document impact/analysis). The following items might be a part of that analysis:

- Impact on scope, resources, cost, quality, schedule, a deliverable, goal, or any other item in the project that will change.

- Any new risks introduced or old risks impacted. What are some of the issues to existing requirements of the service or product that could occur due to the scope change?

- The effect the change will have on other dependencies, such as another project or business processes.

You'll want to document the levels of review and approval for the change and how the change (or reason the change was not accepted) is communicated to everyone (whether affected or not). You might set up a matrix for levels of approval in the scope change plan or in the overall change control plan. The thresholds for approval will vary greatly depending on the complexity of the project. For instance, a five-month project may be able to tolerate a week's slippage and thus may not require a high-level approval. But a one-week slippage for a two-month project is relatively significant. And lastly, indicate how the change will be integrated into the scope and managed and tracked as part of the project management plan.

Provide in the scope management plan the probability of scope changes and their frequency and a plan for regular, consistent reviews of the project scope.   Make sure you document how you will review the project scope throughout the project's life. The best way to stay within scope is to remind your team and stakeholders frequently about what was agreed to. A scheduled project scope review can do this. Also, after you have defined project scope, you might want to provide a confidence factor about its stability. A cookie-cutter, well-defined project scope will change much less than a new, innovative, or risky project that is not similar to anything anyone has ever done. To determine a scope confidence factor, you might want to answer the following questions:

- Has everyone approved your statement?
- Will you have new stakeholders join the project over time?
- Does it still need some clarity?
- Have you been able to thoroughly document its assumptions and constraints?
- Have you been able to easily identify success criteria and create objective measurements for its goal statements?

You could use this information to estimate how much time you will need for project administration of scope changes. You might create a table with various dates on which you will perform a scope review so you can have the team review the scope and its stability and then reflect changing stability after these reviews.

Describe how scope changes will impact the project.   If you are under a very tight schedule, you might describe how any scope addition will change the end date. Or if quality is one of the important driving factors, you might stipulate that additions to the scope will have to also include additional quality assurance.

Communicate the scope management plan and the scope change process to your project team. Have a meeting to describe the scope management plan, and hold a training session to make sure everyone knows how to follow your processes to change scope.

Scenario

You're helping BIC to develop consistent practices in project management planning stages. In particular, a project being managed by Betsy Smith has already been started, but it doesn't have a scope management plan. The project is to create a plan that will increase public awareness and use of an Internet investment program that has existed for six months but is not meeting expected market penetration. She has started to create a project scope statement with your help, but she is not quite done with that. The project budget is $50,000, and the project is expected to take three months and includes deliverables of in-house research and a focus survey. The end result is a plan that the sponsor, Harriet Freeman (the director of marketing), feels must be backed up by excellent marketing research and that can easily be implemented.

During the introduction of the project scope statement, two key stakeholders were missing, and Betsy has tried to get their approval but has not been able to do so yet. The project has already started, and most of the research has been completed. Betsy is finding evidence that some major marketing steps were not originally done in the project, plus the market has changed due to the downturn in the economy, so some extra marketing steps need to be taken, including more Internet and TV advertising.

Creating a Scope Management Plan and Managing Scope Change

1. What process would you recommend to Betsy for creating the project scope statement?

2. What is a process you might recommend to verify the accuracy of the research deliverable?

3. Fred Arlington, the project manager from the original project, thinks that the project needs to include hiring an independent auditor to review the market research findings because he does not think the research team is coming to the right conclusions. Describe how this change might impact schedule, quality, the people, or any other important elements of the project.

4. What must Fred do to request this change? What data do you need to capture for this scope change request?

5. Who do you think needs to approve the change, and when should the change reviews occur?

6. Why is a scope management plan important?

Exercise 3.3: Creating the Project Scope Statement

The objectives for Exercise 3.3 are as follows:

- Describe the need for a project scope statement.
- Describe the parts essential to a project scope statement.
- Create the parts of a project scope statement.

Background

The project scope statement is one of the most important items you can create for your project. Without it, you have a project with no bounds. Additionally, what the project will accomplish can be anything you or your stakeholders decide along the way. If it is not well defined, your project may experience rework, delays, cost increases, and maybe poor morale as you and the team members seem to be trying to hit a moving target.

A scope statement acts as a document of common understanding between your project team and its customer of the project requirements, objectives, and deliverables. As a project manager, perhaps your most important job is to make sure the project scope statement is written, understood, and approved. And it becomes your mission to make sure all parties on the project stay focused on the scope and nothing else. It is also the baseline of the scope, and if things change, you will follow change procedures to document and plan the changes into your project. If you use a vendor, the scope statement can be used to develop a statement of work (SOW) to describe the work the vendor will perform. Note that the project scope statement is a detailed document created in the Planning processes; it's not the preliminary scope statement created during the Initiating processes.

In this exercise, you will learn the elements of a project scope statement and the steps involved with creating the project scope statement by leading BIC through a project scope development process.

Project Scope Statement Elements

You will document the following elements for your project scope statement:

Project objectives   Describes the quantifiable criteria for success and includes at least cost, schedule, and quality measures. Make sure that you can measure the completion of the objective in some kind of numerical form (such as in dollars, percentage, date, etc.).

Product or service scope description   Documents the product or service characteristics. Objectives, deliverables, and requirements are often a decomposition of the product or services scope description. This description should include the business need/justification for the product or service as well.

Project deliverables   Lists summary-level, measurable subproducts that will combine for full delivery of the product and project. This may include a high-level work breakdown structure to show the scope of the project.

Requirements and specifications   Ensures that needs and expectations of stakeholders of the deliverables of the product or service are documented. These usually describe the capabilities and conditions the deliverables must meet.

Product or service acceptance criteria   May include quality measurement criteria such as fitness for use or performance measurements.

Project boundaries   Lists what is and is not included in the scope of the project. Usually, since the rest of the document describes what is in the project, this is extremely useful in describing what is not in the project. In many of your discussions with stakeholders, you will hear them say that something should not be addressed during this project. Start including these items in an "out-of-scope" section.

Assumptions and constraints   Lists all assumptions you are making for the project (such as once committed, resources will not be moved off your project) and constraints that restrict what the project team can do (such as the team has to rely on existing infrastructure network to implement new application software throughout the country).

Project organization   Describes how the project is staffed to undertake and complete the project.

Initial risks   Lists major challenges or opportunities the project team and stakeholders identify for the project. This is covered in more detail in risk management, but the list starts here.

Cost and time estimates   Includes cost estimates, milestones that may constrain the project, and funding limitations.

Project configuration management requirements   Documents project specifications, configuration management, and level of change control.

Approval requirements   Defines who must approve what on the project. This is often similar to a Responsibility Assignment Matrix.

The Scope Statement Process

When creating a scope statement, follow these steps:

1. Review the project charter for any items you can reuse for further detail in the project scope statement.

2. Work with your project team or other stakeholders to write a brief general statement about the purpose of your project or review the one you already have from the project charter. Try to include a general description of what is in the project as well as what is not in the project.

3. Create a product scope description and include a project justification. This may have been completed in a business case, feasibility study, the project charter, or the project selection work that was completed prior to the project's being approved.

4. Create a list of major deliverables and create a high-level work breakdown structure to help show the scope of the work. This is a good time to brainstorm with your project team. You might even think of all the deliverables you can on the way to creating your work breakdown structure and then categorize them into major categories. Make sure each of these deliverables is measurable and has success criteria tied to it. You may have enterprise work breakdown structures to help you accomplish this.

5. List the objectives or goals. This is where you describe the goals that help you measure project success. You might think of what must be done for the project to be complete (critical success factors). This needs to be a quantifiable statement, such as "increase shareholder satisfaction by 10 percent." This could be easily measured with pre- and postimplementation surveys. The surveys, of course, would need to be a deliverable of the project.

6. List your assumptions. These are things that you and your project team expect to hold true throughout the project. Sometimes these are statements you should seemingly not have to say. They are obvious, but by documenting them, you can test them as assumptions and ensure that stakeholders agree with them. Often these assumptions, if they do not hold true, become risks.

7. List your constraints. These are bounds under which your team will work throughout the project. They restrain or dictate the actions of the project team. For instance, if the team needs to follow some particularly strict safety procedure, it will restrict the team from getting the work done as fast it could otherwise.

8. You may include requirements and specifications in the project scope statement or produce them in another document (and then refer to them in the project scope statement). These

requirements are the basis for understanding the amount of work that needs to be done and for creating a statement of work for a vendor if you will need to contract some of the work.

9. Include a description of the project organization, including the major roles and responsibilities needed for the project. Also include approval requirements for the items in the scope statement.

10. Include a schedule estimate for the project (including any milestones that must be met) and a budget, including funding limitations.

11. Include risks and project configuration requirements. Holding a session to identify major risks is sometimes a great way to identify deliverables that the team may have missed when creating a deliverables list.

12. Write the scope statement document, and deliver it to your stakeholders for approval. Do not just send the project scope statement out and ask stakeholders to approve it. Have a meeting to review the major items with the major stakeholders and project team. Make sure you get written approval from each stakeholder who needs to approve the project scope statement, especially your customer.

Scenario

You're helping the Best Investments Company (BIC) develop consistent practices in project management in the planning stages. In particular, since you have been on hand to help advise them of good project management principles, Betsy Smith has realized she needs a documented project scope statement for her project, even though the project has started. Betsy is working on a project to increase public awareness and the use of an Internet investment program that has existed for six months but is not meeting expected market penetration. Her team has been researching the project for a month, but now the team needs a plan for what to do next. The Internet investment project was expected to increase the overall investment penetration by 10 percent.

Right now, no one is sure how much it has increased investment penetration because overall investment activity by the public has gone down 15 percent in the last year. The team has advertised this service on TV and with Internet pop-up ads. This project has a budget of $50,000 to develop the plan, and BIC wants the plan within three months. Betsy has already used up about $4,000 in research efforts. Betsy has a team of researchers, part-time software application developers, and the original Internet investment program project manager to call on for help. She is very excited because she has realized the team did not do any advertising for this project in some of the major magazines, such as *Fortune*, and the TV ads were broadcast at the wrong times for the target audience. She thinks with this knowledge, she can help increase penetration for the Internet service immediately if the team focuses on those areas.

Creating the Scope Statement

1. Write a brief purpose statement for this project. Include a business justification statement. What is the product of this project?

2. What are some of the major deliverables of the project? Is each deliverable you identify a critical success factor? Why or why not?

3. Create some goal/objective statements and make sure they are measurable. State what you will put in place to measure them.

4. Describe some of the assumptions you have for this project.

5. Describe some constraints.

6. Will you need a statement of work? Why or why not?

7. If you were to write what should not be in the scope, what are some of the things that should be "out-of-scope"?

Answers to Section 3 Questions

Answers to Exercise 3.1

Your answers may be somewhat different, but the following answers provide a guide.

1. There is a point in time on a project where all of the planning has been completed and you're ready to start executing the plan. This point is when one of the project integration management processes—Develop Project Management Plan—is performed.

2. Develop Project Management Plan takes the information created in the previous planning processes and integrates it into one comprehensive document that will serve as a guide during project execution and monitoring and control.

3. Pam needs to cover the cost management plan baseline associated with each campaign. She also might want to include the cost baseline for each.

4. The typical sections of a project management plan are as follows: management plans, milestone lists, resource calendars, schedule baselines, cost baselines, quality baselines, and risk register.

Answers to Exercise 3.2

Note that the answers you have do not need to match the answers provided. You may think of other information or justifications besides those given.

1. Since project management is new at BIC, the organization probably does not have any forms or templates for a project. You might introduce some excellent project scope statement templates that exist on the Internet, and you might also provide them with a template that your consulting organization uses. You can suggest that a team of project managers meet to review and approve this template and start using it to create a project scope statement. You can also suggest that the process include multiple drafts, reviews, and walkthroughs with the project team and various stakeholders. The process would also include stipulating who needs to review and who needs to approve the project scope statement, how long it will take to develop it, and when it will be completed.

2. To verify the accuracy of the research deliverable, you might suggest that two non-project subject matter experts review and comment on the research report. You might then also suggest that key stakeholders and project team members attend a walk-through of the research that highlights the key findings. At that time, any questions and issues will be submitted and subsequently addressed. Finally, based on an approval matrix included in the scope management plan, you would ask for sign-off from designated approvers for the research report.

3. Fred's decision to hire an independent auditor would have an impact on the in-house researchers. They may feel their integrity and research methods are under question. This could have an impact on the morale of the project team, who might wonder why indepen-

dent research is necessary and what value it will bring to the project Of course, it would increase the schedule and budget. It will take time to find a firm, define the statement of work, hire the firm, and manage them. This could increase the project's schedule to at least a month or more. It will increase the project budget because it will cost money to hire the firm and time to manage the vendor. It would change the quality of the work—it could actually increase it or decrease it, depending on the standards and reputation of the firm hired.

4. To request the change and hire an independent auditor, Fred needs to go through the formal change request process that Betsy will create in the scope management plan. In that plan, she will describe how people are supposed to submit change requests. The following data should be requested and included in the analysis:

    - What is the requested change?

    - Why is the change needed? Fred will need to document a compelling business justification to find support for this change.

    - What is the impact on schedule, budget, quality, deliverables, or goal? Include any analysis about the change. Include any information about who has reviewed this impact to ensure that a good analysis was completed.

5. Before she can approve the change, Betsy will need to come up with some kind of scope approval authority matrix for estimated impacts. The following table illustrates such a matrix.

Approval/Impact	Cost	Schedule	Quality
Project manager	<$200	< one week	Include or exclude some quality measures
Management stakeholder	$200 to < $500	< one week	No approval needed
Sponsor	= or > $500	> one week	No approval needed
Customer	No approval needed	> one week	Include or exclude some quality measures

This matrix shows the various criteria that a person needs to approve based on a schedule of three months and a budget of $50,000. In this case, the project manager needs to approve everything but could approve a change under $200 without its being approved by anyone else (and if there weren't many of them!). However, if the schedule changes or a cost change is greater than $200, the project manager would need to get a management stakeholder's approval as well.

Betsy might set up biweekly change reviews, based on how often she thinks change might occur and how often she needs a change review board to look at the submitted changes.

6. The scope management plan is important because the project manager and the team need to decide how they will create, review, and accept the project scope. The team will know what the project scope statement and work breakdown structure should contain and thus

be able to understand the work effort involved in creating them. And when the deliverable described in the project scope statement is delivered, if it has been documented how it will be reviewed for accuracy, everyone will know what work effort is needed to confirm that the deliverable is acceptable. They will need to know how to react to requests for change when they occur. The team members will be able to manage change (which is inevitable) rather than let the change manage them. It will describe the criteria needed to analyze the change and the thresholds for approval of the change. In this manner change will be organized, managed consistently, and communicated regularly and equally to all stakeholders.

Answers to Exercise 3.3

Note that the answers you have do not need to match the answers provided. You may think of other information or justifications besides those given.

1.   A sample purpose statement:

The purpose of this project is to create a plan to help increase investment penetration by 10 percent and include a way to measure it. The project will research the market demand for the Internet investment project. The product of the project is actually just a plan based on solid market research and a measurement method to ensure that the market increase can be quantified.

It may appear that the team's purpose is to increase market share, but it is solely *to create a plan* to increase market share.

2.   The following are some possible deliverables. You may think of others.

- A market research report. This would be a critical success factor because without it, you would not know the competition or the market share you could obtain. If research was done for the original project, you would want to update or include it in this document.

- A survey to find out why people aren't using the current program. This survey is not required—your plan could use the research as a baseline, and this might add a great deal to the quality of your plan.

- A recommendation. This could be part of the plan, but the recommendation could supply what steps you would include in the plan, such as particular advertising or improvement of the Internet program and support for why the steps should be taken. This may not be a critical success factor but again would help with the quality of the plan.

- A plan. This is a critical success factor—the product of the project.

- A way to measure the current market share of investment programs, and a way to measure the market share after the plan is implemented. This is a critical success factor.

3.   Some possible objectives:

- Create an implementable plan to increase Internet program market share by 10 percent within three months. You may measure whether the plan is implementable by ensuring that time and resources are applied and that all tasks are approved by possible owners of the tasks. All the tasks should be based on specific research or survey results.

- Create a tool that can be systematically applied to measure market improvement for the program at predefined times during the plan's implementation to show increase or decrease from baseline.

4. Some assumptions:

- The output of this project is only a plan. No steps will be taken to actually improve market share at this time.

- The market research will be as accurate and timely as possible.

- A survey will accurately reflect the attitudes of typical users of the Internet program.

- You have the expertise on the team to know what kind of tasks to implement to increase market share for the program.

5. Some constraints:

- The team is constrained by the remaining budget to do the research, survey, and plan creation.

- The research team must use only the tools and knowledge it has. (Note: This is a good test to see if the stakeholders would consider getting some expert research help for the team.)

6. No, you will probably not need a statement of work (SOW) because you will not be using any outside contractors. Sometimes people call this scope statement an SOW, but it is usually used for contractors. If you use some kind of outside help to perform the survey to gather data about issues with the current Internet program, you would need to create an SOW for their part of the work.

7. Some items that are out-of-scope:

- Performing any of the designs for the deliverables that the report might recommend (such as TV ads marketed to the target audience at the right time) or implementing any of the recommendations.

- Stopping any of the marketing events that are occurring now. The team might make a recommendation, but actually stopping the event is not part of their scope.

- Creating the team that would perform any of the recommended marketing items.

Creating the WBS and Communicating the Plan

The following exercises are presented in this section:

- Exercise 4.1: Creating the Work Breakdown Structure (WBS)
- Exercise 4.2: Planning Communications with Your Stakeholders
- Exercise 4.3: Planning for Quality
- Exercise 4.4: Quality Planning Tools
- Exercise 4.5: Calculating the Cost of Quality

Exercises 4.1: Creating the Work Breakdown Structure (WBS)

The objectives for this exercise are as follows:

- Describe the need for a work breakdown structure.
- Describe the essential elements of a work breakdown structure.
- Create a work breakdown structure.

Background

A work breakdown structure (WBS) is a scope management process used to decompose project scope components into smaller and more manageable components or work packages. The project manager creates it with project team members, and it has many purposes. The WBS helps to identify the major deliverables of the project. It also creates a total view of the project in small, manageable components. Finally, it helps create a common understanding of the project deliverables.

A work breakdown structure is composed of two elements. The first is levels of work, of which there are three. The highest level is usually the project name or the major task. Intermediate levels of work, sometimes called summary tasks, are subcomponents of the highest-level tasks. There can be several levels of intermediate tasks. Intermediate level or summary tasks are used to sum up the type of tasks below them. Summary tasks help you categorize your thoughts. Here are some examples of possible summary level tasks:

- Major Deliverables
- Geographic boundaries
- Phases
- The departments of the organization

You will probably want your first set of summary tasks to be at the deliverable level. The other levels of summary tasks can capture the other three bullet items we just covered. Finally, work packages are the lowest level of work, sometimes just called the work task.

The other element of the WBS is a unique number identifier.

The following shows the three levels of work and the unique number identifiers.

There are eight steps to creating a work breakdown structure:

1. Determine the format used in creating the WBS. You can use either a tree structure or an outline.

2. Determine how many levels of decomposition are appropriate for your project.

3. Determine how the levels of the work breakdown structure will be organized.

4. Label level one the project name.

5. At level two, decompose the project into a set of deliverables.

6. For each subsequent level, decompose the level above into smaller components.

7. Create the lowest level of decomposition. This level, called the work package, should be small enough to easily assign to one person to complete. You also will be able to easily create time and cost estimates for this level.

8. Create a unique numerical identifier for each component on the work breakdown structure. The numbering scheme starts at the left side of the WBS and works the same as a numeric outline (e.g., 1.0, 1.1, 1.1.2, etc.).

In this exercise, you'll guide a TPMP project manager through creating a work breakdown structure in order to help a client reach its goals with the credit card validation project.

Scenario

Your company, Terrific Project Management Partners (TPMP), has just placed you at SystemsDelivery, Inc. as a temporary project manager. You've been assigned the credit card validation project. This project is designed to be the next big thing in credit card fraud prevention. The management of SystemsDelivery believes that this product will be in high demand at every major retailer in the country. Of course, the management needs this product to go to market as quickly as possible. On your first day, the project sponsor hands you several documents about the project. One of these documents is a scope statement the last project manager created before he quit. The scope statement includes the following items:

- The validation system will be housed in a device that attaches to all electronic cash registers.
- The validation system must be updated daily using a telephone line and a special toll-free number.
- The validation system contains both software and hardware components.
- The validation system must validate a credit card in 30 seconds or less.
- The validation system must be ready for the American market first, Canadian second, and European third.
- Different devices and software will be needed for each market.

Creating the Work Breakdown Structure

Follow the scope information provided for the credit card validation project and create the work breakdown structure.

1. There are two possible ways to create your work breakdown structure. Which is the best and why?

2. What is the name of the highest-level component of the work breakdown structure?

3. What are the main project deliverables on the second level of the work breakdown structure? This is high level.

4. Now that you have the main project deliverables defined, analyze each one and determine the substeps that make up each. These new substeps are level three. Draw them.

5. Examine each level as you create it and determine the substeps until you have tasks that are easily assigned to one person. How many levels did you create for this work breakdown structure? Display your work.

6. Uniquely number each component of the work breakdown structure. Draw your answer.

Exercise 4.2: Planning Communications with your Stakeholders

The objectives for this exercise are as follows:

- Use the lines of communication to understand communication complexity.
- Understand how a plan can help you organize your communications.
- Create a detailed communications management plan.
- Create a communications matrix.

Background

As the project manager, one of your primary functions is to consistently and effectively communicate with your stakeholders. People take communication for granted, but once you understand the complexity of communication you will understand why you must control it as best you can to keep people focused on the right information about your project. To do so, you must seriously consider the methods you will use for communicating.

The best way to communicate consistently and in an organized form is to write down your communications management plan. First, you need to perform communications requirements analysis to understand the communication needs of your stakeholders. You have a lot of ways to do this, but one of the best ways is to gather the information directly from your stakeholders when you interview them during some of your stakeholder analysis activities. You will want to include the communications requirements in your communications management plan.

Once you complete the communications requirements analysis, you need to create a plan describing the types of communication you will distribute, to whom you will distribute them, and the methods by which you will distribute them. You will need to describe the strategy and tactics you are using for communication in this plan. For instance, will you use formal or informal methods, and how much will you communicate to your team? You will need to describe how you intend to keep the plan updated as the project goes though its various phases: As the people and activities on the project change, so do the communication needs. If your project is complex and you have many stakeholders, your strategy and tactics for communicating will need to be far more formal and organized than if your project is small and you have few stakeholders. One of the best tools to include in a communications management plan is a communications matrix. In this matrix, you will list all of your communication methods and the stakeholders who will receive the communication. You will describe the communication forms and when they will receive their information.

Lines of Communication

Communication is a very complex activity, often taken for granted. The following formula illustrates the lines of communication (also called communication channels) that can exist based on the number of people involved on a project (n is the number of people on the team who will be communicating):

$$[n \times (n - 1)] \div 2$$

This means if you have 5 people on your project, there are 10 lines of communication. Team members on the project don't just communicate to the project manager, but also with each other. When they communicate with each other, the chances for miscommunication and distortion increase. If you have 20 people on the project, then there are 190 lines of communication—quite an increase for only 10 more people. These lines of communication keep growing exponentially and could become very difficult to manage if you don't have a plan and a consistent method of managing the communication.

Components of a Communications Management Plan

Once you have gathered your communications requirements, you are ready to create a thorough communications management plan. You may include several paragraphs describing your general strategy and tactics to frame your communication philosophy. This helps your team understand what they can expect from you and helps you formalize your thinking on how you will deal with issues as they arise on your project. Then you need to document the details. Determine how and where you will store your project information. You need to decide the structure of the filing methods you will be using: electronic or hard copy. This plan will be published to team members so they know how to get information and where they should store the project information they create. Your plan for storage should also include procedures for documentation and communication management.

Your communications plan should include a communications matrix explaining who receives information, what the information is, who is responsible for distributing it, when it will be distributed, and how it will be distributed. Also, you need to provide your team members with a description of the format and content for each of the kinds of information that will be distributed. For instance, if you listed status report for one of the information types, you would describe the data that will be captured in the status report. This matrix makes you pre-plan all of the formats you will use. You may also include a schedule for each type of information so it's clear when it will be produced.

Your team will need procedures for getting information between regularly scheduled communications and will need to understand how to deal with escalations, and you need to provide the methods for updating the communications management plan itself as the project proceeds.

Creating a Communications Management Plan

Creating a communications plan is absolutely essential on a medium or large project, and by sticking to it you'll prove to your organization that you are consistent and in control of the communication and, by implication, the project itself. Following are the steps you should take to create a communications management plan:

1. Decide on an overall strategy for your communication. You will need to describe how you are going to handle communication and why. For instance, you might state that you are going to manage communication on a very formal basis, with meetings and follow-up documents at all times, because you have a large project. You might state that you will require a part-time communication manager on your project because of its complexity or that you may need help from the public relations staff because you will publish information to the media.

2. Describe how you will store information and how your team will retrieve information. For instance, you might state that you will keep all documents on the network drive and provide the directory name and file structure for all the project information. This policy will keep the directory from becoming unusable because people put documents wherever they think they should. You should also provide procedures as to how the team or stakeholders should use this structure. Or, instead of a network drive, you might state that you will be using a website for all documentation and communication for your project.

3. Create a communications matrix. Make sure you create it thoroughly by answering the basic questions of who, what, where, when, why, and how. You might consider including the following information: what the information is (such as status report), who will use the

information (per stakeholder groups), when it will be published (such as weekly, as needed, or daily), who will be responsible for the communication (the project manager doesn't have to do everything—you can delegate!), and how the stakeholders will receive it (such as via e-mail attachments, presentation, or meeting). You will have an example form to use for your exercise. You might even think about creating the matrix for each phase of the project (concept, design, execution, finish) because the information needs and frequency may change.

4. Create a form and example content for each type of information listed in the matrix, or refer to where the form can be found. For instance, create a status report form. Show all of the fields of data you want to be included, such as dates covered, objectives and accomplishments for the status time frame, hot topics, issues, or action items. Make sure you describe what would go into each field.

5. Describe procedures for how your team and stakeholders will request and obtain information outside of normal distribution times. For instance, by detailing that the media must contact the PR department first if they have a question, everyone on the project will know what to tell the media if they should get a call from a reporter. It's a good idea to describe escalation procedures as well.

6. Describe in the communications management plan how changes will be made and approved for the plan itself. If you have found you need another form of communication as you move into the execution stage, you will need to write a procedure to ensure that your team knows about the new communication form and that you add the information to the plan itself.

Scenario

TPMP is working with an independent, nonprofit organization, Health America, which is creating reports for the status and quality of hospital health care in the United States based on goals created by the president of the United States. Health America is implementing project management processes and TPMP is helping. This is a highly visible program in the government, and it entails working with the major hospitals within the major cities of America and rating whether they are achieving specific goals as identified by the president's program. The research and reporting started about two years ago. You are helping the project manager, Bill Smith, create a communications management plan, including a communications matrix. Your team is made up of researchers, analysts, and writers who will produce the hospital quality report for the Department of Health and Human Services (HHS). Some of the people interested in your project are the media, so they can report on the goals being met/not met; HHS, who is monitoring the project for the president and who is paying for the program; the hospitals throughout the United States; and the public, who needs to understand how this program is helping them.

Creating a Communications Plan

Complete the following matrix to help you answer the questions. When you fill in the Who column, describe the groups receiving the information, not individuals. Also note that you may include another column to state who is responsible for creating the communication (for instance, PR for external media reports), as well as any other columns that can more fully describe how you will manage project communications.

What	Why (Purpose)	Who	When	How	Where (Storage)	Inputs

1. Bill has 17 people on his immediate project team. How many lines of communication does he have with the people directly working on the team? Including the project team, he has around 85 stakeholders he has determined he needs to communicate with or who might communicate with each other. What is the potential number of lines of communication on the entire project?

2. What should Bill's strategy be for communication on this project? Should it be formal or informal, mostly written or verbal? How much time should he spend on communication?

3. Will there be issues if Bill does not receive status updates from his team regularly? Why or why not?

4. Should Bill share the executive and client status reports with his team? Why or why not?

5. What is the purpose of the communications matrix?

6. Will meetings and written status be enough communication for your team members? Why or why not?

7. What kind of data would you include on your status report form? Why is it important to create a form?

Exercise 4.3: Planning for Quality

The objectives for this exercise are as follows:

- Describe the four major inputs into quality planning.
- Describe the only output of the Quality Planning process.

Background

You have probably heard of the triple constraints of project management—time, cost, and quality. These three major areas require constant trade-offs to achieve a project's objectives. The planning process for quality can be just as tricky as schedule or cost planning. In this exercise, we will talk about the inputs to quality planning as well as the major output of quality planning—the quality management plan.

Quality Planning Inputs

There are four inputs in the Quality Planning process. We will cover three of those inputs in depth. The fourth input is the project management plan, which has already been covered.

Organizational process assets   Organizational quality policies and quality guidelines from previous projects can be used as inputs into your Quality Planning process. An organizational quality policy is a key input. A quality policy is a statement (usually provided by top management) regarding the company's beliefs around quality. Your company may have a set quality statement that you can use for your project. If none exists, you will need to create one. This policy will be a guiding light for the people working on the project. If they are in doubt about a quality decision, they can look to the statement to answer their question. A quality policy might look something like this: "Quality will be emphasized in the early stages and throughout the project. It will be planned into the project as work begins, and it will be a part of the fiber of the entire project. We will design quality checkpoints and determine if quality standards have been met."

Project scope statement   This is the same scope statement that was created in Chapter 3. You use the scope statement to verify project deliverables. The scope statement may also spell out quality attributes as part of the objectives of the project.

Enterprise environmental factors   The rules that apply to the creation of your product must also be considered in quality planning. You will want to look for any standards and regulations that may apply. For example, if you are building a shed in your backyard, you would check on standards like homeowner association rules, city and county permits, and easements.

Quality Planning Output

There is one major quality planning output: the quality management plan. The project manager and the project team create the quality management plan. It should detail all quality planning activities and who will perform them. The essence of this plan is how quality will be ensured and how the quality policy will be followed.

TPMP has a new assignment for you. In it, you'll get a chance to begin planning the quality activities for the project.

Scenario

TPMP has just placed you at USRemotes, the largest distributor of remote control devices in the United States. USRemotes has launched a project to redesign the warehouse and shipping areas and processes—the WSAP project. You've been assigned as the temporary project manager.

You have started putting the project schedule and costs together and you know it is time to start working on planning the quality attributes of the project.

Planning for Quality

Using the information provided for the WSAP project, answer the following questions about quality planning.

1. What are the four major inputs into the quality management process?
2. Who should create a quality policy?
3. Why is the project management plan important to quality planning?
4. What is the major output of the Quality Planning process?
5. You have checked throughout USRemotes and cannot find a quality policy statement. Write a short quality policy statement for the WSAP project.

Exercise 4.4: Quality Planning Tools

The objectives for this exercise are as follows:

- Describe the three commonly used quality planning tools.
- Describe the appropriate time to use each quality planning tool.

Background

Many quality gurus like Juran, Crosby, and Deming advocate that quality is planned in, not inspected in. In order to plan in quality, you must use a set of commonly known tools. We are going to review these quality planning tools in this exercise. The three most commonly used tools are benchmarking, cost/benefit analysis, and the cost of quality.

NOTE   The cost of quality is such an important concept, we will cover it in the next exercise.

Benchmarking   Benchmarking is the process of analyzing similar activities as a means of comparison. Say you are able to walk a mile in 20 minutes and you want to walk faster. You would set the benchmark at 20 minutes. The next time you walk a mile, you would time yourself and compare your new time to the benchmark of 20 minutes. Benchmarking is a very effective tool to use when you are working on a project that is improving or changing the way a business currently operates. You can set a benchmark where the company is currently performing and compare the new work environment with the old to see if you are improving. When benchmarking is used as a quality planning tool, it is used to compare project practices or processes to other project practices and processes.

Cost benefit analysis   When you look at the trade-offs involved with an activity, you're probably talking about a cost benefit analysis. Let's go back to our previous example of the 20-minute-mile walker. This walker is trying to burn the most calories or get the maximum benefit from walking. She may want to look at walking faster or perhaps walking on a hilly terrain. These options may burn more calories, but there is a price to be paid in the form of sore muscles or aching feet. She may need to analyze which approach will provide more calories burned and less wear and tear on her body. In quality planning, the same technique is used to determine which quality activities will provide more quality with less cost.

Scenario

TPMP has just placed you at USRemotes, the largest distributor of remote control devices in the United States. USRemotes has launched a project to redesign the warehouse and shipping areas and processes—the WSAP project. You have been assigned as the temporary project manager.

You have started putting the project schedule and costs together and now you know it is time to start planning the quality attributes of the project.

Quality Planning Tools

Using the information provided for the WSAP project, answer the following questions about quality planning tools.

1. What is benchmarking?

2. What are the three most commonly used tools of quality planning?

3. What is cost benefit analysis?

4. Since you are new to USRemotes, it would be a good idea to use what quality planning tool to understand what is currently being done?

5. The reason that USRemotes is redesigning the warehouse and shipping areas and processes is to improve its shipping time to customers. What quality planning tool would be good to use for this project? Why?

6. You have just about completed your quality planning. The team has determined that there are three quality activities to consider for the project. You only have time to perform one of those activities. Which one would you use and why?

Exercise 4.5: Calculating the Cost of Quality

The objectives for this exercise are as follows:

- Define the cost of quality.

- Describe the three types of costs associated with the cost of quality.

- Describe the elements that make up each type of cost.

Background

The cost of quality is a quality planning tool that deserves its own exercise. It is imperative that you understand the components of the cost of quality as well as how it is calculated. The definition of the cost of quality is the total amount of money required to ensure quality. It is composed of three different types of costs—prevention costs, appraisal costs, and failure costs. It is sometimes easier to think of these costs as the costs of conformance and nonconformance, with prevention and appraisal as conformance costs and failure as nonconformance. When project managers speak of conformance, they are talking about conforming to the customer's requirements for the product. Let's spend some time on each of the different costs of quality.

Prevention   Prevention costs cover all activities that must be done to keep errors out of the process of creating the product. These, of course, are preventative activities. These costs should include all quality planning activities, any training that must be done to keep errors out of the process, product validation activities, and process validation activities.

Appraisal   Appraisal costs cover all activities that must be done to keep errors out of the customer's hands. These are the end-of-the-line activities that check the product one more time before it goes to the customer. These costs should include quality audits, evaluations, calibration, inspections, and field testing.

Failure   Failure costs include all of the costs that are incurred due to the failure of the product both internal to the company and external to the company. Internal failures include the costs for rework, repairs to the product before the project is completed, scrap, and additional inventory that had to be purchased because of the failure.

External failures are those that happen after the product leaves the organization. These costs include warranties, complaint handling, product recalls, legal suits, and harm done to the company's reputation.

Computing the cost of quality is as simple as adding the work effort estimate for each activity that is preventative or appraisal in nature to the costs that are incurred because of any type of failure, whether internal or external. The first calculation for cost of quality can be determined during the planning phase. It can also be calculated again during the executing phase when failures occur. The cost of quality can also be calculated after the project is completed when failures finally hit the customer's hands.

Scenario

TPMP has just placed you at USRemotes, the largest distributor of remote control devices in the United States. USRemotes has launched a project to redesign the warehouse and shipping areas and processes—the WSAP project. You have been assigned as the temporary project manager. You have just completed the project planning phase.

USRemotes is very interested in quality and is planning to gain some type of quality certification. Company executives have asked you to calculate the cost of quality for the WSAP project. The network diagram you have completed is depicted here:

Calculating the Cost of Quality

Using the information provided for the WSAP project, answer the following questions about calculating the cost of quality.

1. What are the three types of costs associated with the cost of quality?

2. What type of cost is associated with nonconformance?

3. What is the definition for the cost of quality?

4. What tasks in the network diagram shown earlier should be included in the preventative cost of quality?

5. What tasks in the network diagram shown earlier should be included in the appraisal cost of quality?

6. While the warehouse was being reconfigured, you found out that the new shelving units did not fit the warehouse structure. These shelving units had to be scrapped and new ones purchased. The cost of the shelving units should be included in what cost of quality type?

7. It is a year after the WSAP project completed. You have heard through the grapevine that USRemotes has had to hire several customer service representatives to handle the complaints due to mis-shipped items. These costs are part of what cost of quality type?

Answers to Section 4 Exercises

Answers to Exercise 4.1

1. The tree structure is the best way to set up the work breakdown structure for the credit card validation project because it provides a visual layout of the activities of the project.

2. The highest-level component of the WBS is the name of the project, in this case credit card validation project.

3. The main project deliverables that will be on the second level of the work breakdown structure are American market, Canadian market, and European market.

4. Your answer should look like the following graphic.

5. You should create four levels for this work breakdown structure. The level three substeps should look like the following graphic.

6. If you uniquely number each component of the work breakdown structure, your answer would look like the following graphic.

Answers to Exercise 4.2

1. Using the formula $[n \times (n-1)] \div 2$, Bill has 136 lines of communication for his immediate project team as seen in the following computation:

$[17 \ (17-1)] \div 2 = [17 \times 16] \div 2 = 272 \div 2 = 136$ if you do not include Bill in the communications formula.

Bill has 3,570 potential lines of communication on the entire project, as seen in the following computation.

$[85 \times (85-1)] \div 2 = [85 \times 84] \div 2 = 7,140 \div 2 = 3,570$ if you do not include Bill in the communications formula.

To complete some of these questions, it might help to create a matrix such as the following example. Remember, your answers may be very different, depending on how you see the needs of these stakeholder groups.

What	Why (purpose)	Who	When	How	Where (Storage)	Inputs
Executive status	To gather and check progress and discuss corrective actions	Heath America (HA) executives and lead functional managers	Biweekly	Meetings and written communication	Website and network drive under Status/ Executive	Team status
Team status	Same as executive status but at detailed level.	Team	Weekly	Meetings and written communication	Website and network drive under Status/ Team	Team member updates
Status—escalations	To communicate critical status changes and to get help with corrective actions outside of normal status time frame	HA executives	As needed	Via e-mail with follow-up voicemail if needed; enter on escalation log; might need special meetings	Website and network drive under Status/ Executive/ Escalations	Team status and ad hoc communication
Client status	Same as escalation status but emphasize budget and schedule	HHS	Monthly	Meetings and written communication	Network drive under Status/ Client	Executive and team status
Press	To send information to news agencies	Print media	As needed	Written in press release format	Website and network drive under Press Releases	Newspapers, radio, and TV media
Change request	To communicate changes	Team change board	Weekly	Written, reviewed in meetings, enter in change log	Website and network drive under Change Requests	Anyone filling out a change request form

What	Why (purpose)	Who	When	How	Where (Storage)	Inputs
Project processes and standards	To ensure consistent and organized PM processes	Team and stakeholders	Initially, and when updates are made	Written, e-mail, changes via log	Website, log, and network drive under Project Standards	Tech writer updates
Hospital quality reports	To provide status to HHS of hospital improvements based on team research	HHS	Quarterly	Written	Website for hospitals only; network drive under Quarterly Reports	Research by team members

2. Bill's strategy, due to the high visibility, should support a very formal and well-documented communication methodology. He will need to allot quite a bit of his time to communication. This does not mean that he needs to do it himself. He might hire a communications manager or delegate or distribute some of the work. Bill might indicate the percentage of time he will spend on communication, such as 85 percent. He should also state that he will need some help from the PR or media relations department regularly. He might indicate that they will be responsible for press releases.

3. Status reports to the HHS and to the HA executives depend on regular and accurate updates from the project team. Bill must be sure he has team updates prior to the status reports he must provide to the executives and HHS Also, Bill does not want to be rushing around trying to get status reports just before he must present high-level status reports. If he does not get regular status reports from his team, he may miss issues or escalations that his executives may need to help him overcome project roadblocks. If he reinforces behavior that requires updated status reports from his team members and sets up a status form, he probably will just need to plug in the information regularly.

4. Yes, Bill should share the status reports with his team. If his team members see this information, they will understand the importance of their updates for their project manager and also know the level of information that their executives want. They may also be able to see issues that the executives care about and communicate them more efficiently. Bill might even want to review the executive and client status report format with the team to make sure team members understand it so they can help improve their input.

5. The communications matrix helps the project manager and their team understand what must be communicated in a standardized, consistent form according to regularly scheduled communication. The matrix helps systemize communication so that the project manager can focus on issues and exceptions rather than gathering the information each time someone asks for it. It will help the project manager see the dependencies between the kinds of

communication so they can plan when information should be collected and feed it into follow-up processes and communications.

6. Meetings and written status will probably not be enough communication for your team members. Team members will also need one-on-one time to understand your project status needs as well as communicate possible project issues. Some people will not feel comfortable communicating issues in a public forum. So besides the formal, regularly scheduled communication in group meetings, you will need to schedule regular one-on-one meetings with your team members. You will also probably receive and need to send e-mails and make phone calls to team members.

7. You might include the following information on a status report: date range of status, overall project schedule status (on time, behind schedule, ahead of schedule), upcoming milestone (deliverable) completion progress and accomplishments, issues and progress on solving them, budget status and projections, and accepted changes to the project and how they are being integrated into the project. It is important to create a form so that you collect all the status information you need and make sure you get updates consistently. Without it, you may miss important items from status report to status report.

Answers to Exercise 4.3

1. The four major inputs into the quality management process are enterprise environmental factors, organizational process assets, project scope statement, and the project management plan.

2. The quality policy should come from the leadership of the company. If none exists, the project manager should create one.

3. The project management plan is important to quality planning because it may contain information about the desired level of quality from previous planning activities.

4. The major output of the Quality Planning process is a quality management plan.

5. Your quality policy statement for the WSAP project might be as follows: Quality will be emphasized in the early stages and throughout the project. It will be planned into the project as work begins and it will be a part of the fiber of the entire project. We will design quality checkpoints and determine if quality standards have been met.

Answers to Exercise 4.4

1. Benchmarking is the process of analyzing similar activities as a means of comparison.

2. The three most commonly used tools of quality planning are benchmarking, cost benefit analysis, and the cost of quality.

3. A cost benefit analysis is done by looking at the trade-offs involved with performing an activity.

4. Benchmarking would be a good quality planning tool to use if you are new to the company. You can use benchmarking to analyze what is currently being done before you decide what quality parameters should be set.

5. You would use the benchmarking quality planning tool for projects where you are improving or changing the way a business currently operates.

6. A cost benefit analysis would be a good quality planning tool to use to determine what quality activity will provide the most benefit for the least cost.

Answers to Exercise 4.5

1. The three types of costs of quality are prevention, appraisal, and failure.

2. A failure is the type of cost associated with nonconformance.

3. The definition of the cost of quality is the total amount of money required to ensure quality.

4. Process design training is an activity that should be included in the preventative cost of quality.

5. Validating the new design and testing the warehouse design internally are activities that should be included in the appraisal cost of quality.

6. The cost of scrapping the shelving units should be included in the internal failure cost of quality figures.

7. The cost of the additional customer service representatives should be included in the external failure cost of quality figures.

Risk Planning

The Exercises in this section include:

- Exercise 5.1: Creating Your Risk Management Plan
- Exercise 5.2: Identifying Risks
- Exercise 5.3: Qualitative Risk Analysis
- Exercise 5.4: Quantitative Analysis Tools and Techniques
- Exercise 5.5: Quantitative Risk Analysis—Updating the Risk Impact/Probability Matrix
- Exercise 5.6: Types of Risk Response Strategies
- Exercise 5.7: Risk Responses

Exercise 5.1: Creating Your Risk Management Plan

The objectives for Exercise 5.1 are:

- Introduce risk management.
- Understand what a risk management plan (RMP) does.
- Describe the components of the RMP.
- Practice building parts of an RMP.

Background

Risk management is a project management process that helps defend against the potential damaging events. Risk management also helps you identify opportunities that you may take advantage of on your project. This aspect is an important one in risk planning since a lot of people focus on the negative aspects of risks. Although doing something innovative or new with your project could be a risk if it doesn't work properly, your organization may ultimately revolutionize technology that leads to far more profit or opportunity than expected. In order to manage risk management activities, you need to create a plan. This plan describes the strategy you will use for your project in relation to risk. It describes how much time you will spend, how your team will work on risk, the measurements you will use to describe risk, and why you are taking the time to manage risk.

The major steps of risk management are:

- Creating a risk management plan.
- Identifying risks.
- Analyzing risks (qualitative and quantitative analysis).
- Creating a risk response plan.
- Monitoring and controlling risks throughout the project.

Note that this is the planning that takes place to respond to identified risks, which occurs later in the process.

Components of the Risk Management Plan

A risk management plan should contain at least the following components that will help your project team members understand how they need to manage risk:

Methodology   Describes how you will manage risk management. Your team and stakeholders need to understand the purpose and objectives of the risk management strategy. What are the processes the team will follow to perform risk management? What kind of analysis will you use for your risks? Will you hire consultants? Will you use expert judgment, or will you use sensitivity analysis? Will you keep it simple, or due to the complexity of your project, will you need to put a lot of time and expertise into managing risk, including bringing in outside consultants or the organization's risk management experts? In this section, you will describe in detail how you are going to manage risk and why.

Roles and responsibilities   Describes who will be in charge of the risk management plan, and who will be in charge of risk management responses. This step identifies the overall management team (such as the project manager or independent facilitator being the lead), and who will analyze the risks and implement risk response plans if a negative or positive risk event occurs. This responsible party is often a functional manager, or someone who understands the risk well, who has the subject matter expertise, or who has the authority to be able to gather the resources to analyze and respond appropriately and quickly. Sometimes you might have members on the risk team who are outside of the immediate project team.

Budgeting   Describes how much the risk management methods and process costs on the project. If you are going to hire a risk management expert and have her or him manage the process and have meetings every two weeks, that will cost something toward project management processes. The project may simply by complex enough to warrant a larger budget. In small projects, the risk process might be a part of the weekly status meeting, and the project manager ensures that risk discussions continue regularly in the project team meetings. The budget would be small, but appropriately relative to the complexity of the project. You will include these costs in the overall budget of your project.

Timing   Describe how often the risk management processes will occur on the project. This may also reflect different timing for different phases in the project. For instance, you might meet once a week during the concept phase, once a week during the design phase, and twice a week during the implementation phase. You might also plan some kind of independent Risk Identification to be performed early in the design phase. You would include the activities in your project schedule.

Risk categories   Categories are a way to group the kinds of risks that you may have on a project. You may find these categories from your project's particular application or industry. For instance, some categories may be legal, technical, or managerial. Risks may be identified in a risk breakdown structure (RBS) which organizes risks in overall grouping and sub-groupings. You may look in industry or application publications for a list of risk categories (which often have actual risks identified with them). Based on each of these categories, your team, executives or sponsors, outside experts, customers, or other stakeholders can start identifying risks. Categories will be described in more detail in Exercise 5.2.

Definitions of risk probability and impact   How will you rate and react to risks you identify? You will come up with a method to rate the probability of a risk occurring, and the impact it will have on the project objectives. For instance, will you use definitions of high, medium and low to rate probability and/or impact, or will you use numerical values, such as 1 through 10 or 0 to 100 percent? It is also useful to create a definition for the impact, such as medium impact means it could increase cost of the project by 20 percent or extend the end date of the project by 2 weeks. This process has to be done before you actually start identifying and rating the risks on your project. Completing this step ensures that your team has a consistent understanding so when the risk rating processes occur you are not debating how you will score risks while you are in the midst of the process itself.

Probability and impact matrix   Defines which risks will be addressed. You could have a big list of risks. You cannot work on all of them, or your budget would be astronomical. This process describes the thresholds of risks you will work on. By multiplying the factors of risk probability and impact you will rate and prioritize the risks. For instance, high probability and high impact on a negative risk event means you probably want to do something to try to eliminate or reduce the event's impact or probability, but you may decide you should not do anything with risks with low probability and low impact. You may want to create a matrix or chart in your risk management plan to visually show where you will place the rated risks, so you can quickly see what risks you will work on versus those you will not. You would possibly base this on your organization or stakeholder tolerance for risk.

Revised stakeholders tolerances   When you develop the project charter, you will analyze enterprise environmental factors in your organization that can influence success on your project. One of those factors you should have analyzed was stakeholder risk tolerances. You may have determined that the stakeholder risk tolerances are high: they seem to be willing to take larger risks for success. During the risk planning meetings that are input to the risk management plan, you may find that as more detailed discussions take place, further analysis of the stakeholders indicates they are not quite so tolerant of high risk as originally thought. So this component of the RMP includes a definition (if it was not created in the project charter) or a revision to stakeholder risk tolerances documentation.

Reporting formats   Describes your Risk Identification and response reporting and how you will communicate risk processes and results to your stakeholders. Usually this is a risk register, which allows you to document identified risks, record their probability and impact, and include responses to the risks. You will see more about formats in a later exercise when you finalize the risk register after completing the risk response planning process. This step might also include describing risk performance reporting and its processes, how the report is maintained and updated. You will want to describe how you report risk to your various audiences. For instance your project team may have a detailed risk register, but executives will see a colorful dashboard.

Tracking Describes the process for how you will record your project risks activities. You might describe how your risk management database will contribute to the organization's risk management system and lessons learned. You would include a description of whether you will audit your risk management plan and processes and how you will perform the audit.

Once you understand the components of a risk management plan, you should be ready to learn the steps involved with creating a risk management plan.

Creating a Risk Management Plan

A risk management plan is a road map for how you and your team will deal with risk processes and how you plan to analyze and manage risks. Following are the steps you'll need to take to create a risk management plan.

1. Create a risk management team.

2. Decide on and document your processes and strategy for risk management. Some questions you might ask: Is it new technology? Is it extremely difficult or financially risky? Is it a large project? Is the customer extremely "finicky"? Create a methodology around risk to match the complexity of the project. Don't forget to see if your organization already has risk management processes, guidelines, or expertise.

3. Get input from the team and stakeholders and other risk management experts about best practices and how they would like to see risk managed on the project.

4. Assign risk management roles and responsibilities. You will select leads for each risk, and it is often best to pick a functional manager, or someone with expertise that could help analyze a risk, then put a plan in place to take care of the risk. Create a roles and responsibilities matrix for risk and include it in the plan. The following table provides an example of a risk roles and responsibilities matrix.

Risk Type	Owner	Who	Responsibility
Overall	Risk manager	Myrna Floyd	Ensures overall risk management processes are identified and followed throughout the project lifecycle.
Documentation	Documentation lead	Ted Dimino	Identifies risks, analyzes risks, implements changes in documentation plan, or creates contingencies.

Risk Type	Owner	Who	Responsibility
Project Processes	Project manager	Myrna Floyd	Implements changes in project plan and project schedule.
Operational	Operations manager	Thomas Sing	Identifies risk, analyzes risks, and implements changes in operational processes or systems.
HR system software	HR system manager	Lee Neely	Implements risk response plans or contingencies.

5. Determine the budget for the risk process based on all the work you must do. Include this in the schedule and costs of the project. Describe and justify the budget in the plan.

6. Decide how often you will have risk management meetings and work on risk for the project. PMI recommends that you have risk as an agenda item at every project meeting. Describe this under the heading of risk timing in the plan.

7. Define your risk rating approach. Also create as detailed a definition of probability and impact as possible. An impact of medium might mean that the project will go on, but will be slowed significantly with over $10,000 being spent to deal with the problem. Write these discrete definitions in the plan, and make sure your team understands them.

8. Create a matrix of how you will rate risks. Describe in the plan the thresholds for determining risk. For instance, you might say you will create plans for only the top 50 percent of the risks identified, or those with a high impact and high probability only. Exercise 5.5 will describe this matrix in more detail.

9. Review your project's stakeholder risk tolerance. You might do this via surveys, by observation, or by asking them to rate impact on a risk. You will find that the tolerances you found while creating the charter have become more defined as you are able to start defining specific risks.

10. Create reporting formats for risk (forms that describe all the data you want to collect and record about risk) and tracking methods so you and your team can easily and consistently manage Risk Identification and responses.

11. Publish the plan to your team and stakeholders, get approval, and make sure everyone understands it through review and training.

12. Review the plan throughout the project to see whether you must make updates to the plan.

In Exercise 5.1, you will learn about the components of the risk management plan and help a telecommunications company implementing a large and complex project decide on the important components of the plan.

Scenario

TPMP is helping Mountain Communications (MC), a well-established telecommunications company, create risk management processes. One of your first assignments is to create risk planning for a project that is replacing two old systems with newer systems to reflect modern technological advances. The old systems will need to continue functioning while data is converted. The new systems are provided by a vendor who is asking MC to be one of the first companies to implement them. The MC company has decided to use a gateway program, which will convert the old data into the formats of the new systems. The company has decided to create this program itself, although several are available on the market. The program is critical to both conversion efforts, and a plan has been created for a phased conversion—the data will not be converted all at once—MC has been able to segment the data to be converted over the next couple of years.

The project has around 100 people working on the conversion and implementation of the new systems. Some of the team members are the program manager, Tasha Smith (whom you are advising to establish the risk management processes); the production manager who is responsible for the current systems and will take over the new systems; a development manager responsible for the gateway program; another development manager responsible for implementing the new systems and managing the conversion plan; the client who will need to maintain current service and use the new system during the conversions; and the vendor who is helping to implement both systems.

Creating Your Risk Management Plan

1. Why should Tasha create a risk management plan?
2. Describe components of the methodology you will suggest Tasha use for this project.
3. Describe what Tasha should do to justify a budget for risk management on the project.
4. Describe the risk management processes you would recommend that Tasha implement and describe how often they should be performed.
5. Describe the roles and responsibilities of the stakeholders participating in the risk management process.

Exercise 5.2: Identifying Risks

The objectives for Exercise 5.2 are:

- Understand risk categories.
- Learn how to identify risks.
- Practice identifying risks on a project.

Background

After you have created a plan for managing risk, the next step in risk management is to identify the risks on your project and enter them into your risk register, which is the form you use to start documenting your risks and how you will deal with them. This step can be done in many ways: You can brainstorm with your team to identify everything you can think of. You can review your documentation to help you think of risks. You can get survey and interview experts to discover risk based on their experience (using the Delphi technique). You can look at previous projects that were similar to yours to capture some of their risks. You can look at industry publications to see if they have identified and classified typical risks. This might include finding risk checklists for the industry. You might perform assumptions analysis or use diagramming techniques to identify risks. The main output from this step is to document all the risks you identify and make sure you describe them and their characteristics well. Not only do you identify risks in the Planning process, you do so throughout the life of the project. As the project progresses, you may identify new risks, and also be able to close out risk you have already identified because they didn't occur and will not based on the phase you are in. This exercise will explore some of the various ways you can categorize and identify risk.

To help you identify risks, and also organize them in similar groupings for more efficient risk response plans, you can use risk categories (also called risk sources) based on a risk breakdown structure (RBS) you identify for your project. You may find these categories from your project's particular application or industry. Look in industry or application publications for a list of categories (which often have actual risks identified with them). Based on each of these categories, your team, executives or sponsors, outside experts, customers, or other stakeholders can further breakdown the risks into sub-categories if appropriate and start identifying risks. You may also use these categories to identify who should own the risk for analysis and possible risk response. Some major risk categories are:

Technical, quality, or performance   Sources of risk can come from major technical complexity or new technology. If your project is counting on a new technology, it could be seriously jeopardized if the technology fails or is delayed in some way. However, opportunity can also come from the risk technological risk: if it succeeds, not only may your project succeed, but you can possibly sell or use the new technology for future projects. Risk can come from low quality standards, or even high ones. For instance, for high quality standards, the time and effort to include the steps for quality can create risk for the schedule, especially if something is found to be wrong. Eventually, however, that risk may be better than releasing an inferior product. Performance goals may also cause risk—for instance, the sponsor may have an unrealistic expectation of the product's performance that cannot be met with the expected schedule or budget.

Project management   There may be risks associated with an undeveloped project management methodology, an inexperienced project manager, or lack of training. Also, the organization may not support project management, or give the project manager enough authority to manage the project as needed. For instance, if the project is to provide a complex medical application, using a junior project manager could be very risky.

Organizational   Many of us realize that many of the greatest risks on a project are based on the organization: frequent changes in an organization's management, a culture that does not support the project, downsizing, or a project that does not fit into the overall strategy can cause many risks. For instance, the project may be moved around to two managerial groups within three months, based on an organizational shake-up. The project team has to re-educate each manager, and discuss how it affects their roles and jobs during this time. Productivity could plummet, and the project could go off schedule.

External Projects often overlook examining external risks: those caused by legal changes, government regulations, market changes, or changes in political influences. They are outside of the influence of the project manager, and often of the organization. For instance, if your project's product launch was based on the assumption that your market's niche would continue expanding, what would the risk be if you started seeing a downward trend?

Besides identifying risks, you will want to identify triggers for each risk. If a piece of equipment is not delivered on time, could that be a trigger for a possible schedule delay? You will also want to identify possible root causes for the risk. This may help you understand possible risk responses and who should own managing the risk event and the responses you identify.

To identify risks:

1. Gather a group of people to identify risks. You may have several groups or iterations to complete this process. Having different perspectives can help you get a much more exhaustive list that will cover all aspects of your project. This step might include management, process, methodology, quality, or technical perspectives. Don't forget, you should identify risks throughout your project.

2. Choose a method or methods that you would like to use to identify risks as described in Chapter 5. You might want to use a few techniques to make sure you identify as many risks as you can or to make your team as comfortable as possible with the process.

3. Review industry or application area publications and the project work breakdown structure to create the categories you would use to identify and organize your risks.

4. List the risks and describe them as clearly as possible. Try to identify the root causes for each risk. You may want to perform some root cause identification to do this.

5. Describe the trigger for each risk if you can identify it.

6. While you and your team are identifying risks, you may identify further actions, some possible responses, or issues with the risks you identify. Perhaps you realize you don't have enough information about a particular risk, and you realize you need to research it. However, keep an open mind, and try to keep from jumping to conclusions too fast about how you would respond to this risk. The next step is analysis, and you might find more information during that process.

7. Document the risks, potential risks, triggers, and categories and further action using a risk register. The following table illustrates the initial fields you might use in a risk register to document risks, triggers, categories, and possible responses. You could add further columns, such as root cause identification, or owners if you think you want to start identifying them now. As you continue building the register, you will be adding ratings and prioritizing risks.

In Exercise 5.2, you will learn how to identify risks by helping a telecommunications company examine the risks in a large and complex project converting two old systems to two new systems.

Risk ID	Risk	Category	Trigger	Response or Comments

Scenario

TPMP is helping Mountain Communications (MC), a well-established telecommunications company, create risk management processes. One of your first assignments is to create a risk management process for a project that is replacing two old systems with two newer systems to reflect modern information technological advances. The systems depend on one another and will have telephone and location information for MC's customers. The old systems will need to continue functioning while data is converted. The new systems are provided by a vendor who is asking MC to be one of the first companies to implement them. The company has decided to use a gateway program, which will convert the old data into the formats of the new systems. The company has decided to create the gateway program itself though several are available on the market. The program is critical to both conversion efforts and a plan has been created for a phased conversion—the data will not be converted all at once—MC has been able to segment the data to be converted over the next couple of years.

The project has around 100 people working on the conversion and implementation of the new systems. Some of the team members are the program manager, Tasha Smith (whom you are advising to establish the risk management processes); the production manager who is responsible for the current systems and will take over the new systems; a development manager responsible for the gateway program; another development manager responsible for implementing the new systems and managing the conversion plan; the client who will need to maintain current service while the new systems are converted; and the vendor who is helping to implement both systems.

Identifying Risks

1. What are some of the categories Tasha might use to identify risks and why?
2. Who should be on the risk identification team, and why?
3. What are the risk identification methods Tasha could use for this project?
4. What are some of the risks that Tasha and the team might identify? Use the table below to complete the exercise. This table contains some of the initial fields you will use for your risk register.

Risk	Category	Trigger

Exercise 5.3: Qualitative Risk Analysis

The objectives for Exercise 5.3 are:

- Understand Qualitative Risk Analysis.
- Learn to analyze risks via a rating matrix and decide which risks to perform quantitative analysis on.
- Practice rating risks via qualitative analysis.
- Practice ranking risks.

Background

Qualitative Risk Analysis is the next step in risk management to help you complete your risk register. It is a process in which you and your risk team determine, through subjective analysis, the probability of your identified risk occurring and the impact if it occurs. Again, this step can be done in many ways, including using some of the same methodologies as Risk Identification and may be done at the same time you identify risks. Although a quantitative analysis step follows this step, you might actually decide to stop your risk management analysis process after qualitative analysis based on the thresholds you established in your risk management plan based on cost, risk priorities, risk tolerance, probability, or impact.

Risk Probability

To decide the probability of whether the risk will occur, you can use a scale of high/medium/low, 0 to100 percent, 1 through 10, or whatever scale you think is appropriate. The team will decide on the scale and define the gradations when you set up your risk management plan, as defined described in Chapter 5.You might define that a one in two chance is high, but a one in a million chance is low depending on what you are measuring.

For instance, you have identified a risk on a construction project—that the dump truck you need on March 15 won't be delivered on time. Your team has determined that the equipment company is very reliable. You have used it for all major equipment rentals, and of the 35 times you have rented from the company, it has been able to deliver the equipment on time all but twice. So you might rate the chance of the equipment not being delivered on time as low. If you can get this accurate of probability data, that is terrific. But, usually, this data is based on the experience and feelings of the team. That is okay in qualitative analysis.

Risk Impact

Next, you need to decide on the impact of each risk. You can use a scale of high/medium/low, 1 through 10, or some other kind of scale that ranks the impact. Again, you will need to have set this up prior to the actual impact rating, and it should be defined in your risk management plan. You might define a high impact as one in which the budget will go over 15 percent or the schedule will be delayed by more than two weeks. You might define it as affecting the quality or disappointing the customer so it jeopardizes the project.

To continue with the previous example, let's say your team is trying to rate the impact of the dump truck not being delivered on time. Your team members do this independently of the probability rating they give the risk. Your team decides the impact would be high. The entire project would be delayed based on the delivery being delayed, even by one day.

Risk Rating Matrix and Risk Ranking

Based on these two factors, impact and probability, you create a ranking for the risks. For instance, risks with low probability and low impact would be rated low risk events. But how would you rank something with low probability but high impact? Should you do something specific about it and rate it a high risk event? And what about a high probability but low impact? That sounds like it might be a lower rated risk event, because if it happens, the actual impact to the project is not so important. So when you look at both factors together, you need to figure out how you want to rate the event. So you might come up with a graph to plot the ratings, or you choose the rankings like those displayed in the Risk Impact Scale Table below: This kind of rating creates an impact scale so you can more consistently see the risk's affect on project objectives. This scale should be created during the risk management planning process, but will be used in the qualitative analysis process.

Probability/Impact	Risk Rating
Low/Low	Low
Low/Medium	Low
Low/High	Medium
Medium/Low	Low
Medium/Medium	Medium
Medium/High	High
High/Low	Medium
High/Medium	High
High/High	High

In this case, you may work on all risks that have a rating of medium and high and just monitor those that are rated low.

Risk Data Quality Assessment

Although you can go through this process with a team of experts that help determine probability and impact, a clear definition and rating of the risk is only as good as the quality of data you have. You may perform analysis to determine if the data for each of your risks and judgment has integrity. If not, you may determine that you want to do further analysis and clarification. In fact, you could add a column to the risk register and for each risk, list a confidence factor for risk analysis data integrity. You may determine that anything under a 60 percent confidence factor needs more research and analysis.

Performing Qualitative Risk Analysis

You and your project team will want to perform Qualitative Risk Analysis to document the probability and impact of the risk. You will perform the following steps to analyze your risks.

1. Gather your risk team.

2. Make sure you have a standard definition of probability and impact.

3. List all the risks previously identified and rank the probability of each occurring.

4. Separately, rank the impact if it were to occur.

5. Determine the quality of the risk assessment.

6. Update the risk register with the findings. The additional columns in the register may be similar to the following matrix.

Risk	Probability	Impact	Score

7. Rank those with a high score, then rearrange the tasks from top rated to low rated.

8. Decide on which risks you would like to continue to perform analysis on by moving onto the next step of risk quantification.

In Exercise 5.3, you will learn how to create a probability and impact matrix to update the risk register based on qualitative analysis as you continue to help the MC company develop its own risk register for a systems replacement project.

Scenario

TPMP is helping Mountain Communications (MC), a well-established telecommunications company, create risk management processes. One of your first assignments is to create a risk management process for a project that is replacing two old systems with newer systems to reflect modern technological advances. The old systems will need to continue functioning while data is converted. The new systems are provided by a vendor who is asking MC to be one of the first companies to implement them. The company has decided to use a gateway program, which will convert the old data into the formats of the new systems. The company has decided to create this program itself although several are available on the market. The program is critical to both conversion efforts and a plan has been created for a phased conversion—the data will not be converted all at once—MC has been able to segment the data to be converted over the next couple of years.

The project has around 100 people working on the conversion and implementation of the new systems. Tasha's team has identified 10 possible risks on the project. They are:

- The gateway program will not convert some of the data in time for the new system to go live on the conversion days.

- The new system will not perform a function the old system performed.

- Upon going live, the new system does not work properly, and end customer orders start backing up.

- The order takers cannot properly work the new system.

- The data gets converted but is wrong upon going live.

- The new system is slow.

- The vendor can't fix a system bug in time for the next scheduled conversion.

- The MC sponsor for the project is promoted to another division.

- Another company hires Tasha away from MC.

- The customer is dissatisfied with the performance of the new systems with a few of the conversions completed.

Qualitative Risk Analysis

For each risk laid out in the Scenario, use the following table to enter your answers.

Risk	Probability	Impact	Score

1. For each risk, help Tasha and her team determine the probability. Use a high/medium/low rating scheme. Do this first, without rating the impact.

2. For each risk, help Tasha and her team determine the impact. Use a high/medium/low rating scheme.

3. Use the Risk Impact Scale Table, to score the risks.

4. Which risks should Tasha work on first and which ones might her team just monitor?

Exercise 5.4: Quantitative Analysis Tools and Techniques

The objectives for Exercise 5.4 are:

- Understand the difference between qualitative and quantitative risk analysis.
- Learn about particular quantitative risk analysis methods.
- Practice using a quantitative risk method using expected value and decision tree analysis.

Background

Quantitative Risk Analysis, the next step in risk management, uses several tools and techniques to numerically analyze the probability and impact of your risks to help determine the probability of accomplishing project objectives. The tools and techniques provide a more detailed and objective analysis than you used in Qualitative Risk Analysis. If you decided to perform this analysis based on impact or probability thresholds you established in your risk management plan, you must have planned this work into your schedule because it will take up a lot of your team's time. You may even need to hire someone with expertise in performing this analysis if you or your team does not have it.

Some of the tools and techniques you might use for Quantitative Risk Analysis are:

- Data gathering and representation techniques including, interviewing (for instance, to gather information for PERT analysis), probability distributions, and expert judgment.
- Quantitative risk analysis and modeling techniques, including sensitivity analysis, modeling and simulation, decision tree analysis, and expected monetary value analysis (EVM).

The results of this analysis help you analyze the targeted costs and schedule of the project and assign confidence levels and probability of achieving project success. The further analysis may also help you re-prioritize your risks and help you discover which tasks have the greatest affect on your schedule's critical path and costs. You might also see trends which allow you to see particular trouble areas in the project or the categories of risk your project has.

This exercise describes some of the tools and techniques of Qualitative Analysis while the following exercise describes how you update a probability and impact matrix with the data you have to prioritize our risks.

Data Gathering Techniques

These techniques are similar to the method in which you bring a team together to brainstorm the risks. But in this case, you may be asking particular subject matter experts to determine the probability and consequences of risks on project objectives. The sessions or questions you ask depend on the kind of information you are trying to retrieve for analysis. One particular interviewing session can lead to PERT analysis when you ask your subject matter experts to provide their pessimistic, most likely, and optimistic estimates for how long it will take to perform a particular task.

Sensitivity Analysis

This form of quantification can help you determine which events have the most impact on a project and how the risk can be changed by varying one variable in an equation or in the project schedule if everything else is kept equal. You may have used sensitivity analysis to a certain extent when you used a computer scheduling tool and added a task to the project schedule to see how it would affect the end date or cost of the project.

Modeling and Simulation

This method of quantitative analysis (an example being Monte Carlo Analysis) runs a model over and over again with different variables to see how it might change the overall project and its risks. Many software programs can be added to a computer scheduling application to run this simulation process automatically.

Decision Tree Analysis and Expected Monetary Value

Decision tree analysis is a form of quantitative analysis that represents the decisions that can be made for paths that be taken based on probability on a graphical "tree." It is often used with expected value to determine the various monetary impacts for the decisions you might make on your project. It multiplies probability times impact to create expected value. This exercise will focus on this form of quantitative analysis. The following formula describes expected value:

Risk Probability × Amount at Stake (or Impact) = Expected Value

If you have several possibilities for an outcome, the probability of each of the cases must add up to one. The following table shows you an expected value table when you have four possible choices in a decision.

Probability	Amount at Stake	Expected Value
.3	50,000	15,000
.2	30,000	6,000
.4	(20,000)	(8,000)
.1	75,000	7,500
1	—	20,500

Similarly, you can illustrate expected value for a decision on a decision tree. For instance, you have two choices: You may release your new Easy-Start Snow Blower in January or in March. You know you may have more success of getting all the kinks out of the product in March, whereas you have some doubt you can fix all bugs by January and thus might experience a loss of profits due to poor sales. Your probability of a positive (success) or negative (failure) outcome is calculated on both. If you release in March, the probability of success is .7 with an expected value of $200,000. The expected value of failure is ($30,000). If you release in January, the probability of success is .4 with an expected value of $350,000 (you project more sales in January than March). The expected value of failure is ($75,000). The following figure illustrates a decision tree for the Easy-Start Snow Blower project.

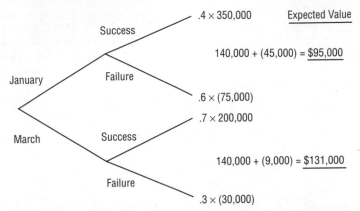

In this case, releasing in March is a better financial projection despite the fact that the sales could be a great deal better in January. If the organization decides to use financial gain as the basis for decisions, then releasing in March is the best decision.

In Exercise 5.4, you will help the MC company use decision tree analysis and expected value to perform quantitative analysis on its new telecommunications system.

Now that you know what a decision tree analysis is and how you can apply expected value, if you need to perform a decision tree analysis, you can follow the steps below:

1. Decide on the risks and decisions you would like to analyze in greater depth based on the work you did in qualitative analysis.

2. Use statistical analysis to determine numerical probability for the decisions. Use market research for possible value/impact for each branch of the decision tree.

3. Create the diagram showing the decision paths with probability and impact.

4. For each branch, multiply probability and impact. Add up the results to achieve expected value for each discrete decision.

5. Review and decide the best path for the decision. Sometimes, risk tolerances for your stakeholders become visible in reviewing this method. For instance, in the above illustration, your stakeholders may actually choose to release in January because of the greater opportunity for sales. This decision would indicate they have a high tolerance for risk.

Scenario

TPMP is helping Mountain Communications (MC), a well-established telecommunications company, create risk management processes. One of your first assignments is to create a risk management process for a project that is replacing two old systems with newer systems to reflect modern technological advances. The company must make a decision regarding the risks of either buying or making a gateway program that will convert the data from the old systems to the new systems. You are helping the program manager, Tasha Smith, create quantitative analysis processes for making decisions. The project team, with the help of market research and company financial analysts, has come up with the following information:

- If the company buys the gateway product, it has a 70 percent change of success with a potential impact of $250,000. The impact of failure is ($20,000).

- If the company makes the gateway project in-house, it has a 50 percent chance of success with a potential impact of $500,000. The impact of failure is ($150,000).

The project team feels that building the gateway product in-house can be a great opportunity for the company, since it is expecting to upgrade several other systems within the next 10 years. The team members feel they may be able to reuse the product for these efforts and perhaps even sell it to other telecommunications companies if it proves efficient and accurate.

Quantitative Analysis Methods

1. Create the expected value table for the exercise above using the following tables.

For Buy Decision:

Probability	Amount at Stake	Expected Value

For Make Decision:

Probability	Amount at Stake	Expected Value

2. Create the decision tree for the exercise above.

3. What is the best decision for making or buying the gateway system based on this analysis and why?

4. What are the quantitative tools and techniques?

Exercise 5.5: Quantitative Risk Analysis—Updating the Risk Probability and Impact Matrix

The objectives for Exercise A5.5 are:

- Understand the quantitative probability and impact matrix updates for Quantitative Risk Analysis.

- Practice rating risks via quantitative analysis.

Background

By using the tools and techniques described in Exercise 5.4, you will be able to apply the numerical probability of your identified risks occurring and the impact on your project cost and schedule objectives. In Exercise 5.3, you learned to create the scales or measurements you will use for probability (such as 0 to 100 percent or high/medium/low) and impact (such as 0 to 10, or high/medium/low). You would update the Risk Register with the information obtained during that process. In Quantitative Risk Analysis, you might use the same probability scales, but one of the most effective means of determining schedule or cost impact is applying dollars or timelines on the impact as gathered from using various Quantitative Analysis tools and techniques.

As a note, you may choose not to perform Quantitative Risk Analysis on all of your risks, but only your most probable or high-impact risks. However, if you do perform this analysis, it will be more precise, and help you determine the true costs of risk response and justify any actions you may take to offset those risks.

Applying Quantitative Risk Data to a Probability and Impact Matrix

Although you may use the same probability scales from qualitative risk analysis, you will put more precise scales on the impact of the risk event. For instance, if a construction team does not receive a bulldozer on time for work to begin, it will cost the wages of everyone on the job not doing anything, and the wages for each day the bulldozer is not on site. Say this is a cost of $1,500 per day. With a probability of 40 percent, this becomes a risk expected value of $600. This tells you much more about the relative cost of the risk occurring (or maybe even the opportunity you could gain), than just rating items high, medium, or low. You can start re-rating the risks with much more substantial emphasis on their real impact to the objectives of the project.

The following tables shows you how you might update the risk probability and impact matrix for the construction project, The team has listed risks and quantified their impact and probability based on more quantitative analysis. The following table shows you the results of the construction team's efforts.

Risk	Probability	Impact	Value
Bulldozer is not delivered on time	40%	$1,500	$600
Rain stops work on any given day	20%	$6,000	$1,200
Customer disapproves the quality of work when first room is being painted	30%	$15,000	$4,500

Risk	Probability	Impact	Value
Permits are not received on time	50%	$6,000	$3,000
Strike occurs (impact per day)	10%	$7,000	$700

With this data, you can start identifying the most important risks. For instance, for each day of rain, the impact is $1,200. With a few days of rain, this amount can easily become one of the biggest impacts. Thus, the team needs to think of things that can be done to lessen the impact. And with a 50 percent possibility of permits not being received on time, the team needs to look at ways of reducing the probability of that happening. But, most important, it looks like the customer's disapproval of the quality can have a big impact. Perhaps, the team will want to build in a customer quality check into the process way before the rooms get painted. You will look at how a team might come up with risk responses to reduce or mitigate these impacts in Exercise 5.7.

Updating the Risk Register for Quantitative Risk Analysis

If your team decides to perform quantitative analysis and update the Risk Register with the analysis data, the following steps will help you create a consistent and organized approach to the analysis.

1. Gather your risk team again.
2. Make sure you have a standard definition of probability and impact and use any quantitative information you might have gained in expected value, sensitivity analysis, Monte Carlo Analysis, simulation, or decision tree analysis you might have performed (see Exercise 5.4).
3. List all the risks previously identified and rank the probability of each occurring using a numerical equivalent for probability.
4. Separately, rank the impact if it were to occur using a numerical equivalent for impact, such as dollars.
5. Enter the findings in the risk matrix and multiply the information to get the expected value.
6. Rank those with a high score, then rearrange the tasks from top rated to low rated.
7. Decide on which risks you would like to continue to create responses for.
8. Determine and document the confidence level and your probability of achieving cost and time objectives of the project.

Scenario

TPMP is helping Mountain Communications (MC), a well-established telecommunications company, create risk management processes. One of your first assignments is to help Tasha Smith, the program manager on the project, create a risk management process for replacing two old systems with newer systems to reflect modern technological advances. The old systems will need to continue functioning while data is converted. The new systems are provided by a vendor who is asking MC to be one of the first companies to implement them. The company has decided to use a gateway program, which will convert the old data into the formats of the new systems. The company has decided to create this program itself although several are available on the market. The program is critical to both conversion efforts and a plan has been created for a phased conversion—the data will not be converted all at once—MC has been able to segment the data to be converted over the next couple of years.

The project has around 100 people working on the conversion and implementation of the new systems. Tasha's team has identified 10 possible risks on the project. They are listed in a matrix created earlier for the Qualitative Risk Analysis and are repeated in the table below for quantitative analysis. The team has completed some quantitative expected value analysis and has decided on the following probabilities/impact.

Quantitative Risk Analysis—Risk Impact/Probability Matrix

1. Complete the expected value in the following table.

Risk	Probability	Impact	Value
1. The gateway program will not convert some of the data in time for the new system to go live on the conversion days.	40%	50,000	
2. The new system will not perform a function the old system performed.	20%	20,000	
3. Upon going live, the new system does not work properly, and customer orders start backing up.	50%	60,000	
4. The order takers cannot properly work the new system.	60%	100,000	
5. The data gets converted but is wrong upon going live.	10%	250,000	
6. The new system is slow.	15%	25,000	
7. The vendor can't fix a system bug in time for the next scheduled conversion.	45%	12,000	
8. The MC sponsor for the project is promoted to another division.	20%	65,000	
9. Another company hires Tasha away from MC.	25%	50,000	
10. The customer is dissatisfied with the performance of the new systems with a few of the conversions completed.	40%	30,000	

2. What are the top three risks Tasha's team should work on and why?
3. Why is quantitative analysis better than qualitative analysis?
4. Should quantitative analysis always be performed?

Exercise 5.6: Types of Risk Response Strategies

The objectives for Exercise 5.6 are:

- Learn the various risk response strategies for threats and opportunities.
- Practice recognizing the risk response strategies.

Background

Once you have identified analyzed and prioritized your risks, you want to do something about your higher priority risks. In fact, while you analyze the risks, you might come up with ways to respond to the risks by reducing the chance of project threats occurring or maximize the chance of opportunities occurring. You can use several strategies to help in the process of reducing threats or enhancing opportunities. You may use the following tools and techniques for creating risk responses:

Avoid　This is a response strategy for a negative risk or threat where you attempt to overcome the risk event by trying to stray away from or eliminate it altogether. You do something to your plan, so that the risk simply won't occur. For instance, if a construction project has a risk that the dump truck won't be delivered on time and the project could be delayed and money lost, perhaps you would reduce the scope of the project to eliminate the elaborate landscaping part of the project that required the dump truck.

Transfer　Most of us understand insurance—you pay someone to protect against the risk of possible losses. Risk transference is a response strategy for a negative risk or threat where you transfer the responsibility for the risk to someone else. In project management, insurance is one response using transference, but you might also transfer the risk by hiring a vendor who is more adept at the particular work itself. For instance, in a construction project, a project manager would probably subcontract with an electrical company who can do the building's wiring. This transfers the risk of doing the work to someone else rather than the construction company hiring or training electricians themselves. Transference does not necessarily eliminate the risk—and in fact, the company who takes on the risk should be insured itself, otherwise, your project could still suffer great consequences if the risk occurs.

Mitigate　This risk strategy for a negative risk or threat is almost like risk avoidance, but in this case, you may only be able to reduce the probability of the risk or the impact to the project or its objectives. For instance, if the risk of rain would delay your project, you would add extra days into your project schedule, to "pad" it for rain days. Many times, this involves building more budget or adding more tasks to your schedule to reduce your risk. That's why risk management is a planning process—by doing it up front, you can get important items built into your schedule before they become difficult to manage.

Exploit　You will want to use the exploit risk strategy for a positive risk or opportunity to ensure an opportunity occurs. For instance, let's say you are developing a movie that relies on a new technical innovation, that if realized, you may win an Oscar for outstanding technical achievement, but you may be able to patent and sell the new technology. If so, you will want to exploit the opportunity by putting the most creative and talented crew on the development of the technology to increase the likelihood of success.

Share   Risk sharing is like the transfer strategy but for a positive risk or opportunity. This is often used in contracts to promote a positive vendor relationship and a sharing of rewards for some aspect of the project. For instance, using the same example of a new technical innovation for moviemaking, you may subcontract the creation of this new technology. The contract may be a joint venture, or contain a profit-sharing clause.

Enhance   As mitigation tries to reduce the probability or impact of a risk, the enhance strategy tries to increase the probability or impact of a positive risk or opportunity by maximizing the cause of the opportunity and supporting its triggers. For instance, for the technological innovation for the movie, you might start marketing the innovation to start seeing if other movie productions would be interested in using it.

Acceptance   There are many positive or negative responses to risks that are so expensive that trying to avoid, insure, mitigate, exploit, share, or enhance them might be as expensive as the project itself. There may be other risks where the expense is so small, and the risk can be so easily handled, it is not worthwhile making major changes to the project plan or schedule. This response strategy is called acceptance: you are willing to take the consequences of the risk were it to occur. For instance, it might be possible that you would have the flood of the century that would wipe out your project, and yet you can't get flood insurance in your city. Since you live in a very dry region, with no major floods, your team might decide to accept the risk of flooding and deal with it if it occurs. Your team would do well, though, to create a contingency plan if flooding does occur, which is discussed next.

Contingent response strategies   Contingency planning is a plan of action if the risk event occurs. You may have created a response strategy using mitigation for the risk event, but the event could still happen anyway. You might have decided to accept the risk, and you need a plan to deal with it when it happens. You and your team will create a plan of action to deal with the risk, but only if the event occurs. For instance, on a construction project, perhaps there is a threat of a strike by dump truck drivers during a time when you are expecting to need numerous dump trucks. You might create a contingency plan to hire temporary workers who have experience driving dump trucks. You decide to do nothing proactively to deal with the risk, but if it happens, you have a plan of action to implement immediately.

Understanding the various risk strategies can help you and your project team create risk responses that can have quite an impact on your project plan. To help you think about what you need to do when creating risk responses, perform the following steps.

1.   After the majority of risk analysis is complete, gather your risk team again.

2.   Identify the risks that you have prioritized to provide responses.

3.   List the risk response strategies to help you think of possible responses. Start detailing the steps you would take for each response based on the response types you have chosen. You may choose more than one response type and plan for a risk.

4.   For each response, also detail the contingency plan(s).

5.   Document the response and contingency plans. Exercise 5.7 will describe this documentation in more detail.

In this exercise, you will help the MC company's project team recognize various risk response strategies as you consult with them on best risk management processes.

Scenario

TPMP is helping Mountain Communications (MC), a well-established telecommunications company, create risk management processes. One of your first assignments is to create a risk management process for a project that is replacing two old systems with newer systems to reflect modern technological advances. The old systems will need to continue functioning while data is converted. The new systems are provided by a vendor who is asking MC to be one of the first companies to implement them. The company has decided to use a gateway program, which will convert the old data into the formats of the new systems. The company has decided to create this program itself although several are available on the market. The program is critical to both conversion efforts and a plan has been created for a phased conversion—the data will not be converted all at once—MC has been able to segment the data to be converted over the next couple of years. The project has around 100 people working on the conversion and implementation of the new systems.

Types of Risk Responses

1. What response strategies does Tasha's team have to choose from?

2. The team has decided that one of the biggest negative risks for this project is that the in-house gateway program will not work. They have decided that they will create a prototype of the gateway, and test it on data they would convert. What kind of risk response strategy is this?

3. The team has decided that there is not much it can do if the office is closed down for several days due to a large snowstorm shutting down the city. What kind of risk response strategy is this?

4. The team has decided that it would be a good idea to hire an outsourcing agency to run the operating systems for the new computer systems since the MC company has decided to reduce computer operations personnel. What kind of risk response strategy is this?

5. The team has decided that although it will accept the risk of the office shutting down for several days, team members could work at home for the days the office is shut down. The team has created steps for taking action if the office does shut down. What kind of response strategy is this?

6. The team has decided that the requirements for the functionality for one of the systems is not very clear. The team has decided to hold another requirements session to eliminate this risk. What type of risk response is this?

7. The team has decided to hire a vendor with a reputation for engineering excellence to develop the gateway system. The contract they create is a joint venture contract. What risk response strategy have they chosen to use?

Exercise 5.7: Risk Responses

The objectives for Exercise 5.7 are:

- Understand how you update a risk register with risk response plan.

- Create risk responses for prioritized risks.

Background

The most important output of the risk management process is the documented risk responses to indicate how you will deal with risks if they occur. While identifying, analyzing, and rating the risks, and deciding which ones to work on, you and your team will continue building your risk register: a documented and living plan for dealing with the risks. Among many possible items you can document on the risk register are:

- Risks, their root causes, triggers, and risk categories
- Owner
- Response strategy
- Actual response steps you would take and budget for the response
- Contingency plan and possible contingency actions
- Secondary risks, which are new risks that might have been identified based on the risk response plans

The owner will be responsible for implementing the response or the contingency. And one of the overlooked processes with the risk register is continual review of it by the project team during execution and control of the project. In fact, as the team members continue to review risks, or come up with new risk responses, they may identify new risks for which they need to create risk responses. For instance, if you decided that you will avoid a risk by creating a prototype system, you may have created a new risk that management will want to use the prototype instead of creating a new system based on the prototype as originally planned.

Creating a documented risk register is the most important aspect of risk planning. The following sample table and suggested steps will help you and your team create a risk register that you can apply to your project.

1. First, decide on how you will document your risk register. You should have done this initially when creating your risk management plan (see Exercise A5.1). The table you create might looks something like the table below:

ID	Risk	Owner	Risk Strategy	Risk Response	Plan Budget	Contingency	Contingency Budget	Secondary Risk

2. Make sure the risks and their analysis are documented, and gather the team to review the list.

3. Discuss with the team the various risk responses you could use for the risk (perhaps using risk strategies to help you do so). Decide on the best response or responses for each risk.

4. Document each risk response in detail. The risk owner may do this or the team may provide input. Don't forget to create a contingency plan for each risk if it is appropriate.

5. Analyze how the risk affects the work breakdown structure, and add appropriate risk responses into the schedule or budget. Change the project plan or other areas of the project as necessary based on the risk responses.

6. Add any secondary risks and risk responses based on any risk responses your team decides to implement.

7. Review the risk responses and contingency plans and ensure the owner and any other implementer understands it and knows what to do.

8. Review the risks and their proposed responses regularly to see if the risk has occurred and if the plans are still applicable.

9. Identify any new risks based on continued risk identification meetings you hold with the project team.

In this exercise, you will help the MC company complete the risk register with responses for some of the risks it has identified through risk management processes you helped it create.

Scenario

TPMP is helping Mountain Communications (MC), a well-established telecommunications company, create risk management processes. One of your first assignments is to create a risk management process for a project that is replacing two old systems with newer systems to reflect more modern technological advances. The old systems will need to continue functioning while data is converted. The new systems are provided by a vendor who is asking MC to be one of the first companies to implement them. The company has decided to use a gateway program, which will convert the old data into the formats of the new systems. The company has decided to create this program itself although several are available on the market. The program is critical to both conversion efforts and a plan has been created for a phased conversion—the data will not be converted all at once—MC has been able to segment the data to be converted over the next couple of years.

The project has around 100 people working on the conversion and implementation of the new systems. Some of the team members are the program manager, Tasha Smith (whom you are advising to establish the risk management processes); the production manager who is responsible for the current systems and will take over the new systems; a development manager responsible for the gateway program; another development manager responsible for implementing the new systems and managing the conversion plan; the client who will need to maintain current service while the new systems are converted; and the vendor who is helping to implement both systems.

Creating a Risk Response Plan

1. What are some of the responses for the risks to Tasha's project? Complete the following table by choosing five of the risks and entering the response strategy, owner, and a possible response for each.

Risk	Owner	Response Strategy	Plan
The gateway program will not convert some of the data in time for the new system to go live on the conversion days.			
The new system will not perform a function the old system performed.			
Upon going live, the new system does not work properly, and customer orders start backing up.			
The order takers cannot properly work the new system.			
The data gets converted but is wrong upon going live.			
The new system is slow.			
The vendor can't fix a system bug in time for the next scheduled conversion.			
The MC sponsor for the project is promoted to another division.			
Another company hires Tasha away from MC.			
The new gateway technology can be sold to other companies.			

2. What are some of the contingency plans for Tasha's project? Complete the following table with at least five contingency plans (they do not need be the same ones for which you chose to create responses).

Risk	Contingency Plan
The gateway program will not convert some of the data in time for the new system to go live on the conversion days.	
The new system will not perform a function the old system performed.	
Upon going live, the new system does not work properly, and customer orders start backing up.	
The order takers cannot properly work the new system.	
The data gets converted but is wrong upon going live.	
The new system is slow.	
The vendor can't fix a system bug in time for the next scheduled conversion.	
The MC sponsor for the project is promoted to another division.	
Another company hires Tasha away from MC.	
The customer is dissatisfied with the performance of the new systems with a few of the conversions completed.	

3. When the team creates a response, it creates a new risk. What does the team need to do with the new risk?

Answers to Section 5 Exercises

Answers to Exercise 5.1

Your answers may be somewhat different, but the following answers provide a guide.

1. Tasha needs to create a risk management plan in order to help her and the team create a strategy and methodology for dealing with risk on the project. The team members and stakeholders need to have common expectations and objectives for what they will be doing, when they will be doing it, why, and who will be involved. By setting the standards up front, the team won't use precious time later trying to figure out the processes and will understand the rating system to objectively rate risks.

2. Since this is a very complex project, with a number of stakeholders, and dependencies for successful conversions, you recommend she consider a highly organized and regular process for risk management. You suggest that the team consider expert risk management consultation in setting up the processes. You might suggest Tasha consider some outside auditing of the technology and conversion approach to determine risks, analyze them, and determine plans for the risks. You might suggest to Tasha that she ask the vendor to implement risk management processes, as well.

3. To justify a budget for risk management on the project, Tasha will need to create a work breakdown structure of all the deliverables from the risk management process and determine resources needed for the activities. For instance, possible deliverables are a risk management plan, Risk Identification, risk analysis, and a risk response plan. She would need to include the deliverables in the schedule, and estimate the budget based on the resources costs and time. In this case, if she brings in expert help, she will need to include the costs of the vendor or consultants. She needs to consider all the team's time in meetings, analysis, and developing risk responses.

4. You might suggest Tasha explore initial risk management planning and team organization: two hours for three weeks. Initial Risk Identification: once a week for a month (during the planning phase). Analysis of the risks: an average of two hours for each selected risk for analysis. Reviewing the risk list (monitoring and controlling risk): 20 minutes in a weekly status meeting.

5. The following might be the roles and responsibilities.
   - Program manager: risk manager (since the project is complex, you might suggest a separate manager responsible for the overall risk process).
   - Production manager: old systems risk analysis and risk response implementer.
   - Vendor: new systems risk analysis and risk response implementer.
   - Gateway manager: gateway risk analysis and risk response implementer.
   - New systems manager and conversion manager: new systems risk analysis and risk response implementer. This particular role is very complex. Tasha might want to look

at ensuring this role is broken into two responsibilities: new systems and conversion, with a different analysis and response manager for each.

Answers to Exercise 5.2

Your answers may be somewhat different, but the following answers provide a guide.

1. Tasha might use risk categories based on data she could find in information technology publications. Since this is a major systems project, you would want to use the expertise and experience of others who have managed complex systems projects. You also might suggest she use the technical category, since the entire project is very complex due to new systems and the gateway program. Tasha would want to organize all identified risks into this category, and she would want some of her most senior technical people to manage those risks. Another category you might use is project management risks since the project has several managers ensuring their portions of the project are completed (the development manager, conversion manager, vendor project manager, etc.).

2. The members of your risk team should include Tasha Smith, the production manager; the gateway development manager; the new systems and conversion development manager; the client; and the vendor. Tasha might also include some technical experts, maybe some folks from other projects that were similar, and functional experts from other parts of the organization. All of these people need to identify risks that are important to their portions of the project or area of expertise.

3. Some of the risk identification methods Tasha could use for this project include documentation reviews, brainstorming, surveying and interviewing experts perhaps using the Delphi technique or the nominal group technique, checklists, assumptions analysis, SWOT analysis (strengths, weaknesses, opportunities, and threats) or diagramming techniques. You might recommend she use a couple of methods to ensure she gets a more exhaustive list than if she uses only one method.

4. Considering some of the risks that Tasha and the team might identify, your answer should look like the table below.

Risk	Category	Trigger
The new system can't perform the same function as the old system.	Technical	Testing shows a function will not be performed.
The vendor decides to stop supporting one of the systems.	Organizational	The vendor starts to "lose interest" in helping with solving issues with the system.
The gateway program does not convert some of the data accurately.	Technical	Testing shows data is not converting properly.

Risk	Category	Trigger
One of the new systems does not allow for data conversion as fast as the other new system.	Technical	Testing shows data cannot be converted as well in one system in the same time frame as the other.
The vendor cannot fix a major bug in one of the systems, which delays the conversion schedule.	Technical	The time frame for a bug to be fixed comes and goes so that the conversion schedule is in jeopardy.

Answers to Exercise 5.3

The following table shows the risk rating matrix that Tasha and her team completed which they will use to update their risk register. Your answers may be somewhat different but the answers provided may be used as a guide.

Risk	Probability	Impact	Score
The gateway program will not convert some of the data in time for the new system to go live on the conversion days.	Medium	High	High
The new system will not perform a function the old system performed.	Low	Medium	Low
Upon going live, the new system does not work properly, and customer orders start backing up.	Medium	High	High
The order takers cannot properly work the new system.	Medium	High	High
The data gets converted but is wrong upon going live.	Low	High	Medium
The new system is slow.	Low	Medium	Low
The vendor can't fix a system bug in time for the next scheduled conversion.	Medium	Low	Low
The MC sponsor for the project is promoted to another division.	Low	High	Medium
Another company hires Tasha away from MC.	Low	Medium	Low
The customer is dissatisfied with the performance of the new systems with a few of the conversions completed.	Medium	Medium	Medium

1. The table above shows you the probability ratings for each risk Tasha faces.
2. The table above shows you impact ratings determined by Tasha's group.
3. The table above shows you the scores determined by Tasha's group.
4. Tasha and her team might now show the risks according to the order below based on the highest to lowest scores. The team may decide to move on to quantitative analysis for the high and medium risks only. They may monitor the low risks without doing quantitative analysis.

Risk	Probability	Impact	Score
The gateway program will not convert some of the data in time for the new system to go live on the conversion days.	Medium	High	High
Upon going live, the new system does not work properly, and customer orders start backing up.	Medium	High	High
The order takers cannot properly work the new system.	Medium	High	High
The data gets converted but is wrong upon going live.	Low	High	Medium
The MC sponsor for the project is promoted to another division.	Low	High	Medium
The customer is dissatisfied with the performance of the new systems with a few of the conversions completed.	Medium	Medium	Medium
The new system is slow.	Low	Medium	Low
The vendor can't fix a system bug in time for the next scheduled conversion.	Medium	Low	Low
Another company hires Tasha away from MC.	Low	Medium	Low
The new system will not perform a function the old system performed.	Low	Medium	Low

Answers to Exercise 5.4

For question 1, your answers should match the table. For the remaining questions, your answers may be somewhat different but the answers provided may be used as a guide.

1. Your answers for creating expected value tables for the make/buy decision for the gateway system should look like the following.

For Buy Decision:

Probability	Amount at Stake	Expected Value
.7	$250,000	$175,000
.3	($20,000)	($6,000)
Total = 1	—	$169,000

For Make Decision:

Probability	Amount at Stake	Expected Value
.5	$500,000	$250,000
.5	($150,000)	($75,000)
Total = 1	—	$175,000

2. Your answer for creating the decision tree analysis for the make/buy decision for the gateway system should look like the following illustration.

3. The best decision is to make the gateway system for two reasons. First, the expected value is higher for the "make" decision, though not significantly. Second, the loss potential is much higher, but the team has decided that the opportunity for future use of the product if they make it in-house is much greater.

4. Quantitative tools and techniques are interviewing, sensitivity analysis, simulation, and decision tree analysis.

Answers to Exercise 5.5

For question 1 and 2, your answers should match the answers provided. For the remaining questions, your answers may be somewhat different but the answers provided may be used as a guide.

1. The following table provides the expected value for the risks.

Risk	Probability	Impact	Value
1. The gateway program will not convert some of the data in time for the new system to go live on the conversion days.	40%	50,000	$20,000
2. The new system will not perform a function the old system performed.	20%	20,000	$4,000
3. Upon going live, the new system does not work properly, and customer orders start backing up.	50%	60,000	$30,000
4. The order takers cannot properly work the new system.	60%	100,000	$60,000
5. The data gets converted but is wrong upon going live.	10%	250,000	$25,000
6. The new system is slow.	15%	25,000	$3,750
7. The vendor can't fix a system bug in time for the next scheduled conversion.	45%	12,000	$5,400
8. The MC sponsor for the project is promoted to another division.	20%	65,000	$13,000
9. Another company hires Tasha away from MC.	25%	50,000	$12,500
10. The customer is dissatisfied with the performance of the new systems with a few of the conversions completed	40%	30,000	$12,000

2. Tasha's team should work on risks 3, 4, and 5. They have the highest expected value of all of the risks. In mitigating or reducing these risks, they could save the company $115,000. All the other risks combined would add up to $70,650.

3. Quantitative analysis is better than qualitative analysis because it provides more objective data. The project team can make better decisions and perhaps achieve more support from management in the risk management process they will need to reduce the risks.

4. Quantitative analysis, although more objective than qualitative analysis, does not always need to be performed, although it is recommended for the top risks of your project. It takes a long time to perform quantitative analysis. Sometimes it's important to invest less time and money. So it depends on what your project team has decided to do.

Answers to Exercise 5.6

Your answers may be somewhat different, but the following answers provide a guide.

1. Tasha's team can choose from the following strategies: avoid, transfer, mitigate, exploit, share, enhance, accept, and contingent response strategy. It also should create a contingency plan for each risk it has chosen to deal with.

2. Creating a gateway prototype is a mitigation risk response type. This would help reduce the probability of the gateway's failure. The team would add tasks to the work breakdown structure and the project schedule to create this prototype.

3. If team members have decided they can do little about the office shutting down for several days, they have chosen acceptance as the risk response type.

4. Since team members have decided that it would be a good idea to hire an outsourcing agency to run the hardware for the new computer systems, they have chosen a risk response strategy of transference because they will transfer the risk of operating the computers to someone else.

5. The team members created a contingency plan as a response when they decided that, although they will accept the risk of the office shutting down for several days, they could work at home for the days the office is shut down.

6. The team has responded with an avoid risk response strategy by holding another requirements session to eliminate the risk of the requirements not being clear.

7. The team has chosen two risk response strategies for the opportunity. They have decided to use the exploit risk strategy to ensure the opportunities' success by having the best talent to produce the software, and they are using the share risk strategy by creating a joint venture with the vendor.

Answers to Exercise 5.7

Your answers may be somewhat different, but the following answers provide a guide.

1. To assign the owner and describe the response strategy and plan for five of the risks, you might complete the table according to the following answers.

Risk	Owner	Response Strategy	Plan
The gateway program will not convert some of the data in time for the new system to go live on the conversion days.	Gateway development manager	Mitigate	Add tasks to the project plan to perform test conversions with the data one month prior to conversion date.
The new system will not perform a function the old system performed.	Production manager	Avoid	Hold a requirements review session to ensure that all functions of the old system will be performed in the new system.

Risk	Owner	Response Strategy	Plan
Upon going live, the new system does not work properly, and customer orders start backing up.	Client	Accept	Use a contingency plan
The order takers cannot properly work the new system.	Program manager	Transfer	Hire a training firm to create a training plan, document, and perform training to help the order takers learn the new system.
The data gets converted but is wrong upon going live.	New systems and conversion manager	Mitigate	Create tasks in the plan to test the first 50 orders, to ensure the data is correct during the weekend before the conversion goes "live." If there are issues, create a rollback plan.
The new system is slow.	New systems and conversion manager	Mitigate	Add tasks to the project plan to create performance testing on the system prior to production.
The vendor can't fix a system bug in time for the next scheduled conversion.	Vendor	Mitigate	Add tasks to the project plan to review test plans early in vendor testing and also schedule a client review for the system functionality testing. Also, create a clause in the contract that penalizes the vendor for delays it causes.
The MC sponsor for the project is promoted to another division.	Program manager	Transfer	Create a "contract" with several executives besides the sponsor on the project to help rally support through this second tier of sponsors.
Another company hires Tasha away from MC.	MC company management	Accept	Create a contingency plan to find a replacement quickly, including identifying some good potential replacements within the company.
The new gateway technology can be sold to other companies.	Marketing department	Enhance	Start marketing the system to see if other organizations would be interested in using it..

2. To describe the contingency plan for the five risks you have chosen, you might have completed the table according to the following possible answers.

Risk	Contingency Plan
The gateway program will not convert some of the data in time for the new system to go live on the conversion days.	Make up the time delay by adding the conversions to a future conversion time frame. This will increase the risk for that future conversion, however.
The new system will not perform a function the old system performed.	Create a manual workaround until the function can be added, if the functioning is not delayed significantly. This may also require hiring of retired employees temporarily if this missing function cannot be implemented in a timely fashion. If the function is significant, the conversions will be delayed until the function is added.
Upon going live, the new system does not work properly, and customer orders start backing up.	Set up extra shifts with retired employees temporarily to help reduce the backlog.
The order takers cannot properly work the new system.	Be ready to send an appropriate number of trainers or employees familiar with the systems to the order taker's site to train on the job.
The data gets converted but is wrong upon going live.	Hire extra employees who can review and clean up the data quickly before the order is completed.
The new system is slow.	Implement a customer education campaign to alert the customers that their orders will take longer than usual when the order takers are processing the orders with the customers.
The vendor can't fix a system bug in time for the next scheduled conversion.	Delay the current conversion and roll it into a future one. Implement the contract clause that penalizes the vendor for delays to conversions due to vendor issues.
The MC sponsor for the project is promoted to another division.	Immediately set up a communication campaign to let management know the importance of the project, and start soliciting a new sponsor from previously identified candidates immediately.

Risk	Contingency Plan
Another company hires Tasha away from MC.	Identify good potential replacements within the company, and have management aligned to make the replacement quickly.
The new gateway technology can be sold to other companies.	Although a contingency plan may not be necessary for an opportunity, to take full advantage of an opportunity if a company should show interested in the gateway technology, you could bring in a marketing team to create a pricing and implementation strategy for out-of-house deployment.

3. When the team identifies a new risk because of a response created for a previously identified risk, the team needs to go through the entire identification, analysis, and risks response planning process that Risk Management Planning requires. Based on the analysis and ranking, the team decides if it warrants response or not.

Resource Planning

The following exercises are presented in this section:

- Exercise 6.1: Deciding on Contract Types
- Exercise 6.2: Creating a Procurement Management Plan
- Exercise 6.3: Creating a Contract Statement of Work (SOW)
- Exercise 6.4: Evaluating and Selecting the Vendor
- Exercise 6.5: Creating a Responsibility Assignment Matrix (RAM)
- Exercise 6.6: Creating a Staffing Management Plan
- Exercise 6.7: Activity Sequencing
- Exercise 6.8: Activity Resource Estimating

Exercise 6.1: Deciding on Contract Types

The objectives for Exercise 6.1 are as follows:

- Introduce contract concepts.
- Understand the most common contract types.
- Practice recognizing contract types.
- Practice applying contract types to different situations.

Background

Often, project teams cannot do all the work that must be performed to accomplish the scope of the work. The project needs someone else to do the work because it might be more cost effective, the organization lacks a particular expertise, or another organization simply has the goods you need for the product. Whenever you have someone outside of your organization (also known as a vendor, contractor, or supplier) provide goods or services on your project, you will need to create processes to manage them and agreements to set expectations for the work they will provide. When the organization is not a part of your own company, the agreements must be made via a contract. A contract provides an agreement that one party will provide goods or services and the other party will pay for them (in money or some other kind of trade of equal value). It also provides for legal recourse for disputes that may occur between the two parties. Most of us don't really think about contracts as anything but a lot of "legalese," but you can actually choose the type of contract for your project to help create the results you want. Your understanding of the different types may help you create the best contract for your project.

Contracts also have a certain amount of risk associated with them for the contractor or the buyer of the services or goods. That is, based on whether it is fixed fee or cost reimbursable, either the contractor or the buyer might have more risk in recouping their costs or making a profit. There are many creative variations of contracts these days, especially if you want to create incentives for your contractors, but most contracts are based on two basic contract types:

fixed price (also known as lump sum) and cost reimbursable. A fixed price contract involves one predetermined fee for the goods or services you and the contractor agree on. You can set incentives or penalties in addition to that fixed price. Cost reimbursable is a floating price contract, based on the costs the contractor incurs. Again, you can set up incentives or penalties in addition to the costs. You can also have a third kind of contract type called time and materials, which is a hybrid of the fixed price and cost reimbursable contract types. Each contract type is described in more detail in the following sections.

Fixed Price or Lump Sum

The fixed price (also known as fixed fee) or lump sum contract sets a fixed fee for the work the contractor will provide. This means that if the fee is $10,000, the contractor must get all the work done before their costs go above that amount. If, for some reason, there are delays and the contractor's costs go above $10,000, the contractor loses money. If the contractor's costs go below $10,000, then the contractor makes even more money than expected. Because of this, most of the risk of the contract is on the contractor. If the kind of work has been done frequently, or the scope of the work is very well understood, this can be a very good contract for the contractor. If the scope of the work is not well defined or this is a research project, it would be very risky for the contractor to bid using a fixed price. And the seller should be wary of such a bid. This is the most common kind of contract, but again, it is used usually for well-defined work.

For this kind of contract, you may add incentives to reward the contractor with earlier delivery or better performance than the agreed-to terms of the contract. You may want the contractor to complete the project sooner but know it may not be possible under normal circumstances. So you motivate the contractor with a bonus of 10 percent of the contract to finish 10 days early. When you add an incentive, you are taking on more risk than a usual fixed price contract, because you may have to pay more (which you are willing to risk) or the work may not be completed when you really hope it will (which you must accept if the contractor cannot make the earlier date). Although not usually a part of a contract type, but often added as a contract clause, you could also add a penalty for the product or service not being delivered on time or with lower than agreed-to quality.

Cost Reimbursable

The cost reimbursable contract reimburses the contractor for all their costs (direct and indirect, with the indirect costs being figured as a percentage of the direct costs) in producing the goods or services for you. Since you don't know how much the total costs will be, this provides a lot of risk to you and your project, and less risk to the contractor, who can just keep working and charging you for all the work they do. You might insert some checkpoints along the way in the contract to audit what is going on—to make sure the project does not keep growing. Although this might seem to be a less than desirable contract type, it is quite necessary for projects with a lot of uncertainty. Good contractors will require a cost reimbursable contract when you require research and development on something never done before or if the scope of your project is poorly defined. You can also add incentives or awards to cost reimbursable contracts. This often helps reduce the risk to the buyer because it motivates the contractor to get done as soon as possible, depending on how the incentive or award is written in the contract. Some major cost reimbursable type contracts are cost plus fee, cost plus fixed fee, and cost plus incentive fee.

Time and Materials

The time and materials contract is a mixture of fixed fee and cost reimbursable. The price of the units is fixed, but the cost is not known when the contract is awarded. Some people use this type to get work started before the contract is awarded since finalizing a contract can take so long but the work must get started.

In order to create the right kind of contract, you and your organization decide on what you expect of your contractors and decide how much risk you need to take on. The following lists the contract types from highest risk to lowest risk to you:

- Cost (highest risk to you)
- Cost reimbursable plus incentive or award
- Time and materials
- Fixed price plus incentive
- Fixed price (lowest risk to you)

In this exercise, you will learn about contract types when you help the Creative Cartoon Company decide on the contract types for the products and services it needs to acquire for creating its first full-length feature film.

Scenario

Recently, the Creative Cartoon Company (CCC) has obtained enough capital to create its first feature-length animated film based on its most recent short film, which won several major entertainment awards. CCC hired TPMP several months ago to help it improve project management processes, and now, because CCC has to subcontract some of the work to outside organizations in order to complete the film, the company executives are asking you and your company, TPMP, to help them with their procurement management processes. For the new feature film, they have decided that they will need outside services for sound production, an overseas cartoon firm to create background artwork, a marketing firm, and an animation software development firm to implement an idea that the producer has for advancing the animation industry to the next level. Marcus Manning is the producer of the film, tentatively titled *Bouncing with Bob*. He and the film's director, Sheila Wong, have high aspirations—they want the feature-length film to win an Oscar for best animated film, and they want their new animation idea to win a technical Oscar. They want you to help them create good vendor relationships so that the vendors can help them create the best possible film.

Deciding on Contract Types

1. Marcus wants to incent the marketing company to create a great marketing campaign for the film. What kind of contract type might you recommend to Marcus and why?

2. After some discussion, you and Marcus have decided that the overseas contract for artwork should be time and materials. Describe how CCC might implement the pricing for the time and materials contract.

3. What is the riskiest contract type for CCC? What is the riskiest type of contract for the contractor, and why?

4. What contract type would you recommend to Marcus for the sound production company? Why?

5. What contract type would you recommend to Marcus for the animation software development firm? Why?

Exercise 6.2: Creating a Procurement Management Plan

The objectives for Exercise 6.2 are as follows:

- Understand the need for a procurement management plan.

- Understand the elements of a procurement management plan.

- Practice creating parts of a procurement management plan.

Background

PMI expects you to create a plan to set the strategy for managing the processes for each knowledge area for your project. With procurement management, you will create a plan to describe how you will manage the different processes and standards for your contracts and vendors. Some of the processes you need to document are how you will manage vendor solicitations, including describing the documents and evaluation criteria; how you will obtain contract vendors; and how you will evaluate proposals and make your final vendor selection. You might also describe how you would like your contracts negotiated and how you will manage and administer your project's contracts. If your project is going to have contracts, this is extremely important so that you can be efficient and objective in selecting your contractors. Also, due to this early planning, you can direct lawyers who might be responsible for reviewing contract documents to include important items in the contract to help make your project successful and to manage the contractors with a more organized approach once they have been chosen. Your plan should accomplish the following.

- Justify why you have decided to purchase the services or goods via a contract.

- Describe the types of contracts your project will have and why you have decided on a contract type for particular goods or services. Describe how you will control the costs/prices of the contracts.

- Describe any organizational policies you have for creating and managing contracts and where you can find standard procurement documents for your organization.

- Describe the documentation/specifications required for each contract, including who will create the contract statement of work (SOW), which describes what will be provided by the vendor under the contract, what format it will use, and to what extent it will be documented and used in the proposals.

- Discuss how processes in procurement and solicitation planning will be managed and integrated with other project processes. You will want to make sure you describe your strategies on the following topics:

  - What procurement documents will you use? Will you need a request for proposal (RFP), invitation for bid (IFB), request for quotation (RFQ), or some other document to receive contract bids?

  - Will you create evaluation criteria for the contract bids, and will you provide the criteria? If you do create evaluation criteria, how will you do it and on what will it be based?

  - How will you solicit bids for your contracts? Will you hold bidder conferences or advertise in industry publications, or will you use some other form? Are you constrained in some way on how you obtain bids?

  - Can you identify prequalified sellers? Who are they?

  - Once you obtain the bids or proposals, what will the evaluation process be, including who will do it and how will you use the evaluation criteria you have prepared? Will you use any screening or weighting systems, or will you use any independent estimates to help you evaluate the bids?

  - How will you handle bid protests if it is possible your organization might receive them?

  - How will you deal with lead time needed for purchases on each contract and expected schedule dates?

  - How will assumptions and constraints be impacted by purchasing, and how will you manage risks for each contract, including insurance, bonds and other ways to protect your organization from the actions of the vendors?

- Describe the management strategies and actions for administering each contract, including the change control and payment systems that should be used for each contract. You should describe how you will coordinate with your regular project performance reporting and metrics, especially for scheduling and performance status. You also might include how you would manage the contracts differently during different phases of the project. Describe how you will manage multiple providers if you have them—will you require joint meetings or separate meetings or a combination of both?

- Document the roles and responsibilities for managing each contract. What authority does your project team have? Will the project manager be the contract manager, or will you have a procurement specialist manage the contract? You might describe the different roles and responsibilities of the procurement department versus the project team duties—what actions can the project team take without working with lawyers or the procurement management department?

- Describe how you would recommend that your project proceed with each contract negotiation, including who would manage the negotiations and who would participate in them. Discuss how disputes might be negotiated.

- Document what will constitute closeout of each contract.

Make sure the procurement management plan is well documented and reviewed by your procurement department if you have one. Although much of the contract is written by lawyers, you can have a great deal of influence on what is expected of the vendor and the product or service to be delivered by setting up this plan early in the project.

In this exercise, you will help the Creative Cartoon Company create portions of a procurement management plan based on the need for different contract types and vendors it will require to produce its first full-length feature film.

Scenario

Recently, the Creative Cartoon Company (CCC) has obtained enough capital to create its first feature-length animated film based on its most recent short film, which won several major entertainment awards. CCC hired TPMP several months ago to help it improve project management processes, and now, because CCC has to subcontract some of the work to outside organizations in order to complete the film, the executives are asking you and your company, TPMP, to help them with their procurement management processes. For the new feature film, they have decided that they will need outside services for sound production, an overseas cartoon firm to create background artwork, a marketing firm, and an animation software development firm to implement an idea that the producer has for advancing the animation industry to the next level. Marcus Manning is the producer of the film, tentatively titled *Bouncing with Bob*. He and the film's director, Sheila Wong, have high aspirations—they want the feature-length film to win an Oscar for best animated film, and they want their new animation advancement idea to win a technical Oscar. They want you to help them create good vendor relationships, so that the vendors can help them create the best possible film.

Creating a Procurement Management Plan

1. Describe how you would recommend that CCC manage the scheduling and performance of the contracts for sound production, overseas artwork production, software development, and marketing in unison.

2. Describe how Marcus should manage CCC's procurement processes for the sound production contract. What procurement document should he use? Should he use evaluation criteria? How should he solicit bids? Once CCC receives the bids, who do you recommend should evaluate the bids and use the evaluation criteria?

3. Describe whether CCC will use evaluation criteria for each contract, what criteria CCC should focus on, and whether CCC should obtain some independent estimates. Explain your reasoning for each of these items.

4. Describe what constitutes closeout for each contract.

5. Who should be in the negotiations for each contract, and what might some general negotiation points be?

6. What are some important items that the project manager needs to consider in administering the contract?

Exercise 6.3: Creating a Contract Statement of Work (SOW)

The objectives for Exercise 6.3 are as follows:

- Justify the need for a contract statement of work (SOW).
- Understand the elements of a contract SOW.
- Practice creating parts of a contract SOW.

Background

The contract statement of work (SOW) is perhaps the single most important output from your project procurement management process. A well-written contract SOW fully describes the services or products the vendor will supply under the contract and can help you obtain the best product or service from your contractor. You need a contract SOW for each product or service that you are procuring for your project. The contract SOW may be derived from the scope statement and, if you are procuring the entire product or service, may actually be the same as the scope statement. Some people may call the contract SOW a scope statement, or they may call it the scope of work, and in fact, the contract SOW is a scope statement focused on just the work required of the vendor. In procurement management, the contract SOW will be written for contractors to understand the expectations of the work you are requesting. The contract SOW often follows the same pattern of information the scope statement provides: objectives, description of the product or service and operational support needed, deliverables required, requirements or specifications, assumption and constraints, and time estimates. The only thing you might not provide is the cost estimate because you usually expect the bidder to provide that. The contract SOW needs to be written well enough so the vendor knows whether they want to bid on it and can actually provide the work. Vagueness sometimes leads to optimism by vendors—because it isn't clear, they think they can take on the work and figure out how to handle it along the way. This could be very dangerous for your project.

As the project manager, it would be useful to get involved in the writing of the contract SOW as soon as possible so you understand the scope and understand how you need to manage the work. Often, though, you may not be involved up front. Whenever you become involved, make sure you read and understand the contract SOW thoroughly. This may require reviews with both your team and the vendor's team to make sure everyone understands the requirements and expectations.

Once you have chosen a contractor, you may use the initial contract SOW you created for the bidding, or you may need to create a more detailed contract SOW for the contract. The closer you can get the contract SOW you create for the bidding to what you end up with in the contract, the closer your contract pricing and contract contents will be.

You or members of your project team may choose to write the contract SOW, but sometimes the vendor is better equipped to write it and you may just review it. It is important that the contract SOW be as clear and detailed as possible. If the vendor or the customer misunderstands any part of it, then disputes are more likely to occur. Initially, if the contract SOW is not well defined, the vendor may underbid, and if a poorly defined contract SOW is used in the contract, it may produce unpredictable results. For instance, if the contract SOW says the widget needs to be slim and economical, the vendor could interpret this requirement as being as slim as a ruler and about $5 each when you were thinking as slim as a measuring tape and about $3 each. At times, the work may simply need creativity and flexibility, so the contract SOW may focus more on the skills, attitude, and technical expertise of the vendor.

You may use a template, a checklist, or previous contracts to help you prepare a good contract SOW. The following are some major elements you need to consider in your contract SOW:

Roles and responsibilities   Make sure that it is clear who is doing what. You need to include who is taking the action (such as who will perform the product testing) and who is participating in reviews (such as who reviews deliverables like specifications). If specific people are needed at certain meetings or in particular roles, make sure it is clear. If you need the architect of the project in a technical review, make sure the SOW states that.

Security   Discuss any security specifications. Will the product or facilities need any specific security processes or procedures during production, transportation, and on delivery?

Location of work   Make sure you describe where the work needs to be done. Can the vendor work on its own premises, work at the project site, or maybe work in both places depending on the work itself or phase of the project? If there are different locations where the work must take place, put it in the SOW.

Milestones/deliverables   List all expected milestones and deliverables.

Quantities   Make sure you list quantities of everything needed. For instance, specify that you need one report that you can copy, or maybe you want the vendor to provide 15 copies. This may seem minor, but for a 750-page report, the difference can be hundreds of dollars.

Vendor payments   Include how the vendor will be paid or should invoice the work. Make sure it is clear how often payment occurs, what constitutes payment, and what constitutes final payment.

Progress reporting   Be specific about when and how you want the work's progress to be reviewed. For instance, state that you want a report every week showing schedule/budget and that you want a monthly review meeting with the major vendor team members attending if you feel that is important for project success.

Testing   Describe the testing requirements for the work, if any. You might indicate that you want an independent testing group or that the vendor can provide the testing but needs to provide testing plans and results for your review.

Quality   Describe the quality required. You may describe that you will accept no more than a .05 percent error rate and leave it up to the vendor to provide that. Or you may require a major quality plan and processes.

Change control   Describe change control requirements, including a general description of the change process.

When you create requests for proposals, invitations to bids, or any procurement documents, always include the contract SOW. Without it, you might not get the kinds of bids that give you a clear understanding of the work the vendor can provide you.

In this exercise, you will help Creative Cartoon Company create parts of a statement of work so that vendors will know the work they are required to do for their first full-length feature film.

You will help CCC understand whether descriptions of their SOW are specific enough for a vendor to bid on or perform their work.

Scenario

Recently, the Creative Cartoon Company (CCC) has obtained enough capital to create its first feature-length animated film based on its most recent short film, which won several major entertainment awards. CCC hired TPMP several months ago to help it improve project management processes, and now, because CCC has to subcontract some of the work to outside organizations in order to complete the film, the executives are asking you and your company, TPMP, to help them with their procurement management processes. For the new feature film, they have decided that they will need outside services for sound production, an overseas cartoon firm to create background artwork, a marketing firm, and an animation software development firm to implement an idea that the producer has for advancing the animation industry to the next level. Marcus Manning is the producer of the film, tentatively titled *Bouncing with Bob*. He and the film's director, Sheila Wong, have high aspirations—they want the feature-length film to win an Oscar for best animated film, and they want their new animation idea to win a technical Oscar. They want you to help them create good vendor relationships so that the vendors can help them create the best possible film.

Creating a Statement of Work (SOW)

1. Describe three elements in the contract SOW that you might recommend that CCC requires from the sound production company. Describe why they would be important in the contract SOW.

2. CCC has provided a description of the quality of work it expects from the marketing firm. It says, "Marketing materials must be of the highest quality as expected in the entertainment industry." Will this be a good enough description of the quality? What might you do to improve this if you could?

3. What three elements of the contract SOW might you recommend as the most important for the animation software development firm? Why?

4. What are some of the deliverables that might be required in the contract SOW for the overseas contractors?

5. Since CCC has never done sound production before, how would you recommend that CCC create the contract SOW for the sound production vendor?

6. For the sound production and overseas artwork contract SOWs, describe any security considerations.

Exercise 6.4: Evaluating and Selecting the Vendor

The objectives for Exercise 6.4 are as follows:

- Introduce evaluation criteria and why you need it.
- Describe how you use evaluation criteria in selecting a vendor.
- Practice creating and using evaluation criteria.

Background

If you are requesting a proposal or bid from a vendor for a complex product or service, your chances of getting what you want are dramatically increased if you have criteria to evaluate the vendors prior to creating the request for proposal, the invitation to bid, or any other kind of procurement document. If you focus on what is important to you, you will be more objective when the proposals or bids are returned to you. You may choose to share the evaluation criteria with the vendors, or you may choose to use it for your internal evaluation processes only. The evaluation criteria may be subjective or objective. You may create the evaluation criteria using weighting factors and scoring to help you decide what is important to you. Note that if you are procuring a product or service that is well established on the market, you may create the evaluation criteria, but in a simplified manner. For instance, the best price may be the only evaluation criteria you have.

When you plan evaluation criteria, first decide on the tools and techniques that you want to use. You may document this information in your procurement management plan as described in Exercise 6.2.

- What criteria are most important to you? Is quality, technical expertise, price, company experience and culture, previous references, or the vendor's understanding your need most important? For each criterion, describe what you want the vendor to deliver.

- Decide if you are going to use an independent estimate for comparison to the estimates you receive from the vendors. If you do not choose to, describe why or how you will be able to know if you have a fair estimate. If you choose to use an independent estimate, describe how you will obtain it and when. Don't forget to put it into your project plan and schedule as an activity.

- Document whether you will use a screening system. This means you will use some kind of minimum level of requirements or threshold you expect in the bid or proposal. For instance, you may only accept companies with a demonstrated annual profit because you do not want to take a chance on a start-up or floundering company. You will want to document what you are screening and eliminate anyone not meeting the requirements immediately. You may or may not want to share this requirement within the request.

- If you decide to weight the criteria, create and document the numerical ratings for each criterion. Again, you may or may not choose to share these weighting factors with the vendors.

Your criteria should be specific to the product or service you are procuring, but the following lists some of the general evaluation criteria you might use:

- Does the vendor demonstrate the best value, lowest price, or some other price comparison advantage? Make sure you distinguish what is more important and evaluate it for the overall life cycle of your project. Don't forget to include operational and maintenance activities in the consideration.

- Does the vendor demonstrate an understanding of your expectations of the product and service, as well as how you expect the vendor to work with you during the project?

- Does the vendor clearly demonstrate the ability to carry out the technical or operational processes needed to perform the work? You will judge this on references, previous performance, skill sets of the employees within the organization assigned to the project, and any awards or technical achievements the vendor can demonstrate.

- Will your project team be able to work with the vendor management team? This criterion is sometimes overlooked. All other qualifications may look terrific, but the management itself might be difficult to work with, or the company processes for invoicing, status reporting, treatment of its employees, and documenting financial transactions may be lax or difficult to deal with. Sometimes contracts are rewarded solely for the relationships between the management personnel of each firm. Although the project manager may have to settle for this kind of decision, it is still important to both document evaluation criteria to ensure that the vendor can fulfill the work and attempt to make sure that a bid or proposal is submitted by the vendor.

- Can the vendor fulfill the obligations of performing the work based on their financial capabilities? If you choose a vendor who is relying on your project to stay afloat, you have a very large risk on hand if they have to lay off employees during the project.

- What intellectual property or proprietary rights does the vendor expect or need, and what do you need from the vendor? Some contracting organizations, especially in creative or services projects, require that the contractor assumes ownership of the product and the vendor keep the work produced for the project confidential. Some vendors have issues with this since they think they should own the intellectual work or be able to discuss the work as part of their marketing strategies. The needs of each party around these issues need to be evaluated up front the issues do not become damaging to the contract during execution or support.

The other evaluation criteria may be on a more personal level; in other words, is this vendor a good match for your organization's culture and personnel? You may also decide that the vendor needs to pass some face-to-face interviews to make sure your project team or organization feels comfortable with the vendor's team and management methods despite how good the proposal or bid looks.

Once you have created these evaluation criteria in the planning processes of your project, you will then use them as in the executing process of source selection. Even if you have rigorous evaluation criteria, it is possible that once you receive the proposals, you may find that some vendors are strong candidates for criteria you did not think of or that are hard to measure, such as levels of creativity or reputation. You may decide that new criteria outweigh the criteria you thought were important.

In this exercise, you will help Creative Cartoon Company create some evaluation criteria for a few of its contracts. You will work with Marcus and Sheila to help them determine what is most important for each criterion and how to input it into their request for proposal as they start to understand what kind of help they need in creating their first full-length feature film.

Scenario

Recently, the Creative Cartoon Company (CCC) has obtained enough capital to create its first feature-length animated film based on its most recent short film, which won several major entertainment awards. CCC hired TPMP several months ago to help it improve project management processes, and now, because CCC has to subcontract some of the work to outside organizations in order to complete the film, the executives are asking you and your company, TPMP, to help them with their procurement management processes. For the new feature film, they have decided that they will need outside services for sound production, an overseas cartoon firm to create background artwork, a marketing firm, and an animation software development firm to implement an idea that the producer has for advancing the animation industry to the next level. Marcus Manning is the producer of the film, tentatively titled *Bouncing with Bob*. He and the film's director, Sheila Wong, have high aspirations—they want the feature-length film to win an Oscar for best animated film, and they want their new animation idea to win a technical Oscar. They want you to help them create good vendor relationships so that the vendors can help them create the best possible film.

Evaluating and Selecting a Vendor

1. List the five general evaluation criteria CCC should consider for each contract.

2. You will help Marcus create criteria for the animation software development vendor. List four of the top criteria and rank them in importance.

3. You will help Marcus create criteria for the overseas artwork vendor. List four of the top criteria and rank them in importance.

4. Why should CCC create evaluation criteria before sending out the requests for proposals?

5. Marcus has a golfing buddy, Davis Neely, one of the co-owners of Thundering Sound Productions. Marcus would like Davis, whom he trusts and has worked with before, to receive the sound production contract. Would you recommend that Marcus still use evaluation criteria?

6. Would you recommend that CCC include its evaluation criteria in each RFP? Why or why not?

Exercise 6.5: Creating a Responsibility Assignment Matrix (RAM)

You've finished four exercises concerning procurement resource planning. Now we are going to look at several exercises that will cover resource planning for all project resources.

The objectives for Exercise 6.5 are as follows:

- Describe a Responsibility Assignment Matrix.
- Describe the components of a RAM.

Background

Previous exercises covered procuring outside resources in a project. Now we continue with exercises on how to plan a project's human resources. The integration of many different types of information is required to plan a project effectively. The Responsibility Assignment Matrix (RAM) is an example of merging two different knowledge areas, integrating them to create a planning output. The RAM combines an organization chart with project tasks and creates a planning tool that describes who will accomplish what on a project. These components are an organization breakdown structure and the work breakdown structure. Let's examine the two components more closely.

Organization breakdown structure   An organization breakdown structure is really nothing more than a project organization chart. It needs to depict who is working on the project and the departments they represent. The following shows a typical organization breakdown structure.

Work breakdown structure   A work breakdown structure is an output from the Create WBS process and includes the decomposed project scope components of smaller and more manageable components or work packages. The project manager creates it with project team members. We covered work breakdown structures in Section 4. The following shows a typical work breakdown structure.

These two charts now come together to create the RAM. The following table shows a RAM based on the previous illustrations.

	IT	Finance	Operations	Legal
Task 1.1	x		x	
Task 1.2	x	x		
Task 1.3				x
Task 2.1			x	
Task 3.1	x			
Task 3.2	x	x	x	x
Task 3.3	x			

You can now see that the RAM explains who will work on what task of the project.

RAMs can also be used to describe the responsibilities of team members on specific tasks. Creating a legend and applying it to the RAM allows team members to understand their roles on the same task. In the following table, we have added the legend of a = accountable, c = creator, u = updater, r = reviewer to our previous table.

	IT	Finance	Operations	Legal
Task 1.1	a		r	
Task 1.2	c	a		
Task 1.3				a
Task 2.1			a	
Task 3.1	a			
Task 3.2	r	r	c	a
Task 3.3	a			

In this exercise, you'll get a chance to answer some questions regarding Responsibility Assignment Matrixes.

Scenario

Terrific Project Management Partners (TPMP) has just placed you at Affordable Sweeping, Inc., an up-and-coming property maintenance company. Affordable Sweeping has just been awarded the contract to get the local NFL stadium ready for the current football season. Affordable Sweeping named the project Operation:NFL and has hired you to project manage. You will have over 100 people working on the project: team leads and sub–team leads who are employees of Affordable Sweeping and many subcontractors. You have created the following RAM for this project.

	Groundskeepers	Turf Prep	Game Operations	Power Washers
Task A.1	a		r	
Task B.2	c	a		
Task A.3				a
Task C.1			a	
Task C.1	a			
Task A.2	r	r	c	a
Task B.3	a			

Creating a Responsibility Assignment Matrix (RAM)

1. What does the acronym RAM stand for?

2. What is a RAM?

3. What two components make a RAM?

4. The RAM created for Operation:NFL is an example of what type of RAM? Why would you use this type of RAM?

Exercise 6.6: Creating a Staffing Management Plan

The objectives for Exercise 6.6 are as follows:

- Describe a staffing management plan.

- Describe the inputs for a staffing management plan.

- Describe contents of a staffing management plan.

Background

The staffing management plan documents for the project team exactly when and how the human resources needs will be managed on a project. A staffing management plan can be general or very detailed. Regardless of the approach you take, you will need to work through the process for creating this plan. In this exercise, we will examine the inputs to creating a staffing management plan as well as the thought process for creating it. Let's start with the inputs.

Inputs for a Staffing Management Plan

There are three pieces of information that the project manager needs to have at their fingertips in order to create a staffing management plan. These inputs are enterprise environmental factors, organizational process assets, and the project management plan. We will cover each of them here.

Enterprise environmental factors   As you think through the staffing management plan, you will need to understand the enterprise environmental factors that affect your project. These factors can be organizational, technical, logistical, political, or interpersonal. Organizational factors involve coordinating project work across multiple vendors, departments, or both. Technical factors involve the way the work of the project must be done. Logistical factors have to do with collocation, time zones, and the countries that the project team may work in. Political factors involve informal power and the alliances of the people on the team and their affect on the project. And, finally, interpersonal factors involve the reporting relationships among all of the project's personnel. Some typical constraints that are found in enterprise environmental factors are the organizational structure, collective bargaining agreements and economic conditions. You will want to document the types of enterprise environmental factors you identify and how you will mange each of them for your staffing management plan.

Organizational process assets   Be on the lookout for templates and checklists that might be of value for you to use to create your staffing management plan. Another organizational process asset is the existence of lessons learned documentation from other projects that might be applied to your project.

Project management plan   Other sections of the project management plan will help you in creating your staffing management plan. Be sure to investigate any sections that refer to the human resources that will be used on the project. You typically will find them in areas such as procurement, quality assurance, and risk management.

Contents of a Staffing Management Plan

Once you have your inputs together, it is time to construct your staffing management plan. These plans can be as individual as your organization or your project. Here are some ideas of sections that might be included in a staffing management plan.

Organization charts   An organization chart is a graphical depiction of the hierarchy of the project team. It is used to depict the reporting relationships of the team members to the project manager. Figure 6.1 shows a sample organization chart:

FIGURE 6.1   Sample organization chart

Responsibility Assignment Matrix (RAM)   A Responsibility Assignment Matrix is a diagram that merges an organization breakdown structure and the work breakdown structure. We dedicated an entire exercise to the RAM in Exercise 6.5.

Roles and responsibilities   A roles and responsibilities matrix would include each team member or resource grouping and a list of their responsibilities. This matrix makes it clear who is accountable for what on the project. In the following table, general responsibilities are noted.

Role	Responsibility
Executive sponsor	Chairs the steering committee
	Champions the project
	Resolves issues escalated from the steering committee
Project manager	Organizes the team structure
	Manages the project
	Tracks progress
	Creates project plan
Project team member	Completes assigned tasks and their associated deliverables
	Adheres to project standards and methodology
	Meets status and time reporting obligations

Staff acquisition   This portion of the staffing management plan should address all of the ways that staff will be added to the project. It should include where the staff will come from—are they internal resources and from what department? Or are they external resources, where they will work, and the costs associated with each level of expertise.

Release criteria   This portion of the staffing management plan explains how all types of project vacancies will be managed. It should cover how key personnel and team members are replaced as well as how all project personnel will be reassigned at the end of the project.

Training needs   You will need to review the credentials of each human resource on your team. You may need to provide training for those individuals that require it in order for them to work effectively on your project. Their training needs should be documented as part of the staffing management plan.

Recognition and rewards   Each project manager should document exactly how rewards and recognition will be handled on their project. This too should be covered in the staffing management plan.

Compliance   Policies, rules, and regulations that impact the treatment of team members should be documented in the staffing management plan.

Safety   Departmental policies regarding how safety is handled at your company may impact how your resources are managed. These concerns should be documented in a staffing management plan.

In this exercise, we'll cover some questions regarding the staffing management plan.

Scenario

TPMP has just placed you at Affordable Sweeping, Inc., an up-and-coming property maintenance company. Affordable Sweeping has just been awarded the contract to get the local NFL stadium ready for the current football season. Affordable Sweeping named the project Operation:NFL and has hired you to project manage. You will have over 100 people working on the project: team leads and sub–team leads who are employees of Affordable Sweeping and many subcontractors. Each of these subcontracting companies has its own project managers and team leads, basically its own organization structure. Also many of these subcontractors are protected by collective bargaining agreements.

Creating a Staffing Management Plan

1.   What is the definition of a staffing management plan?

2.   For the Operation:NFL project, you are running into some issues creating your staffing management plan. What are the three constraints typically found in enterprise environmental factors that hinder a project manager's ability to perform human resource planning? Which two are affecting your ability to plan this project and why?

3.   What are the three inputs into a staffing management plan?

4.   On the Operation:NFL project, why would you include an organization chart in your staffing management plan?

5.   On Operation:NFL, why would you include a roles and responsibilities matrix in your staffing management plan?

Exercise 6.7: Activity Sequencing

We've talked about resource planning in the last two exercises. Now we'll look at how that resource information gets utilized while we determine how the work is sequenced and how resource estimating is accomplished.

The objectives for Exercise 6.7 are as follows:

- Describe the different types of dependencies.

- Describe the differences between the precedence diagramming method (PDM) and the arrow diagramming method (ADM).

- Define the four types of dependency relationships.

- Create a project schedule network diagram.

Background

Once you have completed the human resource planning, you can look at the work that needs to be performed. Activity Sequencing is a time management planning process used to determine how the work of the project will progress. In other words, it is the sequence of the tasks of the project. In Activity Sequencing, you take the activity list created by the work breakdown structure and then use tools and techniques to decide on the progression of the work, which results in the creation of a project schedule network diagram.

Components of Activity Sequencing

In order to begin the sequencing process, you must first understand the elements that make it possible, including activity lists, dependencies, and diagramming methods.

Activity List

In Section 4, we talked about the lowest level of work on the WBS. That lowest level is called a work package. It is also called the activity list.

Dependencies

A tool and technique of Activity Sequencing is determining the dependencies of the work to be done. A dependency is the relationship between two tasks. There are three types of dependencies:

Mandatory dependencies   Dependencies that are inherent in the work to be done. You cannot road-test a new tire until the tire is manufactured.

Discretionary dependencies   Dependencies that are created by the project team. On the new tire you are creating, you want a 1/2-inch tread. Because of the size of the tread, you'll need to use a new tire mold that won't be ready for six weeks. You've just created a discretionary dependency.

External dependencies   Dependencies that come from outside of your project. On your new tire, you are using a special rubber formula that is being shipped from Japan. The next ship to leave for the United States doesn't leave for two more days. You now have an external dependency on that shipment.

Diagramming Methods

Once you understand dependencies, you will need to know which tool and technique to use to depict the sequence of the work. There are two diagramming methods that are most commonly used for sequencing. The first is the precedence diagramming method (PDM), also known as activity on node (AON). In this type of diagram, the nodes (boxes) depict the task and the arrows depict the dependency.

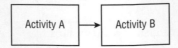

Precedence diagramming uses four types of logical relationships to determine the dependencies between the activities:

- In the finish-to-start relationship, illustrated in the preceding diagram, Activity B cannot start until Activity A is completed.

- In the start-to-finish relationship, illustrated in the following diagram, Activity B cannot finish until Activity A has started.

- In the finish-to-finish relationship, pictured in the following diagram, Activity B cannot be completed until Activity A is completed.

- Finally, in the start-to-start relationship, Activity B cannot start until Activity A starts. The following is an example of the start-to-start relationship.

The other commonly used diagramming method is the arrow diagramming method (ADM), also known as activity on arrow (AOA). In this method, the lines are the activities and the circles are the nodes that depict the relationship. The arrow diagramming method uses a finish-to-start relationship.

The Project Schedule Network Diagram

Once you know the components of Activity Sequencing, you can create a project schedule network diagram, like the following one, that depicts the progression of work on a project. You will need to create a start and finish node so that all nodes on the network diagram are connected. You always connect all tasks on a project schedule network diagram. You need to understand exactly what has to be done in what order. In other words, what is a predecessor for each piece of work? Also, what is the successor to each piece of work? Without this knowledge, you might miss an important step in how the work has to be done, which causes rework and lost time.

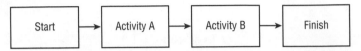

Here are the steps to make a project schedule network diagram using Activity Sequencing:

1. Determine whether the WBS needs to be decomposed into smaller activities, called an activity list. These should be small activities that can be assigned to one person.

2. Understand each activity well enough to determine the dependencies between them. Are they mandatory, discretionary, or external?

3. Determine the method of diagramming you will use: precedence or arrow diagramming.

4. Understand the dependencies well enough to know the type of logical relationship between the activities.

5. Create a start and finish node.

6. Sequence the lowest-level activities or tasks between the start and finish nodes. Do not sequence the higher levels of the work breakdown structure, that is, the summary level activities.

In this exercise, you're going to work with SystemsDelivery on the credit card validation project. This scenario was introduced in Section 4. In this exercise, you'll determine dependencies and logical relationships and choose a diagramming method to create a network diagram.

Scenario

Your company, Terrific Project Management Partners (TPMP), has just placed you at SystemsDelivery, Inc. as a temporary project manager. You've been assigned the Credit Card Validation project. This project is designed to be the next best thing in credit card fraud prevention. The management of SystemsDelivery believes that this product will be in high demand at every major retailer in the country. Of course the management needs this product to go to market as quickly as possible. You have been on the project for two weeks now. You have created the work breakdown structure in the following illustration for producing the Canadian product. This WBS was created at the lowest possible level, the activity list.

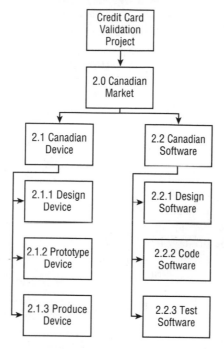

Activity Sequencing

1. How many activities have been created at the lowest level of the work breakdown structure (the activity list level)?

2. Analyze the dependencies between the activities. Are these dependencies mandatory, discretionary, or external?

3. Analyze the dependencies again. This time determine what is the one logical relationship between each activity for the Canadian software?

4. Determine the best method to diagram these activities. Will you use the precedence diagramming method or the arrow diagramming method?

5. Sequence the lowest-level activities between a start and finish node. Draw your answer.

Exercise 6.8: Activity Resource Estimating

The objective for Exercise 6.8 is as follows:

▪   Describe the three types of resources.

Background

Activity Resource Estimating is a Time Management planning process done early in the planning process group to establish the resource costs of a project. Activity Resource Estimating requires that you determine what resources are needed on your project and determine how many of each type of resource are needed.

The Activity Resource Estimating process incorporates the work breakdown structure, the scope statement, and resource pool descriptions. Using expert judgment, alternatives analysis, published estimating data, project management software, and bottom-up estimating, the project manager can determine the resource requirements for the project.

When we talk about resources in Activity Resource Estimating, we are not talking about actual individual people. Instead, with Activity Resource Estimating, we are talking about types of resources. There are three commonly known types of resources: people, equipment, and materials. People can be individuals that work in your department or your company or vendors you hire to complete the work—basically any skilled resource. Equipment refers to items such as a forklift, a dump truck, a computer, or other nonconsumable resources. Materials are things like water, power, and other consumables.

Let's examine each of the primary inputs to the Activity Resource Estimating process. The first input is the activity list from the WBS, which you learned about in Section 4. The following shows a typical WBS with duration estimates in days.

The second input into the Activity Resource Estimating process, organizational process assets, provides the policies concerning staffing or the acquisition of materials and equipment. The last input into the Activity Resource Estimating process is resource availability. Resource availability is sometimes referred to as a resource pool description. This description may or may not exist at your company. You'll want to create or modify it depending on what you find. It should contain a list of the resource types in the company as well as the actual number of resources for each category. The following table shows a sample resource pool description.

Resource Type	Name	Number
Skilled resources	Accountant	2
	Office manager	1
	Forklift operator	4
	Warehouse supervisor	1
	Heavy equipment operator	5
Equipment	Backhoe	2
	Forklift	3
Materials	Water	100 gallons
	Gas	1,000 gallons
	Electricity	10 kilowatt hours

Once you have your three primary inputs together, you are ready to use your expert judgment and other tools and techniques to determine what types of resources should be used on which tasks of your project. When you are through, you might apply the resource type name to your WBS or you might just create a table like the following that shows the assignment. The major output of Activity Resource Estimating is activity resource requirements.

Task	Resource	Number of Resources
1.1	Forklift	1
	Forklift operator	1
1.2	Backhoe	2
	Heavy equipment operator	2
	Water	50 gallons
2.1	Accountant	1
3.1	Office manager	1
3.2	Warehouse supervisor	1
3.3	Forklift	1
	Forklift operator	1

In this exercise, you'll apply what you've learned about Activity Resource Estimating to another scenario.

Scenario

TPMP has just placed you at the Pinnacle Candy Company as a temporary project manager. You have been assigned the EspressoFix Bar project. This project is going to create a new candy that will satisfy every coffee addict's need for coffee all wrapped up in a candy bar. The management at Pinnacle only wants to see if this new candy bar is marketable. Production of the finished product will be another project initiated later. You have been on the job long enough to have created a scope statement and the work breakdown structure that is shown in the following graphic. You and your team have also completed the duration estimates for each task.

You asked the project team if there is a documented resource pool for the company. You find out that nothing exists so you get some reports from human resources and you and your team brainstorm to create the resource pool illustrated in the following table.

Resource Type	Name	Number
Skilled resources	Marketing	5
	Advertising	4
	Legal	2
	Chefs	2
	Employees	35
	Vendor—Focused Marketing, Inc.	Unlimited
Equipment	Test kitchen	1

You have also discovered that the company normally subcontracts the focus group work with Focused Marketing, Inc.

Activity Resource Estimating

1. Activity Resource Estimating is what process step in the Time Management process?
2. What are the three types of resources?
3. What are some examples of a material resource?
4. What are the three primary inputs used in Activity Resource Estimating?
5. What is the major output of Activity Resource Estimating?
6. Create a resource requirement table for the EspressoFix Bar with the resource pool shown in the table earlier.

Task	Resource	Number of Resources

Answers to Section 6 Exercises

Answers to Exercise 6.1

Your answers may be somewhat different, but the following answers provide a guide.

1. To motivate the marketing company to create a great marketing campaign for CCC's film, Marcus might decide to use a fixed price plus incentive contract (also known as Fixed Fee plus incentive). Film marketing is a fairly common service, and so the scope is well understood and a fixed fee would be appropriate. However, if Marcus would like the marketing firm to go above and beyond, perhaps an incentive bonus based on a independent market awareness survey or a target for first week box office returns would help provide an incentive for the marketing firm.

2. You and Marcus have decided that you would like to try a time and materials contract for the overseas contractor. To implement this, CCC and the overseas company would create a fixed unit price for each of the art positions needed, such as senior artist and junior artist. However, the work itself to deliver certain sections of the backgrounds would be based on how long it would take to produce them to the level of quality Marcus and Sheila expect. At this time, CCC is uncertain of how long that would take, and it is possible it may need other kinds of artwork from the firm they hire.

3. The riskiest type of contract for CCC is the cost reimbursable contract because the work could continue indefinitely and end up being very costly for CCC. The fixed price contract is the riskiest type of contract for the contractor because the work might take much longer than planned by the contractor and they would lose all chances for a profit.

4. You might recommend a fixed price contract for the sound production company. The scope of the work is well known for sound production and though the technical expectations for the animation portion of *Bouncing with Bob* are high, the sound can be of the same quality level as most of the major animated features on the market.

5. Marcus and you, after discussing the uncertainty of the idea for the animation software development, might decide that a cost reimbursable contract is the only kind that a good company will take on for such a new and risky technical advancement. You might recommend that CCC include an incentive to the firm it hires. CCC might award the development firm with a percentage of the film's profit if the new technical advancement wins an Oscar or other technical award. CCC might also consider a contract that sets the foundation for a joint partnership for profiting from the new animation advancement if it is successful.

Answers to Exercise 6.2

Your answers may be somewhat different, but the following answers provide a guide.

1. Marcus needs to manage the sound production, overseas production company, and software development firm together with the overall schedule and team status. Each vendor will have deliverables that need to be on schedule and with a quality that matches the rest of the production. Sheila may need to create a schedule in which parts of the deliverables

are provided at certain audit checkpoints, with the entire project team gathering to review quality and progress. Marcus might manage the marketing firm completely separately. He might provide some of the film's scenes for input to the marketing plan. It would be important to treat the vendors as team members so that their work synchs with the rest of the film.

2. You might recommend that Marcus use a request for proposal (RFP) to lay out the requirements and bids from sound production vendors as part of the procurement processes for the sound production contract. CCC should use evaluation criteria to help define the quality and expectations of the sound production company. Marcus might decide to solicit bids via advertisements in film industry and animation publication magazines. The technical division of CCC should evaluate the bids based on the evaluation criteria.

3. The evaluation criteria CCC will use for three of the four contracts the criteria for the project, and whether CCC should obtain some independent estimates are included here. Explanations are given for each.

    Sound production   Yes, CCC should use evaluation criteria. CCC might focus evaluation criteria on quality, previous experience (especially on animated films), and price. CCC should be able to estimate the job without an independent estimate based on previous similar jobs.

    Marketing firm   Yes, CCC should use evaluation criteria. CCC might focus evaluation criteria on successful campaigns in the past and creative capabilities. CCC might request an independent estimate for the work or use previous industry productions to decide if the bids are fair.

    Overseas art contractor   CCC may choose not to use evaluation criteria for this time and materials contract. It may choose to go with the best bid based on comparing prices from various firms and recommendations from other industry peers. It would not need an independent estimate.

    Software development firm   CCC may choose to use evaluation criteria based on the creative capabilities of the software firm and its willingness to take risks and put some of its own "skin in the game." It may want to see previous experience but also base criteria on the skills base of the vendor's employees. An accurate estimate based on an independent company's work might be difficult to obtain since the new animation idea has never been tried before.

4. The following describes what closeout would constitute for each contract. You might recommend to CCC that closeout should consist of a lessons learned document or audit of each contract as well as what is described in the following list.

    Sound production   Closeout would be a technical review of the completed film and positive preview audience reaction for the technical sound qualities of the product. Final payment would be provided during the film's release week since that is when the final audience reaction would be obtained.

    Marketing firm   Closeout would be when the final deliverable is made for the marketing plan. This might consist of the results of a marketing survey or a calculation of the target box office receipts versus actual box office receipts. Payment would occur when the last deliverable is made and when all terms of the contract have been fulfilled.

    Overseas art contractor   Closeout would be when the final artwork is delivered, possibly after the first few audience previews show the work is satisfactory. Payment would be made, however, when the last of the artwork is delivered for integrating with the film and the director/editor have approved the work. If more work is required after the audience preview, an extension to the contract might be required.

Software development firm   Closeout would be when the animation software is at the level of quality to make the animation in the film appear to work seamlessly. Final payment would be made after the preview audience gives the film's animation quality a positive review.

5.   Marcus, Sheila, and appropriate technical subject matter experts from CCC should be involved in the negotiations for the three technical contracts. The marketing contract may need just Marcus and Sheila involved, with a lawyer who is an expert in marketing contracts. In all cases, the procurement department of CCC and lawyers with particular industry expertise should be involved.

6.   Sheila and Marcus need to consider the vendor relationships in administering the contracts and making sure those administration considerations are well detailed in the contract. This might involve creating a contract that ensures regular status reporting and meetings and a good change control process that everyone is trained on and understands. CCC should consider some kind of continuous improvement meetings to work on correcting issues with the vendors. CCC might also consider bringing the vendors in on major team meetings and perhaps a few celebrations after major deliverable completions to make sure they feel a part of the film team.

Answers to Exercise 6.3

Your answers may be somewhat different, but the following answers provide a guide.

1.   You might recommend that the following three elements in the SOW be addressed for the sound production company:

Quality   CCC would need to be very specific about the quality, based on measurable and technical production objectives. This will help the vendor understand the equipment they need to provide and the expertise of the people needed for the work. CCC may need to describe that high quality is not needed for some phases but is needed for the final edit, as measured by an independent technical auditor.

Concise requirements/specifications   CCC would need to be very specific about the requirements, such as when sound production is needed for what deliverables. For instance, will sound production need to be delivered for the storyboards, when proofs are created, or when the animation is three-fourths complete? This is necessary for the sound production vendor to lay out the total scope and schedule of their own project.

Where the work should be done/location of deliverables   It might be important to indicate that the initial work can be done at the sound production company's site but that during production and postproduction, the sound production team may need to be on-site at the animation studio. This will affect the costs, equipment used, and people involved for the vendor.

2.   CCC needs to improve the description of quality for the marketing firm to be more objective. One way to do it is to require a deliverable such as the results of a survey in which the marketing company conducts a marketing preview and asks the audience specific questions about

the production's quality. CCC might also request an independent review of all of the written materials or a focus group to help demonstrate quality levels earlier in the production cycle.

3. The following elements of the SOW are the three most important elements for the animation software development firm:

    Security   Since this is a proprietary project in which CCC is hoping to achieve a new animation technology, CCC might require a high level of security and confidentiality. This is important because the animation vendor will not only need to educate employees to keep work confidential, but may also need to hire special security for delivering trial software.

    Quality   CCC would need to be very specific about the quality of the final software product. It might state something like "based on a survey of a typical audience, 98 percent of the survey participants finds the technology to appear 'real looking.'" The vendor might need to build a schedule in which the vendor has expert reviews often and audience surveys at appropriate milestones as the animation software is developed.

    Roles and responsibilities   CCC may require a lead system engineer to work with the CCC technical folks in weekly meetings and require the vendor project manager to report at status meetings every two weeks.

> **NOTE**   It will be difficult to provide precise requirements. Since this is a new product, the requirements might describe the need for the vendor's flexibility and technical creativity to help solve difficult programming issues.

4. Some of the deliverables that may be required in the SOW for the overseas contractors could be samples of proposed background styles and colors for CCC to review and approve, draft background artwork based on initial storyboards, final backgrounds, and revised backgrounds after animation is added. Deliverables also might include status reports and art reviews.

5. Since CCC has never done sound production before, you might recommend that it actually have the leading sound production vendor candidates write the contract SOW. CCC may send out a request for proposal with a requirement that the sound production company would need to write the contract SOW and deliver it with the proposal.

6. For the sound production vendor, CCC may require vendor employees to sign confidentiality statements and may perform background checks of employees to make sure they have never divulged secrets on previous assignments. For the overseas artwork vendor, CCC may require the proofs to be sent via secure mail or e-mail services. However, since the art backgrounds may give little away about the movie itself, the security may not need be too strict.

Answers to Exercise 6.4

Your answers may be somewhat different, but the following answers provide a guide.

1. The five general evaluation criteria CCC should consider for its contracts are competitive pricing and value, vendor understanding of expectations, capability of vendor to carry out technical or operational work, vendor management team fit, and financial capabilities.

2. The top four evaluation criteria for the animation software development vendor might be in order of importance, technical capability (including expertise of personnel), understanding of need (showing flexibility to work with CCC and its new idea), management team fit, and financial capability. The price of the contract is probably one of the least important evaluation criteria for CCC.

3. The top four evaluation criteria for the overseas artwork vendor might be in order of importance, price (since one of the reasons CCC is sending artwork production overseas is to save money), technical and operational capability of the vendor to ensure that the vendor has the skills to create the artwork, financial capability, and understanding of need. Since the deliverables may be well defined, the management philosophy won't be as important to CCC.

4. The CCC procurement team should create evaluation criteria before sending out the requests for proposals so that they can focus on the specific requirements needed. For instance, since price is the most important aspect of the overseas artwork, CCC can emphasize that the proposal that includes the best price and that demonstrates the highest technical ability will win over other proposals. That way, the vendors can put together proposals that focus on demonstrating those capabilities. Even if CCC does not include the evaluation criteria in the procurement documents for the vendors, CCC can at least write them with more focus and clarity.

5. Marcus should still use evaluation criteria for the Thundering Sound Productions company. Even though Marcus may have good judgment about his buddy, it will help both CCC and Thundering Sound Productions to make sure that each can fulfill the contract. It will also help the teams create a more robust contract SOW and, eventually, a better contract.

6. For each vendor, you might answer whether CCC should share the evaluation criteria or not as follows:

    Sound production   Yes, it's important that each criterion is met.

    Overseas artwork   Yes, it's important that they understand that the price and technical capability are some of the most important aspects. Showing creativity is not important, so the vendor won't waste time trying to be different from everyone else.

    Marketing firm   Possibly, to make sure the vendor demonstrates a proposal that includes the quality they will provide. CCC might find an advantage to judging the vendor on the merit of the vendor's own creative ideas rather than giving them too much direction.

    Animation software development   Perhaps not. Since CCC wants to build a good relationship with the vendor, it might be important for the proposal to demonstrate some of the creativity and flexibility without CCC hinting that is what is needed. CCC might want to see some independent thinking and want the management philosophy to reveal itself in the proposal.

Answers to Exercise 6.5

Your answers may be somewhat different, but the following answers provide a guide.

1. The acronym RAM stands for Responsibility Assignment Matrix.

2. The RAM is the integration of an organization chart and project tasks that creates a planning tool that describes who will accomplish what on a project.

3. A RAM is created by merging an organization breakdown structure with a work break-down structure.

4. The RAM for Operation:NFL is an example of a RAM that utilizes a legend. A RAM with a legend can be used to describe project team roles.

Answers to Exercise 6.6

Your answers may be somewhat different, but the following answers provide a guide.

1. The staffing management plan documents for the project team exactly how the human resources will be assigned to a project, what they will work on, and when they will depart from the project.

2. The three types of constraints found in enterprise environmental factors are the organizational structure, collective bargaining agreements, and economic conditions. On project Operation:NFL, you are probably having problems with organizational structures of the subcontracting companies as well as the collective bargaining agreements that cover those subcontractors.

3. The three inputs into a staffing management plan are enterprise environmental factors, organizational process assets, and the project management plan.

4. You would include an organization chart in a staffing management plan so the project team understands the reporting relationships on the project. On Operation:NFL, you have over 100 people working on the project. You will want to have an organization chart that depicts all 100 people to make sure everyone understands who reports to whom.

5. You would include a roles and responsibilities matrix in your staffing management plan to make it clear who is accountable for what on the project. With 100 people working on Operation:NFL, you will want to make sure everyone understands who is accountable for what pieces of work.

Answers to Exercise 6.7

Your answers may be somewhat different, but the following answers provide a guide.

1. Six activities have been created at the lowest level of the work breakdown structure (the activity list level).

2. The dependencies in all six activities are mandatory because they are inherent in the work to be done. For example, you can't prototype the device until the design is complete.

3. Finish-to-start is the one logical relationship between each activity for the Canadian software. This relationship was used because, for example, the prototype of the device should not start until the design is completed.

4. Precedence diagramming method is the best method to diagram these activities because this technique allows you to have four dependency relationships. For this example, you could have also used the arrow diagramming technique since all of the relationships are finish-to-start relationships

5. If you sequence the lowest-level activities between a start and finish node, your answer should look like the following graphic.

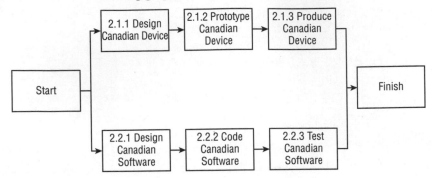

Answers to Exercise 6.8

Your answers may be somewhat different, but the following answers provide a guide.

1. Activity Resource Estimating is the third process step in the Time Management process.

2. The three types of resources are people, equipment, and materials.

3. Some examples of material resources are water and electrical power.

4. The three primary inputs used in Activity Resource Estimating are an activity list of the WBS, organizational process assets, and resource availability or resource pool.

5. Activity Resource requirements are the primary output of Activity Resource Estimating.

6. Your answer should be similar to the following:

Task	Resource	Number of Resources
Market surveys	Marketing	2
Legal clearance on name	Legal	1
Create recipe	Chef	1
Create product	Chef	1
Internal taste testing	Employees	10
Focus group taste testing	Focused Marketing, Inc.	50
Marketing plan	Marketing	4
Ad campaign	Advertising	2
	Marketing	1

Creating the Project Schedule and Budget

The following exercises are presented in this section:

- Exercise 7.1: Estimating Duration Activity
- Exercise 7.2: Calculating Critical Path
- Exercise 7.3: Calculating PERT
- Exercise 7.4: Duration Compression
- Exercise 7.5: Creating Gantt Charts
- Exercise 7.6: Ranges of Cost Estimates
- Exercise 7.7: Cost Estimating
- Exercise 7.8: Creating a Budget and Cost Baseline

Exercise 7.1: Estimating Duration Activity

The objectives for Exercise 7.1 are as follows:

- Describe the meaning of duration.
- Describe the four types of tools and techniques used to create a duration estimate.
- Create duration estimates.

Background

Activity Duration Estimating is a time management planning process that helps determine the amount of time an activity will take. Time in this context means how many work periods (days, weeks, hours, etc.) for the activity to be performed and takes into account elapsed time. For example, you start work at 8:00 AM and begin a task immediately. If you do your normal daily routine, you take a break at 10:00 AM and 2:00 PM and have lunch at noon for an hour. You started the work at 8:00 AM and complete the first draft at 11:00 AM. You have your boss review your work from 11:00 AM till 3:30 PM. At 3:30 PM you put some finishing touches on the report and hand it in at 5:00 PM and go home. You would call this a one-day duration even though you only worked on it from 8:00 AM until 10:00 AM, 10:15 AM until 11:00 AM, and 3:30 PM until 5:00 PM.

To create an activity duration estimate, you take the inputs of enterprise environmental factors, organizational process assets, the project scope statement, the work breakdown structure activity list, the resource calendar, the project management plan, and the activity resource requirements and you then determine the estimated time expected for each activity.

Elements of Duration Estimates

You can use several tools and techniques to determine the duration estimates. The first is called expert judgment. In this technique, you ask the people who will perform the task to provide the estimates.

The second technique is called analogous estimating, sometimes called top-down estimating. In this technique, you find other similar tasks that were performed before and use this historical information to create the estimates.

The next technique is parametric estimating. It uses a unit of work multiplied by the productivity of the worker. Say, for example, you are estimating a street-paving project. You know that one paving truck can pave 100 feet in 2 hours. You also know the length of the street is 300 feet. Therefore the duration for paving this street is 6 hours.

The next technique is called three-point estimating. In this technique you ask your resources to provide three estimates for the work to be performed. They would provide a most likely estimate, meaning all things considered what it would take to do the work. The second estimate is an optimistic estimate, meaning how long it will take if everything to complete the task goes really well. The last estimate in three-point estimating is a pessimistic estimate, meaning how long it will take to complete the task if everything goes very poorly.

The last technique used in activity duration estimating is reserve analysis, also called contingency. Reserve time is a unit of measure that is added to the original estimate to allow for any schedule risk. The unit of measure can be either more hours or a percentage. In our paving example, you know the truck you're using has been having some problems. Because of this you will add 2 more hours to the 6-hour estimate as reserve time. This analysis of how much reserve time should be applied is called reserve analysis.

Creating a Duration Estimate

There are seven steps to creating duration activity estimates.

1. Determine if the WBS needs to be decomposed into smaller activities, called an activity list. Each activity should be small enough to be assigned to one person.

2. Understand the resource requirements for each activity.

3. Determine whether it would be best to use expert judgment, analogous estimating, three-point estimating, or parametric estimating for each activity.

4. Determine the proper duration estimate for each activity.

5. Analyze each activity for schedule risk.

6. Analyze what type of reserve time you might apply: a work unit or percentage.

7. Add reserve time to each activity where appropriate.

In this exercise, we're going to continue building our time management information at SystemsDelivery by creating duration estimates for the credit card validation project.

Scenario

Your company, TPMP, has just placed you at SystemsDelivery, Inc. as a temporary project manager. You've been assigned the credit card validation project. This project is designed to be the next best thing in credit card fraud prevention. The management of SystemsDelivery believes that this product will be in high demand at every major retailer in the country. Of course, the management needs this product to go to market as quickly as possible. You have been on the project for two weeks now. You have created the work breakdown structure (WBS) illustrated in the following figure for producing the Canadian product. This WBS was created at the lowest possible level, the activity list.

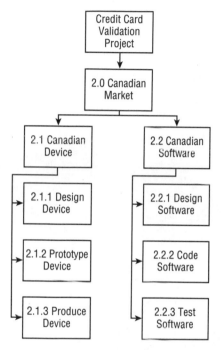

Estimating Duration Activity

Use the work breakdown structure provided in the previous illustration for the credit card validation project and start creating duration estimates.

1. How many activities have been created at the lowest level of the work breakdown structure (the activity list level)?

2. What types of people will be needed to perform these activities?

3. What tool and technique will you use to derive the estimate?

4. Determine the duration estimate for each activity. These estimates will be your "best guess." Please place your answer on the following WBS.

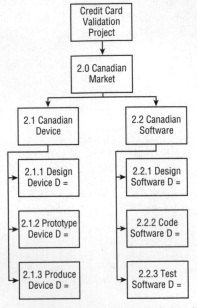

5. Determine what type of reserve time you might apply to the tasks at risk.

6. Add the reserve time to the appropriate estimates. Place new duration estimates on the following WBS.

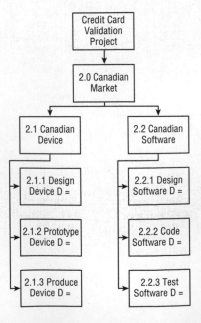

Exercise 7.2: Calculating Critical Path

The objectives for Exercise 7.2 are as follows:

- Describe the meaning of float.
- Understand the three steps of calculating critical path.

Background

When you create a project schedule network diagram, you also create a critical path for your project. The critical path is defined as the longest path through the project and has no float, or slack time—meaning the amount of time you can delay the early start of the project without affecting the planned finish date of the project. Looking at your project schedule network diagram, the critical path or tasks with float may not be obvious. You'll want to manage the critical path because if a task on the critical path slips, the end date of the project slips. To determine the critical path for your project, you use a mathematical analysis tool and technique of the Schedule Development process called Critical Path Method (CPM).

CPM calculates a single critical path for the project. (It is possible for another path to have the exact same estimates and therefore you could have two critical paths, but this rarely happens.) It requires that you perform a forward pass and backward pass and calculate float for the entire project schedule network diagram.

Let's calculate the critical path for the project schedule network diagram illustrated here:

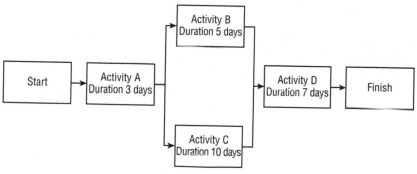

Calculating a Forward Pass

To calculate the critical path for our project schedule network diagram, first we'll have to compute a forward pass. Starting at the earliest point of the project schedule network diagram, a forward pass calculates the early start and early finish for each task. An early start is the earlier time a task can start. An early finish is the earlier time a task can finish. Following are the steps to calculating a forward pass:

1. Starting at the earliest point of the project schedule network diagram, look at Activity A. The earliest time Activity A can start is day 0. Therefore the early start is zero. Add the duration to the early start. The early finish is 3. 0 + 3 = 3. The formula is Early Start + Duration = Early Finish.

2. Continue through the project schedule network diagram and calculate the early start and early finish for each task.

3. When you get to Activity D, use the largest early finish from Activity B or Activity C for the early start of Activity D. The following table illustrates the early start and early finish days for our network diagram.

Activity	Early Start	Early Finish
A	0	3
B	3	8
C	3	13
D	13	20

Calculating a Backward Pass

Calculate the backward pass by starting at the latest point of the project schedule network diagram; a backward pass determines the late start and late finish for each task. The late start is the latest time a task can start for the task to be completed without changing the end date of the project. The late finish is the latest time a task can finish for the task to be completed without changing the end date of the project. Following are the steps for computing a backward pass.

1. Starting at the latest point of the project schedule network diagram, look at the final activity, in this case, Activity D. The latest time it can finish is day 20. Day 20 is the early finish from the forward pass. Therefore, the late finish is 20. Subtract the duration from the late finish. The late start is 13. 20 – 7 = 13.

2. Continue through the project schedule network diagram and calculate the late start and late finish for each task. The formula for the backward pass is Late Finish – Duration = Late Start.

3. When you get to Activity A, use the smallest late start from Activity B or Activity C for the late finish of Activity A. The following table illustrates the late start and late finish for our project schedule network diagram.

Activity	Late Start	Late Finish
D	13	20
C	3	13
B	8	13
A	0	3

Calculating Float

Finally, you can calculate float by subtracting the early start from the late start or subtracting the early finish from the late finish.

1.   Starting at the earliest point of the project schedule network diagram, look at Activity A. The late start is zero and the early start is zero. Subtract the early start form the late start. Therefore the float is zero. $0 - 0 = 0$.

2.   Continue through the project schedule network diagram and calculate the float for each task. The following table depicts the float available for each activity of our network diagram.

Activity	Float
A	0
B	5
C	0
D	0

Using the Critical Path Method

If you look at the project schedule network diagram shown earlier and take into account the forward, backward, and float calculations, you determine the critical path for the project. Here's how you calculate the critical path:

1.   Take the project schedule network diagram for your project. Perform a forward pass. Starting at the earliest point, day 0, determine the early start and early finish for each task.

2.   Perform a backward pass. Starting at the latest point of the project schedule network diagram, determine the late start and late finish for each task.

3.   Subtract the early start from the late start to determine the float.

4.   Determine which tasks have zero float.

The critical path of our project schedule network diagram is Activity A, C, and D because the critical path has zero float. The following figure illustrates the critical path for the project schedule network diagram.

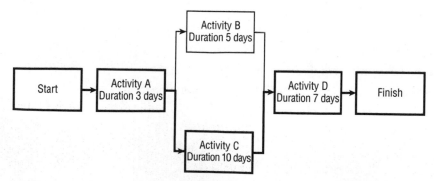

Now it's time to put the critical path method into action. In calculating critical path, TPMP is going to help SystemsDelivery determine the critical path for the credit card validation project.

Scenario

Your company, TPMP, has just placed you at SystemsDelivery, Inc. as a temporary project manager. You've been assigned the credit card validation project. This project is designed to be the next best thing in credit card fraud prevention. The management of SystemsDelivery believes that this product will be in high demand at every major retailer in the country. Of course, the management needs this product to go to market as quickly as possible. You have been on the project for two weeks now. You have created the project schedule network diagram shown in the following figure. You've decided to determine the critical path. You know that this information will help you manage the project more effectively.

Calculating Critical Path

Use the project schedule network diagram provided earlier for the credit card validation project and calculate the critical path.

1. Do a forward pass on the project schedule network diagram. What is the early start for tasks 2.1.1 and 2.2.1?

2. What is the early start for task 2.2.2?

3. Do a backward pass on the project schedule network diagram. What is the largest early finish between tasks 2.1.3 and 2.2.3? It is also the late finish.

4. What is the late finish for task 2.1.2?

5. What is the definition of float?

6. Calculate the float for the project schedule network diagram. What is the float on task 2.1.1?

7. Which tasks make up the critical path?

Exercise 7.3: Calculating PERT

The objectives for Exercise 7.3 are as follows:

- Describe the three types of estimates for a PERT calculation.

- Perform a PERT calculation.

Background

Another mathematical analysis tool and technique that has been used for years even though it is no longer covered in *A Guide to the PMBOK* is the Program Evaluation and Review Technique (PERT). Like CPM, it focuses on determining the project's duration, but it uses expected values or weighted averages for each lowest level activity to perform the calculations instead of a most likely duration estimate as CPM uses. PERT relies heavily on the mathematics of probability and statistical bell curves. PERT can be used to provide more confidence to duration estimates that may be shaky. It can be applied to every task, to certain risky tasks, or to the critical path.

To do a PERT calculation, you must start with the three estimates created in the three-point estimating tool and technique of the Activity Duration Estimating process:

Optimistic   If everything goes well, how long the task will take.

Pessimistic   If everything goes poorly, how long the task will take.

Most likely   The original estimate provided. Sometimes called a best guess.

Once you know the three estimates, you then do a calculation to determine the mean. In statistics, the mean represents the average of all estimates for a particular task. Next, you determine the standard deviation. This calculation will be used to determine the amount of additional time that can be added to the estimates to provide more confidence. Last, you add the mean to as many standard deviations as you need to provide the confidence you are looking for.

Let's take our previous project schedule network diagram and do a PERT calculation for each task using the following steps.

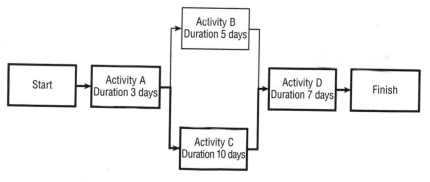

1. Determine the optimistic and pessimistic estimates. The most likely estimates were created in Exercise 7.1 with the three-point estimating tool and technique. Ask the experts who provided the first estimate to determine the optimistic and pessimistic estimates. The following table shows the estimates that our experts created.

Activity	Most Likely	Optimistic	Pessimistic
A	3	2	5
B	5	4	8
C	10	7	15
D	7	5	10

2. Determine the mean for each task. The formula for this calculation is

    Mean = (optimistic + (4 * most likely) + pessimistic) ÷ 6

    The following table illustrates the mean calculations for the network diagram.

Activity	Most Likely	Optimistic	Pessimistic	Mean
A	3	2	5	3.2
B	5	4	8	5.3
C	10	7	15	10.3
D	7	5	10	7.2

3. Determine the standard deviation for each task. The formula for this calculation is

    Standard Deviation (SD) = (pessimistic – optimistic) ÷ 6

    The following table shows the standard deviation for each task.

Activity	Most Likely	Optimistic	Pessimistic	Mean	SD
A	3	2	5	3.2	.5
B	5	4	8	5.3	.7
C	10	7	15	10.3	1.3
D	7	5	10	7.2	.8

4. Determine the confidence level you want to achieve. Add the mean to a standard factor multiplied by the standard deviation. The following table shows the standard factor and formula for each confidence level.

Confidence level	Standard Factor	Formula
50%	0	Mean
60%	0.25	Mean + (.25*SD)
70%	0.53	Mean + (.53*SD)
80%	0.84	Mean + (.84*SD)
90%	1.28	Mean + (1.28*SD)
95%	1.65	Mean + (1.65*SD)
99%	2.33	Mean + (2.33*SD)

Using the 99 percent confidence shown in the preceding table, you would be able to complete your PERT calculation in the following table.

Activity	Most likely	Optimistic	Pessimistic	Mean	SD	New
A	3	2	5	3.2	.5	4.5
B	5	4	8	5.3	.7	7
C	10	7	15	10.3	1.3	13.5
D	7	5	10	7.2	.8	9

NOTE   Values in the table above for the new estimate have been rounded to the nearest .5 value.

Now, you'll get a chance to calculate PERT for the credit card validation project.

Scenario

TPMP has just placed you at SystemsDelivery, Inc. as a temporary project manager. You've been assigned the credit card validation project. This project is designed to be the next best thing in credit card fraud prevention. The management of SystemsDelivery believes that this product will be in high demand at every major retailer in the country. Of course, the management needs this product to go to market as quickly as possible. You have been on the project for a while now. You've been developing your schedule and you're very worried about a couple of the estimates that have been provided. You've decided to use PERT to create some new estimates that will provide more confidence in the completion date of the project. The following figure illustrates the critical path you've created for the Canadian device. You'll use this critical path as the basis for calculating PERT.

Calculating PERT

Use the critical path diagram provided in for the credit card validation project and start a PERT calculation.

1. What are the three types of estimates used for a PERT calculation?
2. What is the most likely estimate for task 2.2.2?
3. You and your team have determined that the pessimistic estimate is 13 and the optimistic estimate is 9. What is the mean?
4. What is the standard deviation for task 2.2.2?
5. What is the standard factor for 80 percent confidence?
6. What is the new estimate for this task using 80 percent confidence?

Exercise 7.4: Duration Compression

The objectives for Exercise 7.4 are as follows:

- Describe the two types of duration compression.
- Describe the steps performed to crash a project.
- Describe the steps performed to fast track a project.

Background

You have put your schedule together, and you now know the end date. Your sponsor requested that the project be completed in the fourth quarter of this year. Your end date is first quarter of next year. This is when you employ another set of Schedule Development process tools and techniques—duration compression. There are two popular techniques to achieve duration compression. The first is crashing. The second is fast tracking. We'll spend some time on each of these topics.

Crashing

Crashing is an analysis method that looks at trade-offs between the schedule and the cost of the project. In crashing, you analyze the critical path and determine what you can do to shorten it. It's best to get your team together to do this activity. You'll need your experts to help analyze the schedule.

Crashing may or may not result in a shorter schedule. You may not be able to apply enough crashing to enough tasks on the critical path to shorten the amount needed to finish the project where the sponsor wants you to. It also may affect the project's budget beyond the acceptable range.

Let's take our previous network diagram illustrated again and do a crashing exercise.

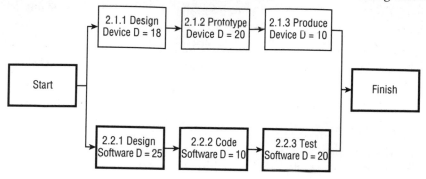

1. If you haven't already determined the critical path, you'll need to do that. You can't shorten the project duration if you don't know the critical path. The critical path we created in Exercise 7.2 is illustrated in here.

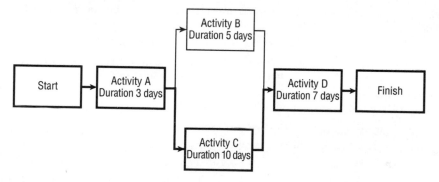

2. Now analyze each task for compression possibilities. You are looking for opportunities to do the following:

    ▪ Add more resources to shorten the task duration.

    ▪ Reduce the scope of the project and subsequently these critical path tasks.

    ▪ Find a different way of sequencing the tasks that will reduce the duration.

3. Determine whether the schedule and cost trade-off are acceptable. For example, you've decided to add another resource to Activity C. Adding the other resource changes the work of the task as illustrated here.

Activity	Duration	Cost
Do 10 days of work with one person	10 days	$1,000
Do 5 days of work per person and 1 day to consolidate the results.	6 days	$1,200

That's it! Adding another $200 to the budget is not a problem since the project manager has the authority to approve this budget change and you've decreased the duration of the project by four days.

Fast Tracking

Fast tracking is another analysis method that may enable you to reduce the duration of your projects. In fast tracking, you look for opportunities to have tasks performed in parallel or partial parallel instead of sequentially. Again, you only look for opportunities on the critical path. It would be best to do this analysis with the people who will perform these tasks. They are the experts and can determine if this technique will work.

Fast tracking may indeed result in a shorter schedule than your original critical path, but it may raise the risks beyond the acceptable range. Let's take our faithful network diagram and run through the steps of fast tracking. Take a look at the network diagram again.

1. Determine the critical path of the project. We did this already in Exercise 7.2, but take another look at the critical path. You won't shorten the project duration if you don't work on the critical path.

2. Analyze each task on the critical path for its ability to be performed at the same time as another task.

3. Determine if the risks associated with your schedule changes are acceptable.

Crashing and fast tracking are effective tools to compress the duration of a project. Now, you'll get a chance now to use those tools on the credit card validation project.

Scenario

TPMP has just placed you at SystemsDelivery, Inc. as a temporary project manager. You've been assigned the credit card validation project. This project is designed to be the next best thing in credit card fraud prevention. The management of SystemsDelivery believes that this product will be in high demand at every major retailer in the country. Of course the management needs this product to go to market as quickly as possible. You have been on the project for a while now. You've completed your schedule and critical path shown in the following figure and realize that the Canadian device won't hit in the market window SystemsDelivery has targeted. You've decided to compress the duration of the project.

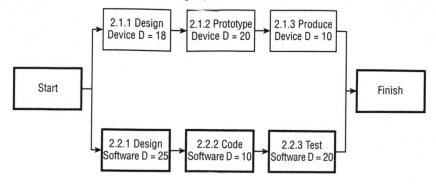

Duration Compression

Use the critical path diagram provided for the credit card validation project and compress the project duration.

1.   What are the two types of duration compression?

2.   Describe crashing.

3.   Describe fast tracking.

4.   Compare the following project schedule network diagram to the one in the scenario. This is an example of which technique?

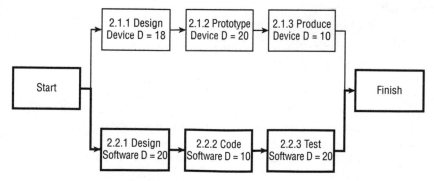

5. Compare the network diagram below to the one in the scenario. This is an example of which technique?

6. What tasks are on the new critical path for the graphic above?

Exercise 7.5: Creating Gantt Charts

The objectives for Exercise 7.5 are as follows:

- Define a Gantt chart.
- Determine the values for the X and Y axes.
- Construct a Gantt chart.

Background

You have put your schedule together and you now need a simple way to communicate the activities of your project over time. You have already created a work breakdown structure and a project schedule network diagram. Those tools have worked well for communicating the work and sequence of the work to your project team. Your next audience is the project sponsor and the executive team. These are people who do not need to know every single task but need to know the general flow of the work. They may be more interested in the bottom line than the details. This is probably the right time to create a Gantt chant, also known as a bar chart. *A Guide to the PMBOK* describes a Gantt chart as a "graphic display of schedule related information." It normally depicts the project elements down the left side of the chart (Y axis) and a time scale across the top or bottom of the chart (X axis). Tasks with a duration are shown as date-placed horizontal bars. Most project managers use a project management software system for creating a Gantt chart.

To create a Gantt chart you must first determine the time scale you will use to display the information. Second, you will determine the level of the tasks that will be displayed. Last, draw the chart and place the tasks on the chart.

Let's take our project schedule network diagram illustrated in here and turn it into a Gantt chart using the following four steps.

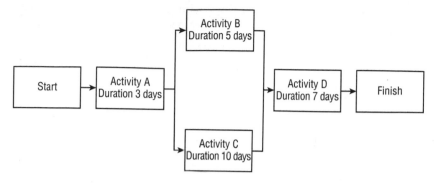

1. Determine the time scale you will use for your Gantt chart. Analyzing the project schedule network diagram, you determine that the time scale used is days. You also look at the critical path. You determine that the critical path is 20 days in length. That should create a chart that fits nicely on one page. Having these two pieces of information, you decide to use a time scale of days for the Gantt chart.

2. Now analyze the tasks for the appropriate level to depict on your chart. If your audience is looking for a summarization of the project progress, you would not show every task in a 200-task project. You would find a way to summarize the information. You may find it helpful to go back to your work breakdown structure and look at the upper levels. These are the levels you used to decompose the rest of the project's tasks. Use these summary tasks or others that you believe will be the best way to depict the information.

3. Draw the chart. The activities should go on the left side of the bar chart and the time scale across the top or bottom. The following graphic illustrates this Gantt chart.

4. Place the tasks on the chart. On the network diagram we are using, Activity A has a three-day duration. You draw that task as a horizontal bar on the chart crossing over days 1, 2, and 3. When you're through, your diagram would look like the one shown here.

Scenario

Your company, Terrific Project Management Partners, has just placed you at SystemsDelivery, Inc. as a temporary project manager. You've been assigned the credit card validation project. This project is designed to be the next best thing in credit card fraud prevention. The management of SystemsDelivery believes that this product will be in high demand at every major retailer in the country. Of course, the management needs this product to go to market as quickly as possible. You have been on the project for a while now. You've completed your schedule, which is shown in the following graphic, and have compressed the duration so that the project will complete in the desired time frame. You have a status presentation in a few days to the project sponsor and the executives in the marketing department. You want to make sure that they understand the sequence of activities and the time line to complete the project. You've decided the best way to communicate the time line is via a Gantt chart.

Creating Gantt Charts

Use the project schedule network diagram provided earlier for the credit card validation project and create a Gantt chart.

1. Gantt charts are sometimes also called what?

2. What is the definition of a Gantt chart?

3. Determine the best time scale for the credit card evaluation project. What is it?

4. How many activities will you show for this audience?

5. Draw your Gantt chart.

Exercise 7.6: Ranges of Cost Estimates

The objectives for Exercise 7.6 are as follows:

- Describe the three ranges of cost estimates.
- Describe when each range is used.

Background

You have completed the project schedule for your project and now you are ready to do cost estimating. Before you do, let's define the different ranges of cost estimates and in what phase of the project they are typically done. There are three types of cost estimates: order of magnitude, budget, and definitive. These types originated in the engineering and construction industries.

Order of magnitude estimates   Order of magnitude estimates are usually done at the very beginning of a project, sometimes as early as the Initiating phase. These estimates are usually derived from information for similar or previous projects. For example, you had a project two years ago that took one year and $1 million to complete. The current project you are estimating is similar, and the same people are available to work on this one. Based on that information, you might use the same estimate on the new project. Order of magnitude estimates can vary greatly in the range they cover. A typical order of magnitude estimate can fall between –25 percent and +75 percent of the actual cost of the project.

Budget estimates   Budget estimates are created during the Cost Budgeting process, which is done during the planning portion of a project. Budget estimates should cover all of the costs of a project including all personnel, equipment, and materials needed for the project. Budget estimating should be done prior to the budget being set for the project. You'll need to work with management to make sure that budgets are set after budget estimates are done. A budget estimate should be more precise than an order of magnitude estimate, falling in the range of –10 percent to +25 percent of the actual cost of the project.

Definitive estimates   Definitive estimates will be the most detailed and therefore the most precise estimate of the three types. A definitive estimate is usually derived from an expert or project team looking at a specific task and determining how long it will take to complete the work. When you add up all of the task estimates, you will have a total project estimate that should fall in the range of –5 percent to +10 percent of the actual cost of the project. Like budget estimates, definitive estimates are also created in the Planning portion of a project.

Getting clear about the range of estimates you are creating will make it easier on your team to create the right estimate at the right time.

Scenario

TPMP has just placed you at the Pinnacle Candy Company as a temporary project manager. You have been assigned the EspressoFix Bar project. This project is going to create a new candy that will satisfy every coffee addict's need for coffee all wrapped up in a candy bar. The management at Pinnacle only wants to see if this new candy bar is marketable. Production of the finished product will be another project initiated later. You have been asked to estimate your project. You are very interested in making sure the estimates are done well because you are going to be held accountable for the costs of the project.

Ranges of Cost Estimates

Using the information provided for the EspressoFix Bar project, answer the following questions about types of cost estimates.

1. What are the three ranges of estimates?

2. Which estimate should be in the –5 percent to +10 percent range of the total cost of the project?

3. Which estimate is sometimes created in the Initiating processes?

4. The Pinnacle Candy Company has asked for you to create an order of magnitude estimate for the project. You have learned that the last time the company looked at creating a new product and its marketability, it spent $500,000 on the project. What should your estimate range be?

5. What is the most precise range of estimate? Why?

6. You have decided to create a definitive estimate for your project. Your team has created the following effort estimate. What will be the total cost of the project?

Task	Effort	Cost per Task Resources
Market surveys	18 days	$28,800
Legal clearance on name	15 days	$18,000
Create recipe	10 days	$4,000
Create product	7 days	$2,800
Internal taste testing	1 day	$2,000
Focus group taste testing	5 days	$250,000
Marketing plan	20 days	$64,000
Ad campaign	20 days	$32,000
Ad campaign	5 days	$4,000

Exercise 7.7: Cost Estimating

The objectives for Exercise 7.7 are as follows:

- Describe the three ways to create a cost estimate.
- Describe the three steps in creating estimates.

Background

Now that you know about order of magnitude, definitive, and budget Cost Estimating ranges, it's time to turn your focus on the three steps for creating estimates. First, you need to choose one of the various methods used for Cost Estimating. Next, you will need to determine the unit of measure for the estimates, and finally, you will actually create the estimates here in this section.

Determining the Estimating Method

Your first step in creating a cost estimate is to pick a method. There are actually eight tools and techniques used in the Cost Estimating process. Here we cover the three most commonly used techniques: analogous estimating, parametric estimating, and bottom-up estimating.

Analogous estimating   This technique uses expert judgment and information from previous projects to create the estimate. The previous projects you use must be very similar to the project you are trying to estimate. Your expert judgment helps you determine whether you will use the previous project's costs as is or extrapolate different portions of information to determine your own estimates. This technique is also sometimes called top-down estimating and is used to create an order of magnitude estimate. Because analogous estimating can be very subjective, it is usually not very accurate.

Parametric estimating   In this method of estimating, you determine what elements should be placed in a mathematical model to help you predict costs. Parametric estimating can be used to create any of the three types of estimates.

Bottom-up estimating   This method is the most precise method because it requires estimating each individual task separately. These estimates look at the effort required to complete a task, not the duration. Effort can be described as the time it takes to complete a task with no breaks or interruptions. Bottom-up estimating is to create definitive estimates.

Determining the Unit of Measure

Your next task, when you are creating estimates, is to determine the time unit of measure the entire team will use. You want all of your estimates in similar time increments (i.e., hours, days, weeks, etc.).

Creating the Estimate

Finally, once you determine the technique to use in creating your estimates, it is time to actually create them. In this step, you will pull together your project team and ask them to determine the estimate. There are times when this might feel like an episode of *Name That Tune,* but you need to provide as much precision as possible. You can apply more precision to your estimates by doing the following:

- Have the person doing the work create the estimate.
- Use task information from other projects.
- Use PERT (described in Exercise 7.3).

Be sure to estimate all tasks for all resources: people, equipment, and materials.

Scenario

TPMP has just placed you at the Pinnacle Candy Company as a temporary project manager. You have been assigned the EspressoFix Bar project. This project is going to create a new candy that will satisfy every coffee addict's need for coffee all wrapped up in a candy bar. The management at Pinnacle only wants to see if this new candy bar is marketable. Production of the finished product will be another project initiated later. You have been asked to estimate your project. You are very interested in making sure the estimates are done well because you are going to be held accountable for the costs of the project. Your team has already created the WBS with duration estimates illustrated in the following figure. They have also provided the resource pool located in the following table.

Resource Type	Name	Number
Skilled resources	Marketing	5
	Advertising	4
	Legal	2

Resource Type	Name	Number
	Chefs	2
	Employees	35
	Vendor—Focused Marketing, Inc.	Unlimited
Equipment	Test kitchen	1

Cost Estimating

Using the information provided for the EspressoFix Bar project, answer the following questions about Cost Estimating.

1. What are the three most commonly used estimating techniques?
2. Top-down estimating is also known as what?
3. Which estimating technique requires that you use a mathematical model?
4. Since you are going to be held accountable for the costs of the project, you have decided to create the most precise estimates possible. Which estimating technique will produce the most precise results?
5. What unit of measure will you use to estimate this project?
6. You have decided to ask the people performing the work to create the estimates. Who should create the estimate for the internal taste testing?
7. What are the three types of resources?

Exercise 7.8: Creating a Budget and Cost Baseline

The objectives for Exercise 7.8 are as follows:

- Describe the three major inputs in the Cost Budgeting process.
- Describe the steps in creating a budget.
- Describe the concept of a cost baseline.

Background

Chances are that sometime in your career you started planning a project and someone handed you the budget before you had completed the planning. You probably learned the hard way that you should be given a budget after the Planning processes and that the project manager is the person who should request the amount. The budgeting process outlined in PMI's *A Guide to the PMBOK, Cost Budgeting,* is the means you should use to create your project budget. In PMI's process, you use the major inputs of the cost estimates you created in Exercise 7.7, the WBS, and the project schedule created in the Schedule Development process. Then, using Cost Budgeting tools and techniques, you create the project budget. We'll walk you through this process here.

Inputs to Cost Budgeting

There are nine inputs for the Cost Budgeting process, three of which are the major inputs. The first is cost estimates. Depending on what Cost Estimating technique you used—analogous estimating, parametric modeling, or bottom-up estimating—your estimate may be very general or very specific. Regardless of the technique, you should have a list of the estimates for your project. The following table shows an example list of estimates for a project using the bottom-up estimating technique.

Task	Resource	Effort Estimate
A	Resource 1	8 hours
B	Resource 16	4 hours
C	Resource 7	6 hours
D	Resource 9	10 hours
	Resource 10	9 hours
	Resource 11	12 hours

The second input of the Cost Budgeting process is the WBS. The WBS is used to determine which tasks will have costs associated with them. You can use a traditional WBS diagram as shown here or you can translate the WBS into a table format like the preceding table.

The last input used to create a project budget is the project schedule. The project schedule is created in the Schedule Development process. It provides the element of time to your budget—

what monies need to be spent at what time. In the example shown in the following figure, you have already calculated the critical path and know that the project is 19 days in length.

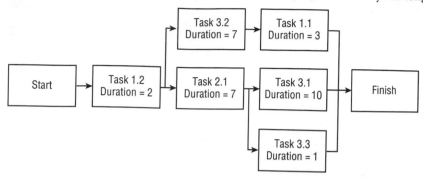

Determining the Budget

Using the cost estimating techniques described in Exercise 7.7 (analogous, parametric estimating, and bottom-up estimating), you will determine your cost budget. Remember to include all resource costs, not just human resources. You also need to include the costs for material and equipment resources.

At this point in the budget process, it's imperative that we introduce reserve analysis, another tool and technique of the Cost Budgeting process. Managerial reserves are additional monies put away to cover situations that are impossible to predict. You can add this pot of money to your budget during the Cost Budgeting process. Managerial reserves are usually controlled by upper management but are available to the project manager if the need arises. These monies are not used to fund bad cost estimates. You will need to determine whether you will add these funds to your budget request based on the risks associated with your project.

The result of your work at this point is the total project budget. In the following table, managerial reserves are a part of the budget Managerial reserves are monies amount put aside for emergencies. This amount was a small percentage of the total amount needed for the project.

Task	Resource	Effort Estimate	Rate	Cost
A	Resource 1	8 hours	$25 per hour	$200
B	Resource 16	4 hours	$100 per hour	$400
C	Resource 7	6 hours	$75 per hour	$450
D	Resource 9	10 hours	$30 per hour	$300
	Resource 10	9 hours	$175 per hour	$1,575

Task	Resource	Effort Estimate	Rate	Cost
	Resource 11	12 hours	$25 per hour	$300
Managerial Reserve				$500
Total Budget				$3,725

Creating a Cost Baseline

Just as you create a schedule baseline at the completion of the Schedule Development process, you also will create a cost baseline. A cost baseline is a copy of the budget prior to work beginning on your project. It is kept for comparison, analysis, and future forecasts. It is also called the planned value (PV), an earned value term. It does *not* include the managerial reserve or any fees that need to be paid on your project. The following table shows a sample cost baseline.

Task	Resource	Effort Estimate	Rate	Cost
A	Resource 1	8 hours	$25 per hour	$200
B	Resource 16	4 hours	$100 per hour	$400
C	Resource 7	6 hours	$75 per hour	$450
D	Resource 9	10 hours	$30 per hour	$300
	Resource 10	9 hours	$175 per hour	$1,575
	Resource 11	12 hours	$25 per hour	$300
Cost Baseline or Planned Value				$3,225

Scenario

TPMP has just placed you at the Pinnacle Candy Company as a temporary project manager. You have been assigned the EspressoFix Bar project. This project is going to create a new candy that will satisfy every coffee addict's need for coffee all wrapped up in a candy bar. The management at Pinnacle only wants to see if this new candy bar is marketable. Production of the finished product will be another project initiated later. The budget of $100,000 was established before you started work on the project. You are just about done with the project planning and wonder whether $100,000 will be enough money to cover the project. Your team has already created the WBS with duration estimates illustrated in the following figure and the project schedule network diagram and effort estimates shown in the following table.

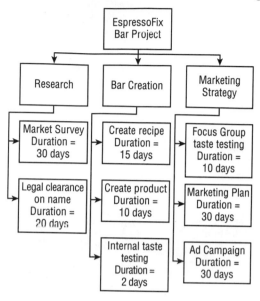

Task	Resource	Effort Estimate	Rate
Market surveys	Marketing	20 days	$1,200 per day
Marketing plan	Marketing	25 days	$1,200 per day
Ad campaign	Advertising	10 days	$1,000 per day
Legal clearance on the name	Legal	10 days	$1,600 per day
Create recipe	Chef	7 days	$800 per day
	Test kitchen	15 days	$1,000 per day
Create product	Chef	6 days	$800 per day
	Test kitchen	10 days	$1,000 per day
Internal taste testing	Employees on break	0	
	Employee cafeteria	0	
Focus group taste testing		Firm fixed price contract	$50,000

Creating a Budget and Cost Baseline

Use the information provided for the EspressoFix Bar project and answer the following questions about creating a budget and cost baseline.

1. What are three major inputs into the Cost Budgeting process?

2. What are three common techniques used to create cost estimates ?

3. What are managerial reserves?

4. A cost baseline is a copy of the budget prior to work beginning on your project. Why do you keep a cost baseline?

5. A cost baseline does not include what?

6. A cost baseline is also known as what?

7. How long is this project?

8. You have decided to not apply any managerial reserves to this project. What is the total budget? Why?

9. What is the cost baseline? Why?

Answers to Section 7 Exercises

Answers to Exercise 7.1

1. Six activities have been created at the lowest level of the work breakdown structure (the activity list level).

2. Programmers and product engineers are the types of people needed to perform these activities.

3. Your best tool and technique to derive the estimate is expert judgment. You use expert judgement when there is no historical information available. This exercise did not state that there was any other information available. Therefore expert judgement would be the best answer.

4. When you determine the duration estimate for each activity, your answer might look like the following graphic.

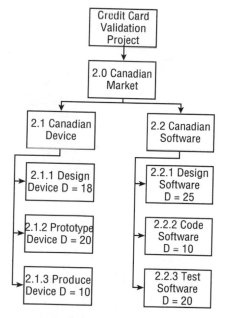

5. The type of reserve time you might apply to the tasks at risk is a work unit. The other option available is a percentage. Either of those methods can be used here.

6. If you add the reserve time to the appropriate estimates, your answer will look like the following graphic.

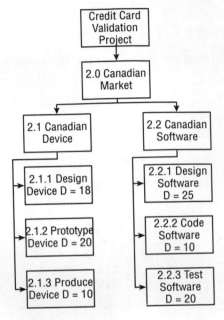

Answers to Exercise 7.2

1. When you do a forward pass on the project schedule network diagram, the early start for tasks 2.1.1 and 2.2.1 is zero.

2. The early start for task 2.2.2 is 25.

3. When you do a backward pass on the project schedule network diagram, the largest early finish between tasks 2.1.3 and 2.2.3 is 55. It is also the late finish.

4. The late finish for task 2.1.2 is 45.

5. Float is the amount of time that an activity may be delayed from the early start without delaying the project finish date.

6. If you calculate the float for the project schedule network diagram, the float on task 2.1.1 is 7.

7. Tasks 2.2.1, 2.2.2, 2.2.3 make up the critical path.

Answers to Exercise 7.3

1. The three types of estimates used for a PERT calculation are most likely, optimistic, and pessimistic.

2. The most likely estimate for task 2.2.2 is 10.

3. When you and your team determine that the pessimistic estimate is 13 and the optimistic estimate is 9, then the mean is 10.3.

4. The standard deviation for task 2.2.2 is .7 (rounded).

5. The standard factor for 80 percent confidence is .84.

6. Using 80 percent confidence, the new estimate for this task is 11.

Answers to Exercise 7.4

1. The two types of duration compression are crashing and fast tracking.

2. Crashing is an analysis method that looks at trade-offs between the schedule and the cost of the project. In crashing, you analyze the critical path and determine what you can do to shorten it.

3. In fast tracking, you look for opportunities to have tasks worked in parallel instead of sequentially.

4. Comparing the project schedule network diagrams, you'll notice that this is an example of crashing.

5. Comparing the project schedule network diagrams, you'll notice that this is an example of fast tracking.

6. The new critical path for the new graphic is 2.1.1, 2.1.2, and 2.1.3.

Answers to Exercise 7.5

1. Gantt charts are sometimes also called bar charts.

2. A Gantt chart is a graphic display of schedule-related information.

3. The best time scale for your project is days because all of the duration estimates are calculated in days.

4. You will show six activities for this audience.

5. Your Gantt chart should look like the following chart.

Answers to Exercise 7.6

1. The three ranges of estimates are order of magnitude, definitive, and budget.

2. A definitive estimate should be in the –5 percent to +10 percent range of the total cost of the project.

3. An order of magnitude estimate is sometimes created in the Initiating phase.

4. You have learned that the last time it looked at creating a new product and its marketability, the company spent $500,000 on the project. Since a typical order of magnitude estimate will fall between –25 percent and +75 percent of the actual cost of the project, your estimate range should be $375,000 to $875,000.

5. A definitive estimate is the most precise range of estimate because it is usually derived by an expert or the project team looking at a specific task and determining how long it will take to complete the work.

6. Given the provided effort estimate, the total cost of the project will be $405,600.

Answers to Exercise 7.7

1. Analogous estimating, parametric modeling, and bottom-up estimating are the three most commonly used estimating techniques.

2. Top-down estimating is also known as analogous estimating.

3. The parametric estimating technique requires that you use a mathematical model.

4. Since you are going to be held accountable for the costs of the project, you create the most precise estimates possible by using the bottom-up estimating technique.

5. You should use hours as your measure for this project because the smaller duration estimate is 2 days. Using hours would be a safe way to guarantee that you have one unit of measure to fit all of the tasks.

6. The chef would be the mostly likely candidate to create the estimate for the internal taste testing since chances are good she has done this type of work before.

7. The three types of resources are people, equipment, and materials.

Answers to Exercise 7.8

1. Cost estimates, WBS, and project schedule are three major inputs into the Cost Budgeting process.

2. Analogous estimating, parametric modeling, and bottom-up estimating are three common techniques that are used to create cost estimates.

3. Managerial reserves are additional monies put away to cover situations that are impossible to predict. These funds are usually controlled by upper management but are available to the project manager if the need arises. These monies are not used to fund bad cost estimates.

4. One reason you should keep a cost baseline is for comparison purposes. You may also use it later for analysis and future forecasts.

5. A cost baseline does not include managerial reserves and fees.

6. A cost baseline is also known as planned value (PV).

7. This is a 90-day project.

8. You create the total budget by adding all of the definitive estimates. Since no managerial reserves have been applied to the project, the total budget is $165,400.

9. The cost baseline is the total project budget minus the managerial reserve. Since this project does not have a managerial reserve, the cost baseline is $165,400.

Developing the Project Team

The following exercises are presented in this section:

- Exercise 8.1: Directing and Managing Project Execution
- Exercise 8.2: Acquiring the Project Team
- Exercise 8.3: Developing the Project Team
- Exercise 8.4: Communicating with the Team and Resolving Conflict
- Exercise 8.5: Deciding on Information Distribution

Exercise 8.1: Directing and Managing Project Execution

The objectives for Exercise 8.1 are as follows:

- Describe seven inputs into the Direct and Manage Project Execution process.
- Describe the executing processes that are integrated into the Direct and Manage Project Executing process.
- Describe the tools and techniques of the Direct and Manage Project Execution process.

Background

It's show time! You have planned a flawless project and you have baselined the schedule, the quality plan, and the budget. Now it's time to start working the plan you have created. At this point in time, you have created your project management plan, and you have approved corrective actions, preventive actions, change requests, and defect repairs. You also have validated defect repairs, and finally, you have an administrative closure procedure. With these inputs, you now execute the plan.

The Direct and Manage Project Execution process is part of the integration management knowledge area. During this process, you will integrate the other executing processes, such as quality assurance, team development, information distribution, and contract administration.

This phase of the project will exercise all of your talents as a project manager. The tools and techniques used in this process are critical to your success. In this exercise, we will spend some time on each of the tools and techniques used to execute the project to successful completion.

Direct and Manage Project Execution Tools and Techniques

The two tools and techniques used to successfully execute the project are a project management methodology and project management information systems.

Project management methodology   This all-encompassing term is used to describe the process used by the project management team to execute the project. The following types of items are covered in this methodology:

- The day-to-day management of the tasks that produce the project objectives.
- Management of the team, the necessary training, and the acquisition of more resources when needed.

- Verification and validation of the project deliverables.

- Management of the risks on the project.

- Management of the changes to the baselines that have been established.

- Collection of data on project performance. Taking corrective action where needed.

- Lessons learned meetings to document and apply the findings.

Project management information systems (PMIS)   A PMIS is any manual or software program that helps the project manager collect, analyze, and integrate information about the project.

Using these tools and techniques effectively produces deliverables that enable the project manager to deliver the objectives of the project as chartered.

Outputs of Direct and Manage Project Execution

Outputs of the Direct and Manage Project Execution process are the deliverables of the project, that is, the reason the project was initiated in the first place.

Additional outputs are the actions that are taken as a result of managing the execution of the project:

- Requested changes: Any inquiry to expand or reduce the scope of the project after it has been set or baselined

- Implemented change requests: An inquiry that requests a change to the scope of the project and that has been accepted and implemented

- Implemented corrective actions: Any activity that the project manager has undertaken to keep the project on track

- Implemented preventive action: Specific activities that the project team has taken on to reduce the consequences of project risks

- Implemented defect repairs: Repairs that have been completed for the product of the project to meet the quality standards that were required

- Work performance information: Any status information that the project manager gathers to monitor the execution of the project

In this exercise, you will test your knowledge about directing and managing the execution of the project as you help the Sensational Advertisement Productions company.

Scenario

TPMP has brought project management processes to an advertising firm, Sensational Advertisement Productions (SAP), and the project managers at SAP are learning how to use the eight knowledge areas of scope, time, cost, quality, human resource, communications, risk, and procurement management. However, you need to help them start using the processes and tools of what is probably their most important function: integration management.

You are working with Pam Rosenbaum, who has been assigned account management functions for a telecommunications client's important new product: a new cell phone that integrates normal service with PDA functions right on the phone, which will be sold at a competitive price with normal cell phone services. The account has several project managers for the various sales campaigns: Michael Harland for the print campaigns, Judy Arakawa for the TV campaigns, and Joseph Matumbo for the telemarketing campaigns. Each project manager is working with marketing managers within the telecommunications company to get direction and approval for the work they will produce.

Because these projects must integrate, Pam has created one integrated project plan. She now knows that she must execute this integrated project plan.

Directing and Managing Project Execution

1. What are the seven inputs for Direct and Manage Project Execution?

2. Pam has found that some tasks are being done out of sequence on the project. She also has found work done that is out of scope. What tool and technique of Direct and Manage Project Execution needs to be put into place?

3. Pam uses spreadsheet software to prepare task assignments. This spreadsheet software is also known as what general project management term?

4. Pam is having difficulty with the team making the same mistakes over and over again. What aspect of the project management methodology might Pam employ to correct this situation?

5. What are the seven outputs of Direct and Manage Project Execution process?

Exercise 8.2: Acquiring the Project Team

The objectives for Exercise 8.2 are as follows:

- Describe the five inputs of Acquire Project Team.
- Describe the four tools and techniques of Acquire Project Team.
- Describe the steps of negotiating for project staff.

Background

Acquire Project Team is a key planning process for completing the human resource management processes. In the Acquire Project Team process, the project manager gathers the following inputs:

- Enterprise environmental factors
- Organizational process assets
- Roles and responsibilities
- Project organization charts
- Staffing management plan

The project manager also uses four tools and techniques to put the project staff into place:

- Negotiations
- Preassignment
- Virtual teams
- Acquisition

We examine each of these in this exercise.

Negotiations

One of the necessary skills a project manager must have is negotiating. This skill is highly utilized during the Acquire Project Team process.

In order to get the right people on your project, you will need to have a negotiating strategy. Here are the steps to effective staff negotiations:

1. Identify your target team.   If you could have the best people for your project, who would they be? Step through your WBS and examine the staffing requirements outlined in your staffing management plan. Determine the right person for each task. Have a fallback plan by identifying one or two people who also could do the task yet may not be as desirable as your first choice.

2. Identify potential barriers to getting your target team.   You will need to understand why you may not be able to get the right people for your project. Examine the following possibilities:

Availability of the people you want   Jose is your top candidate for Task 62. Jose is constantly sought after for projects because of his expertise and work ethic. What strategy will you use if Jose is not available when you need him?

Your relationship with the functional manager   You have found Jose's boss, Mary, to be difficult to work with. How will you work with her to come to a win-win solution that will benefit your project and her?

Your authority as a project manager   Organizations give project managers different levels of authority to run their projects. What is your authority to staff your project? How strong are your influencing skills?

Your organization structure   Organizations can be established as functional or as projectized, with many variations in between. Functional organizations have clear reporting relationships, where a subordinate usually has one supervisor. Projectized organizations are created to support project work and most of the people are doing project work. Projectized organizations tend to provide more authority to project managers by the very nature of the organization. What is your organization structure? How will that structure help or hinder your ability to get the right resources?

3. Build your negotiation strategy.   Spend a little time building your negotiating strategy. Determine your requests and your fallback strategy if you cannot get your requests filled. Understand enough about your barriers to know what will help or hinder your position. Determine the best approach to negotiate your position.

4. Negotiate for your project team.   Start negotiating for the most critical staff first. If you are able to get them assigned to your project, you may not need your first choice candidate for other, less important positions. Work your way negotiating through your dream list until all of your positions are filled.

Preassignment

The second tool and technique of the Acquire Project Team process is preassignment. Preassignment is described as a situation in which a project has certain positions filled as the project is initiated. This can happen in the following situations:

- There is only one resource available who can fill a specific position.

- Projects are "sold" with staff predefined.
- The staff is defined in the charter for the project.

Virtual Teams

As technology advances, the possibility of successful virtual teams becomes greater. It is no longer necessary to completely co-locate the project team because of advances in teleconferencing and videoconferencing. This tool and technique creates new possibilities for nontraditional teams.

Acquisition

The last tool and technique of Acquire Project Team process is acquisition—how you acquire outside resources for your project team. We will not spend any time on this subject here. Procurement is extensively covered in other exercises.

Scenario

TPMP has just placed you at Affordable Sweeping, Inc., an up-and-coming property maintenance company. Affordable Sweeping has just been awarded the contract to get the local NFL stadium ready for the current football season. Affordable Sweeping named the project Operation:NFL and has hired you to project manage. You will have over 100 people working on the project: team leads and sub–team leads who are employees of Affordable Sweeping and many subcontractors.

You are ready to start staffing the project. You have some concerns about getting the right people for the project. Affordable Sweeping has many contracts, and most of the people you need are already assigned to other projects.

In this exercise you'll test your knowledge of this process.

Acquiring the Project Team

1. What are the five inputs to the Acquire Project Team process?
2. What are the four tools and techniques of staff acquisition?
3. Name the four steps to negotiating staff.
4. When the contract for Operation:NFL was signed, Bill was named as the lead of the outside maintenance team. This is an example of what tool and technique of staff acquisition?
5. Why would your organization structure influence your ability to acquire the project team?

Exercise 8.3: Developing the Project Team

The objectives for Exercise 8.3 are as follows:

- Describe the Develop Project Team process.
- Describe the six tools and techniques of team development.
- Describe when team development techniques should be utilized.

Background

Develop Project Team is one of two human resource management processes that are performed in the executing process group. (The other is Acquire Project Team, which we just covered.) Develop Project Team deals with how a project team performs together to create the project deliverables. There are six tools and techniques of the team development process:

- General management skills
- Team-building activities
- Reward and recognition systems
- Collocation
- Ground rules
- Training

We will discuss each of these tools and techniques, as well as how to decide when each should be used.

General Management Skills

There are hundreds of books that describe general management skills. These skills cover communication, managing, and team development, among other things. The project manager will utilize all of these skills and more while developing the project team.

Team-Building Activities

Team-building activities are any type of planned activities that increase the comfort level of the team in working with each other. There is a substantial body of literature published on this subject. Project managers need to be well aware of the types of activities that are available through this literature. Team-building activities can be as simple as a group lunch or as complex as day-long facilitated sessions. Project managers should use team-building sessions at three different points in the team development process:

Initiation   As soon as the project team is assembled, team-building activities should begin. Sufficient time should be devoted to the team-building work at this stage. These activities will serve as a foundation to move the team through progressing stages of development.

New team members   Anytime a new team member joins a project, the dynamics of the team will change. Project managers need to be aware of the effects of adding new staff. It may be necessary to incorporate team-building activities back into the work plan.

Conflict   Conflict is normal and desirable on projects. It allows the team to resolve problems and find the right solutions for successful project completion. There are times, though, when conflict lasts longer than necessary and is a detriment to project completion. This may be a time to use team-building techniques to resolve the conflict and bind the team into a better-performing group.

Reward and Recognition Systems

The next tool and technique of the Develop Project Team process is reward and recognition. This technique describes what you will use to incentivize the team to outstanding performance. You will need to design your reward and recognition systems at the beginning of the project. Communicate the plan to the team members so they understand "what is in it for them" to complete the project successfully. The key to a reward and recognition system is doing what you promised. If you have promised a day off for extra work, be sure to let the person have the day off. The first time you do not reward as you said you would, the system will be destroyed because trust in the system will be lacking. You would then need to redesign and reapply a new system.

Collocation

Another tool and technique of team development is collocation. Collocation is simply moving members of the project team next to each other to facilitate team development. If it is impossible for the team to be together, the project manager needs to find other ways for team interaction. Collocation should be established at the beginning of the project. Replacement collocation activities (when resources leave and new resources are added to the project) must be ongoing through the project's execution.

Ground Rules

This tool and technique of the Develop Project Team process allows team members to establish clear expectations for how they will work together. The meeting where this discussion occurs should be facilitated by the project manager, and each person should be encouraged to participate. Once the ground rules are established, each team member is accountable for adhering to them. This technique should be established early in the project and reinforced during the Executing process group processes.

Training

The last tool and technique of the Develop Project Team process is training. Training is used to enhance the team's management or technical skills. If team members are allowed to attend training together, it can be used as another type of team-building activity. Training should be completed at the beginning of the project where core competencies are missing. Training can be utilized later in the project when specific needs arise.

In Exercise 8.3 you'll spend some time analyzing project team development techniques.

Scenario

TPMP has just placed you at Affordable Sweeping, Inc., an up-and-coming property maintenance company. Affordable Sweeping has just been awarded the contract to get the local NFL stadium ready for the current football season. Affordable Sweeping named the project Operation:NFL and has hired you to project manage. You will have over 100 people working on the project: team leads and sub–team leads who are employees of Affordable Sweeping and many subcontractors.

The staffing is complete and you have heard a lot about team development techniques. You are wondering what techniques you should utilize and when you should use them.

Developing the Project Team

1. Develop Project Team is performed during what phase of a project?

2. What are the six primary tools and techniques of Develop Project Team?

3. Affordable Sweeping has several offices throughout the city. You have acquired the staff and now you are moving them all into the same office. This is an example of which tool and technique of the Develop Project Team process?

4. When the staff acquisition for Operation:NFL was completed, you took the entire team on a tour of the stadium and later to lunch. At lunch you had team members introduce themselves and explain their role on the project. This is an example of what primary tool and technique of the Develop Project Team process?

5. You have been working on Operation:NFL for several months. You have found that the groundskeepers and turf preparation teams are constantly fighting and are running behind schedule. What tool and technique of the Develop Project Team process would you use now? Why?

Exercise 8.4: Communicating with the Team and Resolving Conflict

The objectives for Exercise 8.4 are as follows:

- Identify communication forms and listening skills.

- Learn and practice some conflict resolution methods.

Background

To help you manage team communication, it might help to understand how you use various forms of communication, including listening, to provide information to and receive information from your team. Your communication skills can make a big difference between you getting important information quickly and your team members holding it back. And even if you use communication skills expertly, you will still have conflict on your project. Conflict is a natural part of a project. Team members may not understand their roles clearly, there aren't enough resources to get the work completed, or team members may have differing opinions.

Communication

There is a basic model of communication based on a sender encoding a message and receivers decoding the message. Perhaps the most important aspect of this model is that there needs to be feedback: You can't assume that everyone will understand the information you send out. And the receiver has some responsibility in understanding the message. The receiver needs to do something to confirm that they understand the communication as you intended. So, using the terms of the model, the sender formats the message to be sent (encoding it in a way that can be decoded by the receiver).

During the sending and receiving of the message, noise, such as garbled communication or distance, may get in the way of clear communication, The receiver, or in this case, your team member, might "filter" the message (a form of noise) to perceive the message according to their mindset as learned by culture, language, or emotions. But it is their duty to try to describe what they perceived so you can confirm the communication as you intended it. Important items need to be communicated often, too. People usually don't get the point once. That's why commercials play over and over again—the media has figured out that messages aren't understood the first time. You as a project manager need to remember it too: Important information needs to be repeated. You will need to repeat important information like milestones, quality expectations, changes, the project goals, or job expectations.

You also need to understand the forms of communication—whether they are formal or informal—so you can use them in the appropriate situations: You will make decisions on whether your communication should be verbal, nonverbal (pictures or gestures), or written, depending on the situation. Become aware of your communication habits. You may frown a lot while you listen and folks may interpret this as disapproval even though you may be just listening hard—you may need to change that habit to have a more open look on your face. And as a project manager, you will need to fine-tune your listening skills: You will need to practice active listening (keep an open mind while listening—don't formulate responses in your head), eye contact, gestures showing interest (like nodding), recapping what was said, and not allowing interruptions.

Conflict Resolution

Besides practicing communication skills, you will also get the chance to practice conflict resolution. Most people have some natural reactions to conflict, but as a project manager, you need to actively use problem solving as much as possible. The following five terms describe possible conflict resolution methods you may choose to apply:

Forcing   One person tries to force their point of view on another in order to solve a problem. The opinion is usually imposed by someone with authority. It solves the conflict temporarily, but your team or the person who is on the receiving end may continue to harbor issues.

Smoothing   Smoothing emphasizes agreement, or choosing to ignore the disagreement. Again, this is a temporary solution because you or your team have not worked through the disagreement and solved the issue more thoroughly. The issue may resurface again.

Compromise   This method allows those who disagree to reach some level of satisfaction by each party giving something up. This method provides for a grudging agreement, and although this may be a permanent solution because everyone makes a commitment to it, there might have been a better solution.

Withdrawal   One of the parties avoids conflict by leaving or avoiding it, so the conflict doesn't get resolved. The project manager needs to look out for this kind of situation: You might need to have more discussions with the team to keep working on the issue. This is one of the worst forms of resolution because no one wins and the problem will continue.

Problem solving (confrontation)   This method involves getting to the bottom of the issue and resolving it to everyone's satisfaction. Usually, you use the problem-solving techniques of analysis, alternatives review, recommendations, and finally coming up with the best solution based on fact. This is the best way to resolve conflict.

By looking for the various forms of dealing with conflict, and attempting to facilitate the team to solve the issue through problem solving, you will be performing one of your most important roles as a project manager.

Planning and Managing Team Communications

Knowing that communication, feedback, and conflict resolution are such an important part of maintaining an effective project team, you should keep the following considerations in mind when planning and managing your team and its activities:

1. Take an inventory of your communication skills, and develop your listening skills. Practice active listening regularly.

2. Think about the types of communication you will use and decide on how you will use them. You will probably want to use verbal communication in status meetings as you discuss issues informally, but to record the decisions, you will want to write them down in some kind of weekly report.

3. Study and understand the methods of resolving conflict. When you resolve an issue with a method other than problem solving, ensure that you understand why and the possible consequences.

4. Practice conflict resolution using the problem-solving method as much as possible.

In this exercise you will practice identifying various forms of dealing with conflict on an organization's team.

Scenario

TPMP is working with an independent, nonprofit organization, Health America, that is creating reports for the status and quality of hospital health care in the United States based on goals created by the president of the United States. Health America is implementing project management processes and TPMP is helping. This is a highly visible program in the government, and it entails working with the major hospitals within the major cities of America and rating whether they are achieving specific goals as identified by the president's program.

The research and reporting started about two years ago. You are helping the project manager, Bill Smith, discover some communication methods and techniques he can employ as he manages this very complex project. Bill works for Karen Palmer, and she wants to make sure that project management methodologies are applied to this project. Jeremy Checks, a peer of Karen's, thinks that project management is a waste of time and is hoping the project will turn sour and that project management will be the cause. Bill Smith will have several team members, including Kate Sullivan and Edward Salazar, who think project management will get in the way of getting their work done. Bill will be introducing several project management techniques and methods during the course of the project.

Communicating with the Team and Resolving Conflict

1. Bill is sending an e-mail to his project team telling them that there will be a review of the latest research findings next Monday at 10:00 AM. Identify each of the following: Who is the

sender? What is the message? What is being encoded? Who is the receiver? What is being decoded? What are some of the filters the team members might have about this message?

2. Kate Sullivan has been researching the quality of pre-op procedures in the various hospitals, and she needs help in resolving an issue in the information she has found. She comes to Bill to tell him her problems because she does not think she can produce a report with what she's finding. What are some of the listening techniques Bill could use to help her out?

3. Jeremy Checks has come to Bill to complain. He found out that some of his employees, who are members of Bill's team, will be spending a couple of days on project management training. He doesn't like it all—the time spent on training won't help them get their work done. He said the team members are complaining to him already. Which conflict resolution method should Bill use to help solve the issue with Jeremy and why?

4. Kate and Edward are arguing about the best research method for collecting data about each hospital's use of peer reviews for complex operations on patients. They need to collect this data for one of their reports. Kate feels the Internet will work, whereas Edward knows that at least 20 percent of the hospital staff will respond only to traditional mail. They need to come up with the best method to get this data. What conflict resolution method should Bill use to help facilitate this issue?

Exercise 8.5: Deciding on Methods of Information Distribution

The objectives for Exercise 8.5 are as follows:

- Identify the forms of information.
- Identify information retrieval systems.
- Identify the ways that information can be distributed.
- Decide on methods of information distribution for your project.

Background

You created the communication plan during the planning process, and during the execution process you will distribute the information according to your plan. The Information Distribution process had the following outputs:

- Lessons learned documentation (to record suggestions for future projects or phases)
- Project records
- Project reports
- Project presentations
- Feedback from stakeholders
- Stakeholder notifications
- Requested changes

Make sure you think about these outputs and how you will distribute them as you are planning your communication. For instance, you should plan that lessons learned is a document you will create and distribute at the end of each phase of your project. You will also need to decide when and how you will distribute it: Will you send it out via e-mail or publish it to a project website? Lessons learned documentation is further discussed in the exercise "Closing a Project or Phase, Including Contract Close" in Chapter 11.

So, once you know whom you need to communicate to and something about their needs, you need to decide on what you will distribute and how you will distribute the information. You might take an inventory of what forms of information you can create and the methods your organization has (or the methods you can obtain) for distributing information. First, what kinds of information will you distribute? The list could be almost endless and could include some of the following information: status/progress, escalations, issues, risks and risk response plans, quality standards, project processes and standards, contracts, change requests, scope statements, team directory, work breakdown structure, schedule or budget and their variances, requirements, specifications, user guides, test plans, reports, project charter, responsibility and organization charts, lessons learned, and a project plan.

Next, you will decide on how the information will be distributed, such as via e-mails, written memos, formal or informal meetings, presentations (including charts and graphs), conference or video calls, websites, instant messaging, videos, TV, press releases, faxes, voicemail, articles, brochures, announcements, phone calls, and speeches.

Not only do you need to think about how you push information to your team or other stakeholders, you also need to consider the way your team or stakeholders will pull information when they need to get to it. Do you store all your information on a website or in an electronic database? Or do you store it in project management software files, in an electronic directory, or in hard copy via a file cabinet or notebook? Some of these decisions might be based on the need for archiving files or corporate policies.

The decisions about what and how information is distributed may be based on how often and how formal the information needs are, your organization's capabilities, your team members' skills, and confidentiality and need to know. Do people need information updated frequently, or can they wait for a week? If your team is not trained in reading and using a project schedule, you may need to find a simpler form for communicating status and progress rather than using a Gantt chart. Or you may need to find project management training for the team so they can interpret a Gantt chart.

What's more, you need to match the right kind of information with the right kind of audience at the right time. For instance, although you may create a status report, you may find you need to design two kinds of status reports: a detailed status report for the team involving the status of each person's deliverables for the week and an overview of major deliverables, budget, and escalations for executives. The format for each may also be entirely different so that the team sees the detailed schedule and executives see only a high-level milestone report.

Last but not least, you need to decide how you can get information to people when they request it outside of the regularly scheduled times or when stakeholders have special requests for information you don't normally provide. In other words, you need to create an information distribution strategy. Following are some guidelines on how to create an information distribution strategy:

1. Decide on your major forms of communication for the various types of information you will be creating. For instance, you might have a written status report via presentations for executives and meetings, issues, and updated schedules for your team meetings.

2. Decide on the technology or method you will use to distribute the information: e-mail, Internet, written memos, or a directory structure on the network.

3. Decide how often you will distribute different forms of information. You might start forming a matrix that will eventually be complete in a communications plan.

4. Let the team members know where all the information is, where they can put their information, and how they can get information when it's needed.

In this exercise, you will help Health America decide on the various methods they will use to distribute information for the project.

Scenario

TPMP is working with an independent, nonprofit organization, Health America, who is creating reports for the status and quality of hospital health care in the United States based on goals created by the president of the United States. Health America is implementing project management processes and TPMP is helping them. This is a highly visible program in the government, and it entails working with the major hospitals within the major cities of America and rating whether they are achieving specific goals as identified by the president's program.

The research and reporting started about two years ago. The Department of Health and Human Services (HHS) is your client and needs to keep up-to-date on the budget and the status of the reports you are creating. You are helping the project manager, Bill Smith, decide on his information distribution strategy so he is more consistent in communicating with the team. In preparation for creating the communications plan, he is thinking about all of the kinds information he has been creating and the technologies the organization has. Bill has the extra charge of communicating how the project management techniques are working as well. HHS is the customer and needs up-to-date information on the budget. Health America relies on e-mail for communication, uses the Web to gather information, and has a shared network drive to store files. Karen Palmer, Bill's boss at Health America, and her peer, Jeremy Checks, are very interested in the project management processes being implemented, even though Jeremy is skeptical of project management processes. Bill has a team doing research and creating the reports. In working with his team, Bill realizes several of his teammates use e-mail daily and some check it every now and then. Bill has also been receiving some calls from some national news agencies asking about the new program.

Deciding on Information Distribution

1. What kinds of information would you recommend that Bill Smith distribute?

2. What are some methods you would recommend that Bill use to distribute information at Health America?

3. After consulting with you, Bill has decided to distribute a status report to the team, to Health America executives, and to HHS. He will also create press releases and provide status on an external website that only hospitals can access. How often do you think he should issue or update each of these and why?

4. When someone needs information in between status reports, how would you recommend that Bill set up the information for them to get it?

5. Bill will be training the team next week about how often to expect information and where to store project information. Will this training be enough for the team? What should Bill do to follow up on this training?

Answers to Section 8 Exercises

Answers to Exercise 8.1

Your answers may be somewhat different, but the following answers provide a guide.

1. The seven inputs for Direct and Mange Project Execution are the project management plan, approved preventive action, approved change requests, approved defect repair, validated defect repair, administrative closure procedures, and approved corrective action.

2. Pam needs to put a project management methodology into place. Specifically, she should be looking at how the day-to-day work is being managed and how changes to the baseline are being managed.

3. This spreadsheet software is also known as a project management information system.

4. Pam should employ the project management methodology that addresses conducting lessons learned meetings and documenting and applying the findings

5. The seven outputs of the Direct and Mange Project Execution process are deliverables, requested changes, implemented change requests, implemented corrective actions, implemented preventive actions, implemented defect repairs, and work performance information.

Answers to Exercise 8.2

Your answers may be somewhat different, but the following answers provide a guide.

1. The five inputs of the Acquire Project Team process are enterprise environmental factors, organizational process assets, roles and responsibilities, project organization charts, and the staffing management plan.

2. The four Acquire Project Team tools and techniques are negotiation, preassignment, virtual teams, and acquisition.

3. The four steps to negotiating staff are (1) identifying your target team, (2) identifying potential barriers to getting your target team, (3) building your negotiation strategy, and (4) negotiating for your project team.

4. When the contract for Operation:NFL was signed, Bill was named as the lead of the outside maintenance team. This is an example of the preassignment tool and technique of Acquire Project Team.

5. The organization structure of your company can influence your ability to acquire your project team because projectized organizations are built for executing projects. Project managers should have more power and influence in this type of structure.

Answers to Exercise 8.3

Your answers may be somewhat different, but the following answers provide a guide.

1. Develop Project Team is one of two human resource management processes that is performed in the executing portion of a project.

2. The six tools and techniques of Develop Project Team are team-building activities, reward and recognition, collocation, ground rules, general management skills, and training.

3. Moving staff into the same office is an example of the Develop Project Team technique called collocation.

4. Taking the entire team on a tour of the stadium and having members introduce themselves and talk about their role on the project is an example of the team-building activities tool and technique of the Develop Project Team process.

5. You would use team-building activities to shore up the relationship between the groundskeepers and the turf prep team. These teams do not need additional training; they just need to complete the project on time.

Answers to Exercise 8.4

Your answers may be somewhat different, but the following answers provide a guide.

1. When Bill sends an e-mail to his project team telling them that there will be a review of the latest research findings next Monday at 10:00 AM, the sender is clearly Bill. The message is that there will be a review on Monday at 10:00 AM. The message is being encoded. Bill encodes the message according to the way he is accustomed to communicating. He needs to make his messages as clear as possible. To ensure that the team understands the message, he might want to add more information, perhaps create an agenda that describes why they are meeting, the expected outcome, how long the meeting will be, and who is expected to be there. The receiver is everyone on the team to whom Bill sent the message, including Kate Sullivan and Edward Salazar. The message is being decoded. The team members use their personal or cultural filters. For instance, Kate might think this is just another way to take up her valuable time and Bill is trying to unjustly impose his project management authority on her. Edward might think this is a great idea: they never review the research to make sure they are on the right track, and this will help each team member see what the others are doing to achieve better results.

2. There are many things Bill could do to help Kate out. Bill may not know much about the kind of research that Kate does, but he can help her resolve her issue by listening well. Some techniques he can use are eye contact and nodding to show he is listening and appears interested, not interrupting as she speaks, and not allowing interruptions from the telephone or other people. At appropriate pauses, Bill can restate what he thought he heard Kate say and make sure she confirms that he heard her correctly. He's got to concentrate on the moment and not let other internal thoughts distract him from what Kate has to say.

3. Bill has a few options to help resolve the argument with Jeremy. Bill may try problem solving. He needs to use his listening techniques to account for all of Jeremy's issues and needs. But this may be a situation in which the "status quo" works for Jeremy, and there may be no way to convince him that project management will be effective without showing him. So

this may be a situation in which forcing is used to resolve the conflict. Bill may go to his boss, Karen, and ask for help to make sure he gets management support to reiterate the importance of project management to help achieve greater efficiency. Bill may also remind Jeremy that his project plan calls for the team to be trained in some portions of project management and that it is his plan's budget that is being used, not Jeremy's budget.

4.   Bill has a few options to help resolve the disagreement between Edward and Kate. The best conflict resolution method will be problem solving in this case. Since these team members will continue to work together, and perhaps have similar issues, it will be important to come to a final resolution where both team members agree. Bill should start by having them analyze the best way to get the most responses (via research into marketing surveys or using other objective measurements). He should have them choose some alternatives as to how they could solve the issues and have them resolve the issue together by selecting the most objective method.

Answers to Exercise 8.5

Your answers may be somewhat different, but the following answers provide a guide.

1.   This project has many communication requirements, based on the number of stakeholders. Information that Bill needs to think about distributing are press releases to the media, a regular budget and milestone report to the Health and Welfare Department, and minutes after team meetings. Due to the fact that he also needs to communicate information about the project management processes being implemented, he also might create a small team that meets regularly to discuss those processes, talk about how they are working, and create improvements based on team feedback. You might also recommend that he informally meet with Jeremy Checks and Karen Palmer now and then to get some feedback of their impressions about the project management processes being implemented.

2.   Bill might use e-mail regularly, although, because some of his team members do not check it regularly, he will need to train the team to use e-mail as a form of team communication. For important or timely information, he may need to leave voicemail for the team, or have regular meetings where attendance is required. Since the team members regularly research using the Web, Bill might create a website with the latest status, issues and project schedule to help keep them informed. He might also store the information on the network directory since the company uses that method for storing information.

3.   Bill should distribute the status report to the team weekly and it will be the basis for team status meetings. This method will keep the team up-to-date and focused on the project's progress. He will distribute a status report biweekly to the executives. Since the project is research oriented and deliverables have long time frames, the executives don't need to know the status more often. The status for the Health and Welfare Department will be monthly and might include a meeting. This method lets the department understand progress on deliverables often enough, but not too often, since they have many other projects to monitor. Bill might distribute press releases at important milestones he identifies in this project schedule rather than based on a regular calendar time. This way, the press gets major information in

a timely fashion. He should update the website when he receives new research for the hospitals so that they see that the data they provided is actually being used.

4. Bill's project website can provide the information for anyone to pull if needed. If someone needs information other than what is on the website (which executives always seem to need!), Bill could create a form or checklist to help him qualify the request. This practice will help Bill put the information together faster and may even reveal that the information already exists and just needs to be put in a different format. Here are some ideas for the questions Bill should ask—you may think of more.

- Who is the audience?
- Why do they need the information?
- How current does the data have to be?
- What format does it need to be in?
- What specific kind of information is needed?
- Will this information need to be produced again?

5. Bill needs to follow up at least two more times to train the folks on the communication methods of the project. During the meeting, he needs to provide written information on the communication they can expect and what is expected of them. After the meeting, he might follow up a week later in an e-mail, reminding everyone of the communication methods. Then, two weeks later, he might call another meeting to reiterate the methods and request any feedback on how it is working. Although it might seem that Bill should only have to communicate the distribution methods once, people need to be reminded several times and rewarded for supporting the methods before the information is integrated into team behavior.

Measuring and Controlling Project Performance

The following exercises are presented in this section:

- Exercise 9.1: Creating the Contract
- Exercise 9.2: Perform Quality Assurance
- Exercise 9.3: Understanding Your Stakeholders

Exercise 9.1: Creating the Contract

The objectives for Exercise 9.1 are as follows:

- Introduce concepts for creating a contract.
- Introduce the parts of a contract.
- Discuss some of the most important parts of a contract.
- Practice creating parts of a contract.

Background

Once you finally select your vendor, you will need to create the contract so you and your vendor can work together productively. The contract also legally binds the vendor to provide for the services and the buyer to pay for them. You will start by using templates of your organization's contracts or previous contracts as a basis, collecting the requirements you must include in the contract, and then working with the lawyers and the procurement department (if you have one) to put the contract together. If you need to move more quickly than this process usually takes, you may start the work through a temporary agreement, such as a memorandum of agreement or a time and materials contract.

You may also participate in or have input into negotiations for the contract. It will be in your best interest to get involved early so you can influence the content and quality of the contract. The negotiations can be a prelude to a very good relationship if you go into it with the attitude of creating a good relationship, mutually beneficial agreements with enough detail to be unambiguous, and protections for each party. It can be a difficult and arduous task if the negotiation process is not well managed or if it is confrontational or vague. In such a case, once the contract is signed, the relationship and the contract can end up being difficult to manage. If there is any way you can help influence the attitude and add to the expertise required for the contract negotiations, try to do so, but often it is out of your hands.

You may not understand some of the language in the contract, and you may be even frustrated by it, but it is important that you take the time to try to understand the contract, provide as much input as you can, and then manage it based on your detailed understanding of the work required. The contract explains how you need to manage the contractor, the contractor's work, and your mutual processes, so you will need to know those details.

The contract should include the following content details and may include several more sections based on the particular needs of your product or service (the information may not reside in sections exactly as stated, but the information should be included somewhere in the contract):

Definitions   Define all the technical terms and other terms particular to the contract to indicate agreement on what is meant for the parties. This is not like a glossary—both parties need to understand the definitions and agree on them.

Scope/statement of work   Describe work or the work product you expect from the vendor. You might use the SOW that was in the proposal as a basis, but you will need to review and rewrite the SOW as necessary based on more current knowledge and any details discovered between the vendor solicitation and contract award.

Roles and responsibilities   Describe who does the work, approves the work, administers the contract, and manages the processes described in it. This also might include who supplies the equipment and facilities.

Technical specifications and deliverables   Provide specific measurements, specifications, and other technical requirements, as well as details of all deliverables due for the vendor's work. This might include detailed service-level agreements for operations.

Interpretation of requirements   Give the order of precedence (the order of what is most important) for the project requirements.

Schedule and period of performance   State the general dates for the milestones or deliverables expected from the vendor and time frames for performance of the contract.

Quality assurance/control   Describe the inspections or audits expected. This section might include detailed service level agreements as well as scorecard or testing quality expectations.

Warranty/guarantee and support   Specify how long the product is expected to last (e.g., guaranteed for five years after acceptance) or provide an expectation of meeting a particular standard. This section might include express warranties for equipment, workmanship, performance or process, and design. Another warranty to consider is the implied warranty by the seller that what the seller provides is marketable and can be used by the buyer. This is one of those legal agreements that does not have to be written but that the courts would accept as a good faith agreement. The contract may also have a section describing how a product will be supported.

Contract administration and change control   Describe the processes, time frames, and escalations for contract administration, including the change control procedures.

Price and terms of payment   Include price information and a schedule of invoicing and payments, including the processes for doing so. This may be statements to indicate how the price may be adjusted for inflation or other economic factors.

Laws, regulations, and taxes that might apply   List any legal regulations or restrictions specific to your state or project for administering the project. The lawyers would probably create this section. Similarly, an accountant should probably help determine what taxes will be involved.

Provisions   Include general and special terms and conditions negotiated with the vendor. Lawyers would create this section. It might include incentive/award fee provisions to optimize performance. It might also include who owns what parts of the product or service, especially when it comes to the results of the work, the data involved, or intellectual property.

Provisions for early termination   Describe how the contract would be dissolved and any work produced or payments would be distributed if for some reason the vendor or buyer cannot fulfill the contract.

Liabilities and insurance   Describe liability if the project or product is disrupted, is delayed, or fails. You should take into consideration damages and indemnity of the vendor or buyer as well as force majeure (acts of God) and the results expected if there are any delays due to natural causes or accidents. Plus, as protection, you should know your insurance needs, such as liability and general business insurance required for worker protection or property damage.

Confidentiality, privacy, and security   Describe confidentiality requirements. You need to determine how you will handle confidential information if the company does not already have a policy.

Employee recruiting   Include provisions to protect each party from recruiting each other's employees until after a certain time period.

Disputes   Specify escalations, arbitration, and other ways to settle disputes and the time frames and order in which the escalations should be instigated.

Contract completion/product acceptance   Indicate when the contract is up, which may not be the same as when the product or service is finally delivered. The contract may cover several SOWs or may be extended for new work. But the contract itself might have an eventual end date. Closure should also center on formal acceptance of all deliverables and formal closure of the contract.

In administering the contract, whether you were part of the negotiations or not, you need to know all the parts of the contract and create project procedures to abide by the terms. A good habit for managing each contract is to study each major section in detail and, in your own words, write what the contract is stating. This is a lot of work, but it will help you in the long run. You can share the important parts of the contract with your team members so they too understand its implications and how they need to work with the contractor and review the contractor's work. You might suggest that you review the contract with the contractor's team as well. Since you are managing the project, you need to ensure that the work of the vendor contributes to the success of the project and that all team members understand their contractual obligations.

In this exercise, you will help Creative Cartoon Company (CCC) think about how it needs to approach various contract negotiations and what might be included in parts of the contracts for vendors as CCC starts its first full-length animation feature film production.

Scenario

Recently, the Creative Cartoon Company (CCC) has obtained enough capital to create its first feature-length animated film based on its most recent short film, which won several major entertainment awards. CCC hired TPMP several months ago to help it improve project management processes, and now, because CCC has to subcontract some of the work to outside organizations in order to complete the film, the executives are asking you and your company, TPMP, to help them with their procurement management processes.

For the new feature film they have decided that they will need outside services for sound production, an overseas cartoon firm to create background artwork, a marketing firm, and an animation software development firm to implement an idea that the producer has for advancing the animation industry to the next level. Marcus Manning is the producer of the film, tentatively titled *Bouncing with Bob*. He and the film's director, Sheila Wong, have high aspirations—they want the feature-length film to win an Oscar for best animated film, and they want their new animation idea to win a technical Oscar. They want you to help them create good vendor relationships so that the vendors can help them create the best possible film.

Creating the Contract

1. What might be some specific warranties or guarantees you would recommend that CCC include in its contract for the artwork and sound production vendors?

2. What kind of insurance might CCC require the marketing and software development vendor contractors have??

3. What change control might you recommend be included in the contract?

4. How would you recommend that CCC approach the negotiations for the software development vendor contract?

5. How would you suggest CCC train its team members to work with the contractors and the contract?

Exercise 9.2: Perform Quality Assurance

The objectives for Exercise 9.2 are as follows:

- Describe the tools and techniques used in Perform Quality Assurance.

- Describe the components of a quality audit.

Background

A lot of work goes into the planning of a project. You have done extensive work in planning the quality components of the project. How will you guarantee that the quality will be as good as you planned? This is where the Perform Quality Assurance process comes in. Perform Quality Assurance is the process that focuses on making certain the planned quality will be met. Think of Perform Quality Assurance as a managerial process that is concerned with the process of quality. It assures that the quality system you have planned will work.

There are four different tools and techniques used in the Perform Quality Assurance process. The first tool and technique is called quality planning tools. These tools were covered in Exercise 4.4. They are benchmarking, cost benefit analysis, design of experiments, additional quality planning tools, and the cost of quality. Even though we talked about using these tools in the planning process, they can also be used while the project is being executed to assure that the quality plans are being met.

The second tool and technique of Perform Quality Assurance is process analysis. This means you will examine the processes that are being executed on your project and determine what improvements should be made to guarantee the output of the processes. This analysis also involves problems experienced because of the processes, constraints and bottlenecks that are experienced because of the processes, and finally, any activities that do not add value to completing the processes.

The third tool and technique is quality control tools and techniques. There are 10 tools and techniques in the Perform Quality Control process that can also be used during quality assurance. They are flowcharting, cause and effect diagrams, control charts, histograms, Pareto charts, run charts, scatter diagrams, statistical sampling, inspection, and defect repair review. We will examine these tools and techniques in a future exercise.

The last tool and technique used in Perform Quality Assurance is called a quality audit. A quality audit is a review of the quality management activities that are being performed on the project. This in-depth review will produce findings that should identify lessons learned that can improve project performance. A quality baseline is set when a quality audit is performed after quality planning is completed and before the project begins execution. A quality baseline is used to compare what has been done to what was planned with respect to project quality. Let's look at the components of a quality audit.

Components of a Quality Audit

The components of a quality audit cover who you should use as an auditor, the timeframes when an audit is done and finally the process of an audit.

Determining the auditor   Some companies will hire a highly skilled specialist to perform an audit. Other companies will look for an internal resource to perform the audit to save money. Regardless of whether you use internal or external resources, the auditor must have certain qualities to effectively conduct a quality audit. You need to assign an individual who is independent of the day-to-day project activities. They need to be familiar with the business and the processes used but should be able to take a broad perspective of the project's processes. They should be skilled in project management and know what to look for in a well-managed project.

Time frames to audit   There are three parts to the time frames to audit. They are initial assessment, quality progress review, and quality completion review:

Initial assessment   This first audit should be conducted at the end of the planning process and before the project begins execution. The focus of this review is to evaluate the quality assurance work that is planned. This review also creates a quality baseline for what is to be done on the project. This step also familiarizes the auditor with what to look for in subsequent audits.

Quality progress review   This audit should be planned at regular intervals or at key milestones during the execution of the project. The reviewer will be evaluating whether the quality activities that were outlined are being performed. They will also inspect the quality processes of the project and determine if they are sound. The output of the audit is a lessons learned document that is used for continuous improvement.

Quality completion review This audit is done at the end of the project and should recap the quality assurance effectiveness in light of final project results. The output of this audit is also a lessons learned document that is used to continuously improve the quality assurance processes at the company for the next set of projects.

Quality audit process The quality audit process should include a review log that identifies those points that will be reviewed during the audit. The reviewer should receive relevant materials (e.g., product description, quality policy, project plan, project schedule, status reports, etc.) prior to the review so that questions and suggestions for improvement can be prepared in advance. The review should result in suggested actions for the project manager to enhance the quality of the product. The project manager should follow up on actions with the reviewer according to a schedule established during the audit.

In this exercise, you will analyze how quality can be applied to your project at USRemotes.

Scenario

TPMP has just placed you at USRemotes, the largest distributor of remote control devices in the United States. USRemotes has launched a project to redesign the warehouse and shipping areas and processes—the WSAP project. You have been assigned as the temporary project manager. You have just completed the project planning phase.

USRemotes is very interested in quality and is planning to gain some type of quality certification. Quality is also very important to you. You have been thinking about what you will need to do to assure the quality of the project.

Quality Assurance

1. What are the four tools and techniques of Perform Quality Assurance?

2. On the WASP project, you've just completed the project planning phase of work. You're considering doing a quality audit now. Why is this a good idea?

3. As you continue laying out your plans for quality assurance for the WASP project, you thinking about do a quality audit at the end of the project. Why would this be a good idea?

4. You've now got a quality audit set up for the end of the planning phase for the WASP project and the end of the project. You feel there may be other timeframes that would be good to do a quality audit. You're considering doing a quality audit at a key milestone. What would this be a good idea?

5. Name three quality planning tools.

6. What is a quality baseline used for?

Exercise 9.3: Understanding Your Stakeholders

The objectives for Exercise 9.3 are as follows:

- Identify project stakeholders.
- Learn how to think about the needs of project stakeholders.

- Analyze the needs and expectations of stakeholders.
- Create a stakeholder analysis tool.

Background

Communication management means knowing your stakeholders and communicating with them about their needs and expectations regularly. A project stakeholder is anyone positively or negatively impacted by your project—including project team members. Stakeholders are individuals and organizations, and you will want to identify both kinds to thoroughly identify all needs and expectations. Stakeholders may include the following people or organizations: the project manager, the sponsor, team members, customers, the organization performing the work, functional managers providing team members, operations, and many others.

You also need to think about stakeholders external and internal to the organization, such as contractors, the government, your community, families of team members or company families, and the media. First, you will need to analyze your stakeholders. This will help you identify how to communicate with them. Once you have decided how to communicate with them, you will need to manage communications with them. One of the best ways is to keep issues logs and resolve the issues systematically. The issues log, however, will be lessened if you analyze your stakeholders and execute your communication plan based on that analysis.

Stakeholder Analysis

Once you identify all the stakeholders (and this could be quite a list, depending on the complexity of the project), you need to identify their driving needs and expectations. Some may only need to know about what's going on with the project, whereas others will be decision makers or influence project direction or outcome even if they do not have decision-making power on the project. It's important to understand these needs and expectations early in the project and how they might change over the course of the project. Some people may have different expectations in the planning phase than in the controlling phase of the project. If you do this identification and analysis up front, you will not be as easily swayed or pulled in different directions as the project progresses. Defining stakeholders, depending on the sensitivity of the data gathered, may be a tool only you would use to help define your communication plan (described in an earlier exercise). You will also find that you need to update your analysis throughout the project as the stakeholders change or you get to know them better. The following expectations or needs are among those you need to consider:

- How important is cost and profit to the stakeholder?
- What kind of information will the stakeholder require?
- How important is the schedule to the stakeholder?
- Is quality important to the stakeholder?
- Will the project threaten or enhance the stakeholder's position or organization in any way?
- Is the stakeholder a major player in scope change?
- Does the stakeholder care more for results or more for how people are affected?
- What are the major issues or risks at stake for this stakeholder?

- How much influence does the stakeholder have? Can they threaten the success of your project?
- Is the stakeholder a performer, influencer, decision maker, technical or subject matter expert, or nonessential to the project but interested in it?
- How often do they need information about your project?
- When do they need to be included in the project or when are they most impacted during the project?

You may want to keep your stakeholder analysis to yourself and your sponsor. For instance, some might think they are decision makers on the project but are really nonessential. Such stakeholders may look at the project as something that will enhance their position if they look like they are involved in it. Letting them see a list in which they are categorized as "nonessential" might be counterproductive.

Creating a Stakeholder Needs Matrix

Now that you know some of the criteria behind stakeholder analysis, you can create a stakeholder needs matrix. To do so, follow these steps:

1. Identify criteria as needs and expectations for your stakeholders. You may include the following items:
   - Do they care about quality over everything else?
   - Do they care more about results than they care about other aspects of the project?
   - Do they care more about technology than they care about other aspects of the project?
   - Do they have the ability to impact the project positively or negatively?
   - Do they care about its cost or profit-making potential?
   - Do they require special care? (You might need to indicate that this person might need some special care to help achieve success on the project.)
   - Do they care more about the project making its scheduled date above all else?
   - Do they deal well with change? (If not, you may need to build in some special steps to help them with change.)
   - Do they have scope approval or influence?
   - Do they need special recognition during the course of the project to feel more valued?
   - Are they influencers, decision makers, performers, experts, or nonessential stakeholders who needs information only?
   - Do they demonstrate the ability and desire to help solve problems? (This means you might have someone to call on to help when you need to solve a problem.)
   - Are they people-oriented?
   - Do they need one-on-one meetings to help motivate or clarify project goals and tasks?

2. Decide on ratings (high/medium/low or 1 through 10) for each of the criteria so you can rate its importance to the stakeholder.

3. Identify each and every individual and organizational stakeholder that you and your team can think of. Don't forget to include people who are external to the organization such as the government or media. Include a brief description for each person or organization with this list.

4. Interview as many stakeholders as you can, and find out their expectations and needs for the project. Using a questionnaire with the criteria will help—you may also find you need some additional criteria as you talk with stakeholders.

5. Create a matrix for your stakeholders so you understand their needs better and are able to understand the influence they will have on your project. This matrix will help you make better decisions about how to communicate with them.

6. Create an issues log to help you resolve issues with your stakeholders. Make sure you keep the log updated and close issues regularly.

7. Review and update your stakeholder matrix throughout the length of the project.

In this exercise, you will help an organization create a stakeholder matrix.

Scenario

TPMP is working with an independent, not-for-profit organization, Health America (HA), that is creating reports for the status and quality of hospital health care in the United States based on goals created by the president of the United States. Health America is implementing project management processes and TPMP is helping them. This project is a highly visible program in the government, and it entails working with the major hospitals within major U.S. cities and rating the hospitals' achievement of specific goals as identified by the president's program. Research and reporting started about two years ago.

You are helping the project manager, Bill Smith, identify stakeholders and their expectations so that he can analyze their needs and expectations and thus have a better communications plan. Bill works for Karen Palmer, and she wants to make sure that project management methodologies are applied to this project. Jeremy Checks, a peer of Karen's, thinks that project management is a waste of time and is hoping the project will turn sour and that project management will be the cause. Bill Smith will have several team members, including Kate Sullivan and Edward Salazar, who are researchers on the project. Because this project is so visible at Health America, Edward is hoping his excellent work on this project will help promote him to manager of research one day. Once the research is completed and the program is implemented by all of the hospitals, Fran Freeling will be taking on incidental research and follow-up for the project. You will help Bill create a matrix analysis so he can understand the issues he may have on his project. Some of the people interested in Bill's project are the media, so they can report on the goals being met or not met; the Department of Health and Human Services (HHS) of the government, who is monitoring the project for the president and paying for the program; the hospitals throughout the United States; and the public, who needs to understand how this program is helping them.

Understanding Your Stakeholders

1. What criteria do you want to include to help identify stakeholder expectations and needs?

2. List the stakeholders. Don't hesitate to list any that might not be mentioned in the setup for this exercise.

3. Rate the importance of each criterion for each of the stakeholders.

4. Based on your analysis, how often do you need to communicate with the HHS and what would you communicate?

5. Based on your analysis, is there someone who can adversely affect the program?

6. How often does the public need to be updated about this program?

Answers to Section 9 Exercises

Answers to Exercise 9.1

Your answers may be somewhat different, but the following answers provide a guide.

1. For the artwork vendor, you might recommend that CCC request a warranty/guarantee around the design and workmanship of the artwork. It might include some kind of money-back offer if the work delivered has to be redone more than two times due to quality issues (for instance, the vendor not using agreed-upon color selections or not meeting requirements). For the sound production, CCC might request a warranty/guarantee around the process and workmanship of the sound. If the sound company does not satisfy required sound performance standards that CCC stipulates in the contract, then CCC might request money back if the sound production vendor cannot make it right within a certain time frame.

2. In the contracts for all vendors, CCC would want to require insurance for indirect losses due to contractor problems. For the marketing vendor, you might recommend that CCC require liability insurance in case any of the marketing material creates lawsuits from offended readers or viewers. For the software development vendor, you might recommend that CCC ensures that the vendor has insurance for key employee loss or liability for poor product design or failure. CCC might also require the normal insurance for fire and other property damage as well, in case the software vendor's work is damaged. CCC may want to expressly state in the contract that the vendor must have business insurance to help recover possible losses that CCC could have due to the contractor's problems.

3. You might recommend that CCC provide a general change control process description, including turnaround times for change requests to limit how long vendors and CCC can take to process a request. A change request should not lag in approval processes and should be cancelled if it takes too long to process. You might also include who must approve changes to the schedule or budget and any approval limits they might have. CCC might also stipulate and include in an addendum the change form and log that must be used by both parties to manage and track change. This cannot be overstated. By putting it in the contract, it will be much harder for either group to make changes that can make the budget or schedule get out of hand.

4. The CCC procurement team should make sure they have a well-managed approach for the software development negotiations. Since the work itself is not well defined and CCC wants to create a good relationship with the vendor for possible joint sales of the product, the negotiation should be a forum to create the good relationship and mutually beneficial agreements. CCC might ensure that meetings and status reports are required in the contract administration to help systemize the communication that needs to take place between the companies.

5. You might suggest that the CCC project manager review each part of the contract with the CCC team so that each team member understands what they can and can't do and what is

expected in the relationship. For instance, rather than the CCC project manager describing the change control processes to the team members and giving them the form, it would be best to discuss what is actually in the contract so the team understands that the processes are not just good business but contractual. The CCC project manager may want to do the same thing with the vendor's team, with the agreement of the vendor, so that everyone has a common understanding of the important obligations.

Answers to Exercise 9.2

1. The four tools and techniques of Perform Quality Assurance are quality planning tools, process analysis, quality control tools and techniques, and quality audits.

2. You are concerned with the quality of the project and will be validating the quality of the project all of the way through executing the project You would do a quality audit at the end of the planning phase of the project to set a quality baseline for what you planned to do in regard to quality.

3. You would do a quality audit at the end of the project to create a quality lessons learned document for future projects.

4. You're right, this is a good idea. Quality audits are done at key milestones to assure the quality of the project. Doing an audit at this time gives you a chance to correct problems prior to the product being completed.

5. You should have provided three of these possible five quality planning tools: benchmarking, cost benefit analysis, design of experiments, additional quality planning tools, and the cost of quality.

6. A quality baseline is used to compare what has been done to what was planned with respect to project quality.

Answers to Exercise 9.3

To complete the questions in Exercise 9.3, it might help to create a matrix such as the following to determine the interests and qualifications of your stakeholders. Your matrix may be different, depending on how you see the needs of these people or groups.

Stakeholder	Type	When	Concerns	Change	Special Care
Fran Freeling	I	E, CL, O	P = l, C = l, S = h, Q = h	L	Fran's group must accept turnover when project is complete.
HHS	C, D	A	P = l, C = h, S = h, Q = m	L	Must know all changes to cost and schedule. They will fund a second phase, so Health America needs to impress them.

Stakeholder	Type	When	Concerns	Change	Special Care
Hospitals	I, E	E	P = l, C = l, S = h, Q = h	M	Hospitals do not want to look bad. A bad report will mean having to explain it to the public and to their management.
Jeremy Checks	N	A	P = l, C = l, S = l, Q = l	L	Must keep him informed and slowly win him over to project management. He could be a problem to success of PM methodologies in the project.
State government	I	E, C, CL	P = m, C = h, S = l, Q = l	l	Could enact local legislation to support or block the program.
Health America	D, P, E, I	A	P = h, C = h, S = h, Q = m	l	This is a very high visibility and prestigious project. It could lead to more and bigger projects. It is also important to prove project management methodologies can succeed for other projects.
The public	I	E	P = l, C = m, S = l, Q = l	l	Public is not very aware of program. Will need clear, concise data and information needs to be compelling.

The following key explains each header in the table:

Type   The kind of stakeholder: C = customer, D = decision maker, I = influencer, P = performer, E = expert, N = nonessential

When   When in the project they might be affected most: P = planning, E = execution, C = controlling, CL = closing, O = operating A = equally in all phases

Concerns   The major concerns the person has, with each rated according to their view (h = high, m = medium, l = low): P = how the project will affect the project team and people at Health America, C = cost, Q = quality, S = schedule

Change   A rating as to how well this stakeholder deals with change: H = able to deal with change easily, M = has some ability to deal with change, L = does not deal with change well

Special care   A column to enter text to describe special needs or expectations the stakeholder might have.

The following answers to Exercise 9.3 questions may be different depending upon how you complete your stakeholder matrix.

1. To help identify stakeholder expectations and needs, you could include the criteria as listed in the top row of the table. You might also include how much the stakeholder cares about improved health care and financial hardship on the hospitals trying to implement the improvements.

2. Stakeholders are listed in the matrix. Note that state government has been added because it might support or block the program based on local legislation.

3. The importance of each criterion for each of the stakeholders is documented in the matrix. Note that not all criteria have ratings. For instance, "Type" is a designation, and should not include a rating.

4. The HHS is the main customer of this project and the funder. It would need a report frequently, at least every two weeks. Bill would need to provide a status report on progress emphasizing schedule and cost and perhaps using earned value performance reporting.

5. There are many people who could adversely affect the project: Since Jeremy Checks is more interested in the project management failing, he could start emphasizing issues with project management that could jeopardize the project itself. Edward Salazar could possibly take some action to bring attention to himself but harm the project. The hospitals, if not kept informed of their status, could get very angry if they are blindsided by any of the data reported in the research. And the media could report too early or present false information if they are given inaccurate reports at inappropriate times in the project. Based on this analysis, you can plan ways to provide each stakeholder with the best information and involve them at the right time to help reduce the risk of a stakeholder adversely affecting the project.

6. The public needs to be updated about this project at key milestones and after the more influential stakeholders have been informed. Possible milestones include when the planning is completed, several times during execution to understand progress, and at the end when the final report is issued. HHS may provide advice as to when the public should be informed. Bill may also want to direct team members to perform regular research about any local legislation that may be related to the program: Bill may need to communicate the project's intent and progress during those times to garner support from the public for the project.

Monitoring and Controlling Change

The following exercises are presented in this section:

- Exercise 10.1: Change Control
- Exercise 10.2: Performance Reporting, Including Earned Value Technique
- Exercise 10.3: Controlling Cost Changes
- Exercise 10.4: Controlling Schedule Changes

Exercise 10.1: Change Control

The objectives for Exercise 10.1 are as follows:

- Introduce concepts for integrated project change control.
- Understand why change control is important.
- Practice creating change control procedures.

Background

One of the most common problems that project managers complain about on their projects is how changes affect their projects, drastically inflating, extending, or reducing their original scope, schedule, budget, or quality plan. A change to the original project plan, whether the client requests it or team members decide to implement it, can change any number of factors on the project. Although change is inevitable, and even welcome if appropriate, in order for the project to stay under control, one of your main jobs is to help the team learn how to recognize and manage change and to create good change control processes. You might use or establish systems to help manage the change, and you should create processes and change forms that all of your team members understand and use.

The first thing you must do, and one of the most important, is to baseline your project plan. That is, you need to set a stake in the ground that declares the project's scope, budget, schedule, and quality. This needs to be reviewed and approved by your project stakeholders. Second, you need to identify the process for project changes. You need to take the following questions into consideration:

- How does someone request a change and who can request a change?
- Where does the request go and how is it documented? What is the system you will use to record and archive your changes?
- How is change analyzed and reviewed?
- What constitutes a change that must be made and how should changes be prioritized?
- Who approves the request? Will you have meetings to manage change within your team and will you also have a configuration control board (also known as a change control board in some organizations) to approve the changes? Does the project manager have the authority

to approve change that can be handled within the current schedule and budget, or will all changes need to be managed and approved by the change board?

- How is change implemented if approved and what happens if it is not? How will you communicate the changes to project stakeholders?

- How will you monitor the project to ensure that no unapproved changes are implemented in the project?

During development of the change process, you also need to document what kind of data you must capture to help you organize and make decisions about the change requests. The following lists some of the data you need to capture for a change request. Some of the data can be recorded immediately, but much of it cannot be determined until analysis:

- Request description (short title and longer description)

- Date request opened and date that the requestor would like to see the change implemented

- Originator and information about how to contact them

- Justification for change

- Change request number (must be assigned via a change control process and should never change)

- Status of the change (for instance, has it just been opened, is it in review, has it been approved, or has it been implemented?)

- Priority (high, medium, low)

- Analysis, which might include the following items:

  - Alternatives or trade-offs

  - How functionality is affected

  - Cost and work estimates to implement

  - Risks to project and impacts to quality, scope, budget, and schedule

  - Plans to implement change (including what must be changed, such as requirements, project schedule, scope statement, or test plan updates) and date the change can actually be implemented

  - Dependent project impacts

- Approval, denial, modifications, and short reason for each

- Sign-offs

To manage this process, you need a log that briefly describes the change request and refers to the change request ID you have established so someone can find the change request easily. The log should include information about the status of the change and the final disposition of the change. You might use a mechanized change request system or keep a log and notebooks to house the changes. You might even use both methods for ease of use. If you establish and document your change processes, your project has a much better chance of success and you will manage change instead of change managing you and your team.

In this exercise, you will practice change control processes as you help the Sensational Advertisement Productions company create a system for its advertising campaign for the new cell phone service. You will help the account manager learn how to implement change control processes and documentation for all the project managers on her account's projects.

Scenario

TPMP has brought project management processes to an advertising firm, Sensational Advertisement Productions (SAP), and the project managers at SAP are learning how to use the eight knowledge areas of scope, time, cost, quality, human resource, communications, risk, and procurement management. However, you need to help them start using the processes and tools of what is probably their most important function: integration management. You are working with Pam Rosenbaum, who has been assigned account management functions for a telecommunications client's important new product: a new cell phone that integrates normal service with PDA functions right on the phone, which will be sold at a competitive price with normal cell phone services. The account has several project managers for the various sales campaigns: Michael Harland for the print campaigns, Judy Arakawa for the TV campaigns, and Joseph Matumbo for the telemarketing campaigns. Each project manager is working with marketing managers within the telecommunications company to get direction and approval for the work they will produce.

Because these projects must integrate and a change in one campaign could affect the other, Pam knows she must create a change control process for the overall program, as well as for each individual project. Even though the telecommunications company is putting a lot of money into the campaign, SAP still has a tight budget for all its advertising. You will help Pam put together an integrated change control process that works for both SAP and its client.

Practicing Change Control

1. What is one of the first steps that you will tell Pam to perform to create a change control process?

2. What kinds of analysis should be performed on the change requests that Pam and her project managers receive?

3. Joseph has baselined his project plan and received approval from his client, Bessie Phillips. Days later, Bessie comes to him saying that the president of the company has come up with an idea that must be implemented: they need to add a survey and have the telemarketers call customers to ask them to participate. After the customer answers the survey questions, the telemarketer will try to sell them this cell phone. What should Joseph do?

4. Why will you recommend that Pam create a change log for the change requests?

5. Should each project have a separate log and its own change request management?

6. Who should be on the configuration change board?

Exercise 10.2: Performance Reporting, Including Earned Value Technique

The objectives for Exercise 10.2 are as follows:

- Understand the importance of performance measurement analysis for performance reviews.
- Decide on the best methods for performance reporting.
- Understand the earned value technique.
- Practice the earned value technique.

Background

Once your project gets underway, you need to communicate where it stands and how it is progressing to your sponsor and other executives on the project. It's important to provide the executives with objective measurements. You need to measure progress objectively based on the major elements of the project: cost, schedule, and quality (performance) within the current scope. You may also report on procurement and risk. You might have regularly scheduled performance reviews showing progress with reports, graphs, and charts.

Performance Reporting

There are various methods to choose from for reporting performance against the original estimate (baseline). The following methodsmay use bar charts, S curves, histograms, and tables to help present results to management.:

- Project status
- Forecasting
- Variance analysis
- Trend analysis
- Perform earned value analysis technique

We will briefly discuss variance analysis and trend analysis in this section; however, in this exercise, we will stress earned value techniques as a major performance review method. We will discuss earned value techniques in detail separately.

One form of Performance Reporting that you might consider during a performance review is to show schedule progress via a milestone report. This report will help show graphically if your project is on track, provided you show the original, baseline targets. The following illustrates a milestone report chart. The project was originally baselined to complete on March 7 but now shows a finish date of March 12. You can look at the individual tasks that have made the project move out.

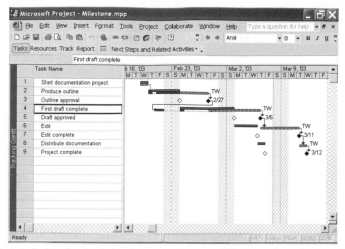

This project is behind schedule. As you can see, extra days have been added to the original end date for producing the outline (maybe someone left something out of the scope). The performance reviewers might ask the tech writer to work overtime, or maybe the performance reviewers accepted the changed dates because making sure everything is in the document is more important than getting the manual produced on time.

Besides the milestone report, you might have a budget report. You might show how much you've spent in relation to the total budget and gauge if you have spent too much in relation to how much more work you have to complete.

During performance reviews you might use variance analysis reports to show you are ahead, behind, or on target for the scheduled end date or budget. The following diagram shows a schedule variance report for the documentation project. This report shows you overall variance for completing the project is +3.1 days over the original target.

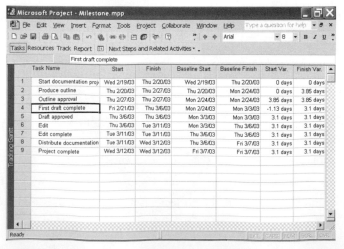

You might use trend analysis (possibly using scatter diagrams) to show quality (number of defects) and progress toward reducing them or schedule or budget trends.

Earned Value Technique (EVT)

If you use earned value analysis, then you show variance and trends in cost and schedule at the same time, and it is especially powerful if displayed graphically. Earned value analysis is one of the best ways to provide performance reporting, and PMI emphasizes it as the primary performance reporting methodology for project management.

There are many terms and formulas you need to learn to be able to describe and use earned value analysis:

Planned value (PV, also known as BCWS)   Budgeted cost of work scheduled. This is what most of us understand as our budget. It is the estimated cost of what you thought it would take to get the task or WBS component done.

Actual cost (AC, also known as ACWP)   Actual cost of work performed. This is what most of us think of as actual work and the rate applied to the work. It is the cost incurred up to a particular point in time in the project for a task or WBS component. You capture this from labor performed and include expenses if they have been applied.

Earned value (EV, also known as BCWP)   This is the value of a task or WBS component completed at the time of measurement compared to the estimate. The work accomplished is worth something even if it is not completely done. Note that you have to initially establish how you are going to measure earned value. Some organizations decide work would have an earned value of zero until it is at least 20 percent or 50 percent done. Some have decided it needs to be 100 percent done before value can be applied.

The following formulas are what you will use to calculate variances and forecast completions using planned value, actual cost, and earned value:

Cost variance (CV)   This formula tells you if costs are higher or lower than budgeted. The formula is $CV = EV - AC$. For instance, if the earned value for the documentation project is $1,605 (the outline and some writing have some earned value as of the status date) and the actual costs are $2,120 on the status date, the CV is <$515>. If the cost variance is a negative number (as shown with the angle brackets <>), the project is over budget. If it is a positive number, the project is under budget. Zero is right on target.

Schedule variance (SV)   This formula tells us if the project schedule is behind or ahead of its estimate. The formula is $SV = EV - PV$. For instance, if the earned value for the documentation project is $1,605, and the planned value is $1,550, the SV is $55. If the schedule variance is a negative number, the project is behind schedule. If it is a positive number, the project is ahead of schedule. Zero is right on target.

There are some basic truths about looking at these variances in concert:

- If CV is positive and SV is positive, the project is under budget and ahead of schedule.
- If CV is negative and SV is negative, the project costs are over budget and the schedule is slipping.

- If CV is positive and SV is negative, some project tasks may not have started or they've started but not enough resources have been assigned to them.

- If CV is negative and SV is positive, then extra money may have been spent to shorten (crash) the schedule.

Performance index (CPI and SPI)   The cost performance index formula is CPI = EV ÷ AC. If this calculation comes out higher than 1, your cost performance is great. If it is less than 1, your cost performance is poor. If it is zero, you are on target. This is a ratio that can tell you how well you are doing for a particular activity.

For instance, on the First Draft task for the documentation project, EV = 965.50 and AC = 1,000. The CPI would be 965.5 ÷ 1,000. CPI would then be .97. Since this is less than 1, we have a cost overrun for the First Draft task.

In addition to these calculations, you can use another one, called cumulative CPI (CPI^C). This sums the periodic earned values divided by the sum of the individual actual costs. This calculation is CPI^C = EV^C ÷ AC^C. This also helps project what the costs will actually be at the end of the project.

Using the documentation project (EV^C = 1,605 and AC^C = 2,120), CPI^C = 1,605 ÷ 2,120 = .76. Our cumulative performance index is .76 (less than 1) and indicates that we have a cost overrun. You could take the original budget calculation (in this case, $8,800) and divide it by .76 and the forecasted budget is now $11,579.

The formula for schedule performance index is SPI = EV ÷ PV. If this calculation comes out higher than 1, your schedule performance is great. If it is less than 1, your schedule performance is poor. If it is zero, you are on target. Again, using the documentation project (EV = 1,605 and PV = 1,550), SPI = 1,605 ÷ 1,550 = 1.04. Our performance index is showing 1.04, which means we are about .04 days ahead of schedule at the point of time for this measurement. You can use this to show trends over time each time you take this measurement.

The following chart shows earned value taken for our documentation project, showing various earned value calculations both for individual tasks and for the entire project.

> You will also see the terms *estimate at completion (EAC), budgeted at completion (BAC), variance at completion (VAC),* and *estimate to completion (ETC),* which you should learn but will not be covered in this exercise.

One of the best ways to show earned value variances and trends is to use a cumulative cost curve, illustrated here, and continue to measure it over the life of your project. Depending on how long your project is, you might measure it weekly, biweekly, or monthly.

Once you take these measurements and report them, you may discuss with the team how you are taking corrective action. The executive team may also help you take some kind of corrective action if you still need help. For instance, with the documentation project, the review team might ask you to reduce the scope of the documentation to help reduce the budget and time to complete the work.

Creating a Performance Report

Now that you know the types of performance reports and what goes into them, you can use the following list to create a performance report.

1. Decide on information that needs to be communicated: schedule, budget, quality, risk, procurement activities, or scope changes.

2. Decide on the kinds of measurements and when you will take them. You will need to make sure you baseline your schedule.

3. If you're using earned value technique, use tools that will help you generate the data regularly. Find a scheduling tool with an earned value reporting capability to capture earned value regularly.

4. Decide on the best form to communicate the information based on the needs of the audience. You will probably want to create a combination of status report, text, and charts or graphs. Executives usually prefer charts and graphs, so you would want to create a standard chart/graph for your performance reports.

5. Schedule performance review meetings regularly, discuss the variances, and decide on corrective action if it is required.

In this exercise, you will help TPMP analyze earned value through performance reporting.

Scenario

TPMP is working with an independent, nonprofit organization, Health America, who is creating reports for the status and quality of hospital health care in the United States based on goals created by the president of the United States. Health America is implementing project management processes and TPMP is helping. This is a highly visible program in the government, and it entails working with the major hospitals within the major cities of America and rating whether they are achieving specific goals as identified by the president's program.

The research and reporting started about two years ago. You are helping the project manager, Bill Smith, set up performance reporting using earned value and other performance reporting methods. The performance reports will go to HA executives and the Department of Health and Human Services (HHS). Bill is reporting earned value performance to both groups of stakeholders for the first time. You have determined that earned value for the current reporting period is $1.9 million. Your planned value is $2.5 million. Your actual costs are $1.8 million.

Performance Reporting, Including Earned Value Analysis

1. What are SV and CV for this project? What do the results mean?
2. What are SPI and CPI ^{C} for this project? What do the results mean?
3. If Bill wanted to show quality improvements over time for the hospitals, what kind of performance reporting might he use?
4. Why is Performance Reporting important?
5. What are some of the kinds of Performance Reporting that Bill could choose from?

Exercise 10.3: Controlling Cost Changes

The objectives for Exercise 10.3 are as follows:

- Describe the similarities in cost and schedule change control processes.
- Describe the three most popular EAC formulas.

Background

The project planning is done and you have been executing your project for over a month. It's time to manage the costs of your project using the Cost Control process. The Cost Control process is very similar to the Schedule Control process that is discussed in Exercise 10.4. Both processes use some of the same inputs, such as their respective baselines, performance reports, and change requests. Both processes use tools and techniques like change control systems and performance measurements to control the changes. Both processes produce outputs like baseline updates, performance measurements, requested changes, corrective action, and project management plan updates.

The one major thing that differentiates these two processes is a tool and technique called forecasting. Forecasting is making a prediction on the outcome of the costs of the project. One of the areas that this forecast concentrates on is called estimate at completion (EAC). EAC is a calculation that is done at any point in the project execution and forecasts the likely final costs of the project. There are three different ways to calculate estimate at completion. We'll spend some time on each:

EAC = AC^C + ETC   This calculation for EAC is used if your original estimates were flawed. You must first determine the estimate to completion (ETC). The ETC is the amount of money you'll need to complete the project. You add the ETC to what has actually been spent or the actual cost (AC^C) to determine the estimate at completion. Here's an example: Your project is 50 percent complete and it is running over budget. The original budget is $15,000. At this point you should have spent $7,500. Based on the performance reports that you have received, you know you need $7,500 more to complete the project (ETC). When you review the budget reports, you know you have spent $9,000 so far ($AC^C$).

EAC	=	AC^C + ETC
$16,500	=	$9,000 + $7,500

The estimate at completion is $16,500.

EAC = AC^C + BAC – EV   This formula is used when the current variances are not typical and are not expected to continue. In this calculation, you take the total budget for the project (BAC) and add it to the actual cost (AC^C). You then subtract the work accomplished (EV), giving you the estimate at completion. Your project is 60 percent complete. You have spent $10,000 ($AC^C$) so far. The total budget for the project was $25,000 (BAC). Based on the performance reports, you know you have an earned value (EV) of $18,000.

EAC	=	AC^C + BAC – EV
$17,000	=	$10,000 + $25,000 – $18,000

The estimate at completion is $17,000.

EAC = (AC^C + ((BAC – EV) ÷ CPI^C)   This calculation is used when the variances you are seeing are typical and you expect them to continue. In this calculation, you take the work accomplished (EV) and subtract it from the total budget for the project (BAC). Add that figure to the actual monies spent to date (AC^C). Then divide that figure by the cumulative cost performance index (CPI^C). Your project is 33 percent complete and the total budget for the project was $17,000 (BAC). Based on the performance reports, you know that you have an earned value of $5,000 (EV). The actual costs of the project to date are $7,000 ($AC^C$). The cumulative cost performance index is 1.10 (CPI^C).

EAC	=	AC^C + ((BAC – EV) ÷ CPI^C)
$23,901	=	$7,000 + (($17,000 – $5,000) ÷ - .71)

The estimate at completion is $17,909.

You are probably wondering what the estimate to completion is on your Pinnacle Candy Company project. In this exercise you will get a chance now to calculate the estimate to completion.

Scenario

TPMP has just placed you at the Pinnacle Candy Company as a temporary project manager. You have been assigned the EspressoFix Bar project. This project is going to create a new candy that will satisfy every coffee addict's need for coffee all wrapped up in a candy bar. The management at Pinnacle only wants to see if this new candy bar is marketable. Production of the finished product will be another project initiated later. The budget of $100,000 was established before you started work on the project. You have completed the planning and have spent 19 days executing the project. You have had some problems with the test kitchen and the chef creating the recipe and the product. Your earned value reports show an earned value of $40,000 and the actual costs of the project are $65,000. You have done the calculation for the cost performance index. The CPI is .6.

Controlling Cost Changes

1. What are two common tools and techniques that are used in the Schedule and Cost Control processes?

2. What are five common outputs that are produced in both the Schedule Control and Cost Control processes?

3. What is the EAC calculation to use if your original estimates were flawed?

4. What is the EAC calculation used when the current variances are not typical and are not expected to continue?

5. What is the calculation used when the variances you are seeing are typical and you expect them to continue?

6. You have decided that the problems with the chef are a fluke and you don't foresee any additional variances. What is your estimate at completion?

7. You have decided that the original estimates on the Pinnacle Candy Company project were flawed. Your ETC is $50,000. What is your estimate at completion?

8. You have realized that you did not use the right resources to estimate the costs of the EspressoFix Bar project. The variances you are seeing are typical and you expect the rest of the project to go as poorly. What is your estimate at completion?

Exercise 10.4: Controlling Schedule Changes

The objectives for Exercise 10.4 are as follows:

- Describe the steps required to control schedule changes.
- Describe the key elements of a schedule management plan.
- Describe the concept of a baseline.

Background

You have completed putting your schedule together and have gotten approval from the executive sponsor. Now it's time to work the plan you've created. You know that if you execute the schedule exactly as you have planned, you will complete this project on time, on budget, and with the quality the sponsor has requested. Now, how do you keep that schedule from changing? First, you must determine the status of your project; second plan for change; third, you must determine whether the schedule has changed; and fourth, you must manage the actual changes that happen on your project. These steps describe the *Guide to the PMBOK* process, Schedule Control. Schedule Control is in the Monitoring and Controlling process group. Monitoring and Controlling processes describe how you monitor and measure project results and what actions you take so the project completes as planned. Schedule Control is highly related to another Monitoring and Controlling process called Integrated Change Control. You need to know how these two processes interrelate for the PMP exam. Integrated Change Control was covered previously.

Let's go back to the components of Schedule Control and spend some time on each of them.

Determine the Status of your Project

Before you begin to execute your project plan, you need to determine how you will track what has been accomplished. This tracking is usually done via some type of status update where the people working on the project report the time worked on specific tasks. This status update is called a performance report and is an input into the Schedule Control process. This time reporting can be done in several ways:

- Report percentage complete on a task.
- Report the time spent on task.
- Report the time spent and the time remaining on a task.

You should determine the frequency of the status reports. Here is a rule of thumb for establishing the frequency. Ask yourself, "How long can a task be out of control and the project manager not know it?" Based on the answer to this question, you might set the frequency at once a week, once every two weeks, or once a month. Applying the actual time to the schedule is how you determine where you are.

Plan for Change

As you were developing your schedule, you were aware of many factors that influenced it. Some of those items were assumptions and constraints. You also know that some of those assumptions may not be true and will possibly disrupt your plan. As you finalize the schedule, you need to create a schedule management plan. This plan will document the assumptions and constraints. The schedule management plan is a subset of the larger project management plan. It documents how you will control the changes that impact the schedule. The schedule management plan can be as detailed or as simple as you need. The key here is to plan for change and determine how you will react when those changes occur. Your plan should cover items like the following:

- Who can request a change?
- How will you determine the impact of the change to the schedule?

- Is there a specific form for requesting a change?
- Who can approve the change?
- What is the reason for the change?
- If the change is denied, how is the requestor notified?
- What are the advantages or disadvantages for allowing the change?
- If the change is approved, how is the schedule updated?
- Will the change be logged and tracked?
- If the change is approved, how are the team and the requestor notified?
- Who will review the change?

Once the schedule management plan is set, you are ready to begin executing your schedule.

Has the Schedule Changed?

The third step in Schedule Control is determining whether the schedule has changed. In order for you to know if the schedule has changed, you must know the following:

- What you planned on doing (in other words, the original schedule for the project)
- Where you currently are in the process
- The variance between the two

WHAT YOU PLANNED ON DOING

Just before you begin the execution of the schedule, you must set the baseline. The baseline is a copy of your plan that shows the original schedule for the project. You set aside this copy as a reference point to be used for analysis across the remainder of the project. Most project managers use a project management software system to plan and track their projects. Almost all systems have a simple command that saves a baseline for comparison purposes. If you are creating and tracking your project manually, you need to keep a copy of your project prior to execution. The schedule baseline is an input into the Schedule Control process.

THE VARIANCE BETWEEN THE TWO

You have created a baseline of what you planned to do. You have also applied the actual time spent to your project schedule. Now it's time to compare the two to each other. This is called variance analysis. Variance analysis is a tool and technique of the Schedule Development process. In variance analysis, you look at several factors and determine whether your project will complete on time. There are several areas that you should examine:

Late starts and late finishes   Have any of the tasks on the critical path started late or finished late?

Early starts and early finishes   Have any of the tasks on the critical path changed their early start and early finish dates?

Remaining work   Do any of the tasks on the critical path have remaining work that will force them to finish late?

Completion date   Is the completion date for the project the same one you had planned?

Managing Changes

The fourth and last component of Schedule Control is managing the actual changes on your project. In this final step, you will take action to keep your project on track. Managing changes proactively will help you respond to these items:

- Requested changes to your project
- Variances to schedule completion

If you plan for change and assess how the schedule has changed appropriately, then managing changes will be easy. You are simply working the processes that you defined. For requested changes, you will use the change control process that you defined earlier in this exercise. For variances, you are using the process established when assessing how the schedule has changed. Your analysis, decisions, and corrective actions regarding changes and variances will help you manage the project to a successful completion.

In this exercise, you'll get a chance to practice controlling changes to your credit card validation project.

Scenario

TPMP has just placed you at SystemsDelivery, Inc. as a temporary project manager. You've been assigned the Credit Card Validation project. This project is designed to be the next best thing in credit card fraud prevention. The management of SystemsDelivery believes that this product will be in high demand at every major retailer in the country. Of course, the management needs this product to go to market as quickly as possible. You have been on the project for a while now. You've completed your schedule and have compressed the duration so that the project will complete in the desired time frame. You've just gotten approval from your executive sponsor on your plan. He is pleased with your delivery date and has told you that you will receive a bonus if you deliver on schedule. You know you're going to need to control the schedule to get that bonus.

Controlling Schedule Changes

1. Name four of the key elements of a schedule management plan.
2. What are the two things you must know to determine if the schedule has changed?
3. A copy of your plan that shows exactly what you planned on doing is also called a _____ _____.
4. What are the four steps of Schedule Control?

Answers to Section 10 Exercises

Answers to Exercise 10.1

Your answers may be somewhat different, but the following answers provide a guide.

1. You will recommend that Pam instruct all of her project managers to baseline their project plans. Pam should also create a change control process and change request forms with appropriate fields to collect relevant data that all of her project managers must use once they have baselined their projects.

2. To complete change requests, Pam and her project managers need to analyze alternatives or trade-offs; how functionality is affected; cost and work estimates to implement; risks and impacts to quality, scope, budget, and schedule; plans to implement if the change is approved; and dependent project impacts.

3. When Joseph's client asks him to include a new deliverable for his baselined telemarketing campaign, he needs to take out the change request form and review the change processes with this client. It does not matter who the change request comes from; the change process needs to be followed and the request needs to be documented and approved.

4. You will recommend that Pam use a change control log so that the change requests can be managed in an organized fashion so people can look up and find change requests quickly. It would be difficult to go through each change request, which could be several pages long, to review them all and their dispositions.

5. Pam should manage the account from an overall perspective, which means the projects should not have separate change request processes. Because these projects are highly dependent on one another, the project managers need to know the changes being considered for each project so that impacts may be analyzed for the entire program. Although the projects may have several requests that do not impact the other projects, it is important to allow a forum and process to ensure communication. Pam needs to ensure that she is the change control process owner and overall manager. Project managers can manage the change requests within their own project but make sure they are discussed in this overall forum.

6. The client, Pam, and the project managers should be on the configuration change board. Both SAP and the telecommunications company need to consider the changes to scope, budget, quality, or schedule. You might recommend that an executive from SAP and an executive from the telecommunications client also sit on the board to help ensure that change is prioritized and agreed to.

Answers to Exercise 10.2

1. For the Health and Welfare Department project, $SV = EV - PV$. $SV = 1.9M - 2.5M = <.6M>$ This means you are behind schedule. The $CV = EV - AC$. $CV = 1.9M - 1.8M = .1M$. This means your costs are lower than expected. Looking at these variances together, this might mean Bill did not apply enough resources to the project and that's why it's behind. However,

because it is behind, the team may decide that applying some extra resources for a short time will get it back on track.

2. For the Health and Welfare Department project, the SPI = EV ÷ PV. SPI = 1.9M ÷ 2.5M = .76. This means the project is behind schedule. The CPI^C = EV^C ÷ AC^C. CPI^C = 1.9M ÷ 1.8M = 1.05. This means the project is below expected cost. Although Bill has just started using this index, he can start showing a trend, and at this point it means the project is about 76 percent of where it needs to be according to the schedule. He is underrunning costs by about 5 percent. To change this trend, he will have to make some major changes on the project.

3. If Bill wanted to show quality improvements over time for the hospitals, he might he use trend analysis to show improvement for the hospital quality reports. He could show the number of errors/problems via a scatter diagram.

4. Performance Reporting is important to provide objective measurements to a project's executives, sponsors, or customers to show project progress, variances, and trends. Objective measurements allow the project manager and the reviewers to discuss corrective actions.

5. Bill could choose from performance reviews, variance analysis, trend analysis, and earned value technique analysis.

Answers to Exercise 10.3

1. Change control systems and performance measurements are two tools and techniques that are used in the Schedule and Cost Control processes.

2. Baseline updates, performance measurements, requested changes, corrective actions, and project management plan updates are the five common outputs that are produced in both the Schedule Control and Cost Control processes.

3. EAC = AC^C + ETC is the EAC calculation used if your original estimates were flawed.

4. EAC = AC^C + BAC – EV is the EAC calculation used when the current variances are not typical and are not expected to continue.

5. EAC = AC^C + ((BAC – EV) ÷ CPI^C) is the calculation used when the variances you are seeing are typical and you expect them to continue.

6. Your estimate at completion should be as follows:

EAC	=	AC^C + BAC – EV
$125,000	=	($65,000 + $100,000) – $40,000
EAC	=	$125,000

7. If your ETC was $50,000, your estimate at completion should be as follows:

EAC	=	AC^C + ETC
$115,000	=	$65,000 + $50,000
EAC	=	$115,000

8. If the variances you are seeing are typical and you expect the rest of the project to go as poorly, your estimate at completion should be as follows:

EAC	=	AC^C + ((BAC - EV) ÷ CPI^C)
$208,333	=	$65,000 + (($100,000 - $40,000) ÷ .6)
EAC	=	$165,000

Answers to Exercise 10.4

1. Four key elements of a schedule management plan may include the following:

Who can request a change?

Is there a specific form for requesting a change?

What is the reason for the change?

What are the advantages or disadvantages for allowing the change?

Will the change be logged and tracked?

Who will review the change?

How will you determine the impact of the change to the schedule?

Who can approve the change?

If the change is denied, how is the requestor notified?

If the change is approved, how is the schedule updated?

If the change is approved, how are the team and the requestor notified?

2. The two things you must know to determine if the schedule has changed are what you planned on doing where you currently are in the process and the variance between the two.

3. A copy of your plan that shows exactly what you planned on doing is also called a baseline.

4. The four steps of Schedule Control are determining the current status of your project, planning for change, determining if the schedule has changed, and managing the actual changes that happen on your project.

Controlling Work Results and Closing Out the Project

The following exercises are presented in this section:
- Exercise 11.1: Quality Control
- Exercise 11.2: Closing a Project or Phase, including Contract Close

Exercise 11.1: Quality Control

The objectives for Exercise 11.1 are as follows:
- Define the Perform Quality Control process.
- Describe the tools and techniques used in Perform Quality Control.

Background

The Quality Management Knowledge Area contains a process from the Monitoring and Controlling process group called Perform Quality Control. This process establishes the framework to monitor project results to guarantee that the project will achieve the desired quality. Where Perform Quality Assurance is a management process, Perform Quality Control is a technical process that is concerned with the quality of the product or service that is being created. In this process, you measure the performance of the project by collecting data.

Ten tools and techniques are used in Perform Quality Control. We will spend time on each of them.

- Control charts
- Flowcharting
- Histogram
- Pareto chart
- Run chart
- Scatter diagram
- Cause and effect diagram
- Statistical sampling
- Inspection
- Defect repair review

Inspection   Inspections are used to review or verify the quality of the product you are creating in your project. Inspections can be done on a single component or part of the product or it can be done on the entire finished product. For example, when you buy a new piece of clothing, you usually look the garment over carefully. You look at the seams, buttons, and button holes to make sure the garment is well constructed. This type of review is also known as an inspection.

Control chart   A control chart is a graphic display that shows measurements of a specific process over time. This type of chart creates an upper control limit—a boundary that shows when a product is made with very few defects and therefore more expensive than the product the manufacturer wants to create. It also shows a lower control limit—a boundary that shows that the product has too many defects and will probably not be accepted by the consumer. The middle line on a control chart shows the mean, or the area where the best product should be created. The diagram in Figure 11.1 shows a control chart for a tire manufacturing process. The third batch created would probably be melted and manufactured again because the quality is not within the accepted parameters.

FIGURE 11.1   Tire manufacturing control chart

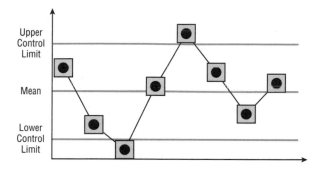

Pareto chart   A Pareto chart is used to rank order problems from larger to smallest. A Pareto chart is a type of histogram. The Pareto chart is based on the Pareto Principle, which says that the majority of defects are caused by a few problems (the 80/20 rule). This chart is useful in the Perform Quality Control process in determining where the most problems lie, therefore rank ordering what step of the process should be fixed first. The following is a typical Pareto chart.

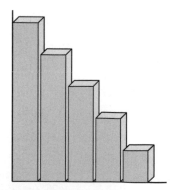

Statistical sampling   If you have many products to inspect as part of your project and you have very little time, you might decide to use statistical sampling. Statistical sampling involves gathering a subset of the total set of units and randomly selecting items to be inspected or reviewed.

This method can be very cost effective. In the following example, you'll see a pie chart that can be used to depict the results of a statistical sampling.

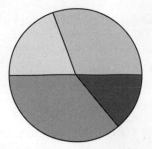

Flowcharting   Flowcharting is a way of depicting the way work proceeds from beginning to end. This technique is used in Perform Quality Control to show the interrelationship of a series of activities, thus giving the project team information about where problems may occur. The following shows a simple flowchart for building a shed in your backyard.

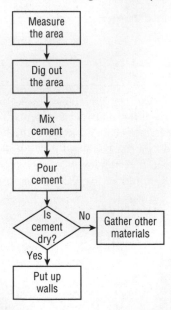

Run charts   A run chart depicts a pattern and the history of a series of events or activities. In trend analysis, the run chart is used to understand the pattern of occurrences. Trend analysis is a set of mathematical computations that allow you to determine what the future outcome will be for a product you are creating. In simple terms, if you have a process that is creating 100 defects per 10 products and you do nothing to correct the defects, you will have a trend of 100 defects per 10 products. If you have a process that is creating 100 defects per 10 products in March, you fix some process problems, and then have 85 defects per 10 products in April, you know the trend is improving.

Cause and effect diagrams   These diagrams are also known as Ishikawa or fishbone diagrams. They are used to depict how various elements(causes) can potentially create an output (effect).

Histogram   A histogram is also called a bar chart. The Pareto chart is a type of histogram. Each column of the histogram depicts the frequency of a problem or variable. This tool and technique is used in Perform Quality Control as a means of showing the severity of types of problems.

Scatter diagrams   In a scatter diagram, you use two variables to show a pattern of relationship. Say, for instance you wished to measure the relationship between how many defective products were released to customers and how many mechanized test cases were used per product as depicted in the following diagram. This scatter diagram would provide you with information on whether you produced a better product using mechanized test cases.

Defect repair review   The last tool and technique of Perform Quality Control is defect repair review. This is an action that is taken by the project team responsible for quality control to verify that defect repair has been performed satisfactorily.

In this exercise you will analyze how quality can be applied to a project at USRemotes.

Scenario

TPMP has just placed you at USRemotes, the largest distributor of remote control devices in the United States. USRemotes has launched a project to redesign the warehouse and shipping areas and processes—the WSAP project. You have been assigned as the temporary project manager. You have just completed the project planning phase.

USRemotes is very interested in quality and is planning to gain some type of quality certification. Quality is also very important to you. You have been thinking about what data you will need to gather to control the quality of the project.

Perform Quality Control

Using the information provided for the WSAP project, answer the following questions about quality control.

1. What is the definition of the Perform Quality Control process?

2. List the 10 Perform Quality Control tools and techniques.

3. You have determined that the most cost-effective timetable for shipping products from USRemotes is 24 hours. It is too expensive to ship earlier than 12 hours, and customers call to complain after 36 hours. What tool and technique of Perform Quality Control would you use to measure the shipping times? Why?

4. A Pareto chart is based on what rule?

5. What is a cost-effective tool and technique of Perform Quality Control?

Exercise 11.2: Closing a Project or Phase, including Contract Close

The objectives for Exercise 11.2 are as follows:

- Understand why project close and phase close is important.

- Describe project and phase close tools.

- Practice creating lessons learned documentation for a project.

Background

Closing is one of the most neglected activities in project management. Project managers are often assigned the next project or are ready to move to the next phase of a project and just can't take the time to properly verify all the activities of the phase or do what's necessary to close down the phase or project. So it is important to actually plan closing into your project schedule and set up the verification and measurement deliverables around the closing activities. A project is not the only thing that should be closed. You should also close each phase of a project.

In this exercise, we will explore closing for both projects and phases. Closing includes both administrative and contract closure. Contract closure is following the particular obligations stated in the contracts with the vendors of the project and archiving and auditing their portions of the project. Administrative closure includes performing activities such as documenting formal acceptance, performing lessons learned sessions, and filing all project documents and records. This exercise will focus on the activities of administrative closure, especially lessons learned.

Closing a Phase

First, a closing process ensures that you have performed all activities for a project phase. You might pass through a phase gate, a stage gate, or a kill point according to your industry practices. After the work of the phase is complete and measurements have been reviewed, a group of decision makers decides to move on to the next phase, possibly make some corrections to the current phase, and sometimes, cancel the project entirely if warranted. You may have moved on to the next phase already because the team needed to get started, but you still need to close out the previous phase. At this point, you might also conduct a lessons learned sessions to explore what you could have done better. This information can be used for another project going through the same type of project phase. Completing one phase of a project is also a good place to celebrate with the team. Here are some specific steps you can take to close a phase in a project:

1. Make sure you understand all of the deliverables and quality audits that must be passed to move out of a phase. The deliverables should be in your project plan. This should include any deliverables expected from vendors as well.

2. Gather measurements and reports that describe project or phase performance. This may include earned value analysis or other kinds of performance reporting outputs.

3. Create a checklist based on the deliverables and associated measurements completed showing their success. Prove completion or provide justification for why the deliverable was not needed.

4. Receive approval from the customer or sponsor for the end of the phase and to move on to the next phase.

5. Store the documents from the phase in your project files. If they are to be changed, make sure you have a good process and justification for the changes.

6. Hold lessons learned as soon after the phase completion as possible. Try to get participation from as many stakeholders as possible.

7. Document the lessons learned in a nonjudgmental way, and share with the rest of your organization. Try to implement as many improvements in other projects as possible.

Closing a Project

There are two kinds of project closings: a closing when the project is terminated before all work is completed and a closing when all the work of the project is completed. In the project closing process, you will verify that all the work has been completed that needed to be completed according to the project's requirements. You will archive the project's data, receive formal acceptance for the project, perform a project lessons learned, and release the resources on the project (including the project manager!). You do this even when a project has terminated early—the process establishes a record of where it ended, and if by some chance it gets picked up again (yes, it can happen), it will be much easier to restart. If the project is terminated early, it is especially important to perform a lessons learned session.

You can use the following steps to close a project:

1. Review the project plan to ensure that all phases have been completed to satisfaction. You might also conduct an independent audit for the project.

2. Gather measurements and reports that describe project performance. Again, this may include earned value analysis and any other kinds of items you set up for performance reporting.

3. Prove project completion or provide justification for why the deliverable was not needed or the phase did not complete with all expected deliverables.

4. Receive approval from the customer or sponsor for project closure.

5. Archive the project files.

6. Hold a lessons learned session as soon as possible near project close. Try to get participation from as many stakeholders as possible. You might have to request time from team members who may have already been reassigned to another project.

7. Document the lessons learned in a nonjudgmental way, and share the information with the rest of your organization. Try to implement as many improvements in other projects as possible. If you found tasks or processes that should be added to other projects, think about including those tasks or processes to project schedule templates or project plans.

Contract closeout is part of Procurement Management but it is also a part of project closing. You would perform many of the same functions to close the contract as the project itself, but you would ensure that the terms of the contract are completed, including final payment and written approval to ensure formal acceptance of the work of the vendor. You will make sure you keep a contract file (especially if there could be legal repercussions at some point), and you might perform a procurement audit to create a lessons learned document on the contract and to help rate the vendor for future considerations. Contract closeout would be performed prior to the full project closure and contract documentation is one of the inputs to the Close Project process.

Lessons Learned

Perhaps the most important part of closure is lessons learned. Note that the process is a part of the Information Distribution tools and techniques. This process should occur throughout the project at important junctures and if something in particular goes very wrong. But it is best performed at the end of a phase or project and as soon as possible after the phase or project ends so ideas are fresh and the project stakeholders are available to participate.

One of the most important aspects of a lessons learned session is that it be conducted in an atmosphere that does not place blame. The project manager or an independent facilitator should create an atmosphere in which the team approaches it as, "If we had it all to do again, what would we do better?"—not "What did we do wrong?" You can't change the past, but you can do better in the future. Your team should look at lessons learned as an opportunity to take the improvements into the next project. This attitude toward improvement is critical to ensure the best lessons learned input from your stakeholders. Depending on the make-up of your team, you may hold one lessons learned session with as many stakeholders participating as possible. You may also need to consider holding several sessions. For instance, team members might be more likely to bring up improvements with other team members but not in front of the customer because it looks like admitting mistakes or problems.

You also need to capture the right data for lessons learned. You can cover both product processes and project processes. You might include the following in your lessons learned documentation:

- A brief description of something discrete that could be improved. If possible, make this description positive. For instance, instead of saying, "Reports were incomplete," you might state, "Add more relevant data to reports." Then you can actually state what the data should be.

- Analysis of the lesson (perhaps root cause or some reason why the issue occurred).

- Recommendations (sometimes this happens without the analysis because a team member has already figured out the solution).

- A record of who originated the lessons learned in case you need to get clarification later.

- How you might implement the improvement in a future project or future phase.

In this exercise, you'll explore some important processes you should consider for closing and practice some of the elements of lessons learned as TPMP helps one of its clients implement improved project management processes.

Scenario

TPMP is working with an independent, nonprofit organization, Health America, that is creating reports for the status and quality of hospital health care in the United States based on goals created by the president of the United States. Health America is implementing project management processes and TPMP is helping them. This is a highly visible program in the government, and it entails working with the major hospitals within the major cities of America and rating whether they are achieving specific goals as identified by the president's program.

The design phase for how the reports will be created is coming to a close soon. You are helping the project manager, Bill Smith, set up closing processes for his project. These processes may be used for future projects. During the design phase, the budget was exceeded by about 15 percent; he lost several team members to promotions, which disrupted the project; and the scope of the design changed several times. His team feels that the design phase went on for too long, and some team members have already started many implementation tasks. The team wants to move on quickly. Many of his team members have told Bill they can make design changes anyway as they start implementing the project.

Closing a Project or Phase

1. What closing processes will you suggest that Bill create for the end of his design phase?

2. What are some lessons learned that the team might come up with? Remember to keep the descriptions positive.

3. Bill had a contractor design the report format that would be used in his project for the government. What will Bill need to do to close the contract?

4. What deliverables or milestones should Bill add to his project schedule for the closing processes?

5. Are closing processes important? Why or why not?

Answers to Section 11 Exercises

Answers to Exercise 11.1

1. Perform Quality Control monitors project results to guarantee that the project will achieve the desired quality.

2. The 10 Perform Quality Control tools and techniques are run charts, flowcharting, statistical sampling, Pareto charts, control charts, cause and effect diagrams, histograms, scatter diagrams, defect repair review, and inspection.

3. A control chart would be a good tool and technique to use for this measurement because it allows you to set an upper and lower control limit as well as a mean. Since you have these parameters, determining whether the process is in control or out of control could be measured with this tool.

4. The Pareto chart is based on the 80/20 rule.

5. A cost-effective tool and technique of Perform Quality Control is statistical sampling.

Answers to Exercise 11.2

1. Bill should complete all processes for design: Don't give into the team's desire to skip any design deliverables, although it might be fine to move on to steps in the next phase. File design documents, take time for lessons learned, and get acceptance of the design phase. Schedule a go/no go meeting for the next phase. Have a design closeout party.

2. Here are examples of some lessons learned: Report on budget progress weekly to make adjustments sooner so the team won't go over budget quite as much. Bill or other project managers might consider building a team of both junior and senior folks so that promotions won't disrupt the team as much. Also, project managers might consider ensuring that team members are trained as backups for the important tasks. Because the budget went over, all project managers want to make sure they have a good scope change control process. In the future, the schedule might include some checkpoints. At the checkpoints, the team can determine whether they are on track for completing the phase and discuss corrections to the work of the project if it is going on for too long.

3. Bill will need to review the contract terms and, in written format, verify that all deliverables and expectations have been met. Bill might use one of the organization's lawyers to help with that task. Bill will need to ensure that final payment is made to the contractor. He should also have lessons learned sessions with the team and the contractor and perform a procurement audit. He will then need to file the contract documents according to company standards. TPMP would advise that Bill make sure that, in the future, all of these tasks are included in project schedules and plans.

4. Bill needs to add the following regular tasks to the end of each phase: review and approvals, gathering and filing of the documents approved during the phase, lessons learned sessions, procurement audits (optional), and team celebration.

5. Although you could possibly have success without great closing processes, they are important because, by having them, you will ensure that you've done everything required on the project. You make sure you cover everything the customer wanted. Having closing processes is also an excellent way to show phase or milestone completion to the team throughout the project—you need incremental success points to motivate the team. Most important, though, you can help future projects. Most project management process improvements have come from project managers sharing their knowledge with others and making consistent and standardized processes so everyone has a chance for even greater success on their next project.

Professional Responsibility

The following exercise is presented in this section:

- Exercise 12.1: Professional Responsibility

Exercise 12.1: Professional Responsibility

The objectives for Exercise 12.1 are as follows:

- Introduce the major concepts of professional responsibility.

- Understand why you need to include professional responsibility in your everyday project choices and management.

- Practice making professional responsibility decisions.

Background

Within the past few years, the Project Management Institute (PMI) added a section to the PMP exams about professional responsibility. Although project managers might know how to perform all the required technical processes of project management, if they do not work ethically, with regard for customer fairness, and with the latest project management knowledge, then they may still not be doing the best job for their customer. Professional responsibility is based on the *Project Management Professional Code of Professional Conduct*. Read and understand the items listed on the code of conduct. The following list includes the major elements of the code of conduct:

- Adherence to the code of conduct, including supporting it and sharing it with others, acting ethically when taking the PMP exam, and cooperating with PMI in gathering ethics violations information

- Disclosing what could look like conflict of interest or impropriety to customers and ensuring that a conflict of interest does not compromise your judgment or duties to the customer

- Advertising your qualifications truthfully

- Complying with all applicable laws wherever you are performing your project management duties

- Respecting intellectual property

- Providing accurate cost and service estimates and expected results of the project

- Sticking to and satisfying the scope of your objectives (unless changed by the customer)

- Protecting confidential information

- Refraining from taking gifts or payments for personal gain (unless conforming to the customs where you are practicing yet still not violating your own customary practices)

There are a few other areas that you need to think about that are not expressly mentioned in the code of conduct:

- Seek growth opportunities in your knowledge of project management practices, including taking classes, reading articles, and attending seminars.

- Stay on top of your industry's practices because your project management skills are coupled with your knowledge of your industry.

- Deal with issues on your project as quickly and with as much fairness as possible, making sure you use problem-solving techniques if you can. If you have competing stakeholder or customer needs, make sure you try to resolve the differences fairly and with regard to the objectives of the project.

- Use all your project management knowledge, and make sure you use the most significant processes and create the most important outputs from the nine PMI knowledge areas as appropriate for your projects.

- Respect cultural differences by learning about them as needed, following local customs, and making sure your team is trained on cultural issues as appropriate.

- Communicate as accurately and fairly as possible with your stakeholders. This means accurately reporting status—if it is bad news, report it. Your customers or management cannot make good decisions or help you get back on track if they do not know they need to.

- Protect the community as needed. Although you may be following the requirements of your customer, if you think the project could harm the community in any way, you need to work with your customer to change what could be harmful. If the customer will not change the project, then you may need to report the issue to the community.

To perform ethically in project management, you need to follow general business ethics and, on top of those, items specific to project management. You must work with honesty, integrity, and fairness; show concern for client, stakeholder, and community interests; continue pursuing professional growth and education; and protect intellectual property and confidential information. You will make sure no conflict of interest clouds your professional judgment and actions as you manage each of your projects. This added piece of project management helps round out your full success in your project management career.

In this exercise, you will help the project managers of SAP identify and understand the individual elements of professional responsibility. These elements will help them think about their professional responsibility in their daily jobs as they manage the projects for their telecommunications client.

Scenario

TPMP has brought project management processes to an advertising firm, Sensational Advertisement Productions (SAP), and the project managers at SAP are learning how to use the eight knowledge areas of scope, time, cost, quality, human resource, communications, risk, and procurement management. However, you need to help them start using the processes and tools of what is probably their most important function: integration management. You are working with Pam Rosenbaum, who has been assigned account management functions for a telecommunications client's important new product: a new cell phone that integrates normal service with PDA functions right on the phone, which will be sold at a competitive price with normal cell phone services. The account has several project managers for the various campaigns: Michael Harland for the print campaigns, Judy Arakawa for the TV campaigns, and Joseph Matumbo for the telemarketing campaigns. Each project manager is working with marketing managers within the telecommunications company to get direction and approval for the work they will produce.

Professional Responsibility

1. What are five professional responsibility elements the SAP project managers need to understand?

2. Last week, Judy found out that the time frame for one of her most important TV commercials might not be available during a major golf tournament when everyone felt it would be most effective. Judy thinks she can recover by working some deals with other advertisers. Should she report this issue to Pam and the client or wait until she knows for sure what will happen?

3. One of Michael's deliverables is to create a test print advertisement campaign in various markets of Europe. His team will be working with a subcontractor in Europe who will help SAP create the campaign. What does Michael need to do to prepare for that deliverable?

4. The telecommunications company has shared with Joseph some of the projected sales of the cell phone product. Joseph is thinking that he might make a great amount of money if he were to invest in the company's stocks at this time. What should Joseph do?

5. What could TPMP do to help support the educational growth opportunities of the project managers of SAP?

Answers to Section 12 Exercises

Answers to Exercise 12.1

Your answers may be somewhat different, but the following answers provide a guide.

1. Elements that TPMP needs to review with SAP project managers are as follows: respecting confidential information and intellectual property, continued professional and industry knowledge growth, respecting cultural differences and following the cultural norms, protecting the community, not accepting gifts or payments for personal gain that can cloud professional judgment or actions, complying with the applicable laws, and reporting budget and status truthfully.

2. Judy needs to report the possible loss of her TV spot to Pam and the client. It is possible that they could either decide the advertisement spot is not as important as previously thought or think of ways that Judy has not thought of to help secure the spots. Also, they may need to consider what they might lose if they do not get the advertising spot and the impacts to the campaign's objectives. Judy needs to deal with the issues sooner rather than later when the consequences might be much more serious.

3. You will advise Michael to have people on his advertising team study the cultural norms of the test markets they will be in. You will also suggest that his sales team take training in the cultural norms of the European culture they will be working with. They need to be especially sensitive to the culture to help ensure the most productive teamwork possible.

4. During your training on professional responsibility, you have taught Joseph and the other project managers that confidential information must be protected and not used for personal gain. Joseph needs to keep this in mind because he has insider information because he could profit from the insider information. It is not appropriate for Joseph to do anything with this information.

5. To help promote the project managers' continued educational growth, TPMP could create a curriculum or suggested growth path for SAP. This might include a project management tier structure (something like project coordinator, project manager, program manager, senior program manager, project management office director) with educational achievements and certifications required for each tier, participation in local PM activities and seminars, and joining PMI for the professional magazines and information it provides.

Glossary

Numbers

360-degree review   360-degree reviews are a form of project performance appraisal (a tool and technique of the Manage Project process) that solicit feedback from everyone the team member interacts with, including the stakeholders, customers, project manager, peers, subordinates, and others.

A

acceptance   Acceptance is a strategy for threats or opportunities and is a tool and technique of the Risk Response Planning process. This strategy implies that the organization is willing to accept the consequences of the risk should it occur.

acceptance criteria   Acceptance criteria refers to the product of the project and includes the process and the criteria that will be used to determine if the deliverables and the final product or service of the project are acceptable and satisfactory.

Achievement Theory   This motivational theory says people are motivated by the need for three things: achievement, power, and affiliation.

Acquire Project Team   This process involves attaining human resources and assigning them to the project. Human resources may come from inside or outside the organization. Acquire the Project Team belongs to the Executing process group.

activity attributes   Activity attributes describe the characteristics of the activities such as the activity identifier or code, descriptions, constraints and assumptions associated with the activity, predecessor activities, successor activities, resource requirements, the individual responsible for completing the work, and so on. The activity attributes are an extension of the activity list and are used in the schedule model tool and technique of the Schedule Development process.

Activity Definition   This process identifies the activities of the project that need to be performed to produce the product or service of the project.

activity duration estimates   Activity duration estimates are quantifiable estimates of the number of work periods needed to complete the schedule activities listed. They are an output of the Activity Duration Estimating process.

Activity Duration Estimating   This process assesses the number of work periods needed to complete the project activities. Work periods are usually expressed in hours or days. Large projects might express duration in weeks or months.

activity list   An extension of the WBS that contains all the activities of the project and a description of each activity. The activity list is an output of the Activity Definition process.

activity on arrow (AOA)   A diagramming method that places activities on arrows, which connect to dependent activities using nodes. This is also known as the *arrow diagramming method*.

activity on node (AON)   A diagramming method that places activities on nodes, which connect to dependent activities using arrows. This is also known as the *precedence diagramming method*.

Activity Resource Estimating   This process determines the types of resources needed (both human and materials) and in what quantities for each schedule activity within a work package.

Activity Sequencing   This process sequences activities in logical order and determines if dependencies exist among the activities.

actual cost (AC)   The actual cost of work to date or during a given time period, including direct and indirect costs.

addition   A type of project ending where the project evolves into an ongoing operation.

administrative closure procedure   Administrative closure procedures is a document that outlines how administrative closure will occur on the project, the activities needed to perform this procedure, and the essential roles and responsibilities. This is an output of the Direct and Manage Project Execution process.

advertising   Informing potential vendors that an RFP, RFQ, and so on is available. This is a tool and technique of the Request Seller Responses process.

alternatives identification   A technique used to discover different methods or ways of accomplishing the project. Alternatives identification is a tool and technique of the Scope Definition process.

analogous estimating   This technique uses the actual duration of a similar, completed activity to determine the duration of the current activity. This is also called top-down estimating and uses both expert judgment and historical information.

appeals   See *contested changes*.

approval requirements   Approval requirements refer to how the objectives, deliverables, project management documents, and other outcomes and results of the project will be approved.

arbitration   A negotiation technique used to settle contract disputes. All parties come to the table with a third, disinterested party who is not a participant in the contract to try to reach an agreement. The purpose of arbitration is to reach an agreement without having to go to court.

arrow diagramming method (ADM)   A diagramming method that places activities on arrows, which connect to dependent activities using nodes. This is also known as *activity on arrow*.

assumption   An event or action believed to be true. Project assumptions should always be documented.

attributes   Measurements of deliverables (or certain characteristics of the deliverable) that meet one of two options: conforming or nonconforming. Conforming meets the requirement; nonconforming does not. This is an inspection technique (which is a tool and technique) of the Perform Quality Control process.

avoid   The avoid strategy is used for risks that pose threats to the project or have negative impacts. It's a tool and technique of the Risk Response Planning process. This strategy requires changes to the project plan in order to avoid or eliminate risk events and their impacts to the project objectives.

B

backward pass   A calculation used in CPM to determine late start and late finish dates for activities.

balanced matrix   A type of organizational structure where power is balanced between project managers and functional managers.

bar charts   A method of displaying schedule activities. See also *Gantt charts*.

benefit measurement methods   A category of project selection methods, which are a tool and technique of the Develop Project Charter process. They employ various forms of analysis and comparative approaches to make project decisions and include cost-benefit analysis, scoring models, benefit contribution methods, and economic models.

bidder conferences   Meetings with prospective vendors or sellers are held prior to the completion of their response proposal to clarify project objectives and answer questions. Bidder conferences are a tool and technique of the Select Seller process.

brainstorming   This is an information-gathering technique that is a tool and technique of the Risk Identification process. It involves assembling together in one place subject matter experts, team members, risk management team members, and anyone else who might benefit the process and querying them on possible risk events.

budget at completion (BAC)   The remaining budget less the work that's been done to date. This figure is used in earned value analysis calculations.

buffer   See *reserve time*.

C

calculation methods   A category of selection methods outlined in the project selection methods tool and technique of the Initiation process. Calculation methods provide a way to calculate the value of the project. This value is used in the project selection decision-making process.

cardinal scale   Values that are linear or nonlinear and referenced in the Qualitative Risk Analysis process.

cause-and-effect diagram   This diagram shows the relationship between the effects of problems and their causes. It depicts every potential cause and subcause of a problem and the effect that each proposed solution will have on the problem. This diagram is also called a fishbone diagram or an Ishikawa diagram.

change control system   Documented procedures that describe how to submit change requests and how to manage change requests. The change control system tracks the status of change requests and defines the level of authority needed to approve changes. It describes the management impacts of the changes as they pertain to project performance. Change control systems are a subset of the configuration management system.

claims   See *contested changes.*

claims administration   Claims administration involves documenting, monitoring, and managing changes to the contract.

Close Project   This process is concerned with gathering and disseminating information to formalize project closure. The completion of each project phase requires administrative closure also.

Closing   The last of the five project management process groups. Closing brings a formal, orderly end to the activities of a project phase or to the project itself. All the project information is gathered and archived for future reference. Contract closeout occurs here, and formal acceptance and approval are obtained from project stakeholders.

collocated   Team members physically working at the same location or holding project meetings in a common area such as a war room.

collocation   Team members physically working at the same location or holding project meetings in a common area such as a war room.

common causes of variances   Process variances seen in run charts (a tool and technique of the Perform Quality Control process) that are a result of random variances, known or predictable variances, or variances that are always present in the process.

communication   The process of exchanging information. There are three elements to all communication: the sender, the message, and the receiver. Communication can be written or verbal and formal or informal. A project manager spends 90 percent of their time communicating.

compromise   Compromise is a conflict resolution technique. Compromise is achieved when each of the parties involved in the conflict gives up something to reach a solution.

configuration control board (CCB)   A team that is established by the organization and given the authority to review all change requests and approve them or deny them. This is also known as a *change control board.*

configuration management   Documented procedures that describe how to submit change requests and how to manage change requests. Configuration management tracks the status of change requests and defines the level of authority needed to approve changes. It describes the characteristics of the product of the project and ensures that the description is accurate and complete. Configuration management controls changes to the characteristics of an item and tracks the changes made or requested and their status.

conflict   The incompatibility of goals, which often leads to one party resisting or blocking the other party from attaining their goals.

conflict of interest   Conflict of interest occurs when personal interests are put above the interests of the project. It also occurs when personal influence is used to cause others to make decisions in favor of the influencer without regard for the project outcome.

confrontation   Confrontation is a conflict resolution technique also known as problem solving. This technique involves discovering all the facts related to the conflict. Once all the facts are known, a solution will become clear. This is the preferred method of conflict resolution.

constrained optimization methods   See *mathematical models*.

constraint   Anything that either restricts the actions of the project team or dictates the actions of the project team.

contested changes   Contract changes that cannot be agreed upon. They usually involve a disagreement about the compensation to the vendor for implementing the change.

contingency planning   This is a risk response strategy that involves planning alternatives to deal with the risks should they occur. Contingency planning is a tool and technique of the Risk Response Planning process.

contingency reserves   Contingency reserves hold project funds, time, or resources in reserve to offset any unavoidable threats that might occur to project scope, schedule, cost overruns, or quality. This is a tool and technique of the Risk Response Planning process.

contingency time   See *reserve time*.

contract   A legally binding agreement between two or more parties used to acquire products or services. Contracts can be made between two or more parties, and money is typically exchanged for goods or services. They are enforceable by law and require an offer and an acceptance.

Contract Administration   This process involves monitoring vendor performance and ensuring that all the requirements of the contract are met.

contract change control system   This describes the processes needed to make contract changes and is a tool and technique of the Contract Administration process.

Contract Closure   This process is concerned with completing and settling the terms of the contract and determines if the work described in the contract was completed accurately and satisfactorily. This process is performed after Close Project but its output (contract file) becomes an input to the Close Project process (contract documentation).

contract file   A file of all the contract records and supporting documents. This is part of the organizational process asset output of the Contract Closure process.

contract negotiation   Contract negotiation occurs when all parties discuss the terms of the contract and reach an agreement.

contract statement of work (SOW)   A detailed, concise description of the work of the project included with the contract. This can be written by either the buyer or the seller. See also *statement of work*.

control chart   A tool and technique of the Quality Control process that measures the results of processes over time and displays them in graph form. Control charts measure variances to determine if process variances are in control or out of control.

corrective actions   Taking action to align the anticipated future project outcomes with the project plan.

cost baseline   The expected cost for the project. Cost baselines are produced during the Cost Budgeting process and are represented as S curves.

Cost Budgeting   This process assigns cost estimates to activities and is used to create the cost baseline, which measures the variance and performance of the project throughout the project's life.

Cost Control   This process manages the changes to project costs using the cost change control system.

Cost Estimating   This process develops an approximation of the cost of resources needed for each project activity.

cost performance index (CPI)   An earned value analysis technique that is used to calculate cost performance efficiencies. $CPI = EV \div AC$

cost plus fee (CPF)   Cost plus fee contracts reimburse the seller for all allowable costs and include a fee that's calculated as a percentage of total costs. This is also called a cost plus percentage of cost contract.

cost plus fixed fee (CPFF)   Cost plus fixed fee contracts charge back all allowable project costs to the seller and include a fixed fee upon completion of the contract.

cost plus incentive fee (CPIF)   This type of contract charges the allowable costs associated with producing the goods or services of the project to the buyer and includes an incentive for exceeding the performance criteria laid out in the contract.

cost plus percentage of cost (CPCC)   See *cost plus fee (CPF)*.

cost reimbursable contract   This type of contract charges the allowable costs associated with producing the goods or services of the project to the buyer.

cost variance (CV)   An earned value analysis technique that determines if costs are higher or lower than budgeted during a given period of time. $CV = EV - AC$

cost-benefit analysis   This compares the financial benefits to the company of performing the project to the costs of implementing the project.

crashing   Crashing is a compression technique that looks at cost and schedule trade-offs. One of the things you might do to crash the schedule is add resources, from either inside or outside the organization, to the critical path tasks.

critical chain method   This is a tool and technique from the Schedule Development process that allows for modifying the project schedule due to limited or restricted resources. This is a technique that's designed to help manage the uncertainties of a project. It combines deterministic and probabilistic approaches.

critical path (CP)   The longest path through the project. It's made up of activities with zero float.

Critical Path Method (CPM)   Determines a single early and late start date and early and late finish date for each activity on the project to determine both the longest path of the project schedule network diagram and the finish date of the project.

critical success factors   Those elements that must be completed in order for the project to be considered complete.

culture shock   A disorienting experience that occurs when working in foreign surroundings or cultures that you are not familiar with.

cumulative cost performance index (CPI^c)   An earned value analysis technique that is used to calculate cost performance efficiencies. $CPI^c = EV^c \div AC^c$

D

decision models   A category of selection methods outlined in the project selection methods tool and technique of the Develop Project Charter process. Decision models are used to examine different criteria to help make a decision regarding project selection. (See also *calculation methods*.)

decision trees   These are diagrams that show the sequence of interrelated decisions and the expected results of choosing one alternative over the other. This is a Quantitative Risk Analysis modeling technique, which is a tool and technique of this process.

deliverable   A measurable outcome, measurable result, or specific item that must be produced to consider the project or project phase completed. Deliverables are tangible and can be measured and easily proved.

deliverable   An output that must be produced to bring the phase or project to completion. Deliverables are tangible and can be measured and easily proved.

Delphi technique   A Risk Identification technique used to gather information. Similar to brainstorming, except participants don't usually know each other, nor do they have to be present at the same location.

dependencies   See *logical relationships*.

Develop Project Management Plan   This is the first process in the Planning process group. The purpose of this process is to define, coordinate, and integrate all subsidiary project plans. The subsidiary plans may include the following: project scope management plan, schedule management plan, cost management plan, quality management plan, process improvement plan, staffing management plan, communication management plan, risk management plan, procurement management plan, milestone list, resource calendar, schedule baseline, cost baseline, quality baseline, and the risk register.

Develop Project Team   This process concerns creating an open, encouraging environment for team members as well as developing them into an effective, functioning, coordinated group.

develop qualified sellers lists   Lists of prospective sellers who have been preapproved or prequalified to provide contract services (or provide supplies and materials) for the organization. Qualified seller lists are an output of the Request Seller Responses process.

Direct and Manage Project Execution   This process involves carrying out the project plan. Activities are clarified, the work is authorized to begin, resources are committed and assigned to activities, and the product or service of the project is created. The largest portion of the project budget will be spent during this process.

discounted cash flow   Compares the value of the future cash flows of the project to today's dollars using time value of money techniques.

discretionary dependencies   Dependencies defined by the project management team. Discretionary dependencies are usually process or procedure driven. They are also known as preferred logic, soft logic, and preferential logic. See also *logical relationships*.

disputes   See *contested changes*.

E

earned value (EV)   A measurement of the project's progress to date, or the value of the work completed to date.

earned value technique (EVT)   The most commonly used performance measurement method. It looks at schedule, cost, and scope project measurements and compares their progress as of the measurement date against what was expected. The three measurements needed to perform earned value analysis are *planned value (PV)*, *actual cost (AC)*, and *earned value (EV)*.

enhance   Enhance is a Risk Response Planning strategy used for risks that pose an opportunity to the project.

estimate at completion (EAC)   An earned value analysis technique that forecasts the expected total cost of a work component, schedule activity, or the project at its completion.

estimate to complete (ETC)   An earned value analysis techniques that determines the additional expected costs to complete the schedule activity, WBS component, or control account (or project).

evaluation criteria   A method of rating and scoring vendor proposals. Evaluation criteria are an output of the Select Sellers process.

Executing   The third of the project management process groups. The Executing process group involves putting the project management plan into action, including coordinating and directing project resources to meet the objectives of the project plan. The Executing processes ensure the project plan stays on track and that future execution of project plans stays in line with project objectives.

Expectancy Theory   A motivational theory that states that the expectation of a positive outcome drives motivation and that people will behave in certain ways if they think there will be good rewards for doing so. The strength of the expectancy drives the behavior.

expected monetary value (EMV)   EMV is a statistical technique that calculates the average, anticipated impact of the decision. This is a Quantitative Risk Analysis modeling technique, which is a tool and technique of this process.

expected value   The value calculated by using the three-point estimates for activity duration (most likely, pessimistic, and optimistic) and then finding the weighted average of those estimates.

expert judgment   Expert judgment is a tool and technique of several processes. Expert judgment relies on individuals or groups of people who have training, specialized knowledge, or skills about the inputs you're assessing.

exploit   Exploit is a Risk Response Planning strategy used for risks that pose an opportunity to the project.

external dependencies   Dependencies that are external to the project. See also *logical relationships*.

extinction   A type of project ending where the work of the project is completed and accepted by the stakeholders.

F

fait accompli   Fait accompli happens during contract negotiation when one party tries to convince the other party discussing a particular contract term that it is no longer an issue. It's a distraction technique because the party practicing fait accompli tactics is purposely trying to keep from negotiating an issue and claims the issue cannot be changed.

fast tracking   A schedule compression technique where two activities that were previously scheduled to start sequentially start at the same time. Fast tracking reduces schedule duration if applied to the critical path.

fast tracking   A schedule compression technique where two activities that were previously scheduled to start sequentially start at the same time. Fast tracking reduces schedule duration.

feasibility study   Feasibility studies are undertaken to determine if the project is a viable project, the probability of project success, and the viability of the product of the project.

fixed price contract   This type of contract sets a specific, firm price for the goods or services rendered based on a well-defined deliverable agreed upon by the buyer and seller. The biggest risk is borne by the seller with a fixed price contract.

fixed price plus incentive contract   This type of contract sets a specific, firm price for the goods or services rendered (like the fixed price contract) and includes an extra incentive for exceeding agreed-upon performance criteria.

float   The amount of time you can delay the early start of a task without delaying the finish date of the project. This is also known as *slack time.*

float time   See *float.*

force majeure   Catastrophic risks that are outside the scope of risk management planning such as earthquakes, meteorites, volcanoes, floods, civil unrest, and terrorism. This is referenced in the risk categories section of the Risk Identification process.

forcing   A conflict resolution technique where one person forces a solution on the other parties.

formal acceptance and closure   Formal acceptance and closure involves providing formal notice to the seller—usually in written form—that the contract is complete. It's the organization's way of formally accepting the product of the project from the vendor and closing out the contract. This is an element of both the Close Project and Contract Closure processes.

forward pass   A calculation used in CPM to determine early start and early finish dates for activities.

free float   The amount of time the start of a task can be delayed without delaying the early start of a successor task.

functional organization   A form of organizational structure. Functional organizations are traditional organizations with hierarchical reporting structures. The functional manager traditionally has more authority in this type of organization than the project manager has.

G

Gantt charts   A method of displaying schedule activities. Gantt charts might also show activity sequences, activity start and end dates, resource assignments, activity dependencies, and the critical path.

H

hammocks   Summary-level activities or aggregate activities shown as a summary activity on a project schedule network diagram.

handoffs   The process of ending one project life cycle phase and beginning the next.

hard dependencies   See *mandatory dependencies*.

hard logic   See *mandatory dependencies*.

historical information   An input to several Planning processes that refers to information or records regarding past projects and their performance. Records are available for reference on the existing project.

Human Resource Planning   This process documents the roles and responsibilities of individuals or groups for various project elements and then documents the reporting relationships for each.

Hygiene Theory   This theory was developed by Fredrick Herzberg. It's also known as the Motivation-Hygiene Theory. Hygiene factors and motivators contribute to motivation. Hygiene factors prevent dissatisfaction and deal with work environment issues.

I

impact   The amount of damage or opportunity a risk event poses to a project.

impact scale   A scale in which a value is assigned to depict the severity of a potential risk impact using a cardinal value or actual numeric value.

independent estimates   Comparing the costs of a vendor proposal with outside sources or other vendor prices to determine if estimates are reasonable. This is a tool and technique of the Select Sellers process.

influence diagrams   A diagramming technique referenced in the Risk Identification process that shows the causal influences among project variables, the timing or time order of events, and the relationships among other project variables and their outcomes.

Information Distribution   This process is concerned with providing stakeholders with information regarding the project in a timely manner via status reports, project meetings, review meetings, e-mail, and so on. The communications management plan is put into action during this process.

information distribution methods   A tool and technique of the Information Distribution process that involves getting the project information to the project team or stakeholders.

information gathering and retrieval systems   A tool and technique of the Information Distribution process, information gathering and retrieval systems describe ways that project information is stored and shared among project team members.

Initiating   This is the first project management process group and generally the first phase of a project life cycle. It acknowledges that the project, or the next phase in an active project, should begin.

inspection   A tool and technique of the Scope Verification, Perform Quality Control, and Contract Administration processes that involves physically looking at, measuring, or testing results to determine if they conform to the requirements or quality standards.

Integrated Change Control   This process is concerned with influencing the things that cause change, determining that change is needed or has happened, and managing change. All other change control processes are integrated with this process.

integration   A type of project ending where the financial or human resources assigned to the project are diverted or reassigned elsewhere in the organization.

internal rate of return (IRR)   The discount rate when the present value of the cash inflows equals the original investment. Projects with higher IRR values are generally considered better than projects with lower IRR values. IRR assumes that cash inflows are reinvested at the IRR value.

interviews   Interviews are question-and-answer sessions held with other project managers, subject matter experts, stakeholders, customers, the management team, project team members, and users. Typically these folks have previous experience on projects similar to the current project, or they have specialized knowledge or industry expertise.

iterative   To repeat processes more than once. The five process groups are repeated throughout the project's life due to change requests, responses to change, corrective action, and so on.

L

lags   Lags delay successor activities and require the dependent activity to have time added either to the start date or to the finish date of the activity.

leaders   Leaders impart vision, gain consensus for strategic goals, establish direction, and inspire and motivate others.

leads   Leads speed up successor activities and require time to be subtracted from the start date or the finish date of the dependent activity.

lessons learned   Information gained throughout the course of the project that can be used to benefit the current project, future projects, or other projects currently being performed by the organization. Lessons learned should be documented and may include positive as well as negative lessons.

logical relationships   Dependencies between two project activities whereby one activity must do something (finish or start) before another activity can do something (start or finish). Logical relationships can also exist between an activity and a milestone. These are also known as precedence relationships. The four types of logical relationships are finish-to-start, finish-to-finish, start-to-start, start-to-finish.

lump sum contracts   See *fixed price contracts*.

M

make-or-buy analysis   A tool and technique of the Plan Purchases and Acquisitions process that determines whether it's more cost effective for the organization to purchase goods and services or to produce the goods and services itself. Make-or-buy analysis can also include capacity issues, skills, availability, trade secrets, and so on.

Manage Project Team   Manage Project Team is concerned with tracking and reporting on the performance of individual team members and preparing performance appraisals.

Manage Stakeholders   Manage Stakeholders is concerned with satisfying the needs of the stakeholders by managing communications with them, resolving issues, and improving project performance by implementing requested changes.

managers   Managers focus on results and are concerned with getting the job done according to the requirements.

mandatory dependencies   Dependencies that are directly related to the nature of the work being performed. This is also known as hard dependencies or hard logic. See also *logical relationships*.

Maslow's hierarchy of needs   A motivational theory that hypothesizes that people have five basic needs and they fall in hierarchical order: basic physical needs, safety and security needs, social needs, self-esteem needs, and self-actualization.

mathematical models   Mathematical models, also called constrained optimization methods, are a category of project selection methods, which are a tool and technique of the Develop Project Charter process. They are complex mathematical models that use linear, dynamic, integer, nonlinear, and/or multi-objective programming in the form of algorithms, or in other words, a specific set of steps to solve a particular problem.

matrix organization   A form of organizational structure. Employees in a matrix organization report to one functional manager and at least one project manager. Functional managers assign employees to projects and carry out administrative duties, while project managers assign tasks associated with the project to team members and execute the project.

milestone   A major deliverable or key event in a project used to measure project progress.

milestone chart   A method to display project schedule information that shows the start and/or finish date of milestones.

mitigate   This is a strategy for negative risks or threats, which is a tool and technique of the Risk Response Planning process. Mitigation reduces the probability of a risk event and its impacts to an acceptable level.

Monitor and Control Project Work   Monitor and Control Project Work is concerned with monitoring all the processes in the Initiating, Planning, Executing, and Closing process groups. Collecting data, measuring results, and reporting on performance information are some of the activities performed during this process.

Monitoring and Controlling   This is the fourth project management process group. The Monitoring and Controlling process group involves taking performance measurements and analyzing them to determine if the project is staying true to the project plan. Corrective action is applied where necessary to get the project activities realigned with the project plan.

Monte Carlo analysis   This is a simulation technique that is discussed in the modeling and simulation tool and technique of the Quantitative Risk Analysis and Schedule Development processes. Monte Carlo typically simulates schedule and cost variables many times to calculate a distribution of probable duration results.

motivational theories   Motivational theories present ideas on why people act the way they do and how they can be influenced to act in certain ways to get the results desired.

Motivation-Hygiene Theory   See *Hygiene Theory*.

N

net present value (NPV)   Net present value evaluates the cash inflows using the discounted cash flow technique, which is applied to each period the inflows are expected. The total present value of the cash flows is deducted from the initial investment to determine NPV. NPV assumes that cash inflows are reinvested at the cost of capital. Similar to *discounted cash flow*.

nominal group technique   An information-gathering technique similar to the Delphi technique that can be used during the Risk Identification process.

O

objectives   Describe the purpose of the project. They are the quantifiable criteria used to measure project success. All project work is directed at completing the objective of the project. Describe the results and/or the product or service the project intends to produce. Objectives should be stated in tangible terms that are specific, measurable, accurate, realistic, and time bound.

operations   An ongoing endeavor typically involving repetitive processes that produce the same results.

ordinal scale   Values that are rank-ordered such as high, medium, or low. They are referenced in the Qualitative Risk Analysis process.

organization breakdown structure (OBS)   Relates the WBS elements to the organizational unit responsible for completing the work.

P

parametric estimating   Parametric estimating is a quantitatively based estimating method that multiplies the quantity of work by the rate.

Pareto charts   Pareto charts are a tool and technique of the Perform Quality Control process. They rank-order the most important factors such as delays, costs, or defects by their frequency over time and are displayed as histograms.

passive acceptance   Passive acceptance means that no plans will be made to avoid or mitigate the risk. The consequences of the risk event are accepted should the risk event occur.

payback period   The length of time it takes a company to recover the initial cost of producing a product or service of a project.

payment system   A payment system is the tool and technique of Contract Administration that is used to issue payment based on the input of seller invoices.

Perform Quality Assurance   This process involves performing systematic quality activities and uses quality audits to determine which processes should be used to achieve the project requirements and to assure that they are performed efficiently and effectively.

Perform Quality Control   This process is concerned with monitoring work results to see if they fulfill the quality standards set out in the quality management plan. The Perform Quality Control process determines if the end product conforms to the requirements and product description defined during the Planning processes.

performance measurement baseline   The project plan baseline, schedule baseline, and cost baseline are collectively known as the performance measurement baselines.

Performance Reporting   This process concerns collecting information regarding project progress and project accomplishments and reporting it to the stakeholders, project team members, management team, and other interested parties. It also makes predictions regarding future project performance.

Plan Contracting   This process prepares the documents used in the Request Seller Responses and Select Sellers processes.

Plan Purchases and Acquisitions   This process involves identifying the goods or services that will be purchased from outside of the organization, the quantity needed, and when they need to be purchased. It also involves identifying the project needs that can be met by the project team.

planned value (PV)   The cost of work that's been budgeted for an activity during a certain time period. (Note: *PV* also stands for *present value.*)

Planning   This is the second project management process group. The Planning process group consists of processes that involve formulating and revising project goals and objectives and creating the project management plan that will be used to achieve the goals the project was undertaken to address. Planning involves determining alternative courses of action and selecting from among the best of those to produce the project's goals. The Planning process group is where the project requirements are determined and stakeholders are identified.

politics   A technique used to influence people to perform. It involves getting groups of people with different interests to cooperate creatively even in the midst of conflict and disorder.

portfolio   Collections of projects or programs that meet a specific business goal or objective

portfolio management   The management of collections of programs and projects to meet and maximize the strategic objectives of the business. Involves monitoring active projects, balancing the portfolio among other investments, assuring efficient use of resources, and assessing the value of projects and potential projects against the portfolio's strategic objectives.

power   A technique used to influence people to perform. It's the ability to get people to do things they wouldn't do otherwise, to change minds and the course of events, and to influence outcomes.

preassignment   This is a tool and technique of the Acquire Project Team process. This occurs when a project is put out for bid and specific team members are promised as part of the proposal or when internal project team members are promised and assigned as a condition of the project.

precedence diagramming method (PDM)   A diagramming method that places activities on nodes, which connect to dependent activities using arrows. This is also known as *activity on node*.

precedence relationships   See *logical relationships*.

preferential logic   See *discretionary dependencies*.

preferred logic   See *discretionary dependencies*.

preliminary scope statement   A definition of what the project entails, including a high-level look at the project objectives and deliverables. It provides a brief background of the project and describes the business opportunity the company is attempting to benefit from. It also describes the business objectives the project should meet.

prevention   Keeps errors from occurring in the process. Prevention is a quality concern.

preventive action   Preventive action involves anything that will reduce the potential impacts of risk events should they occur. Contingency plans and risk responses are examples of preventive action. These are inputs to the Direct and Manage Project Execution process.

probability   The likelihood that an event will occur.

probability and impact matrix   The probability and impact matrix defines the combination of probability and impact that helps determine which risks need detailed risk response plans. It's defined during the Risk Management Planning process and included in the risk management plan. The matrix is used in the Qualitative Risk Analysis process to assign an overall risk rating to each of the project's identified risks. The combination of probability and impact results in a classification usually expressed as high, medium, or low. High risks are considered a red condition, medium risks are considered a yellow condition, and low risks are considered a green condition.

process analysis   Process analysis is a tool and technique of the Perform Quality Assurance process. It looks at process improvement from an organizational and technical perspective. Process analysis steps are documented in the process improvement plan and examine problems experienced while conducting the project, the constraints of the project, and inefficient and ineffective processes identified during process operation.

procurement audits   A tool and technique of the Contract Closure process that examines the procurement processes to determine the effectiveness of the processes. Procurement audits are performed on all the Project Procurement Management Knowledge Area processes except the Contract Closure process.

procurement documents   Procurement documents are prepared in the Plan Contracting process and are used to solicit vendors and suppliers to bid on project procurement needs. They might be called request for proposal (RFP), request for information (RFI), invitation for bid (IFB), or request for quotation (RFQ).

procurement management plan   This details how the procurement process will be managed throughout the project and includes elements like the types of contracts used, the authority of the project team, and where to find standard procurement documents.

product analysis   A description of the product of the project that might include performing value analysis, function analysis, quality function deployment, product breakdown analysis, systems engineering techniques, value engineering, and function deployment techniques to further define and better understand the product or service of the project. This is a tool and technique of the Scope Definition process.

product description   See *product scope description.*

product scope   See *product scope description.*

product scope description   A description of the product features typically documented in the product description.

product verification   This determines if the work described in the contract was completed accurately and satisfactorily. It's one of the purposes of the Contract Closure process.

Program Evaluation and Review Technique (PERT)   PERT uses expected value—or weighted average—of critical path tasks to determine project duration by establishing three estimates: most likely, pessimistic, and optimistic. PERT is used when activity duration estimates are highly uncertain.

program   A grouping of projects that are managed together. The individual projects are usually part of one bigger project and are therefore related.

program management   The central management and coordination of groups of related projects and operations work to obtain benefits and administer controls that aren't possible when the projects and operations are managed individually to achieve the program's strategic objectives.

progressive elaboration   The process of taking incremental steps to examine and refine the characteristics of the product of the project. Processes may be progressively elaborated as well.

project   Projects are temporary in nature; have definite start and end dates; create a unique product, service, or result; and are completed when the goals and objectives of the project have been met and signed off on by the stakeholders.

project boundaries   Define what is and what is not included in the work of the project. Should specifically state what is excluded from the work of the project. This is an element of the project scope statement.

project calendars   Project calendars are an input to the Schedule Development process. They concern all the resources involved in the project and specify the working periods for all resources.

project charter   An official, written acknowledgment and recognition that a project exists. The project charter is issued by senior management and gives the project manager the authority to assign organizational resources to the work of the project.

Project Communications Management   One of the nine knowledge areas of project management. Project Communications Management ensures proper and timely communications and includes these processes: Communications Planning, Information Distribution, Performance Reporting, and Manage Stakeholders.

Project Cost Management   One of the nine knowledge areas of project management. Project Cost Management ensures proper cost planning, budgets, and controls and includes these processes: Cost Estimating, Cost Budgeting, and Cost Control.

Project Human Resource Management   One of the nine knowledge areas of project management. Project Human Resource Management ensures effective use of human resources and includes these processes: Human Resource Planning, Acquire Project Team, Develop Project Team, and Manage Project Team.

Project Integration Management   One of the nine knowledge areas of project management. Project Integration Management involves coordinating all aspects of the project and includes these processes: Develop Project Charter, Preliminary Project Scope Statement, Develop Project Management Plan, Direct and Manage Project Execution, Monitor and Control Project Work, Integrated Change Control, and Close Project.

project life cycle   The grouping of project phases in a sequential order from the beginning of the project to the close.

project management knowledge areas   These nine project management groupings—known as knowledge areas—bring together common or related processes.

project management office (PMO)   Office established by organizations to create and maintain procedures and standards for project management methodologies to be used throughout the organization.

project management plan This plan defines how the project is executed, how it's monitored and controlled, and how it's closed and also documents the outputs of the Planning group processes. The size and complexity of the project will determine the level of detail contained in this plan.

Project Management Professional Code of Professional Conduct An ethical code established by PMI to ensure personal and professional conduct on the part of PMPs.

project management The process that's used to initiate, plan, execute, monitor, control, and close out projects by applying skills, knowledge, and project management tools and techniques to fulfill the project requirements.

project manager The person responsible for applying the skills, knowledge, and project management tools and techniques to the project activities in order to successfully complete the project objectives.

project performance review Project performance reviews are similar to status reviews. Their purpose is to examine schedule activities, work packages, or cost account status and their progress to date. The three types of analyses associated with performance reviews are variance analysis, trend analysis, and earned value technique.

project plan An assortment of documents (outputs from the Planning process group) that constitutes what the project is, what the project will deliver, and how all the processes will be managed. The project plan is used as the guideline throughout the project Executing and Controlling process groups to track and measure project performance and to make future project decisions. It's also used as a communication and information tool for stakeholders, team members, and the management team.

project presentations Project presentations are part of the organizational process assets updates, which is an output of the Information Distribution process. These concern presenting project information to the stakeholders and other appropriate parties.

Project Procurement Management One of the nine knowledge areas of project management. Project Procurement Management concerns procurement and contract oversight. The processes included in this knowledge area are Plan Purchases and Acquisitions, Plan Contracting, Request Seller Responses, Select Sellers, Contract Administration, and Contract Closure.

Project Quality Management One of the nine knowledge areas of project management. Project Quality Management ensures that the quality requirements of the project are satisfied. The processes included in this knowledge area are Quality Planning, Perform Quality Assurance, and Perform Quality Control.

project records Project records are all information regarding the project, including project reports, memos, project schedules, project plans, and other documents.

project reports An element of the organizational process assets update output of the Information Distribution process that includes project information such as the project status reports and minutes from project meetings.

Project Risk Management   One of the nine knowledge areas of project management. Project Risk Management is concerned with identifying and planning for potential risks that may impact the project. Its processes include Risk Management Planning, Risk Identification, Qualitative Risk Analysis, Quantitative Risk Analysis, Risk Response Planning, and Risk Monitoring and Control.

project schedule   The project schedule determines the start and finish dates for project activities and assigns resources to the activities.

project scope   The project scope describes the work required to produce the product or the service of the project. This includes the requirements of the product, which describe the features and functionality of the product or service.

Project Scope Management   One of the nine knowledge areas of project management. Project Scope Management is concerned with the work of the project and only the work that is required to complete the project. Its processes include Scope Planning, Scope Definition, Create WBS, Scope Verification, and Scope Control.

project scope management plan   The project scope management plan has a direct influence on the project's success and describes the process for defining project scope and verifying the work of the project. It facilitates the creations of the WBS, describes how the product or service of the project is verified and accepted, and documents how changes to scope will be handled. It is an output of the Scope Planning process.

project scope statement   The project scope statement documents the project objectives, deliverables, and requirements, which are used as a basis for future project decisions. It also includes other elements, such product scope description, project boundaries, product acceptance criteria, constraints, assumptions, project organization, risks, milestones, fund limitations, cost estimate, configuration management requirements, project specifications, and approval requirements.

project sponsor   Usually an executive in the organization. The project sponsor has the authority to assign resources and enforce decisions regarding the project.

project statement of work (SOW)   Describes the product or service the project was undertaken to complete. It is an input to several processes. (See also *contract statement of work*.)

Project Time Management   One of the nine knowledge areas of project management. Project Time Management is concerned with estimating the duration of the project plan activities, devising a project schedule, and monitoring and controlling deviations from the schedule. Its processes include Activity Definition, Activity Sequencing, Activity Resource Estimating, Activity Duration Estimating, Schedule Development, and Schedule Control.

projectized organization   A type of organizational structure focused on projects. Project managers generally have ultimate authority over the project. Sometimes, supporting departments like human resources and accounting might report to the project manager. Project managers are responsible for making project decisions and acquiring and assigning resources.

Q

qualified seller lists   See *develop qualified seller lists*.

Qualitative Risk Analysis   This process determines what impact the identified risks will have on the project and the probability that they'll occur and puts the risks in priority order according to their effect on the project objectives.

quality audits   Quality audits are independent reviews performed by trained auditors or third-party reviewers. The purpose of a quality audit is to identify ineffective and inefficient processes used on the project. Audits may also examine and uncover inefficient processes and procedures.

Quantitative Risk Analysis   This process assigns numeric probabilities to each identified risk and examines their potential impact to the project objectives.

R

RACI chart   A matrix-based chart that shows the type of resource and their responsibility on the project. RACI stands for responsible, accountable, consult, and inform. This is a tool and technique of the Human Resource Planning process.

recognition and rewards   A tool and technique of the Develop Project Team process, recognition and rewards systems are formal ways for the management team and the project manager to recognize and promote desirable behavior.

records management system   A records management system is a tool and technique of the Contract Administration process and involves documenting policies, control functions, and automated tools used to manage project documents and contract documents. A records management system is part of the project management information system.

Request Seller Responses   This process involves obtaining bids and proposals from vendors in response to RFPs and similar documents prepared during the Plan Contracting process.

requirements   The specifications of the objective or deliverable that must be met in order to satisfy the needs of the project. Requirements may also describe results or outcomes that must be produced in order to satisfy a contract, specification, standard, or other project document (typically the scope statement). Requirements quantify and prioritize the wants, needs, and expectations of the project sponsor and stakeholders.

reserve time   A practice of adding a portion of time (percentage of total time or number of work periods) to an activity to account for schedule risk.

residual risk   A risk that remains after implementing a risk response strategy.

resource breakdown structure (RBS)   A hierarchical chart of resources that breaks down the work of the project according to the types of resources needed.

resource calendars   Calendars are an input to the Schedule Development process. Resource calendars refer to specific resources—or categories of resources—and their individual (or group) availability.

resource leveling   Resource leveling attempts to smooth out the resource assignments so that tasks are completed without overloading the individual and without negatively affecting the project schedule. Some ways to perform resource leveling include delaying the start of a task to match the availability of a key team member or giving more tasks to underallocated team members. Resource leveling is also known as resource-based method.

resource-based method   See *resource leveling*.

resources   The people, equipment, and materials needed to complete the work of the project.

Responsibility Assignment Matrix (RAM)   The RAM ties roles and responsibilities with the WBS elements to ensure that each element has a resource assigned.

reverse resource allocation scheduling   A resource-leveling technique used when key resources are required at a specific point in the project and they are the only resources available to perform these activities. Reverse resource allocation scheduling requires that the resources be scheduled in reverse order, that is, from the end date of the project rather than from the beginning, in order to assign key resources at the correct time.

revisions   Adjustments to approved schedule start and end dates for activities to coincide with approved changes and/or corrective actions. This is another term for *schedule updates*.

rework   Failing to meet quality requirements or standards may result in rework (performing the work again to make it conform). Rework may increase the project schedule.

risk breakdown structure (RBS)   An RBS is a graphical way to display risk categories and their subcategories. The RBS is an element of the risk management plan.

risk categories   Risk categories systematically identify risks and provide a foundation for understanding. The use of risk categories helps improve the Risk Identification process by giving everyone involved a common language or basis for describing risk. Risk categories are an element of the risk management plan.

risk identification   This process identifies the potential project risks and documents their characteristics.

risk management plan   Describes how risks are defined, monitored, and controlled throughout the project. The risk management plan is a subsidiary of the project management plan and it's the only output of the Risk Management Planning process.

Risk Management Planning   This process determines how risks will be managed for a project.

Risk Monitoring and Control   This process involves responding to risks as they occur. The risk management plan details how risk is managed, and the risk response plan details how risk response strategies are implemented in the event of an actual risk event. This process implements risk response according to the plan.

risk register   The output of the Risk Identification process that contains the list of identified risks. The risk register is updated and its update becomes an output of every remaining Risk process. At the end of the Risk Response Planning process, the risk register contains these elements: list of identified and prioritized risks, risk owners and their responsibilities, risk triggers, response plans and strategies, cost and schedule activities needed to implement risk responses, contingency reserves for cost and time, contingency plans, fallback plans, residual and secondary risks, probabilistic analysis of the project, and other outputs of the Qualitative and Quantitative Risk Analysis processes.

Risk Response Planning   This process defines what steps to take to reduce threats and take advantage of opportunities and assigns departments or individual staff members the responsibility of carrying out the risk response plans developed in this process.

risk tolerance   Risk tolerance is the level at which stakeholders are comfortable taking a risk because the benefits to be gained outweigh what could be lost or at which risks are avoided because the cost is too great.

run chart   Run chart is a tool and technique of the Perform Quality Control process that are used to show variations in the process over time. They may also show trends in the process.

S

Scatter diagrams   Scatter diagrams are a tool and technique of the Perform Quality Control process. They use two variables, an independent variable, which is an input, and a dependent variable, which is an output, to display the relationship between these two elements as points on a graph.

schedule baseline   The approved project schedule serves as the schedule baseline that will be used in the Executing and Monitoring and Controlling processes to measure schedule process.

schedule change control system   Defines how changes to the schedule are made and managed. Tracks and records change requests, describes the procedures to follow to implement schedule changes, and details the authorization levels needed to approve the schedule changes.

schedule compression   A form of mathematical analysis that's used to shorten the project schedule without changing the project scope. Compression is simply shortening the project schedule to accomplish all the activities sooner than estimated. Crashing and fast tracking are two examples of schedule compressions.

Schedule Control   This process involves documenting and managing changes to the project schedule.

Schedule Development   This process calculates and prepares the schedule of project activities, which becomes the schedule baseline. It determines activity start and finish dates, finalizes activity sequences and durations, and assigns resources to activities.

schedule network analysis   This technique of Schedule Development creates the project schedule. It uses a schedule model and other analytical techniques such as critical path and critical chain method, what-if analysis, and resource leveling (all of which are other tools and techniques in this process) to help calculate these dates and the project schedule.

schedule performance index (SPI)   A performance index that calculates schedule performance efficiencies. SPI = EV ÷ PV

schedule updates   Schedule updates are an output of the Schedule Control process and involve adjusting activities and dates to coincide with approved changes and/or corrective actions.

schedule variance (SV)   An earned value analysis technique that determines if the project schedule is ahead or behind what was planned for a given period of time. SV = EV – PV

scope   All of the components that make up the product or service of the project and the results the project intends to produce.

Scope Control   This process involves documenting and managing changes to project scope. Any modification to the agreed-upon WBS is considered a scope change. Changes in product scope will require changes to the project scope. (See also *product scope* and *project scope*.)

Scope Definition   This Planning process further elaborates the objectives and deliverables of the project into a project scope statement that's used as a basis for future project decisions.

scope management plan   See *project scope management plan*.

Scope Planning   The primary purpose of the Scope Planning process is to document the scope management plan. This is a planning tool that documents how the project team will go about defining project scope, how the work breakdown structure will be developed, how changes to scope will be controlled, and how project scope will be verified.

scope statement   See *project scope statement*.

Scope Verification   This process formalizes the acceptance of the project scope and is primarily concerned with the acceptance of work results.

scoring model   A project selection method used to score and rank project proposals. Project selection methods are a tool and technique of the Develop Project Charter process. Scoring models may also be used in the Select Seller process.

screening systems   A set of predetermined performance criteria used to screen vendors. Screening systems are a tool and technique of the Select Sellers process.

secondary risks   A risk that comes about as a result of implementing a risk response.

Select Sellers   This process involves the receipt of bids or proposals and choosing a vendor to perform the work or supply the goods or services.

seller invoices   A request for payment of goods or services that should describe the work that was completed or the materials that were delivered. Seller invoices are part of the Contract Administration process.

seller rating systems   Seller rating systems are a tool and technique of the Select Sellers process. These systems use information about the sellers—such as past performance, delivery, contract compliance, and quality ratings—to determine seller performance.

sensitivity analysis   A quantitative method of analyzing the potential impact of risk events on the project and determining which risk events have the greatest potential for impact by examining all the uncertain elements at their baseline values. This is a Quantitative Risk Analysis modeling technique.

share   Share is a Risk Response Planning strategy for risks that pose an opportunity to the project.

should cost estimates   See *independent estimates*.

slack time   The amount of time you can delay the early start of a task without delaying the finish date of the project. This is also known as *float time*.

smoothing   Smoothing is a conflict resolution technique that is a temporary way to resolve conflict where someone attempts to make the conflict appear less important than it is. This is a temporary solution.

soft logic   See *discretionary dependencies*.

stakeholder   A person or organization who has a vested interest in the project and stands to gain or lose something as a result of the project.

starvation   A type of project ending where financial or human resources are cut off from the project.

statistical sampling   Taking a sample number of parts from the whole population and examining them to determine if they fall within the variances outlined by the quality control plan. Statistical sampling is a tool and technique of the Perform Quality Control process.

status review meetings   Status meetings are a tool and technique of the Project Plan Execution process. The purpose of status meetings is to provide updated information regarding the progress of the project. They are not show-and-tell meetings.

steering committee   A group of high-level managers or executives in the organization who manage project prioritization and various project decisions. The steering committee typically represents functional areas or departments within the organization.

successor activities   Activities that follow predecessor activities.

T

tailoring   Determining which processes and process groups should be performed for the project. The project manager and project team should take into consideration the size and complexity of the project and the various inputs and outputs of each of the processes when determining which ones to perform. It's generally accepted that performing all five process groups is good practice for any project.

team building   Team building activities are a tool and technique of the Develop Project Team process. They involve getting a diverse group of people to work together in the most efficient and effective manner possible.

technical performance measurements   These measurements are usually determined during trend analysis (which is used with the run chart tool and technique of the Perform Quality Control process) to compare the technical accomplishments of project milestones completed to the technical milestones defined in the project Planning processes.

Theory X   A motivational management theory that proposes that most people do not like work and will try to steer clear of it. It postulates that people have little to no ambition, need constant supervision, and won't actually perform the duties of their job unless threatened.

Theory Y   A motivational management theory that proposes that people are interested in performing their best given the right motivation and proper expectations.

three-point estimates   Three-point estimates are a tool and technique of the Activity Duration Estimating process used to determine activity estimates. The three estimates are the most likely estimate, an optimistic estimate, and a pessimistic estimate.

time and materials (T&M) contract   A type of contract that is a cross between the fixed price contract and the cost reimbursable contract. Preset unit rates are agreed to at contract signing, but costs are charged to the buyer as they're incurred.

tolerable results   Quality measurements that fall within a specified range. Tolerable results are a concern of the Perform Quality Control process. These are also known as *tolerances*.

top-down estimating   See *analogous estimating*.

tornado diagram   This is a diagramming method for sensitivity analysis data. The variables with the greatest effect on the project are displayed as horizontal bars at the top of the graph and decrease in impact as they progress down through the graph. This gives a quick overview of how much the project can be affected by uncertainty in the various elements and which risks have the greatest impact on the project.

total float   The amount of time the earliest start of a task can be delayed without delaying the ending of the project.

training   A tool and technique of the Develop Project Team process that improves the competencies of the project team members.

transfer   Transference is a strategy for negative risks or threats, which is a tool and technique of the Risk Response Planning process. This strategy transfers the consequences of a risk to a third party. Insurance is an example of transference.

triggers   Risk symptoms that imply a risk event is about to occur.

V

variance at completion (VAC)   An earned value analysis technique that calculates the difference between the budget at completion (BAC) and the estimate at completion (EAC).
VAC = BAC − EAC

virtual teams   Virtual teams are teams that don't necessarily work in the same location but all share the goals of the project and have a role on the project. This type of team allows the inclusion of resources from different geographic locations, those who work different hours or shifts from the other team members, those with mobility limitations, and so on.

W

weighted scoring model   See *weighting system*.

weighting system   A way to rank and score vendor proposals or project proposals. Weighting systems assign numerical weights to evaluation criteria and then multiply this by the weight of each criteria factor to come up with total scores for each project or vendor. These systems keep personal biases to a minimum. Weighting systems are a tool and technique of the Selecting Sellers process and a project selection method, which is a tool and technique of the Develop Project Charter process.

withdrawal   This conflict resolution technique occurs when one of the parties gets up and leaves and refuses to discuss the conflict. This never results in resolution.

work authorization systems   Work authorization systems clarify and initiate the work of each work package or activity. This is a formal procedure that authorizes work to begin in the correct sequence and at the right time. Work authorization systems are usually written procedures defined by the organization. These are used in the Executing processes of the project.

work performance information   Work performance information is an input to the Contract Administration process. Work performance information is used to monitor work results and examine the vendor's deliverables and compares their work results against the project management plan. It also makes certain activities are performed correctly and in sequence.

workaround   An unplanned response to a risk event that was unknown and unidentified or an unplanned response to a risk that was previously accepted. Workaround plans are an element of the Risk Monitoring and Control process.

Index

Note to the reader: Throughout this index boldfaced page numbers indicate primary discussions of a topic. Italicized page numbers indicate illustrations.

Numbers

A

Q

Taking the lead in project management!

A quintessential model for project management—a landmark reference

This is the *Ninth Edition* of the best selling "bible" of project management. The last edition re-focused the content on the critical "project management" topics, added pedagogy, and streamlined the book for use in both college level and training courses. This *Ninth Edition* maintains the streamlined approach but moves the content closer to PMI's *Project Management Body of Knowledge* (PMBOK) which just published in its 3rd edition. As of October 2005, the PMBOK 3E will become the mandated source of the PMP Exam training. This text uses sidebars throughout to further align the books. The 9th edition is again supplemented by a Student Workbook, an Instructor's Manual, and a book of case studies to help students learn and prepare for the Project Management Professional (PMP) certification exam.

ABOUT THE AUTHOR:

Dr. Harold Kerzner is Executive Director for Project Management at the International Institute of Learning (IIL), is Professor of Systems Management at Baldwin-Wallace College in Ohio and President of Project Management Associates, a consulting and training firm that conducts seminars for leading U.S. and international corporations.

ADDITIONAL RESOURCES:

Project Management Workbook and PMP Exam Study Guide, 9th Edition
HAROLD KERZNER, Frank P. Saladis
ISBN: 0-471-76076-5, Cloth, 400 pages, $50.00, December 2005

Project Management Case Studies, 2nd Edition
HAROLD KERZNER
ISBN: 0-471-75167-7, Paper, 624 pages, $50.00, December 2005

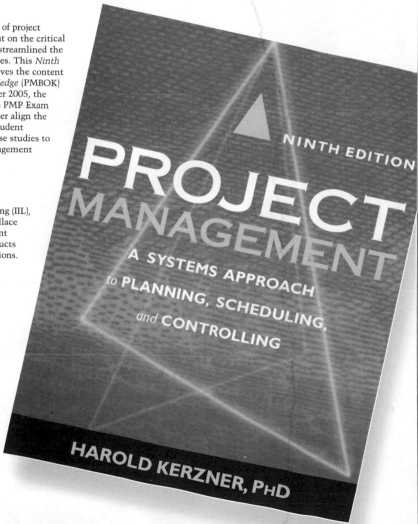

NINTH EDITION

PROJECT MANAGEMENT

A SYSTEMS APPROACH to PLANNING, SCHEDULING, and CONTROLLING

HAROLD KERZNER, PhD

WILEY

Now you know.

wiley.com

ISBN: 0-471-74187-6, Cloth, 1024 pages,
$85.00, December 2005

TELL US WHAT YOU THINK!

Your feedback is critical to our efforts to provide you with the best books and software on the market. Tell us what you think about the products you've purchased. It's simple:

1. Go to the Sybex website.
2. Find your book by typing the ISBN or title into the Search field.
3. Click on the book title when it appears.
4. Click **Submit a Review**.
5. Fill out the questionnaire and comments.
6. Click **Submit**.

With your feedback, we can continue to publish the highest quality computer books and software products that today's busy IT professionals deserve.

www.sybex.com

SYBEX Inc. • 1151 Marina Village Parkway, Alameda, CA 94501 • 510-523-8233

The Best PMP Study Combination Available!

Prepare yourself for PMP 2005 exam with hundreds of challenging sample test questions!

- Chapter-by-chapter review questions from the book.
- A total of eight bonus exams available only on the CD. Six for the PMP exam, as well as two additional CAPM exams.
- Supports question formats found on actual exam.

Reinforce understanding of key topics with flashcards for your PC, Pocket PC, or Palm handheld!

- Contains over 150 flashcard questions.
- Runs on multiple platforms for usability and portability.
- Quiz yourself anytime, anywhere!

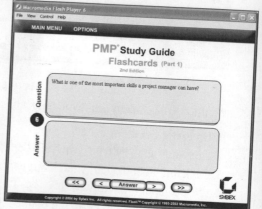

Access the entire book in PDF!

- Full search capabilities let you quickly find the information you need.
- Complete with tables and illustrations.
- Adobe Acrobat Reader included.

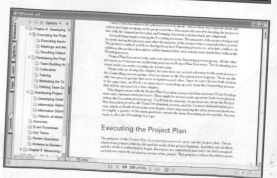